Trading
Price
Action
TRADING
RANGES

Founded in 1807, John Wiley & Sons is the oldest independent publishing company in the United States. With offices in North America, Europe, Australia, and Asia, Wiley is globally committed to developing and marketing print and electronic products and services for our customers' professional and personal knowledge and understanding.

The Wiley Trading series features books by traders who have survived the market's ever changing temperament and have prospered—some by reinventing systems, others by getting back to basics. Whether a novice trader, professional, or somewhere in-between, these books will provide the advice and strategies needed to prosper today and well into the future.

For a list of available titles, please visit our Web site at www.WileyFinance.com.

Trading
Price
Action
TRADING
RANGES

TECHNICAL ANALYSIS of PRICE CHARTS
BAR by BAR for the SERIOUS TRADER

AL BROOKS

WILEY

John Wiley & Sons, Inc.

The first edition of this book, titled *Reading Price Charts Bar by Bar: The Technical Analysis of Price Action for the Serious Trader*, was published in 2009.

Published by John Wiley & Sons, Inc., Hoboken, New Jersey.
Published simultaneously in Canada.

All charts were created with TradeStation. © TradeStation Technologies, Inc. All rights reserved.

For general information on our other products and services or for technical support, please contact our Customer Care Department within the United States at (800) 762-2974, outside the United States at (317) 572-3993 or fax (317) 572-4002.

Wiley also publishes its books in a variety of electronic formats. Some content that appears in print may not be available in electronic books. For more information about Wiley products, visit our web site at www.wiley.com.

Library of Congress Cataloging-in-Publication Data:

Brooks, Al, 1952–
  Trading price action trading ranges : technical analysis of price charts bar by bar for the serious trader / Al Brooks.
      p. cm. – (The Wiley trading series)
  "The first edition of this book titled, Reading price charts bar by bar : the technical analysis of price action for the serious trader, was published in 2009"–T.p. verso.
  Includes index.
  ISBN 978-1-118-06667-6 (cloth); ISBN 978-1-118-17231-5 (ebk);
  ISBN 978-1-118-17232-2 (ebk); ISBN 978-1-118-17233-9 (ebk)
  1. Stocks–Prices–Charts, diagrams, etc.   I. Brooks, Al, 1952– Reading price charts bar by bar.   II. Title.
  HG4638.B757 2012
  332.63'2042–dc23

                                                                                           2011029299

Printed in the United States of America

SKY10087394_101024

I would like to dedicate this book to my daughter, Skylar Brooks, who is tender, sweet, sensitive, incredibly accomplished, trusting, and persistently hopeful. She wants the world to be a better place and is doing far more than the rest of us to make it happen.

Contents

Acknowledgments

My primary goal is to present a series of comprehensive books on price action, and the greatest concern among readers was how difficult my earlier book, *Reading Price Charts Bar by Bar*, was to read. I am deeply appreciative of all of the constructive comments that readers have provided and those from the participants in my daily live webinars. Many of these comments were incredibly insightful and I have incorporated them in this current edition. I am also thankful to all of the traders who have been in my live trading room, because they have given me the opportunity to say things repeatedly until I could clearly articulate what I am seeing and doing. They have also asked many questions that have helped me find the words to communicate more effectively, and I have put those words in these books.

I would like to give a special thank-you to Victor Brancale, who spent long hours proofreading the manuscripts and providing hundreds of very helpful edits and suggestions, and to Robert Gjerde, who built and administers my website and has given me candid feedback on the chat room and the website. Finally, I want to thank Ginger Szala, the Group Editorial Director of *Futures* magazine, for giving me ongoing opportunities to publish articles and speak in webinars, and for regularly giving me very helpful advice on how to become more involved with the trading community.

List of Terms Used in This Book

All of these terms are defined in a practical way to be helpful to traders and not necessarily in the theoretical way often described by technicians.

always in   If you have to be in the market at all times, either long or short, this is whatever your current position is (always in long or always in short). If at any time you are forced to decide between initiating a long or a short trade and are confident in your choice, then the market is in always-in mode at that moment. Almost all of these trades require a spike in the direction of the trend before traders will have confidence.

barbwire   A trading range of three or more bars that largely overlap and one or more is a doji. It is a type of tight trading range with prominent tails and often relatively large bars.

bar pullback   In an upswing, a bar pullback is a bar with a low below the low of the prior bar. In a downswing, it is a bar with a high above that of the prior bar.

bear reversal   A change in trend from up to down (a bear trend).

blown account   An account that your losses have reduced below the minimum margin requirements set by your broker, and you will not be allowed to place a trade unless you deposit more money.

breakout   The high or low of the current bar extends beyond some prior price of significance such as a swing high or low, the high or low of any prior bar, a trend line, or a trend channel.

breakout bar (or bar breakout)   A bar that creates a breakout. It is usually a strong trend bar.

breakout mode   A setup where a breakout in either direction should have follow-through.

breakout pullback   A small pullback of one to about five bars that occurs within a few bars after a breakout. Since you see it as a pullback, you are expecting the breakout to resume and the pullback is a setup for that resumption. If instead you thought that the breakout would fail, you would not use the term *pullback* and instead would see the pullback as a failed breakout. For example, if there was a five-bar breakout above a bear trend line but you believed that the bear trend would continue, you would be considering shorting this bear flag and not looking to buy a pullback immediately after it broke out to the downside.

breakout test   A breakout pullback that comes close to the original entry price to test a breakeven stop. It may overshoot it or undershoot it by a few ticks. It can occur within a bar or two of entry or after an extended move or even 20 or more bars later.

bull reversal   A change in trend from a downtrend to an uptrend (a bull trend).

buying pressure   Strong bulls are asserting themselves and their buying is creating bull trend bars, bars with tails at the bottoms, and two-bar bull reversals. The effect is cumulative and usually is eventually followed by higher prices.

candle   A chart representation of price action in which the body is the area between the open and the close. If the close is above the open, it is a bull candle and is shown as white. If it is below, it is a bear candle and is black. The lines above and below are called tails (some technicians call them wicks or shadows).

chart type   A line, bar, candle, volume, tick, or other type of chart.

climax   A move that has gone too far too fast and has now reversed direction to either a trading range or an opposite trend. Most climaxes end with trend channel overshoots and reversals, but most of those reversals result in trading ranges and not an opposite trend.

countertrend   A trade or setup that is in the opposite direction from the current trend (the current always-in direction). This is a losing strategy for most traders since the risk is usually at least as large as the reward and the probability is rarely high enough to make the trader's equation favorable.

countertrend scalp   A trade taken in the belief that there is more to go in the trend but that a small pullback is due; you enter countertrend to capture a small profit as that small pullback is forming. This is usually a mistake and should be avoided.

day trade   A trade where the intent is to exit on the day of entry.

directional probability   The probability that the market will move either up or down any number of ticks before it reaches a certain number of ticks in the opposite direction. If you are looking at an equidistant move up and down, it hovers around 50 percent most of the time, which means that there is a 50–50 chance that the market will move up by X ticks before it moves down X ticks, and a 50–50 chance that it will move down X ticks before it moves up X ticks.

doji   A candle with a small body or no body at all. On a 5 minute chart, the body would be only one or two ticks; but on a daily chart, the body might be 10 or more ticks and still appear almost nonexistent. Neither the bulls nor the bears control the bar. All bars are either trend bars or nontrend bars, and those nontrend bars are called dojis.

double bottom   A chart formation in which the low of the current bar is about the same as the low of a prior swing low. That prior low can be just one bar earlier or 20 or more bars earlier. It does not have to be at the low of the day, and it commonly forms in bull flags (a double bottom bull flag).

double bottom bull flag   A pause or bull flag in a bull trend that has two spikes down to around the same price and then reverses back into a bull trend.

double bottom pullback   A buy setup composed of a double bottom followed by a deep pullback that forms a higher low.

double top   A chart formation in which the high of the current bar is about the same as the high of a prior swing high. That prior high can be just one bar earlier or 20 or more bars earlier. It does not have to be at the high of the day, and it commonly forms in bear flags (a double top bear flag).

double top bear flag   A pause or bear flag in a bear trend that has two spikes up to around the same price and then reverses back into a bear trend.

double top pullback   A sell setup composed of a double top followed by a deep pullback that forms a lower high.

early longs   Traders who buy as a bull signal bar is forming rather than waiting for it to close and then entering on a buy stop at one tick above its high.

early shorts   Traders who sell as a bear signal bar is forming rather than waiting for it to close and then entering on a sell stop at one tick below its low.

edge   A setup with a positive trader's equation. The trader has a mathematical advantage if he trades the setup. Edges are always small and fleeting because they need someone on the other side, and the market is filled with smart traders who won't allow an edge to be big and persistent.

EMA   See *exponential moving average (EMA)*.

entry bar   The bar during which a trade is entered.

exponential moving average (EMA)   The charts in these books use a 20-bar exponential moving average, but any moving average can be useful.

fade   To place a trade in the opposite direction of the trend (for example, selling a bull breakout that you expect to fail and reverse downward).

failed failure   A failure that fails, resuming in the direction of the original breakout, and therefore a breakout pullback. Since it is a second signal, it is more reliable. For example, if there is a breakout above a trading range and the bar after the breakout is a bear reversal bar, if the market trades below that bar, the breakout has failed. If the market then trades above the high of a prior bar within the next few bars, the failed breakout has failed and now the breakout is resuming. This means that the failed breakout became a small bull flag and just a pullback from the breakout.

failure (a failed move)   A move where the protective stop is hit before a scalper's profit is secured or before the trader's objective is reached, usually leading to a move in the opposite direction as trapped traders are forced to exit at a loss. Currently, a scalper's target in the Emini of four ticks usually requires a six-tick move, and a target in the QQQQ of 10 ticks usually requires a move of 12 cents.

false   Failed, failure.

five-tick failure   A trade in the Emini that reaches five ticks beyond the signal bar and then reverses. For example, a breakout of a bull flag runs five ticks, and once the bar closes, the next bar has a low that is lower. Most limit orders to take a one-point profit would fail to get filled since a move usually has to go one tick beyond the order before it is filled. It is often a setup for a trade in the opposite direction.

flat   Refers to a trader who is not currently holding any positions.

follow-through   After the initial move, like a breakout, it is one or more bars that extend the move. Traders like to see follow-through on the next bar and on the several bars after that, hoping for a trend where they stand to make more profit.

follow-through bar   A bar that creates follow-through after the entry bar; it is usually the next bar but sometimes forms a couple of bars later.

fractal   Every pattern is a fractal of a pattern on a higher time frame chart. This means that every pattern is a micro pattern on a higher time frame and every micro pattern is a standard pattern on a smaller time frame.

gap   A space between any two price bars on the chart. An opening gap is a common occurrence and is present if the open of the first bar of today is beyond the high or low of the prior bar (the last bar of yesterday) or of the entire day. A moving average gap is present when the low of a bar is above a flat or falling moving average, or the high of a bar is below a flat or rising moving average. Traditional gaps (breakout, measuring, and exhaustion) on daily charts have intraday equivalents in the form of various trend bars.

gap bar   See *moving average gap bar*.

gap reversal   A formation in which the current bar extends one tick beyond the prior bar back into the gap. For example, if there is a gap up open and the second bar of the day trades one tick below the low of the first bar, this is a gap reversal.

HFT   See *high-frequency trading (HFT)*.

higher high   A swing high that is higher than a previous swing high.

higher low   A swing low that is higher than a previous swing low.

higher time frame (HTF)   A chart covering the same amount of time as the current chart, but having fewer bars. For example, compared to the day session 5 minute Emini chart on an average day, examples of higher time frame charts include a 15 minute chart, a tick chart with 25,000 ticks per bar, and a volume chart with 100,000 contracts per bar (each of these charts usually has fewer than 30 bars on an average day, compared to the 81 bars on the 5 minute chart).

high-frequency trading (HFT)   Also known as algorithmic trading or black box trading, it is a type of program trading where firms place millions of orders a day in thousands of stocks to scalp profits as small as a penny, and the trading is based on statistical analysis rather than fundamentals.

high/low 1 or 2   Either a high 1 or 2 or a low 1 or 2.

high 1, 2, 3, or 4   A high 1 is a bar with a high above the prior bar in a bull flag or near the bottom of a trading range. If there is then a bar with a lower high (it can occur one or several bars later), the next bar in this correction whose high is above the prior bar's high is a high 2. Third and fourth occurrences are a high 3 and 4. A high 3 is a wedge bull flag variant.

HTF   See *higher time frame (HTF)*.

ii   Consecutive inside bars, where the second is inside the first. At the end of a leg, it is a breakout mode setup and can become a flag or a reversal setup. A less reliable version is a "bodies-only ii," where you ignore the tails. Here, the second body is inside the first body, which is inside the body before it.

iii   Three inside bars in a row, and a somewhat more reliable pattern than an ii.

inside bar   A bar with a high that is at or below the high of the prior bar and a low that is at or above the low of the prior bar.

institution   Also called the smart money, it can be a pension fund, hedge fund, insurance company, bank, broker, large individual trader, or any other entity that trades enough volume to impact the market. Market movement is the cumulative effect of many institutions placing trades, and a single institution alone usually cannot move a major market for very long. Traditional institutions place trades based on fundamentals, and they used to be the sole determinant of the market's direction. However, HFT firms now have a significant influence on the day's movement since their trading currently generates most of the day's volume. HFT firms are a special type of institutional firm and their trading is based on statistics and not fundamentals. Traditional institutions determine the direction and target, but mathematicians determine the path that the market takes to get there.

ioi   Inside-outside-inside—three consecutive bars where the second bar is an outside bar, and the third bar is an inside bar. It is often a breakout mode setup where a trader looks to buy above the inside bar or sell below it.

ledge   A bull ledge is a small trading range with a bottom created by two or more bars with identical lows; a bear ledge is a small trading range with a top created by two or more bars with identical highs.

leg   A small trend that breaks a trend line of any size; the term is used only where there are at least two legs on the chart. It is any smaller trend that is part of a larger trend and it can be a pullback (a countertrend move), a swing in a trend or in a sideways market, or a with-trend move in a trend that occurs between any two pullbacks within the trend.

likely   At least 60 percent certain.

long   A person who buys a position in a market or the actual position itself.

lot   The smallest position size that can be traded in a market. It is a share when referring to stocks and a contract when referring to Eminis or other futures.

lower high   A swing high that is lower than a previous swing high.

lower low   A swing low that is lower than a previous swing low.

low 1, 2, 3, or 4   A low 1 is a bar with a low below the prior bar in a bear flag or near the top of a trading range. If there is then a bar with a higher low (it can occur one or several bars later), the next bar in this correction whose low is below the prior bar's low is a low 2. Third and fourth occurrences are a low 3 and 4. A low 3 is a wedge bear flag variant.

major trend line   Any trend line that contains most of the price action on the screen and is typically drawn using bars that are at least 10 bars apart.

major trend reversal   A reversal from a bull to a bear trend or from a bear trend to a bull trend. The setup must include a test of the old trend extreme after a break of the trend line.

meltdown   A sell-off in a bear spike or a tight bear channel without significant pullbacks and that extends further than the fundamentals would dictate.

melt-up   A rally in a bull spike or a tight bull channel without significant pullbacks and that extends further than the fundamentals would dictate.

micro   Any traditional pattern can form over one to about five bars and still be valid, although easily overlooked. When it forms, it is a micro version of the pattern. Every micro pattern is a traditional pattern on a smaller time frame chart, and every traditional pattern is a micro pattern on a higher time frame chart.

micro channel   A very tight channel where most of the bars have their highs and lows touching the trend line and, often, also the trend channel line. It is the most extreme form of a tight channel, and it has no pullbacks or only one or two small pullbacks.

micro double bottom   Consecutive or nearly consecutive bars with lows that are near the same price.

micro double top   Consecutive or nearly consecutive bars with highs that are near the same price.

micro measuring gap   When the bar before and the bar after a strong trend bar do not overlap, this is a sign of strength and often leads to a measured move. For example, if there is a strong bull trend bar and the low of the bar after it is at or above the high of the bar before it, the midpoint between that low and that high is the micro measuring gap.

micro trend channel line   A trend channel line drawn across the highs or lows of three to five consecutive bars.

micro trend line breakout   A trend line on any time frame that is drawn across from two to about 10 bars where most of the bars touch or are close to the trend line, and then one of the bars has a false breakout through the trend line. This false breakout sets up a with-trend entry. If it fails within a bar or two, then there is usually a countertrend trade.

money stop   A stop based on a fixed dollar amount or number of points, like two points in the Eminis or a dollar in a stock.

moving average   The charts in this book use a 20-bar exponential moving average, but any moving average can be useful.

moving average gap bar (gap bar)   A bar that does not touch the moving average. The space between the bar and the moving average is the gap. The first pullback in a strong trend that results in a moving average gap bar is usually followed by a test of the trend's extreme. For example, when there is a strong bull trend and there is a pullback that finally has a bar with a high below the moving average, this is often a buy setup for a test of the high of the trend.

nesting   Sometimes a pattern has a smaller version of a comparable pattern "nested" within it. For example, it is common for the right shoulder of a head and shoulders top to be either a small head and shoulders top or a double top.

news   Useless information generated by the media for the sole purpose of selling advertising and making money for the media company. It is unrelated to trading, is impossible to evaluate, and should always be ignored.

oio   Outside-inside-outside, an outside bar followed by an inside bar, followed by an outside bar.

oo   Outside-outside, an outside bar followed by a larger outside bar.

opening reversal   A reversal in the first hour or so of the day.

outside bar   A bar with a high that is above or at the high of the prior bar and a low that is below the low of the prior bar, or a bar with a low that is below or at the low of the prior bar and a high that is above the high of the prior bar.

outside down bar   An outside bar with a close below its open.

outside up bar   An outside bar with a close above its open.

overshoot   The market surpasses a prior price of significance like a swing point or a trend line.

pause bar   A bar that does not extend the trend. In a bull trend, a pause bar has a high that is at or below the prior bar, or a small bar with a high that is only a tick or so higher than the previous bar when the previous bar is a strong bull trend bar. It is a type of pullback.

pip   A tick in the foreign exchange (forex) market. However, some data vendors provide quotes with an extra decimal place, which should be ignored.

pressing their longs   In a bull trend, bulls add to their longs as in a bull spike and as the market breaks out to a new high, because they expect another leg up to about a measured move.

pressing their shorts   In a bear trend, bears add to their shorts in a bear spike and as the market breaks out to a new low, because they expect another leg down to about a measured move.

price action   Any change in price on any chart type or time frame.

probability   The chance of success. For example, if a trader looks back at the most recent 100 times a certain setup led to a trade and finds that it led to a profitable trade 60 times, then that would indicate that the setup has about a 60 percent probability of success. There are many variables that can never be fully tested, so probabilities are only approximations and at times can be very misleading.

probably   At least 60 percent certain.

pullback   A temporary pause or countertrend move that is part of a trend, swing, or leg and does not retrace beyond the start of the trend, swing, or leg. It is a small trading range where traders expect the trend to resume soon. For example, a bear pullback is a sideways to upward move in a bear trend, swing, or leg that will be followed by at least a test of the prior low. It can be as small as a one-tick move above the high of the prior bar or it can even be a pause, like an inside bar.

pullback bar   A bar that reverses the prior bar by at least one tick. In an uptrend, it is a bar with a low below that of the prior bar.

reasonable   A setup with a favorable trader's equation.

reversal   A change to an opposite type of behavior. Most technicians use the term to mean a change from a bull trend to a bear trend or from a bear trend to a bull trend. However, trading range behavior is opposite to trending behavior, so when a trend becomes a trading range, this is also a reversal. When a trading range becomes a trend, it is a reversal but is usually called a breakout.

reversal bar   A trend bar in the opposite direction of the trend. When a bear leg is reversing up, a bull reversal bar is a bull trend bar, and the classic description includes a tail at the bottom and a close above the open and near the top. A bear reversal bar is a bear trend bar in a bull leg, and the traditional description includes a tail at the top and a close below the open and near the bottom.

reward   The number of ticks that a trader expects to make from a trade. For example, if the trader exits with a limit order at a profit target, it is the number of ticks between the entry price and the profit target.

risk   The number of ticks from a trader's entry price to a protective stop. It is the minimum that the trader will lose if a trade goes against him (slippage and other factors can make the actual risk greater than the theoretical risk).

risk off   When traders think that the stock market will fall, they become risk averse, sell out of volatile stocks and currencies, and transition into safe-haven investments, like Johnson & Johnson (JNJ), Altria Group (MO), Procter & Gamble (PG), the U.S. dollar, and the Swiss franc.

risk on   When traders think that the stock market is strong, they are willing to take more risks and invest in stocks that tend to rise faster than the overall market, and invest in more volatile currencies, like the Australian dollar or the Swedish krona.

risky   When the trader's equation is unclear or barely favorable for a trade. It can also mean that the probability of success for a trade is 50 percent or less, regardless of the risk and potential reward.

scalp   A trade that is exited with a small profit, usually before there are any pullbacks. In the Emini, when the average range is about 10 to 15 points, a scalp trade is usually any trade where the goal is less than four points. For the SPY or stocks, it might be 10 to 30 cents. For more expensive stocks, it can be $1 to $2. Since the profit is often smaller than the risk, a trader has to win at least 70 percent of the time, which is an unrealistic goal for most traders. Traders should take trades only where the potential reward is at least as great as the risk unless they are extremely skilled.

scalper   A trader who primarily scalps for small profits, usually using a tight stop.

scalper's profit   A typical amount of profit that a scalper would be targeting.

scratch   A trade that is close to breakeven with either a small profit or a loss.

second entry   The second time within a few bars of the first entry where there is an entry bar based on the same logic as the first entry. For example, if a breakout above a wedge bull flag fails and pulls back to a double bottom bull flag, this pullback sets up a second buy signal for the wedge bull flag.

second moving average gap bar setup   If there is a first moving average gap bar and a reversal toward the moving average does not reach the moving average, and instead the move away from the moving average continues, it is the next reversal in the direction of the moving average.

second signal   The second time within a few bars of the first signal where there is a setup based on the same logic as the first signal.

selling pressure   Strong bears are asserting themselves and their selling is creating bear trend bars, bars with tails at the tops, and two-bar bear reversals. The effect is cumulative and usually is eventually followed by lower prices.

setup   A pattern of one or more bars used by traders as the basis to place entry orders. If an entry order is filled, the last bar of the setup becomes the signal bar. Most setups are just a single bar.

shaved body   A candle with no tail at one or both ends. A shaved top has no tail at the top and a shaved bottom has no tail at the bottom.

short   As a verb, to sell a stock or futures contract to initiate a new position (not to exit a prior purchase). As a noun, a person who sells something short, or the actual position itself.

shrinking stairs   A stairs pattern where the most recent breakout is smaller than the previous one. It is a series of three or more trending highs in a bull trend or lows in a bear trend where each breakout to a new extreme is by fewer ticks than the prior breakout, indicating waning momentum. It can be a three-push pattern, but it does not have to resemble a wedge and can be any series of broad swings in a trend.

signal bar   The bar immediately before the bar in which an entry order is filled (the entry bar). It is the final bar of a setup.

smaller time frame (STF)   A chart covering the same amount of time as the current chart, but having more bars. For example, compared to the day session 5 minute Emini chart on an average day, examples of smaller time frame charts include a 1 minute chart, a tick chart with 500 ticks per bar, and a volume chart with 1,000 contracts per bar (each of these charts usually has more than 200 bars on an average day, compared to the 81 bars on the 5 minute chart).

smart traders   Consistently profitable traders who are usually trading large positions and are generally on the right side of the market.

spike and channel   A breakout into a trend in which the follow-through is in the form of a channel where the momentum is less and there is two-sided trading taking place.

stair A push to a new extreme in a trending trading range trend or a broad channel trend where there is a series of three or more trending swings that resembles a sloping trading range and is roughly contained in a channel. After the breakout, there is a breakout pullback that retraces at least slightly into the prior trading range, which is not a requirement of other trending trading ranges. Two-way trading is taking place but one side is in slightly more control, accounting for the slope.

STF See *smaller time frame (STF)*.

strong bulls and bears Institutional traders and their cumulative buying and selling determine the direction of the market.

success Refers to traders achieving their objective. Their profit target was reached before their protective stop was hit.

swing A smaller trend that breaks a trend line of any size; the term is used only when there are at least two on the chart. They can occur within a larger trend or in a sideways market.

swing high A bar that looks like a spike up on the chart and extends up beyond the neighboring bars. Its high is at or above that of the bar before it and that of the bar after it.

swing high/low Either a swing high or a swing low.

swing low A bar that looks like a spike down on the chart and extends down beyond the neighboring bars. Its low is at or below that of the bar before it and that of the bar after it.

swing point Either a swing high or a swing low.

swing trade For a day trader using a short-term intraday chart like the 5 minute, it is any trade that lasts longer than a scalp and that the trader will hold through one or more pullbacks. For a trader using higher time frame charts, it is a trade that lasts for hours to several days. Typically, at least part of the trade is held without a profit target, since the trader is hoping for an extended move. The potential reward is usually at least as large as the risk. Small swing trades are called scalps by many traders. In the Emini, when the average range is about 10 to 15 points, a swing trade is usually any trade where the goal is four or more points.

test When the market approaches a prior price of significance and can overshoot or undershoot the target. The term *failed test* is used to mean opposite things by different traders. Most traders believe that if the market then reverses, the test was successful, and if it does not and the move continues beyond the test area, the test failed and a breakout has occurred.

three pushes Three swing highs where each swing high is usually higher or three swing lows where each swing low is usually lower. It trades the same as a wedge and should be considered a variant. When it is part of a flag, the move can be mostly horizontal and each push does not have to extend beyond the prior one. For example, in a wedge bull flag or any other type of triangle, the second push down can be at, above, or below the first, and the third push down can be at, above, or below either the second or the first, or both.

tick   The smallest unit of price movement. For most stocks, it is one penny; for 10-Year U.S. Treasury Note Futures, it is 1/64th of a point; and for Eminis, it is 0.25 points. On tick charts and on time and sales tables, a tick is every trade that takes place no matter the size and even if there is no price change. If you look at a time and sales table, every trade is counted as one tick when TradeStation charting software creates a tick chart.

tight channel   A channel where the trend line and trend channel line are close together, and the pullbacks are small and last for only one to three bars.

tight trading range   A trading range of two or more bars with lots of overlap in the bars and in which most reversals are too small to trade profitably with stop entries. The bulls and bears are in balance.

time frame   The length of time contained in one bar on the chart (a 5 minute time frame is made of bars that close every five minutes). It can also refer to bars not based on time, such as those based on volume or the number of ticks traded.

tradable   A setup that you believe has a reasonable chance of leading to at least a scalper's profit.

trader's equation   To take a trade, you must believe that the probability of success times the potential reward is greater than the probability of failure times the risk. You set the reward and risk because the potential reward is the distance to your profit target and the risk is the distance to your stop. The difficulty in solving the equation is assigning a value to the probability, which can never be known with certainty. As a guideline, if you are uncertain, assume that you have a 50 percent chance of winning or losing, and if you are confident, assume that you have a 60 percent chance of winning and a 40 percent chance of losing.

trading range   The minimum requirement is a single bar with a range that is largely overlapped by the bar before it. It is sideways movement and neither the bull nor the bears are in control, although one side is often stronger. It is often a pullback in a trend where the pullback has lasted long enough to lose most of its certainty. In other words, traders have become uncertain about the direction of the breakout in the short term, and the market will have repeated breakout attempts up and down that will fail. It will usually ultimately break out in the direction of the trend, and is a pullback on a higher time frame chart.

trailing a stop   As the trade becomes increasingly profitable, traders will often move, or trail, the protective stop to protect more of their open profit. For example, if they are long in a bull trend, every time the market moves to a new high, they might raise the protective stop to just below the most recent higher low.

trap   An entry that immediately reverses to the opposite direction before a scalper's profit target is reached, trapping traders in their new position and ultimately forcing them to cover at a loss. It can also scare traders out of a good trade.

trapped in a trade   A trader with an open loss on a trade that did not result in a scalper's profit, and if there is a pullback beyond the entry or signal bars, the trader will likely exit with a loss.

trapped out of a trade   A pullback that scares a trader into exiting a trade, but then the pullback fails. The move quickly resumes in the direction of the trade, making it difficult emotionally for the trader to get back in at the worse price that is now available. The trader will have to chase the market.

trend   A series of price changes that are either mostly up (a bull trend) or down (a bear trend). There are three loosely defined smaller versions: swings, legs, and pullbacks. A chart will show only one or two major trends. If there are more, one of the other terms is more appropriate.

trend bar   A bar with a body, which means that the close was above or below the open, indicating that there is at least a minor price movement.

trend channel line   A line in the direction of the trend but drawn on the opposite side of the bars compared to a trend line. A bull trend channel line is above the highs and rising to the right, and a bear trend channel line is below the lows and falling to the right.

trend channel line overshoot   One or more bars penetrating a trend channel line.

trend channel line undershoot   A bar approaches a trend channel line but the market reverses away from the line without reaching or penetrating it.

trend from the open   A trend that begins at the first or one of the first bars of the day and extends for many bars without a pullback, and the start of the trend remains as one of the extremes of the day for much if not all of the day.

trending closes   Three or more bars where the closes are trending. In a bull trend, each close is above the prior close, and in a bear trend, each close is lower. If the pattern extends for many bars, there can be one or two bars where the closes are not trending.

trending highs or lows   The same as trending closes except based on the highs or lows of the bars.

trending swings Three or more swings where the swing highs and lows are both higher than the prior swing highs and lows (trending bull swings), or both lower (trending bear swings).

trending trading ranges Two or more trading ranges separated by a breakout.

trend line A line drawn in the direction of the trend; it is sloped up and is below the bars in a bull trend, and it is sloped down and is above the bars in a bear trend. Most often, it is constructed from either swing highs or swing lows but can be based on linear regression or just a best fit (eyeballing).

trend reversal A trend change from up to down or down to up, or from a trend to a trading range.

20 moving average gap bars Twenty or more consecutive bars that have not touched the moving average. Once the market finally touches the moving average, it usually creates a setup for a test of the trend's extreme.

undershoot The market approaches but does not reach a prior price of significance like a swing point or a trend line.

unlikely At most 40 percent certain.

unreasonable A setup with an unfavorable trader's equation.

usually At least 60 percent certain.

vacuum A buy vacuum occurs when the strong bears believe that the price will soon be higher so they wait to short until it reaches some magnet above the market. The result is that there is a vacuum that sucks the market quickly up to the magnet in the form of one or more bull trend bars. Once there, the strong bears sell aggressively and turn the market down. A sell vacuum occurs when the strong bulls believe that the market will soon be lower so they wait to buy until it falls to some magnet below the market. The result is that there is a vacuum that sucks the market down quickly to the magnet in the form of one or more bear trend bars. Once there, strong bulls buy aggressively and turn the market back up.

wedge Traditionally, a three-push move with each push extending further and the trend line and trend channel line at least minimally convergent, creating a rising or descending triangle with a wedge shape. For a trader, the wedge shape increases the chances of a successful trade, but any three-push pattern trades like a wedge and can be considered one. A wedge can be a reversal pattern or a pullback in a trend (a bull or bear flag).

wedge flag A wedge-shaped or three-push pullback in a trend, such as a high 3 in a bull trend (a type of bull flag) or a low 3 in a bear trend (a type of bear flag). Since it is a with-trend setup, enter on the first signal.

wedge reversal A wedge that is reversing a bull trend into a bear trend or a bear trend into a bull trend. Since it is countertrend, unless it is very strong, it is better to take a second signal. For example, if there is a bear trend and then a descending wedge, wait for a breakout above this potential wedge bottom and then try to buy a pullback to a higher low.

with trend   Refers to a trade or a setup that is in the direction of the prevailing trend. In general, the direction of the most recent 5 minute chart signal should be assumed to be the trend's direction. Also, if most of the past 10 or 20 bars are above the moving average, trend setups and trades are likely on the buy side.

Trading
Price
Action
TRADING
RANGES

Introduction

There is a reason why there is no other comprehensive book about price action written by a trader. It takes thousands of hours, and the financial reward is meager compared to that from trading. However, with my three girls now away in grad school, I have a void to fill and this has been a very satisfying project. I originally planned on updating the first edition of *Reading Price Charts Bar by Bar* (John Wiley & Sons, 2009), but as I got into it, I decided instead to go into great detail about how I view and trade the markets. I am metaphorically teaching you how to play the violin. Everything you need to know to make a living at it is in these books, but it is up to you to spend the countless hours learning your trade. After a year of answering thousands of questions from traders on my website at www.brookspriceaction.com, I think that I have found ways to express my ideas much more clearly, and these books should be easier to read than that one. The earlier book focused on reading price action, and this series of books is instead centered on how to use price action to trade the markets. Since the book grew to more than four times as many words as the first book, John Wiley & Sons decided to divide it into three separate books. This first book covers price action basics and trends. The second book is on trading ranges, order management, and the mathematics of trading, and the final book is about trend reversals, day trading, daily charts, options, and the best setups for all time frames. Many of the charts are also in *Reading Price Charts Bar by Bar*, but most have been updated and the discussion about the charts has also been largely rewritten. Only about 5 percent of the 120,000 words from that book are present in the 570,000 words in this new series, so readers will find little duplication.

My goals in writing this series of three books are to describe my understanding of why the carefully selected trades offer great risk/reward ratios, and to present ways to profit from the setups. I am presenting material that I hope will be interesting to professional traders and students in business school, but I also hope that even traders starting out will find some useful ideas. Everyone looks at price charts but usually just briefly and with a specific or limited goal. However, every chart has an incredible amount of information that can be used to make profitable trades, but much of it can be used effectively only if traders spend time to carefully understand what each bar on the chart is telling them about what institutional money is doing.

Ninety percent or more of all trading in large markets is done by institutions, which means that the market is simply a collection of institutions. Almost all are profitable over time, and the few that are not soon go out of business. Since institutions are profitable and they are the market, every trade that you take has a profitable trader (a part of the collection of institutions) taking the other side of your trade. No trade can take place without one institution willing to take one side and another willing to take the other. The small-volume trades made by individuals can only take place if an institution is willing to take the same trade. If you want to buy at a certain price, the market will not get to that price unless one or more institutions also want to buy at that price. You cannot sell at any price unless one or more institutions are willing to sell there, because the market can only go to a price where there are institutions willing to buy and others willing to sell. If the Emini is at 1,264 and you are long with a protective sell stop at 1,262, your stop cannot get hit unless there is an institution who is also willing to sell at 1,262. This is true for virtually all trades.

If you trade 200 Emini contracts, then you are trading institutional volume and are effectively an institution, and you will sometimes be able to move the market a tick or two. Most individual traders, however, have no ability to move the market, no matter how stupidly they are willing to trade. The market will not run your stops. The market might test the price where your protective stop is, but it has nothing to do with your stop. It will only test that price if one or more institutions believe that it is financially sound to sell there and other institutions believe that it is profitable to buy there. At every tick, there are institutions buying and other institutions selling, and all have proven systems that will make money by placing those trades. You should always be trading in the direction of the majority of institutional dollars because they control where the market is heading.

At the end of the day when you look at a printout of the day's chart, how can you tell what the institutions did during the day? The answer is simple: whenever the market went up, the bulk of institutional money was buying, and whenever the market went down, more money went into selling. Just look at any segment of the chart where the market went up or down and study every bar, and you will soon notice many repeatable patterns. With time, you will begin to see those patterns unfold in real time, and that will give you confidence to place your trades. Some of the price action is subtle, so be open to every possibility. For example, sometimes when the market is working higher, a bar will trade below the low of the prior bar, yet the trend continues higher. You have to assume that the big money was buying at and below the low of that prior bar, and that is also what many experienced traders were doing. They bought exactly where weak traders let themselves get stopped out with a loss or where other weak traders shorted, believing that the market was beginning to sell off. Once you get comfortable with the idea that strong trends often have pullbacks and big money is buying them rather than selling them, you will be in a position to make some great trades that you previously thought were exactly the wrong thing to do. Don't think too hard about it. If the market is going up, institutions are buying constantly, even at times when you think that you should stop yourself out of your long with a loss. Your job is to follow their behavior and not use too much logic to deny what is happening right in front of you. It does not matter if it seems counterintuitive. All that matters is that the market is going up and therefore institutions are predominantly buying and so should you.

Institutions are generally considered to be smart money, meaning that they are smart enough to make a living by trading and they trade a large volume every day. Television still uses the term *institution* to refer to traditional institutions like mutual funds, banks, brokerage houses, insurance companies, pension funds, and hedge funds; these companies used to account for most of the volume, and they mostly trade on fundamentals. Their trading controls the direction of the market on daily and weekly charts and a lot of the big intraday swings. Until a decade or so ago, most of the trade decisions were made and most trading was done by very smart traders, but it is now increasingly being done by computers. They have programs that can instantly analyze economic data and immediately place trades based on that analysis, without a person ever being involved in the trade. In addition, other firms trade huge volumes by using computer programs that place trades based on the statistical analysis of price action. Computer-generated trading now accounts for as much as 70 percent of the day's volume.

Computers are very good at making decisions, and playing chess and winning at *Jeopardy!* are more difficult than trading stocks. Gary Kasparov for years made the best chess decisions in the world, yet a computer made better decisions in 1997 and beat him. Ken Jennings was heralded as the greatest *Jeopardy!* player of all time, yet a computer destroyed him in 2011. It is only a matter of time before computers are widely accepted as the best decision makers for institutional trading.

Since programs use objective mathematical analysis, there should be a tendency for support and resistance areas to become more clearly defined. For example, measured move projections should become more precise as more of the volume is traded based on precise mathematical logic. Also, there might be a tendency toward more protracted tight channels as programs buy small pullbacks on the daily chart. However, if enough programs exit longs or go short at the same key levels, sell-offs might become larger and faster. Will the changes be dramatic? Probably not, since the same general forces were operating when everything was done manually, but nonetheless there should be some move toward mathematical perfection as more of the emotion is removed from trading. As these other firms contribute more and more to the movement of the market and as traditional institutions increasingly use computers to analyze and place their trades, the term *institution* is becoming vague. It is better for an individual trader to think of an institution as any of the different entities that trade enough volume to be a significant contributor to the price action.

Since these buy and sell programs generate most of the volume, they are the most important contributor to the appearance of every chart and they create most of the trading opportunities for individual investors. Yes, it's nice to know that Cisco Systems (CSCO) had a strong earnings report and is moving up, and if you are an investor who wants to hold stock for many months, then do what the traditional institutions are doing and buy CSCO. However, if you are a day trader, ignore the news and look at the chart, because the programs will create patterns that are purely statistically based and have nothing to do with fundamentals, yet offer great trading opportunities. The traditional institutions placing trades based on fundamentals determine the direction and the approximate target of a stock over the next several months, but, increasingly, firms using statistical analysis to make day trades and other short-term trades determine the path to that target and the ultimate high or low of the move. Even on a macro level, fundamentals are only approximate at best. Look at the crashes in 1987 and 2009. Both had violent selloffs and rallies, yet the fundamentals did not change violently in the same short period of time. In both cases, the market got sucked slightly below the monthly trend line and reversed sharply up from it. The market fell because of perceived fundamentals, but the extent of the fall was determined by the charts.

There are some large patterns that repeat over and over on all time frames and in all markets, like trends, trading ranges, climaxes, and channels. There are also lots of smaller tradable patterns that are based on just the most recent few bars. These books are a comprehensive guide to help traders understand everything they see on a chart, giving them more opportunities to make profitable trades and to avoid losers.

The most important message that I can deliver is to focus on the absolute best trades, avoid the absolute worst setups, use a profit objective (reward) that is at least as large as your protective stop (risk), and work on increasing the number of shares that you are trading. I freely recognize that every one of my reasons behind each setup is just my opinion, and my reasoning about why a trade works might be completely wrong. However, that is irrelevant. What is important is that reading price action is a very effective way to trade, and I have thought a lot about why certain things happen the way they do. I am comfortable with my explanations and they give me confidence when I place a trade; however, they are irrelevant to my placing trades, so it is not important to me that they are right. Just as I can reverse my opinion about the direction of the market in an instant, I can also reverse my opinion about why a particular pattern works if I come across a reason that is more logical or if I discover a flaw in my logic. I am providing the opinions because they appear to make sense, they might help readers become more comfortable trading certain setups, and they might be intellectually stimulating, but they are not needed for any price action trades.

The books are very detailed and difficult to read and are directed toward serious traders who want to learn as much as they can about reading price charts. However, the concepts are useful to traders at all levels. The books cover many of the standard techniques described by Robert D. Edwards and John Magee (*Technical Analysis of Stock Trends*, AMACOM, 9th ed., 2007) and others, but focus more on individual bars to demonstrate how the information they provide can significantly enhance the risk/reward ratio of trading. Most books point out three or four trades on a chart, which implies that everything else on the chart is incomprehensible, meaningless, or risky. I believe that there is something to be learned from every tick that takes place during the day and that there are far more great trades on every chart than just the few obvious ones; but to see them, you have to understand price action and you cannot dismiss any bars as unimportant. I learned from performing thousands of operations through a microscope that some of the most important things can be very small.

I read charts bar by bar and look for any information that each bar is telling me. They are all important. At the end of every bar, most traders ask themselves, "What just took place?" With most bars, they conclude that there is nothing worth trading at the moment so it is just not worth the effort to try to understand. Instead, they choose to wait for some clearer and usually larger pattern. It is as if they believe that the bar did not exist, or they dismiss it as just institutional program activity that is not tradable by an individual trader. They do not feel like they are part of the market at these times, but these times constitute the vast majority of the day. Yet, if they look at the volume, all of those bars that they are ignoring have as much volume as the bars they are using for the bases for their trades. Clearly, a lot of trading is taking place, but they don't understand how that can be and essentially pretend that it does not exist. But that is denying reality. There is always trading taking place, and as a trader, you owe it to yourself to understand why it's taking place and to figure out a way to make money off of it. Learning what the market is telling you is very time-consuming and difficult, but it gives you the foundation that you need to be a successful trader.

Unlike most books on candle charts where the majority of readers feel compelled to memorize patterns, these three books of mine provide a rationale for why particular patterns are reliable setups for traders. Some of the terms used have specific meaning to market technicians but different meanings to traders, and I am writing this entirely from a trader's perspective. I am certain that many traders already understand everything in these books, but likely wouldn't describe price action in the same way that I do. There are no secrets among successful traders; they all know common setups, and many have their own names for each one. All of them are buying and selling pretty much at the same time, catching the same swings, and they all have their own reasons for getting into a trade. Many trade price action intuitively without ever feeling a need to articulate why a certain setup works. I hope that they enjoy reading my understanding of and perspective on price action and that this gives them some insights that will improve their already successful trading.

The goal for most traders is to maximize trading profits through a style that is compatible with their personalities. Without that compatibility, I believe that it is virtually impossible to trade profitably for the long term. Many traders wonder how long it will take them to be successful and are willing to lose money for some period of time, even a few years. However, it took me over 10 years to be able to trade successfully. Each of us has many considerations and distractions, so the time will vary, but a trader has to work though most obstacles before becoming consistently profitable. I had several major problems that had to be corrected, including raising three wonderful daughters who always filled my mind with thoughts of them and what I needed to be doing as their father. That was solved as they got older and more independent. Then it took me a long time to accept many personality traits as real and unchangeable (or at least I concluded that I was unwilling to change them). And finally there was the issue of confidence. I have always been confident to the point of arrogance in so many things that those who know me would be surprised that this was difficult for me. However, deep inside I believed that I really would never come up with a consistently profitable approach that I would enjoy employing for many years. Instead, I bought many systems, wrote and tested countless indicators and systems, read many books and magazines, went to seminars, hired tutors, and joined chat rooms. I talked with people who presented themselves as successful traders, but I never saw their account statements and suspect that most could teach but few, if any, could trade. Usually in trading, those who know don't talk and those who talk don't know.

This was all extremely helpful because it showed all of the things that I needed to avoid before becoming successful. Any nontrader who looks at a chart will invariably conclude that trading has to be extremely easy, and that is part of the appeal. At the end of the day, anyone can look at any chart and see very clear entry and exit points. However, it is much more difficult to do it in real time. There is a natural tendency to want to buy the exact low and never have the trade come back. If it does, a novice will take the loss to avoid a bigger loss, resulting in a series of losing trades that will ultimately bust the trader's account. Using wide stops solves that to some extent, but invariably traders will soon hit a few big losses that will put them into the red and make them too scared to continue using that approach.

Should you be concerned that making the information in these books available will create lots of great price action traders, all doing the same thing at the same time, thereby removing the late entrants needed to drive the market to your price target? No, because the institutions control the market and they already have the smartest traders in the world and those traders already know everything in these books, at least intuitively. At every moment, there is an extremely smart institutional bull taking the opposite side of the trade being placed by an extremely smart institutional bear. Since the most important players already know price action, having more players know it will not tip the balance one way or the other. I therefore have no concern that what I am writing will stop price action from working. Because of that balance, any edge that anyone has is always going to be extremely small, and any small mistake will result in a loss, no matter how well a person reads a chart. Although it is very difficult to make money as a trader without understanding price action, that knowledge alone is not enough. It takes a long time to learn how to trade *after* a trader learns to read charts, and trading is just as difficult as chart reading. I wrote these books to help people learn to read charts better and to trade better, and if you can do both well, you deserve to be able to take money from the accounts of others and put it into yours.

The reason why the patterns that we all see do unfold as they do is because that is the appearance that occurs in an efficient market with countless traders placing orders for thousands of different reasons, but with the controlling volume being traded based on sound logic. That is just what it looks like, and it has been that way forever. The same patterns unfold in all time frames in all markets around the world, and it would simply be impossible for all of it to be manipulated instantaneously on so many different levels. Price action is a manifestation of human behavior and therefore actually has a genetic basis. Until we evolve, it will likely remain largely unchanged, just as it has been unchanged for the 80 years of charts that I have reviewed. Program trading might have changed the appearance slightly, although I can find no evidence to support that theory. If anything, it would make the charts smoother because it is unemotional and it has greatly increased the volume. Now that most of the volume is being traded automatically by computers and the volume is so huge, irrational and emotional behavior is an insignificant component of the markets and the charts are a purer expression of human tendencies.

Since price action comes from our DNA, it will not change until we evolve. When you look at the two charts in Figure I.1, your first reaction is that they are just a couple of ordinary charts, but look at the dates at the bottom. These weekly Dow Jones Industrial Average charts from the Depression era and from World War II have the same patterns that we see today on all charts, despite most of today's volume being traded by computers.

If everyone suddenly became a price action scalper, the smaller patterns might change a little for a while, but over time, the efficient market will win out and the votes by all traders will get distilled into standard price action patterns because that is the inescapable result of countless people behaving logically. Also, the reality is that it is very difficult to trade well, and although basing trades on price action is a sound approach, it is still very difficult to do successfully in real time.

FIGURE I.1 Price Action Has Not Changed over Time

There just won't be enough traders doing it well enough, all at the same time, to have any significant influence over time on the patterns. Just look at Edwards and Magee. The best traders in the world have been using those ideas for decades and they continue to work, again for the same reason—charts look the way they do because that is the unchangeable fingerprint of an efficient market filled with a huge number of smart people using a huge number of approaches and time frames, all trying to make the most money that they can. For example, Tiger Woods is not hiding anything that he does in golf, and anyone is free to copy him. However, very few people can play golf well enough to make a living at it. The same is true of trading. A trader can know just about everything there is to know and still lose money because applying all that knowledge in a way that consistently makes money is very difficult to do.

Why do so many business schools continue to recommend Edwards and Magee when their book is essentially simplistic, largely using trend lines, breakouts, and pullbacks as the basis for trading? It is because it works and it always has and it always will. Now that just about all traders have computers with access to intraday data, many of those techniques can be adapted to day trading. Also, candle charts give additional information about who is controlling the market, which results in a more timely entry with smaller risk. Edwards and Magee's focus is on the overall trend. I use those same basic techniques but pay much closer attention to the individual bars on the chart to improve the risk/reward ratio, and I devote considerable attention to intraday charts.

It seemed obvious to me that if one could simply read the charts well enough to be able to enter at the exact times when the move would take off and not come back, then that trader would have a huge advantage. The trader would have a high winning percentage, and the few losses would be small. I decided that this would be my starting point, and what I discovered was that nothing had to be added. In fact, any additions are distractions that result in lower profitability. This sounds so obvious and easy that it is difficult for most people to believe.

I am a day trader who relies entirely on price action on the intraday Emini S&P 500 Futures charts, and I believe that reading price action well is an invaluable skill for all traders. Beginners often instead have a deep-seated belief that something more is required, that maybe some complex mathematical formula that very few use would give them just the edge that they need. Goldman Sachs is so rich and sophisticated that its traders must have a supercomputer and high-powered software that gives them an advantage that ensures that all the individual traders are doomed to failure. They start looking at all kinds of indicators and playing with the inputs to customize the indicators to make them just right. Every indicator works some of the time, but for me, they obfuscate instead of elucidate. In fact, without even looking at a chart, you can place a buy order and have a 50 percent chance of being right!

I am not dismissing indicators and systems out of ignorance of their subtleties. I have spent over 10,000 hours writing and testing indicators and systems over the years, and that probably is far more experience than most have. This extensive experience with indicators and systems was an essential part of my becoming a successful trader. Indicators work well for many traders, but the best success comes once a trader finds an approach that is compatible with his or her personality. My single biggest problem with indicators and systems was that I never fully trusted them. At every setup, I saw exceptions that needed to be tested. I always wanted every last penny out of the market and was never satisfied with a return from a system if I could incorporate a new twist that would make it better. You can optimize constantly, but, since the market is always changing from strong trends to tight trading ranges and then back again and your optimizations are based on what has recently happened, they will soon fail as the market transitions into a new phase. I am simply too controlling, compulsive, restless, observant, and untrusting to make money in the long term off indicators or automated systems, but I am at the extreme in many ways and most people don't have these same issues.

Many traders, especially beginners, are drawn to indicators (or any other higher power, guru, TV pundit, or newsletter that they want to believe will protect them and show their love and approval of them as human beings by giving them lots of money), hoping that an indicator will show them when to enter a trade. What they don't realize is that the vast majority of indicators are based on simple price action, and when I am placing trades, I simply cannot think fast enough to process what several indicators might be telling me. If there is a bull trend, a pullback, and then a rally to a new high, but the rally has lots of overlapping bars, many bear bodies, a couple of small pullbacks, and prominent tails on the tops of the bars, any experienced trader would see that it is a weak test of the trend high and that this should not be happening if the bull trend was still strong. The market is almost certainly transitioning into a trading range and possibly into a bear trend. Traders don't need an oscillator to tell them this. Also, oscillators tend to make traders look for reversals and focus less on price charts. These can be effective tools on most days when the market has two or three reversals lasting an hour or more. The problem comes when the market is trending strongly. If you focus too much on your indicators, you will see that they are forming divergences all day long and you might find yourself repeatedly entering countertrend and losing money. By the time you come to accept that the market is trending, you will not have enough time left in the day to recoup your losses. Instead, if you were simply looking at a bar or candle chart, you would see that the market is clearly trending and you would not be tempted by indicators to look for trend reversals. The most common successful reversals first break a trend line with strong momentum and then pull back to test the extreme, and if traders focus too much on divergences, they will often overlook this fundamental fact. Placing a trade because of a divergence in the absence of a prior countertrend momentum surge that breaks a trend line is a losing strategy. Wait for the trend line break and then see if the test of the old extreme reverses or if the old trend resumes. You do not need an indicator to tell you that a strong reversal here is a high-probability trade, at least for a scalp, and there will almost certainly be a divergence, so why complicate your thinking by adding the indicator to your calculus?

Some pundits recommend a combination of time frames, indicators, wave counting, and Fibonacci retracements and extensions, but when it comes time to place the trade, they will do it only if there is a good price action setup. Also, when they see a good price action setup, they start looking for indicators that show divergences, different time frames for moving average tests, wave counts, or Fibonacci setups to confirm what is in front of them. In reality, they are price action traders who are trading exclusively off price action on only one chart but don't feel comfortable admitting it. They are complicating their trading to the point that they certainly are missing many, many trades because their overanalysis takes too much time for them to place their orders and they are forced to wait for the next setup. The logic just isn't there for making the simple so complicated. Obviously, adding any information can lead to better decision making and many people might be able to process lots of inputs when deciding whether to place a trade. Ignoring data because of a simplistic ideology alone is foolish. The goal is to make money, and traders should do everything they can to maximize their profits. I simply cannot process multiple indicators and time frames well in the time needed to place my orders accurately, and I find that carefully reading a single chart is far more profitable for me. Also, if I rely on indicators, I find that I get lazy in my price action reading and often miss the obvious. Price action is far more important than any other information, and if you sacrifice some of what it is telling you to gain information from something else, you are likely making a bad decision.

One of the most frustrating things for traders when they are starting out is that everything is so subjective. They want to find a clear set of rules that guarantee a profit, and they hate how a pattern works on one day but fails on another. Markets are very efficient because you have countless very smart people playing a zero-sum game. For a trader to make money, he has to be consistently better than about half of the other traders out there. Since most of the competitors are profitable institutions, a trader has to be very good. Whenever an edge exists, it is quickly discovered and it disappears. Remember, someone has to be taking the opposite side of your trade. It won't take them long to figure out your magical system, and once they do, they will stop giving you money. Part of the appeal of trading is that it is a zero-sum game with very small edges, and it is intellectually satisfying and financially rewarding to be able to spot and capitalize on these small, fleeting opportunities. It can be done, but it is very hard work and it requires relentless discipline. Discipline simply means doing what you do not want to do. We are all intellectually curious and we have a natural tendency to try new or different things, but the very best traders resist the temptation. You have to stick to your rules and avoid emotion, and you have to patiently wait to take only the best trades. This all appears easy to do when you look at a printed chart at the end of the day, but it is very difficult in real time as you wait bar by bar, and sometimes hour by hour. Once a great setup appears, if you are distracted or lulled into complacency, you will miss it and you will then be forced to wait even longer. But if you can develop the patience and the discipline to follow a sound system, the profit potential is huge.

There are countless ways to make money trading stocks and Eminis, but all require movement (well, except for shorting options). If you learn to read the charts, you will catch a great number of these profitable trades every day without ever knowing why some institution started the trend and without ever knowing what any indicator is showing. You don't need these institutions' software or analysts because they will show you what they are doing. All you have to do is piggyback onto their trades and you will make a profit. Price action will tell you what they are doing and allow you an early entry with a tight stop.

I have found that I consistently make far more money by minimizing what I have to consider when placing a trade. All I need is a single chart on my laptop computer with no indicators except a 20-bar exponential moving average (EMA), which does not require too much analysis and clarifies many good setups each day. Some traders might also look at volume because an unusually large volume spike sometimes comes near the end of a bear trend, and the next new swing low or two often provide profitable long scalps. Volume spikes also sometimes occur on daily charts when a sell-off is overdone. However, it is not reliable enough to warrant my attention.

Many traders consider price action only when trading divergences and trend pullbacks. In fact, most traders using indicators won't take a trade unless there is a strong signal bar, and many would enter on a strong signal bar if the context was right, even if there was no divergence. They like to see a strong close on a large reversal bar, but in reality this is a fairly rare occurrence. The most useful tools for understanding price action are trend lines and trend channel lines, prior highs and lows, breakouts and failed breakouts, the sizes of bodies and tails on candles, and relationships between the current bar to the prior several bars. In particular, how the open, high, low, and close of the current bar compare to the action of the prior several bars tells a lot about what will happen next. Charts provide far more information about who is in control of the market than most traders realize. Almost every bar offers important clues as to where the market is going, and a trader who dismisses any activity as noise is passing up many profitable trades each day. Most of the observations in these books are directly related to placing trades, but a few have to do with simple curious price action tendencies without sufficient dependability to be the basis for a trade.

I personally rely mainly on candle charts for my Emini, futures, and stock trading, but most signals are also visible on any type of chart and many are even evident on simple line charts. I focus primarily on 5 minute candle charts to illustrate basic principles but also discuss daily and weekly charts as well. Since I also trade stocks, forex, Treasury note futures, and options, I discuss how price action can be used as the basis for this type of trading.

As a trader, I see everything in shades of gray and am constantly thinking in terms of probabilities. If a pattern is setting up and is not perfect but is reasonably similar to a reliable setup, it will likely behave similarly as well. Close is usually close enough. If something resembles a textbook setup, the trade will likely unfold in a way that is similar to the trade from the textbook setup. This is the art of trading and it takes years to become good at trading in the gray zone. Everyone wants concrete, clear rules or indicators, and chat rooms, newsletters, hotlines, or tutors that will tell them when exactly to get in to minimize risk and maximize profit, but none of it works in the long run. You have to take responsibility for your decisions, but you first have to learn how to make them and that means that you have to get used to operating in the gray fog. Nothing is ever as clear as black and white, and I have been doing this long enough to appreciate that anything, no matter how unlikely, can and will happen. It's like quantum physics. Every conceivable event has a probability, and so do events that you have yet to consider. It is not emotional, and the reasons why something happens are irrelevant. Watching to see if the Federal Reserve cuts rates today is a waste of time because there is both a bullish and bearish interpretation of anything that the Fed does. What is key is to see what the market does, not what the Fed does.

If you think about it, trading is a zero-sum game and it is impossible to have a zero-sum game where rules consistently work. If they worked, everyone would use them and then there would be no one on the other side of the trade. Therefore, the trade could not exist. Guidelines are very helpful but reliable rules cannot exist, and this is usually very troubling to a trader starting out who wants to believe that trading is a game that can be very profitable if only you can come up with just the right set of rules. All rules work some of the time, and usually just often enough to fool you into believing that you just need to tweak them a little to get them to work all of the time. You are trying to create a trading god who will protect you, but you are fooling yourself and looking for an easy solution to a game where only hard solutions work. You are competing against the smartest people in the world, and if you are smart enough to come up with a foolproof rule set, so are they, and then everyone is faced with the zero-sum game dilemma. You cannot make money trading unless you are flexible, because you need to go where the market is going, and the market is extremely flexible. It can bend in every direction and for much longer than most would ever imagine. It can also reverse repeatedly every few bars for a long, long time. Finally, it can and will do everything in between. Never get upset by this, and just accept it as reality and admire it as part of the beauty of the game.

The market gravitates toward uncertainty. During most of the day, every market has a directional probability of 50–50 of an equidistant move up or down. By that I mean that if you don't even look at a chart and you buy any stock and then place a one cancels the other (OCO) order to exit on a profit-taking limit order X cents above your entry or on a protective stop at X cents below your entry, you have about a 50 percent chance of being right. Likewise, if you sell any stock at any point in the day without looking at a chart and then place a profit-taking limit order X cents lower and a protective stop X cents higher, you have about a 50 percent chance of winning and about a 50 percent chance of losing. There is the obvious exception of X being too large relative the price of the stock. You can't have X be $60 in a $50 stock, because you would have a 0 percent chance of losing $60. You also can't have X be $49, because the odds of losing $49 would also be minuscule. But if you pick a value for X that is within reasonable reach on your time frame, this is generally true. When the market is 50–50, it is uncertain and you cannot rationally have an opinion about its direction. This is the hallmark of a trading range, so whenever you are uncertain, assume that the market is in a trading range. There are brief times on a chart when the directional probability is higher. During a strong trend, it might be 60 or even 70 percent, but that cannot last long because it will gravitate toward uncertainty and a 50–50 market where both the bulls and bears feel there is value. When there is a trend and some level of directional certainty, the market will also gravitate toward areas of support and resistance, which are usually some type of measured move away, and those areas are invariably where uncertainty returns and a trading range develops, at least briefly.

Never watch the news during the trading day. If you want to know what a news event means, the chart in front of you will tell you. Reporters believe that the news is the most important thing in the world, and that everything that happens has to be caused by their biggest news story of the day. Since reporters are in the news business, news must be the center of the universe and the cause of everything that happens in the financial markets. When the stock market sold off in mid-March 2011, they attributed it to the earthquake in Japan. It did not matter to them that the market began to sell off three weeks earlier, after a buy climax. I told the members of my chat room in late February that the odds were good that the market was going to have a significant correction when I saw 15 consecutive bull trend bars on the daily chart after a protracted bull run. This was an unusually strong buy climax, and an important statement by the market. I had no idea that an earthquake was going to happen in a few weeks, and did not need to know that, anyway. The chart was telling me what traders were doing; they were getting ready to exit their longs and initiate shorts.

Television experts are also useless. Invariably when the market makes a huge move, the reporter will find some confident, convincing expert who predicted it and interview him or her, leading the viewers to believe that this pundit has an uncanny ability to predict the market, despite the untold reality that this same pundit has been wrong in his last 10 predictions. The pundit then makes some future prediction and naïve viewers will attach significance to it and let it affect their trading. What the viewers may not realize is that some pundits are bullish 100 percent of the time and others are bearish 100 percent of the time, and still others just swing for the fences all the time and make outrageous predictions. The reporter just rushes to the one who is consistent with the day's news, which is totally useless to traders and in fact it is destructive because it can influence their trading and make them question and deviate from their own methods. No one is ever consistently right more than 60 percent of the time on these major predictions, and just because pundits are convincing does not make them reliable. There are equally smart and convincing people who believe the opposite but are not being heard. This is the same as watching a trial and listening to only the defense side of the argument. Hearing only one side is always convincing and always misleading, and rarely better than 50 percent reliable.

Institutional bulls and bears are placing trades all the time, and that is why there is constant uncertainty about the direction of the market. Even in the absence of breaking news, the business channels air interviews all day long and each reporter gets to pick one pundit for her report. What you have to realize is that she has a 50–50 chance of picking the right one in terms of the market's direction over the next hour or so. If you decide to rely on the pundit to make a trading decision and he says that the market will sell off after midday and instead it just keeps going up, are you going to look to short? Should you believe this very convincing head trader at one of Wall Street's top firms? He obviously is making over a million dollars a year and they would not pay him that much unless he was able to correctly and consistently predict the market's direction. In fact, he probably can and he is probably a good stock picker, but he almost certainly is not a day trader. It is foolish to believe that just because he can make 15 percent annually managing money he can correctly predict the market's direction over the next hour or two. Do the math. If he had that ability, he would be making 1 percent two or three times a day and maybe 1,000 percent a year. Since he is not, you know that he does not have that ability. His time frame is months and yours is minutes. Since he is unable to make money by day trading, why would you ever want to make a trade based on someone who is a proven failure as a day trader? He has shown you that he cannot make money by day trading by the simple fact that he is not a successful day trader. That immediately tells you that if he day trades, he loses money because if he was successful at it, that is what he would choose to do and he would make far more than he is currently making. Even if you are holding trades for months at a time in an attempt to duplicate the results of his fund, it is still foolish to take his advice, because he might change his mind next week and you would never know it. Managing a trade once you are in is just as important as placing the trade. If you are following the pundit and hope to make 15 percent a year like he does, you need to follow his management, but you have no ability to do so and you will lose over time employing this strategy. Yes, you will make an occasional great trade, but you can simply do that by randomly buying any stock. The key is whether the approach makes money over 100 trades, not over the first one or two. Follow the advice that you give your kids: don't fool yourself into believing that what you see on television is real, no matter how polished and convincing it appears to be.

As I said, there will be pundits who will see the news as bullish and others who will see it as bearish, and the reporter gets to pick one for her report. Are you going to let a reporter make trading decisions for you? That's insane! If that reporter could trade, she would be a trader and make hundreds of times more money than she is making as a reporter. Why would you ever allow her to influence your decision making? You might do so only out of a lack of confidence in your ability, or perhaps you are searching for a father figure who will love and protect you. If you are prone to be influenced by a reporter's decision, you should not take the trade. The pundit she chooses is not your father, and he will not protect you or your money. Even if the reporter picks a pundit who is correct on the direction, that pundit will not stay with you to manage your trade, and you will likely be stopped out with a loss on a pullback.

Financial news stations do not exist to provide public service. They are in business to make money, and that means they need as large an audience as possible to maximize their advertising income. Yes, they want to be accurate in their reporting, but their primary objective is to make money. They are fully aware that they can maximize their audience size only if they are pleasing to watch. That means that they have to have interesting guests, including some who will make outrageous predictions, others who are professorial and reassuring, and some who are just physically attractive; most of them have to have some entertainment value. Although some guests are great traders, they cannot help you. For example, if they interview one of the world's most successful bond traders, he will usually only speak in general terms about the trend over the next several months, and he will do so only weeks after he has already placed his trades. If you are a day trader, this does not help you, because every bull or bear market on the monthly chart has just about as many up moves on the intraday chart as down moves, and there will be long and short trades every day. His time frame is very different from yours, and his trading has nothing to do with what you are doing. They will also often interview a chartist from a major Wall Street firm, who, while his credentials are good, will be basing his opinion on a weekly chart, but the viewers are looking to take profits within a few days. To the chartist, that bull trend that he is recommending buying will still be intact, even if the market falls 10 percent over the next couple of months. The viewers, however, will take their losses long before that, and will never benefit from the new high that comes three months later. Unless the chartist is addressing your specific goals and time frame, whatever he says is useless. When television interviews a day trader instead, he will talk about the trades that he already took, and the information is too late to help you make money. By the time he is on television, the market might already be going in the opposite direction. If he is talking while still in his day trade, he will continue to manage his trade long after his two-minute interview is over, and he will not manage it while on the air. Even if you enter the trade that he is in, he will not be there when you invariably will have to make an important decision about getting out as the market turns against you, or as the market goes in your direction and you are thinking about taking profits. Watching television for trading advice under any circumstances, even after a very important report, is a sure way to lose money and you should never do it.

Only look at the chart and it will tell you what you need to know. The chart is what will give you money or take money from you, so it is the only thing that you should ever consider when trading. If you are on the floor, you can't even trust what your best friend is doing. He might be offering a lot of orange juice calls but secretly having a broker looking to buy 10 times as many below the market. Your friend is just trying to create a panic to drive the market down so he can load up through a surrogate at a much better price.

Friends and colleagues freely offer opinions for you to ignore. Occasionally traders will tell me that they have a great setup and want to discuss it with me. I invariably get them angry with me when I tell them that I am not interested. They immediately perceive me as selfish, stubborn, and close-minded, and when it comes to trading, I am all of that and probably much more. The skills that make you money are generally seen as flaws to the layperson. Why do I no longer read books or articles about trading, or talk to other traders about their ideas? As I said, the chart tells me all that I need to know and any other information is a distraction. Several people have been offended by my attitude, but I think in part it comes from me turning down what they are presenting as something helpful to me when in reality they are making an offering, hoping that I will reciprocate with some tutoring. They become frustrated and angry when I tell them that I don't want to hear about anyone else's trading techniques. I tell them that I haven't even mastered my own and probably never will, but I am confident that I will make far more money perfecting what I already know than trying to incorporate non-price-action approaches into my trading. I ask them if James Galway offered a beautiful flute to Yo-Yo Ma and insisted that Ma start learning to play the flute because Galway makes so much money by playing his flute, should Ma accept the offer? Clearly not. Ma should continue to play the cello and by doing so he will make far more money than if he also started playing the flute. I am no Galway or Ma, but the concept is the same. Price action is the only instrument that I want to play, and I strongly believe that I will make far more money by mastering it than by incorporating ideas from other successful traders.

The charts, not the experts on television, will tell you exactly how the institutions are interpreting the news.

Yesterday, Costco's earnings were up 32 percent on the quarter and above analysts' expectations (see Figure I.2). COST gapped up on the open, tested the gap on the first bar, and then ran up over a dollar in 20 minutes. It then drifted down to test yesterday's close. It had two rallies that broke bear trend lines, and both failed. This created a double top (bars 2 and 3) bear flag or triple top (bars 1, 2, and 3), and the market then plunged $3, below the prior day's low. If you were unaware of the report, you would have shorted at the failed bear trend line breaks at bars 2 and 3 and you would have sold more below bar 4, which was a pullback that followed the breakout below yesterday's low. You would have reversed to long on the bar 5 big reversal bar, which was the second attempt to reverse the breakout below yesterday's low and a climactic reversal of the breakout of the bottom of the steep bear trend channel line.

FIGURE I.2 Ignore the News

Alternatively, you could have bought the open because of the bullish report, and then worried about why the stock was collapsing instead of soaring the way the TV analysts predicted, and you likely would have sold out your long on the second plunge down to bar 5 with a $2 loss.

Any trend that covers a lot of points in very few bars, meaning that there is some combination of large bars and bars that overlap each other only minimally, will eventually have a pullback. These trends have such strong momentum that the odds favor resumption of the trend after the pullback and then a test of the trend's extreme. Usually the extreme will be exceeded, as long as the pullback does not turn into a new trend in the opposite direction and extend beyond the start of the original trend. In general, the odds that a pullback will get back to the prior trend's extreme fall substantially if the pullback retraces 75 percent or more. For a pullback in a bear trend, at that point, a trader is better off thinking of the pullback as a new bull trend rather than a pullback in an old bear trend. Bar 6 was about a 70 percent pullback and then the market tested the climactic bear low on the open of the next day.

Just because the market gaps up on a news item does not mean that it will continue up, despite how bullish the news is.

As shown in Figure I.3, before the open of bar 1 on both Yahoo! (YHOO) charts (daily on the left, weekly on the right), the news reported that Microsoft was

FIGURE I.3 Markets Can Fall on Bullish News

looking to take over Yahoo! at $31 a share, and the market gapped up almost to that price. Many traders assumed that it had to be a done deal because Microsoft is one of the best companies in the world and if it wanted to buy Yahoo!, it certainly could make it happen. Not only that—Microsoft has so much cash that it would likely be willing to sweeten the deal if needed. Well, the CEO of Yahoo! said that his company was worth more like $40 a share, but Microsoft never countered. The deal slowly evaporated, along with Yahoo!'s price. In October, Yahoo! was 20 percent below the price where it was before the deal was announced and 50 percent lower than on the day of the announcement, and it continues to fall. So much for strong fundamentals and a takeover offer from a serious suitor. To a price action trader, a huge up move in a bear market is probably just a bear flag, unless the move is followed by a series of higher lows and higher highs. It could be followed by a bull flag and then more of a rally, but until the bull trend is confirmed, you must be aware that the larger weekly trend is more important.

The only thing that is as it seems is the chart. If you cannot figure out what it is telling you, do not trade. Wait for clarity. It will always come. But once it is there, you must place the trade and assume the risk and follow your plan. Do not dial down to a 1 minute chart and tighten your stop, because you will lose. The problem with the 1 minute chart is that it tempts you by offering lots of entries with smaller bars and therefore smaller risk. However, you will not be able to take them all and you will instead cherry-pick, which will lead to the death of your account because you will invariably pick too many bad cherries. When you enter on a 5 minute chart, your trade is based on your analysis of the 5 minute chart without any idea of what the 1 minute chart looks like. You must therefore rely on your five-minute stops and targets, and just accept the reality that the 1 minute chart will move against you and hit a one-minute stop frequently. If you watch the 1 minute chart, you will not be devoting your full attention to the 5 minute chart and a good trader will take your money from your account and put it into his account. If you want to compete, you must minimize all distractions and all inputs other than what is on the chart in front of you, and trust that if you do you will make a lot of money. It will seem unreal but it is very real. Never question it. Just keep things simple and follow your simple rules. It is extremely difficult to consistently do something simple, but in my opinion, it is the best way to trade. Ultimately, as a trader understands price action better and better, trading becomes much less stressful and actually pretty boring, but much more profitable.

Although I never gamble (because the combination of odds, risk, and reward are against me, and I never want to bet against math), there are some similarities with gambling, especially in the minds of those who don't trade. Gambling is a game of chance, but I prefer to restrict the definition to situations where the odds are slightly against you and you will lose over time. Why this restriction? Because without it, every investment is a gamble since there is always an element of luck and a risk of total loss, even if you buy investment real estate, buy a home, start a business, buy a blue-chip stock, or even buy Treasury bonds (the government might choose to devalue the dollar to reduce the real size of our debt, and in so doing, the purchasing power of the dollars that you will get back from those bonds would be much less than when you originally bought the bonds).

Some traders use simple game theory and increase the size of a trade after one or more losing trades (this is called a martingale approach to trading). Blackjack card counters are very similar to trading range traders. The card counters are trying to determine when the math has gone too far in one direction. In particular, they want to know when the remaining cards in the deck are likely overweighed with face cards. When the count indicates that this is likely, they place a trade (bet) based on the probability that a disproportionate number of face cards will be coming up, increasing the odds of winning. Trading range traders are looking for times when they think the market has gone too far in one direction and then they place a trade in the opposite direction (a fade).

I tried playing poker online a few times without using real money to find similarities to and differences from trading. I discovered early on that there was a deal breaker for me: I was constantly anxious because of the inherent unfairness due to luck, and I never want luck to be a large component of the odds for my success. This is a huge difference and makes me see gambling and trading as fundamentally different, despite public perception. In trading, everyone is dealt the same cards so the game is always fair and, over time, you get rewarded or penalized entirely due to your skill as a trader. Obviously, sometimes you can trade correctly and lose, and this can happen several times in a row due to the probability curve of all possible outcomes. There is a real but microscopic chance that you can trade well and lose 10 or even 100 times or more in a row; but I cannot remember the last time I saw as many as four good signals fail in a row, so this is a chance that I am willing to take. If you trade well, over time you should make money because it is a zero-sum game (except for commissions, which should be small if you choose an appropriate broker). If you are better than most of the other traders, you will win their money.

There are two types of gambling that are different from pure games of chance, and both are similar to trading. In both sports betting and poker, gamblers are trying to take money from other gamblers rather than from the house, and therefore they can create odds in their favor if they are significantly better than their competitors. However, the "commissions" that they pay can be far greater than those that a trader pays, especially with sports betting, where the vig is usually 10 percent, and that is why incredibly successful sports gamblers like Billy Walters are so rare: they have to be at least 10 percent better than the competition just to break even. Successful poker players are more common, as can be seen on all of the poker shows on TV. However, even the best poker players do not make anything comparable to what the best traders make, because the practical limits to their trading size are much smaller.

I personally find trading not to be stressful, because the luck factor is so tiny that it is not worth considering. However, there is one thing that trading and playing poker share, and that is the value of patience. In poker, you stand to make far more money if you patiently wait to bet on only the very best hands, and traders make more when they have the patience to wait for the very best setups. For me, this protracted downtime is much easier in trading because I can see all of the other "cards" during the slow times, and it is intellectually stimulating to look for subtle price action phenomena.

There is an important adage in gambling that is true in all endeavors, and that is that you should not bet until you have a good hand. In trading, that is true as well. Wait for a good setup before placing a trade. If you trade without discipline and without a sound method, then you are relying on luck and hope for your profits, and your trading is unquestionably a form of gambling.

One unfortunate comparison is from nontraders who assume that all day traders, and all market traders for that matter, are addicted gamblers and therefore have a mental illness. I suspect that many are addicted, in the sense that they are doing it more for excitement than for profit. They are willing to make low-probability bets and lose large sums of money because of the huge rush they feel when they occasionally win. However, most successful traders are essentially investors, just like an investor who buys commercial real estate or a small business. The only real differences from any other type of investing are that the time frame is shorter and the leverage is greater.

Unfortunately, it is common for beginners to occasionally gamble, and it invariably costs them money. Every successful trader trades on the basis of rules. Whenever traders deviate from those rules for any reason, they are trading on hope rather than logic and are then gambling. Beginning traders often find themselves gambling right after having a couple of losses. They are eager to be made whole again and are willing to take some chances to make that happen. They will take trades that they normally would not take, because they are eager to get back the money they just lost. Since they are now taking a trade that they believe is a low-probability trade and they are taking it because of anxiety and sadness over their losses, they are now gambling and not trading. After they lose on their gamble, they feel even worse. Not only are they even further down on the day, but they feel especially sad because they are faced with the reality that they did not have the discipline to stick to their system when they know that discipline is one of the critical ingredients to success.

Interestingly, neurofinance researchers have found that brain scan images of traders about to make a trade are indistinguishable from those of drug addicts about to take a hit. They found a snowball effect and an increased desire to continue, regardless of the outcome of their behavior. Unfortunately, when faced with losses, traders assume more risk rather than less, often leading to the death of their accounts. Without knowing the neuroscience, Warren Buffett clearly understood the problem, as seen in his statement, "Once you have ordinary intelligence, what you need is the temperament to control the urges that get other people into trouble in investing." The great traders control their emotions and constantly follow their rules.

One final point about gambling: There is a natural tendency to assume that nothing can last forever and that every behavior regresses toward a mean. If the market has three or four losing trades, surely the odds favor the next one being a winner. It's just like flipping a coin, isn't it? Unfortunately, that is not how markets behave. When a market is trending, most attempts to reverse fail. When it is in a trading range, most attempts to break out fail. This is the opposite of coin flips, where the odds are always 50–50. In trading, the odds are more like 70 percent or better that what just happened will continue to happen again and again. Because of the coin flip logic, most traders at some point begin to consider game theory.

Martingale techniques work well in theory but not in practice because of the conflict between math and emotion. That is the martingale paradox. If you double (or even triple) your position size and reverse at each loss, you will theoretically make money. Although four losers in a row is uncommon on the 5 minute Emini chart if you choose your trades carefully, they will happen, and so will a dozen or more, even though I can't remember ever seeing that. In any case, if you are comfortable trading 10 contracts, but start with just one and plan to double up and reverse with each loss, four consecutive losers would require 16 contracts on your next trade and eight consecutive losers would require 256 contracts! It is unlikely that you would place a trade that is larger than your comfort zone following four or more losers. Anyone willing to trade one contract initially would never be willing to trade 16 or 256 contracts, and anyone willing to trade 256 contracts would never be willing to initiate this strategy with just one. This is the inherent, insurmountable, mathematical problem with this approach.

Since trading is fun and competitive, it is natural for people to compare it to games, and because wagering is involved, gambling is usually the first thing that comes to mind. However, a far more apt analogy is to chess. In chess, you can see exactly what your opponent is doing, unlike in card games where you don't know your opponent's cards. Also, in poker, the cards that you are dealt are yours purely by chance, but in chess, the location of your pieces is entirely due to your decisions. In chess nothing is hidden and it is simply your skill compared to that of your opponent that determines the outcome. Your ability to read what is in front of you and determine what will likely follow is a great asset both to a chess player and to a trader.

Laypeople are also concerned about the possibility of crashes, and because of that risk, they again associate trading with gambling. Crashes are very rare events on daily charts. These nontraders are afraid of their inability to function effectively during extremely emotional events. Although the term *crash* is generally reserved for daily charts and applied to bear markets of about 20 percent or more happening in a short time frame, like in 1927 and 1987, it is more useful to think of it as just another chart pattern because that removes the emotion and helps traders follow their rules. If you remove the time and price axes from a chart and focus simply on the price action, there are market movements that occur frequently on intraday charts that are indistinguishable from the patterns in a classic crash. If you can get past the emotion, you can make money off crashes, because with all charts, they display tradable price action.

Figure I.4 (from TradeStation) shows how markets can crash in any time frame. The one on the left is a daily chart of GE during the 1987 crash, the middle is a 5 minute chart of COST after a very strong earnings report, and the one on the right is a 1 minute Emini chart. Although the term *crash* is used almost exclusively to refer to a 20 percent or more sell-off over a short time on a daily chart and was widely used only twice in the past hundred years, a price action trader looks for shape, and the same crash pattern is common on intraday charts. Since crashes are so common intraday, there is no need to apply the term, because from a trading perspective they are just a bear swing with tradable price action.

Created with TradeStation

FIGURE I.4   Crashes Are Common

Incidentally, the concept that the same patterns appear on all time frames means that the principles of fractal mathematics might be useful in designing trading systems. In other words, every pattern subdivides into standard price action patterns in smaller time frame charts, and trading decisions based on price action analysis therefore work in all time frames.

HOW TO READ THESE BOOKS

I tried to group the material in the three books in a sequence that should be helpful to traders.

Book 1: *Trading Price Action Trends: Technical Analysis of Price Charts Bar by Bar for the Serious Trader*

- *The basics of price action and candles.* The market is either trending or in a trading range. That is true of every time frame down to even an individual bar, which can be a trend bar or a nontrend bar (doji).
- *Trend lines and trend channel lines.* These are basic tools that can be used to highlight the existence of trends and trading ranges.
- *Trends.* These are the most conspicuous and profitable components of every chart.

Book 2: *Trading Price Action Trading Ranges: Technical Analysis of Price Charts Bar by Bar for the Serious Trader*

- *Breakouts.* These are transitions from trading ranges into trends.
- *Gaps.* Breakouts often create several types of intraday gaps that can be helpful to traders, but these gaps are evident only if you use a broad definition.
- *Magnets, support, and resistance.* Once the market breaks out and begins its move, it is often drawn to certain prices, and these magnets often set up reversals.
- *Pullbacks.* These are transitions from trends to temporary trading ranges.
- *Trading ranges.* These are areas of largely sideways price activity, but each leg is a small trend and an entire trading range is usually a pullback in a trend on a higher time frame chart.
- *Order and trade management.* Traders need as many tools as possible and need to understand scalping, swing trading, and scaling into and out of trades, as well as how to enter and exit on stops and limit orders.
- *The mathematics of trading.* There is a mathematical basis for all trading, and when you see why things are unfolding the way they do, trading becomes much less stressful.

Book 3: *Trading Price Action Reversals: Technical Analysis of Price Charts Bar by Bar for the Serious Trader*

- *Trend reversals.* These offer the best risk/reward ratios of any type of trade, but since most fail, traders need to be selective.
- *Day trading.* Now that readers understand price action, they can use it to trade. The chapters on day trading, trading the first hour, and detailed examples show how.
- *Daily, weekly, and monthly charts.* These charts have very reliable price action setups.
- *Options.* Price action can be used effectively in option trading.
- *Best trades.* Some price action setups are especially good, and beginners should focus on these.
- *Guidelines.* There are many important concepts that can help keep traders focused.

If you come across an unfamiliar term, you should be able to find its definition in the List of Terms at the beginning of the book.

Some books show charts that use the time zone of the location of the market, but now that trading is electronic and global, that is no longer relevant. Since I trade in California, the charts are in Pacific standard time (PST). All of the charts were created with TradeStation. Since every chart has dozens of noteworthy price action events that have not yet been covered, I describe many of them immediately after the primary discussion under "Deeper Discussion of This Chart." Even though you might find this incomprehensible when you first read it, you will understand it on a second reading of the books. The more variations of standard patterns that you see, the better you will be able to spot them as they are developing in real time. I also usually point out the major one or two trades on the chart. If you prefer, you can ignore that supplemental discussion on your first read and then look at the charts again after completing the books when the deeper discussion would be understandable. Since many of the setups are excellent examples of important concepts, even though not yet covered, many readers will appreciate having the discussion if they go through the books again.

At the time of publication, I am posting a daily end-of-day analysis of the Emini and providing real-time chart reading during the trading day at www.brookspriceaction.com.

All of the charts in the three books will be in a larger format on John Wiley & Sons' site at www.wiley.com/go/tradingtrends. (See the "About the Website" page at the back of the book.) You will be able to zoom in to see the details, download the charts, or print them. Having a printout of a chart when the description is several pages long will make it easier to follow the commentary.

SIGNS OF STRENGTH: TRENDS, BREAKOUTS, REVERSAL BARS, AND REVERSALS

Here are some characteristics that are commonly found in strong trends:

- There is a big gap opening on the day.
- There are trending highs and lows (swings).
- Most of the bars are trend bars in the direction of the trend.
- There is very little overlap of the bodies of consecutive bars. For example, in a bull spike, many bars have lows that are at or just one tick below the closes of the prior bar. Some bars have lows that are at and not below the close of the prior bar, so traders trying to buy on a limit order at the close of the prior bar do not get their orders filled and they have to buy higher.
- There are bars with no tails or small tails in either direction, indicating urgency. For example, in a bull trend, if a bull trend bar opens on its low tick and trends up, traders were eager to buy it as soon as the prior bar closed. If it closes on or near its high tick, traders continued their strong buying in anticipation of new buyers entering right after the bar closes. They were willing to buy going into the close because they were afraid that if they waited for the bar to close, they might have to buy a tick or two higher.

- Occasionally, there are gaps between the bodies (for example, the open of a bar might be above the close of the prior bar in a bull trend).
- A breakout gap appears in the form of a strong trend bar at the start of the trend.
- Measuring gaps occur where the breakout test does not overlap the breakout point. For example, the pullback from a bull breakout does not drop below the high of the bar where the breakout occurred.
- Micro measuring gaps appear where there is a strong trend bar and a gap between the bar before it and the bar after it. For example, if the low of the bar after a strong bull trend bar in a bull trend is at or above the high of the bar before the trend bar, this is a gap and a breakout test and a sign of strength.
- No big climaxes appear.
- Not many large bars appear (not even large trend bars). Often, the largest trend bars are countertrend, trapping traders into looking for countertrend trades and missing with-trend trades. The countertrend setups almost always look better than the with-trend setups.
- No significant trend channel line overshoots occur, and the minor ones result in only sideways corrections.
- There are sideways corrections after trend line breaks.
- Failed wedges and other failed reversals occur.
- There is a sequence of 20 moving average gap bars (20 or more consecutive bars that do not touch the moving average, discussed in book 2).
- Few if any profitable countertrend trades are found.
- There are small, infrequent, and mostly sideways pullbacks. For example, if the Emini's average range is 12 points, the pullbacks will all likely be less than three or four points, and the market will often go for five or more bars without a pullback.
- There is a sense of urgency. You find yourself waiting through countless bars for a good with-trend pullback and one never comes, yet the market slowly continues to trend.
- The pullbacks have strong setups. For example, the high 1 and high 2 pullbacks in a bull trend have strong bull reversal bars for signal bars.
- In the strongest trends, the pullbacks usually have weak signal bars, making many traders not take them, and forcing traders to chase the market. For example, in a bear trend the signal bars for a low 2 short are often small bull bars in two or three bar bull spikes, and some of the entry bars are outside down bars. It has trending "anything": closes, highs, lows, or bodies.
- Repeated two-legged pullbacks are setting up with trend entries.
- No two consecutive trend bar closes occur on the opposite side of the moving average.

- The trend goes very far and breaks several resistance levels, like the moving average, prior swing highs, and trend lines, and each by many ticks.
- Reversal attempts in the form of spikes against the trend have no follow-through, fail, and become flags in the direction of the trend.

The more of the following characteristics that a bull breakout has, the more likely the breakout will be strong:

- The breakout bar has a large bull trend body and small tails or no tails. The larger the bar, the more likely the breakout will succeed.
- If the volume of the large breakout bar is 10 to 20 times the average volume of recent bars, the chance of follow-through buying and a possible measured move increases.
- The spike goes very far, lasts several bars, and breaks several resistance levels, like the moving average, prior swing highs, and trend lines, and each by many ticks.
- As the first bar of the breakout bar is forming, it spends most of its time near its high and the pullbacks are small (less than a quarter of the height of the growing bar).
- There is a sense of urgency. You feel like you have to buy but you want a pullback, yet it never comes.
- The next two or three bars also have bull bodies that are at least the average size of the recent bull and bear bodies. Even if the bodies are relatively small and the tails are prominent, if the follow-through bar (the bar after the initial breakout bar) is large, the odds of the trend continuing are greater.
- The spike grows to five to 10 bars without pulling back for more than a bar or so.
- One or more bars in the spike have a low that is at or just one tick below the close of the prior bar.
- One or more bars in the spike have an open that is above the close of the prior bar.
- One or more bars in the spike have a close on the bar's high or just one tick below its high.
- The low of the bar after a bull trend bar is at or above the high of the bar before the bull trend bar, creating a micro gap, which is a sign of strength. These gaps sometimes become measuring gaps. Although it is not significant to trading, according to Elliott Wave Theory they probably represent the space between a smaller time frame Elliott Wave 1 high and a Wave 4 pullback, which can touch but not overlap.

- The overall context makes a breakout likely, like the resumption of a trend after a pullback, or a higher low or lower low test of the bear low after a strong break above the bear trend line.
- The market has had several strong bull trend days recently.
- There is growing buying pressure in the trading range, represented by many large bull trend bars, and the bull trend bars are clearly more prominent than the bear trend bars in the range.
- The first pullback occurs only after three or more bars of breaking out.
- The first pullback lasts only one or two bars, and it follows a bar that is not a strong bear reversal bar.
- The first pullback does not reach the breakout point and does not hit a breakeven stop (the entry price).
- The breakout reverses many recent closes and highs. For example, when there is a bear channel and a large bull bar forms, this breakout bar has a high and close that are above the highs and closes of five or even 20 or more bars. A large number of bars reversed by the close of the bull bar is a stronger sign than a similar number of bars reversed by the high.

The more of the following characteristics that a bear breakout has, the more likely the breakout will be strong:

- The breakout bar has a large bear trend body and small tails or no tails. The larger the bar, the more likely the breakout will succeed.
- If the volume of the large breakout bar is 10 to 20 times the average volume of recent bars, the chance of follow-through selling and a possible measured move down increases.
- The spike goes very far, lasts several bars, and breaks several support levels like the moving average, prior swing lows, and trend lines, and each by many ticks.
- As the first bar of the breakout bar is forming, it spends most of its time near its low and the pullbacks are small (less than a quarter of the height of the growing bar).
- There is a sense of urgency. You feel like you have to sell but you want a pullback, yet it never comes.
- The next two or three bars also have bear bodies that are at least the average size of the recent bull and bear bodies. Even if the bodies are relatively small and the tails are prominent, if the follow-through bar (the bar after the initial breakout bar) is large, the odds of the trend continuing are greater.
- The spike grows to five to 10 bars without pulling back for more than a bar or so.

- As a bear breakout goes below a prior significant swing low, the move below the low goes far enough for a scalper to make a profit if he entered on a stop at one tick below that swing low.
- One or more bars in the spike has a high that is at or just one tick above the close of the prior bar.
- One or more bars in the spike has an open that is below the close of the prior bar.
- One or more bars in the spike has a close on its low or just one tick above its low.
- The high of the bar after a bear trend bar is at or below the low of the bar before the bear trend bar, creating a micro gap, which is a sign of strength. These gaps sometimes become measuring gaps. Although it is not significant to trading, they probably represent the space between a smaller time frame Elliott wave 1 low and a wave 4 pullback, which can touch but not overlap.
- The overall context makes a breakout likely, like the resumption of a trend after a pullback, or a lower high or higher high test of the bull high after a strong break below the bull trend line.
- The market has had several strong bear trend days recently.
- There was growing selling pressure in the trading range, represented by many large bear trend bars, and the bear trend bars were clearly more prominent than the bull trend bars in the range.
- The first pullback occurs only after three or more bars of breaking out.
- The first pullback lasts only one or two bars and it follows a bar that is not a strong bull reversal bar.
- The first pullback does not reach the breakout point and does not hit a breakeven stop (the entry price).
- The breakout reverses many recent closes and lows. For example, when there is a bull channel and a large bear bar forms, this breakout bar has a low and close that are below the lows and closes of five or even 20 or more bars. A large number of bars reversed by the close of the bear bar is a stronger sign than a similar number of bars reversed by its low.

The best-known signal bar is the reversal bar and the minimum that a bull reversal bar should have is either a close above its open (a bull body) or a close above its midpoint. The best bull reversal bars have more than one of the following:

- An open near or below the close of the prior bar and a close above the open and above the prior bar's close.
- A lower tail that is about one-third to one-half the height of the bar and a small or nonexistent upper tail.
- Not much overlap with the prior bar or bars.

- The bar after the signal bar is not a doji inside bar and instead is a strong entry bar (a bull trend bar with a relatively large body and small tails).
- A close that reverses (closes above) the closes and highs of more than one bar.

The minimum that a bear reversal bar should have is either a close below its open (a bear body) or a close below its midpoint. The best bear reversal bars have:

- An open near or above the close of the prior bar and a close well below the prior bar's close.
- An upper tail that is about one-third to one-half the height of the bar and a small or nonexistent lower tail.
- Not much overlap with the prior bar or bars.
- The bar after the signal bar is not a doji inside bar and instead is a strong entry bar (a bear trend bar with a relatively large body and small tails).
- A close that reverses (closes below) the closes and extremes of more than one bar.

Here are a number of characteristics that are common in strong bull reversals:

- There is a strong bull reversal bar with a large bull trend body and small tails or no tails.
- The next two or three bars also have bull bodies that are at least the average size of the recent bull and bear bodies.
- The spike grows to five to 10 bars without pulling back for more than a bar or so, and it reverses many bars, swing highs, and bear flags of the prior bear trend.
- One or more bars in the spike have a low that is at or just one tick below the close of the prior bar.
- One or more bars in the spike have an open that is above the close of the prior bar.
- One or more bars in the spike have a close on the high of the bar or just one tick below its high.
- The overall context makes a reversal likely, like a higher low or lower low test of the bear low after a strong break above the bear trend line.
- The first pullback occurs only after three or more bars.
- The first pullback lasts only one or two bars, and it follows a bar that is not a strong bear reversal bar.
- The first pullback does not hit a breakeven stop (the entry price).
- The spike goes very far and breaks several resistance levels like the moving average, prior swing highs, and trend lines, and each by many ticks.

- As the first bar of the reversal is forming, it spends most of its time near its high and the pullbacks are less than a quarter of the height of the growing bar.
- There is a sense of urgency. You feel like you have to buy but you want a pullback, yet it never comes.
- The signal is the second attempt to reverse within the past few bars (a second signal).
- The reversal began as a reversal from an overshoot of a trend channel line from the old trend.
- It is reversing a significant swing high or low (e.g., it breaks below a strong prior swing low and reverses up).
- The high 1 and high 2 pullbacks have strong bull reversal bars for signal bars.
- It has trending "anything": closes, highs, lows, or bodies.
- The pullbacks are small and sideways.
- There were prior breaks of earlier bear trend lines (this isn't the first sign of bullish strength).
- The pullback to test the bear low lacks momentum, as evidenced by its having many overlapping bars with many being bull trend bars.
- The pullback that tests the bear low fails at the moving average or the old bear trend line.
- The breakout reverses many recent closes and highs. For example, when there is a bear channel and a large bull bar forms, this breakout bar has a high and close that are above the highs and closes of five or even 20 or more bars. A large number of bars reversed by the close of the bull bar is a stronger sign than a similar number of bars reversed by only its high.

Here are a number of characteristics that are common in strong bear reversals:

- A strong bear reversal bar with a large bear trend body and small tails or no tails.
- The next two or three bars also have bear bodies that are at least the average size of the recent bull and bear bodies.
- The spike grows to five to 10 bars without pulling back for more than a bar or so, and it reverses many bars, swing lows, and bull flags of the prior bull trend.
- One or more bars in the spike has a high that is at or just one tick above the close of the prior bar.
- One or more bars in the spike has an open that is below the close of the prior bar.
- One or more bars in the spike has a close on its low or just one tick above its low.
- The overall context makes a reversal likely, like a lower high or higher high test of the bull high after a strong break below the bull trend line.

- The first pullback occurs only after three or more bars.
- The first pullback lasts only one or two bars and it follows a bar that is not a strong bull reversal bar.
- The first pullback does not hit a breakeven stop (the entry price).
- The spike goes very far and breaks several support levels like the moving average, prior swing lows, and trend lines, and each by many ticks.
- As the first bar of the reversal is forming, it spends most of its time near its low and the pullbacks are less than a quarter of the height of the growing bar.
- There is a sense of urgency. You feel like you have to sell, but you want a pullback, yet it never comes.
- The signal is the second attempt to reverse within the past few bars (a second signal).
- The reversal began as a reversal from an overshoot of a trend channel line from the old trend.
- It is reversing at a significant swing high or low area (e.g., breaks above a strong prior swing high and reverses down).
- The low 1 and low 2 pullbacks have strong bear reversal bars for signal bars.
- It has trending "anything": closes, highs, lows, or bodies.
- The pullbacks are small and sideways.
- There were prior breaks of earlier bull trend lines (this isn't the first sign of bearish strength).
- The pullback to test the bull high lacks momentum, as evidenced by it having many overlapping bars with many being bear trend bars.
- The pullback that tests the bull high fails at the moving average or the old bull trend line.
- The breakout reverses many recent closes and lows. For example, when there is a bull channel and a large bear bar forms, this breakout bar has a low and close that are below the lows and closes of five or even 20 or more bars. A large number of bars reversed by the close of the bear bar is a stronger sign than a similar number of bars reversed by only its low.

BAR COUNTING BASICS: HIGH 1, HIGH 2, LOW 1, LOW 2

A reliable sign that a pullback in a bull trend or in a trading range has ended is when the current bar's high extends at least one tick above the high of the prior bar. This leads to a useful concept of counting the number of times that this occurs, which is called bar counting. In a sideways or downward move in a bull trend or a trading range, the first bar whose high is above the high of the prior bar is a high 1, and this ends the first leg of the sideways or down move, although this leg may become a small leg in a larger pullback. If the market does not turn into a bull swing and instead continues sideways or down, label the next occurrence of a bar with a high above the high of the prior bar as a high 2, ending the second leg.

A high 2 in a bull trend and a low 2 in a bear trend are often referred to as ABC corrections where the first leg is the A, the change in direction that forms the high 1 or low 1 entry is the B, and the final leg of the pullback is the C. The breakout from the C is a high 2 entry bar in a bull ABC correction and a low 2 entry bar in a bear ABC correction.

If the bull pullback ends after a third leg, the buy setup is a high 3 and is usually a type of wedge bull flag. When a bear rally ends in a third leg, it is a low 3 sell setup and usually a wedge bear flag.

Some bull pullbacks can grow further and form a high 4. When a high 4 forms, it sometimes begins with a high 2 and this high 2 fails to go very far. It is instead followed by another two legs down and a second high 2, and the entire move is simply a high 2 in a higher time frame. At other times, the high 4 is a small spike and channel bear trend where the first or second push down is a bear spike and the next pushes down are in a bear channel. If the high 4 fails to resume the trend and the market falls below its low, it is likely that the market is no longer forming a pullback in a bull trend and instead is in a bear swing. Wait for more price action to unfold before placing a trade.

When a bear trend or a sideways market is correcting sideways or up, the first bar with a low below the low of the prior bar is a low 1, ending the first leg of the correction, which can be as brief as that single bar. Subsequent occurrences are called the low 2, low 3, and low 4 entries. If the low 4 fails (a bar extends above the high of the low 4 signal bar after the low 4 short is triggered), the price action indicates that the bears have lost control and either the market will become two-sided, with bulls and bears alternating control, or the bulls will gain control. In any case, the bears can best demonstrate that they have regained control by breaking a bull trend line with strong momentum.

PART I

Breakouts: Transitioning into a New Trend

The market is always trying to break out, and then the market tries to make every breakout fail. This is the most fundamental aspect of all trading and is at the heart of everything that we do. One of the most important skills that a trader can acquire is the ability to reliably determine when a breakout will succeed or fail (creating a reversal). Remember, every trend bar is a breakout, and there are buyers and sellers at the top and bottom of every bull and bear trend bar, no matter how strong the bar appears. Since every trend bar is a breakout and trend bars are common, traders must understand that they have to be assessing every few bars all day long whether a breakout will continue or fail and then reverse. This is the most fundamental concept in trading, and it is crucial to a trader's financial success to understand it. A breakout of anything is the same. Even a climactic reversal like a V bottom is simply a breakout and then a failed breakout. There are traders placing trades based on the belief that the breakout will succeed, and other traders placing trades in the opposite direction, betting it will fail. The better traders become at assessing whether a breakout will succeed or fail, the better positioned they are to make a living as a trader. Will the breakout succeed? If yes, then look to trade in that direction. If no (and become a failed breakout, which is a reversal), then look to trade in the opposite direction. All trading comes down to this decision.

Breakout is a misleading term because *out* implies that it refers only to a market attempting to transition from a trading range into a trend, but it can also be a buy or sell climax attempting to reverse into a trend in the opposite direction. The most important thing to understand about breakouts is that most breakouts fail. There is a strong propensity for the market to continue what it has been doing, and therefore there is a strong resistance to change. Just as most attempts to end a trend fail, most attempts to end a trading range and begin a trend also fail.

A breakout is simply a move beyond some prior point of significance such as a trend line or a prior high or low, including the high or low of the previous bar. That point becomes the breakout point, and if the market later comes back to test that point, the pullback is the breakout test (a breakout pullback that reaches the area of the breakout point). The space between the breakout point and the breakout test is the breakout gap. A significant breakout, one that makes the always-in position clearly long or short and is likely to have follow-through for at least several bars, almost always appears as a relatively large trend bar without significant tails. "Always in" is discussed in detail in the third book, and it means that if you had to be in the market at all times, either long or short, the always-in position is whatever your current position is. The breakout is an attempt by the market either to reverse the trend or to move from a trading range into a new trend. Whenever the market is in a trading range, it should be considered to be in breakout mode. There is two-sided trading until one side gives up and the market becomes heavily one-sided, creating a spike that becomes a breakout. All breakouts are spikes and can be made up of one or several consecutive trend bars. Breakouts of one type or another are very common and occur as often as every few bars on every chart. As is discussed in Chapter 6 on gaps, all breakouts are functionally equivalent to gaps, and since every trend bar is a breakout (and also a spike and a climax), it is also a gap. Many breakouts are easily overlooked, and any single one may be breaking out of many things at one time. Sometimes the market will have setups in both directions and is therefore in breakout mode; this is sometimes referred to as being in an inflection area. Traders will be ready to enter in the direction of the breakout in either direction. Because breakouts are one of the most common features of every chart, it is imperative to understand them, their follow-through, and their failure.

The high of the prior bar is usually a swing high on some lower time frame chart, so if the market moves above the high of the prior bar, it is breaking above a lower time frame swing high. Also, when the market breaks above a prior swing high on the current chart, that high is simply the high of the prior bar on some higher time frame chart. The same is true for the low of the prior bar. It is usually a swing low on a lower time frame chart, and any swing low on the current chart is usually just the low of the prior bar on a higher time frame chart.

It is important to distinguish a breakout into a new trend from a breakout of a small trading range within a larger trading range. For example, if the chart on your screen is in a trading range, and the market breaks above a small trading range in the bottom half of the screen, most traders will assume that the market is still within the larger trading range, and not yet in a bull trend. The market might simply be forming a buy vacuum test of the top of the larger trading range. Because of this, smart traders will not buy the closes of the strong bull trend bars near the top of the screen. In fact, many will sell out of their longs to take profits and others will short them, expecting the breakout attempt to fail. Similarly, even though buying a high 1 setup in strong bull spike can be a great trade, it is great only in a bull trend, not at the top of a trading range, where most breakout attempts will fail. In general, if there is a strong bull breakout, but it is still below the high of the bars on the left half of the screen, make sure that the there is a strong trend reversal underway before looking to buy near the top of the spike. If you believe that the market might still be within a trading range, only consider buying pullbacks, instead of looking to buy near the top of the spike.

Big traders don't hesitate to enter a trend during its spike phase, because they expect significant follow-through, even if there is a pullback immediately after their entry. If a pullback occurs, they increase the size of their position. For example, if there is a strong bull breakout lasting several bars, more and more institutions become convinced that the market has become always-in long with each new higher tick, and as they become convinced that the market will go higher, they start buying, and they press the trades by buying more as the market continues to rise. This makes the spike grow very quickly. They have many ways to enter, like buying at the market, buying a one- or two-tick pullback, buying above the prior bar on a stop, or buying on a breakout above a prior swing high. It does not matter how they get in, because their focus is to get at least a small position on, and then look to buy more as the market moves higher or if it pulls back. Because they will add on as the market goes higher, the spike can extend for many bars. A beginning trader sees the growing spike and wonders how anyone could be buying at the top of such a huge move. What they don't understand is that the institutions are so confident that the market will soon be higher that they will buy all of the way up, because they don't want to miss the move while waiting for a pullback to form. Beginners are also afraid that their stops would have to be below the bottom of the spike, or at least below its midpoint, which is far away. The institutions know this, and simply adjust their position size down to a level where their dollars at risk are the same as for any other trade.

At some resistance level, the early buyers take some profits, and then the market pulls back a little. When it does, the traders who want a larger position quickly buy, thereby keeping the initial pullback small. Also, the bulls who missed the earlier entries will use the pullback to finally get long. Some traders don't like to buy spikes, because they don't like to risk too much (the stop often needs to be below the bottom of the spike). They prefer to feel like they are buying at a better price (a discount) and therefore will wait for a pullback to form before buying. If everyone is looking to buy a pullback, why would one ever develop? It is because not everyone is looking to buy. Experienced traders who bought early on know that the market can reverse at any time, and once they feel that the market has reached a resistance area where they think that profit taking might come in or the market might reverse, they will take partial profits (they will begin to scale out of their longs), and sometimes will sell out of their entire position. These are not the bulls who are looking to buy a few ticks lower on the first pullback. The experienced traders who are taking partial profits are scaling out because they are afraid of a reversal, or of a deeper pullback where they could buy back many ticks lower. If they believed that the pullback was only going to last for a few ticks, and then the bull was going to resume, they would never have exited. They always take their profits at some resistance level, like a measured move target, a trend line, a trend channel line, a new high, or at the bottom of a trading range above. Most of the trading is done by computers, so everything has a mathematical basis, which means that the profit taking targets are based on the prices on the screen. With practice, traders can learn to spot areas where the computers might take profits, and they can take their profits at the same prices, expecting a pullback to follow. Although trends have inertia and will go above most resistance areas, when a reversal finally does come, it will always be at a resistance area, whether or not it is obvious to you.

Sometimes the spike will have a bar or a pattern that will allow aggressive bears to take a small scalp, if they think that the pullback is imminent and that there is enough room for a profit. However, most traders who attempt this will lose, because most of the pullbacks do not go far enough for a profit, or the trader's equation is weak (the probability of making a scalp times the size of the profit is smaller than the probability of losing times the size of the protective stop). Also, traders who take the short are hoping so much for their small profit that they invariably end up missing the much more profitable long that forms a few minutes later.

Traders enter in the direction of the breakout or in the opposite direction, depending on whether they expect it to succeed or to fail. Are they believers or nonbelievers? There are many ways to enter in the direction of the breakout. Once traders feel a sense of urgency because they believe that a significant move might be underway, they need to get into the market. Entering during a breakout is difficult for many traders because the risk is larger and the move is fast. They will often freeze and not take the trade. They are worried about the size of the potential loss, which means that they are caring too much to trade. They have to get their position size down to the "I don't care" size so that they can quickly get in the trade. The best way for them to take a scary trade is to automatically trade only a third or a quarter of their normal trade size and use the wide stop that is required. They might catch a big move, and making a lot on a small position is much better than making nothing on their usual position size. It is important to avoid making the mistake of not caring to the point that you begin to trade weak setups and then lose money. First spot a good setup and then enter the "I don't care" mode.

As soon as traders feel that the market has had a clear always-in move, they believe that a trend is underway and they need to get in as soon as possible. For example, if there is a strong bull breakout, they can buy the close of the bar that made them believe that the trend has begun. They might need to see the next bar also have a bull close. If they wait and they get that bull close, they could buy as soon as the bar closes, either with a limit order at the level of the close of the bar or with a market order. They could wait for the first pause or pullback bar and place a limit order to buy at its close, a tick above its low, at its low, or a tick or two below its low. They can place a limit order to buy any small pullback, like a one- to four-tick pullback in the Emini, or a 5 to 10 cent pullback in a stock. If the breakout bar is not too large, the low of the next bar might test the high of the bar before the breakout, creating a breakout test. They might place a limit order to buy at or just above the high of that bar, and risk to the low of the breakout bar. If they try to buy at or below a pause bar and they do not get filled, they can place a buy stop order at one tick above the high of the bar. If the spike is strong, they can look to buy the first high 1 setup, which is a breakout pullback. Earlier on, they can look at a 1, 2, or 3 minute chart and buy at or below the low of a prior bar, above a high 1 or high 2 signal bar, or with a limit order at the moving average. Once they are in, they should manage the position like any trend trade, and look for a swing to a measured move target to take profits and not exit with a small scalp. The bulls will expect every attempt by the bears to fail, and therefore look to buy each one. They will buy around the close of every bear trend bar, even if the bar is large and closes on its low. They will buy as the market falls below the low of the prior bar, any prior swing low, and any support level, like a trend line. They also will buy every attempt by the market to go higher, like around the high of a bull trend bar or as the market moves above the high of the prior bar or above a resistance level. This is the exact opposite of what traders do in strong bear markets, when they sell above and below bars, and above and below both resistance and support. They sell above bars (and around every type of resistance), including strong bull trend bars, because they see each move up as an attempt to reverse the trend, and most trend reversal attempts fail. They will sell below bars (and around every type of support), because they see each move down as an attempt to resume the bear trend, and expect that most will succeed.

Since most breakout attempts fail, many traders enter breakouts in the opposite direction. For example, if there is a bull trend and it forms a large bear trend bar closing on its low, most traders will expect this reversal attempt to fail, and many will buy at the close of the bar. If the next bar has a bull body, they will buy at the close of the bar and above its high. The first target is the high of the bear trend bar, and the next target is a measured move up, equal to the height of the bear trend bar. Some traders will use an initial protective stop that is about the same number of ticks as the bear trend bar is tall, and others will use their usual stop, like two points in the Emini. Information comes fast during a breakout, and traders can usually formulate increasingly strong opinions with the close of each subsequent bar. If there is a second strong bear trend bar and then a third, more traders will believe that the always-in position has reversed to down, and the bears will short more. The bulls who bought the bear spike will soon decide that the market will work lower over the next several bars and will therefore exit their longs. It does not make sense for them to hold long when they believe that the market will be lower in the near future. It makes more sense for them to sell out of their longs, take the loss, and then buy again at a lower price once they think that the bull trend will resume. Because the bulls have become sellers, at least for the next several bars, there is no one left to buy, and the market falls to the next level of support. If the market rallied after that first bear bar, the bears would quickly see that they were wrong and would buy back their shorts. With no one left to short and everyone buying (the bulls initiating new longs and the bears buying back their shorts), the market will probably rally, at least for several more bars.

Traders have to assess a breakout in relation to the entire chart and not just the current leg. For example, if the market is breaking out in a strong bull spike, look across the chart to the left side of the screen. If there are no bars at the level of the current price, then buying closes and risking to below the bottom of the spike is often a good strategy. Since the risk is big, trade small, but because a strong breakout has at least a 60 percent chance of reaching a measured move that is approximately equal to the size of the spike, the trader's equation is good (the probability of success times the potential reward is greater than the probability of failure times the risk). However, when you look to the left side of the screen, if you see that the current breakout is still below the high from 20 or 30 bars earlier, the market might still be in a trading range. Trading ranges regularly have sharp bull spikes that race to the top, only to reverse. The market then races to the bottom and that breakout attempt also fails. Because of this, buying the closes of strong bull trend bars near the top of the trading range is risky, and it is usually better to look to buy pullbacks instead. Traders should trade the market like a trading range until it is clearly in a trend.

A move above a prior high in a bull trend will generally lead to one of three outcomes: more buying, profit taking, or shorting. When the trend is strong, strong bulls will press (add to) their longs by buying the breakout above the old high and there will be a measured move up of some kind. If the market goes up far enough above the breakout to enable a trader to make at least a profitable scalp before there is a pullback, then assume that there was mostly new buying at the high. If it goes sideways and the breakout shows signs of weakness (discussed further on), assume that there was profit taking and that the bulls are looking to buy again a little lower. If the market reverses down hard, assume that the strong bears dominated at the new high and that the market will likely trade down for at least a couple of legs and at least 10 bars.

In the absence of some rare, dramatic news event, traders don't suddenly switch from extremely bullish to extremely bearish. There is a gradual transition. A trader becomes less bullish, then neutral, and then bearish. Once enough traders make this transition, the market reverses into a deeper correction or into a bear trend. Every trading firm has its own measure of excess, and at some point enough firms decide that the trend has gone too far. They believe that there is little risk of missing a great move up if they stop buying above the old high, and they will buy only on pullbacks. If the market hesitates above the old high, the market is becoming two-sided, and the strong bulls are using the new high to take profits.

Profit taking means that traders are still bullish and are looking to buy a pullback. Most new highs are followed by profit taking. Every new high is a potential top, but most reversal attempts fail and become the beginning of bull flags, only to be followed by another new high. If a rally to test the high has several small pullbacks within the leg up, with lots of overlapping bars, several bear bodies, and big tails on the tops of the bars, and most of the bull trend bars are weak, then the market is becoming increasingly two-sided. The bulls are taking profits at the tops of the bars and buying only at the bottoms of the bars, and the bears are beginning to short at the tops of the bars. Similarly, the bulls are taking profits as the market approaches the top of the bull trend and the bears are shorting more. If the market goes above the bull high, it is likely that the profit taking and shorting will be even stronger.

Most traders do not like to reverse, so if they are anticipating a reversal signal, they prefer to exit their longs and then wait for that signal. The loss of these bulls on the final leg up in the trend contributes to the weakness of the rally to the final high. If there is a strong reversal down after the market breaks above the prior high, the strong bears are taking control of the market, at least for the near term. Once that happens, then the bulls who were hoping to buy a small pullback believe instead that the market will fall further. They therefore wait to buy until there is a much larger pullback, and their absence of buying allows the bears to drive the market down into a deeper correction lasting 10 or more bars and often having two or more legs. Whenever there is a new trend, traders reverse their mind-set. When a bull trend reverses to a bear trend, they stop buying above bars on stops and buying below bars on limit orders, and begin selling above bars on limit orders and selling below bars on stops. When a bear trend reverses to a bull trend, they stop selling below bars on stops and selling above bars on limit orders, and begin buying above bars on stops and buying below bars on limit orders.

There is one situation where the breakout in a bull trend is routinely met by aggressive shorts who will usually take over the market. A pullback is a minor trend in the opposite direction, and traders expect it to end soon and for the larger trend to resume. When there is a pullback in a strong bear trend, the market will often have two legs up in the minor bull trend. As the market goes above the high of the first leg up, it is breaking out above a prior swing high in a minor bull trend. However, since most traders will see the move up as a pullback that will end very soon, the dominant traders on the breakout will usually be aggressive sellers, instead of aggressive new buyers, and the minor bull trend will usually reverse back down into the direction of the major bear trend after breaking out above the first or second swing high in the pullback.

The same is true of new lows in a bear trend. When the bear trend is strong, strong bears will press their shorts by adding to their positions on the breakout to a new low and the market will continue to fall until it reaches some measured move target. As the trend weakens, the price action at a new low will be less clear, which means that the strong bears are using the new low as an area to take profits on their shorts rather than as an area to add to their shorts. As the bear trend further loses strength, the strong bulls will eventually see a new low as a great price to initiate longs and they will be able to create a reversal pattern and then a significant rally.

As a trend matures, it usually transitions into a trading range, but the first trading ranges that form are usually followed by a continuation of the trend. How do the strong bulls and bears act as a trend matures? In a bull trend, when the trend is strong, the pullbacks are small because the strong bulls want to buy more on a pullback. Since they suspect that there may not be a pullback until the market is much higher, they begin to buy in pieces, but relentlessly. They look for any reason to buy, and with so many big traders in the market, there will be some buying for every imaginable reason. They place limit orders to buy a few ticks down and other limit orders to buy a few ticks above the low of the prior bar, at the low of the prior bar, and below the low of the prior bar. They place stop orders to buy above the high of the prior bar and on a breakout above any prior swing high. They also buy on the close of both any bull or bear trend bar. They see the bear trend bar as a brief opportunity to buy at a better price and the bull trend bar as a sign that the market is about to move up quickly.

The strong bears are smart and see what is going on. Since they believe, just like the strong bulls, that the market is going to be higher before long, it does not make sense for them to be shorting. They just step aside and wait until they can sell higher. How much higher? Each institution has its own measure of excess, but once the market gets to a price level where enough bear firms believe that it might not go any higher, they will begin to short. If enough of them short around the same price level, more and larger bear trend bars form and bars start to get tails on the tops. These are signs of selling pressure, and they tell all traders that the bulls are becoming weaker and the bears are becoming stronger. The strong bulls eventually stop buying above the last swing high and instead begin to take profits as the market goes to a new high. They are still bullish but are becoming selective and will buy only on pullbacks. As the two-sided trading increases and the sell-offs have more bear trend bars and last for more bars, the strong bulls will want to buy only at the bottom of the developing trading range and will look to take profits at the top. The strong bears begin to short at new highs and are now willing to scale in higher. They might take partial profits near the bottom of the developing trading range if they think that the market might reverse back up and break out to a new high, but they will keep looking to short new highs. At some point, the market becomes a 50–50 market and neither the bulls nor the bears are in control; eventually the bears become dominant, a bear trend begins, and the opposite process unfolds.

A protracted trend will often have an unusually strong breakout, but it can be an exhaustive climax. For example, in a protracted bull trend, all strong bulls and bears love to see a large bull trend bar or two, especially if it is exceptionally large, because they expect it to be a brief, unusually great opportunity. Once the market is close to where the strong bulls and bears want to sell, like near a measured move target or a trend channel line, especially if the move is the second or third consecutive buy climax, they step aside. The absence of selling by the strongest traders results in a vacuum above the market. The programs that detect the momentum early on in a bar see this and quickly buy repeatedly until the momentum slows. Since few strong traders are selling, the result is one or two relatively large bull trend bars. This bull spike is just the sign that the strong traders have been waiting for, and once it is there, they appear as if out of nowhere and begin their selling. The bulls take profits on their longs and the bears initiate new shorts. Both sell aggressively at the close of the bar, above its high, at the close of the next bar (especially if it is a weaker bar), and at the close of the following bar, especially if the bars are starting to have bear bodies. They also short below the low of the prior bar. When they see a strong bear trend bar, they short at its close and below its low. The momentum programs also take profits. Both the bulls and the bears expect a larger correction, and the bulls will not consider buying again until at least a 10-bar, two-legged correction, and even then only if the sell-off looks weak. The bears expect the same sell-off and will not be eager to take profits too early.

Weak traders see that large bull trend bar in the opposite way. The weak bulls, who had been sitting on the sidelines hoping for an easy pullback to buy, see the market running away from them and want to make sure they catch this next leg up, especially since the bar is so strong and the day is almost over. The weak bears, who shorted early and maybe scaled in, were terrified by the rapidity with which the bar broke to a new high. They are afraid of relentless follow-through buying, so they buy back their shorts. These weak traders are trading on emotion and are competing against computers, which do not have emotion as one of the variables in their algorithms. Since the computers control the market, the emotions of the weak traders doom them to big losses on big bull trend bars at the end of an overdone bull trend.

Once a strong bull trend begins to have pullbacks that are relatively large, the pullbacks, which are always small trading ranges, behave more like trading ranges than like bull flags. The direction of the breakout becomes less certain, and traders begin to think that a downside breakout is about as likely as an upside breakout. A new high is now a breakout attempt above a trading range, and the odds are that it will fail. Likewise, once a strong bear trend begins to have relatively large pullbacks, those pullbacks behave more like trading ranges than like bear flags, and therefore a new low is an attempt to break below a trading range and the odds are that it will fail.

Every trading range is within either a bull or a bear trend. Once the two-sided trading is strong enough to create the trading range, the trend is no longer strong, at least while the trading range is in effect. There will always be a breakout from the range eventually, and if it is to the upside and it is very strong, the market is in a strong bull trend. If it is to the downside and strong, the market is in a strong bear trend.

Once the bears are strong enough to push a pullback well below the bull trend line and the moving average, they are confident enough that the market will likely not go much higher and they will aggressively short above the old high. At this point, the bulls will have decided that they should buy only a deep pullback. A new mind-set is now dominant at the new high. It is no longer a place to buy, because it no longer represents much strength. Yes, there is profit taking by the bulls, but most big traders now look at the new high as a great opportunity to initiate shorts. The market has reached the tipping point, and most traders have stopped looking to buy small pullbacks and instead are looking to sell rallies. The bears are dominant and the strong selling will likely lead to a large correction or even a trend reversal. After the next strong push down, the bears will look for a lower high to sell again or to add to their short positions, and the bulls who bought the pullback will become concerned that the trend might have reversed or at least that there will be a much larger pullback. Instead of hoping for a new bull high to take profits on their longs, they will now take profits at a lower high and not look to buy again until after a larger correction. Bulls know that most reversal attempts fail, and many who rode the trend up will not exit their longs until after the bears have demonstrated the ability to push the market down hard. Once these bulls see this impressive selling pressure, they will then look for a rally to finally exit their longs. Their supply will limit the rally, and their selling, added to the shorting by aggressive bears and the profit taking by bulls who saw the sell-off as a buying opportunity, will create a second leg down.

If the market enters a bear trend, the process will reverse. When the bear trend is strong, traders will short below prior lows. As the trend weakens, the bears will take profits at new lows and the market will likely enter a trading range. After a strong rally above the bull trend line and the moving average, the bears will take profits at a new low and strong bulls will aggressively buy and try to take control of the market. The result will be a larger bear rally or possibly a reversal into a bull trend.

A similar situation occurs when there is a pullback that is large enough to make traders wonder if the trend has reversed. For example, if there is a deep, sharp pullback in a bull trend, traders will begin to wonder if the market has reversed. They are looking at moves below prior swing lows, but this is in the context of a pullback in a bull trend instead of as part of a bear trend. They will watch what happens as the market falls (breaks out) below a prior swing low. Will the market fall far enough for bears, who entered on a sell stop below that swing low, to make a profit? Did the new low find more sellers than buyers? If it did, that is a sign that the bears are strong and that the pullback will probably go further. The trend might even have reversed.

Another possibility on the breakout to a new low is that the market enters a trading range, which is evidence that the shorts took profits and that there was unimpressive buying by the bulls. The final alternative is that the market reverses up after the breakout to a new low. This means that there were strong bulls below that swing low just waiting for the market to test there. This is a sign that the sell-off is more likely just a big pullback in an ongoing bull trend. The shorts from higher up took profits on the breakout to the new low because they believed that the trend was still up. The strong bulls bought aggressively because they believed that the market would not fall further and that it would rally to test the bull high.

Whenever there is any breakout below a swing low, traders will watch carefully for evidence that the bulls have returned or that the bears have taken control. They need to decide what influence is greater at the new low, and will use the market's behavior to make that decision. If there is a strong breakout, then new selling is dominant. If the market's movement is uncertain, then profit taking by the shorts and weak buying by the bulls are taking place, and the market will likely enter a trading range. If there is a strong reversal up, then aggressive buying by the longs is the most important factor.

Sometimes, when the market is in a weak trend, there is a large breakout bar in the direction of the trend. That breakout bar often acts as a spike, and it is usually followed by several more trend bars, but they usually overlap and have tails. These bars create a tight bull channel. Like with any spike and channel trend, the market often tests back to the start of the channel, which in this case is the breakout gap area. For example, if there is a relatively weak bull swing and then the market breaks to the upside with a large bull trend bar, and this is followed by three or four more smaller bull trend bars, these bars usually act as a channel. Once the market trades down to the area of the first of those channel bars, it often goes slightly below its low, and that puts the market in the gap area that was created by the breakout bar. The gap is both a measuring gap and a breakout gap, and the test of the gap is usually followed by a resumption of the trend rather than the start of a reversal down.

An inflection is a mathematical term that means that there has been a change of direction. For example, if there is a horizontal wave that goes up and down repeatedly, when the wave is going down, at some point the slope changes from steeply down to less steeply down as it begins to form a bottom. For example, the middle of the letter *S* is the inflection point in the curve, because it is the point where the slope begins to change direction. In trading, an inflection is just an area where you expect a trend reversal, which may or may not develop. Since the move can go in either direction, the market is in breakout mode and traders will be ready to enter in the direction of the breakout. In either case, the market will often make a measured move, which is a move that covers about the same number of points as the pattern that led up to it. For example, a double top often leads to a breakout to the upside or downside. After the breakout, the market often runs beyond the breakout point to a measured move target that is about the same number of points away as the distance from the bottom to the top of the double top. There is often a gap between the breakout point and the first pullback, and the middle of the gap often leads to a measured move (measuring gaps are discussed in Chapter 6 on gaps).

Breakout mode situations can behave in an opposite way in a trading range. For example, if there is a breakout mode setup in the middle of a trading range, there may be more buyers than sellers below the bar and more sellers than buyers above. If the situation is too uncertain to make traders believe that they have a good trader's equation, it is usually better to wait for clarity. At the extremes of a trading range, three things can happen: there can be (1) a reversal, (2) a breakout that fails and is followed by a reversal, or (3) a successful breakout. Only one of the three leads to a trend. This is consistent with the concept that most breakout attempts fail.

When there is a breakout against a trend, the countertrend traders are trying to create a channel (a spike and channel trend) or some other form of a new trend after their spike. However, the trend traders are usually able to reverse the breakout within a few bars, turning it into a flag. For example, if there is a bear channel that has a large bull trend bar or two breaking above the channel, the bulls are hoping to form a bull channel after a pullback. However, they will usually fail and the bull spike will end up as simply part of a bear flag. The bears saw the spike as a great opportunity to add to their shorts at a brief, high price, which represented correctly value to them.

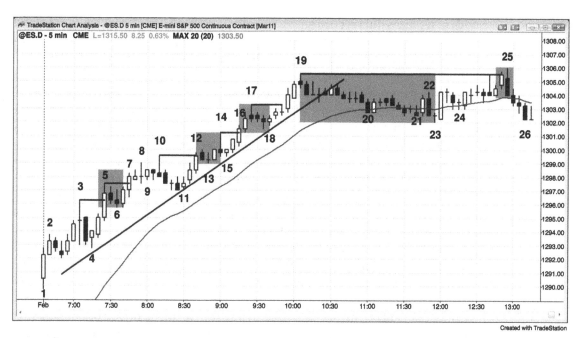

FIGURE PI.1   New Highs Find New Buyers, Profit Takers, and Shorts

When a bull trend breaks above a prior swing high, there will be new buyers, profit takers, and shorts (see Figure PI.1). If the trend that preceded the breakout is starting out and is very strong, there will be some profit taking, like after bars 5, 12, and 17, but the new buyers will overwhelm the bears, and the trend will quickly resume. Later in the trend, there will be much less new buying and much more profit taking, like after bar 19. There are many measures of excess, and once enough trading firms believe that the bull trend is overdone, they will take profits on their longs and buy again only after about a 10-bar, two-legged correction. I use the phrase "10-bar, two-legged" often, and my intention is to say that the correction will last longer and be more complex than a small pullback. That usually requires at least 10 bars and two legs, and sometimes can result in a trend reversal.

Whenever there is a breakout, it might fail and lead to a trend reversal. The chance of a successful reversal is greater if the context is right and the reversal bar is strong. If the breakout bar and spike leading to the breakout is stronger than the reversal bar, and the chance of a climactic reversal is not great, the odds are that the reversal attempt will fail within a few bars and form a breakout pullback setup that will lead to a resumption of the trend. For example, bar 12 was a small bear reversal bar, but it followed a much stronger three-bar bull spike and the market was trending up in a tight channel all day following a large gap up. This made the odds of a successful reversal small, so bulls bought at and below the low of bar 12. The next bar was a doji and therefore a weak entry bar for the bears, so there were almost certainly going to be more buyers than sellers above its high. It became a breakout pullback buy signal bar (here, a high 1 buy setup). The next bar was a bull bar, and more buyers bought above its high. In general, the odds of a successful buy signal are greater when traders wait to enter above a bull bar. Bar 14 was the breakout bar, but it closed on its low and formed a bear doji reversal bar, which is a weak sell signal in the face of such a tight bull channel. The bulls were so aggressive that they did not want the short to trigger. They placed limit orders at and above the low of the bear bar, and there were enough buy orders to overwhelm the bears. The short never triggered and the market continued to rally. Bar 14 was simply another pullback from the breakout (and it was also the breakout), and traders bought above the high of bar 15, which was another breakout pullback buy signal.

Another example of comparing the strength of the breakout with that of the reversal occurred on the bar 5 breakout. The bear bar after bar 5 was the signal bar for the failed breakout of the bar 4 one bar bull flag and the breakout above bar 3. The bear signal was small compared to the 3 bar bull spike up from bar 4, and was therefore unlikely to reverse the trend. The next bar was a breakout pullback buy setup, but had a bear body, which is not a strong buy signal bar. The bar after had a bull body and therefore buying above its high had a higher probability of success.

Bar 10 was a breakout of an ii bull flag, but the breakout bar was a bear reversal bar, which is a weak breakout bar. This increased the chances that the breakout would fail. The breakout bar was also the signal bar for the failed breakout.

The correction sometimes breaks the bull trend line and creates enough selling pressure for the bears to become aggressive at the next new high, as they were at bar 25. There was still some profit taking by the bulls, but very little new buying. The bears took control going into the close.

Both the strong bulls and bears looked forward to the final, strong breakout up to bar 19. They liked seeing a large bull spike after a protracted bull trend, because the expected correction provided both of them with a temporary trading opportunity. It was the third consecutive bull climax without a correction since the bar 11 low (bars 11 to 12 and 15 to 17 were the first two), and consecutive buy climaxes often lead to a two-legged correction lasting about 10 bars and falling below the moving average. Both the strong bulls and bears sold at the close of the two-bar bull spike before bar 19, above its high, at the close of bar 19 (especially since it had a bear body), and below its low. The bulls didn't look to buy again and the bears did not take profits on their shorts until after the two-legged correction was complete, which was in the bar 21 to bar 24 area. The sell-off was strong enough for both to think that the market might have a trend reversal into a bear trend after a lower high or higher high test of the bar 19 bull high, and this resulted in the sell-off from bar 25 into the close.

Since most reversal attempts fail, traders often fade them. Bar 22 was a strong bear trend bar in a bull trend, and many traders bought its close. Their first target was a move to the high of the bar, which occurred two bars later, and then a measured move up, which was reached by the end of the day.

The bear bar after bar 5 was a breakout mode setup. Since it was a bear bar after a bull breakout above the bar 3 swing high, it was a failed breakout short setup. It was also a one-bar pullback in a bull breakout, so it was a high 1 breakout pullback buy setup. In this case, since the three-bar bull spike was so strong, it was more likely that the bulls would outnumber the bears both below and above the bar. Some bought at the low of the bear inside bar with limit orders, whereas others bought above it and above bar 6 with stop orders.

FIGURE PI.2   Low-Volume Bull Breakout in a Bear Trend

As shown in Figure PI.2, the Emini was in a bear trend on the 60 minute chart on the left and many traders looked to buy a measured move down, based on the height of the initial spike down from bar 1 to bar 2. The bears bought back their shorts to take profits, and aggressive bulls bought to initiate longs, expecting a possible trend reversal and test of the start of the bear channel (the lower swing high after bar 2). The chance of at least two legs up was increased by the reversal down from the bar 3 moving average gap bar and break above the bear trend line (reversals are covered in the third book).

The 5 minute chart on the right reversed up after falling one tick below the 60 minute measured move target (bar 4 is the same time on both charts). Bar 5 was a large bull reversal bar with a small tail, and bulls were hopeful for a strong reversal up. However, the bar had only 23,000 contracts, or about three times as many as an average 5 minute bar. When the average 5 minute bar has 5,000 to 10,000 contracts, most bull reversals with protracted follow-through have about 5 to 10 times that volume, or at least 40,000 to 50,000 contracts. The most reliable bars have over 100,000 contracts. Traders do not have to worry about volume because the chart will tell them what they need to know, but seeing huge volume on a large trend bar that is breaking out increases the chances that there will be follow-through and usually at least some kind of measured move. When there is a strong bear trend and the reversal up goes for only two bars and then pulls back, and the second bar up has a large tail, the reversal is not strong. More experienced traders can look at the volume and see it as another sign that the reversal is not strong, or they can look at the 60 minute chart and see the strong bear trend. However, all day traders need to see is the 5 minute chart to place their trades. They would have bought bar 5 as it was forming, as it closed, and above its high. They would have also bought the bar 7 ioi (inside-outside-inside) pattern, high 4 bull flag at the moving average. Since they were buying a strong bull move, they should have assumed that they had at least a 60 percent chance of making a reward that was at least as large as their risk. They could have chosen a two-point stop, since that worked well lately, and then used a two-point profit target. Another trader who bought at the bar 5 close might have been willing to risk to below the bar 5 low (about four points), and his profit taking target might have been as many points as he had to risk. The stop for the trader who bought above bar 7 would have been below the low of bar 7 or below the bar before it. Her risk was about two points, and she could have held for either two points or for a move above the bar 6 high (here, it was also about two points).

CHAPTER 4

Example of How to Trade a Breakout

M any beginners find breakouts difficult to trade because the market moves fast, requiring quick decisions, and often has large bars, which means that there is more risk and traders then have to reduce their position size. However, if a trader learns to identify one that is likely to be successful, the trader's equation can be very strong.

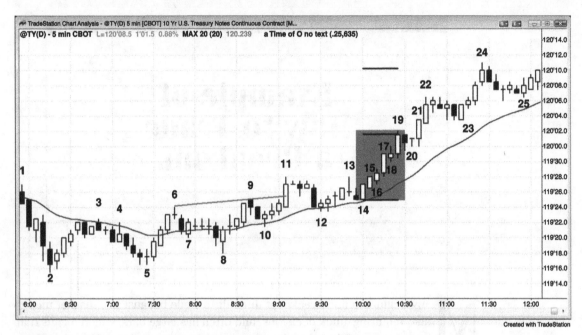

FIGURE 1.1 Breakouts Are Reliable Setups

When a chart discussion runs for multiple pages, remember that you can go to the Wiley website (www.wiley.com/go/tradingtrends) and either view the chart or print it out, allowing you to read the description in the book without having to repeatedly flip pages back to see the chart.

Successful breakouts, like the bull breakouts in Figure 1.1, have excellent math, but can be emotionally very difficult to trade. They happen quickly and traders instinctively know that the risk is to the bottom of the spike (they put their protective stop at one tick below the low of the lowest bar in the bull spike, like below bar 14), which is often more than their usual risk tolerance. They want a pullback but know it will likely not come until the market is higher, and they are afraid to buy at the market because they are buying at the top of a spike. If the market reverses on the next tick, they will have bought at the top of a spike and their protective stop is very far away. However, what they often fail to appreciate is that the math is on their side. Once there is a strong spike in a breakout like this, the probability of at least a measured move up based on the height of the spike is at least 60 percent and may even sometimes be 80 percent. This means that they have at least a 60 percent chance of making at least as much as their initial risk, and if the spike continues to grow after they enter, their risk stays the same but the measured move target gets higher and higher. For example, if traders bought at the close of bar 15 on the 5 minute chart of the 10-Year U.S. Treasury Note Futures in Figure 1.1, they would risk to one tick (one 64th of a point) below the bottom of the two-bar spike, which is one tick below the bar 14 low, or seven ticks below the entry price. At this point, since the traders believed that the market was always-in long, they thought that there was at least a 60 percent chance of it being higher within a few bars. They should also have assumed that there would be at least a measured move up. Since the spike was six ticks tall, the market had at least a 60 percent chance of trading up at least six ticks before falling to their protective stops.

At the close of bar 19, the spike had grown to 17 ticks tall and since it was still a breakout spike, there was still at least a 60 percent chance of at least a measured move up. If traders were flat at this point, they could have bought small positions at the market and risked to one tick below the bar 14 bottom of the spike, or 18 ticks, to make 16 ticks (if the market went 17 ticks higher, they could get out with 16 ticks of profit). The traders who bought the bar 15 close were still risking seven ticks to below the bar 14 low, but now had a 60 percent chance of the market trading 17 ticks above the bar 19 high, which would be about a 28-tick profit (14 32nds). The spike ended at bar 19, once the next bar was a bear inside bar instead of another strong bull trend bar. This was the first in a series of pullbacks in the channel phase of the bull trend. Bar 24 went above the measured move target, and the market traded even higher about an hour later.

In practice, most traders would have tightened their stops as the spike grew, so they would have risked less than what was just discussed. Many traders who bought the bar 15 close might have raised their stops to below bar 17 once it closed because they would not have wanted the market to fall below such a strong bull trend bar. If it did, they would have believed that their premise was wrong and they would not want to risk a larger loss. When bar 19 closed and traders saw that it was a strong bull trend bar, many might have put their protective stops in the micro measuring gap created by the bar 17 breakout. The low of bar 18 was above the high of bar 16, and this gap is a sign of strength. Traders would want the market to continue up and not trade below bar 18 and into the gap, so some traders would have trailed their stop to below the bar 18 low. Many experienced traders use spikes to press their trades. They add to their longs as the spike continues up, because they know that the spike has an exceptional trader's equation and that the great opportunity will be brief. A trader needs to be aggressive when the market is offering trades with strong trader's equations. He also needs to trade little or not at all when it does not, like in a tight trading range.

The bull spike up from bar 5 flipped the market to always-in long for most traders. When the market traded above the bar 11 wedge bear flag high, it was likely to have approximately a measured move up. Bar 15 was a second consecutive strong bull trend bar and confirmed the breakout in the minds of many traders. Both bars 14 and 15 were strong bull trend bars with good-sized bodies and without significant tails. There was good buying pressure all of the way up from the bar 5 low, as seen by many strong bull trend bars, little overlap, and only a few bear trend bars and the absence of consecutive strong bear trend bars. The market might have been in the early stages of a bull trend, and smart traders were looking for a bull breakout. They were eager to get long once bars 14 and 15 broke out, and traders kept buying relentlessly in pieces all the way up to the bar 19 high.

The most important thing that traders must force themselves to do, and it is usually difficult, is as soon as they believe that there is a reliable breakout spike, they must take at least a small position. When they feel themselves hoping for a pullback but fearing that it won't come for many more bars, they should assume that the breakout is strong. They must decide where a worst-case protective stop would be, which is usually relatively far away, and use that as their stop. Because the stop will be large, their initial position should be small if they are entering late. Once the market moves in their direction and they can tighten their stop, they can look to add to their position, but should never exceed their normal risk level. When everyone wants a pullback, it usually will not come for a long time. This is because everyone believes that the market will soon be higher but they do not necessarily believe that it will be lower anytime soon. Smart traders know this and therefore they start buying in pieces. Since they have to risk to the bottom of the spike, they buy small. If their risk is three times normal, they will buy only one-third of their usual size to keep their absolute risk within their normal range. When the strong bulls keep buying in small pieces, this buying pressure works against the formation of a pullback. The strong bears see the trend and they, too, believe that the market will soon be higher. If they think it will be higher soon, they will stop looking to short. It does not make sense for them to short if they think that they can short at a better price after a few more bars. So the strong bears are not shorting and the strong bulls are buying in small pieces, in case there is no pullback for a long time.

What is the result? The market keeps working higher. Since you need to be doing what the smart traders are doing, you need to buy at least a small amount at the market or on a one- or two-tick pullback and risk to the bottom of the spike. Even if the pullback begins on the next tick, the odds are that it won't fall too far before smart bulls see it as value and they buy aggressively. Remember, everyone is waiting to buy a pullback, so when it finally comes it will only be small and not last long. All of those traders who have been waiting to buy will see this as the opportunity that they wanted. The result is that your position will once again be profitable very soon. Once the market goes high enough, you can look to take partial profits or you can look to buy more on a pullback, which will probably be at a price above your original entry. The important point is that as soon as you decide that buying a pullback is a great idea, you should do exactly what the strong bulls are doing and buy at least a small position at the market.

Some traders like to buy breakouts as the market moves above a prior swing high, entering on a buy stop at one tick above the old high. In general, the reward is

Figure 1.1   EXAMPLE OF HOW TO TRADE A BREAKOUT   **57**

greater, the risk is smaller, and the probability of success is higher when entering on pullbacks. If traders buy these breakouts, they usually will then have to hold through a pullback before they can make much profit. It is usually better to buy the pullback than the breakout. For example, rather than buying above bar 6 as the market moved up to bar 9, the trader's equation was probably stronger for a buy above the bar 10 pullback instead.

The same is true for the bar 11 move above bar 9. With every breakout, traders have to decide if it will succeed or fail. If they believe that it will succeed, they will look to buy the close of the breakout or follow-through bars, at and below the low of the prior bar, and above the high of the prior bar. If they believe that it will fail, they will not buy and if they are long, they will exit their positions. If they believe that the failure will trade down far enough for a scalp, they might go short for a scalp. If they think that the failure will lead to a trend reversal, they might look to swing a short down. In this particular case, as the market moved strongly above the bar 9 and bar 11 double top, it was reasonable to buy the breakout, but traders who bought the close of bar 15 entered around the same price and had a more sound reason to take the trade (buying the close of a strong bull trend bar in a strong bull spike).

If any bull trend or breakout that does not look quite strong enough to buy near the top of the spike, like on the close of the most recent bar, the trader's equation is stronger if traders instead wait to buy pullbacks. Bar 22 was the second bar of a breakout from an ii pattern and therefore the beginning of a possible final flag reversal setup. This was likely a minor buy climax (discussed in book 3 in the chapter on climax reversals). At this point, the trader's equation was stronger for buying a pullback than for buying the close of bar 22. The same was true for bar 24. As a trend becomes more two-sided, it is better to look to buy pullbacks. Once the two-side trading becomes strong enough and the prior pullbacks have been deeper and lasted for more than five bars or so, traders can begin to short for scalps, like at the two bar reversal at bar 24 (shorting below the low of then bear bar that followed). After the market has transitioned into a trading range, the bears will begin to short for swing trades, expecting deeper pullbacks and a possible trend reversal.

Other examples of breakout pullback buy setups in this bull trend include the bar 8 high 2 bull flag (a pullback from the rally to bar 6, which broke out of the bear channel from bar 3 to bar 5), the bar 12 high 2 at the moving average (bar 11 broke above the trading range and out of the bar 10 high 1 bull flag; the first push down was the bear bar that formed two bars after bar 11), the bar 14 outside up bar (traders could have bought as it went outside up, but the probability of success was higher if they bought above bar 14, because it was a bull trend bar), the bar 20 ii, the high 2 at bar 23 (bar 23 was the entry bar), and the bar 25 high 2 (all double bottoms are high 2 patterns). The signal bar is more reliable when it has a bull body.

In general, whenever there is an initial pullback in a trend that has just become strongly always-in long, a trader should immediately place a buy stop to buy above the high of the spike. This is because many traders are afraid to buy below the low of the prior bar or above a high 1, thinking that the market might have a two-legged pullback. However, if they wait for a two-legged pullback, they will miss many of the very strongest trends. To prevent themselves from being trapped out of a strong trend, traders need to get into the habit of placing that last-ditch buy stop. If they buy the high 1, they can cancel their buy stop. But if they miss the earlier entries, at least they will get into the trend, which is what they need to do. By bar 19, the trend was clearly very strong and was likely to continue up for about a measured move based on the height of the spike. As soon as the market gave a sign of a possible pullback, traders needed to place their worst-case entry buy stop orders above the spike high. The bar after bar 19 was a bear trend bar and a possible start of a pullback. They needed to place a buy stop at one tick above the bar 19 high, in case the trend quickly resumed. If they instead bought the bar 20 ii high 1 setup, they would have canceled the buy stop above bar 19. However, if they missed buying the high 1 for any reason, at least they would have been swept into the trend as the market moved to the new high. Their initial protective stop would have been below the most recent minor pullback, which was the bar 20 low.

Bar 24 was a two-bar bull spike and the third consecutive buy climax without a correction. There was not enough time left in the day for a 10-bar, two-legged correction, so not many bears were willing to short it, especially since the move up from bars 5 and 12 had had so little selling pressure. However, some bulls used it as an opportunity to take profits, which turned out to be a reasonable decision, since the market did not get back above its high for the rest of the day.

Traders know that most attempts to reverse a trend fail, and many like to fade the attempts. The bar before bar 12 was a large bear trend bar, which was a break below the trend line and an attempt to reverse down from the bar 11 bull breakout. Bulls bought the close of the bear trend bar, expecting a move back up to its high, and probably a measured move up equal to the height of the bar. Once they saw that bar 12 had a bull close, they bought the close of bar 12 and above its high. A successful bear breakout usually is followed by another bear trend bar or at least a doji bar, and if there is instead a bull body, even a small one, the odds of a failed breakout attempt become higher, especially when the bar is at the moving average in a bull trend. The bears wanted a bear channel after the bear spike, or some other type of bear trend, but the bulls saw the bear spike as an opportunity to buy during a brief discount. Bear spikes, especially on daily charts, can be due to news items, but most fail to have follow-through, and the longer-term bullish fundamentals win out, leading to a failed bear breakout and a resumption of the bull trend. The bears get excited and hopeful because of the terrible news, but the news is usually a one-day minor event and trivial compared to the sum of all of the fundamentals.

Figure 1.2   EXAMPLE OF HOW TO TRADE A BREAKOUT   **59**

FIGURE 1.2 Breakout Pullback

Figure 1.2 shows that when a bull swing has a breakout to the upside, the market usually tests back into the breakout gap. The market sold off down to bar 8 and then reversed up. Bar 12 was a second-entry moving average gap bar short, but it failed. Instead of testing the bear low, the market broke to the upside on bar 13. The low of the bar after the breakout bar and the high of the bar 11 breakout point created a breakout gap. Either its middle or the high of the first leg up to bar 11 could lead to a measured move up. After the bar 13 spike up, there was a tight four-bar channel that ended at bar 15 and then a test down to the bottom of the channel. The bar 19 test also tested into the breakout gap, which usually happens in these situations.

The selloff from bar 5 to bar 8 had no pullbacks, and the bar after bar 8 was the first bar that traded above the high of the prior bar. Why would experienced traders ever buy back their highly profitable shorts when the first pullback in a strong trend usually fails? They have learned that they should always look for reasons to take partial or full profits, especially when they are large, because those profits can vanish quickly, especially after a possible sell climax. Here, there were three consecutive sell climaxes (the moves down to bars 6, 7, and 8), and the inside bar after bar 7 was a potential final flag (these patterns are discussed in book 3). The odds were high that the market would correct up for about 10 bars, probably to the moving average, the bar 4 low, or even the bar 5 high. The bears saw this as a great opportunity to lock in their profits around bar 8, expecting at least a 10-bar rally, and then look to sell again much higher, if a sell setup developed. The move up was so strong that there was no sell pattern, and the bears were happy that they wisely took their profits, and they were not concerned about the absence of another good chance to short. Had they held onto their shorts, all of their profits would have turned into losses. Profit taking is the cause of the first pullback in any strong trend. The bears who missed the selloff were hoping for a pullback that would allow them to short, but they never got that opportunity.

The bears who missed the selloff to bar 4, or who took profits at bar 4 and were looking to sell again on a pullback, got their chance at the bar 5 low 2 at the moving average. It had a bear body and was also a 20-gap bar short setup (discussed later in this book).

CHAPTER 2

Signs of Strength in a Breakout

The minimum criterion for a breakout to be successful is that a trader could enter on the breakout and make at least a scalper's profit. The strongest breakouts will result in strong trends that can last for dozens of bars. There are early signs that increase the likelihood that a breakout will be strong enough to run to one or more measured move targets. For example, the more of the following characteristics that a bull breakout has, the more likely the breakout will be strong:

- The breakout bar has a large bull trend body and small tails or no tails. The larger the bar, the more likely the breakout will succeed.
- If the volume is 10 to 20 times the average volume of recent bars, the chance of follow-through buying and a possible measured move increases.
- The spike goes very far, lasts several bars, and breaks several resistance levels like the moving average, prior swing highs, and trend lines, and each by many ticks.
- As the first bar of the breakout bar is forming, it spends most of its time near its high and the pullbacks are small (less than a quarter of the height of the growing bar).
- There is a sense of urgency. You feel like you have to buy but you want a pullback, yet it never comes.
- The next two or three bars also have bull bodies that are at least the average size of the recent bull and bear bodies. Even if the bodies are relatively small and the tails are prominent, if the follow-through bar (the bar after the initial breakout bar) is large, the odds of the trend continuing are greater.

- The spike grows to five to 10 bars without pulling back for more than a bar or so.
- As a bull breakout goes above a prior significant swing high, the move above the high goes far enough for scalpers to make a profit if they entered on a stop at one tick above that swing high.
- One or more bars in the spike has a low that is at or just one tick below the close of the prior bar.
- One or more bars in the spike has an open that is above the close of the prior bar.
- One or more bars in the spike has a close on its high or just one tick below its high.
- The low of the bar after a bull trend bar is at or above the high of the bar before the bull trend bar, creating a micro gap, which is a sign of strength. These gaps sometimes become measuring gaps. Although it is not significant to trading, they probably represent the space between a smaller time frame Elliott wave 1 high and a wave 4 pullback, which can touch but not overlap.
- The overall context makes a breakout likely, like the resumption of a trend after a pullback, or a higher low or lower low test of the bear low after a strong break above the bear trend line.
- The market has had several strong bull trend days recently.
- There was growing buying pressure in the trading range, represented by many large bull trend bars, and the bull trend bars were clearly more prominent than the bear trend bars in the range.
- The first pullback occurs only after three or more bars of breaking out.
- The first pullback lasts only one or two bars and it follows a bar that is not a strong bear reversal bar.
- The first pullback does not reach the breakout point and does not hit a breakeven stop (the entry price).
- The breakout reverses many recent closes and highs. For example, when there is a bear channel and a large bull bar forms, this breakout bar has a high and close that are above the highs and closes of five or even 20 or more bars. A large number of bars reversed by the close of the bull bar is a stronger sign than a similar number of bars reversed by its high.

The more of the following characteristics that a bull breakout has, the more likely it will fail and lead to either a trading range or a reversal:

- The breakout bar has a small or average-size bull trend body and a large tail on top.
- The next bar has a bear body and is either a bear reversal bar or a bear inside bar; that bar closes on or near its low, and the body is about the size of the

average bodies of the bars before the breakout (not just a one-tick-tall bear body).

- The overall context makes a breakout unlikely, like a rally to test the high of a trading range day, but the rally has bear bars, many overlapping bars, bars with prominent tails, and a couple of pullbacks along the way.
- The market has been in a trading range for several days.
- The bar after the breakout bar is a strong bear reversal bar or a bear inside bar.
- The bar after a bull trend bar has a low that is below the high of the bar before the bull trend bar.
- The first pullback occurs two bars after the reversal.
- The pullback extends for several bars.
- The trend resumption after the pullback stalls and the market forms a lower high with a bear signal bar.
- The spike breaks above a resistance level like a swing high, a bear trend line, or a bull trend channel line by only a tick or so and then reverses down.
- The spike barely breaks above a single resistance level but pulls back before breaking above other levels that are just a little higher.
- A trader who bought on a stop above a prior swing high would not be able to make a scalper's profit before there was a pullback.
- As the breakout bar is forming, it pulls back more than two-thirds of the height of the bar.
- As the breakout bar is forming, it pulls back for at least a third of its height two or more times.
- The pullback falls below the breakout point. There are no gaps between the low of any bar and the high of the bar two bars earlier.
- The pullback falls below the low of the first bar of the spike.
- The pullback hits the breakeven stop.
- There is a sense of confusion. You feel like you are not certain whether the breakout will succeed or fail.

The opposite of all of the preceding is true for bear breakouts. The more of the following characteristics that a bear breakout has, the more likely the breakout will be strong:

- The breakout bar has a large bear trend body and small tails or no tails. The larger the bar, the more likely the breakout will succeed.
- If the volume is 10 to 20 times the average volume of recent bars, the chance of follow-through selling and a possible measured move down increases.
- The spike goes very far, lasts several bars, and breaks several support levels like the moving average, prior swing lows, and trend lines, and each by many ticks.

- As the first bar of the breakout bar is forming, it spends most of its time near its low and the pullbacks are small (less than a quarter of the height of the growing bar).
- There is a sense of urgency. You feel like you have to sell but you want a pullback, yet it never comes.
- The next two or three bars also have bear bodies that are at least the average size of the recent bull and bear bodies. Even if the bodies are relatively small and the tails are prominent, if the follow-through bar (the bar after the initial breakout bar) is large, the odds of the trend continuing are greater.
- The spike grows to five to 10 bars without pulling back for more than a bar or so.
- As a bear breakout goes below a prior significant swing low, the move below the low goes far enough for scalpers to make a profit if they entered on a stop at one tick below that swing low.
- One or more bars in the spike has a high that is at or just one tick above the close of the prior bar.
- One or more bars in the spike has an open that is below the close of the prior bar.
- One or more bars in the spike has a close on its low or just one tick above its low.
- The high of the bar after a bear trend bar is at or below the low of the bar before the bear trend bar, creating a micro gap, which is a sign of strength. These gaps sometimes become measuring gaps. Although it is not significant to trading, they probably represent the space between a smaller time frame Elliott wave 1 low and a wave 4 pullback, which can touch but not overlap.
- The overall context makes a breakout likely, like the resumption of a trend after a pullback, or a lower high or higher high test of the bull high after a strong break below the bull trend line.
- The market has had several strong bear trend days recently.
- There was growing selling pressure in the trading range, represented by many large bear trend bars, and the bear trend bars were clearly more prominent than the bull trend bars in the range.
- The first pullback occurs only after three or more bars of breaking out.
- The first pullback lasts only one or two bars and it follows a bar that is not a strong bull reversal bar.
- The first pullback does not reach the breakout point and does not hit a breakeven stop (the entry price).
- The breakout reverses many recent closes and lows. For example, when there is a bull channel and a large bear bar forms, this breakout bar has a low and close that are below the lows and closes of five or even 20 or more bars. A large number of bars reversed by the close of the bear bar is a stronger sign than a similar number of bars reversed by its low.

The more of the following characteristics that a bear breakout has, the more likely it will fail and lead to either a trading range or a reversal:

- The breakout bar has a small or average-size bear trend body and a large tail on the bottom.
- The next bar has a bull body and is either a bull reversal bar or a bull inside bar; that bar closes on or near its high, and the body is about the size of the average bodies of the bars before the breakout (not just a one-tick-tall bull body).
- The overall context makes a breakout unlikely, like a sell-off to test the low of a trading range day, but the sell-off has bull bars, many overlapping bars, bars with prominent tails, and a couple of pullbacks along the way.
- The market has been in a trading range for several days.
- The bar after the breakout bar is a strong bull reversal bar or a bull inside bar.
- The bar after a bear trend bar has a high that is above the low of the bar before the bear trend bar.
- The first pullback occurs two bars after the reversal.
- The pullback extends for several bars.
- The trend resumption after the pullback stalls, and the market forms a higher low with a bull signal bar.
- The spike breaks below a support level like a swing low, a bull trend line, or a bear trend channel line by only a tick or so and then reverses up.
- The spike barely breaks below a single support level but pulls back before breaking below other levels that are just a little lower.
- A trader who shorted on a stop below a prior swing low would not be able to make a scalper's profit before there was a pullback.
- As the breakout bar is forming, it pulls back more than two-thirds of the height of the bar.
- As the breakout bar is forming, it pulls back for at least a third of its height two or more times.
- The pullback rallies above the breakout point. There are no gaps between the high of any bar and the low of the bar two bars earlier.
- The pullback rallies above the high of the first bar of the spike.
- The pullback hits the breakeven stop.
- There is a sense of confusion. You feel like you are not certain whether the breakout will succeed or fail.

To a trader, the breakout implies strength and a possible new trend. It follows a period of two-sided trading where the bulls and bears both agree that there is value and both are willing to take positions. During the breakout, they both now agree that the market should find value at another price and the breakout is a fast move in search of that new price. The market prefers uncertainty and quickly moves in search of it. A breakout is a period of certainty. Bulls and bears are certain that the prices within the breakout are too high in a bear breakout or too low in a bull breakout, and the odds of follow-through are usually about 60 to 70 percent. The market moves quickly in search of a price level where both the bulls and bears agree there is value for them to initiate trades. This means that there is once again uncertainty, and no one knows which side will win and succeed in creating the next breakout. Uncertainty is the hallmark of a trading range, so a breakout is a search for a trading range, for uncertainty, and a 50 percent directional probability of an equidistant move. The channel that follows the spike usually creates an approximate top and bottom of the trading range that typically follows. As the market is moving up in the channel, the directional probability of an equidistant move erodes and it actually favors a reversal when it reaches the end of the channel. This is because trading range breakouts generally fail and the odds favor a move back into the middle of the range where the directional probability is neutral. That middle of the range is the target of the breakout, and its location is unknown until after it forms.

A breakout begins with a trend bar, which can be large or small, but it is usually at least somewhat large compared to the size of the recent bars. Remember, all trend bars should be viewed as breakouts, spikes, gaps, and climaxes. When it is small, it is easy to dismiss its importance, but if it is followed by some sideways price action and then a steady directional move, a breakout is underway. The easiest breakouts to spot occur when an unusually large trend bar quickly moves the market out of a trading range and it is soon followed by other trend bars in the same direction. Whether the breakout is a single trend bar or a series of trend bars, it is a spike. As mentioned earlier, almost all trends can be considered to be some type of spike and channel trend. For example, if a bull breakout bar has a strong close and the next several bars also have strong closes, small or nonexistent tails, and trending highs and lows (no pullback bars), and there is very little overlap between the bodies of consecutive bull trend bars, then the market will likely be higher than it is at the current moment at some point before the market reverses back beyond the start of the breakout move. If the trend continues, eventually its momentum will slow and there will generally be some type of channel.

One of the most important concepts in trading is that most breakouts fail. Because of this, entering on every breakout in the direction of the breakout is a losing strategy. However, there are often price action events that increase the likelihood that a breakout will succeed. For example, if there is a strong bear trend and then a two-legged rally to the moving average, going short on the downside breakout of this bear flag is a sensible trade. However, if the market is not in a trend and there are lots of overlapping bars and many bars with large tails, the market is in balance. Both the bulls and the bears are comfortable taking positions and a trading range is developing. If the market then has a bull trend bar that extends to the top of or even above the trading range, the bears who were happy to sell in the middle of the range are going to be even more aggressive at this better price. Also, the bulls who were happy to buy in the middle of the range will become hesitant to buy higher and instead will be quick to exit at the top of the range. This behavior by the bulls and the bears creates a magnetic pull in the middle of the range, and the result is that most of the trading will be in the middle of the range. Even once the market successfully breaks out and travels for maybe a measured move equal to the height of the range, the magnetic pull will still tend to draw the market back into the range. This is what makes final flag reversals so reliable (discussed in book 3).

If you look at any chart, you will notice lots of bull and bear trend bars with relatively large bodies and small tails. Each of these is a breakout attempt and almost all fail to lead to a trend, and instead the trading range continues. On a 5 minute Emini chart, these probably represent buy and sell programs trying to move the market. Some algorithms are designed to fade these trend bars, expecting most to fail. Experienced traders will do this as well when they believe that the breakout will probably fail. For example, if there is a breakout in the form of a large bull trend bar, these programs might short on the close of the bar, above its high, on the close of the next bar or two, or below their lows. If enough program trading dollars come in on the fade side (the sell side), they will overwhelm those programs that are trying to initiate the bull trend, and the trading range will continue. Eventually, a breakout will succeed. The breakout bar will be large, the pullbacks as the bar is forming will be small, and the breakout will have good follow-through over the next several bars. The programs that are trying to fade the move are failing and they will cover their losing positions and drive the trend further. The strength will attract other trend traders, many of whom are momentum traders and quickly enter whenever they see momentum.

Once everyone is convinced that the market is now trending, it might go far before there is a pullback. Why is that? Consider an example of a market breaking into a strong bull trend with a spike formed by three strong bull trend bars. Traders believe that the market will be higher at some point before long and they are not confident that it will be lower within the next few bars. This makes bears buy back their shorts, lifting the market even more. Bulls who are underinvested believe the market is going higher in the near term and that they will make more money by simply buying at the market or on a two- or three-tick pullback than they would if they waited for an eight- or 10-tick pullback or a pullback to the moving average. This also lifts the market. Since bulls and bears are both essentially buying at the market as it is going up, the pullback never comes, or at least it does not come for five or more bars after the market is well above the current price.

This is discussed in more detail in Chapter 8, but traders are willing to buy at the market at any time in a breakout because they believe that the odds are better than 50–50 that they will make at least as many points as they are risking. When the breakout is strong, the probability is usually 60 to 70 percent or more. If they buy the 5 minute Emini on the high tick when the top of the spike is four points above the low of the spike, they believe that the odds are probably 60 percent or better that the market will go up four more points before their four-point stop is hit. How can you be sure of this? Because it is mathematically unwise to have your risk equal your reward if the chance of success is much less than 60 percent, and institutions would therefore not be taking this trade. Since the market is still going up, then institutions are taking the trade. Since the trade remains valid as long as the market stays above the bottom of the spike, they are risking to the bottom of the spike. They know that the spike usually goes up to about a measured move, so their profit target, which is their reward, is equal to their risk. If the spike grows another two points before pausing, the spike is then six points tall. If that is the end of the spike, they will assume that there is about a 60 percent chance that the market will go another six points higher before it falls six points. This means that all of the bulls who bought lower have a 60 percent chance that the market will go another six points higher before their four-point stop is hit. For example, the bulls who bought when the spike was four points tall are now risking four points to make a total of eight points on a 60 percent bet, which is a great mathematical situation. They expect that the market has a 60 percent chance of testing six points above the close of the spike, which is two points above their entry, giving them an eight-point profit target.

When a breakout is successful and leads to a trend, the momentum slows after the initial fast move, and signs of two-sided trading develop, like overlapping bars, increasing tails, trend bars in the opposite direction, and pullback bars. Even though the trend may continue for a long time, this part of the trend usually gets retraced and becomes part of a trading range. For example, in a spike and channel bull trend pattern, the spike is the breakout and the channel usually becomes the first leg of a trading range and therefore will usually be retraced. Typically, the market eventually pulls back all the way to the start of the channel, completing the second leg of the incipient trading range. In the example of that bull breakout, the market will then usually try to bounce off that support. This results in a double bottom bull flag that sometimes leads to a breakout above the new range, and other times it evolves into a protracted trading range like a tight trading range or a triangle. Less often, it is followed by a reversal.

On the 5 minute Emini chart, there are usually many attempts to break out every day but most fail after one or two trend bars. They most likely represent the start of a program trade by some institution, but they get overwhelmed by opposite programs by other institutions. When enough institutions have programs running in the same direction at the same time, their programs will be able to move the market to a new price level and the breakout will be successful. However, nothing is ever 100 percent certain and even the strongest breakouts fail about 30 percent of the time.

When a breakout is very strong, there will be three or more trend bars with small tails and very little overlap. This means that traders are not waiting for a significant pullback. They are afraid that there might not be a pullback until after the market has run a long way, and they want to be certain to capture at least part of the trend. They will enter at the market and on tiny pullbacks of one or two ticks, and their relentless orders will give the trend strength and work against the formation of a significant pullback.

The breakout bars often have large volume and sometimes they will have 10 to 20 times the volume of an average bar. The higher the volume and the more bars in the spike, the more likely it is that there will be significant follow-through. Prior to the breakout, both the bulls and the bears were scaling into their positions, fighting over control of the market and each trying to create a successful breakout in their direction. Once there is a clear breakout, the losing side will cover their large position quickly with a loss, and the winning side will enter even more aggressively. The result is one or more trend bars, often with high volume. Volume is not always especially high but when it is 10 or more times the average of the recent bars, the probability of a successful breakout, meaning that there will be follow-through for many bars, is higher. Also, volume can be unusually high on breakouts that fail within a few bars, but this is less common. Volume is not reliable enough to warrant following it, and the large trend bars that comprise the spike will already tell you whether the breakout is likely to be successful. Trying to think about the volume in addition will, more often than not, distract you and hinder your ability to trade at your best.

All successful breakouts should be viewed as spikes, since most are followed by channels and create a spike and channel trend pattern. However, the breakout can also fail and the trading range that preceded it then becomes a final flag, if it was a flag in a trend. In fact, most breakouts do fail but the breakout bar is so unremarkable that most traders don't even realize that there was an attempted breakout. Less commonly, the market can enter a tight trading range after the breakout, and this is usually followed by trend resumption, but sometimes the breakout of that tight trading range can be in the other direction, resulting in a reversal.

A breakout can be a single large trend bar or a series of large or small trend bars, and the breakout usually becomes part of one of the trend patterns previously discussed. For example, if there is a "trend from the open" bear trend, it is likely a breakout below a pattern from the previous day. If the trend is orderly, it might be followed by a tight trading range for several hours and then the day could turn into a trend resumption bear into the close. If instead the breakout is accelerating to the downside with each bar resulting in a steeper slope, and the chart assumes a parabolic and therefore climactic look, it might be followed by a pullback and then a channel. The day could become a spike and channel bear trend day.

Sometimes, after the market has been in a strong trend for many bars, it creates an unusually large trend bar in the direction of the trend. That large bar typically either becomes a breakout into an even steeper, stronger trend, or at least another leg in the trend, or can signify a climactic end of the trend. If the market pulls back for a few bars and does not retrace too much of the breakout bar, the odds of the breakout being successful are good, and traders will enter on the high 1 breakout pullback if this was a bull breakout (or short a low 1 in a bear breakout).

The trend can continue even if the pullback retraces beyond the breakout point, but the deeper the pullback, the more likely it is that the breakout will fail and the market will reverse. In this case, the large bar will represent a climactic end of the trend rather than a breakout. If the pullback is fairly deep, traders might hesitate to enter with the trend for an hour or so. For example, if there is a large bull trend bar that breaks above a swing high or trading range but the pullback is fairly deep, maybe a little below the top of the swing high, traders will not be certain if the breakout has failed or if the rally is just a little overdone. The bulls in this case often will not buy for about 10 bars or so and the market will frequently enter a small trading range. Instead of buying a high 1, they will likely wait for a high 2, especially if it forms after an hour or so. If the trading range is holding above the moving average and about an hour has passed, bulls will look to buy a two-legged sideways or down pullback. Sometimes the sideways move is followed by a second leg down. That second leg can lead to a new high, or to a trend reversal and more selling.

Once there is a pullback, which is a small trading range, traders will look for the trend to resume. The breakout from the pullback has an initial target of an approximate measured move equal to about the height of the trading range. Many traders will take partial or total profits in that area, and aggressive countertrend traders will initiate new positions.

The easiest breakout failures to spot are those where the market quickly reverses direction and does not make any significant attempt to continue in the direction of the breakout. This is more likely to happen when there is other evidence of a possible reversal, like a breakout above a trend channel line and then a reversal down with a strong signal bar.

The breakout can be of anything, such as a trend line, a trading range, or the high or low of the day or yesterday. It does not matter because they are all traded the same. Fade it if it fails and reenter in the direction of the breakout if the reversal attempt fails and therefore becomes a breakout pullback. Enter on the breakout only if it is very strong. An example of this is if there is a strong bull trend and then a two-bar pullback to a high 1 buy setup. Traders can buy at one tick above the high of the prior bar, and they can buy more on a breakout to a new high by placing an order to buy on a stop at one tick above the old high. Usually, however, it is better to buy a pullback or to look to short a failed breakout.

On most days, traders look at new swing highs and lows as possible fade setups. On a strong trend day, however, the breakouts are usually on huge volume and there is very little pullback even on a 1 minute chart. It is clear that the trend traders are in control. For example, when a bull trend is that strong, price action traders will be buying on high 1 and high 2 pullbacks instead of waiting for a breakout above the prior high of the trend. They are always trying to minimize the risk of the trade. However, once a strong trend is underway, entering with the trend for any reason is a good trade. In a strong trend, every tick is a with-trend entry, so you can simply enter at the market at any point and use a reasonable stop.

If there is a breakout with a large trend bar and the bar has not yet closed, you have a decision to make. If you just scalped out of part of your trade and are now thinking about swinging the remainder, always consider how much risk you have. One way to help decide if you should continue to hold your swing position is to ask yourself what you would do at this moment if you were not holding a position. If you would be willing to enter at the market using a swing-size position and the swing protective stop, then you should stay in your current swing position. If instead you think that it would be too risky to enter at the market with that amount of risk, then you should exit your swing position at the market.

When there is a breakout, both buyers and sellers see it as an opportunity. For example, if the market has a swing high and then pulls back, both bulls and bears will enter as the market moves above that prior swing high. Bulls will be buying the breakout because they see it as a sign of strength and they believe the market will go high enough above their entry for them to exit with a profit. Bears will also see the breakout as an opportunity to make money. For example, bears might sell on a limit order at the level of that prior high or maybe a few ticks above it. If the market reverses and comes down, they will look to exit with a profit. If, however, the market continues up, they will look to add to their short position if they think the market might pull back to test the breakout. Since most pullbacks come all the way back to the prior swing high, they can exit on that breakout test at about breakeven on their first entry and with a profit on their second, higher entry.

When traders think of breakouts they usually immediately have the image of a trading range. However, the breakout can be of anything. One common breakout that many traders overlook is a flag breaking out in the unexpected direction, like a bear flag breaking out of the top or a bull flag breaking out of a bottom. For example, if there is a reasonably strong bear trend and traders are not sure if a tradable low is in and they see a bear flag forming, they might start buying below the low of the prior bars, expecting a low 1 and then a low 2 or even a low 3 to fail. Sometimes the bear flag will have a good shape and trigger the low 2 short or the wedge bear flag short and then immediately reverse up into one or two bull trend bars. This breakout usually creates a measuring gap that leads to a measured move up. Traders will enter on the breakout and on any small pullback; and since bears were trapped, they will likely not be eager to short again until the market has had at least two legs up. The opposite is true of bull flags in bull trends.

There is a special type of breakout that sometimes occurs on trend days in the final hour. For example, if the market is trending down with no sign of a pullback, there can be one or two large bear trend bars that break out of the bottom of the bear channel. There may be a small pullback and then a second brief breakout to a new low. At other times, the market just moves down into the close relentlessly without large bear trend bars. What is likely happening in both cases is that risk managers at trading firms are telling their traders who have been bottom picking that they are on the wrong side of the market and that they have to sell out of their positions at the market. The plunges usually do not have much follow-through since they are mostly due to forced selling. There are likely some smart programmers who anticipate this and try to capitalize on it by designing programs to go short briefly, increasing the size of the sell climax. Momentum programs are also part of the strong trend. There may or may not be a bounce into the close after the one or two sell climaxes. The opposite is true on days that end with strong bull spikes or channels. The risk managers are telling their traders to buy back their losing shorts before the close, and as the market is rising quickly, momentum programs detect this and also buy relentlessly as long as the momentum continues.

One of the goals of traders is to do what the institutions are doing. Many breakouts are made of large trend bars that have the biggest volume of the day. These are times when the institutions are trading most heavily, and they are doing so because they expect the move to have protracted follow-through. As scary and emotional as the market can feel during a big breakout, the institutions see it as a great opportunity, as indicated by the volume, and so should you. Try to learn to trade breakouts because they have an excellent trader's equation. If you have to, simply trade only a quarter-size position ("I don't care" size), just to get experience. The move will often be large enough that you can make as much as you do on a routine trade using your full position size.

Figure 2.1   SIGNS OF STRENGTH IN A BREAKOUT   **73**

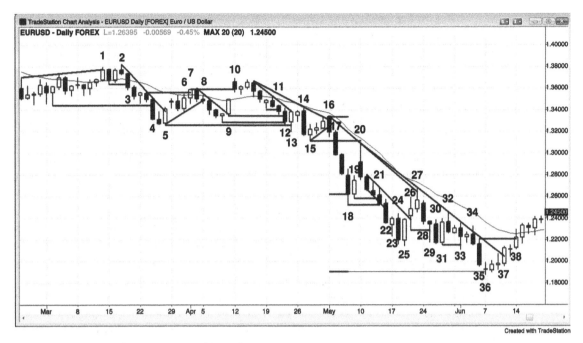

FIGURE 2.1   Breakouts Happen Many Times Every Day

Breakouts of some type occur every few bars on every chart, as shown in Figure 2.1 in the daily chart of the Euro/U.S. Dollar Forex. Strictly speaking, if the high of a bar is above the high of any prior bar or the low of the bar is below the low of any prior bar, it is a breakout of that bar. Also, every trend bar is a breakout (remember from book 1, every trend bar is a spike, breakout, gap, and climax). Many different types of breakouts and failures are highlighted on this chart.

Bar 1 broke above a trend channel line and was followed by a breakout below its low on the next bar, setting up a two-bar reversal, which was triggered on the bar 3 entry bar. Bar 2 was a second attempt to break out above the bull channel and it broke out above another two-bar reversal but the breakouts failed and the market reversed down.

Bar 4 was a breakout below a swing low and it was the sixth bar is a sell climax down from bar 2. Since the range of the bar was large and it had small tails, it might represent a sell climax that needed a correction before there was follow-through selling. This turned out to be the case, because bar 5 was a strong bull reversal bar that turned bar 4 into a failed breakout.

There was a two-legged pullback to the moving average and bar 8 broke out of the bear flag.

Bar 9 broke above the bear trend line.

Bar 10 broke above a swing high but the breakout failed when the next bar traded below its low.

Bar 12 fell below the bar 9 entry bar and below the signal bar just before it.

Bar 13 tried to reverse back up and create a failed breakout, but that failed breakout failed on the bar 14 reversal back down. Bar 14 was also a reversal down from the failed breakout above a micro trend line and above a bull reversal bar. When a failed breakout fails to reverse the market, it becomes a breakout pullback.

The bar 16 break above the bear trend line failed and the bar reversed down into an outside down reversal, falling below the bear flag trend line of the prior three bars.

Bars 16 to 18 created a four-bar breakout composed of strong bear trend bars with large bodies, small tails, and very little overlap. The bulls who scaled into longs within the trading range finally capitulated and not only stopped buying, but had to sell out of their large long positions quickly without waiting for a pullback. They were not confident that a pullback would come soon and were confident that the market would be lower within a few bars. This means that getting out at the market or on a tiny pullback within the bar was their best option. Their long liquidation and their lack of buying for several bars contributed to the strength of the sell-off. When a breakout is that strong, it usually is followed by a channel and often leads to a measured move from the open of the first bar to the close of the final bar in the spike. The bar 36 low was just below that measured move projection, and that ended the channel. The market then usually works its way back up to test the first reasonable buy signal after the spike, which was the high of the bar 19 bull inside bar. If it gets there, it next tries to test the start of the bear channel, which was the bar 20 high.

Bar 20 was an attempt to make the four-bar breakout fail but when a breakout is that strong, there is usually follow-through and the failure will typically fail and just become a breakout pullback, as it did here. The market reversed back down just shy of the bar 15 breakout point and the moving average. Whenever a market turns back down without touching a resistance level, the bears are very strong because they are not waiting for the resistance to be touched. The bears are afraid that the bulls might not be able to get the market up there, so the bears have limit orders just below. This is a sign of urgency by the bears. That gap between the breakout point (the bar 15 low) and the breakout pullback (the bar 20 high) usually becomes a measuring gap and often is the approximate midpoint of the move. The start of the bear trend was the bar 2 high, and the market ultimately fell below the gap by more than the number of points between the bar 2 high and the middle of the measuring gap. The breakout and the strong reversal down on the breakout test established the bear trend as very strong, and traders should only look for shorts for the rest of the day. There might be a long scalp or two, but a trader should take

Figure 2.1   SIGNS OF STRENGTH IN A BREAKOUT   **75**

them only if the trader is able to immediately reverse back to short as soon as a bar falls below the low of the prior bar, indicating that the small pullback might be ending. Incidentally, Elliott Wave traders see the pullback as the top of wave 4 and the breakout point as the bottom of wave 1. The two cannot overlap if the downward wave 3 in between is in fact wave 3, which is usually the strongest wave of the trend.

Bar 22 was a large-range bear bar that broke below the bottom of a four-bar channel. It was arguably the third consecutive sell climax (the first was bar 14 and the second was the four-bar spike down to bar 18). The market usually has at least a 10-bar, two-legged correction after two or three consecutive climaxes. Here, however, that four-bar bear spike was the overwhelming feature of the day and was the beginning of a strong breakout. Yes, it was a spike and therefore a sell climax, but it was so large that the character of the market changed and any counting has to start all over. Once it formed, traders decided that there was going to be a strong move down, and a channel is the most common pattern that follows a strong spike. Channels often have three pushes before they correct, and this one did as well. The three pushes were bars 18, 25, and 36, and they were followed by a weak rally into the close.

Bar 23 was a reversal attempt after the bar 22 sell climax and overshoot through the bottom of the three-bar bear channel. However, it is a mistake to be looking for a long based on these few bars when the big picture is so bearish. The market is always trying to reverse trends, and it is easy to get caught up in the emotion of a bottoming pattern as it happens in real time; but you should never lose sight of the big picture. That four-bar bear spike was very strong, and the always-in position is still short. Any attempt at a bottom at this point will almost certainly result in a bear flag, as it did here. The market always has inertia, and when it is trending, expect all reversal attempts to fail.

Bar 25 was a second attempt to reverse up after the breakout below the bars 20 to 21 channel. Since the signal bars for both attempts had strong bull bodies, the market might test the moving average. Most traders should not take this trade and instead should stay short. Too often, traders will scalp the countertrend trade for a point and then do not reverse back to short, and they miss out on making four or more points on the with-trend trade. It can be difficult to change your mind-set quickly back to short if you just went long, and if you cannot do this easily, do not take the countertrend scalp and then miss the swing down.

Bar 26 broke out of the top of the channel, as expected.

Bar 27 broke above the bear trend line and above the bar 18 breakout point but failed and reversed down on the next bar.

Bar 28 was a breakout of a three-bar bear flag.

Bar 29 broke below the bar 26 long entry bar but it found buyers, as seen by the large tail.

Bar 32 was another test of a bear trend line and therefore an attempted breakout, but it failed.

Bar 35 was another large bear trend bar and therefore another possible sell climax. When the market begins to form second and third sell climaxes within a short time, it is likely to reverse for at least a two-legged correction.

Bar 36 broke below the measured move but did not find sellers. Instead, it found quiet trading, which might be signaling a failed breakout of the bars 22 to 34 bear flag. A horizontal bear flag after a long bear trend often becomes a final flag and is typically followed by at least two legs sideways to up. Bar 36 was also the third push down in the bear channel and that usually leads to at least a reversal attempt.

The bar after bar 36 broke above the bar 36 high and became the entry bar for the long.

Bar 37 was a bull breakout bar above the bear trend line.

Bar 38 broke above the strong bar 35 bear trend bar, and there were certainly many buy stops for shorts above this bar because its large bear body represented strong selling. Once the market got above its high, lots of bears decided that there was no longer enough strength to stay short and they bought back their shorts (short covering) into the close.

Figure 2.2   SIGNS OF STRENGTH IN A BREAKOUT   **77**

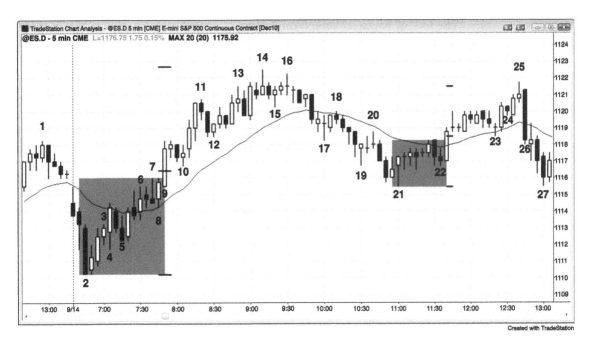

FIGURE 2.2   Flags Can Break Out in the Less Likely Direction

Flags can sometimes break out in the unexpected direction and lead to measured moves. In Figure 2.2, there was a failed wedge bear flag that broke to the upside on bar 9. The measuring gap between the high of the bar 7 breakout point and the bar 10 breakout test led to an almost perfect measured move up.

Bar 3 was a low 1 short setup, but after three strong bull bodies and the bar 2 sell climax, it was likely to fail. Aggressive traders would have gone long on limit buy orders at and below the bar 3 low. Bar 5 was an entry bar for a low 2 short, but after the strong bar 4 outside up bar the market might have been making a low of the day. Again, aggressive traders would have gone long at or below the low of the low 2 signal bar. Bar 7 was a signal bar for a wedge bear flag short, but the market was in a bull channel and the bar 4 outside up bar made the always-in trade long. Rather than short below bar 7, bears should have waited to see if the market formed a lower high. Bulls went long above bar 8, expecting a measured move up from the failed wedge bear flag.

There was then a failed low 2 bear flag buy setup above bar 22 and the entry bar was a bull trend bar. This breakout also led to a measured move up. Bar 21 was the bottom of a bear channel on a bull day and bar 22 was the breakout pullback from that channel breakout, so alert traders thought that the low 2 had an excellent chance of failing and leading to a test of the high of the day.

The low of bar 26 reversed the lows of the past 12 bars (it was below those lows) and the closes of the past 13 bars. Its close reversed these same lows, which is significant because a close below a low is more of a sign of strength than simply a low that is below a prior low. The more lows and closes that are reversed, the stronger the reversal. Every trader who bought during those prior 12 bars is now holding a loser and will look for any small bounce to sell out of his longs. Many sold on the next bar and created the tail on the top of the bar. Also, those bulls will not likely look to buy again for at least a few bars.

Figure 2.3   SIGNS OF STRENGTH IN A BREAKOUT   **79**

FIGURE 2.3 Small Breakout Bar

As shown in Figure 2.3, although big breakout bars like bars 3 and 19 often lead to big trends, sometimes a small breakout bar like bar 12 can be the start of a protracted move. After the bar 9 bear spike, traders wondered if the rally to bar 11 might become a low 2 bear flag at the moving average (bars 10 and 11 were two pushes up). However, instead of breaking to the downside, the market broke above the bar 10 and bar 11 double top (this made the rally a final flag, since it was the final flag of the bear trend, even though it never broke to the downside). The bar 12 breakout bar was small, but it was enough to make traders begin to discard the notion that the move to bar 11 was a bear flag, and they began to wonder if bar 9 was an exhaustive sell climax, which could correct for 10 or more bars. The bar after bar 12 was also small, but it had two signs of strength: a bull body and a low that did not fall below the bar 11 high (the breakout point). Although the rally to bar 14 did not cover many points, it was a relentless bull trend and became the first of two legs up (the second began with the bar 18 double bottom with bar 15, and the triangle formed by the lows of bars 13, 15, and 18).

CHAPTER 3

Initial Breakout

On 5 minute charts of most markets, there are usually at least a couple of successful significant breakouts every day. Most breakouts begin with a single trend bar that is usually larger than the previous bars and has no tails or only small tails. In the strongest breakouts, there will be a series of trend bars with very little overlap. For example, in a strong bull breakout on the 5 minute Emini chart, as soon as the breakout bar closes, some traders will place limit orders to buy at the closing price of that bar. If the next bar opens at that price and immediately trades up without going below that price, the limit orders will likely not get filled and these bullish traders will be trapped out of the market. They will experience a sense of urgency because they are afraid of missing the move and will look to get long as soon as possible, using either a market order or a limit order to buy any one- or two-tick or small pullback, or they will switch to a smaller time frame chart like a 1 or 2 minute, and then enter on a high 1 or high 2 pullback. This is often hard to do emotionally and it is comparable to jumping off a high diving board. What might work in both situations is to just do it: pinch your nose, close your eyes tightly, tense up every muscle in your body, and trust that you won't get hurt too badly and that the bad feelings will end quickly. If you are trading the Emini, you simply buy the small pullback and rely on your stop. If the breakout is good, your stop will not be hit and you will have a good chance of making two to even six or more points over the next many bars while risking about two points.

If, instead of having several strong bull trend bars in a row, the bar after a one- or two-bar breakout is a small bar, a doji, an inside bar, a bar with large tails, or a bear trend bar, the breakout might fail. This could lead to a reversal back into the trading range, a trend reversal into a bear trend, or a failed reversal, which is simply a one- or two-bar pullback that is followed by a resumption of the upward move. When the breakout is successful, it will create some version of a spike and channel trend.

A breakout entry appears deceptively easy to take when you see it on the chart at the end of the day. However, in real time, the setups tend to be either unclear or clear but scary. Entering on the breakout or after the breakout bar closes is difficult to do, because the breakout spike is often large, and traders have to quickly decide to risk much more than they usually do. As a result, they often end up choosing to wait for a pullback. Even if they reduce their position size so that the dollar risk is the same as with any other trade, the thought of risking two or three times as many ticks frightens them. Entering on a pullback is difficult because every pullback begins with a minor reversal, and traders are afraid that the pullback might be the start of a deep correction. If the reversal is just for a bar to two and sets up a breakout pullback entry, they are afraid to enter because they are concerned that the market might be entering a trading range and they do not want to buy at the top if the market is having a bull breakout, or sell at the bottom if there is a bear breakout. Trends do everything that they can to keep traders out, which is the only way they can keep traders chasing the market all day. When a setup is easy and clear, the move is usually a small, fast scalp. If the move is going to go a long way, it has to be unclear and difficult to take, to keep traders on the sidelines and force them to chase the trend.

You will regularly hear pundits discuss a one- or two-day sell-off in a stock that resulted from a bad report, like a disappointing earnings report or a change in management. They are deciding if the news is just a one-day event in an otherwise strong bull trend, or if it will change the outlook for the stock for the next several months. If they conclude that the odds favor the bull trend, they will buy around the bottom of the bear spike. If they think that the news was so severe that the stock will remain under pressure for months, they will not buy, and in fact will look to sell out of their longs on the next rally. Technical traders see the sell-off as a bear breakout and evaluate the stock in terms of the strength of the breakout. If the spike looks strong, they will short rallies, and maybe even the close of the bar, expecting a bigger spike, a spike and channel, or some other type of bear trend. If it looks weak relative to the bull trend, they will buy around the close and low of the bear trend bar, expecting a failed breakout and for the trend reversal attempt to become just another bull flag.

Figure 3.1   INITIAL BREAKOUT   **83**

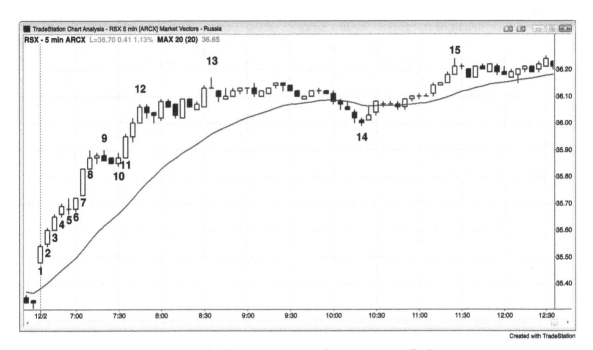

FIGURE 3.1   Breakouts with Many Consecutive Trend Bars Are Usually Strong

The strongest breakouts have a sense of urgency and have several trend bars in a row, as happened in the trend from the open bull trend day in RSX, the Market Vectors exchange-traded fund (ETF) for Russia shown in Figure 3.1. The market broke above the trading range that formed in the final hour of yesterday. Notice how the lows of several of the bars in the breakout did not drop below the close of the prior bar. This means that bulls who waited for the bar to close and then immediately placed limit orders to buy at the level of that close would likely not have their orders filled and they would be trapped out of the market. The market was running away from them and they knew it and would then take any reason to get long. This urgency caused the market to rise sharply. This series of bars should be considered to be a bull spike. A bull spike is usually followed by a bull channel, and together they constitute a spike and channel bull trend.

Bar 6 was an inside bar and the first pause, and this is usually a reliable high 1 long entry in a trend from the open bull trend day. However, when the trend is this strong, you can just buy at the market or buy for any reason at all. Did it rain somewhere in the Amazon last year? Then buy. Did someone on your kid's high school basketball team score a point last year? Then buy more. You need to get long and stay long because there is probably better than a 70 percent chance that the market will make a measured move up equal to or greater than the approximate height of the spike (the low or open of bar 1 to the close or high of bar 4 or 8, and add this many points to the closes of those bars). The exact probability is never knowable, but from experience this is a very strong breakout and the probability of the measured move is likely greater than 70 percent here. The measured move up from the open of bar 1 to the close of bar 4 was the price level where the market paused at the top of bar 8. The measured move based on the open of bar 1 to the close of bar 8 was exceeded by 3 cents on the close of the day (not shown).

Figure 3.2   INITIAL BREAKOUT   **85**

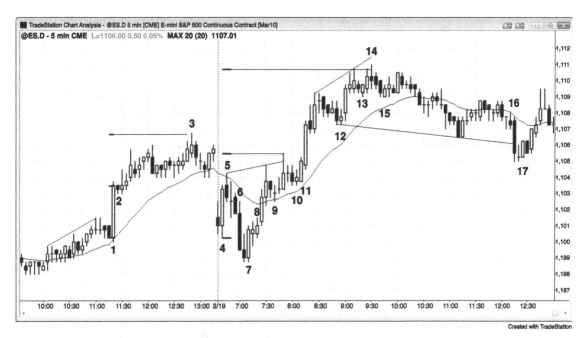

FIGURE 3.2   Successful Breakouts Need Follow-Through

Breakouts are common on the 5 minute Emini chart, but strong, successful ones that have several bars of follow-through, like at bar 1 and bar 11 in Figure 3.2, usually happen only one to three times a day.

Bar 1 broke above the top of a small wedge, and it had a small tail at the top and bottom and was a large bull trend bar.

Bar 2 was a small bear inside bar and is a signal bar both for a failed breakout short and a breakout pullback long. Remember that an inside bar is a one-bar trading range and a setup for a breakout in either direction. Breakouts often lead to measured moves, and one common pattern is a measured move from the open or low of the spike to the close or high of the spike, and then projected up from the close or high of the spike. Here, the move to the bar 3 high of the day was a measured move from the open to the close of the bar 1 breakout bar.

The opening range often leads to a breakout to a measured move, but there are usually several possibilities for the measurement points and it is best to watch the nearest target first. Traders should look at the low of bar 4 to the high of bar 5. Once that measured move was exceeded, traders should look at other possibilities. A failed wedge often leads to a measured move, but traders need to consider every option that they can see. For example, they might look at the low of bar 7 to the high of the wedge (two bars after bar 9). However, the wedge began at bar 4, and the bar 7 lower low might be viewed as an overshoot of the actual bar 4 low. The market tried to form a wedge bear flag beginning at the bar 4 low, and it had three pushes up (bar 5, and the spikes before and after bar 9). Using the bar 4 low to the top of the wedge for the measurement projected a move that was exceeded by only one tick at the bar 14 high of the day. The purpose of finding these measured move targets is to find reasonable areas to take profits, and, if there is a strong countertrend setup, to initiate trades in the opposite direction.

Bar 6 was a strong breakout to a new low of the day, but it was reversed up by the bar 7 outside up bull trend bar. When traders saw the sideways action to bar 8, they were thinking that this was a possible breakout pullback (a bear flag) and it could be followed by another move down. You must always consider both bull and bear alternatives. Instead of more selling, the market moved up quickly. How can such a strong bear trend bar be reversed up so quickly? If the institutions had a huge number of buy orders, they would like to fill them at the best prices, and if they thought that the market was likely to test below the bar 4 low before going up, they would wait to buy until after that test. As the market is getting close to their buy zone, it does not make sense for them to buy because they believe the market will be a little lower over the next several minutes. So these very eager bulls are stepping aside. The absence of the strongest buyers creates an imbalance to the sell side, so the market has to fall quickly for the shorts to find someone willing to take the other side of their trade. The result is a large bear trend bar. Once the market is at a level where the bulls think it will not fall further, they appear out of nowhere and begin to buy heavily and relentlessly, overwhelming the bears. The bears realize what is going on and they stop shorting and begin to buy back their shorts. This means that both the bulls and the bears believe that the market will go up, and this creates a directional probability of an equidistant move of 60 percent or more in favor of the bulls. In other words, there is a 60 percent or more chance that the market will go up two points before falling two points, and up three points before falling three points. In fact, there is probably better than a 60 percent chance that the market will break out above the opening range and have a measured move up before there is a two-point pullback, and this is a great trade for the bulls.

Bars 9 and 10 were breakout pullbacks after new highs of the day.

Bar 11 was a breakout of the wedge that began with the bar 5 high. It was a strong two-bar bull spike, and it was followed by two more pushes up. Bull channels after spikes often have three pushes up, where the top of the spike is the first push up.

Bar 12 was a two-legged high 2 breakout pullback in a strong bull trend and is a great buy setup.

Bar 13 was another breakout pullback but since it would lead to a third push up, bulls had to be cautious. Once bar 14 hit five ticks above the long entry, many bulls moved their stops to breakeven because they were wondering if the bar 14

Figure 3.2   INITIAL BREAKOUT   **87**

wedge high would lead to a lengthy (10 bars or more) two-legged pullback or even a trend reversal. Therefore, bar 15 was a bad signal for longs, who expected that any rally would end below the bar 14 wedge high and be followed by at least one more leg down. Aggressive traders shorted above its high, because a buy signal that is likely to fail means that traders could go short where inexperienced traders just went long and they would have about a 60 percent chance of the market falling two points to the protective stop of the weak longs before the market hit their profit-taking limit order six ticks higher. They are risking six ticks to make eight ticks and are 60 percent confident that they will win, and this is a logical bet.

Bar 16 was a bear breakout below a head and shoulders top, but since most topping patterns are really just bull flags, there was a good chance that the breakout would fail. Bulls could have bought above the small doji inside bar that followed, but this would be somewhat risky because doji bars are not reliable signal bars. Once they saw the bar 17 bull trend bar, buying the wedge bull flag became a more reliable pattern. Buying above a strong bull bar increases the odds for success because the market has already shown some strength. Since strong breakouts usually have several trend bars in a row and not a small doji bar for the next bar, traders saw this as a warning that the bear breakout was weak.

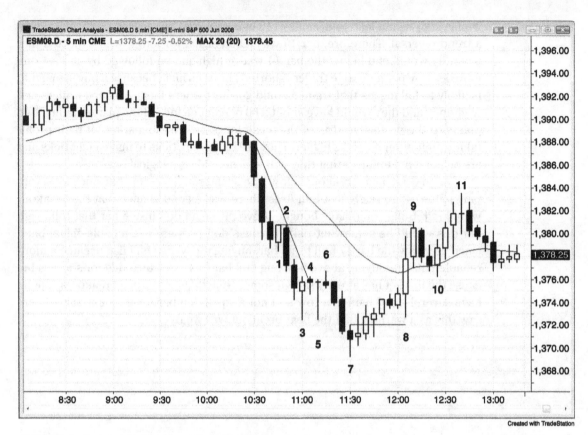

FIGURE 3.3 Watch Charts and Not the News

As shown in Figure 3.3, some news must have been released that led to a sharp sell-off at 10:30 a.m. PST. You should never pay attention to the news, aside from knowing when it will be released, because it creates a distance between you and what you have to do. It requires thought that you then have to reconcile with the chart, which can only reduce your profit. The chart tells you all that you need to know. Something happened that made the institutions sell aggressively, and that is all the information that a trader needs. It is time to look for short setups.

Bar 1 was a strong bull trend bar that trapped early buyers who bought the candle pattern or a smaller time frame reversal. A buy was not even triggered on this 5 minute chart, since the next bar did not go above the bar 1 high. These bulls would exit below the low of bar 1 and wouldn't look to buy again until more price action unfolds. Place an order to short on a stop at one tick below the low of bar 1, which is where those longs will have their protective stops, and as they cover they will provide plenty of downside fuel. If it gets hit, you know the trapped longs will

Figure 3.3

INITIAL BREAKOUT **89**

get out and not want to buy again soon, and the smart bears will be adding to their shorts. With no one left to buy, the market will almost certainly provide a scalper's profit and likely much more.

Bar 5 is the third overlapping bar and at least one of the bars was a doji (all three were). This is barbwire, which is usually a continuation pattern and, like with any trading range, you should never buy at its high or sell at its low. You can fade small bars at its extremes and, since all horizontal trading ranges are magnets and often become final flags, you can wait for a trend bar breakout to fail and look for a reversal back into the range. Here, bar 7 closed above its midpoint and therefore met the minimum requirement for a reversal bar, and it followed a third consecutive sell climax. This is usually followed by at least a 10-bar, two-legged correction.

Bars 3 and 5 were classic candle pattern traps. Traders who memorize candle reversal patterns will be eager to buy these very large candles with long bull tails because they will see the long tails and the closes near the highs as evidence that the bulls were gaining control. When you see a big bar with a long tail and a small body in a bear trend, it tells you that if you buy above its high, you are paying way too much. In a bear trend, you want to buy low, not at the top of a huge bar with a small body when the market is in a tight bear channel and there has been no prior bull strength or trend line break. Bar 5 was an even better candle pattern trap than bar 3 since it was a gravestone doji, which candle novices worship. Also, the market traded above the high of the bar, seeming to confirm the strength of the bulls, and it was a second attempt at a bottom (a double bottom with bar 3). But what went wrong? When you see these small-bodied big candles in a strong trend where there has yet to be a trend line break, you should get excited because they are great traps and therefore perfect short setups. Just wait for the small bar that usually follows. Its lack of upside follow-through makes these early bulls very scared. Everyone knows where those bulls are putting their protective stops, so that is exactly where you should be putting your entry stop to go short. When you see those big doji candles, you, too, see bullish strength, but then assume that since the price was hovering at the high of those bars and the bulls were now in balance with the bears, the highs of those bars are likely to be in the middle or top of a trading range and not at a bottom.

The two-legged sideways move to bar 6 broke a trend line. Traders then knew that the bulls were getting eager to buy, so a perfect long setup would be a failed breakout to new lows. Smart traders just waited for a one- or two-bar break below bars 3 and 5 and then started placing buy orders at one tick above the high of the prior bar. They were prepared to keep moving the orders down if they didn't get filled. If the move continued too far down, they would have waited for another trend line break before looking to buy again because the trend would have resumed and this setup would have failed to trigger. The earlier bulls with two or three losses would wait for confirmation this time and enter late, and this would provide additional fuel for the upward move after the price action longs got in.

Even though bar 7 had a bear body, at least it closed above its midpoint, indicating some strength. Presumably, bulls were a little cautious after losing on entries from bars 1, 3, and 5. Also, it was a failed breakout from barbwire, which often forms the final flag of a trend. The odds were high that this would be a profitable long and smart traders would have been anticipating it, so there was no excuse to miss it.

The entry bar had a bull body, albeit small, which was constructive. Also, it was an inside body variant (its body was inside the body of the signal bar, which is a weaker version of an inside bar), which meant that the bears did not take control. At this point, longs were feeling confident because their protective stop was not hit on the bar after entry, as was the case for the earlier bulls.

The next three bars were all bull trend bars with closes above the prior close, so the closes were in a bull trend. It is reasonable to assume that there will be two legs up, but almost certainly there will be a stop run down before the second leg. The breakeven stop was not hit on the violent move down in bar 8, which turned into a bullish outside bar and the start of the second leg up (a higher low). Whenever there is a strong outside up bar that breaks the market into a new trend, its low is the start of the trend and all bar counting gets reset. For example, the two-bar reversal at bar 9 was a low 1 setup and not a low 2.

The targets for the rally were the bull signal bar highs in the bear (the highs of bars 3 and 5 and possibly bar 2). Bar 9 exceeded the final target by one tick. The momentum was so strong that the bar 8 low was likely just part of the first leg up and not the start of the second leg up, and there instead should be a bigger pullback and then a second leg up (it ended at bar 11).

Bar 11 set up a low 2 short from the rally up from the bar 8 low.

CHAPTER 4

Breakout Entries in Existing Strong Trends

W hen a trend is strong and there is a pullback, every breakout beyond a prior extreme is a valid with-trend entry. The breakout usually has strong volume, a large breakout bar (a strong trend bar), and follow-through over the next several bars. Smart money is clearly entering on the breakout. However, that is rarely the best way to trade a breakout, and price action traders almost always find an earlier price action entry like a high 1 or 2 in a bull trend. It is important to recognize that when a trend is strong, you can enter at any time and make a profit if you use an adequate stop. Once traders see that a trend is strong, some traders do not take the first entries because they are hoping for a larger pullback, like a two-legged pullback to the moving average. For example, if the market just became clearly always-in long and the initial bull spike has three good-sized bull trend bars with small tails, a trader might be afraid that the move was a little climactic and decide that he wants to wait for a high 2 buy setup. However, when a trend is very strong like this, the first couple of entries are usually just high 1 buy setups. Aggressive traders will place limit orders to buy below the low of the prior bar, expecting any reversal attempt to fail. Once the market trades below the low of the prior bar, they will expect a high 1 buy setup to lead to at least a new high and probably a measured move up, based on the height of the bull spike. If traders fail to take either of these two early entries, they should train themselves to guarantee that they get into this strong trend. When they are looking at the pullback beginning, they should put a buy stop at one tick above the high of the spike, in case the pullback is only one bar and reverses up quickly. If they fail to take either of the early pullback entries and the market begins to race up without them, they will be swept into the trade and not be left behind. On the strongest trades, you will usually see that the bar that breaks above the bull spike is usually a large bull trend bar, and this tells you that many strong bulls believe that there is value buying the new high. If it is a great entry for so many of them, it is a great entry for you as well.

One quick way to determine the strength of a trend is to see how it reacts after it breaks beyond prior trend extremes. For example, if a bull trend has a pullback and then breaks above the high of the day, does it find more buyers or sellers on the breakout? If the market moves far enough up for the breakout buyers to make at least a scalper's profit, then the breakout found more buyers than sellers. That is one of the hallmarks of a strong trend. By contrast, if the market raced to a new swing high but then reversed down within a bar or two, then the breakout found more sellers than buyers, which is more characteristic of trading ranges, and the market could be transitioning into a trading range. Watching how the market behaves at a new high gives a clue as to whether there is a still strong trend in effect. If not, even though the trend may still be in effect, it is less strong and longs should be taking profits at the new extreme and even looking to go short, instead of buying the breakout to the new high or looking to buy a small pullback. The opposite is true in bear trends.

In general, if you are entering on a stop at a new extreme, you should scalp most or all of your trade unless the trend is especially strong. If so, you can swing most or all of your position. For example, if the market is in a strong bull trend, bulls will buy above the most recent high on a stop but most will scalp out of their trade. If the market is extremely strong, they might swing most of their position. If not, bears will be shorting on every new swing high with a limit order at the old swing high or slightly above, and they will add on higher. If the market drops after their first entry, they will exit with a profit. If instead the market continued up, they expect the old high to be tested by a pullback within a few bars, and this would allow them to exit their first entry at breakeven and to exit their higher entry with a profit.

Figure 4.1   BREAKOUT ENTRIES IN EXISTING STRONG TRENDS   **93**

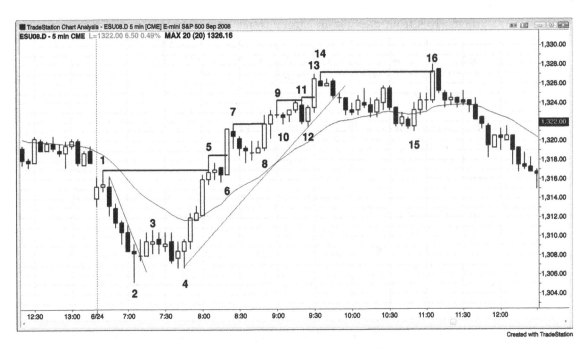

FIGURE 4.1   Strong Breakouts Have Many Consecutive Strong Trend Bars

As shown in Figure 4.1, the rally from the bar 4 higher low became a strong bull trend (higher low after a trend line break), with seven bull trend bars in a row as the market reversed through the bar 1 high of the day. With that much momentum, everyone was in agreement that bar 5 would be exceeded before there was a sell-off below the start of the bull trend at bar 4. The market was in always-in mode and would likely have approximately a measured move up based on the bull spike from bar 4 to bar 5 or from the opening range from bar 1 to bar 2, and therefore bulls could buy at the market, on any pullback, at or below the low of any bar, above the high of any pullback, on the close of any bar, and on a stop above the most recent swing high.

Breakout traders would have bought above every prior swing high, such as on bars 5, 6, 8, 11, 13, and 16. By bar 5, the market was clearly strongly always-in up. Aggressive bulls placed limit orders to buy at the low of the prior bar, expecting the initial pullback to only be a bar or so long and for the market to reverse up in a high 1. Buying below the prior bar is usually a lower entry than buying above the high 1. If traders preferred to enter on stops and did not buy at the low of the bar after bar 5, they would have bought on the bar 6 high 1 entry as it moved above the prior bar. If they instead were hoping for a deeper pullback like a high 2 at the moving average and did not take either of these two entries, they needed to protect themselves from missing the strong trend. They should never let themselves get trapped out of a great trend. The way to do this would be by placing a worst-case buy stop at one tick above the high of the bar 5 bull spike. The entry would be worse, but at least they would get into a trade that was likely to continue for at least a measured move up based on the height of the bull spike. Bar 6 was a large bull trend bar with no tails, which indicated that many strong bulls bought on that same bar. Once traders saw that the strong bulls bought the breakout to the new high, they should have been reassured that the trade was good. Their initial protective stop was below the most recent minor swing low, which was the high 1 signal bar before bar 6.

Pullback traders would have entered earlier in every instance, on the breakout pullbacks, which were bull flags—for example, at the bar 6 high 1, the bar 8 high 2, the bar 10 failed wedge reversal, the bar 12 high 2 and failed trend line break (not shown), and the bar 15 high 2 test below the moving average (first moving average gap bar buy setup) and double bottom with bar 12 (the high 2 was based on the two clear, larger legs down from bar 14). Breakout traders are initiating their longs in the exact area where price action traders are selling their longs for a profit. In general, it is not wise to be buying where a lot of smart traders are selling. However, when the market is strong, you can buy anywhere, including above the high, and still make a profit. However, the risk/reward ratio is much better when you buy pullbacks than it is when you buy breakouts.

Blindly buying breakouts is foolish, and smart money would not have bought the bar 11 breakout because it was a possible third push up after the exceptionally strong bar 6 breakout bar reset the count and formed the first push up. Also, they would not have bought the bar 16 breakout, which was a higher high test of the old bar 14 high after a trend line break, since there was too much risk of a trend reversal. It is far better to fade breakouts when they fail or enter in the direction of the breakout after it pulls back. When traders think that a breakout looks too weak to buy, they will often instead short at and above the prior high.

Bears can make money on breakouts above prior swing highs by shorting the breakout and adding on higher. Then, when the market comes back to test the breakout, they can exit their entire short position and make a profit on their second entry and get out around breakeven on their first short. This strategy would have been possible if a bear shorted as the market moved above bars 5, 7, 9, and 14. For example, as the market pulled back from the bar 7 swing high, bears could place orders to go short at or slightly above that high. Their shorts would be filled during bar 8. They would then add to their short positions when they thought that the market might begin to pull back again or at a couple of points higher. They would then try to exit all their short trades on a limit order at the original entry price, at the bar 7 high. Because bears are buying back their shorts on that breakout test and

Figure 4.1   BREAKOUT ENTRIES IN EXISTING STRONG TRENDS   **95**

because bulls are adding to their longs in that same area, the pullback often ends at that price and the market once again goes up.

The reversal up at bar 4 was a breakout of the final flag of the bear trend. Sometimes final flag reversals come from higher lows and not lower lows. The test of the old extreme can exceed the old extreme or fall short. Bar 15 was the end of the final flag in the bull trend, and the reversal at bar 16 was from a new extreme (a higher high).

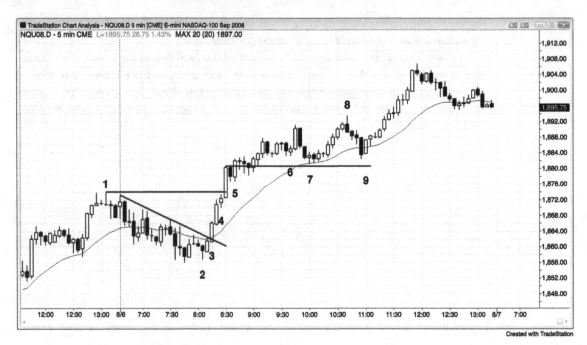

FIGURE 4.2   A Strong Trend Usually Has Follow-Through on the Next Day

As shown in Figure 4.2, yesterday (only the final hour is visible) was a strong trend from the open bull trend day, so the odds were high that there would be enough follow-through today to close above the open, and even if there was a pullback on the open today, the bull trend would likely reach at least a nominal new high. Traders were all watching for a buy setup.

Bar 2 was a small higher low after a high 4 buy setup, and a double bottom with the final pullback of yesterday. The signal bar had a bear close but at least its close was above its midpoint. Traders who missed that entry saw the market form a strong bull spike over the next two and three bars and decided that the market was now always-in long. Smart traders bought at least a small position at the market, just in case there was no pullback until after the market went much higher.

There were two large bull trend bars on the breakout, each with strong closes and small tails. Had you gone long at the close of bar 3, you would be swinging a portion of your trade at this point. This means that if you were instead flat, you could buy that same position size at the market and use the stop that you would have used had you bought earlier. That stop would now be below the bar 3 strong bull trend bar.

Bar 4 was a pause bar just below yesterday's high, and buying one tick above its high is another good entry. A pause bar is a possible reversal setup, so buying

Figure 4.2   BREAKOUT ENTRIES IN EXISTING STRONG TRENDS   **97**

above its high will be going long where the early bears are buying back their shorts and where the longs who exited early would also be buying back their longs.

At this point, the trend was clear and strong and you should be buying every pullback.

Bar 6 was followed by a two-bar reversal and a third push up and was an acceptable short setup for a pullback to the moving average.

Bar 8 was a reasonable countertrend scalp (a failed breakout to a new high after a trend line break) since it was a strong bear reversal bar and an expanding triangle top, but the trend was still up. Note that there had not yet been a close below the moving average and the market had been above the moving average for more than 20 bars, both of which are signs of strength. If you were thinking about taking a countertrend scalp, you would do so only if you would immediately look to get long again as the trend reversed back up. You do not want to exit a long, take a short scalp, and then miss out on a swing up as the trend resumes. If you cannot process the two changes of direction reliably, do not take the countertrend trade; simply hold long.

Bar 9 was a bull inside bar after the first close below the moving average and the second bar of a two-bar reversal, so a breakout above the setup was expected to test the bull high at a minimum.

CHAPTER 5

Failed Breakouts, Breakout Pullbacks, and Breakout Tests

T he sequence of breakout, failed breakout, either trend reversal or breakout pullback and then trend resumption is one of the most common aspects of price action, and most trades every day can be interpreted as some variation of this process. On a larger scale, it is the basis for a major trend reversal, which is discussed in book 3, where there is a trend line break and then a breakout pullback that tests the trend's extreme. The sequence occurs with all breakouts, but most often with a breakout of a bull or bear flag, which is a small trend in the opposite direction of the main trend on the screen.

Whenever there is a breakout, the market eventually pulls back and tests previous significant prices. The start of the pullback converts the breakout into a failure, and you should look at all breakouts as failing at this point, even if they subsequently resume. If the failure succeeds in reversing the trend, the breakout will have failed and the reversal will have succeeded. If the reversal only goes for a bar or two and the breakout resumes, the reversal attempt will simply become a pullback from the breakout (all failed breakouts that fail to reverse the market are breakout pullback setups for trades in the direction of the breakout). For example, if there is a bull breakout and then the market pulls back to around the entry price, forms a buy signal bar, and triggers the long, this pullback tested the breakout (it is a breakout test), and set up a long above the high of the most recent pullback bar. If the trend resumes, the breakout bar usually becomes a measuring gap, and if the trend reverses, the bull trend bar becomes an exhaustion gap, and the bear trend bar becomes a breakout gap (gaps are discussed in Chapter 6). Tests can be on the bar after the breakout or 20 or more bars later. What exactly got tested? The test is whether the breakout will succeed or fail. The market pulls back from the breakout because of selling. The bulls are selling to take partial profits on their longs, and the bears are selling in an attempt to make the breakout fail and flip the direction of the always-in trade to down. Both the bulls and the bears assess the strength of the breakout. If the setup and the entry bar are strong, traders will expect higher prices. When the market pulls back to the area of the breakout, bulls who are already long, whether or not they scalped out of some of their position on the breakout, will use the pullback as an opportunity to buy again. Bulls who missed the original entry will also use this pullback to get long. Bears who shorted prior to the breakout, below the entry price, will believe that the market has flipped to always-in long and it will trend higher. They will therefore use the pullback to buy back their shorts with a small loss. The bears who shorted the breakout will see that the breakout was strong and that the attempt to make the breakout fail was weak, and they will buy back their shorts with either a small profit or loss, or at breakeven. Since the bears now believe the breakout will be successful and that the market will rally, they will not want to short again until the market is higher, and only if a sell signal develops.

If the setup or the breakout was weak, and if a strong bear reversal bar developed shortly after the breakout, traders will expect the breakout to fail and for the bear trend to begin or resume. The bulls will sell out of their longs and not look to buy again for at least several bars, and the bears will initiate new shorts or add to their current shorts. The result will be that the market will fall below the bull breakout entry price, the test of that level will have failed, and the bear trend will have at least one more leg sideways to down.

If the breakout and the reversal are about equally strong, traders will then look at the bar after the bear reversal signal bar. If it has a strong bear close and is a strong bear trend bar, the chances that the reversal will continue down increase. If instead it is a strong bull reversal bar, chances are the failed breakout will not succeed, and this bull reversal bar then becomes a signal bar for a breakout pullback buy at one tick above its high.

Remember, the single most important determination that a trader makes, and he makes this after the close of every bar, is whether there will be more buyers or sellers above and below the prior bar. This is particularly true with breakouts and failed breakouts, because the move that follows usually determines the always-in direction and therefore lasts for many bars, and is not just a scalp.

This same process is repeated many times every day on all time frames. The breakout might simply be a quiet push above the high of the prior bar, and the pullback can begin on the next bar; when that is the case, the breakout might be a 10-bar breakout on a smaller time frame chart. The breakout can also be huge, like a 10-bar bull spike, and the pullback can occur 20 or more bars later. When the process involves many bars, it is a small breakout on a higher time frame chart, with the breakout and pullback on that chart simply lasting a few bars.

Following a bull breakout, these are some of the common areas that often get by the pullback:

- The breakout point (the price where the breakout began).
- The top of a spike in a spike and channel bull trend. Once the market breaks below the channel, it usually tests down to the top of the spike, and eventually to the bottom of the channel.
- The top of the spike in a final flag breakout. Once the market begins to pull back after breaking out of a potential final flag, it usually tests the swing high that preceded the flag.
- The most recent swing high in a stairs pattern. Bull stairs usually have pullbacks that fall at least a little below the most recent swing high.
- The top of the lower trading range in a bull trending trading range day. If it does not reverse back up, it can retrace to the bottom of that lower trading range.
- After the market rallies to the third push up in a potential wedge (a rising convergent channel), the odds are very high that it will test the top of the second push up. Once it reverses, it usually tests to the bottom of the wedge (the bottom of the first pullback, which is the bottom of the wedge channel).
- The high of the signal bar. Even if the breakout bar breaks out above a swing high from 10 bars earlier, there will often be a test of the high of the bar just before the breakout bar.
- The low of the entry bar. If the market falls below the entry bar, it often does so in a strong bear trend bar, and the move down from there is usually big enough for at least a scalp.
- The bottom of the swing low at the start of the leg up. The market sometimes falls below the entry bar and signal bar and retraces to the bottom of the bull leg, where it often will form a double bottom bull flag.
- Any support area like the moving average, a prior swing low, a trend line, or a trend channel line (like if the market forms a wedge bull flag).

Whenever there is a breakout, traders have to decide whether it will be followed by a trend or it will fail and reverse. Since there are many breakouts on every chart, it is important to become proficient at this. The breakout may continue for several bars, but at some point there will be a pullback. The countertrend traders will see the pullback as a sign that the breakout has failed, and they will enter on the assumption that the market will reverse, at least enough for a scalp. The with-trend traders will be taking some profits, but they expect that the failed breakout won't go far before it sets up a breakout pullback and then the trend will resume. For example, if there is a bull breakout, the first bar with a low below the low of the prior bar is a pullback. However, traders need to decide if instead it is a failed breakout and about to lead to a reversal back down. The more that the breakout has characteristics of a strong trend, the more likely it will have follow-through. If it has few or none of those characteristics, the odds of it failing and reversing back down increase. Characteristics of strong trends are detailed in the first book, *Trading Price Action Trends*, but important features of a strong bull trend are several consecutive bull trend bars with very little overlap of the bodies, small tails, and bull strength earlier in the day. If, however, the second bar is a relatively strong bear reversal or a bear inside bar, the breakout bar is not too large, the breakout is the third push up, and that bar reverses back below the trend channel line, the odds of a failed breakout and a tradable short are better. If you short below the low of that bar and the next bar is a strong bull reversal bar, you usually should reverse back to long because that failed breakout might be failing and instead setting up a breakout pullback buy setup.

After a breakout, eventually there will be a pullback to test the strength of the traders who initiated the breakout, and the success of the test will be determined by whether the traders enter in this area for a second time. The strongest breakouts usually do not come all the way back to the breakout point, but some pullbacks can retrace well beyond the breakout point and still be followed by a strong trend. For example, in a bull stair pattern, each breakout to a new swing high is followed by a deep breakout pullback. That breakout pullback stays above the prior higher low, creating a bull trend of higher highs and lows, and then is followed by another higher high. If the breakout pullback comes back to within a few ticks of the entry price, it is a breakout test. The test can occur on the bar after the breakout or even 20 or more bars later, or both. This test bar is a potential signal bar, and smart traders look to place a buy stop entry order at one tick above it in case the test is successful and the trend resumes. It is a particularly reliable breakout pullback setup.

In an upside breakout, there was probably heavy buying in the area of the breakout price and the buyers overwhelmed the sellers. On the breakout pullback, the market is coming back down to that price area to see if the buyers will once again overwhelm the sellers. If they do, the result will likely be at least two legs up, with the breakout being the first leg up. If, however, the sellers overpower the buyers, then the breakout failed and there will likely be a tradable move down since the remaining longs will be trapped and new longs will be hesitant to buy again after the failure. The buyers will have made two attempts to go up from this price area and failed, so the market will now likely do the opposite and have at least two legs down.

If there is a pullback within a bar or two of the breakout, the breakout has failed. However, even the strongest breakouts will have a one- or two-bar failure that in fact becomes just a breakout pullback instead of a reversal. Once the trend resumes, the failed breakout will have failed, which is the case in all breakout pullbacks. A breakout pullback is simply a failed attempt to reverse the breakout.

Consecutive failures are second entries and therefore have an excellent chance of setting up a profitable trade. A breakout pullback is also referred to as a cup and handle, and it is one of the most reliable with-trend setups.

Breakout pullbacks can happen in the absence of an actual breakout. If the market strongly runs close to the old extreme but does not exceed it, and then quietly pulls back for one to four bars or so, this will likely function exactly like a breakout pullback and it should be traded as if the pullback followed an actual breakout. Remember that when something is close to a textbook pattern, it will usually behave like a textbook pattern.

If there was a strong move or a first leg of a trend earlier in the day, then a with-trend breakout later in the day is more likely to be successful; a failure will likely not succeed in reversing the trend, and it will become a breakout pullback. However, if most of the day has been trendless with one- or two-bar breakouts in both directions, the odds of a failure leading to a reversal are increased.

After an initial run, many traders will take partial profits and then place a breakeven stop on the balance. The breakeven stop is not necessarily exactly at the entry price on every trade. Depending on the stock, a trader might be willing to risk 10 or even 30 or more cents and it is still basically considered a breakeven stop, even though the trader will be losing money. For example, if Google (GOOG) is trading at $750 and a trader just took partial profits on half and wants to protect the rest, but GOOG has recently been running breakeven stops by 10 to 20 cents but rarely by 30 cents, the trader might place a breakeven stop at 30 cents beyond the breakout, even though it would result in at least a 30 cent loss and not an exactly breakeven trade.

In the past year or so, Apple (AAPL) and Research in Motion (RIMM) have been very respectful of exact breakeven stops, and most breakout pullback tests in fact end about 5 cents shy of the entry price. Goldman Sachs (GS), in contrast, routinely runs the stops before the pullback ends, so traders would have to be willing to risk a little if they are trying to hold on to their positions. Alternatively, they could exit at breakeven and then reenter on a stop at one tick beyond the test bar, but they will invariably be getting back in at 60 or more cents worse than their initial entry. If the price action is still good, it makes more sense to hold through the breakout test and risk maybe 10 cents rather than getting out and then back in at 60 cents worse.

Most major trend reversals can be thought of as breakout pullback trades. For example, if the market has been in a bear trend and then there is a rally above the bear trend line, the pullback to a lower low or higher low is a breakout pullback buy setup. It is important to realize that the pullback from the breakout can exceed the old extreme, so in a bull reversal, after the breakout to the upside, the pullback can fall below the bear low and the bull reversal can still be valid and controlling the price action.

Sometimes the final pullback of a trend can also function as the first leg of a new trend in the opposite direction. For example, if there is a bear trend, followed by a slow rally that may last 10 to 20 bars or more and then a sell climax and a reversal up into a bull trend, the channel that contained the final bear flag, if projected up and to the right, will sometimes also approximately contain the new bull trend. That final bear flag can in fact in hindsight be viewed as actually the first move up in the new bull trend. The plunge down can be thought of as a lower low pullback in the new bull trend. If you recognize this pattern, you should look to swing more of your position and not be too quick to exit. Once the new bull trend surpasses the bear flag high, it will hit the protective stops of the shorts who saw the bear flag as a weak attempt to rally and therefore likely not the final lower high of the bear trend. After the market reverses above that high, the bears will not look for new shorting opportunities for a while. This often leads to little or no pullback after the bear flag is surpassed, and the move up can be protracted. This same phenomenon is common as a wedge flag is forming. For example, a wedge bear flag has three pushes up. It will often have a breakout down to a lower low after the first push up. It will then have two more pushes up after that low to complete the wedge bear flag. Once the bear flag is complete, the market then usually will break out of the downside of the wedge bear flag and form a new trend low.

Breakouts often fail, and the failure can happen at any point, even after just the first bar. A one-bar breakout of a tight trading range is as likely to fail and reverse back into the range as it is to continue into a trend. Sharp breakouts on the open that last for a few bars often fail and lead to a trend day in the opposite direction. This is discussed in book 3 in the chapter on the first hour of trading.

On daily charts, there are often sharp countertrend breakouts due to surprising news events. However, instead of the spike having follow-through (like a channel) and becoming a successful breakout, the breakout usually fails and the spike becomes just part of a brief pullback. For example, if a stock is in a strong bull trend and it had a surprisingly bad earnings report after the close yesterday, it might fall 5 percent today, making traders wonder if the trend was in the process of reversing. In most cases, bulls will aggressively buy around the low and close of the bear spike, which is always down to a support area like a trend line. They are correctly betting that the odds are that the bear breakout will fail and the bull trend will resume. They see the sell-off as a brief fire sale, allowing them to buy more at a great discount that will be gone in a few days. Within a week or so, everyone will have forgotten about the terrible news and the stock will usually be back above the top of the bear spike, en route to a new high.

Figure 5.1   FAILED BREAKOUTS, BREAKOUT PULLBACKS, AND BREAKOUT TESTS   **105**

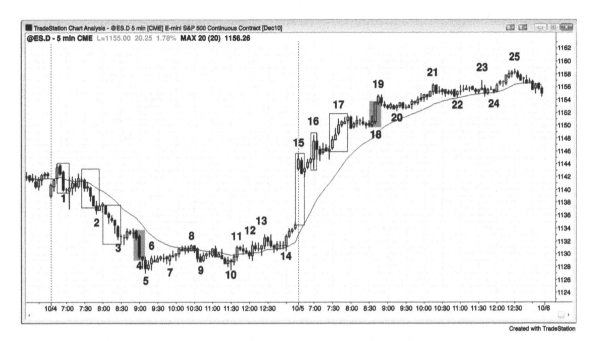

FIGURE 5.1   A Late Breakout in a Trend Can Lead to Reversal or a New Leg

Sometimes a breakout at the end of a trend can be an exhaustive climax and lead to a reversal, and at other times it can be a breakout and lead to another channel. All climaxes end with a trading range, which can be as brief as a single bar. During the trading range, the bulls and bears continue to trade, and both try to get follow-through in their direction. In Figure 5.1, in both the sell climax down to bar 5 and the buy climax up to bar 19, the bulls won the struggles.

Bars 1, 2, 3, and 5 ended bear spikes, and consecutive sell climaxes often lead to a correction that lasts at least 10 bars and has at least two legs. Bar 4 was the largest bear trend bar of the bear trend and it could therefore represent the last weak longs finally giving up and exiting at any price. This was probably the case, and the market corrected up in two legs into the close, with the first leg ending at bar 8 and the second leg ending with the last bar of the day.

The next day, bars 15, 16, 17, and 19 were buy climaxes. The market successfully broke out of the downside of the bull channel that followed the gap spike up to bar 15 and ended with the three pushes up to bar 17. However, whenever a correction is sideways instead of down, the bulls are strong, and they were able to create a breakout above the three-push top. Although the large bull bar could have been caused by the last bears finally giving up, in this case it was created by aggressive bulls successfully breaking the market above the wedge top. This bull spike was followed by a channel that tried to end at bar 21 but was able to extend up to bar 25.

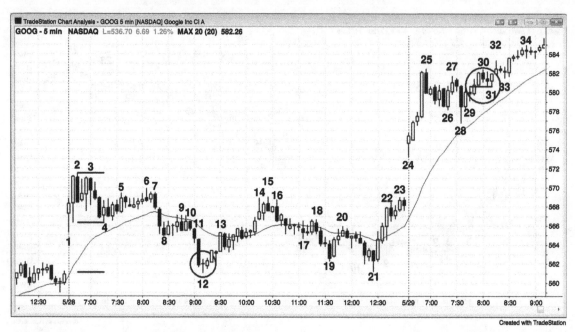

FIGURE 5.2 Breakout Pullbacks

As shown in Figure 5.2, bar 8 was a potential failed breakout but the breakout was strong, made up of three bear trend bars that covered most of the day's range and had small tails and little overlap. The market pulled back to the moving average and led to a low 2 short (or a small wedge bear flag) signal at bar 10, which was the second bear trend bar and the end of the second leg of the pullback to the moving average. A breakout pullback is one of the most reliable setups.

Bar 12 again was a potential failed breakout to a new low of the day. This is a reversal up from a second consecutive sell climax, and reversals from consecutive climaxes usually lead to pullbacks that have at least 10 bars and two legs. Even though the bar 12 signal bar was a doji and not a bull reversal bar, it had a bigger bull tail than bear tail, indicating some buying and some weakening of the bears. Also, the bar 8 to bar 10 bear flag was a tight trading range and therefore had a magnetic pull, increasing the chances that any breakout would get pulled back up to that level. Bar 11 was a breakout bar and therefore it created a breakout gap. Breakout gaps usually get tested, as do breakout points. The bar 1 low was the breakout point. The bears wanted the pullback to stay below bar 1, and the bulls wanted the opposite. At a minimum, the bulls wanted the market to get back above the bar 1 low and stay there so that most traders would see the breakout as a failure. This would have probably ended the bear trend. Finally, the trading range of the first couple of hours was about half of an average daily range, and this increases

Figure 5.2   FAILED BREAKOUTS, BREAKOUT PULLBACKS, AND BREAKOUT TESTS   **107**

the odds that any breakout up or down would be followed by a trading range of about the same size, creating a trending trading range day. Therefore, bulls should be expected to come in around the bar 12 price level, which was a measured move down from the first leg down on the day (bar 2 to bar 4).

Bar 31 is a pullback from a small rally that broke above a minor swing high and almost broke to a new high of the day. When the market almost breaks out and then pulls back, it will trade as if it actually broke out and is therefore a type of breakout pullback. This bar 31 breakout pullback traded down to only 2 cents below the top of the bar 29 signal bar, and when a stock is trading at $580, it is just about a perfect breakout test and therefore a reliable long setup. The market once again found strong buyers at the price where it broke out three bars earlier. A pullback from the breakout of a flag is one of the most reliable setups.

Once the actual breakout to the new high for the day occurred, there was a breakout pullback long entry setup at bar 33.

Although it is not worth looking at lots of different time frames during the day, smaller time frames often have reliable breakout test setups that are not apparent on the chart that you are using for trading. For example, if you were trading the 3 minute chart, you would have seen that the bar 6 high was a breakout test of the 3 minute bar that formed the high at bar 3 above. This means that if you looked at the 3 minute chart, you would have discovered that the bar that corresponds to bar 6 on the 5 minute chart formed a perfect breakout test of the low of the bar on the 3 minute chart that corresponds to bar 3 on the 5 minute chart.

Bar 28 was a strong bear bar and an attempt to break the market to the downside. As it was forming, it briefly was a large bear trend bar with a last price on its low and below the lows of the prior eight bars, creating a strong bear breakout and reversal. However, by the time the bar closed, its close was above the bar 26 trading range low. Most attempts to breakout against the trend fail and are faded by strong trades; they understand that bear spikes in bull trends are common and usually are followed by new highs. At the moment that bar 28 was at the low of its bar, beginners saw it as a very large bear trend bar and assumed that the trend was reversing sharply into a strong bear. They lost sight of all of the other bars on the chart. Experienced traders saw the bear spike as a brief markdown in price and great opportunity to buy a discount in a bull trend. When a bear spike like this occurs on daily charts, it is usually due to some news event, which seemed huge at the time, but experienced bulls know that it is tiny compared to all of the other fundamentals in the stock, and that it is just one bear bar in a strong bull trend.

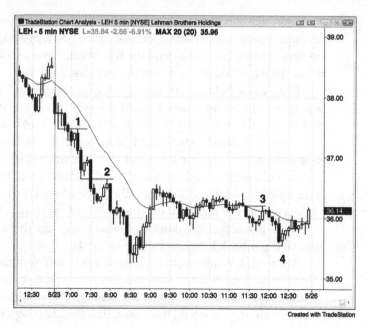

FIGURE 5.3   Breakout Tests

Many stocks are often well behaved and will come back to test the breakout to the exact tick, as Lehman Brothers Holdings (LEH) did four times in one day (see Figure 5.3). Since many traders will enter a breakout on a stop at one tick beyond the signal bar, exact pullbacks like these will run any breakeven stop by one tick. However, reentering at one tick beyond the test bar is usually a good trade (for example, shorting at one penny below the low of bar 2). Alternatively, traders could risk a few cents on the pullback, avoiding getting stopped out by the breakout test. After the trend resumes, they can move their stop to just above that test bar.

Sellers came in once again at the highs of bars 1, 2, and 3. Buyers again asserted themselves in bar 4 when the market came down to where the buyers originally overwhelmed the sellers at the low of the day. This higher low was the second attempt for the buyers to take control of the market in this price area and they succeeded, so there should be at least two legs up.

Figure 5.4   FAILED BREAKOUTS, BREAKOUT PULLBACKS, AND BREAKOUT TESTS   **109**

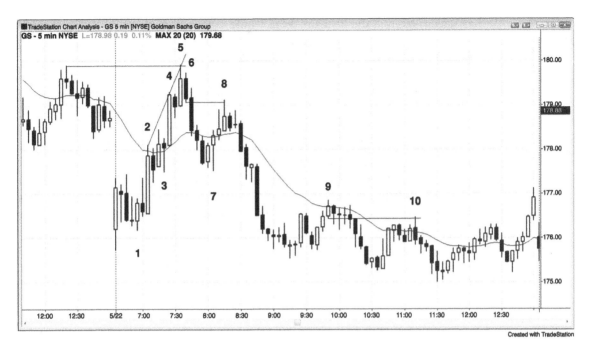

FIGURE 5.4   Breakout Tests Can Hit Breakeven Stops

GS has been notorious for running breakeven stops over the past year, but as long as you are aware of the tendencies of the market you are trading, you can make profitable adjustments (see Figure 5.4).

Bar 8 extended 6 cents above the low of the bar 6 signal bar.

Bar 10 hit 2 cents above the bar 9 signal bar low, running an exact breakeven stop by 3 cents. Traders could avoid being stopped out and having to short again 50 cents lower by risking about 10 cents until after there is a successful breakout test. Once the market falls below the breakout test bar, move the protective stop to 1 cent above its high.

The bar 5 high exceeded the swing high of the final hour of yesterday by 2 cents before reversing down for the second time in this price area. The buyers made two attempts to go above this area and failed both times, creating a double top, so the market should have at least two legs down. It also overshot the trend channel line drawn across bars 2 and 4, and the bull trend line break down to bar 7 was followed by the bar 8 lower high test of the bull extreme (bar 5), leading to a bear swing.

Bar 8 was a pullback from the spike formed by four bear bars that broke below the bull trend line (not shown). Traders debated whether the breakout would fail or succeed. The bulls saw the bar 7 outside up bar, which was a double bottom with bar 3, as a sign that the bear breakout would fail, and bought as it went outside up and above the bar 7 high. The bears saw the bear spike as strong and were looking to short a pullback. They sold below the low of the bear inside bar that followed bar 8 (it formed a two-bar reversal with bar 8).

Bar 1, the bar after bar 2, bar 3, and the bar after bar 4 were one-bar breakout pullback buy setups.

As strong as the three bar bull spike up to bar 9 was, traders cannot lose site of the much stronger sell-off from bar 8 that preceded it. Beginners often only see the most recent few bars and tend to ignore the much more impressive bars just a little to the left. Bar 9 was just a low 2 test of the moving average in a bear trend. Bar 10 was a double top (with the high of the bar from four bars earlier) at the moving average and therefore another low 2 short. Beginners again probably saw the three strong bull bar rally to the moving average as a trend reversal, and again lost sight of the strong bear trend that was in effect. Bar 10 was just another lower high test of the moving average that followed another lower low in a bear trend.

Figure 5.5   FAILED BREAKOUTS, BREAKOUT PULLBACKS, AND BREAKOUT TESTS   **111**

FIGURE 5.5   A Breakout Pullback at a Top Can Be a Higher High

After a breakout from a wedge top, the pullback does not have to be a lower high. In Figure 5.5, there were two wedge tops that broke to the downside, and in both cases the market pulled back to a higher high (at bar 6 and bar 11).

The market was in a trading range from August to October before breaking to the upside, and it had a lot of two-sided trading. This was a trending trading range pattern and the odds were high that once it reversed down, it would at least test the bar 6 high of the lower range. Once the market fell into the lower range and did not immediately reverse back up, the next test point was the bottom of the lower range.

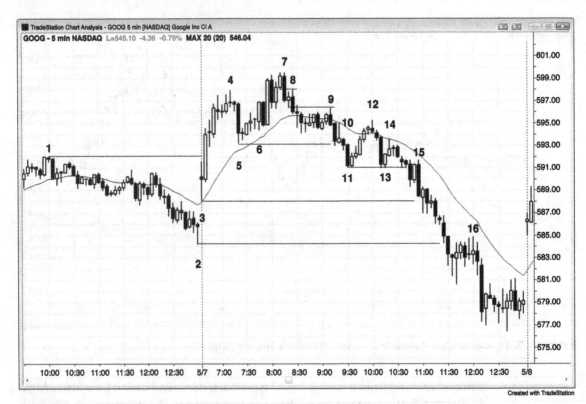

FIGURE 5.6 Breakout Pullback Setups

GOOG formed a series of breakout pullback entries in the chart shown in Figure 5.6. The sharp rally off the open broke above the bar 1 swing high of yesterday, and the pullback at bar 5 could not even reach the moving average or the breakout point. When there is strong momentum, buying a high 1 pullback is a good trade. The signal bar is a small doji inside bar, indicating a loss of selling power following the large bear trend bar. The bear breakout below the bull micro trend line failed and became a pullback from the breakout above yesterday's high. There was a second long entry at bar 6, which was a high 2. In strong trends, sometimes the high 2 entry is higher than that of the high 1 (here, three bars earlier).

Bar 7 was the third strong bear spike in the move up to the higher high. This represented selling pressure, which is always cumulative, and indicated that the bears were becoming increasingly strong.

Bar 8 was a breakout test that missed the low of the signal bar by 2 cents. Bar 9 was a breakout test that missed the signal bar low for the bar 8 short by 4 cents. These are just observations and not needed to take the breakout pullback shorts at bars 8 and 9.

Bar 9 was a low 2 short setup at the moving average and it was a bear trend bar, which is a reliable combination. This was followed by an inside bar, creating another breakout pullback short entry on bar 10. It was also the first clear lower high and the possible start of a bear trend.

Bar 11 broke below the bar 5 pullback and resulted in a breakout pullback short at the moving average at bar 12. Bar 12 was another lower high and a double top bear flag with bar 9. Double tops do not have to be exact. Bar 12 was also the pullback from the bear spike down to bar 11 and the start of a bear channel, which had several more bear spikes in it.

Bar 13 broke only 5 cents below bar 11 but quickly gave a breakout pullback short entry at the bar 14 low 1. Since bar 14 had a bull body, a more cautious trader would have waited for a second entry. The doji bar following bar 14 was an acceptable entry bar, but selling the outside bar that followed this doji bar was even better because it was a low 2. Why was it a low 2? Because it followed two small legs up. Bar 14 was the first leg up, and the outside bar two bars later traded above that small doji bar, creating a second leg up (and the low 2 short entry).

Bar 15 was also an outside bar short entry for the pullback following the breakout below bars 11 and 13. It was especially good because there were trapped longs who had bought the two bar-bull reversal, thinking that it was a failed breakout below the bar 11 and bar 13 double bottom. Whenever a breakout below a double bottom tries to reverse up and fails, it is a failed wedge pattern and often has about a measured move down. The double bottom creates the first two pushes down, and the breakout below the double bottom is the third push down. Since there were four bear trend bars down from bar 14, and smart traders would have wanted a higher low pullback before going long.

Bar 16 was a low 2 pullback after the breakout below yesterday's bar 2 swing low.

Many of these trades were tiny scalps and should not be the focus of the majority of traders. Their significance is that they illustrate a common behavior. Traders should concentrate on trading the bigger turning points, like bars 4, 7, 9, and 12.

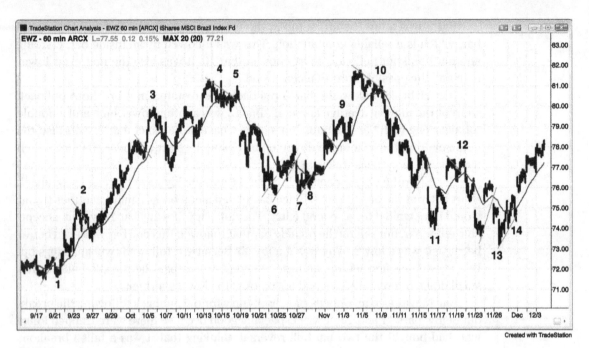

FIGURE 5.7 Failed Breakouts

As shown in Figure 5.7, there were several failed breakouts from bull and bear flags on this 60 minute chart of EWZ, the iShares MSCI Brazil Fund ETF. Once there is a trend and then a flag that has a breakout that fails and is followed by a reversal, that flag is the final flag of the trend.

A final bull flag can reverse down after a higher high, like at bars 3 and 9 or after a lower high, like at bars 5 and 10. A final bear flag can reverse up after a lower low, like at bars 6, 11, and 13, or after a higher low, like at bars 1, 8, and 14.

Figure 5.8   FAILED BREAKOUTS, BREAKOUT PULLBACKS, AND BREAKOUT TESTS   **115**

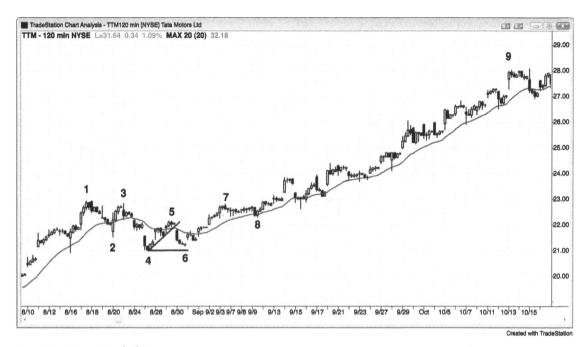

FIGURE 5.8 Final Flag

Sometimes the final bear flag is also the first leg up of the next bull trend (see Figure 5.8). This 120 minute chart of Tata Motors Ltd. (TTM), a carmaker in India, had a bear flag that ended at bar 5 and became the final flag of the sell-off. The bar 6 higher low led to a sharp rally to bar 7, which was above the bar 5 lower high and was therefore a higher high and a sign of bull strength. As discussed in the section on final flags in book 3, the breakout from the final bear flag does not have to fall below the bear low.

FIGURE 5.9 Double Bottom

As shown in Figure 5.9, the 5 minute Emini was in a strong bear trend down to bar 1, and this was followed by a low-momentum, rounded bear flag that ended at bar 2. Next came a sharp sell-off to bar 3 that tested the bar 1 low. Although it was a couple of ticks higher, it was a double bottom test of the bear low. The rally to bar 2 in hindsight was the final bear flag and effectively the first leg up of the new bull trend, and the sell-off to bar 3 was a breakout pullback from that rally and a failed breakout of the bear flag. The bull spike up from bar 3 had so much momentum that it soared above the bar 2 bear flag without a pause. This usually indicates that there is more to go, so traders should not be quick to exit their entire long positions. The first pullback was a high 1 at bar 4, well above the bar 2 high.

Figure 5.10   FAILED BREAKOUTS, BREAKOUT PULLBACKS, AND BREAKOUT TESTS   **117**

FIGURE 5.10   The Final Flag Slope Can Predict Slope of New Trend

Sometimes the slope of the final flag of a trend is about the same as the slope of the new trend after the reversal (see Figure 5.10). This 60 minute chart of GS had a final bull flag from bar 1 to bar 2, and its general slope was about the same as the bear trend that followed the reversal. The market knew the approximate rate of descent that the sell-off would have, but the sell-off was briefly interrupted by one final higher high to bar 3. The entire pattern from bar 1 to bar 9 is a downward channel, which is a bull flag. The move up to bar 3 was a false breakout to the upside.

CHAPTER 6

Gaps

A gap is simply space between two prices. On daily, weekly, and monthly charts, traditional gaps are easy to spot. For example, if the market is in a bull trend and today's low is above the high of yesterday, then today gapped up. These traditional gaps are called breakaway or breakout gaps when they form at the start of a trend, measuring gaps when they are in the middle of a trend, and exhaustion gaps when they form at the end of a trend. When a gap forms at other times, like within the spike phase of a trend or within a trading range, it is simply called a gap. Traders usually cannot classify a gap until after they see what the market does next. For example, if the market is breaking out of the top of a trading range on the daily chart and the breakout bar is a large bull trend bar with a low above the high of the prior bar, traders will see the gap as a sign of strength and will think of it as a potential breakaway gap. If the new bull trend continues for dozens of bars, they will look back at the gap and definitively call it a breakaway gap. If instead the market reverses down into a bear trend within a few bars, they will call it an exhaustion gap.

If the bull trend goes for five or 10 bars or so and gaps again, traders will think that this second gap might become the middle of the bull trend. They will see it as a possible measuring gap, and many traders will look to take profits on their longs once the market makes a measured move up. The measured move is based on the height from the bottom of the bull trend to the middle of the gap, and this height is added to the middle of the gap. This type of gap usually is in the spike phase of a trend, and it gives traders confidence to enter at the market or on small pullbacks because they believe that the market will work its way toward a measured move target.

After the bull trend has gone on for dozens of bars, reaches a resistance area, and is beginning to show signs of a possible reversal, traders will pay attention to the next gap up, if there is one. If one forms, they will see it as a potential exhaustion gap. If, before going much higher, the market trades back down to below the high of the bar before the gap, traders will see that as a sign of weakness and will think that the gap might represent exhaustion, which is a type of buy climax. They will often not look to buy again until after the market has corrected for at least 10 bars and two legs. Sometimes an exhaustion gap forms before a trend reversal, and because of that, whenever there is a possible exhaustion gap, traders will look at the overall price action to see if the trader's equation warrants a short position. If there is a reversal, the trend bar that creates it is then a breakout gap (a bar can function like a gap) and a possible start of a trend in the opposite direction.

Because all trend bars are gaps, traders can see intraday equivalents of the traditional gaps that are so common on daily charts. If there is a bull trend that is at a resistance area and is likely to reverse down (reversals are discussed in book 3), but has one final breakout, that bull trend bar might become an exhaustion gap. The bar is sometimes a very large bull trend bar that closes near its high, and occasionally the final breakout will be made of two very large bull trend bars. This is a potential buy climax, and it alerts astute traders to sell. The bulls sell to grab profits, since they believe that the market will likely trade down for a couple of legs and about 10 bars, possibly allowing them to buy again much lower. They also are aware of the possibility of an exhaustive buy climax and trend reversal, and do not want to risk giving back any of their profits. Aggressive bears are aware of this as well, and they will sell to initiate shorts. If a strong bear trend bar forms within the next few bars and the always-in direction flips to down, that final bull trend bar becomes a confirmed exhaustion gap, and the bear trend bar becomes a breakout gap. The bull trend bar followed by the bear trend bar is a climactic reversal, and a two-bar reversal. If there are one or more bars between the two trend bars, those bars form an island top. The bottom of that island top is the top of the bear breakout gap and, like all gaps, might get tested. If it does and the market turns down again, that breakout test forms a lower high. If the initial reversal down was strong, both bulls and bears will sell as the market tests the island top and as the market turns down again, since both are more confident that the market will fall for about 10 or more bars. The bulls will sell to lock in profits or to minimize losses, if they bought higher as the bull trend breakout bars were forming. The bears will sell to initiate shorts. Once the market trades down for many bars, profit takers (bears buying back their shorts) will come in and create a pullback or a trading range. If the market again has a bear trend bar that breaks below the trading range, that bar is then a possible measuring gap, and traders will try to hold onto part of their shorts until the market approaches that target.

As the market turns down, traders will look at the strength of the bear bars. If there are one or two large bear trend bars closing near their lows, traders will assume that the always-in direction might be flipping to short. They will watch the next few bars to see if a high 1 buy signal bar develops. If one forms and it is weak (relative to the selloff), like a small bull doji or a bear bar, more traders will look to short above its high than to buy. Remember, this is a high 1 pullback in what has been a bull trend, but now traders are looking for about 10 bars sideways to down, so more will look to short above the high 1 buy signal bar than to buy. If they are right, the high 1 buy signal will fail and form a lower high. If the reversal down is strong, traders will also short below the lower high and below the high 1 buy signal bar. If the market goes more sideways to down and then forms a high 2 buy setup, the bears will assume that it, too, will fail, and will place limit orders at and above its high to go short. Other bears will place stop orders to go short below the high 2 buy signal bar, because that is where the bulls who bought the high 2 will have their protective stops. Once these bulls get stopped out, they will likely not look to buy again for at least a couple of bars, and the absence of bulls and the presence of bears can lead to a bear breakout. If it is weak, the bulls might be able to create a wedge bull flag (a high 3 buy setup). If the breakout is strong, the move down will likely go for at least a couple of small legs, and reach a measured move, based on the height of the trading range (the bull high to the bottom of the high 2 bull signal bar). The breakout bar then becomes a measuring gap. If the bulls are successful in turning the market up at the high 3 (a wedge bull flag), then the bear measuring gap will close and become an exhaustion gap.

This process happens many times a day on every chart, and traders are always asking themselves whether a breakout will likely succeed (and turn the breakout bar into a measuring gap), or will it more likely fail (and turn the trend bar that formed the breakout into an exhaustion gap). The labels are not important, but the implications are. This is the single most important decision that traders make, and they make it whenever they consider any trade: Will there be more buyers or sellers above and below the prior bar? Whenever they believe that there is an imbalance, they have an edge. In the case of that bull breakout, when there finally is a signal bar for a failed breakout, traders will decide if there will be more buyers or sellers below that bar. If they think that the breakout is strong, they will assume that there will be more buyers, and they will buy below the bar. Others will wait to see if the next bar only falls for a few ticks. If so, they will place stop orders to buy above it, and they will consider it to be a breakout pullback buy setup. The gap will then likely become a measuring gap. The bears will see that signal bar for the failed breakout as a strong sell signal, and they will short below its low. If they are right, the market will sell off, and close the bull gap (turning it into an exhaustion gap), and soon move below the low of the bull breakout bar, and they hope that it will continue much lower.

"All gaps will get filled" is a saying that you sometimes hear, but this saying only rarely helps traders. The market is always coming back to test prior prices, so the saying would be more precise if it were "all prior prices get tested." However, enough traders pay attention to gaps so that they act as magnets, especially when the pullback gets close to them. The closer the market gets to any magnet, the stronger the magnetic field and the more likely the market will reach the magnet (this is the basis for buy and sell vacuums). For example, if there is a gap up in a bull trend, once there is finally a correction or a reversal, the market might be only slightly more likely to go below the high of the bar before the gap (and therefore fill the gap) than it is to go below the high of any other bar in the rally. However, since gaps are magnets, traders can look for trading opportunities as the market approaches them, just as they should as the market approaches any magnet.

Gaps where the low of a bar is above the high of the prior bar, or where the high of a bar is below the low of the prior bar, are rare on an intraday chart of a highly liquid instrument, except on the first bar of the day, when they are common. However, if one uses a broad definition, gaps of other types occur many times every day on a 5 minute chart, and they can be useful in understanding what the market is doing and in setting up trades. Occasionally, the open of a bar on a 5 minute chart will be above the close of the prior bar, and this is often a subtle indication of strength. For example, if there are two or three of these gaps on consecutive bull trend bars, the bulls are likely strong. All of these gaps have the same significance on daily, weekly, and monthly charts as well.

Because gaps are important elements of price action, intraday traders should use a broad definition of a gap and look at trend bars as an intraday equivalents because they are functionally identical. If the volume was thin enough, there would be actual gaps on every intraday chart whenever there was a series of trend bars. Remember, all trend bars are spikes, breakouts, and climaxes, and a breakout is a variant of a gap. When there is a large gap up on the first bar of the day on the Emini, there will be a large bull trend bar on the Standard & Poor's (S&P) 500 cash index. That is an example of how a gap and a trend bar represent the same behavior. When there is a large trend bar at the start of a trend, it creates a breakout gap. For example, if the market is reversing up from a low or breaking out of a trading range, the high of the bar before the trend bar and the low of the bar after it create the breakout gap. You can simply think of the entire trend bar's body as the gap as well, and there may be other recent swing highs that some traders will consider as the bottom of the gap. There is often not a single choice, but that does not matter. What does matter is that there is a breakout, which means that there is a gap, even though a traditional gap is not visible on the chart. The market will often dip a tick or two below the high of the bar before the trend bar, and traders will still think that the breakout is in effect as long as the pullback does not fall below the low of the trend bar. In general, if the market falls more than a couple of ticks below the high of the bar before it, traders will lose confidence in the breakout and there might not be much follow-through, even if there is no reversal.

Whenever there is a trend bar in a potential bull breakout, always look at the high of the bar before it and the low of the bar after it. If they do not overlap, the space between them might function as a measuring gap. If the trend continues up, look for profit taking at the measured move (based on the low of the bull leg to the middle of the gap). Sometimes the bottom of the gap will be a swing high that formed several bars earlier, or a high within the spike, but a couple of bars before the trend bar. The low of the gap might be a swing low that forms many bars after the breakout bar. The same is true of a bear trend bar that is breaking out in a bear leg. Always look for potential measuring gaps, the most obvious one being the one between the low of the bar before the bear trend bar and the high of the bar after it.

If the bull trend has been going on for 5 to 10 or more bars and then there is another bull trend bar, it might become just an unremarkable gap, a measuring gap, or an exhaustion gap. Traders will not know until they see the next several bars. If there is another strong bull trend bar, the odds of a measuring gap are greater and bulls will continue to buy with the expectation of the rally continuing up for about a measured move, based on the middle of the gap.

Another common gap is between the high or low of a bar and the moving average. In trends, these can set up good swing trades that test the extreme of the trend, and in trading ranges, they often set up scalps to the moving average. For example, if there is a strong bear trend and the market finally rallies above the moving average, the first bar in that rally that has a low above the moving average is a first moving average gap bar. Traders will place a sell stop order at one tick below the low of that bar to go short, looking for a test of the bear market low. If the stop is not triggered, they will keep moving the stop up to one tick below the low of the bar that just closed until their short is filled. Sometimes they will get stopped out by the market moving above the signal bar, and if that happens, they will try one more time to reenter their shorts at one tick below the low of the prior bar. Once filled, the signal bar is a second moving average gap bar short signal.

Moving average gaps happen many times a day every day, and most of the time they occur in the absence of a strong trend. If traders are selective, many of these gap bars can set up fades to the moving average. For example, assume that the day is a trading range day and that the market has been above the moving average for an hour or so. If it then sells off to below the moving average but is followed by a strong bull reversal bar with a high that is below the moving average, traders will often go long above that bar if there enough room between the high of that bar and the moving average for a long scalp.

Breakouts on all time frames, including intraday and daily charts, often form breakout gaps and measuring gaps that are different from the traditional versions.

The space between the breakout point and the first pause or pullback after the breakout is a gap, and if it appears early in a possible strong trend, it is a breakaway gap and is a sign of strength. Although it will lead to a measured move from the start of the leg, the target is usually too close for traders to take profits and they should therefore ignore the measured move projection. Instead, they should look at the gap as only a sign of strength and not a tool to use to create a target for taking profits. For example, if the average daily range in the Emini has been about 12 points and after about an hour into the day the range is only three points, the gap formed by a breakout would lead to a target that would result in a range for the day of only six points. If a trend is just beginning, it is more likely that the range will reach about the average of 12 points and not just six points, and therefore traders should not be taking profits at the measured move target.

When the distance from the start of the leg to the breakout gap (breakaway gap) is about a third to a half of an average daily range, its middle often leads to a measured move projection where traders might take profits or even reverse their positions. For example, if the market is in a trading range and then the market forms a large bull trend bar that breaks out above the trading range, the swing high at the top of the range is the breakout point. If the market moves sideways or up on the next bar, the low of that bar is the first price to consider as the breakout test; the midpoint between its low and the breakout point often becomes the middle of the bull leg, and the gap is a measuring gap. If the range is about a third to a half of the recent average daily range, use the bottom of the leg as the starting point for the measured move; measure the number of ticks between that low and the middle of the measuring gap, and project that same number of ticks up above that midpoint. Then look to see how the market behaves if it moves up to a tick or so of the measured move. If within a few bars of the breakout the market pulls back into the gap but then rallies, use that pullback low as the breakout test, and then the measuring gap is between that low and the breakout point. This is a sign of strength. Once the market rallies to the measured move projection, many traders will take partial or total profits on their longs. If the move up was weak, some traders might even place limit orders to short at the measured move target, although only very experienced traders should consider this.

Elliott Wave traders see most of these gaps as being formed by a small wave 4 pullback that is staying above the high of wave 1, and expect a wave 5 to follow. Not enough volume is being traded based on Elliott Wave Theory to make this a significant component of the price action, but whenever a pullback does not fall below the breakout point, all traders see this as a sign of strength and expect a test of the trend high. The pullback is a breakout test.

If the pullback falls a little below the breakout point, this is a sign of a lack of strength. You can still use the middle between that low and the breakout point even though the pullback is below the breakout. When that happens, I refer to this type of gap as a negative gap, since the mathematical difference is a negative number. For example, in a bull breakout, if you subtract the high of the breakout point from the low of the breakout test bar, the result is a negative number. Negative measuring gaps lead to projections that are less reliable, but still can be very accurate and therefore are worth watching. Incidentally, stairs patterns have negative gaps after each new breakout.

Small measuring gaps can also form around any trend bar. These micro measuring gaps occur if the bar before and the bar after the trend bar do not overlap and, like any gap, can lead to a measured move. The measured move will usually be more accurate if the trend bar was acting as a breakout. For example, look at any strong bull trend bar in any bull leg where the trend bar is breaking into a strong bull leg. If the low of the bar after it is at or above the high of the bar before it, the space between is a gap and it can be a measuring gap. Measure from the start of the leg to the middle of the gap, and project up to see how high the market would have to go if the gap was in the middle of the leg. This is an area where longs might take profits. If there are other reasons to short up there, bears will short there as well. When these micro gaps occur in the first several bars of a trend, the market will usually extend much further than a measured move based on the gap. Don't use the gap to find an area in which to take profits, because the market will likely go much further and you don't want to exit early in a great swing. However, these gaps are still important in the early stages of a trend because they give trend traders more confidence in the strength of the trend.

Breakouts occur many times every day, but most of them fail and the market reverses. However, when they succeed, they offer a potential reward that can be several times as large as the risk with an acceptable probability of success. Once a trader learns how to determine if a breakout is likely to be successful, these trades should be considered. There are other examples of measuring gaps in Chapter 8 on measured moves.

Using this broad definition of a gap allows traders to discover many trading opportunities. A very common type of gap occurs in any three consecutive trending bars on any chart. For example, if these three bars are trending up and the low of bar 3 is at or above the high of bar 1, there is a gap and it can act as a measuring gap or a breakaway gap. The high of bar 1 is the breakout point and it is tested by the low of bar 3, which becomes the breakout test. On a smaller time frame chart, you can see the swing high at the top of bar 1 and the swing low at the bottom of bar 3. It is easy to overlook this setup, but if you study charts you will see that these gaps often get tested within the next many bars but not filled, and therefore become evidence that the buyers are strong.

A related gap occurs after the market has been trending for many bars but now has an unusually large trend bar. For example, if the market has been going up for the past couple of hours but now suddenly forms a very large bull trend bar with a close near its high, especially if the high of this bar or that of one of the next couple of bars extends above a trend channel line, one or more important gaps with one or more breakout points and breakout tests are created. Rarely, this bar is the start of a new, even steeper bull trend, but much more commonly it represents a buy climax in an overdone, exhausted bull trend and will be followed within a few bars by a sideways to down correction that could last about 10 bars or so, and may even become a trend reversal. Experienced traders wait for these bars, and their waiting removes sellers from the market and creates a buy vacuum that sucks the market up quickly. Once they see it, the bulls take profits and the bears short on the close of the bar, above the bar, on the close of the next bar or two if they are weak, or on a stop below those bars. Look at the bars before and after the buy climax bar. The first gap to consider is that between the low of the bar after it and the high of the bar before it. If the market continues to go up for a few bars and then pulls back and rallies again, the breakout test is now the low of that pullback. If the market trades down below the high of the bar before the buy climax bar, the gap is then closed (filled). If the market continues down into a large leg down, the gap becomes an exhaustion gap.

Also, look at the bars before the bull breakout for other possible breakout points. These usually are swing highs and there might be several to consider. For example, there might have been a small swing high a few bars earlier but another couple of higher swing highs that formed even a couple of hours earlier. If the breakout bar broke strongly above all of them, they are all possible breakout points that could lead to a measured move up and you might have to consider the projections up from the midpoint of each of these gaps. If there is a confluence of resistance at one of the projections, like a trend channel line, a higher time frame bear trend line, or a couple of other measured move targets based on other calculations, like the height of the trading range, profit takers will come in at that level and there will also be some shorts. Some of the shorts will be scalping, but others will be establishing swings and will add on higher.

There is a widely held belief that most gaps get filled or at least the breakout point gets tested, and this is true. Whenever something is likely to happen, there is a trading opportunity. When there is a bear spike and channel, the market often corrects back up to the top of the channel, which is the bottom of the gap, and tries to form a double top for a test down. When there is a buy climax bar that breaks out above a significant swing high, there will usually be a pullback that tests that swing high, so traders should look for short setups that could lead to the test. However, do not be too eager, and make sure that the setup makes sense and that there is other evidence that the pullback is likely to be imminent. This might be a sideways bull flag that breaks out and runs for a couple bars and then has a strong reversal bar, turning that bull flag into a possible final flag. Final flags usually are followed by at least a two-legged correction that tests the bottom of the flag; they often drop for a measured move down from the top to the bottom of the flag, and sometimes lead to a trend reversal. All of the preceding is true for bear breakouts as well.

Besides the breakout gaps that form at the start of trends and the measuring gaps that form in the middle, exhaustion gaps form when a trend is trying to reverse. When there is a gap late in a trend and then the market reverses and closes the gap, the gap becomes an exhaustion gap and, like all signs of exhaustion (discussed in book 3 on reversals), it is usually followed by a trading range, but it sometimes leads to a reversal. These are more important to traders who are trading off of daily charts, but day traders see them all the time on gap openings that lead to opening reversals. Day traders think of them as just failed gap openings, but they are a type of exhaustion gap. On the daily chart, if there is an exhaustion gap followed by a breakout gap in the opposite direction and that gap remains open after the bar closes, this creates an island reversal pattern. For example, if there is a bull trend and then there is a gap up that is followed by a gap down on the next bar or even a dozen bars later, the bars between the two gaps are considered to be the island top. Figure 18.4 (in Chapter 18) shows an example of an island bottom on a daily chart.

Whenever there is a channel and then a trend bar that closes beyond the extreme of the prior bar, traders should watch to see if a gap forms. For example, if there is a bull channel or a bear flag and the next bar closes several ticks above the high of the prior bar, this breakout bar might become a measuring gap. Watch the low of the next bar to see if it stays above the high of the prior bar. If so, the breakout bar might be a measuring gap. If the gap closes, the trend bar might be an exhaustion gap and the bull spike could lead to a reversal down.

Breakout gaps are discussed further in the first book in Chapter 23 on trends from the open and in the third book in the chapter on gap openings.

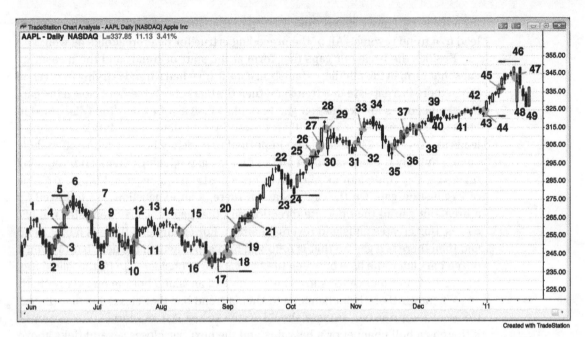

FIGURE 6.1 Many Types of Gaps on a Daily Chart

Traditional gaps on a daily chart are classified as breakout gaps (breakaway gaps), measuring gaps, exhaustion gaps, and just ordinary gaps. For the most part, the classification is not important, and a gap that appears as one type initially can be seen as a different type later on. For example, gap 5 on the daily chart of AAPL shown in Figure 6.1 might have been a measuring gap but ended up as an exhaustion gap. Also, when a market is in a strong trend, it often has a series of gaps and any can become a measuring gap. Traders need to be aware of each possibility. For example, gaps 4, 21, 25, 26, 27, and 45 were potential measuring gaps. Gap 4 was a measuring gap, and the bar 6 high was almost a perfect measured move. The bar 2 bottom of the leg to the middle of the gap had about as many ticks as the middle of the gap to the top of bar 6, where profit takers came in, as did new strong bears. Profit taking came in just below the targets based on gaps 26 and 45.

Breakout gaps often flip the always-in direction and therefore are an important sign of strength. Most traders would classify the following as breakout gaps: gaps 3, 7, 11, 15, 18, 29, 32, 36, 44, and 47. When there is a breakout and a gap, look at the gap as a sign of strength and not as a tool to create a measured move target. When a trend is just beginning, it is a mistake to take profits too early. Do not use a reasonable candidate for a breakout gap as a measuring gap.

Figure 6.1   GAPS   **129**

The rally to bar 22 broke out above the bar 6 high, and the pullbacks to bars 23 and 24 were breakout tests. The space between the bar 24 low, where the market turned up again, and the bar 6 high is the breakout gap. Here, because the bar 24 low was below the bar 6 high, the breakout gap was negative. Since it was a breakout from a large trading range, it had a good chance of also being a measuring gap.

Some experienced traders would have faded the breakout and shorted below bar 22, looking for a test of the breakout point and a quick scalp down. The bulls were looking for the same thing and were ready to eagerly buy at the market or on limit orders when the pullback tested into the gap. The bulls originally bought the breakout in the move up to bar 22, and their eagerness to buy again at the same price enabled the new bull trend to resume and go for at least some kind of measured move up (for example, it might have been based on the height of the pullback from the bar 22 high to the bar 23 low).

After a trend has gone on for a while, traders will begin to look for a deeper pullback. A gap often appears before the correction, and that gap is an exhaustion gap, like gaps 5, 16, 27, 33, and 45.

When a gap occurs as part of a series in a spike or within a trading range, it is usually not classified and most traders refer to it simply as a gap, like gaps 19, 20, 37, and 38.

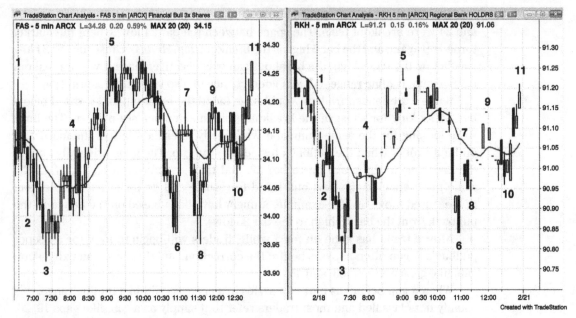

FIGURE 6.2 Trend Bars Are the Same as Gaps

Traditional gaps on intraday charts can usually be seen on 5 minute charts only if the volume is extremely light. Figure 6.2 shows two related exchange-traded funds (ETFs). The FAS on the left traded 16 million shares today, and the RKH on the right traded only 98,000 shares. All of the gaps on the RKH chart were trend bars on the FAS chart, and many of the large trend bars on the FAS chart were gaps on the RKH chart, demonstrating that a trend bar is a variant of a gap.

Figure 6.3   GAPS   **131**

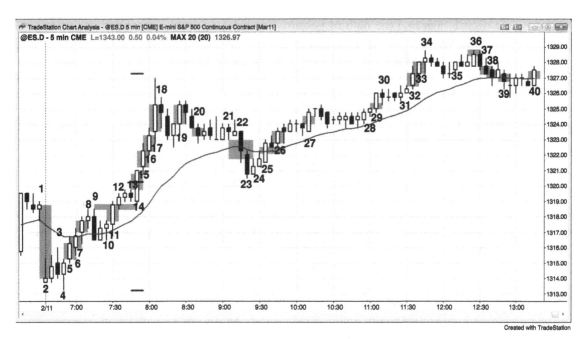

FIGURE 6.3 Trend Bars Are Gaps

Intraday charts have their own versions of gaps. Every trend bar is a spike, a breakout, and a climax, and since every breakout is a variant of a gap, every trend bar is a type of gap. Gaps on the open are common on most 5 minute charts. In Figure 6.3, bar 2 gapped beneath the low of the final bar of yesterday, creating an opening gap.

The market reversed up on bar 5, and at the time of the reversal, the odds of it being the start of a bull trend were good, given the strong bottom. Because it was the start of a bull trend, it was a breakout gap. Some traders saw its body as the gap, and others thought that the gap was the space between the high of bar 4 and the low of bar 6.

Bar 6 and bar 7 were also trend bars and therefore also gaps. It is common for trends to have gaps along the way and are a sign of strength.

Bar 11 was a breakout of the bull flag from bar 9 to bar 10 and a breakout above the opening range. Since the opening range was about half of the size of an average daily range, traders were looking for a doubling of the range, and that made bar 11 a likely measuring gap as well as a breakout gap.

The market hesitated for three bars between bar 12 and bar 13, in the area of yesterday's high, going into the close. Some traders saw this as the top of today's opening range. Bar 13 was a bear reversal bar, and since the market might have traded below it, the bears saw it as a signal bar for a failed breakout (of both the bar 9 high and the high of yesterday's close). Since the breakout was so strong, far more traders assumed that the failed breakout sell signal would not succeed, and therefore placed limit orders to buy at and below its low. Those aggressive bulls were able to turn the market up quickly on bar 14. The low of 14 then formed the top of the measuring gap, and the high of bar 9 was the bottom. Since bar 14 was an outside up bar, it was a breakout pullback buy entry that triggered the buy as the market went above the high of the prior bar (bar 13). The bull trend went far beyond the measured move target. Had the bears succeeded in reversing the market down, bar 11 would have become an exhaustion gap instead of a measuring gap. As long as the pullback did not fall more than a tick or so below the bar 9 high, traders would have still looked at the gap as a measuring gap, and they would have considered taking partial profits at the measured move target (the market raced up so sharply that many would not have exited at the target). If the market fell further, traders would not have trusted any measured move up based on the bar 11 gap, and instead would have looked for other ways to calculate measured move targets. At that point, referring to bar 11 as either a measuring or exhaustion gap would have been meaningless, and traders would no longer have thought of it in those terms. As long as the selloff did not fall below the bar 10 high, the bulls would have considered the breakout to be successful. If it fell below the high of bar 10, or the low of bar 10, traders would have then saw the market as in a trading range, or possibly even a bear trend, if the selloff was strong. Bar 14 was a breakout test of the bar 11 gap. It missed the bar 9 breakout point by a tick and turned back up. By not letting the market fall below the bar 9 high or the bar 12 low, the bulls were showing their strength.

The market broke out again on bar 15, which meant that bar 15 was a breakout gap and a potential measuring gap. Some traders would have used the height of the opening range for the measured move (the bar 4 low to the bar 13 high), and others would have used the middle of the gap between the bar 13 breakout point and the bar 15 pullback.

Bars 15 and 16 were also gaps in a bull trend, and therefore signs of strength.

Bar 17 was an especially large bull trend bar in a trend that had gone on for 10 or 20 bars, and therefore it was likely to function as an exhaustion type of trend bar and a possible exhaustion gap. Buy climaxes sometimes lead to reversals but more often just lead to corrections that last about 10 bars and often have two legs.

Bar 19 was another potential breakout gap, since it was the breakout above a small bull flag, but after a buy climax, more of a correction was likely.

Bar 20 was an attempt at a bear breakout gap, but the body was too small; the bar did not break below the bottom of the developing trading range (the low of the bar before bar 19).

Bar 22 was a breakout gap, and the bears hoped that it would lead to a measured move down (and therefore become a measuring gap). It had a large bear body

Figure 6.3   GAPS   **133**

and it broke below a five-bar ledge and the bottom of the trading range. However, in a strong bull trend, it could simply have been part of a test of the moving average, and it might simply have been due to a sell vacuum, with strong bulls and bears just waiting for slightly lower prices. The bulls were waiting to buy to initiate new longs, and the bears were waiting to take profits on their shorts.

Bar 23 extended the breakout, but there was no follow-through, and like most reversal attempts and most bear breakout attempts in bull trends, it failed. Most traders wanted to see one more bear trend bar before they would have considered the market as having flipped to always-in short. This is a common situation, which is why aggressive bulls buy the closes of bars like 23, expecting that the bears would be unable to flip the market to short. This allows those bulls to get long near the very bottom of the correction.

Bar 24 was a bull moving average gap bar and a signal bar for the end of two legs down from the bar 17 buy climax. Although bar 22 could be considered to be an exhaustion gap, since it was the end of a small bear trend, most traders still saw the market as always-in long and the trend as still up, so there was no significant bear trend to exhaust. This was a pullback in a bull trend and not a new bear trend. Bar 22 was therefore just a failed breakout.

Bar 25 was another breakout, since the market was reversing up from a pullback in a bull trend and therefore breaking above a bull flag (the bull inside bar after bar 23 was the signal bar for the bull flag entry). Bar 25 was a potential bear flag after the bear spike down to bar 23. Once bar 25 closed well above the bar 24 high, the bears probably gave up on their premise that a second leg down would follow. That close created the possibility that bar 25 was a measuring gap, which it was once bar 26 turned the market up again after a one-bar pause. The rally went well above the measured move target and 25 became a breakaway gap.

Some traders still wondered whether a bear channel might be underway, but when bar 26 went above the bear trend bar before it and above the top of bar 22 (the bear breakout gap), the bear theory was untenable for most traders.

Bars 27, 29, 32, and 40 were also bull breakout gaps.

Bar 36 was a breakout gap but the next bar reversed down. Some traders then saw bar 36 as an exhaustion gap and a possible end of the rally and the start of either a trading range or a larger correction.

Bars 37, 38, and 39 were bear gaps and signs of strength on the part of the bears (selling pressure).

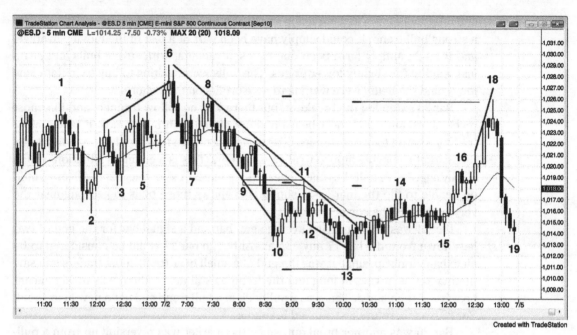

FIGURE 6.4   Intraday Gaps

This 5 minute Emini chart in Figure 6.4 illustrates a number of gaps. The only traditional gap occurred on the open when the low of the first bar of the day gapped above the high of the final bar of yesterday. However, since the first bar did not gap above the high of yesterday, there was no gap on the daily chart.

The market trended down to bar 13 and then rallied above the moving average, breaking the bear trend line. Notice how the low of bar 14 is above the moving average and it is the first such bar in over a couple of hours. This is a moving average gap, and these gaps often lead to a test of the bear low and then a two-legged move up, especially if the move up to the gap bar breaks above the bear trend line as it did here. Here, it led to a higher low trend reversal at bar 15 and then a second leg up to bar 18.

Bar 6 broke out above the highs of bars 1 and 4, which became breakout points. The space between those highs and the low of bar 6 was a gap, and it was filled on the bar after bar 6. Day traders think of this as simply a gap up and an opening reversal down, but it is a form of an exhaustion gap.

The bear trend bar before bar 10 opened near its high, closed near its low, and had a relatively large range. Since it formed after the market had trended down for many bars, it was a sell climax where there was a last gasp of selling with no one left who would be willing to sell until after a pullback, which often has two legs. That breakout bar broke below many swing lows (bars 2, 3, 5, 7, and 9), and bar 11

Figure 6.4

GAPS **135**

became the breakout test. There was also a large gap between the bar 10 high and the moving average, and that gap was filled by a two-legged move that formed a low 2 short setup.

The middle of the gap between the bar 9 breakout point and the bar 11 breakout test led to a measured move down from the bar 8 top of the channel down to bar 9. The hash mark below and one bar to the right of the bar 10 low is the projection down from the two higher hash marks. This gap became a measuring gap. Instead of reversing up, as is common after a reversal up from a trend channel line overshoot, the market broke to the downside and the bottom was at the measured move to the tick. Since you never know in advance which, if any, of the possible measured move targets will work, it is good to draw all that you can see and look for a reversal at any of them. These are reasonable areas to take profits on shorts. If there are other reasons to initiate a long, the chance of a profitable reversal trade increases if it occurs at a measured move. Here, for example, the market broke below a trend channel line and the prior low of the day and reversed up at an exact measured move.

Although the rally to bar 11 was close to the bars 7 and 9 breakout points, the gap was not filled. That is a sign that the bears were strong, and it was followed by a new bear low.

Bar 13 was another big bear bar after a protracted bear trend and therefore a second sell climax. The next bar filled the gap below the bar 10 low.

Bar 14 was a second breakout test of the bars 7 and 9 double bottom, which was the breakout point. However, instead of the market falling, it went sideways to bar 15 and formed a wedge bull flag. This led to a rally and a closure of the gap, and the breakout below bars 7 and 9 failed. The day tried to become a reversal day, as trending trading range days sometimes do, but the bull trend could not maintain control late in the day.

Bar 17 was a breakout pullback that tested the high of the bar 14 breakout point and led to a strong rally that stopped two ticks above the measured move from the bottom of bar 13 to the top of bar 11. The measured move hash marks are just to the right of the bar 13, and the distance from the bottom one to the middle one led to the projection up to the top one.

Bar 18 is another example of a large moving average gap, and the gap was filled within a couple of bars.

There are many other minor gaps as well, like between the low of bar 6 and the high bar 8. Even though that high is at the same price as the low of bar 6, it is a gap and it is the breakout test of the breakout below bar 6. Similarly, the bar 15 reversal bar high was the breakout point for the breakout test bar that occurred two bars later.

Note that the three bars with the largest bodies, bar 7, the bar before bar 10, and two bars before bar 18, all led to reversals. Remember, most breakouts fail to go very far and usually reverse, at least into a pullback. When a large trend bar occurs after a trend has been going for a while, it usually represents capitulation or exhaustion. For example, that large bull trend bar that formed two bars before bar 18 was in a very strong bull leg. Shorts were desperate to get out and were worried that the market might go much higher before a pullback would come and let them out at a lower price. Other traders who were flat were panicking, afraid that they were missing a huge trend into the close, so they were buying at the market, also afraid that a pullback would not come. This intense buying was caused by traders with tremendous urgency, and after they bought, the only traders left who were willing to buy were traders who would only buy a pullback. With no one left to buy at these high prices, the market could only go sideways or down.

There were several micro measuring gaps. For example, the bear trend bar after bar 6 set up one, as did the bull trend bar after bar 10 and the bull trend bar after bar 15. All of the moves went beyond the measured move targets.

The low of the bar after bar 6 and the high of the bar before bar 7 formed a micro measuring gap, and the bar 7 low was an exact measured move down. The trend bar in the middle was a breakout to a new low of the day and a strong bear trend bar, closing on its low.

The bar after bar 15 broke out of a small wedge bull flag. The low of the bar after it tested the high of bar 15, which was the breakout point. The test was exact, and as long as the low of the breakout test does not fall more than a tick or so below the breakout point, the test is a sign of strength. If the breakout test fell more, it would be a sign that the breakout was not strong and was more likely to fail. The space between the breakout point and the breakout test is a micro gap. Since it is a breakout gap, it should be used only as an indication of the strength of the breakout and not as a basis for a measured move. Initial breakouts generally lead to big moves, and traders should not be looking to take profits prematurely. Micro gaps are often negative gaps, meaning that the low of the breakout test bar is a tick or two below the low of the breakout point bar. Once the breakout bar closes, an aggressive trader can place a limit order to buy one tick above the high of the prior bar and risk just three ticks or so. The chance of success might be only about 40 percent, but the reward is many times the risk, so the trader's equation is very favorable.

Figure 6.5   GAPS   **137**

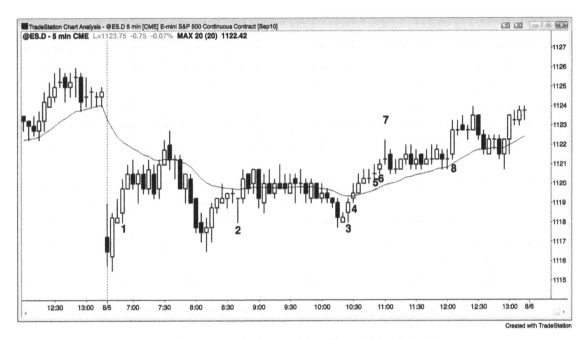

FIGURE 6.5 Gap between the Open of a Bar and the Close of the Prior Bar

If the open of the bar is above or below the close of the prior bar, there is a gap. Sometimes it can be entirely due to low volume (for example, when there are many dojis), but other times it can signify strength. Seven of the eight gaps in Figure 6.5 were bullish; only on bar 2 was the gap to the downside. When there are two or more successive gaps in the same direction and the bars have trending bodies, it is a sign of strength. In those seven bull gaps, a large number of traders placed market orders on the close of the bar and the orders got filled at the offer, indicating that the market had to go up to find enough sellers to fill those orders. If sellers are only willing to sell higher and bulls are willing to buy the offer, the market will likely continue up, at least for a while.

Bar 1 set up a micro measuring gap with the high of the bar before it and the low of the bar after it. The move up to the 7:35 a.m. PST swing high was an exact measured move from the open of the second bar of the day. Measured moves often begin with the open of the first trend bar of a spike. If the market goes above that target, then use the bottom of the spike to see if the market begins to correct at that target.

The downside gap reversed up on the second bar and it was therefore an exhaustion gap. Day traders would instead just think of it as a failed gap down opening and an opening reversal up.

PART II

Magnets: Support and Resistance

There are two types of magnets: support and resistance. When a magnet is below the market, it is a support level, which means that it is an area where bulls will initiate positions and bears will take profits on their shorts. When a magnet is above the market, it is a resistance level, which means that it is an area where bulls will take profits on their longs and bears will initiate shorts. Support and resistance are magnets that draw the market toward them. When you become aware of a magnet not too far from the current price, trade only in the direction of the magnet until after it is reached. At that point, you will have to decide if it looks like the market will reverse, go sideways, or ignore the magnet and keep trending. Magnets tell you the likely destination, but not the path, and there may be big pullbacks along the way. Also, the market might be in a trading range for dozens of bars, but within striking distance of a magnet. Although you should be aware of the magnet, there still can be reliable trades in both directions as the market decides if it will test the magnet and how it will get there.

Traders are constantly looking at support and resistance. The market has inertia and a strong propensity to continue what it has been doing. When it is trending, most attempts to reverse the trend will fail. For example, if the market is trending down, most support levels will fail to hold or reverse the market. However, all bull reversals happen at support levels (and all bear reversals happen at resistance levels), so if the market begins to reverse up, the potential reward is often many times larger than the risk. Even though the probability of success is often only 40 percent, the trader's equation is still positive and the reversal trade is therefore mathematically sound. Inertia also means that when the market is in a trading range, most attempts to break out will fail, and the market will repeatedly reverse up from the support created by the bottom of the range, and reverse down from the resistance at the top. Even though most attempts to reverse a trend will fail, all trend reversals and all pullbacks begin at support and resistance levels, so knowing where they are can lead traders to take profits and to enter reversal trades at optimal locations.

Most Emini trading is done by computers, and their algorithms are based on logic and numbers. When they buy a falling market or sell a rally, they are doing so because they calculated that the particular price was a logical location for them to place their trades. If enough algorithms are using similar prices, the market can reverse, at least for a bar or two, and often enough for a profitable trade. Although some algorithms use numbers that are not directly based on the Emini price chart (for example, they might use data based on the options markets or other related markets), unless many programs are coming up with similar numbers, it is unlikely that there will be enough force to change the direction of the market. When the market reverses, it always does so at support and resistance levels; with practice, an individual trader can usually spot them. Because some of these reversals lead to profitable trades, and because these levels are sensible areas to take profits, it is useful to know where possible turning points are.

One of the important reasons to look for magnets is that they are logical areas to take partial or full profits. You should always be faster to take profits on a trade than you should be to look for an entry in the opposite direction. This means that you need a stronger setup to initiate a trade in the opposite direction than you need to take profits. If the move toward the magnet is weak and if it is against the direction of a larger trend, you can also look to initiate a trade in the opposite direction, expecting a reversal. The market will usually overshoot the magnet, at least by a small amount, and if the move toward the magnet is not a strong trend, the market will usually reverse, at least for a bar or two. If the trend resumes and goes even further past the magnet and then reverses a second time, this is usually a reliable setup for a trade in the opposite direction, especially if there is a strong reversal bar.

Any significant type of price action can form support or resistance, and common examples include:

- Trend lines.
- Trend channel lines.
- Any type of moving average on any time frame.
- Measured move targets.
- Prior swing highs or lows.
- Bull entry bar lows and bear entry bar highs.

- Bull signal bar highs and bear signal bar lows.
- Yesterday's high, low, open, and close.
- The high, low, open, or close of any bar, especially if the bar is a large trend bar.
- Daily pivots.
- Fibonacci retracement levels and projections.
- Any type of band.

Support and *resistance* are terms created by traders to describe any price as having enough of a mathematical edge for a trader to place a profitable trade. These terms were created by traders to help them spot trades. The high of every bar on every time frame is at some resistance level, the low of every bar is at support, and the close is where it is and not one tick higher or lower because computers put it there for a reason. The support and resistance may not be obvious, but since computers control everything and they use logic, everything has to make sense, even if it is often difficult to understand. Every price on the chart has some mathematical edge, but the edges are usually too small to be tradable except by high-frequency trading (HFT) programs, many of which are designed to scalp for a penny of profit. By definition, a price is support or resistance only if it has a directional probability imbalance. For example, if a market falls to a level of support, traders believe that there is about a 60 percent chance or better that there will be at least a bounce big enough for a scalp, which is every trader's minimal trade. If the chance was only 52 or 53 percent, traders would probably not consider that high enough to use the term and instead would just consider the price as unremarkable. If the market is in the middle of a trading range, the low of the prior bar is always at least a minimal area of support in the general sense of the word, but that does not mean the expected bounce is big enough to place a profitable trade. If the expected bounce is only a couple of ticks, it is not support from a trader's perspective. If the current bar is still forming and it is on its low and is one tick above the low of the prior bar, there might be a 53 percent chance of the market bouncing two ticks before it falls two ticks. However, that is too small an edge and too small a price movement for traders to place a trade (although a high-frequency program might make that trade), and therefore traders would not call it support. The opposite is true for resistance.

Support and resistance exist because the market has memory. Once the market returns to a prior price, it will tend to do the same thing that it did the last time it was there. For example, if the market falls through the bottom of a trading range and then rallies back to the bottom of the range, it will usually sell off again because that's what it did when it was last at that price level. The traders who failed to exit their longs and rode through the bear leg will be eager to get a second chance to exit them with a smaller loss, and they will hold until the market rallies back and tests the breakout. At that point, they will sell out of their longs and this will create selling pressure. Also, the shorts who took profits at the bottom of the sell-off will be eager to short again on the rally. The combined selling by the bears and the liquidating bulls will create resistance to a further rally and usually drive the market back down.

When the market falls back to a price and hits it several times and bounces each time, it is finding support at that price level. If the market rallies to a price level and keeps falling back, the area is resistance. Any area of support or resistance acts as a magnet, drawing the market to the price. As the market approaches, it enters the magnetic field, and the closer it gets, the stronger the magnetic pull is. This increases the odds of the market touching the price. That greater magnetic pull in part is generated by the vacuum effect. For example, if the market is having a bear rally toward a bear trend line but has not yet hit it, the sellers will often step aside and wait for the test. If they believe the market will touch the line, it does not make sense for them to sell just below the line when they can soon sell higher. The absence of selling creates a buy imbalance and therefore a vacuum effect that quickly sucks the market up. The result is often a bull trend bar. Then, the bull scalpers sell out of their longs for a profit and the bears sell to initiate new shorts. Since there was no clear bull reversal at the low, most of the bulls bought for scalps, expecting only a pullback and then a resumption of the bear trend.

Once the market gets to the target, traders think that the market will now more likely go down far enough to place a profitable trade, and they appear out of nowhere and short aggressively and relentlessly, driving the market down. The weak bulls who bought at the top of that strong bull trend bar are stunned that there is no follow-through, but they misunderstood the significance of the bull trend bar. They thought that traders were suddenly convinced that the market was going to break above the trend line and a bull leg would begin. They were oblivious to the vacuum effect and did not consider that the bears were just waiting for the market to get a little higher. The strong bull trend bar was due to the bears briefly stepping aside rather than the bears buying back their shorts. The bulls who kept buying needed to find bears to take the other side of their trades and they could only find them higher, where the bears thought the market would begin to reverse. The market will continue down to an area of neutrality and usually beyond to the point that the bulls now have a mathematical edge. This is because the market never knows that it has gone far enough until it goes too far. Then it trades up and down above the area of neutrality, which becomes tighter and tighter as the bulls and bears are better able to define it. At some point, both perceive that the value is wrong and the market then breaks out again and begins a new search for value.

Every countertrend spike should be considered to be a vacuum effect pullback. For example, if there is a sharp bear spike on the 5 minute chart and then the market suddenly reverses into a bull leg, there was an area of support at the low, whether or not you saw it in advance. The bulls stepped aside until the market reached a level where they believed that value was considerable, and the opportunity to buy at this great price would be brief. They came in and bought aggressively. The smart bears were aware of that magnet, and they used it as an opportunity to take profits on their shorts. The result was a market bottom on the 5 minute chart. That bottom, like all bottoms, occurred at some higher time frame support level, like a bull trend line, a moving average, or a bear trend channel line at the bottom of a large bull flag. It is important to remember that if the 5 minute reversal was strong, you would buy based on that reversal, regardless of whether you saw support there on the daily or 60 minute chart. Also, you would not buy at that low, even if you saw the higher time frame support, unless there was evidence on the 5 minute chart that it was forming a bottom. This means that you do not need to be looking at lots of different charts in search of that support level, because the reversal on the 5 minute chart tells you that it is there. If you are able to follow multiple time frames, you will see support and resistance levels before the market reaches them, and this can alert you to look for a setup on the 5 minute chart when the market reaches the magnet. However, if you simply follow the 5 minute chart carefully, it will tell you all that you need to know.

In general, if the market tests an area of support four or five times, the likelihood of breaking through that support increases and, at some point, the breakout becomes more likely than not. If the buyers who lifted the market at this level fail repeatedly to do so again, they will give up at some point and be overwhelmed by sellers. For example, if the market is resting above a flat moving average, traders will buy every touch of the moving average, expecting a rally. If instead the market continues sideways and they don't even get enough of a rally to allow for a profitable scalp, at some point they will sell their longs, thereby creating selling pressure. They will also stop buying touches of the moving average. This absence of buying will increase the probability that the market will fall through the moving average. The bulls have decided that the moving average was not enough of a discount for them to buy aggressively, and they will do so only on a further discount. If it does not find those buyers within 10 to 20 bars after falling below the moving average, the market will usually either trend down or continue in a trading range, but now below the moving average. Traders will begin shorting rallies to the moving average, which will increase the chances that the market will begin to form lower highs and that the moving average will start to trend down. Once the market falls through support, it usually becomes resistance; and once the market breaks above resistance, it usually becomes support.

This can also happen with a trend line or a trend channel line. For example, if a bull market pulls back to a trend line four or more times and it does not rally far above the trend line, at some point the bulls will stop buying tests of the trend line and they will begin to sell their longs, creating selling pressure. This is added to the selling of the bears, and since the bulls have stopped buying, the market will fall through the trend line. Sometimes, however, the market will instead suddenly accelerate to the upside and the bears will stop shorting every small bounce and instead will buy back their shorts, driving the market higher.

Institutional trading is done by discretionary traders and computers, and computer program trading has become increasingly important. Institutions base their trading on fundamental or technical information, or a combination of both, and both types of trading are done by traders and by computers. In general, most of the discretionary traders base their decisions primarily on fundamental information, and most of the computer trades are based on technical data. Since the majority of the volume is now traded by HFT firms, and most of the trades are based on price action and other technical data, most of the program trading is technically based. In the late twentieth century, a single institution running a large program could move the market, and the program would create a micro channel, which traders saw as a sign that a program was running. Now, most days have a dozen or so micro channels in the Emini, and many have over 100,000 contracts traded. With the Emini currently around 1200, that corresponds to $6 billion, and is larger than a single institution would trade for a single small trade. This means that a single institution cannot move the market very far or for very long, and that all movement on the chart is caused by many institutions trading in the same direction at the same time. Also, HFT computers analyze every tick and are constantly placing trades all day long. When they detect a program, many will scalp in the direction of the program, and they will often account for most of the volume while the micro channel (program) is progressing.

The institutions that are trading largely on technical information cannot move the market in one direction forever because at some point the market will appear as offering value to the institutions trading on fundamentals. If the technical institutions run the price up too high, fundamental institutions and other technical institutions will see the market as being at a great price to sell out of longs and to initiate shorts, and they will overwhelm the bullish technical trading and drive the market down. When the technical trading creates a bear trend, the market at some point will be clearly cheap in the eyes of fundamental and other technical institutions. The buyers will come in and overwhelm the technical institutions responsible for the selloff and reverse the market up.

Trend reversals on all time frames always happen at support and resistance levels, because technical traders and programs look for them as areas where they should stop pressing their bets and begin to take profits, and many will also begin to trade in the opposite direction. Since they are all based on mathematics, computer algorithms, which generate 70 percent of all trading volume and 80 percent of institutional volume, know where they are. Also, institutional fundamental traders pay attention to obvious technical factors. They see major support and resistance on the chart as areas of value and will enter trades in the opposite direction when the market gets there. The programs that trade on value will usually find it around the same areas, because there is almost always significant value by any measure around major support and resistance. Most of the programs make decisions based on price, and there are no secrets. When there is an important price, they all see it, no matter what logic they use. The fundamental traders (people and machines) wait for value and commit heavily when they detect it. They want to buy when they think that the market is cheap and sell when they believe it is expensive. For example, if the market is falling, but it's getting to a price level where the institutions feel like it is getting cheap, they will appear out of nowhere and buy aggressively. This is seen most dramatically and often during opening reversals (the reversals can be up or down and are discussed in the section on trading the open in book 3). The bears will buy back their shorts to take profits and the bulls will buy to establish new longs. No one is good at knowing when the market has gone far enough, but most experienced traders and programs are usually fairly confident in their ability to know when it has gone too far.

Because the institutions are waiting to buy until the market has become clearly oversold, there is an absence of buyers in the area above a possible bottom, and the market is able to accelerate down to the area where they are confident that it is cheap. Some institutions rely on programs to determine when to buy and others are discretionary. Once enough of them buy, the market will usually turn up for at least a couple of legs and about 10 or more bars on whatever time frame chart where this is happening. While it is falling, institutions continue to short all the way down until they determine that it has reached a likely target and it is unlikely to fall any further, at which point they take profits. The more oversold the market becomes, the more of the volume is technically based, because fundamental traders and programs will not continue to short when they think that the market is cheap and should soon be bought. The relative absence of buyers as the market gets close to a major support level often leads to an acceleration of the selling into the support, usually resulting in a sell vacuum that sucks the market below the support in a climactic selloff, at which point the market reverses up sharply. Most support levels will not stop a bear trend (and most resistance levels will not stop a bull trend), but when the market finally reverses up, it will be at an obvious major support level, like a long term trend line. The bottom of the selloff and the reversal up is usually on very heavy volume. As the market is falling, it has many rallies up to resistance levels and selloffs down to support levels along the way, and each reversal takes place when enough institutions determine that it has gone too far and is offering value for a trade in the opposite direction. When enough institutions act around the same level, a major reversal takes place.

There are fundamental and technical ways to determine support (and resistance). For example, it can be estimated with calculations, like what the S&P 500 price earnings multiple should theoretically be, but these calculations are never sufficiently precise for enough institutions to agree. However, traditional areas of support and resistance are easier to see and therefore more likely to be noticed by many institutions, and they more clearly define where the market should reverse. In the crashes of both 1987 and 2008–2009, the market collapsed down to slightly below the monthly trend line and then reversed up, creating a major bottom. The market will continue up, with many tests down, until it has gone too far, which is always at a significant resistance level. Only then can the institutions be confident that there is clear value in selling out of longs and selling into shorts. The process then reverses down.

The fundamentals (the value in buying or selling) determine the overall direction, but the technicals determine the actual turning points. The market is always probing for value, which is an excess, and is always at support and resistance levels. Reports and news items at any time can alter the fundamentals (the perception of value) enough to make the market trend up or down for minutes to several days. Major reversals lasting for months are based on fundamentals and begin and end at support and resistance levels. This is true of every market and every time frame.

It is important to realize that the news will report the fundamentals as still bullish after the market has begun to turn down from a major top, and still bearish after it has turned up from a major bottom. Just because the news still sees the market as bullish or bearish does not mean that the institutions do. Trade the charts and not the news. Price is truth and the market always leads the news. In fact, the news is always the most bullish at market tops and most bearish at market bottoms. The reporters get caught up in the euphoria or despair and search for pundits who will explain why the trend is so strong and will continue much longer. They will ignore the smartest traders, and probably do not even know who they are. Those traders are interested in making money, not news, and will not seek out the reporters. When a reporter takes a cab to work and the driver tells him that he just sold all of his stocks and mortgaged his house so that he could buy gold, the reporter gets excited and can't wait to find a bullish pundit to put on the air to confirm the reporter's profound insight in the gold bull market. "Just think, the market is so strong that even my cabbie is buying gold! Everyone will therefore sell all of their other assets and buy more, and the market will have to race higher for many more months!" To me, when even the weakest traders finally enter the market, there is no one left to buy. The market needs a greater fool who is willing to buy higher so that you can sell out with a profit. When there is no one left, the market can only go one way, and it is the opposite of what the news is telling you. It is difficult to resist the endless parade of persuasive professorial pundits on television who are giving erudite arguments about how gold cannot go down and in fact will double again over the next year. However, you have to realize that they are there for their own self-aggrandizement and for entertainment. The network needs the entertainment to attract viewers and advertising dollars. If you want to know what the institutions are really doing, just look at the charts. The institutions are too big to hide and if you understand how to read charts, you will see what they are doing and where the market is heading, and it is usually unrelated to anything that you see on television.

Most major tops do not come from climaxes made of huge bars and volume, which are more common at major bottoms. More often, a top comes from a trading range, like a double top or a head and shoulders top, followed by a breakout in the form of a bear spike. However, tops can be climactic, and bottoms can be trading ranges.

The chapters on trading ranges (further on) and channels (in book 1) describe how to use support and resistance to place trades. For example, traders will buy near the bottom of a channel or other type of trading range and short near the top, and then take profits and reverse on the test of the other side of the channel or trading range.

In a strong trend, the market extends beyond most magnets. For example, in a bull trend, beginning traders will discover that the rally continues up far beyond every measured move target and trend channel line that they draw. These beginners will mistakenly be shorting at every perceived resistance level, finding their losses growing all day long. They incorrectly keep shorting tops that look great but are bad, and refuse to buy pullbacks that look bad but are great. However, once there finally is a pullback or a reversal, it will always occur at a resistance level. Even in strong trends, measured move targets often work precisely to the tick. Obviously, this is in part because computers can calculate them accurately. Computers control the market and their profit taking has to be at some calculated level, which is always at some magnet. Additionally, if a trade is minimally "good," meaning that the strategy is profitable, the reward has to be at least as large as the risk to create a positive trader's equation. This usually results in some profit taking once the reward reaches the size of the risk, because this is the minimum level that the market has to reach to make the strategy profitable. Minor swings often end precisely at measured move projections, and many strong trends end exactly at, or within a tick, of a significant measured move target, as the price gets vacuumed to the magnet.

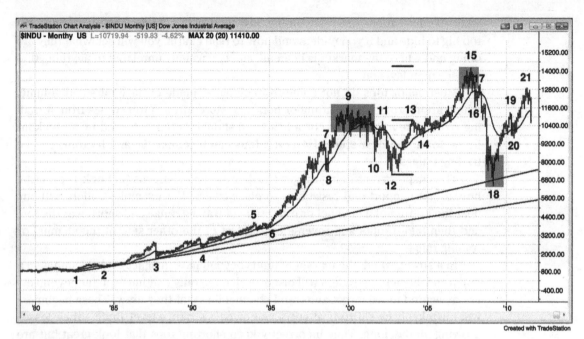

FIGURE PII.1   Dow Jones Industrial Average Monthly Chart

The monthly chart of the Dow Jones Industrial Average (Figure PII.1) shows several types of support and resistance (all are magnets).

Trend lines and trend channel lines are important support and resistance areas. The bar 18 bottom of the 2009 crash reversed up from below a monthly trend line drawn from the 1987 crash low to the October 1990 pullback. It also was at the trend channel line created by bars 8 and 12 (creating a dueling lines pattern, discussed in a later section). All major reversals up from bear markets occur at support and all tops occur at resistance, but most support and resistance do not stop trends. However, if there is a strong reversal pattern and it forms at a support or resistance level, institutions will take profits and many will even enter in the other direction. Market bottoms more often come from sell climaxes, like the crashes of 1987 and 2009. Market tops more often come from trading ranges, like around bars 9 and 15.

The bar 15 high was close to a measured move up based on the height of the bar 12 to bar 13 bull spike.

The moving average repeatedly acted as support, like at bars 3, 4, 6, 8, 14, and 20, and resistance, like at bars 11 and 17.

Trading ranges act as support and resistance. The breakout below the bar 9 trading range was resistance to the bar 11 rally, and the bar 15 trading range was resistance to the bar 17 rally. Once the market rallied up to bar 15, bar 16 found support at the top of the bar 9 trading range.

Swing highs and lows act as support and resistance. Bar 12 found support at the bar 8 low and formed a double bottom. Bar 13 formed a double top with bar 11, but the market went sideways and soon broke above that resistance.

FIGURE PII.2 Support Can Become Resistance, and Resistance Can Become Support

Support became resistance and resistance became support in the 5 minute Emini chart shown in Figure PII.2. This was true for both the moving average and for trend lines.

Bars 1, 2, 5, 6, 17, 18, 19, and 20 found sellers on rallies to the moving average, and bars 7, 8, 13, 15, and 16 found buyers on minor pullbacks to the moving average.

Bars 12, 13, 15, and 16 were repeated tests of the moving average, and the buyers were not getting rewarded and soon stopped buying the pullbacks. The market then fell below the moving average and the bears began to short small rallies up to the moving average, creating a series of lower highs and lows.

The bull trend line was a best fit line drawn with the objective of having as many bars as possible test it. Buyers were clearly buying in the area of the trend line, and it was tested more than a dozen times without a sharp rally away from the trend line. This lack of acceleration made the bulls more cautious over time, and eventually they became unwilling to buy in the area of the trend line. Once the market fell below the trend line, bulls became even more hesitant to buy, and began to sell out of their longs, and bears became more aggressive. Lower highs and lows formed and traders began to draw bear trend lines where they shorted rallies.

Incidentally, any upward-sloping channel should be thought of as a bear flag, even if it is part of a bull market, because eventually there will be a break below the trend line and the market will behave as if the channel was a bear flag for trading purposes. Likewise, any downward-sloping channel should be thought of as a bull flag and its eventual breakout should be traded as if a bull leg is underway.

CHAPTER 7

Measured Moves Based on the Size of the First Leg (the Spike)

A measured move is a swing that is equal in size to a prior swing in the same direction. You estimate how far the market will go on its second attempt based on how far it went on its first. Why do measured moves work? If you are looking for a measured move, then you believe that you know the always-in direction, which means that you are probably at least 60 percent certain that the move will occur. The measured move is usually based on the height of a spike or trading range, and the initial protective stop is usually beyond the beginning of the first move. For example, if there is a strong buy spike, then the initial protective stop is one tick below the low of the spike. If the spike is huge, traders will rarely risk that much, and will usually still have a profitable trade, but the theoretical stop is still below the spike. Also, the probability is often more than 60 percent. If the spike is about four points tall, then the risk is about four points. Since you believe that the measured move will occur and that the strategy of buying at the top of the spike is sound, then you are risking four points on a 60 percent bet. Mathematics dictates that your belief (that the strategy will be profitable when the probability is 60 percent) will be true only if the reward is at least as big as the risk. This is discussed in Chapter 25 about the mathematics of trading. This means that for the strategy to work, you need to have a 60 percent chance of making at least four points, which is the measured move target. In other words, the only way that the strategy works is if the measured move target is hit about 60 percent of the time. Since trading a trend is the most reliable form of trading, if there ever are strategies that work, then this has to be one. Is this the reason why measured moves work? No one knows for sure, but it is a plausible explanation, and the best that I have imagined.

Most measured moves are based either on spikes or on trading ranges. When one is based on a spike, it usually leads to a trading range; and when it is based on a trading range, it usually leads to a spike. For example, if there is a double top, which is a type of trading range, traders will often take partial profits once the breakout up or down reaches a measured move. Traders look for a breakout, which is a spike, and they usually expect some profit taking once the spike has reached the measured move area. If the breakout was with a strong spike and there is no significant pause at the measured move target, the spike itself often leads to a measured move based on the height of the spike. Once the market gets there, traders will often begin to take profits and the result will usually be a trading range.

Once there is a pullback from a strong move, there is usually a second leg in the same direction, and it is often approximately the same size as the first leg. This concept is the basis for a few reliable techniques to project a possible target for the end of that second leg. That measured move area is a reasonable place to take profits on your trend position, and then you can wait for another pullback to reestablish your position. If there is a strong reversal setup, you can also consider a countertrend trade.

When a market makes a sharp move and then has a pullback, it will likely have a second leg and the second leg is frequently approximately the same size as the first. This is a leg 1 = leg 2 move, but it is also called an ABC move or an AB = CD. This alphabetical terminology is confusing, and it is simpler to just refer to the two moves as leg 1 and leg 2, and the pullback after leg 1 as simply the pullback. The confusion with the alphabetical labeling is that in the AB = CD pattern, the B, C, and D correspond to the A, B, and C of the ABC move. The B leg of an ABC is the pullback and it creates a thick area on a Market Profile (CME Group's graph of price and time information). The middle of any thick area often leads to a measured move, and here the target is the same as the one based on AB = CD. For example, for the AB = CD in a bull trend, if you start at point A and add the length of the AB leg (which is B − A), then add that to C, you get C + (B − A). For the thick area, you start at A and then add the length of the AB leg (which is B − A), then move back down to one-half of the thick area (so subtract half of the BC leg), and then add the height of B minus one-half of the BC thick area to get the measured move up from the middle of the BC thick area. Both equations equal C + (B − A) and therefore give the same measured move projection. This is way too complicated, and it is of minor importance because you should not be fading the move with a limit order solely based on Fibonacci extensions or measured moves or any other magnet. They just provide a guide to keep you trading with the trend until they are approached, and at that point you can consider countertrend setups as well.

In addition to clear pullback entries that set up measured moves, sometimes there is a more subtle situation that is equally valid. When a market has a strong trend move and then a fairly strong pullback leg, and then a trading range, traders can use the approximate middle of the range to project where the second leg of the pullback might reach. As the trading range unfolds, keep adjusting the line to where you estimate the midpoint is, and that will usually be around the midpoint of the pullback once the move has finally completed its second leg. This just serves as a guide to where you should be anticipating the two-legged pullback to end and for the market to set up a trade for a resumption of the trend. You can also simply use a leg 1 = leg 2 measurement. For example, in a two-legged bull flag, take the length of the first leg down and subtract that height from the top of the pullback to find a reasonable location for where the second leg down of the pullback might end.

There is a variation of this in spike and channel trends where the height of the channel is often about the same as the height of the spike. This is especially true when the spike is strong, like one with exceptionally large trend bars or several strong trend bars with little overlap and small tails. When there is a strong spike, the market often makes a measured move in either direction, but usually in the with-trend direction based on some combination of the open, close, high, or low of the first and last bars of the spike. For example, if there is a huge bull spike, take the number of points from the open of the first bar of the spike to the close of the final bar of the spike and add that to the close of that final bar of the spike. The channel that follows usually will find some resistance in that area and the market will often then correct down to the bottom of the channel. This measured move target is an area where you can take profits on your long position. Sometimes the market might make a measured move from the low of the first bar of the spike to the close or high of the final bar of the spike, or from the open of the first bar to the high of the final bar, so it is prudent to look at all the possibilities. Less often, the market will not form much of a channel up and will reverse to below the bottom of the spike, and then make a measured move down.

It is important to remember that most of the time the market is in some kind of trading range and therefore the directional probability of an equidistant move is 50 percent. This means that the market is as likely to go up X number of points as it is to go down that same number of points. When there is a trend, the odds are better in the trend direction. When there is a strong spike, the odds of follow-through might be 60 percent and sometimes even 70 percent if the overall chart pattern is consistent with a strong trend move. Also, when the market is at the bottom of a trading range, the probability favors a move up; and when it is at the top of the range, the probability favors a move down. This is because of market inertia, which means that the market tends to continue what is has been doing. If it is trending, the odds favor more trending, and if it is in a trading range, the odds favor that breakout attempts will fail. In fact, about 80 percent of trend reversal attempts fail, and that is why you should wait for them to evolve into pullbacks and then enter in the direction of the trend. Also, 80 percent of attempts to break out of a trading range fail, and it makes far more mathematical sense to fade the tops and bottoms of the trading range than it does to buy large bull trend bars near the top and short large bear trend bars near the bottom.

Here is an example of a measured move that uses several assumptions. There was a strong bull spike made of three bull trend bars that broke out of a trading range. The next bar was a small doji bar, and this pause meant that the spike ended on the prior bar, which was the last of the consecutive bull trend bars. The breakout was strong because there was very little overlap between the bars, with the open of each bar at or above the close of the prior bar. The biggest tail on any bar was only two ticks, and a couple of bars had no tail on the bottom. The first bar was three and a half points (14 ticks) tall, the second bar was 10 ticks tall, the third bar was eight ticks tall, and the fourth bar had a one-tick bull body but a three-tick tail on the bottom and a two-tick tail on the top. That doji was the first bar that lacked momentum and it therefore told you that the spike had ended on the previous bar. The open of the first bar was eight points below the close of the third and final bull trend bar in the spike, so the spike should be thought of as being eight points tall, at a minimum. You could use the low of the first bar to the high of the third bar or even the high of the doji fourth bar, but it is more conservative to use the smaller figure for your initial projection. If the second leg surpasses this target, then look at other targets.

As that spike was forming, if you bought at any point, your stop on your trade might have to be below the bottom of the spike. For argument's sake, assume that you would risk to one tick below the open of the first bar of the spike. If you bought at the market at the highest tick when the spike was three points tall, then you would be risking about three points to make at least three points. At that moment, you believed that the market would have a measured move up equal to the height of the spike, which was three points tall. You knew where your stop was, and you didn't yet know where the top of the spike would be, but you knew that it would be at least as high as where you bought. Since you believed that the market was trending, you felt that the odds were better than 50–50 that the market would go up three points before it fell and hit that stop three points below.

After the spike continued to grow to seven points, you changed your assessment. You now believed that since the market was still trending, the odds were at least 50–50 that the market would go up seven more points before it fell seven points. At the moment, you already had four points of open profit on a trade where you were hoping for three while you risked three. If you wanted, you could have bought more at the high tick of the spike, which was still forming, and then your risk would have been seven points (maybe a few ticks more since you would probably have wanted to risk to one tick below the bottom of the first bar of the spike), and your profit target would be seven points higher. However, on your initial long, you were still risking three points but now had better than a 50 percent chance of making a total of 11 points (the four from your entry to the current top of the spike, and then seven more).

Once that fourth bar formed, which was a doji, you then knew that the spike up had ended at the close of the prior bar, eight points above the open of the first bar of the spike. At that point, you would have concluded that the market had more than a 50 percent chance of going up eight more points above the close of the spike before falling eight points to below the open or bottom of the spike (maybe a tick or two more than eight points on the downside, since the safest stop was beyond the start of the spike). Since the spike was so strong, the probability was likely more than 60 percent.

As soon as the spike ended, two-sided trading began, and at that point uncertainty increased. The market corrected sideways to down and then the channel up began. Although the market might have made a leg 1 = leg 2 move up from the bottom of this pullback, where the spike was leg 1 and the channel was leg 2, when a spike is very strong, the more reliable target is the one based on the open of the first bar of the spike to the close of the final bar of the spike. As the market rallies, the probability of higher prices slowly erodes. When the bull channel reached about half of the distance to the measured move target, the directional probability of an equidistant move fell back to around 50 to 55 percent and uncertainty once again was very high. Remember, a bull channel is usually followed by a move back down to the bottom of the channel and then at least a bounce, so the bull channel was actually the first leg of a trading range that had not yet formed. Once the market made it to the measured move target area, it was likely the high end of that incipient range, and the odds favored a move down. This is true of all trading ranges. This is an excellent area to take profits on your longs, and because so many traders take profits in the area of the measured move, the market begins to pull back. Most traders will not look to buy aggressively again until the market retraces to around the bottom of the channel, where a double bottom usually forms. This area is also a magnet. The bulls begin to buy again and the bears who shorted at the top of the channel will take profits. Since the market is now around the bottom of the developing trading range, the directional probability slightly favors the bulls.

Once the market enters the trading range, the directional probability of an equidistant move is again 50–50 whenever the market is near the middle of that range. If your risk is X points, you have a 50 percent chance of making X points before your stop is hit, and a 50 percent chance of losing X points before your profit target is reached. This is a by-product of the markets being relatively efficient. Most of the time, they are efficient and the odds of making X points before losing X points are close to 50–50. The best trading occurs when the odds are better than 50–50, but this often occurs during spikes, which are emotional, fast moving, and difficult to enter. Traders understand this and that is why the spike grows so quickly without any pullbacks. Traders keep adding to their positions all the way up because they know that until the spike ends, the odds of making as much as they are risking are better than 50–50, and the odds fall to about 50–50 only once the channel is well underway. When that spike is forming, they do not know if there will be a pullback before the market goes higher, but they are confident that it will go higher in the near term. Rather than waiting for a pullback that may never come and therefore missing out on a strong trade, they buy at the market or on one- to four-tick pullbacks and risk to around the bottom of the spike. This urgency is behind the formation of spikes, and the increased risk keeps many traders away. Most beginners are unwilling to risk the three to seven points. Instead, they should simply buy a small position, maybe one-quarter of their normal size, and take the risk, because that is what the institutions are doing. They understand the math and therefore are not afraid to take the trade.

This move toward a 50–50 market is the basis of all measured move trades. The odds are out of balance, and the rally to the measured move is an attempt to restore uncertainty. The market invariably overshoots and has to backtrack to home in on a 50–50 market. The measured move area is an overshoot of the odds, and they then briefly favor the bears. Once the market retraces to the bottom of the channel, the odds again overshoot, but this time in favor of the bulls. When the market bounces back up toward the middle of the developing trading range, the odds are once again around 50–50 and the market is in balance.

FIGURE 7.1   Leg 1 = Leg 2

Exxon Mobil (XOM) had a strong first leg up from bar A to bar B on the daily chart shown in Figure 7.1, so traders bought the bar C higher low for a possible leg 1 = leg 2 rally. Bar D slightly undershot the target (the top of the dashed line). Once in the area of the target, many traders saw what they thought might be two-legged bear rally after the sell-off to bar A. If you were to use ABC labeling, bar B is point A, bar C is point B, and bar D is point C, and because of this confusion, it is better to simply refer to the move up to bar B as leg 1, the sell-off down to C as the pullback, and the rally up to D as leg 2.

Once there was a higher low at bar E and the rally broke above bar D, a trader could look at AD as a first leg that contains two smaller legs (AB and CD), and then stay long until there was a measured move up (AD = EF, and the target is the top of the solid line).

Fibonacci traders also look to other extensions (138 percent, 150 percent, 162 percent, etc.) as valid areas in which to look for reversals, but this is too complicated and approximate. Once the market has clearly two-sided behavior, it is just as reliable to look to buy low and sell high whenever there is a strong signal.

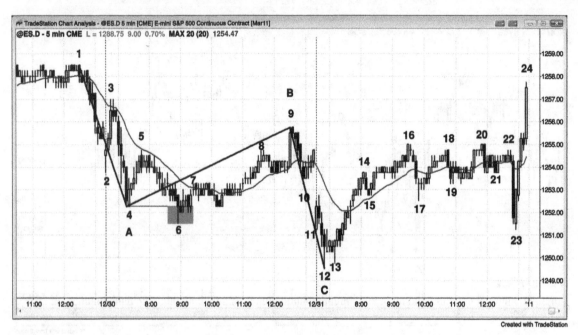

FIGURE 7.2   Variant of Leg 1 = Leg 2

Sometimes a leg 1 = leg 2 measured move has a leg 1 that is not the absolute low
of the initial sell-off. The correction up from the first leg down is usually a two-
legged move or a wedge bear flag, but the pullback from either often falls below
the beginning of the corrective leg, as it did in Figure 7.2 at bar 6. By the time bar 9
formed what appeared to be the end of the pullback from the first leg down, astute
traders were open to the possibility that the correction up to bar 9 began at bar 4
and not bar 6, and therefore thought that the second leg down might be equal to the
bar 1 to bar 4 first leg down instead of the bar 1 to bar 6 first leg down. The bottom
of bar 12 was a perfect leg 1 = leg 2 measured move to the tick based on the bar 4
end of the first leg. If the market instead continued down, then traders would have
watched to see what happened once it fell to the area of the leg 1 = leg 2 based on
a leg 1 ending at bar 6.

Why did it make sense to consider the possibility that leg 1 ended at bar 4?
Traders were looking for a two-legged pullback up before the second leg down began, and the move up from bar 6 to bar 9 was in a channel and therefore likely
just one leg. Elliott Wave traders know that upward corrections can include a pullback that goes below the bottom of the initial move down, and they call this sideways type of correction a flat. The flat here would be the move up to bar 5, the
move down to bar 6, and the move up to bar 9. Also, the move up to bar 5 was a

reasonably strong bull spike and therefore it was a possible start of the correction. The pullback to bar 6 from that spike up was a lower low pullback, and lower low pullbacks are common. Therefore, as the correction was unfolding, traders were not troubled by this interpretation.

Bars 5 and 8 formed a potential double top bear flag, but the breakout to bar 9 eliminated that possibility. However, whenever there is a breakout above a double top, traders watch to see if it fails. If so, this effectively is a wedge top. The three pushes up are the bar 5 and bar 8 double top followed by the failed breakout to bar 9.

Once the market spiked down to bar 10 after the failed breakout, traders believed that the second leg down from the bar 1 high had begun.

There were some other noteworthy features on this chart. Bar 12 was an expanding triangle bottom with bars 4, 6, and 12 being the three pushes down.

The first day opened with a sharp rally up to bar 3 and then a sharp sell-off down to bar 6 that extended about as far below the open as bar 3 did above it. Even though the range was small, it was about average for the recent days (the end of December often has small days). Whenever a day has an average range and the open is in the middle of the range, the market often tries to close around the open. Traders know this, and that is why the tight trading range that followed bar 7 had a good chance of having a breakout that tested the open of the day. The day closed at one tick above the open, and this formed an almost perfect doji candle on the daily chart.

The rally to bar 9 was a breakout test of the sell-off below bar 3. The sell-off to bar 23 was a breakout test of the rally above bar 13, and it missed the breakeven stops by one tick. It was also an exact test of the open of the day.

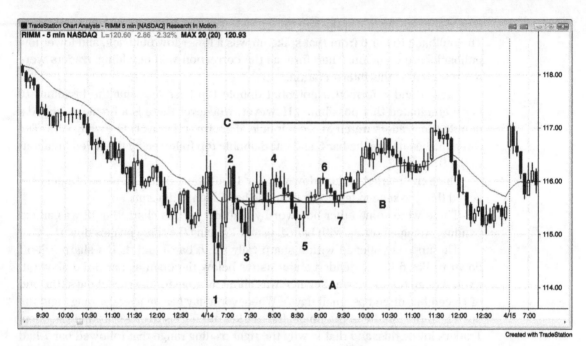

FIGURE 7.3   Measured Move Based on Middle of Trading Range

In Figure 7.3, Research in Motion (RIMM) had a sharp move up to bar 2 after an opening reversal from below yesterday's low, and then a pullback to bar 3. Since a second leg up was likely after a strong three-bar bull spike, if traders were interested in knowing where it might end, they could keep adjusting line B to be in the middle of the developing range. Once the market breaks out, they could make a parallel and drag it equidistantly up from line A for a measured move, where they could expect to take profits. Even though the market was in a trading range, there was a slight bias toward an upside breakout because the move before the trading range was up and most of the bars in the trading range were bull trend bars, representing buying pressure.

Until the market broke out of the triangle by going above bar 6, traders could have traded in both directions, as they can in any trading range. Since a trading range is an area where both the bulls and the bears have agreed that there is value, most probes away from the middle fail and the market will get drawn back into the range. Eventually, the market will break away from the magnetic field and find value at a different price.

FIGURE 7.4 Measured Move Based on Bear Spike

When there is a news release that creates a spike, the spike often leads to a measured move where traders can look to take profits. In Figure 7.4, at bar 1 the market was surprised by an announcement about the president proposing new banking regulations, and this led to two large bear trend bars. Once there is a pause bar like a doji, a bar with a large tail on the bottom, or a bar with a bull body, then you know that the spike had ended on the prior bar. Here, the spike lasted two bars and traders looked for a measured move down from the close of the final bar of the spike. They expected it to be about the same number of ticks as there were from the open of the first bar of the spike down to the close of the final bar of the spike. Sometimes the high of the first bar to the low of the final bar of the spike becomes the height of the measured move, but traders will always look at the nearest possibility first and look for bigger moves only if the first target failed to contain the market. This target is a good place to take your final profit on a swing short and then look for a pullback to short again. If there is a strong reversal signal at that test area, a countertrend trade can be considered.

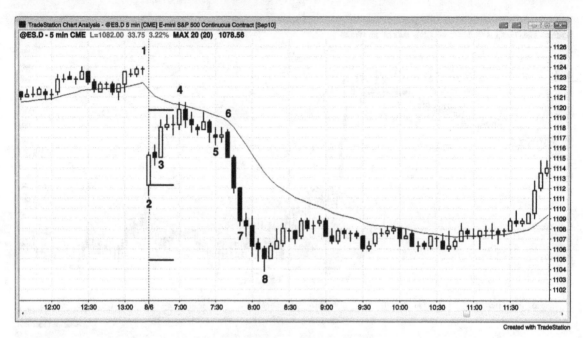

FIGURE 7.5   A Spike Can Lead to a Measured Move Up or Down

A spike can be followed by a measured move in either direction. In Figure 7.5, there was a strong six-bar rally on the open, but the market failed at the moving average on this large gap down day and ultimately reached a measured move to the downside. The move was based on the open of the first bar of the spike to the close of the final bar of the spike. Although most spikes end as soon as there is any pause bar, if the move continues up after the pause, you should consider the possibility that it will function like a spike, which it probably is on a higher time frame chart.

CHAPTER 8

Measured Moves Based on Gaps and Trading Ranges

Gaps are common on daily charts where the low of one bar is above the high of the prior bar or the high of a bar is below the low of the prior bar. If there is conviction about the direction of the market, the middle of the gap often becomes the middle of the trend. As the market gets near the measured move target, traders will look carefully at the exact target and often take partial or total profits in that area, and some traders will begin to take positions in the opposite direction. This often leads to a pause, a pullback, or even a reversal.

When a breakout occurs on an intraday chart, only rarely will this kind of gap appear. However, there is often something just as reliable, which is a gap between the breakout point and the first pause or pullback. For example, if the market breaks out above a swing high and the breakout bar is a relatively large bull trend bar and the low of the next bar is above the breakout point, then there is a gap between that low and the breakout point and that often becomes a measuring gap. If the bar after the breakout is also a large bull trend bar, then wait for the first small bull trend bar, bear trend bar, or doji bar. Its low is then the top of the gap. If the breakout point or the breakout pullback is unclear, the market will often just use the middle of the breakout bar as the middle of the gap. In this case, the measured move is based on the start of the rally to the middle of the breakout bar. The market would then be expected to rally for about the same number of ticks above that level.

If the market pulls back within a few bars of breaking out and the low of the pullback is in the gap, then the gap is now smaller but its midpoint still can be used to find a measured move target. If the market pulls back further, even to a little below the gap, the midpoint between the breakout point and that pullback can still be used for the projection. Since the difference between the breakout pullback and the breakout point is then a negative number, I call this a negative gap. Measured move projections are less reliable when they are based on a negative gap.

On a Market Profile, these intraday measuring gaps where the market moves quickly are thin areas between two distributions, and represent prices where the market is one-sided. The distributions are "fat" areas and are simply trading ranges where there is two-sided trading taking place. A trading range is an area of agreement on price, and its middle is the middle of what bulls and bears think is fair. A gap is also an area of agreement. It is an area where the bulls and bears agree that no trading should take place, and its middle is the midpoint of that area. In both cases, on a simplistic level, if those prices are a midpoint of agreement between bulls and bears, then they are a rough guide to the midpoint of the leg that contains them. Once they form, swing part or all of your with-trend entries. As the target is approached, consider countertrend entries if there is a good setup. Most traders use the height of the prior trading range for measuring, which is fine because the exact distance is only approximate no matter how you do it (unless you are a Fibonacci or Elliott Wave trader and have the uncanny ability to convince yourself that the market almost always creates perfect patterns, despite the overwhelming evidence to the contrary). The key is to trade only with the trend, but once the market is in the area of the measured move, you can begin to look for countertrend entries. However, the best countertrend trades only follow an earlier countertrend move that was strong enough to break the trend line.

If the market pauses after the measured move is reached, the two strong trend legs might be simply the end of a higher time frame correction, and if that appears to be the case, then swing part of any countertrend entry. Two legs often complete a move, and the move is usually followed by at least a protracted countertrend move that has at least two legs, and it sometimes becomes a new, opposite trend. The countertrend move will often test all the way back to the breakout point.

Sometimes the projections are exact to the tick, but most of the time the market undershoots or overshoots the target. This approach is only a guideline to keep you trading on the correct side of the market.

Figure 8.1   MEASURED MOVES BASED ON GAPS AND TRADING RANGES   **167**

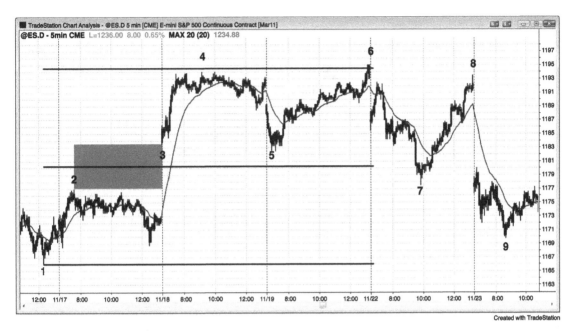

FIGURE 8.1   Measuring Gap

The middle of a gap often leads to a measured move. In Figure 8.1, the Emini had a gap up at bar 3, above the bar 2 high of the previous day, and the middle of that gap was a possible middle of the move up. Traders measured from the bar 1 bottom of the rally to the middle of the gap and then projected that same number of points upward. Bar 4 came within a couple of ticks of the projection, but many traders believe that a target in the Emini has not been adequately tested unless the market comes to within one tick of it. This gave traders confidence to buy the sharp sell-off on the open of the next day down to bar 5. The high of the day was two ticks above the measured move projection. The market sold off on the next day down to bar 7 but rallied again to test just below the target. On the following day, the bulls gave up and there was a large gap down and then a sell-off. There were certainly news announcements that the television pundits used to explain all of the moves, but the reality was that the moves were based on math. The news was just the excuse for the market to do what it was already going to do.

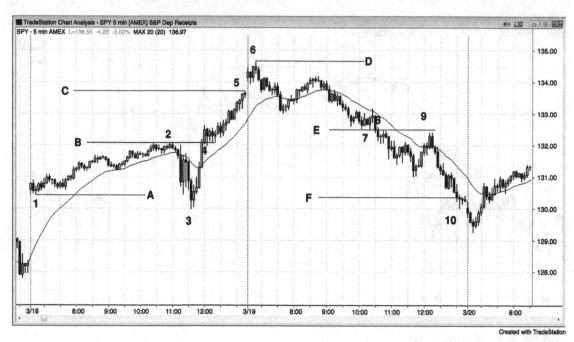

FIGURE 8.2   Measuring Gaps

Figure 8.2 shows two days that have measured moves based on thin areas. A thin area is a breakout area where there is very little overlap of the bars.

The market had a sharp move up from bar 3 on the Federal Open Market Committee (FOMC) report at 11:15 a.m. PST, and broke above the bar 2 high of the day. The flag at bar 4 tested the breakout with a two-legged sideways correction, and there was a small negative gap between the top of bar 2 and the bottom of the bar 4 breakout test. If you subtract the high of the bar 2 breakout point from the low of the bar 4 pullback, you get a negative number for the height of the gap. Although the middle of a negative gap sometimes yields a perfect measured move, more commonly the end of the measured move will be equal to the top of the breakout point, here the bar 2 high, minus the bottom of the initial trading range, here the bar 1 low. You could also use the low of bar 3 to calculate the measured move, but it is always better to look at the nearest target first and to consider further targets only if the market trades through the lower ones. The market reached the line C target from the line A (bar 1) to line B measured move exactly on the last bar of the day, and poked above the line D target using the bar 3 to line B projection on the open

Figure 8.2   MEASURED MOVES BASED ON GAPS AND TRADING RANGES   **169**

of the next day. Even though bar 1 is higher than bar 3, it can still be considered the bottom of the measured move by thinking of the sell-off to bar 3 as just an overshoot of the bar 1 actual low of the leg.

On the second day, there was a gap below bar 7 and above bar 8, and the line F target was exceeded just before the close.

Incidentally, there was also a double top bear flag at bars 8 and 9.

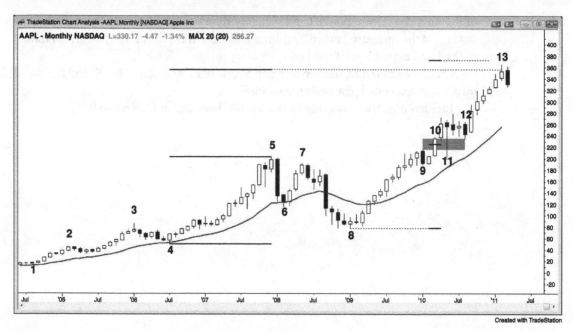

FIGURE 8.3 Profit Taking at Measured Move Targets

Apple (AAPL) was in a strong bull trend on the monthly chart shown in Figure 8.3. Whenever there is a trend, traders look for logical levels where they can take partial or full profits. They usually turn to measured moves. Bar 13 was just above the measured move based on the strong rally from bar 4 to bar 5.

Bar 10 was a bull trend bar that broke out above the bar 9 pullback from the attempted breakout above bar 5. Every trend bar is a breakout bar and a gap bar, and here bar 10 functioned as a breakout gap and a measuring gap. Although bar 11 spiked below bar 10, the move down was unlikely to have much follow-through as a failed breakout bar, because the signal bar was the third consecutive strong bull trend bar. This was too much momentum to be a reliable short. The market tested into the gap above bar 9 again at bar 12, and this pullback gave traders a potential measuring gap. The market turned down at bar 13, about 3 percent below the target based on the move up from the bar 8 low to the middle of that gap. It might be in the process of forming a two-bar reversal, which could lead to a deeper correction that could have a couple of legs and last for 10 or more bars. Since bar 13 was the sixth consecutive bull trend bar, the momentum up was still strong. When this much strength occurs after a protracted bull trend, it sometimes represents a climactic exhaustion of the trend and is followed by a large correction. This is a reasonable area to take partial or full profits on longs, but not yet a strong enough setup for traders to be initiating shorts based on this monthly chart. However, since there is

Figure 8.3   MEASURED MOVES BASED ON GAPS AND TRADING RANGES   **171**

not yet a clear top, the market might have another push up to the measured move target based on the bar 10 gap.

Although it is too early to tell, traders might be using the bar 8 low to the bar 9 high to create a measured move target. Although not shown, that target is just slightly below the target based on the bar 4 to bar 9 bull spike, which the market already exceeded. Traders need to see more bars before they know whether the high is in or it will reach the target based on the bar 10 gap. If it does, it may or may not find profit takers and shorts, but since it is a clear measured move magnet, it is a logical area for both to be present.

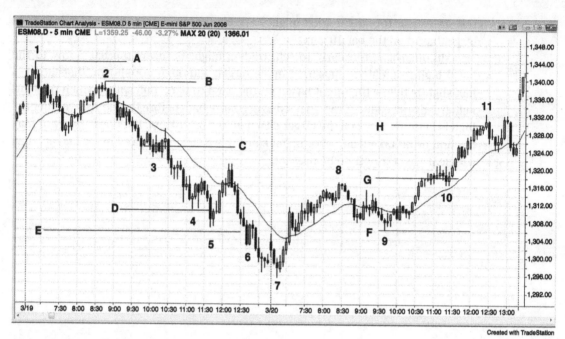

FIGURE 8.4   Measured Moves

As shown in Figure 8.4, the move down to the breakout pullback bear flag around bar 3 was steep, and a reasonable target for a measured move down is from the top of the leg (bar 2) to the approximate middle of the flag (line C). This projected to line D, which was overshot and led to a moving average test. You could also have used the bar 1 high for a measurement, but you should generally look at the start of the current leg for your first target. After the line D target was reached, the line E target based on the bar 1 starting point was hit soon afterward. Note that the move down to bar 4 from bar 2 was a strong bear trend with no significant trend line break, so it was best to stick to with-trend setups.

The small wedge bear flag around bar 4 was mostly horizontal and therefore a possible final bear flag, but since there had yet to be a sharp rally (like a gap bar above the exponential moving average), countertrend trades had to be scalps (if you took them at all). You should take them only if you are a good enough trader to then switch to with-trend trades as soon as one developed. If you are not, you should not be trading countertrend and instead you should be working hard to take with-trend entries. Just being in the area of a measured move is not enough reason for a countertrend entry. You need some earlier countertrend strength.

On the second day, there was a flag around bar 10, after the breakout above bar 8. This breakout above the double bottom bull flag projected up to line H.

The first bottom was the one-bar pullback in the spike up from bar 7. If instead you used the bar 7 low of the day, the target would have been reached shortly after the gap up on the following day.

Once there is a breakout flag, it is wise to swing part of your with-trend trade until the measured move is reached. At that point, consider a countertrend trade if there is a good setup.

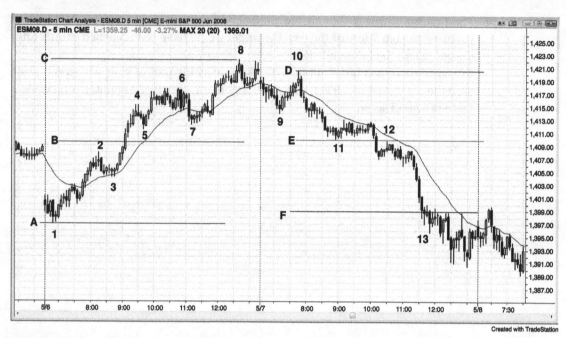

FIGURE 8.5   Measuring Gaps

As shown in Figure 8.5, line B is the midpoint of the thin area in between the breakout (the high of bar 2) and the low of the first pullback (the low of bar 5). The measured move was hit to the exact tick at bar 8.

Line E was the midpoint of a thin area and the market greatly overshot its line F projection. The breakout from the bar 12 bear flag had a huge thin area down to bar 13, but it was so late in the day that a measured move from its midpoint was unlikely to be reached. However, at that point the day was clearly a bear trend day and traders should only be shorting unless there was a clear and strong long scalp (there were a couple in the final hour). The five-bar spike down to bar 13 led to a measured move down, and the low of the day missed it by a tick.

Incidentally, the move to bar 7 broke a trend line, indicating that the bears were getting stronger, and the move to bar 9 broke a major trend line, setting up the bar 10 lower high test of the trend extreme (bar 8), and the subsequent bear trend that followed.

CHAPTER 9

Reversals Often End at Signal Bars from Prior Failed Reversals

The entry price of an early reversal that failed is often a magnet for a later, successful reversal. For example, if there is a bear trend and there have been several bull entries that failed as the market continued to sell off, each of these entry prices and the highs of every signal bar will be targets once a reversal up finally succeeds. The market will often rally all the way to the highest signal bar's high before having a significant pullback. It is likely that some traders who entered on those higher signals scaled in as the market went against them and they then used their initial entry as their final profit target, exiting breakeven on their worst entry and taking profits on all of the lower entries. It might just be that smart traders believe this to be the case and will dump their longs at those targets, or it might simply be one of the many secret handshakes that all great traders know, and they exit there simply because they know that it is a reliable recurring pattern for pullbacks to end near earlier entry points. It can also be something of a "Thank you, God, I will never do this again!" price for traders. They did not exit a losing trade, and their loss kept growing while they kept hoping for the market to come back to their entry. When it finally does, they exit and swear that they will never make that mistake again.

There is a mathematical basis for just about everything that happens in trading, especially since so much of the volume is generated by software algorithms that are based on statistical analysis. In the example of that bear trend that reversed up, that earliest buy signal is often at the start of a bear channel. When a bear channel begins, the directional probability of an equidistant move is at least 60 percent. That means that the market had about a 60 percent chance of falling 10 ticks before rallying 10 ticks. It can be any size move that is within reasonable reach based on the recent swings, but the key point is that the market has a downside bias. As the market falls and the momentum slows, the directional probability falls to around 50 percent when the move down is about half over, but the price of this neutral area is usually not knowable until after the market forms a trading range. As it continues to fall down to some significant magnet, the directional probability overshoots neutrality and actually shifts in favor of the bulls. In the middle of the trading range, there is uncertainty; but once the market hits the bottom, there is agreement that the market went too far. At this point, the directional probability favors the bulls. It will then rally and begin to form a trading range. The directional probability always favors the bulls at the bottom of a trading range, and that bottom will be at some key technical price. There are many to choose from as the market is falling, and most do not lead to a clear buy setup. Some firms will write programs based on one or more technical support levels, and other firms will use others. When enough key technical areas occur in close proximity, there will be enough volume betting on a reversal to change the direction. At that point, the math is on your side because you are buying at what will be the bottom of a trading range. The reversal point is never known with certainty in advance, but it will happen with some kind of reversal pattern; it is important to watch for these patterns when the market is at key technical levels, like at measured move targets, trend lines, and even higher time frame moving averages and trend lines. This is discussed further in the chapter on reversals in book 3. It is usually not necessary to look at lots of charts in search of setups because there will be a reasonable setup on every chart if you are patient, vigilant, and aware of the patterns.

Once the market turns up, it will usually try to form a trading range, and the first possibilities for the top of the incipient trading range are those earlier long entry prices. The market will try to rally to the top of those bull signal bars. As it is going up, the directional probability falls back to 50 percent, and it continues to fall further as the market gets near the top of the range. Since that top is never known in advance and the middle of the trading range where the directional probability is neutral is never known in advance, the market overshoots until it hits some technical level where traders believe it is clearly overdone. This is often at the level of those earlier buy signals. Remember, the directional probability favored the bears when the price was last there, and when it gets there another time it usually favors the bears once more; that is why the market typically turns down there again. It is a price where the sellers took control. The rally often forms a double top with one of those earlier entry bars and then turns down, at least briefly, as the trading range evolves. The market will often go up and down as it searches for uncertainty, which means a neutral directional probability of 50 percent. At some point, the market will decide that this area no longer represents value for both the bulls and the bears and that it is a bad price for one side. The market will then trend again until it finds a price that both the bulls and the bears see as a good price at which to initiate positions.

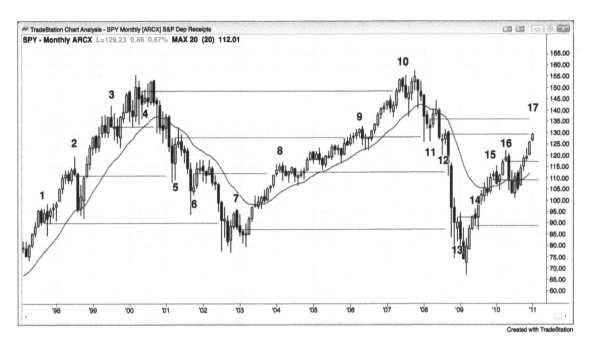

FIGURE 9.1   Earlier Entry Points Are Targets for Pullbacks

The monthly chart of the SPY (an exchange-traded fund that is comparable to the Emini) had a strong bull trend that ended in 2000, but there were several attempts to reverse into a bear trend as the market continued up (see Figure 9.1). Each of the bear signal bar lows (bars 1, 2, and 3) was a target for any correction on the way down.

Likewise, the bear trend that ended in 2003 had several failed bull reversal attempts along the way (bars 4, 5, and 6) and the high of each bull signal bar was a target for any subsequent rally.

Also, the rally from 2003 had several failed bear attempts (bars 7, 8, 9, and 10), and each one was a target in the bear trend that ended in early 2009. That sell-off had several bottom attempts, and the high of each of those buy signal bars (bars 11, 12, and 13) is a target for the current rally. Finally, the rally up to bar 17 had several attempts at a top (bars 14, 15, and 16), and the bottom of each of those sell signal bars is a magnet on any sell-off.

None of the targets ever has to be reached, but each is a strong magnet that frequently draws the market back to its level.

CHAPTER 10

Other Magnets

There are many other price magnets that will tend to draw the market toward them for a test. Here is a list of some. Many of these are discussed elsewhere in the books. When a market is trending toward a magnet, it is prudent to trade with the trend until the magnet is tested and preferably overshot. Do not trade countertrend at the magnet unless there has been some prior countertrend strength like a trend line break, or unless the move is a pullback in a higher time frame trend.

- Trend lines.
- Trend channel lines.
- Any measured move target including a leg 1 = leg 2 projection.
- Spike and channel: the start of the channel is usually tested before long.
- High, low, open, and close of yesterday.
- Swing highs and lows of the past few bars or even days, often setting up double bottom bull flags and double top bear flags.
- Breakout points.
- Gaps of any kind, including moving average gaps.
- The extreme of a trend after every type of pullback (see Chapter 11 on the first pullback sequence).
- Trading ranges from earlier in the day or prior days, including tight trading ranges and barbwire: the extremes and the middle often get tested.
- The approximate middle of the range on a trading range day, especially if there is an intraday trading range in that area (a fat area).

- Final flags: after the breakout from the flag, the market comes back to the flag and usually breaks out of the other side.
- Barbwire.
- Entry bar and signal bar protective stops.
- Entry price (breakout test).
- Huge trend bar opposite extreme (the low of a huge bull trend bar and the high of a huge bear trend bar).
- Common profit targets for scalp and swing positions: in AAPL, 50 cents and a dollar; in the 5 minute Emini, five to six ticks for a four-tick scalp, and three, four, and 10 points for a swing.
- A move equal to the size of the required protective stop: if an Emini trade required you to use a 12-tick protective stop to avoid getting stopped out, expect the move to ultimately reach 12 ticks in your favor.
- Daily, weekly, and monthly swing highs and lows, bar highs and lows, moving averages, gaps, Fibonacci retracements and extensions, and trend lines.
- Round numbers like hundreds in stocks (e.g., AAPL at $300) and thousands in the Dow Jones Industrial Average (Dow 12,000). If a stock quickly moves from $50 to $88, it will likely try to test $100 and usually go to $105 or $110 before pulling back.

Figure 10.1   OTHER MAGNETS   **181**

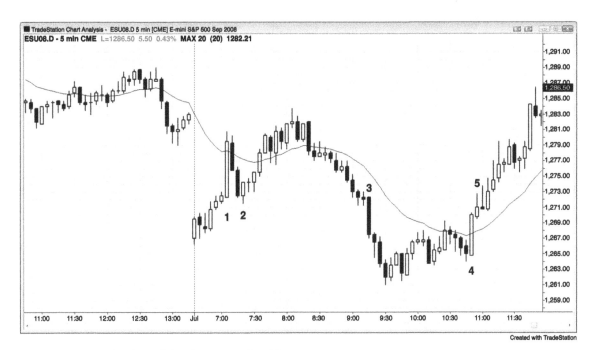

FIGURE 10.1   Big Trend Bar Extremes Are Magnets

When there is a huge trend bar with small tails, traders who enter on the bar or soon afterward will often put their protective stops beyond the bar. It is fairly common for the market to work its way to those stops and then reverse back in the direction of the trend bar.

Bar 1 in Figure 10.1 is a huge bull trend bar with a shaved bottom. The market reversed down off the bear inside bar that followed and formed a higher low, but not before running the protective stops below the low of the trend bar. Smart traders would have shorted the inside bar, but they were ready to go long above the bar 2 bull reversal bar that hit the stops and then turned the market back up.

Bars 3 and 4 were also huge trend bars with small tails, but neither was followed by an immediate pullback that ran stops.

PART III

Pullbacks: Trends Converting to Trading Ranges

E ven when a chart is in a strong trend, it will have periods of two-sided trading, but as long as traders believe that the trend will resume, these are only pullbacks. These trading ranges are small enough for traders to view them as just brief pauses in the trend, rather than the dominant feature of the chart. All pullbacks are small trading ranges on the chart that you are viewing, and all trading ranges are pullbacks on higher time frame charts. However, on the chart in front of you, most attempts to break out of a trading range fail, but most attempts to break out of a pullback succeed. On higher time frame charts, the trading range is a simple pullback, and if you are trading on that chart, you can trade it like any other pullback. Since the bars are larger on a higher time frame chart, your risk is greater, and you have to reduce your position size. Most traders prefer to trade off a single time frame and not switch back and forth taking different-sized positions and using different-sized stops and profit targets depending on the time frame.

If the market is in a strong trend and everyone expects the trend to continue, why would a pullback ever happen? To understand why, consider the example of a bull trend. The reversal down into the pullback is due to profit taking by the bulls and, to a lesser extent, scalping by the bears. Bulls will take profits at some point because they know that it is the mathematically optimal thing to do. If they hold forever, the market will almost always work back down to their entry price and will eventually go far below, creating a large loss. They never know for certain where the optimum place is to take profits, and they use resistance levels as their best estimate. These levels may or may not be obvious to you, but because they offer opportunities to traders, it is important to look for them constantly. Trend scalpers and swing traders, as well as countertrend scalpers, expect the pullback and trade accordingly. When the market reaches a target where enough bulls think that they should take profits, their lack of new buying and their selling out of their longs will cause the market to pause. The target can be any resistance level (discussed in the chapters on support and resistance in Part II of this book), or a certain number of ticks above an important signal bar (like six, 10, or 18 in the Emini). The bar might have a bull body that is smaller than the bull body of the prior bar, it might have a tail on the top, or the next bar might be a small bar with a bear body. These are all signs that the bulls are less willing to buy at the top of the swing, that some bulls are taking profits, and that bears are beginning to short for scalps. If enough bulls and bears sell, the pullback will become larger and the current bar might fall below the low of the prior bar. In a strong bull spike, traders will expect that the bull trend will immediately resume, so both the bulls and bears will buy around the low of the prior bar. This creates a high 1 buy signal and is usually followed by a new high. As a bull trend matures and weakens, more two-sided trading will develop, and both the bulls and the bears will expect a pullback to fall for more ticks and last for more bars. The market might form a high 2 buy signal, a triangle, or a wedge bull flag. This creates a small downtrend, and when it reaches some mathematical target, the bulls will begin to buy again, and the bears will take profits and buy back their shorts. Neither will sell again until the market rallies far enough for the process to repeat.

Some of the buying also begins to dry up as bulls become unwilling to continue buying only one- to three-tick dips. They grow cautious and suspect that a larger pullback is imminent. Because they believe that they will be able to buy six to 10 ticks or more below the high, there is no incentive for them to buy any higher. Also, there is an incentive for them to take partial or full profits because they believe that the market will soon be lower, where they can buy again and make additional profits as the market rallies to test the most recent high. Momentum programs sense the loss of momentum and will also take profits and not enter again until momentum in either direction returns. Bears also see the weakening of the trend and begin to sell above the highs of bars and above swing highs for scalps, and they scale in higher. Once they see more selling pressure, they will also short below the lows of bars, expecting a deeper pullback.

Most bulls will exit their longs on a weaker sell signal than they would need to take short positions. They initially look to take profits on strength, like above a swing high or the high of the prior bar or on the close of a large bull trend bar. After taking profits on strength, they will then look to take profits on the remainder of their positions on weakness, and begin to sell out of their longs below bear reversal bars; they suspect that the pullbacks will become larger. Most will not join the bears in shorting, because most traders are unable to reverse a trade consistently well. They have been thinking that the market was going up, and usually need to get out of their longs for several minutes before they can convince themselves that they should take a trade in the opposite direction. If they believe that the market is only pulling back and not reversing, they will instead look to buy back their longs once they think that the pullback has ended. Since most cannot or will not reverse, they don't want to be short when they are looking to buy. If they took the short scalp, they would most likely not be able to reverse back to long, and they would find themselves trapped out of a bull swing because they tried to make a small bear scalp. It does not make mathematical sense to try to make one point on a low-probability short and end up missing two to four points on a high-probability long.

In a bull trend, there is a series of higher highs and higher lows. When the trend is strong, bulls will buy for any reason, and many will trail their protective stops. If the market makes a new high, they will raise their stops to below the most recent higher low. If enough bears short and enough bulls take profits, the reversal can be stronger than what traders initially expected. This often happens later in a trend, after several prior pullbacks were followed by new bull highs. However, both the bulls and the bears believe that the market will turn back up above the most recent swing low, and both will usually buy at or above that low. This results in either a double bottom bull flag or another higher low. The sell-off can be sharp, but as long as enough traders believe that the bull trend is intact, traders will buy and the market will test the old high, where bulls will take partial or full profits, and the bears will short again.

As the bull trend matures, traders will only look to buy a deeper correction, and they expect the market to make two-legged corrections, where the second leg falls below the low of the first. The price action tells traders when a deeper correction like this is likely, and when they believe that it is, they will no longer trail their protective stops below the most recent swing low. They will look to take profits higher, like above the most recent swing high, and then look to buy again around that low, reestablishing their longs. It does not make sense for them to rely on a stop below the most recent higher low once they believe that the market is likely to have a two-legged correction and, therefore, fall below that low. They will exit most or all of their position before that happens, but still remain bullish. The bull trend is no longer forming higher highs and higher lows. However, this lower low is usually still above the most recent higher low on a higher time frame chart, so the larger bull trend is still intact. This two-legged pullback is a large high 2 buy setup, and as the trend matures, these pullbacks get larger and have subdivisions. If the trend has truly reversed, there will be a series of lower highs and lows, but there is usually a clear reversal (reversals are discussed in book 3). In the absence of a clear reversal, a two-legged down move is just a type of bull flag and is usually followed by a new bull high. For example, the first leg down might be a small bear spike and the second leg down is a small bear channel. If the move down is strong, even if it is in a tight, complex channel and is not a bear spike, traders will expect it to be the first of at least two legs down. Bulls who bought the pullback will take profits below the trend high, and bears will begin to short aggressively below the old high, expecting a lower high and second leg down.

Once the market begins to make lower highs, the bulls will usually only look to buy deeper pullbacks, and their absence of buying helps to create those deeper pullbacks. The bears see the same price action, and transition to holding on to their shorts for larger profits, expecting the sell-offs to become larger. The market repeatedly sells off around (slightly above, at, or below) the old high, but continues to rally from around the old low. Upside and downside breakout attempts fail, and the market loses its direction, creating near-term uncertainty. This is the hallmark of a trading range. There will be repeated attempts by the bulls to resume the trend and by the bears to reverse the trend, and 80 percent of both fail. Since a trading range in a bull trend is just a bull flag on a higher time frame chart, the odds favor an upside breakout. There will always be some pattern that the bulls and bears will recognize as a sign that the bull trend is about to resume. When a credible one appears, fewer bears will be willing to scalp shorts on the rally, and the bulls will begin to continue to buy toward the top of the range. With fewer bears willing to short and fewer bulls willing to sell out of their longs, the rally will break above the trading range. If the breakout is strong, the bears who were building a swing position, expecting a larger correction or a reversal, will buy back their shorts and not look to short again for at least several more bars. With neither the scalping nor the swinging bears now shorting and the bulls not taking profits, the market usually runs for about a measured move up, equal to about the height of the trading range. Bulls will then begin to take profits and bears will again short. If the selling is strong, there will be a pullback, a trading range, or even a reversal down.

The opposite happens in a bear trend. The pullbacks are initially due to bears taking profits on new lows, but there is always some buying by aggressive bulls who think that the market will rally far enough for them to make a profitable scalp. Once the market has rallied to some resistance level, usually in a low 2 or low 3 pattern, the bulls will sell out of their longs as they take profits, and the bears will short again. The bears want the market to continue to make lower highs and lows. Whenever they see a sharp rally, they will aggressively short when it approaches the most recent lower high. They sometimes don't short heavily until the market reaches the most recent swing high, which is why double top bear flags are so common. As long as the market continues to make lower highs, they know that most traders will see the bear trend as being intact, and therefore likely to be followed by another lower low, where they can take partial or full profits on their shorts. Eventually a pullback will evolve into a trading range, and there will be some rallies above the most recent lower highs. On a higher time frame chart, there will still be lower highs and lows, but on the chart that you are trading, this higher high is a sign that the bear trend has lost some of its strength. As bear trends mature and weaken, they often form two-legged rallies where there is both a higher low and a higher high, but the bear trend is still intact. This is the basis for a low 2 short setup, which is simply a two-legged rally. There will be some pattern within the range that will tell both bulls and bears that the bear trend is likely to resume, and it will always be at a resistance level, like a measured move or a trend line. This will make bulls less willing to buy near the bottom of the range and bears more willing to continue to sell all the way to the bottom. The market then breaks to the downside, the bull scalpers stop buying, and the bull swing traders sell out of their longs. The market then falls for about a measured move, where the bears will begin to take profits and the aggressive bulls will once again begin to buy. If the buying by the bulls and the bears is strong enough, there will be a pullback, a trading range, or a trend reversal up.

The final leg of a pullback is often a micro channel against the trend (a bear micro channel at the end of a bull flag or a bull micro channel at the end of a bear flag). The breakout of a micro channel usually only goes for a bar or two before there is a pullback, especially if the micro channel has four or more bars. If the trend is strong, there is often no pullback and therefore entering on the breakout of the micro channel is a reasonable trade. When the trend is not very strong, the breakout from the micro channel usually has a failure attempt within a bar or two. As is the case with all breakouts, traders have to assess the strength of the breakout compared to the strength of the signal bar for the failed breakout. If the breakout is significantly stronger, especially if the underlying trend is strong, the reversal attempt will likely fail and lead to a breakout pullback setup that will give traders a second chance to enter in the direction of the breakout. If the breakout is relatively weak, like a small trend bar with big tails, and the reversal bar is strong, especially if the context is likely to lead to a reversal (like a bull flag just below the top of a trading range), the reversal attempt will probably succeed and traders should take the reversal entry. If the breakout and reversal are about equally strong, and there is no strong underlying trend, traders will assess the strength of the next bar. For example, if there is a bull flag in the middle of a trading range, and the bull trend bar that breaks out of the flag is followed by an equally strong bear reversal bar, and the market trades below the low of that bar, traders will evaluate the appearance of that bear entry bar. If it becomes a bull reversal bar, they will assume that the market is just forming a pullback from the breakout of the bull flag, and will buy above the high of the bar. If instead it is a strong bear trend bar, especially if it closes on its low and below the low of the bull breakout bar, traders will see the pattern as a bear breakout and look to get short, if they did not already short below the bear reversal bar.

In the strictest sense, a pullback is a bar that moves against the trend enough to take out the prior bar's extreme. In a bull trend, a pullback is a move where a bar extends at least one tick below the low of the prior bar. However, a broader definition is more useful, and any pause (including an inside bar, an opposite trend bar, or a doji bar) in a trend's momentum should be considered to be a pullback, even though there may be only sideways action and not an actual move backward. As even the strongest trend progresses, it at some point begins to give evidence of how deep a pullback will be. Most commonly, it will be an area of two-sided trading. For example, after the spike in a spike and channel bull trend, the market has a pause or pullback that creates the start of the channel. Once the trend channel ends and a sell-off (pullback) begins, it will usually test down to the bottom of the channel. That is where bears started selling, and as the bull channel goes above their short entry price, they begin to worry. They and other bears sell more as the bull trend advances, but once the trend turns down into a pullback, those bears will be very happy to exit all of their entries at their earliest and lowest short entry price, which was the start of the channel. Once they are flat, they will not look to sell in that area, because they saw how far the market rallied after their earlier short trade. However, if they are still bearish, they will short again on a rally. If the rally ends below the prior high, it will create a lower high and usually leads to a second leg down. If the bears are particularly strong, that lower high could be the start of a new bear trend and not just a second pullback in an incipient trading range.

The same is true for a wedge at the end of a trend. If a bear trend forms a downward-sloping wedge, the market will try to correct to the top of the wedge where the earliest bulls began to buy. If the market can reach their earliest entry price, then they can exit that trade at breakeven and with a profit on all of their lower entries, and they will likely not want to buy until the market falls again. They learned from their first trade that they bought at too high a price; they did not like riding through the open losses of their long positions as the market continued to fall and do not want to experience that again. This time, they will wait for a pullback and hope the market forms a higher low or even a lower low. They expect that the original low of the wedge will be support on any subsequent pullback and that buying near that level with a stop a little below that price gives them an entry with a defined and limited risk, and they like that.

The tendency of the market in a trend to test the earliest area of two-sided trading allows perceptive traders to anticipate when a pullback might form and how far it will likely extend. They won't want to enter countertrend at the first sign of two-sided trading, but that two-sided trading tells them that countertrend traders are beginning to take positions and at some point before too long the market will likely pull back to that price level. After the trend channel or wedge or stairs pattern begins to develop signs of a reversal (see the chapter on trend reversals in book 3), they will take countertrend trades and look to exit with a profit in the area where the two-sided trading began (the start of the channel).

Since a pullback is a trend, even though it is usually small compared to the larger trend from which it is pulling back, like all trends it will commonly have at least two legs. One-legged and three-legged pullbacks are also common, as are small channels and triangles, but all pullbacks are relatively brief, and traders will expect the trend to resume soon. Sometimes the legs are visible only on a smaller time frame chart, and other times they are large and each leg breaks down into smaller legs, each of which also has two legs. Because traders expect the major trend to resume soon, they will fade breakouts in a pullback. For example, if there is a strong bear trend that finally has a pullback with two legs up, there will usually be far more bears than bulls as the market breaks out above the high of the first leg up. Even though the market is breaking out above a swing high in a bull trend, the bulls buying the breakout will usually be overwhelmed by bears who will short it, because they expect the breakout to fail and for the bear trend to resume very soon. They will short on limit and market orders at and above the swing high. They see this breakout as a brief opportunity to reestablish shorts at a high price. Since 80 percent of attempts to reverse a trend will fail, the odds strongly favor the bears. This is especially true for the first two-legged pullback in a strong trend.

Any move that has two legs should be traded as if it is a pullback, even if it is with the trend. Sometimes the final leg in a trend is a two-legged, with-trend move to a higher or lower high in a bull trend or a lower or higher low in a bear trend. For example, if there is a bull trend that has a sell-off that falls through the bull trend line and this trend line breakout is followed by a two-legged pullback, that pullback simply tests the prior extreme and can even exceed the old extreme. This means that the pullback from that trend line breakout can result in either a lower high or even a higher high and still be part of a transition into a new bear trend. Strictly speaking, the bear trend does not begin until after the final high, but that final high is often just a higher high pullback from the breakout below the bull trend line.

What qualifies as two legs? You can create a line chart based on closes and often clearly see a two-legged move. If you are using bar or candle charts, the easiest two-legged move to see is one in which there is a countertrend move, then a smaller with-trend move, and then a second countertrend move (a textbook ABC pullback). So why does the move often reverse after the second leg? Look at a two-legged pullback in a bull trend as an example. Bulls will buy the new low (the C leg), thinking that the second leg down will be the end of the trend. Also, short scalpers who were looking for a two-legged correction will be buying back their shorts. Finally, aggressive bulls who bought the low of the first leg down (the A leg) will now be adding to their long positions on the move to a lower low. If all of these buyers overwhelm the new bears who shorted on the breakout below the first leg down, a rally will ensue and it will usually test the old high at a minimum.

However, oftentimes the two legs are clearly visible only on a smaller time frame chart and have to be inferred on the chart that you are viewing. Since it is easier to use a single chart for trading than to be checking multiple charts all day long, traders have an advantage if they can see the two legs on the chart in front of them, if only by inference.

In a bull market, when there is a series of bull trend bars, a bear trend bar can be assumed to be the first leg of a pullback (the A leg) even if the low of the bar is above the low of the prior bar. If you examined a smaller time frame chart, a countertrend leg would likely be evident. If the next bar has a with-trend close but a high below that of the bar that ended the bull swing, then this is the B leg. If there is then a bear bar or a bar with a low below the low of the prior bar, this will create the second leg down (the C leg).

The more that has to be inferred, the less reliable is the pattern, since fewer traders will see it or have confidence in it. Traders will likely commit less capital and be quicker to exit.

There is an obvious point here. If the trend that is now pulling back ended in a climax or any significant trend reversal pattern, the trend has changed and you should not be looking to enter pullbacks in the old trend. It is over, at least for maybe 10 bars or so and maybe for the rest of the day. So after a strong rally, if there is a wedge top or a lower low after a break of the bull trend line, you should now be looking for setups to short and not pullbacks in the old bull trend to buy. When it is not clear that there was a probable trend reversal, setups in both directions are likely to work, at least for scalps. The more likely it is that a trend reversal has taken place, the more important it becomes to avoid trades in the old direction, since it is now likely that there will be at least two legs in the new direction. Also, the amount of time and number of points in this move will usually be roughly proportional to the clarity of the reversal. When you have a great reversal setup, you should swing part or, rarely, even all of your position.

All pullbacks begin with a reversal pattern of some type. It is usually strong enough to entice countertrend traders into taking a position against the trend, but not strong enough to be a reliable countertrend setup. Since the setup and the pullback are not strong enough to change the direction of the always-in trade, traders should not be looking for a countertrend trade. Instead, they should be looking for a setup that signifies a possible end of the pullback and then enter in the direction of the trend. However, since the pullback began with a reversal, many traders would be overly cautious and talk themselves out of a great trade. You are never going to be 100 percent certain of any trade, but when you are reasonably confident that a trade looks good, you have to trust the math, take the trade, and simply accept the reality that you will lose some of the time. That is just the nature of the business, and you cannot make a living as a trader unless you are willing to take losses. Remember, a major league baseball hitter who fails 70 percent of the time is considered to be a superstar and makes millions off that other 30 percent.

When the market is in a weak trend, or in the early stages of transitioning from a trading range into a trend, it will sometimes have a flag, and then a flag breakout, and then a pullback, and that pullback becomes another flag. The market will sometimes do this several times before a strong breakout materializes.

One- and two-bar pauses are more difficult to trade than pullbacks that last many bars and actually pull back from the extreme. For example, if there is a strong bull move in which the last bar was a small bar with a high just a tick or two below the prior bar's high and that bar was a large bull trend bar and followed one or two other large bull trend bars, if you buy one tick above this bar, you are buying at the high of the day. Since lots of institutions fade every new high, there is a substantial risk that the move might reverse and hit your stop before your profit target is reached. However, if the trend is very strong, this is an important trade to take. Part of what makes this trade so difficult is that you have very little time to analyze the strength of the trend and to look for possible trend channel line overshoots or other reasons why the trade might fail.

An even more difficult pause is a small doji with a high one tick above the high of the prior strong bull trend bar. Buying above the high of the doji is sometimes a good trade, but for most traders, it is too difficult to assess risk quickly enough and it is better to wait for a clearer setup. A reason against buying a pause bar breakout is if the last trend bar or two had fairly large tails, which indicates that countertrend traders were able to assert some influence. Also, if the prior with-trend entry followed a larger pullback, like a high 2, you should be hesitant since each pullback usually gets deeper, not shallower. However, if the market just broke out and had three bull trend bars with closes near their highs, then the chance of a successful scalp when you buy above the pause bar that follows these bars is good. In general, these high 1 longs (or low 1 shorts in bear trends) in the early stages of a strong bull trend are the only pause bars entries that most traders should consider. Also, remember that a pause bar after a one-bar breakout is just as likely to be an entry in the opposite direction, since one-bar breakouts often fail, especially if they are countertrend.

If a pullback is small compared to the trend, it is usually safe to enter as soon as it ends. If it is large enough to be a tradable, strong countertrend move, it is better to wait until a second signal sets up. For example, if there is a protracted bear channel in a strong bull trend, rather than buying the first reversal back up, it is safer to wait for a pullback from that breakout and buy the breakout pullback.

All bull pullbacks end for a reason, and that reason always is that the market has reached some kind of support. Sometimes they end quietly and other times with strong trend bars against the main trend and come close to reversing the trend. This is true of large pullbacks, and one- or two-bar pullbacks from breakouts of small flags. Even the 1987 and 2009 stock market crashes ended at the monthly bull trend line, and were therefore just pullbacks in a bull trend. Most end at a cluster of support levels, even though many traders may not see some or all of them. Some traders will buy a pullback in a bull trend because they are focused on one support level, whether it is a bull trend line, a channel line along the bottom of the bull flag, a prior high or low, some moving average, or any other type of support, and others will buy because they see a different support level in the same area. Once there are enough buyers coming in to overwhelm the bears, the trend will resume. The same is true of bear pullbacks. They always end at a cluster of resistance levels, although it is often easy to not see the resistance that the market is seeing. Once the market gets close to the key price, the vacuum effect often dominates. For example, if buyers believe that the market is getting close to an important support level, they will often step aside and wait for that level to be hit. This can result in a very strong bear spike, but once the support is hit, the bulls come in and buy aggressively and relentlessly. The same is true for the bears who created the pullback. They, too, see the support level, and the closer the market gets to it, the more confident they are that the market will get there. The result is that they sell aggressively and re- lentlessly until the level is reached, and then they suddenly stop selling and quickly buy back their shorts. The pullback can end with a large bear trend bar that looks like it might flip the always-in trade to short, but the follow-through selling over the next bars does not develop. Instead, the bull trend resumes, sometimes slowly at first. With both the bulls and the bears buying, the reversal can be sharp and go a long way. The vacuum effect is always present, even during the most dramatic reversals, like the 1987 and the 2009 stock market crashes. In both instances, the market was in a free fall, but strongly reversed up once the market fell a little below the monthly trend line. As dramatic as both crashes were, they were just examples of the vacuum effect at work.

This same behavior happens on a one- or two-bar pullback from the breakout of a flag. For example, if there is a low 2 bear flag at the moving average in a strong bear trend and it triggers a short, the entry bar might be followed by a bull trend bar. This represents a failed breakout and could be the start of a bull trend or a larger bear rally. However, it usually fails, and when a failure fails, it becomes a pullback in the larger trend. Here, it becomes a breakout pullback short setup. Traders will expect it to fail, and aggressive bears will short on its close and just below and above its high. More conservative traders will wait for confirmation that this bear trend bar is just a pullback from the breakout of the bear flag. They will short on a stop below the low of the bear bar, or the next bar or two, if the pullback continues a little longer.

Since a pullback is only a pause in a trend and not a reversal, once you identify what you believe is a pullback, you believe that the trend will resume and there will be a test of the trend's extreme. For example, if there is a bull trend and then the market sells off for several bars and if you see that sell-off as a buying opportunity, then you believe that it is just a pullback in the bull trend. You are expecting a test of the bull trend's high. It is important to note that the test does not have to reach a new high. Yes, it is often a higher high, but it can be a double top or a lower high. After the test, you will then decide whether the bull trend is intact or has transitioned into a trading range or even a bear trend.

Pullbacks are often strong spikes that make traders wonder if the trend has reversed. For example, in a bull trend, there might be a large bear trend bar or two that break below the moving average and maybe several ticks below a trading range. Traders will then wonder if the always-in direction is in the process of flipping to down. What they need to see is follow-through selling in the form of maybe just one more bear trend bar. Everyone will watch that next bar closely. If it is a large bear trend bar, most traders will believe that the reversal has been confirmed and will start shorting at the market and on pullbacks. If the bar instead has a bull close, they will suspect that the reversal attempt has failed and that the sell-off is just a brief, but sharp, markdown in price and therefore a buying opportunity. Beginning traders see the strong bear spike and ignore the strong bull trend in which it is occurring. They sell the close of the bear trend bar, below its low, any small bounce over the next few bars, and below any low 1 or low 2 sell setup. Smart bulls are taking the opposite side of those trades because they understand what is happening.

The market is always trying to reverse, but 80 percent of those reversal attempts fail and become bull flags. At the time the reversal attempt is occurring, the two or three bear bars can be very persuasive, but without follow-through selling, the bulls see the sell-off as a great opportunity to get long again near the low of a brief sell climax. Experienced bulls and bears wait for these strong trend bars and sometimes step aside until one forms. Then they come into the market and buy because they view it as the climactic end of the selling. The bears buy back their shorts and the bulls reestablish their longs. This is the opposite of what happens at the end of a trend when the strong traders are waiting for one large trend bar. For example, in a strong bear trend near a support area, there will often be a late breakout in the form of an unusually large bear trend bar. Both the bulls and the bears stopped buying until they saw it form. At that point, both buy the sell climax, because the bears see it as a great price to take profits on their shorts and the bulls see it as a brief opportunity to buy at a very low price.

If traders see what they believe is just a pullback, then they believe that the trend is still intact. When they are evaluating the trader's equation, the probability is never known with certainty, but since they are making a trade in the direction of the trend, they can assume that the directional probability of an equidistant move is 60 percent. It might be higher but it is unlikely to be much lower. Otherwise, they would have concluded that the pullback had lasted so long that it had lost its predictive value and had become an ordinary trading range, which has about an equal probability of the eventual breakout being up or down. Once they determine their risk, they can then set a profit target that is at least as large as the risk and reasonably assume that they have about a 60 percent chance or better of being successful. For example, if they are buying a breakout of a bull flag in Goldman Sachs (GS) and their protective stop is below the bull flag, about 50 cents below their entry, they can assume that they have at least a 60 percent chance of making at least a 50 cent profit on their long. Their profit target might be a test of the bull high. If it is and that high is $2.00 above their entry, they likely still have about a 60 percent chance of success, but now their potential reward is four times their risk, and this creates a very favorable result from the trader's equation.

Once you believe that the market has reversed, it usually will pull back to test the prior trend's extreme before the new trend unfolds. For example, assume that there is a bear trend and that the prior pullback was strong enough to break above the bear trend line and now the market is reversing up from a lower low test of the bear trend's bottom. This is a possible trend reversal into a bull trend. If that first leg up is in the form of a strong spike, you then believe that the odds of a reversal are now even greater. The pullback from that first strong leg up will usually result in a higher low, but it can also result in a double bottom with the bear's low or even a lower low. How can it be that you believe that the trend has reversed up into a bull trend, yet the market has now fallen to a lower low? A lower low is one of the hallmarks of a bear trend, and it can never be a part of a bull trend. Yes, that is the conventional wisdom, but you stand to make more money as a trader if you use broader definitions. You might stop yourself out of your long if the market falls below the old bear low, but you might still believe that the bulls really control the market. That spike up was a breakout of the old bear trend and converted the market into a bull trend. It does not matter if the pullback from the breakout falls below the bear low. Suppose the market stopped exactly at the old low instead of going one tick lower. Do you really think that is of major importance? Sometimes it is but usually close is close enough. If two things are similar, they will behave the same. It also does not matter if you consider the bottom of the bull spike or the pullback to the lower low as the start of the bull trend. Strictly speaking, the spike was the first attempt at a reversal and it failed once the market fell below the bottom of the spike. However, it was still the breakout that showed that the bulls took control over the market, and it really does not matter that the pullback fell to a lower low and that the bears briefly regained control. All that matters is that the bulls are in control and will likely be so for many bars, so you need to be looking to buy pullbacks, even that first pullback to the lower low.

Pullbacks to lower lows in bull trends or higher highs in bear trends are common in the small legs that take place on every chart. For example, assume that there is a bear trend and then there is a tight channel rally to the moving average that lasts about eight bars. Since the channel is tight, it is strong and this means that the first bear breakout will likely fail, even though it is in the direction of the trend. Traders usually wait for a pullback back up before looking to short. However, that pullback will often be in the form of a higher high, creating an ABC pullback in the bear trend. They will short below the low of the prior bar, confident that a low 2 short at the moving average is a great trade in a strong bear trend. Many traders do not think of this ABC as a bear breakout (the B leg is the breakout below the channel that constitutes the A leg) and then a breakout pullback to a higher high (the C leg), but that is what it actually is, if you think about it.

There is a special type of higher high or lower low pullback that is common in major trend reversals, which are discussed in book 3. For example, if there is a bull trend that has a strong move down below the bull trend line, and then a weak rally (for example, a wedge) to a new high, this higher high is sometimes the start of a new bear trend. If the trend then reverses down into a bear trend, this weak rally to the higher high is simply a pullback from the bear spike that broke the bull trend line. That bear spike was the actual start of the bear trend, even though the pullback from the spike rallied to above the top of the bear spike and created a new high in the bull trend. After the bear trend has gone on for 20 or more bars, most traders will look back at the higher high and see it as the start of the bear trend, and that is a reasonable conclusion. However, as the trend was forming, astute traders were wondering if the market had reversed into a bear trend, and they did not care if the rally up from the bear spike tested the bull high as a lower high, a double top, or a higher high. From a strictly technical perspective, the trend began once the bears took control of the market during the bear spike and not with the test of the bull high. The confirmation of the trend reversal came once the market sold off strongly from the higher high. Although the higher high is actually simply a pullback from the bear spike, it does not matter which of the two highs you think is the start of the bear trend, because you would trade the market the same way and look to short below the higher high. The same is true when a bear trend reverses into a bull trend from a lower low after a strong rally breaks above the bear trend line. The bulls took control of the market on the spike that broke above the bull trend line, but most traders would say that the new bull began with the lower low. However, that lower low was simply a pullback from the strong bull spike.

Any trend that covers a lot of points in very few bars, meaning that there is some combination of large bars and bars that overlap each other only minimally, will eventually have a pullback. These trends have such strong momentum that the odds favor resumption of the trend after the pullback and then a test of the trend's extreme. Usually the extreme will be exceeded, as long as the pullback does not turn into a new trend in the opposite direction and extend beyond the start of the original trend. In general, the odds that a pullback will get back to the prior trend's extreme fall substantially if the pullback retraces 75 percent or more. For a pullback in a bear trend, at that point, a trader is better off thinking of the pullback as a new bull trend rather than a pullback in an old bear trend.

The most frustrating thing about waiting for a pullback is that sometimes it never seems to come. For example, when there is a rally and you are now confident that it would be smart to buy a pullback, the market goes up bar after bar and does not pull back until it has gone so far that now you think it might reverse instead of pulling back. Why is that? Every bull trend is created by buy programs that use every imaginable algorithm, and strong trends occur when many firms are running programs in the same direction. Once you are confident that the bull trend is strong, so is everyone else. Experienced traders understand what is going on, and they realize that any pullback will almost certainly be bought and it will be followed by a new high. Because of that, instead of waiting for a pullback, they are doing just what the institutions are doing. They are buying at the market and on tiny pullbacks that are not evident on the chart in front of them. Maybe they are buying on a one- or two-tick pullback. The programs will keep buying because the probability is that a trend will continue until it reaches some technical level. At that point, the math will favor a reversal. In other words, the math overshot neutrality and now favors a reversal, and because it does, the firms will aggressively trade in the opposite direction and the new trend will continue until once again it overshoots neutrality and the odds again favor a move in the opposite direction.

For example, if AAPL is up $4.00 at $280 and it has gone up for seven straight bars on the 5 minute chart, it will probably go up for the eighth bar and even more. Traders are willing to buy at $280 because they understand the logic of the directional probability of an equidistant move. Since they are confident that at some point soon the market will be higher than it is right now and they are not confident that it will be lower soon, they buy at the market and on small dips. Although they may not think in terms of directional probability, all trend trading is based on it. When AAPL is trending up strongly, they would rather buy at $280 because they believe that the market will reach $281 before it falls back to $279. They also likely believe that it will reach $282 and maybe $283 before it falls back one dollar. They may not think of this in terms of math and the exact probability is never certain, but in this situation, there is probably about a 70 percent chance that AAPL will go two or three dollars higher before it pulls back one dollar. That means that if you take this trade 10 times, you will make two dollars in seven cases for $14 profit and you will lose one dollar three times. Your net profit is $11, or more than a dollar per trade.

If instead they wait for the $1.00 pullback, it might not come until AAPL is at $283. They then could buy it at $282, but that is two dollars worse than what they could have paid earlier if they just bought at the market.

If after they bought at $280, AAPL fell to $279, many traders would buy more because they believe that the odds are probably better than 70 percent that it would rally to a new high and they could get out of their first long at breakeven and have a dollar profit on their lower entry.

This is important for traders who are waiting to enter on pullbacks. When the trend is strong, it is often better to enter at the market than to wait for a pullback.

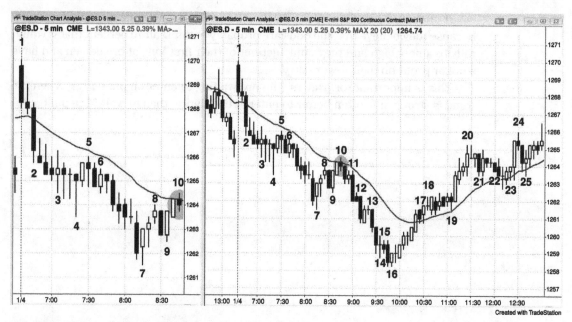

FIGURE PIII.1   Pullbacks Begin with Reversals

All pullbacks begin with a reversal, and it is often strong enough so that traders are too afraid to take the with-trend signal when it finally develops. In Figure PIII.1, the chart on the left shows what the 5 minute chart looked like at the time of the bar 10 low 2 sell setup at the moving average, and the chart on the right shows the entire day. Bar 7 was a strong bull reversal bar, and it was followed by a strong two-bar reversal and higher low at bar 9. However, the market had not touched the moving average in more than 20 bars, so the bear trend was strong and the bears were likely going to look to short a two-legged rally to the moving average, especially if there was a bear signal bar. When the perfect setup finally formed, many beginners were so focused on bars 7 and 9 that they ignored the bear trend that preceded them, and the reality that a low 2 short at the moving average where there is a bear signal bar is a reliable sell setup. The rally was created by profit-taking bears and scalping longs, and both planned to sell into strength on a two-legged pullback to around the moving average. The longs took profits and the bears reestablished their shorts. Nothing is ever going to be 100 percent certain, but a low 2 at the moving average in a bear trend where there is a bear signal bar is usually at least 60 percent likely to be a successful short for bears who shorted on a stop at one tick below bar 10. In this particular case, the signal bar was only three ticks tall, so a bear would have been risking five ticks for a test of the bear low, which was about two points lower. Many bears shorted this first pullback to the moving average with a limit order located one tick below the moving average. Other bears saw this as the first two-legged bear rally, and therefore expected it to fail. When they saw the bar 9 bull reversal, they placed limit orders to short at or above the bar 8 high and were filled on the rally to bar 10. They expected any reversal to be the start of a bear flag and thought that any breakout to the upside would be a brief opportunity to reestablish shorts at a higher price; they aggressively seized that opportunity, overwhelming bulls who bought the breakout above bar 8.

The bar 10 low 2 bear flag broke out with a strong bear trend bar, but was followed by a bar with a bull body. This was an attempt to have the breakout fail. The bulls wanted the market to form a failed low 2 and then a rally, and flip to always-in long. However, traders know that most reversal attempts fail, and many shorted the bull close and had limit orders to short above its high. Because the bears did not know whether the market would trade above the high of this bull bar, if they were hoping to short at or above the bar but wanted to guarantee getting short even if their limit orders up there did not get filled, many also placed stop orders at one tick below its low. If their limit orders at the high of the bar were filled, many would have canceled their stop entry orders. If their limit orders were not filled, the stop below the bar would have ensured that they got short. Most would have already shorted the low 2 breakout, but some would have added on as the market went their way. This is particularly true of computerized program trading where many programs continue to short as the market continues to fall.

Incidentally, one of the cardinal rules about trading reversals is to exit on the market's second attempt to resume the trend. In this case, it was premature to expect bar 7 to be a lasting bottom. Once the market formed a low 2 at the moving average, and especially with the bar 10 signal bar having a bear body, all the longs must exit. Very few had the ability to reverse to short, and those who did not have that ability exited their small long scalps and missed a big short trade. It is far better to wait patiently to short a rally to the moving average in a bear trend than it is to scalp a long.

Once the bull trend was clear, traders expected the first two-legged pullback to fail. When they saw the bull trend bar after bar 21, they placed buy limit orders at the bar 21 low, since they expected that the breakout below bar 21 would fail. It would have been the first two-legged move down in a strong bull trend, and most firsts against a strong trend fail. They also believed that the moving average would be support and that there would be aggressive buyers there. Their buy limit orders were filled as the market fell to the moving average. Other bulls entered on a buy stop above the bar 23 high, since it was a high 2 buy setup in a bull trend with a bull signal bar at the moving average, which is a very strong buy setup.

The bar 24 bear reversal bar had a tail on the bottom and was slightly less strong than the bull breakout of the bear micro channel from bar 20 to the bar before bar 23. The breakout bar was a large bull trend bar, and it followed two bull bars. Some traders shorted below bar 24, expecting the bull breakout to fail. Others waited to see what the next couple of bars would look like. The short entry bar was a strong bear bar but held above the low of the bull breakout bar, so the market did not yet flip to always in short. The next bar had a bull body, and therefore did not confirm the selling. Bulls bought above its high, believing that it was a reasonable breakout pullback buy setup at the moving average in a bull trend, or in a bull leg in a developing trading range.

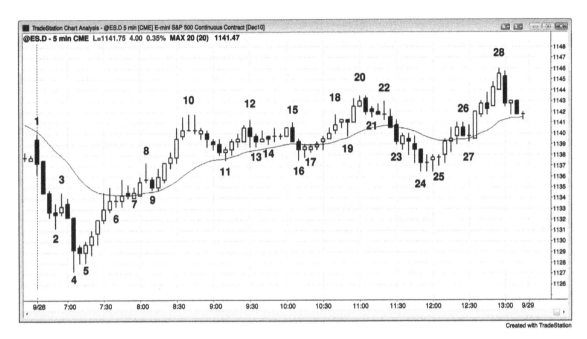

FIGURE PIII.2 Every Pullback Begins with a Reversal

Every pullback begins with some kind of reversal setup. The reversal is needed for many with-trend traders to begin to take profits, and for countertrend trades to initiate trades. Yes, institutions create the reversal pattern as the with-trend institutions take profits and the countertrend institutions begin to scale into reversal trades. However, lots of other institutions and traders wait for the early signs of a reversal before initiating their trades, and the cumulative effect of all traders creates the pullback. If the trend is strong and the reversal setup is weak, the pullback sometimes lasts only a bar or two, like at bars 3, 9, and 19 in Figure PIII.2. Sometimes it is just a pause and creates a sideways pullback, like bar 7.

There was a four-bar bear spike down to bar 2, but the third and fourth bars had shrinking bear bodies, indicating a loss of momentum. The tails on bar 2 are a sign of two-sided trading. Some traders thought that this could be signaling an opening reversal and the low of the day and they bought above bar 2.

The five-bar bull spike up from bar 5 was enough to make most traders believe that the always-in trade had flipped to long. They expected higher prices, and they believed that any sell-off would be bought aggressively and result in a higher low. However, there were three pushes up to bar 8, and this wedge top could have two legs down. This resulted in a one-bar pullback that was followed by another strong leg up. Since the rally up from bar 5 was so strong, many traders believed that any pullback would be bought.

Once everyone believes that there are strong buyers below, they just buy at the market. They don't know if the market will pull back soon but they do believe that whether or not it does, it will soon be higher. Rather than risk missing too much of the trend, they start buying at the market, and they keep buying until they think that the market might finally be starting to pull back.

Bar 10 had a couple of doji bars after a parabolic move in a spike and climax bull trend. The five bars up from bar 5 formed the bull spike. It was also a new high of the day. Some traders began to short what they thought could be the high of the day, but it resulted in only another pullback.

Some traders saw bar 18 as a possible double top with bar 10, and they shorted below the inside bar signal bar. Since there were seven consecutive bull bodies, most traders expected more uptrend so they bought below the low of that signal bar instead of shorting there.

Bar 26 was a bear reversal bar and a possible lower high after a reversal down through the bar 16 bottom of the trading range. However, more traders believed that the day was a strong bull trend day and they bought at and below the low of bar 26.

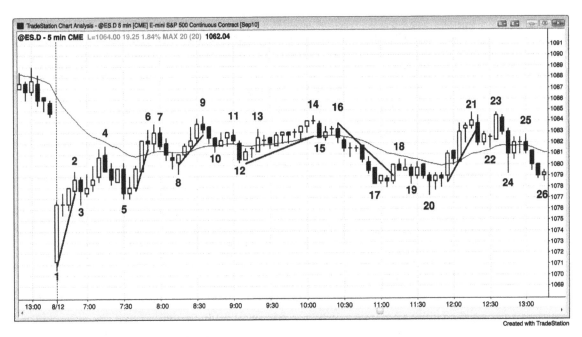

FIGURE PIII.3   Breakout Pullbacks

When a channel is steep, it is better not to enter a reversal trade on the breakout through the trend line and instead wait to see if there is a breakout pullback that sets up a second signal. In Figure PIII.3, the spike up to bar 2 was too steep to short the first breakout below the trend line. Instead, traders should consider shorting only if there is a breakout pullback that tests the high of the spike. The test can be a lower high, a double top, or a higher high. Here, there was a higher high just below the moving average at the bar 4 bear reversal bar.

The spike up to bar 6 was also too strong to short on the breakout below bar 6. The bears were hoping for a successful breakout below the bull trend line with good follow-through to the downside. Instead, traders should wait for a breakout pullback before considering going short. Here, the bar after bar 6 became an outside up bar, and it was a higher high test of the high of the tight channel from bar 5 up to bar 6. It was followed by a bear inside bar, forming an ioi (inside-outside-inside) higher high short setup.

The channel from bar 8 up to bar 9 had four consecutive bull trend bars and was therefore too strong to short the first breakout below the channel. Instead, traders should wait to see what the breakout pullback looked like. It was a lower high at bar 11, and they could go short at one tick below its low.

The bull channel from bar 12 to bar 14 was very tight and therefore traders should not short the breakout below the trend line. Instead, they should wait to see if there was a good breakout pullback short setup. Bar 16 formed a lower high test of the channel high, and traders could short as bar 16 fell below the low of the prior bar and became an outside down bar. Alternatively, they could wait for the bar to close. Once they saw that it had a bear body and it closed below the low of the prior bar, they could short below the low of the bar 16 outside down bar, which is a higher-probability short since that bear close gave them additional confirmation that the bears were strong.

The sell-off down to bar 17 was in a tight channel and there were seven bars without a bull close. This is too strong to buy the first attempt to break out to the upside. The breakout pullback was to a lower low at bar 20, and the buy setup was an ii (inside-inside) pattern.

The rally to bar 21 was in a steep bull channel with seven bars with higher lows and highs. This is too strong to short the first breakout below the bull channel. The breakout pullback to bar 23 formed a double top with the bar 21 channel high. The following bar was a strong bear inside bar, which was a good signal bar for the breakout pullback short.

The move down to bar 5 was a bull flag, and it was followed by a breakout and then a pullback to bar 8, which was at the bottom of another bull flag. It then broke out to bar 9 and formed another pullback to bar 12, which was another bull flag buy setup. The market often has breakouts that lead to pullbacks that become flags. This usually happens in weaker trends and in trading ranges, as it did here.

Although bars 5 and 12 were strong bear trend bars and attempts to flip the always-in position to short, they did what most such attempts do—they failed. The bears needed one more strong bear trend bar before they could convince traders that the short-term trend was down and lower prices were likely over the next several bars. When it became clear that the bulls were buying relentlessly and the bears could not push the market down, they bought back their shorts. Their buying, combined with the continued buying by the bulls who saw the strong bear trend bars as great opportunities to buy at a low price, resulted in the resumption of the bull trend. Bulls like to see strong bear trend bars into support. They know that they represent attempts by the bears to reverse the trend and that most will be brief and fail. They often step aside and wait for one to form, and they see it as a likely end of the pullback. This gives them a brief opportunity to buy at a low price. Experienced traders can buy at the close of the bear trend bar, at and below its low, and at the close of the next couple of bars. Most traders should instead wait for a bull reversal bar and buy above its high, or wait for the reversal up, and then buy above a pullback from the breakout of the bull flag (like above the two-bar sideways pullback that followed the bar 13 breakout of the bar 12 high 2 bull flag).

CHAPTER 11

First Pullback Sequence: Bar, Minor Trend Line, Moving Average, Moving Average Gap, Major Trend Line

There are many types of pullbacks that can occur in a trend, some shallow and others deep, and they can be classified and ranked in terms of their extent. The first time any one of them appears is a first pullback for that type of pullback. Each subsequent pullback will be the first one of a larger variety, and each one will usually be followed by a test of the trend extreme since strong moves generally have at least two legs. Each type of first countertrend move will therefore likely be followed by another leg in the trend. The pullbacks don't have to occur in the exact same order. For example, sometimes a high 1 will occur after a high 2 if the trend accelerated after the high 2.

As a bull trend progresses, it eventually loses momentum, becomes more two-sided, and starts to have pullbacks. The pullbacks become larger and evolve into a trading range, and eventually a trading range will reverse into a bear trend. Prior to the final reversal, each countertrend move is usually followed by another high in the trend. Therefore, each sign of weakness is theoretically a buy setup, and each can occur several times before any other on the following list develops. Also, one can occur and then occur again later after others have occurred.

Here is the general order in which signs of weakness in a bull trend develop:

- The bull bodies become smaller.
- Tails start to form on the tops of bars, and the tails become larger on subsequent bars.
- Bars overlap their respective prior bars more than they did earlier.
- A bar has a very small body or a doji body.
- A bar has a bear body.
- The high of the current bar is at or below the high of prior bar.

- The low of the current bar is at or just above the low of the prior bar.
- The low of the current bar is below the low of the prior bar.
- There is a one-legged pullback (a high 1 buy setup), where the high of the bar is below the high of the prior bar.
- There is a two-legged pullback (a high 2 buy setup) lasting only five to about 10 bars.
- There is a three-legged pullback (a wedge bull flag or a triangle) lasting only five to about 15 bars.
- There is a break of a minor bull trend line.
- A bar touches the moving average (a 20 gap bar buy setup).
- The next rally to a new high has one or more bear trend bars and a pullback or two.
- A bar has a close below the moving average.
- A bar has a high below the moving average (a moving average gap bar).
- There is a break of a major bull trend line.
- Once there is a bar with a high below the moving average, there is a second leg down before the market gets back above the moving average.
- The rally to the new high has two or more pullbacks, each lasting two or three bars and having more prominent bear bodies.
- There is a larger two-legged pullback, lasting more than 10 bars, with the second leg down falling below a prominent higher low, forming a lower low.
- The market enters a trading range, and the bull and bear bars are about equally prominent.
- The market breaks above the trading range and comes back into the trading range, forming a larger trading range.

This is the sequence of weakening of a bear trend:

- The bear bodies become smaller.
- Tails start to form on the bottoms of bars, and the tails become larger on subsequent bars.
- Bars overlap their respective prior bars more than they did earlier.
- A bar has a very small body or a doji body.
- A bar has a bull body.
- The low of the current bar is at or above the low of prior bar.
- The high of the current bar is at or just below the high of the prior bar.
- The high of the current bar is above the high of the prior bar.
- There is a one-legged pullback (a low 1 sell setup), where the low of the bar is above the low of the prior bar.
- There is a two-legged pullback (a low 2 sell setup) lasting only five to about 10 bars.

- There is a three-legged pullback (a wedge bear flag or a triangle) lasting only five to about 15 bars.
- There is a break of a minor bear trend line.
- A bar touches the moving average (a 20 gap bar sell setup).
- The next rally to a new low has one or more bull trend bars and a pullback or two.
- A bar has a close above the moving average.
- A bar has a low above the moving average (a moving average gap bar).
- There is a break of a major bear trend line.
- Once there is a bar with a low above the moving average, there is a second leg up before the market gets back below the moving average.
- The sell-off to the new low has two or more pullbacks, each lasting two or three bars and having more prominent bull bodies.
- There is a larger two-legged pullback, lasting more than 10 bars, with the second leg up reaching above a prominent lower high, forming a higher high.
- The market enters a trading range, and the bull and bear bars are about equally prominent.
- The market breaks below the trading range and comes back into the trading range, forming a larger trading range.

Most of the first pullbacks are minor and are still part of the larger trend's first leg. However, each pullback tends to be greater as the countertrend traders become more willing to take positions and the with-trend traders become quicker to take profits. Countertrend traders start to take control at new extremes. For example, in a bull trend, traders will start to be able to make profitable trades by shorting reversals from new highs, and with-trend traders will begin to lose when they buy breakouts to new highs. At some point, the countertrend traders will overwhelm the with-trend traders and the trend will reverse.

The first minor pullback in a strong trend is a one- or two-bar pullback, which almost always is followed by a new extreme. For example, if there is a bull spike that goes on for four bars and there is little overlap between the bars and the tails are small, the trend is strong. If the next bar has a low below the low of the prior bar, this is the first pullback in this bull trend. Traders will place a buy stop above its high, since they expect at least one more push up. If their order is filled, this is a high 1 long entry, which is discussed in detail in Chapter 17 in this book. Aggressive traders will buy on a limit order below the low of the prior bar, expecting the pullback to be brief and wanting to get in at a lower price than the traders who are waiting to buy on a stop above the pullback bar or bars. The next pullback might be three to five bars long and will likely break a minor trend line and then be followed by another new extreme. If this pullback has two small legs, then the buy entry is a high 2 long (a two-legged pullback, commonly called an ABC pullback).

Although this second pullback can be a high 2 setup, if the trend is very strong, it can be another high 1 (a one-legged pullback). If the market went from one or two high 1 entries and then a high 2 entry, and it appeared to be setting up another high 1, it is wise to wait. After a series of winning trades, you should be suspicious of renewed strength without first seeing a larger pullback, since this strength might be a trap setting up (like a final flag, discussed in book 3). It is better to wait for more price action and miss a possible trap than to feel invincible and fearless because you fooled yourself into believing that you are playing with someone else's money. If you trade, it will likely become someone else's money.

The opposite is true in a strong bear trend, where the first pullback is usually a brief one- or two-bar low 1 short entry and later pullbacks have more bars and more legs. For example, an ABC pullback has two legs and sets up a low 2 short entry.

If the trend is strong, it might stay away from the moving average for two hours or more, but once it hits the moving average, it will likely form another with-trend setup that will lead to another new extreme, or at least a test of the old extreme. In a pullback to the moving average in a bull trend, many traders believe that the price is at a good enough discount for them to buy. The bears who shorted above will buy back their shorts to take profits; the bulls who took profits higher will look to buy again; and the traders who had been on the sidelines, waiting for lower prices, will see the moving average as support and a sufficient discount for them to initiate new longs. If the market cannot move above the moving average after about 10 to 20 bars, it is probably because traders want more of a discount before aggressively buying. The price is not low enough yet to attract sufficient buyers to lift the market. The result is that the market will have to fall further before enough buyers return to lift the market up to test the old highs. This same process happens at all support levels.

If a pullback goes beyond the moving average, it will have the first moving average gap bar setup (for example, in a strong bull trend, there is finally a pullback that has a bar with a high below the exponential moving average). This is usually followed by a test of the extreme and likely a new extreme. Eventually, there will be a countertrend move that will break a major trend line, and it often is the pullback to the first moving average gap bar. It will be followed by a test of the extreme, which may undershoot (higher low in a bear trend or lower high in a bull trend) or overshoot (lower low in a bear trend or higher high in a bull trend) the old extreme. This is then usually followed by at least a two-legged countertrend move, if not a trend reversal. Each pullback prior to the reversal is a with-trend entry, because each is a first pullback of one type or another (bar, minor trend line, moving average, moving average gap, or major trend line), and any type of first pullback is usually followed by at least a test of the extreme and usually a new extreme until after the major trend line is broken.

Although it is not worth the effort to pay attention to higher time frame charts when trading on a 5 minute chart, it is likely that the larger 5 minute pullbacks end at 15, 30, or 60 minute, or even daily, weekly, or monthly chart points of significance like exponential moving averages (EMAs), breakout points, and trend lines. Also, there is often a tendency for the first pullback to the 15 minute moving average to be followed by a test of the trend extreme, and then a pullback to the 30 or 60 minute moving average, which would likely be followed by another test of the extreme. With higher time frame points of significance occurring relatively infrequently, spending time looking for tests of those points will be a distraction and cause traders to miss too many 5 minute signals.

If a trend is strong and you have made several profitable trades but there are now several sideways bars, be cautious about further entries because this is effectively a trading range. In a bull trend, you can buy if there is a setup near the low of the range, but be careful buying a breakout of the high of the trading range, because bears might be willing to sell a new high and bulls might be beginning to take profits at the high.

The same is true in a bear flag after a protracted down move. Sideways bars mean that both buyers and sellers are active, so you do not want to be shorting on a breakout of the low of the flag. However, if there is a short setup near the top of the flag, your risk is small and the trade is worth taking.

FIGURE 11.1   Subsequent Pullbacks Tend to Get Larger

In a trend there will always be pullbacks, and they tend to get larger the longer the trend extends. However, until there is a reversal, each pullback should at least test the prior extreme (in Figure 11.1, in a bear trend, the prior low of the day), and the test will usually create a new extreme.

Bar 1 was a two-legged higher high after a bull trend line break. It reversed down in a two-bar reversal. At that point, smart traders were looking for short entries in the potential new bear trend instead of long entries in the prior bull trend.

Bar 3 was a short after a two-bar pullback to the moving average, which was the first pullback after the two-bar bear spike that started the reversal down from above yesterday's high. It was a breakout pullback following the breakout below yesterday's swing low.

Bar 4 was the first break of a bear trend line and of the moving average, albeit by only a tick or so, and was followed by a new low. It went above a minor swing high, and therefore was a small higher high, but it failed to get above the moving average, the top of the bear spike that followed bar 3, or the swing high before bar 3. Most traders saw this as a simple two-bar reversal and a low 2 short setup at the moving average. There were only two or three bars in each of the legs of this ABC, and that is rarely enough for traders to see this small rally as a trend reversal.

Figure 11.1   FIRST PULLBACK SEQUENCE   **211**

Bar 5 was another test of the moving average, and this time there were two closes above the moving average, but barely, and the pullback was followed by a new low. Instead of moving above the small swing high that followed bar 4, it failed one tick shy and formed a double top. Traders saw bar 4 as a significant lower high because it was followed by a new bear low. Once the market fell to a new low after bar 5, bar 5 became the most recent lower high of significance. Bears moved their protective stops from above bar 4 to above bar 5.

Bar 8 broke a major trend line and formed the first moving average gap bar (a bar with a low above the EMA). The first gap bar is usually followed by a test of the low, but sometimes there is a second entry. The break of a major trend line might be the first leg of a new trend but will usually be followed by a test of the low that can either overshoot or undershoot the low before a countertrend move of at least two legs unfolds (here, in a bear trend, a rally). At this point, traders needed to be looking to buy instead of continuing to trade the old bear trend. The pause bar after bar 8 set up a short because it led to a failed breakout above the bear trend line.

The rally to bar 8 also broke above the minor highs between bars 6 and 7, creating a minor higher high at bar 8. However, bar 8 was still a lower high in the larger bear trend. The market fell for many bars to bar 9, where it tested the bar 6 bear low. However, instead of reaching a new bear low, bar 9 formed a higher low. Most bears would have moved their protective stops to just above the bar 8 high. They would likely have exited sooner, because they decided that the market had reversed to always-in long on the two-bar bull spike up from the bar 9 higher low, or when it went above the two-bar bull flag that formed two bars later. Once the market went above bar 8 and formed a higher high, they expected higher prices.

The market formed a double bottom bull flag at bars 7 and 9. Bar 9 dipped one tick below bar 7, running stops, but it was not able to put in a new low. The bulls were defending their longs and were aggressively buying the dips (accumulation). The second leg up was completed the next day.

Compare the bars 4, 5, and 8 tests of the moving average and notice that bar 5 penetrated it more than bar 4, and bar 8 had more penetration than bar 5. This is to be expected, and when this is the case be careful about placing a short trade, because there will be many smart bears who will short only at a higher price, and many bulls who will be confident enough to buy dips. This reduces the selling pressure and makes your short entry risky.

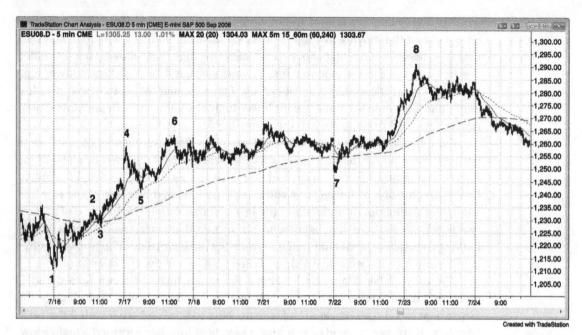

FIGURE 11.2   Moving Average Pullbacks

The market reversed at the bar 1 lower low in Figure 11.2. There were several pull-backs to the 20-bar exponential moving average that led to new highs on the move up to bar 4.

Bar 4 was a trend channel line overshoot that led to a sharp correction to bar 5, which tested the 15 minute 20-bar EMA (dotted line) and was then followed by a test of the trend high (bar 6 was a higher high).

The market gapped down to bar 7, and, although the market initially appeared bearish, the move down was the first pullback to the 60 minute 20-bar EMA (dashed line) and it was followed by the bar 8 new high.

CHAPTER 12

Double Top Bear Flags and Double Bottom Bull Flags

A bull trend often ends with a double top, and a bear trend often ends with a double bottom. Since a pullback in a bull trend is a small bear trend, this small bear trend can end in a double bottom. Because it is a pullback in a bull trend, it is a bull flag and can be referred to as a double bottom bull flag. It is two legs down in a bull trend, and therefore a high 2 buy setup. It is a particularly reliable type of high 2 buy setup, so I generally refer to it as a double bottom to distinguish it from other high 2 patterns. Likewise, a pullback in a bear trend is a bear flag and it is a small bull trend, and that small bull trend can end with a double top. If it does, that double top is a double top bear flag.

In a bull trend, bulls often trail their protective stops below the most recent higher low, because they want the trend to continue to make higher lows and higher highs. A double bottom bull flag is, in part, due to bulls defending their trailing stops below the most recent swing low. If the market falls below the most recent swing low, traders will see the bull trend as weaker, and possibly over. That would be a lower low, and they would be concerned that it might be followed by a lower high instead of a new high. If so, the market might be forming a two-legged correction (a large high 2 buy setup), or even a trend reversal. Because of this, if the bulls have a lot of conviction in the trend, they will buy heavily at and just above the most recent swing low, creating a double bottom bull flag. The opposite is true in a bear trend, where the bears want the market to keep forming lower highs and lows. Many will trail their protective stops just above the most recent lower high, and strong bears often short aggressively on any rally up to that most recent lower high. This can result in a double top bear flag.

Any pullback in a bull or bear trend can turn into either a double bottom bull flag or a double top bear flag. Sometimes both are present within the same pullback, and then this small trading range puts the market in breakout mode. If the market breaks to the upside, traders will see the pattern as a double bottom bull flag, and if it breaks to the downside, they will see it as a double top bear flag. If there is significant momentum up or down before the pattern, that momentum increases the odds that the trading range will just be a continuation pattern. For example, if there was a strong move up just before the trading range, an upside breakout is more likely and traders should look to buy the reversal up from a double bottom at the bottom of the range. If there is then an upside breakout, traders will see the pattern as a double bottom bull flag. If instead the market was in a bear spike just before the trading range, traders should look to sell the reversal down from a double top within the pattern and expect a downside breakout. If that happens, traders will see the trading range as a double top bear flag.

When there is a bull trend and then a two-legged pullback where either of the down legs is a bear spike, which might appear unremarkable, the bears will want the market to stay below the lower high that followed the first leg down. They will short in an attempt to reverse the trend into a bear trend. The bulls always want the opposite because trading is a zero-sum game—what's good for the bears is bad for the bulls and vice versa. The rally up from the second leg down often will stall at or just below the lower high. The bulls want the rally to go above the lower high, run the protective stops of the bears, and then reach a new high. The bears will short aggressively to keep that from happening and are often willing to short heavily at a tick or two below the lower high and at the lower high. This is why the rally often goes all the way up to the lower high before the market turns down. It is the final defense of the bears, and they will be at their absolute strongest at the lower high. If the bears win and the market turns down, this creates a double top bear flag, and a bear channel often follows. After the lower high and the double top test of the lower high, the bears next want a lower low and then a series of lower highs and lows.

Whether or not the rally up from the second leg down stalls at the lower high, above it, or below it, if the market then sells off again, it can form a double bottom with the bottom of the pullback. If there is a reasonable buy setup, traders will buy it, looking for this double bottom to be a bull flag that will be followed by a new high in the bull trend. Many bulls who bought at the bottom of the two legs down will have their protective stops just below the pullback. If the market starts up and comes back down again, the bulls will buy aggressively at a tick or two above the bottom of the first leg down in an attempt to turn the market up. They don't want the market to create a lower low after the lower high, because this is a sign of strength by the bears and it would increase the chances that the market would trade either further down or sideways instead of up. If they succeed, they might be able to resume a bull trend. If the market falls a tick or two below the bottom of that first leg down, it might run the protective stops of the bulls and then break out into a measured move down.

Two-legged pullbacks are common in any trend, and they are often horizontal with both legs ending around the same price. Sometimes the pullback can last for dozens of bars before the trend resumes. The sideways move often begins and ends with small legs that have extremes that are very close in price (the second spike can slightly overshoot or undershoot the first one). The trend resumption from each of the legs is an attempt to extend the trend. For example, if there is a bear trend and then a pullback, and then the market sells off again, the bears are pushing for a lower low and an extension of the bear trend. However, if instead the market finds more buyers than sellers above the bear low and forms a higher low, the bears have failed to drive the market down to a new low. If this second leg up does not result in a new bull trend and the bears are able to regain control and create a low 2 short entry, they will drive the market down again in an attempt to have the market break out to a new low. If again the bulls overwhelm the bears around the same price as they did earlier, the bears will have failed twice at the same price level. When the market fails twice in an attempt to do something, it usually then tries to do the opposite. Those two pushes down that ended around the same price, just above the bear low, create a double bottom bull flag. It is a higher low that has two bottoms instead of one. It is a type of failed low 2, and is a reliable buy signal in this situation.

Similarly, if there is a sell-off in a bull trend but then the bulls regain control of the market and try to rally it up beyond the old high and fail, then the bears were successful in driving the market down again and they created a lower high. If the bulls once again take control and once more push the market up as they try for a new bull high, and again the bears overwhelm them around the same price as they did earlier, there will be a double top. Since the market twice tried to break out to a new bull high and failed, it will likely try to go in the opposite direction. There aren't enough bulls near the old high to create a new high, so the market will have to go lower to find more bulls. Instead of being a successful ABC pullback (a high 2 buy setup) in the bull trend, the pullback failed to find enough bulls to create a new high and the result was a lower high, which was made of a double top.

A common form of this occurs in spike and channel trends. For example, if there is a spike up and then a pullback that leads to a bull channel, the market usually eventually corrects down to test the bottom of the channel, where it tries to turn up again. This test of the bottom of the channel creates a double bottom with the bottom of the channel, which might have been dozens of bars earlier, and since it is in a bull trend (a spike and channel bull trend), it is a double bottom bull flag.

A head and shoulders continuation pattern is another variation, with the spikes on either side of the right shoulder forming a double top or bottom.

Unlike a double top that is a reversal pattern at the top of a bull move, a double top bear flag is a continuation pattern in a bear trend that is already underway.

Both double tops lead to a sell-off. Since a double top bear flag functions like any other double top, many traders simply call it a double top and think of it as the top of a corrective move up in a market that has already turned down. Similarly, a double bottom bull flag is a continuation pattern in a move up and not a reversal pattern at the bottom of a bear trend. A double bottom bull flag is simply a double bottom, and like all double bottoms, it is a buy setup.

The first higher low in a new bull trend often takes the form of a double bottom bull flag, and the first lower high of a new bear trend often is a double top bear flag.

When a double top bear flag or a double bottom bull flag fail and the market breaks out in the wrong direction, watch to see if the breakout is successful. If it is not and it fails within a bar or two, the market usually sets up a variation of a wedge flag. For example, if a double bottom bull flag sets up but the market immediately reverses and falls below the double bottom, there might be a downside measured move based on the height of the failed double bottom. This is often a short setup where traders enter on a sell stop at one tick below the double bottom. However, if the downside breakout fails within a bar or two and the market trades above the high of the prior bar, then this is a three-push bottom entry (functionally the same as a wedge). The two bars that formed the double bottom formed the first two pushes down, and the failed breakout is the final push down. The critical feature of any wedge is the three pushes, not a perfect wedge shape.

Figure 12.1   DOUBLE TOP BEAR FLAGS AND DOUBLE BOTTOM BULL FLAGS   **217**

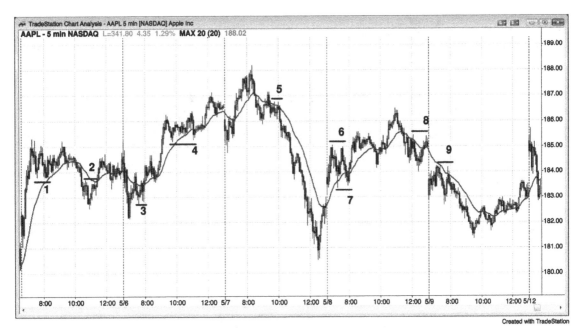

FIGURE 12.1 Bull Flags

A with-trend bull flag sets up a long entry on a buy stop order at one tick above the high of the previous bar, and the initial protective stop is one tick below the low of that signal bar. After the entry bar closes, the stop is moved to one tick below the entry bar if it is a trend bar. If it is a small bar, don't tighten the stop until there is a trend bar in your direction.

Although double bottoms are well-known reversal patterns at the bottom of bear markets, these flags are with-trend setups in bull markets. By ending the pullback, which is a small bear trend, they are reversing it, but it is better to think of them as with-trend patterns.

As shown in Figure 12.1, the double top bear flag at bar 2 failed and resulted in a tradable long (and became a small head and shoulders bottom).

Bar 7 was a setup for a double bottom bull flag within a small trading range that had just formed a double top bear flag. Since the momentum leading up to the trading range was strongly up, the odds favored that the pattern would break to the upside and become a double bottom bull flag, instead of breaking to the downside and becoming a double top bear flag. The minimum target after the breakout up or down is a measured move based on the height of the small trading range.

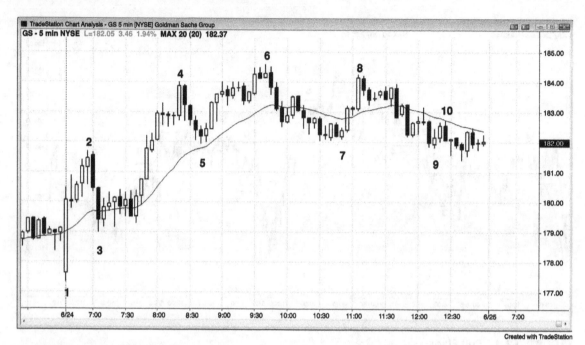

FIGURE 12.2   Double Bottom Bull Flag

As shown in Figure 12.2, Goldman Sachs (GS) had a bull spike up from bar 3 to bar 4 and then a pullback to bar 5. This was followed by a channel up to bar 6 and a pullback to around the bottom of the channel. This created a double bottom bull flag with bars 5 and 7, even though there was the bar 6 higher high in between. Bar 5 was the last higher low of the bull trend, and bar 7 was possibly the first swing low of a bear trend or trading range. In this situation, the market could have formed a head and shoulders top if bar 6 was not exceeded by the rally off bar 7. In any case, a double bottom bull flag is a reliable setup for at least a scalp. Also, since most head and shoulders tops, like all tops, turn into failures and become continuation patterns, it is always wise to keep buying near the bottom of any trading range in a bull trend. In a trend, most reversal patterns fail and most continuation patterns succeed.

There was also a small double bottom bull flag after the bar 3 low formed by the third and seventh bars that followed bar 3. This was a failed low 2 short setup, which often becomes a double bottom bull flag.

Deeper Discussion of This Chart

Bar 1 in Figure 12.2 was a strong bull reversal bar that reversed the breakout below the moving average and the small trading range into yesterday's close. There was a

Figure 12.2   DOUBLE TOP BEAR FLAGS AND DOUBLE BOTTOM BULL FLAGS   **219**

two-bar bear spike down to bar 3 and then the market went sideways as the bulls and bears fought over the direction of the channel. Because the bull spike was bigger (some traders saw the spike ending at the high of bar 1 and others saw it as ending at bar 2), the odds favored that the bulls would create a bull channel and that the bears would fail in their attempt to get follow-through after their spike down. The double bottom bull flag after bar 3 was a higher low buy setup that led to a wedge channel that ended at bar 6. Since it was a wedge, two legs down were likely, and since it was a bull spike and channel, a test of the bar 3 area where the channel began was also likely. Sometimes the test takes more than a day, but once it forms, the market usually tries to form a double bottom with the low of the channel. Because the spikes up to bar 2 and to bar 6 were so strong, the market might not come down to the bar 3 area, and instead might form a wedge bull flag with bars 5 and 7 being the first two pushes down. In fact, that is what happened, and GS gapped up on the following day.

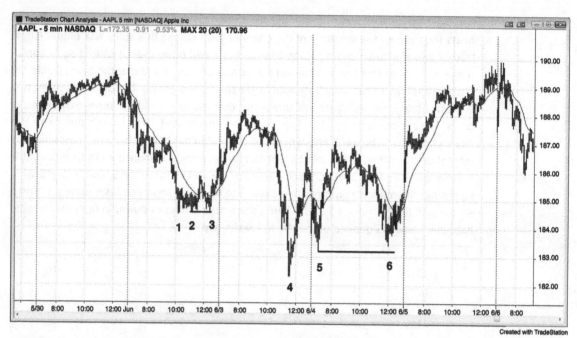

FIGURE 12.3   Double Bottom Bull Flags

Bars 2 and 3 and bars 5 and 6 formed double bottom bull flags in Figure 12.3. Both bars 3 and 6 slightly undershot their first legs, but patterns are rarely perfect.

When the double bottom forms right near the trend low as it did with bars 2 and 3, the pattern is often a small spike up and trading range, and it is often an ii pattern on a higher time frame chart.

The move up from bar 4 was almost vertical and therefore a spike. The move up from bar 5 was the channel, even though it also was nearly vertical. This is a spike and climax type of spike and channel bull trend. After the channel phase of a bull spike and channel pattern, the market usually tests to the bottom of the channel and sets up a double bottom bull flag, as it did here, at bar 6. From there, the market usually bounces up to at least about a quarter of the trading range. After that, the pattern has played out and traders should look for the next pattern.

The move up from bar 5 stalled around the top of the move up from bar 4. Some traders saw this as a double top bear flag and shorted. The market then sold off and found support at bar 6 around the level of the bar 5 pullback. Many of the double top shorts took profits on the test of the bar 5 low, and strong bulls defended that low by buying aggressively. This set up a double bottom bull flag signal. The upside breakout went for an approximate measured move up.

Figure 12.4 DOUBLE TOP BEAR FLAGS AND DOUBLE BOTTOM BULL FLAGS **221**

FIGURE 12.4 Head and Shoulders Top or Double Bottom

The daily chart of GS was forming either a head and shoulders bear flag or a possible double bottom pullback, as shown in Figure 12.4. The market had a spike up to bar 2 and then a pullback to a higher low at bar 3, which was retested a couple of weeks later at bar 4. Then the market had a bull channel up to bar 5 and then a test to the bottom of the channel at bar 6, where it set up a double bottom bull flag with the bar 4 low. The minimum objective is a bounce of about 25 percent of the height of the sell-off from bar 5 to bar 6.

For the bears, the left shoulder is bar 2 and the right shoulder is bar 7. The bears want the market to break below the neckline drawn across the lows of bars 3, 4, and 6. The bulls, however, see the double bottom formed by bars 4 and 6 and want a rally. They will buy the pullback down to bar 8, and if they are successful in turning the market up, this would become a double bottom pullback long trade.

The early bears shorted below the bar 7 right shoulder instead of waiting for the breakout below the neckline, and they would buy back their shorts if the market went above the bar 7 right shoulder. That would create a failed head and shoulders top, and the minimum objective to the upside would be a measured move up from the bar 6 low to the bar 7 high.

The rally up to bar 2 was strong enough for most traders to believe that the market would soon be higher (they believed that the market had flipped to always-in long). This made traders hesitant to short the double top bear flag that formed a couple of weeks later. However, because they were looking for higher prices after the possible bottom at bar 1 and the strong rally to bar 2, they bought the bar 4 double bottom bull flag.

Figure 12.5   DOUBLE TOP BEAR FLAGS AND DOUBLE BOTTOM BULL FLAGS   **223**

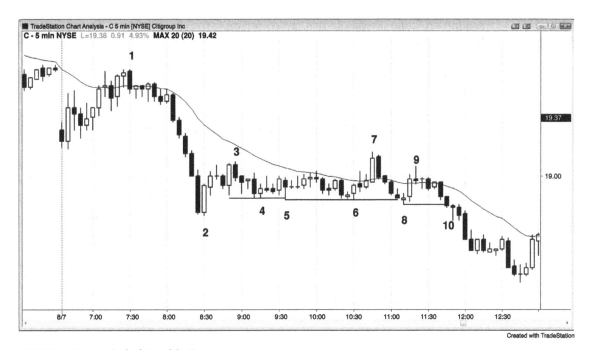

FIGURE 12.5   Failed Double Bottom

In Figure 12.5, the market formed a five-bar bear spike that was followed by a two-bar bull spike at bar 2.

Bar 4 attempted to form a double bottom bull flag with the bar before bar 3 and with the bull entry bar after bar 2. Bars 5 and 6 also tried to complete the base. Often the market breaks below the first bottom by a tick or so, trapping bulls out and bears in, as was the case at bar 5. Bar 6 was an exact test of the bar 5 false breakout of the bar 4 low, and was an outside up entry bar or signal bar for a double bottom bull flag. It led to the bar 7 breakout of the top of the range, which quickly failed in a two-bar reversal.

The market made a second one-tick breakout below the trading range at bar 8. It is important to realize that if the market falls below that low by even a tick, traders will start to assume that the bears are taking control. They will see this as effectively a failed attempt at a wedge bottom, where bar 4 was the first push down, the one-tick breakout at bar 5 was the second, and the next one-tick breakout at bar 8 was the third. Once the market fell below bar 8, the target was an approximate measured move down using either the height of the wedge (the bar 6 low to the bar 3 high) or the height of the trading range (the bar 8 low to the bar 7 high). This type of three-push pattern can take place in any market, and the downside breakouts don't have to be exactly one tick. For example, in a stock that is trading around $200, the breakouts that are comparable to bars 5 and 8 in this chart might be 20 cents or more.

Some traders would see the reversal up from bar 6 as a failed breakout of the bottom of the range, and then bar 7 as a failed breakout of the top of the range. Many would short below the two-bar reversal at the top, where bar 7 was the first bar, because they know that trading ranges often have strong breakouts that quickly fail. Some would exit at breakeven on the rally to bar 9 but then would have taken the second entry short below the lower high at bar 9.

Other traders would trade the market in breakout mode, looking to sell on a stop below bar 6 and buy on a stop above bar 7. There were trapped bears on the failed downside breakout and then trapped bulls on the failed upside breakout, and when there are trapped bulls and bears, the next breakout usually results in a decent swing. Although the rally to bar 9 was strong, the bears would short below it because they would see it as a pullback from the bar 8 breakout.

Compare this to Figure 11.1 in Chapter 11, where there was a similar trading range after an early strong bear spike, but the potential trend resumption bear day failed and the market reversed up.

Figure 12.6   DOUBLE TOP BEAR FLAGS AND DOUBLE BOTTOM BULL FLAGS   **225**

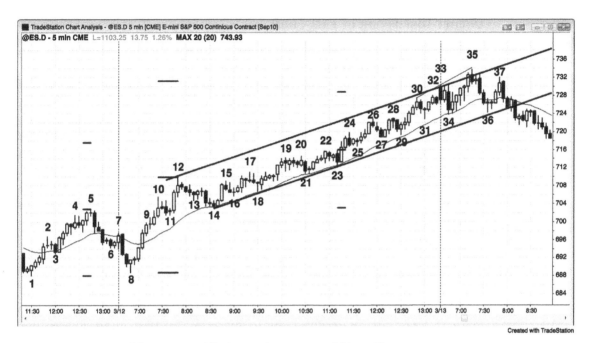

FIGURE 12.6   Double Bottom Bull Flag and a Measured Move Up

A double bottom followed by a sharp move off the second low and then a pause after the breakout often leads to a very strong trend. Even though the chart in Figure 12.6 does not show it, yesterday was a bull trend day. Although the expectation for the behavior is the same for any double bottom whether it is a reversal or a continuation pattern as it was here, bars 1 and 8 formed a double bottom bull flag. The move up to bar 10 was much stronger than the move down to bar 8, with every bar's open, close, high, and low above those of all of the prior bars. This strength alerted traders that this double bottom bull flag could lead to a strong move up. After breaking out above bar 5, the market went sideways instead of pulling back, and this setup is very strong and fairly common. After the spike up to bar 12, there was a pullback to bar 14 and it formed a double bottom bull flag with bar 11. This was followed by a bull channel that lasted for the rest of the day.

Bar 18 formed a double bottom bull flag with bar 16. Remember, the lows don't have to be exactly the same. If a pattern resembles a textbook setup, it will likely behave in a similar way. Bar 29 formed another with bar 27, and again set up a high 2 buy in a strong bull channel. A high 2 is simply a two-legged pullback, which all double bottoms are.

Deeper Discussion of This Chart

As shown in Figure 12.6, yesterday closed with a strong bull run and then a pullback to just below the moving average, where bulls would be looking for a higher low and then a second leg up. The channel down to bar 6 was steep enough so that traders should not buy the bar 7 outside up breakout on the open. Bar 8 was a strong bull reversal bar, as well as a higher low and a high 2 in a large trading range. It was also a reversal up from consecutive sell climaxes. The first sell climax was the three-bar bear spike that followed the bar 5 bull channel, and the second sell climax was formed by the two strong bear trend bars that followed the bar 7 attempt to reverse up. Consecutive climaxes are usually followed by at least a two-legged countertrend move and often a reversal. Since this was occurring within the first hour, it could be setting up the low of the day and bulls should swing much of their long position.

The spike up to bar 10 was followed by a large bull trend bar, creating a spike and climax type of spike and channel bull trend. The market corrected down to the bar 14 start of the brief channel, where it formed the expected double bottom bull flag.

The protracted bull channel from bar 14 followed a bull spike. Some traders saw the spike as the move from bar 8 to bar 10 and the pullback as the move from bar 10 to bar 11, where a micro trend line high 1 long set up. The small breakout below that tight channel down to bar 11 was followed by a higher high pullback to bar 12 and then a second leg down to bar 14.

Other traders, especially those using a higher time frame chart, saw the move from bar 8 to bar 12 as the spike, and the two-legged moving average test at bar 14 as the pullback that led to the large bull channel.

The short below bar 12 was also a reversal from the bar 11 final flag, and a second reversal from yesterday's high.

There was a large bear trend bar two bars before bar 14, and this was therefore a spike down. Since it followed a spike up relatively soon (nine bars earlier), it created a buy climax (a bull trend bar followed by a bear trend bar). Although it may not be obvious, you could look at different time frames and find one where this entire pattern is just a two-bar reversal (in fact, it was one on the 30 minute chart). This is never necessary because you can infer it from the 5 minute chart. Whenever there is any climax, the market soon becomes uncertain because both the bulls and bears will add to their positions as they attempt to create a channel in their direction. Uncertainty means that the market is in a trading range, and some traders saw the two-legged move up from bar 14 to the slightly higher high at bar 17 as simply a higher high pullback from the bar 14 bear spike. This is a plausible interpretation, given that the move had many doji bars. The bulls, however, created a two-bar bull spike up from bar 14, and this created a sell climax with the bear bar that formed two bars before bar 14. Again, a bear trend bar followed soon after by a bull trend bar is a sell climax, and you can find some time frame where it is a two-bar reversal up.

Figure 12.6 DOUBLE TOP BEAR FLAGS AND DOUBLE BOTTOM BULL FLAGS **227**

Bar 18 set up a failed low 2 buy, and then traders had to evaluate the momentum of the upside breakout to determine whether it was more likely to have at least two more legs up or simply to have one more push up and form a wedge top (a low 3). Since the price action since bar 10 has been two-sided, this was trading range behavior and it was reasonable to be looking for low 2 short setups (you should not do that in a strong bull trend).

The market had a large bull trend bar breakout up to bar 19, and this increased the odds of at least two legs up from the bar 18 failed low 2. The bull channel from bar 18 to bar 19 was tight, with six consecutive bull bodies. When the channel is strong, it is better not to look to short the breakout below the channel, which means that it was better not to look to short a low 3 (a wedge top) and instead look to see if there was a breakout pullback that looked like a good short setup. A breakout pullback would be a second-entry short signal. The move up to bar 20 could have been that setup but it, too, was too strong, since it had five consecutive bull trend bars. At this point, most traders would see the move up from bar 14 as a strong bull trend, even though it was still in a channel, and they would trade it like any strong bull channel, buying for any reason and not getting trapped out by pullbacks.

Whenever there is a strong spike, you should expect follow-through and you can use measured move projections to find reasonable locations for profit taking. Since they are so often reliable, the institutions must be using them as well. The first measurements should be based on the double bottom. Look for a possible profit-taking area by adding the height from bar 1 to bar 5, or from bar 5 to bar 8, to the high of bar 5. Both of these projections were exceeded at bar 24. Since the channel was still steep at that point, more of a rally was likely so bulls should still hold some of their longs and should be looking for opportunities to buy more. They can buy using the techniques described in the section on channels in book 1.

The next higher target comes from doubling the height of the spike, using either bar 10 or bar 12 as the top of the spike. If you add the number of points from bar 8 to bar 12 to the top of bar 12, that projection was minimally exceeded on the first hour of the next day and it was followed by a 16-point pullback over the next couple of hours.

Bar 24 was the fourth push up in the channel, and when the market failed to reverse on the low 4 after bar 24, it broke out to the upside. In general, traders should not be using the low 4 terminology here since this is a bull market and not a trading range or a bear trend, but the breakout after bar 23 indicates that there were many traders who used the failed low 4 as a reason to cover their longs. The breakout created a gap between the breakout point at the bar 22 high and the breakout pullback at the bar 25 low. A gap that occurs after a strong move often becomes a measuring gap, as it did here. The current leg began at the bar 24 channel low and you can take the number of points from that low to the middle of the gap and add it to the middle of the gap to find the measured move projection where bulls might take profits. The market missed the target by two ticks on the rally to the close, but turned down briefly from it on the open of the next day.

Traders should be looking for trend lines and trend channel lines and redrawing them as the channel progresses. If you see a failed breakout of the top of the channel, it can lead to a reversal. A second failed breakout is an even more reliable short setup. if you draw a bull trend line from the bar 14 to bar 23 lows and create a parallel that you then anchor to the top of the bar 12 spike, you then have a channel that contains the price action. Bar 35 was a second failed breakout of the top of the range and a reasonable short setup. The minimum objective is a poke below the bottom of the channel and then a measured move down using the height of the channel and subtracting it from the location of the breakout below the channel.

Channels often correct after a third push. Bars 15, 17, and 19 were three pushes, but the channel was so steep that you should look for a short trade only if there first was a strong downside breakout and then a pullback. The same is true for the three pushes up at bars 24, 26, and 28. The failure to reverse set up the high 2 long above bar 29, which was followed by five bull trend bars that formed a spike.

Bars 30, 33, and 35 set up another three-push top pattern, and this one was worth taking for a possible high of the day. In the first hour, a reversal can be the high of the day, so you should be willing to be more aggressive. The move down to bar 34 had two strong bear trend bars, so the bears were getting stronger. Bar 35 was a strong bear reversal bar and the second reversal down from a breakout of the top of the bull channel, and it was a little above a measured move up using the height of the bar 8 to bar 12 spike.

Today is a good example of how strong trend channels can have lots of two-sided trading, and pullbacks never look quite strong enough to buy. It had lots of bear trend bars that trapped bears into shorts as they looked for a second leg down. However, buyers returned on every test of the moving average and there was never a good breakout pullback to short. This told experienced traders to only look to buy. There were only a couple of countertrend scalps, but traders should consider taking them only if they then get right back in on the long side with the next buy setup. If they miss that next buy, they are not good enough to be shorting a day like this, because they are likely missing too many long winners as they wait and wait for a rare profitable short scalp. They are on the wrong side of the math and are not maximizing their profit potential because of a lack of discipline.

The entire channel was so steep that you should assume that the spike formed a large spike up on a higher time frame chart as well (in fact, it formed a strong, eight-bar bull spike on the 60 minute chart), and should therefore be followed by a higher time frame bull channel. This means that there would likely be follow-through buying on the 5 minute chart over the next two or three days, and there was. When a 5 minute channel is part of a higher time frame spike, the pullback that eventually follows usually tests only the channel low on the higher time frame chart but not the channel low on the 5 minute chart.

Figure 12.6   DOUBLE TOP BEAR FLAGS AND DOUBLE BOTTOM BULL FLAGS   **229**

There were many breakout tests that tested the earlier breakout to the tick, running stops on traders using a breakeven stop on their swing portion of their long trades. For example, if traders bought the bar 11 high 2 and held long through the bar 12 failed flag (not recommended, because this was a decent short setup at this point of the day), they would have been stopped out to the tick if they used a breakeven stop. However, traders who recognized this strong double bottom pattern would have used a wider stop on the swing portion of their trades after going long above the bar 14 two-legged moving average test, expecting a strong bull trend day. Look at the moving average. There were no closes below it after the initial bull spike to bar 10, so do not use a tight stop out of fear of losing a tick or two on your trade. In fact, a trader should be ready tomorrow to buy the first close below the moving average, and then buy again above the first moving average gap bar below the moving average.

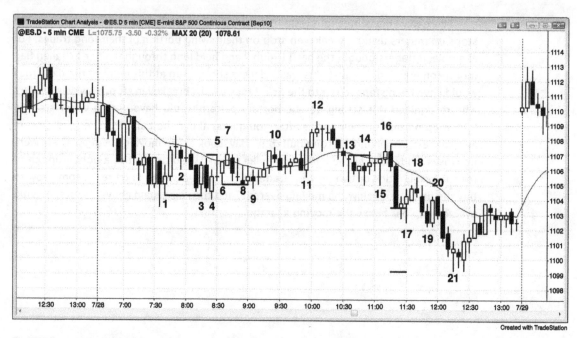

FIGURE 12.7   Failed Double Bottom Breakout Is a Wedge Variant

If a double bottom bull flag breaks to the downside but immediately reverses back up, it becomes a variant of a wedge bull flag. In Figure 12.7, bar 3 formed a double bottom with the bar 1 signal bar, but the market immediately reversed down. However, the breakout below the bottom of the double bottom failed and the market reversed up again at bar 4, creating a wedge bull flag (you could also call it a triangle). The three pushes down are the tails at the bottom of bar 1, bar 3, and bar 4. In this particular case, bar 2 is also an acceptable first push down. Since the market was in a trading range between bars 1 and 3, it was risky to buy at the top of bar 1 because it was so tall that you would be buying near the top of a trading range. A large bull reversal bar does not function as a reversal bar when it is in a trading range where there is nothing to reverse. In situations like this, it is always better to wait to see if there is a breakout pullback and then a second-entry opportunity. Bar 4 was a pullback to a lower low and a safer signal bar for a long.

Bars 6 and 8 tried to set up a double bottom bull flag but it never triggered. Instead, it broke to the downside at bar 9 and then reversed back up a couple of bars later. This is another wedge bull flag, and the three pushes down are bars 6, 8, and 9. However, the bear bar after bar 7 was an alternative first push down. For any wedge, it does not matter if there are multiple choices as long as there are at least three pushes down.

Bars 13 and 14 set up a double top, even though bar 14 was one tick higher. The market reversed up at bar 15 but the upside breakout failed and bars 13, 14, and 16 became a wedge bear flag short setup.

Deeper Discussion of This Chart

The bars 13 and 14 double top in Figure 12.7 formed in barbwire just below the moving average. Bear barbwire often has a failed low 2, and traders can buy below the low 2 signal bar in anticipation of the downside breakout failing. This is a scalp. Since the first trend bar to break out of barbwire usually fails, traders could look to short below bar 16.

Bar 19 was arguably a high 2 long setup (it was a two-bar bull reversal, but the market never traded above the bull bar), but since the market might now be in a bear trend on the strong breakout below the trading range, you should not be looking for high 2 buy setups, which are setups only in bull trends and in trading ranges. The trading range was mostly below the moving average, and since the market was falling before entering the trading range, a downside breakout was more likely (trend resumption). Traders would expect the high 2 buy to fail and trap bulls, and these traders would then look to short below the bar 20 low 2 setup, where the trapped bulls would sell out of their longs.

The bear channel ended with a third push down to bar 21 and the next day gapped up well above the bar 18 start of the bear channel. The channel was preceded by a strong two-bar bear spike after bar 16. There was a perfect measured move down, using the height of the spike and projecting down from the bottom of the spike.

Bar 19 was another two-bar-spike down, and it led to the bear channel down from bar 20 to bar 21. The channel was parabolic because it had an acceleration phase in the form of a large bear bar and then a deceleration phase in the form of bodies that became smaller, and the final one even had an up close. The three bear trend bars starting at bar 20 formed a bear spike, which is a sell climax. It was the third consecutive sell climax, and this is usually followed by at least a two-legged correction that lasts at least 10 bars. The two-bar bear spike after bar 16 was the first sell climax, and the three-bar bear spike that ended with bar 19 was the second sell climax.

CHAPTER 13

Twenty Gap Bars

When the market stays on one side of the moving average without touching it for 20 consecutive bars or more, the trend is strong, but it is also overdone and will likely soon pull back to the moving average, creating a 20 gap bar setup. If there was no clear trend reversal before the pullback, the first touch is a high-probability scalp for a test of the trend's extreme. There are traders who will enter at or just above or below the moving average with limit and market orders, but it is better to wait for a price action entry (a reversal back in the direction of the trend and an entry on a stop) in case the pullback goes well beyond the moving average. There is nothing magical about 20 bars. It is just a guideline that is useful to remind you that a trend is strong. You can arbitrarily pick any large number of bars and generate a setup that will usually be the same, and it will also work on other time frames. A trend can be extremely strong and still touch the moving average every 30 minutes, and a trend can be away from the moving average for four hours, only to suddenly reverse into an opposite trend. When it occurs on a 5 minute chart and the market has not touched the moving average for at least two hours, I used to refer to it as a two hours from the moving average setup, or a 2HM. Since the same concept works on all time frames, it is more useful to refer to the number of bars instead of the number of hours. The 20 bars can be at any time during the day and not necessarily during the first two hours.

Once you become aware that 20 consecutive gap bars are present, look to fade all touches of the moving average. After one or more moving average tests, there will likely be a test that goes through the moving average and forms a moving average gap bar where the bar is completely on the other side of the moving average so that there is a gap between the bar and the moving average. Look to fade the first gap bar (in a bull trend, buy one tick above the high of the previous bar if the high is below the exponential moving average). If the first entry fails, buy again on the second entry, if there is one. As with all setups, it is not worth buying a third time if the first two setups fail since the market at that point is likely in a channel and not forming a reversal. Since you are trading with the trend, you should swing part of your position because the market may run much further than you thought possible. Moving average tests are particularly reliable in stocks, and often provide great entries all day long. However, if the first moving average gap bar forms after a strong trend reversal, it will likely fail because the trend has now reversed and that gap bar is a setup for the prior trend, which now has ended.

Figure 13.1   TWENTY GAP BARS   **235**

FIGURE 13.1 Twenty Gap Bars

When a trend is so strong that no bar touches the moving average for 20 or more bars, many traders will look to enter on the first pullback to the moving average and hold for a test of the trend's extreme. In Figure 13.1, bar 11 was the first bar to touch the moving average in over 20 bars and, since there was no clear bottom to the bear trend, traders had limit orders just below, at, and just above the moving average to enter short positions. Even though the move up to bar 11 was composed of six consecutive bull trend bars, there was no clear bottom at bar 10 so traders were looking for shorts around the moving average. The shorting resulted in a small bear inside bar after bar 11 instead of a strong bear trend bar, and this meant that most traders believed that the rally at this point was too strong to short. However, the bears became aggressive on the second-entry short below bar 13 (the first entry opportunity was one bar earlier). Because the move up to bar 13 was so strong, traders were looking for a higher low and then a second test up, so most of the shorts exited around the bar 14 higher low test of the bar 10 bear trend low.

Bar 8 did not touch the moving average but was still a two-legged test of the moving average. The bears were so eager to get short that they placed their limit orders at two or three ticks below the moving average because they were not confident that the rally would touch the moving average. If they were confident, they could have placed their limit orders to go short at one tick below the moving average and they then would have become short on the touch of the moving average.

When the market turns down just below the moving average, the bears are very aggressive. This is especially evident when the test turns into a large bear trend bar as it did here.

Bars 7, 9, and 10 formed a bear wedge, and this is a reversal pattern. The bar 10 signal bar was not strong enough to convince traders that the market was reversing up, so they were still looking for short setups around the moving average. The bottom was strong enough to have a second leg up to bar 15, where it formed a double top bear flag with bar 13.

Deeper Discussion of This Chart

The market gapped down with a bear trend bar in Figure 13.1, so the breakout might have become a trend from the open bear trend. Two bars later, the breakout failed, but the setup was not strong enough to buy. Instead, the bears should exit and wait. Bar 4 formed a double top bear flag with bar 3 and a two-bar reversal with the following bar. Traders could short the double top on a stop below bar 4 or they could wait. The next bar was a bear trend bar that traded below bar 4, making bar 4 a swing high. Since there was now both a swing low and a swing high and the opening range was less than a third of the recent average daily range, the market was in breakout mode. Bulls would go long on a stop above the trading range, and bears would go short on a stop one tick below the range. The breakout should have follow-through and the day often becomes a trend day, as it did here.

Despite the bear strength in the first half of the day, the bulls broke several bear trend lines. They were able to move the market up after the stop run plunge down to bar 25 that formed a double bottom with bar 21 after a break of the bear trend line on the rally to bar 13. It was also a final flag buy setup for the breakout of the bar 21 to bar 24 bear flag. Bar 13 was also the first gap bar above the moving average in a bear trend, and therefore a sell setup (see next chapter).

Figure 13.2   TWENTY GAP BARS   **237**

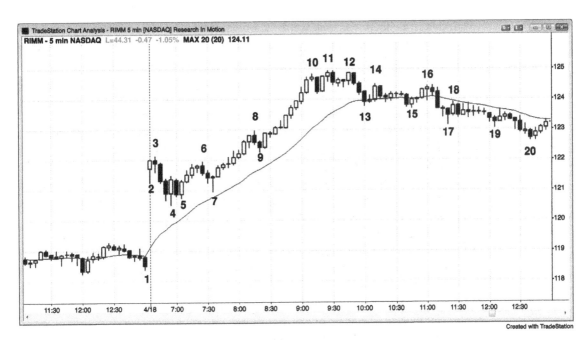

FIGURE 13.2   Twenty Gap Bars Are Not Always a Buy Setup

If the market has not touched the moving average for 20 or more bars but there was first a climax, the 20 gap bar setup may not lead to a bounce and a test of the extreme. As shown in Figure 13.2, Research in Motion (RIMM) had a parabolic bull trend up to bar 10. Since a parabolic move is not sustainable, it is a type of climax, and any climax is usually followed by at least a two-legged correction that lasts at least 10 bars, and it can even be followed by a trend reversal. This makes a one-legged correction to the moving average a risky long.

Deeper Discussion of This Chart

Although bulls could have scalped a small profit on a long in Figure 13.2 based on a limit order at the moving average on bar 13, buying a bear spike after a climax is risky, since at least two legs down should be expected. Bar 15 was a better setup since it was a second leg down and it had a good bull reversal bar, but it failed at the bar 16 low 2. Bar 16 was also a double top bear flag with bar 14. Since the market was in a tight trading range, this was not a strong short setup.

The move up to bar 10 had bars that overlapped very little and closed near their highs. The entire rally from bar 7 to bar 10 was so vertical that it was a bull spike. A spike is followed by a pause or a pullback. Here, the pullback began with three bear trend bars forming a spike down to bar 13. When there is a bull spike and then a bear spike, this is a climax reversal, which is a type of two-bar reversal (but this might be evident only on a higher time frame chart). The market usually goes sideways for a while as the bulls keep buying in an attempt to generate a bull channel, and the bears keep selling as they try to push the market down in a bear channel. Here, the bears won and the market fell below the bars 13 and 15 double bottom for a measured move down. When the market fails twice to do something, it usually does the opposite.

Although it is not shown, the bulls were able to create a strong bull channel from the bar 20 low, and the leg up from bar 20 was the exact same height as the bar 4 to bar 10 first leg, forming a leg 1 = leg 2 measured move. The bull spike up to bar 10 was much larger than the bear spike down to bar 13, and it was also a bull spike on a higher time frame. The bear spike got its channel on this 5 minute chart, and then the bull spike got its channel on a higher time frame chart the next day (not shown).

The climax also had a small wedge top. Even though bar 12 was below bar 11, this still functioned like a wedge where arguably the bears were so aggressive that they prevented the third push from exceeding the second. Some traders would see the bear bar after bar 10 as the first breakout below the bull channel and then bar 11 as the breakout pullback to a higher high. This is not strong enough to short, but it is strong enough for bulls to lighten up or exit. Bar 12 was the first bar of a two-bar reversal, which was a lower high or double top with bar 11. Traders could short below that second bar, which was a strong bear trend bar, and the minimum target was a test of the moving average. Bar 17 was the first gap bar below the moving average, but the bull trend had evolved into a trading range (the market had been sideways for 20 to 30 bars), and this was no longer a reliable buy setup.

CHAPTER 14

First Moving Average Gap Bars

U sually a 20 gap bar setup is followed by a test of the extreme, and the next test of the moving average probes even deeper. A bar may form that is entirely on the other side of the moving average. This is a moving average gap bar, and it sometimes can also be also a 20 gap bar pullback setup. A *gap* is a general term that simply means that there is a space between two points on the chart. For example, if today's open is above yesterday's close, there is a gap up. If the open is above yesterday's high, there will be a gap on the daily chart. A broader use of the term opens up other trading opportunities. For example, if the high of a bar is below the moving average, then there is a gap between that bar and the moving average. In a bull market or sideways market, there is a good chance that the market will move to fill that gap. Sometimes a bar will go above the high of the previous bar, but then, within a bar or two, the pullback continues down again. If the market again goes above the high of a prior bar, this is a second moving average gap bar setup, or a second attempt to fill a moving average gap in a bull trend, and the odds are excellent that there will be a tradable rally off this setup. Likewise, gaps above the moving average will tend to get filled in a bear trend or sideways market.

If there is a strong trend and this is the first moving average gap bar in the trend, it is usually followed by a test of the trend's extreme. This pullback to the gap bar is typically strong enough to break the trend line and after the test of the trend's extreme, the market will generally form a two-legged correction or even a major trend reversal (discussed in book 3). For example, if there is a strong bull and it finally has a bar that has a high below the moving average and then the next bar trades above the high of that bar, the market will try to form a higher high or lower high test of the bull's extreme. Traders will buy for a swing trade, expecting the market to get near or above the old high. Some traders will scale into additional longs if the pullback below the moving average falls some more (this is discussed in Chapter 31 on scaling into and out of trades). If the market rallies to test the old high but there is then a reversal down, there will usually be a more protracted correction that typically has at least two legs and often leads to a trend reversal.

Most bars on most charts are moving average gap bars because most bars do not touch the moving average. However, if there is not a strong trend and a trader fades one (for example, selling one tick below the low of a bar above the moving average), the trader is often just looking for a scalp to the moving average where he will take profits. A trader will take the trade only if there is enough room to the moving average to make an acceptable profit and only if the trade makes sense in the context of the current price action. So if there is a strong trend, a first moving average gap tends to set up swing trades, and if there is not a strong trend and a trader takes a moving average gap bar trade, she is more likely looking for a scalp.

Figure 14.1   FIRST MOVING AVERAGE GAP BARS   **241**

FIGURE 14.1   Moving Average Gaps, Second Signals

In Figure 14.1, bar 2 was a second attempt to fill the gap below the moving average in a sideways market. The downward momentum was somewhat strong, which arguably means that the market is not sideways today, but the moving average was basically flat because of yesterday's strong close. Also, there were several bars that overlapped with the bar or two bars before, and bar 2 was the third push down after the two-bar bear spike created by the third and fourth bars of the day. Bulls placed buy stops to go long at one tick above the high of bar 2 and looked to take a scalper's profit on a test of the moving average.

Bars 3, 4, and 8 were also second attempts (the first attempt can be simply a bull trend bar), or second moving average gap bar entries.

Bar 5 was a moving average gap bar, but traders would not short it for a scalp to the moving average both because there was not enough room for a scalp and because it followed a strong reversal up and a higher low and a second leg up was likely after the bar 4 lower low reversal up.

Bars 6 and 9 were second moving average gap bar short setups. Once the market broke above bar 9, there was then a bull trend because two attempts to go down failed (bar 9 was a second moving average gap bar setup, which means that it was a second attempt to close the gap to the moving average).

Bar 7 was a moving average gap bar setup, but since there was so little room to the moving average, traders would be less likely to buy it for a scalp solely based on its being a moving average gap bar.

Deeper Discussion of This Chart

The market broke to the upside in Figure 14.1, but the first bar of the day was small and therefore not a reliable signal bar for a failed breakout short. The third bar was a strong bar and therefore a better setup for a possible trend from the open bear trend.

Bar 6 was an outside down reversal from a spike and channel bull trend that began with the spike up after bar 4.

Bar 8 was the signal bar for the small expanding triangle that began with the bar 7 low. It can also be viewed as a wedge, since it was a breakout below a small double bottom and the breakout failed. Bar 8 was also a wedge bull flag after the bar 4 bottom; the three pushes down were the bar after bar 5, bar 7, and bar 8. Finally, bar 8 was the higher low after the spike up to bar 5 that followed the bar 4 lower low.

The breakout above bar 9 was a failed wedge bear flag, and therefore a measured move up was likely. The three pushes up were two bars before bar 8, the swing high before bar 9, and bar 9.

Figure 14.2 FIRST MOVING AVERAGE GAP BARS **243**

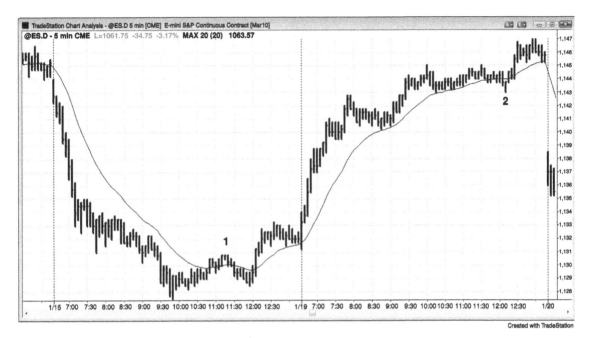

FIGURE 14.2 Moving Average Gap and Test of Extreme

A first moving average gap bar can lead to tests of the trend extreme. In Figure 14.2, both bars 1 and 2 were first moving average gap bars in strong trends and were followed by tests of the trend extreme. Bar 1 was the first bar in the bear trend where the low of the bar was above the moving average (a gap between the bar and the moving average), and it was followed by a higher low test of the bear low. Bar 2 was followed by a new trend extreme.

CHAPTER 15

Key Inflection Times of the Day That Set Up Breakouts and Reversals

The market often breaks out or reverses within a bar before or after 7:00 a.m. and 7:30 a.m. PST on economic reports, at 11:30 a.m. PST, and less often around 11 a.m. and noon PST. Very commonly on strong trend days there will be a strong countertrend panic move that will scare people out of their positions, and this normally happens between 11:00 and 11:30 a.m., although it can come earlier or later. Once it is clear that you were fooled by a strong countertrend move, the trend will usually have gone a long way back toward its old extreme, and you and the other greedy traders who were trapped out will chase it, making it go further. What causes the move? Institutions benefit from the sharp countertrend spike because it allows them to add on at much better prices, expecting the trend to resume into the close. If you were an institutional trader who wanted to load up going into the close and you wanted to enter at much better prices, you would be looking to create or contribute to any rumor that could cause a brief panic that ran stops and briefly caused the market to spike beyond some key level. It doesn't matter what the rumor or news item is or whether some institution spreads it to make some money. All that matters is that the stop run gives traders who understand what is going on an opportunity to piggyback on the institutions and make a profit off the failed trend reversal.

The stop-run pullback usually breaks a significant trend line, so the run to the new extreme (a higher high or lower low test following a trend line break) prompts smart traders to look for a trade in the opposite direction in the first hour of the next day.

This type of trap is common on trading range days as well, where the market has been hovering near one extreme for a couple of hours in what appears to be an incipient breakout, only to make a sharp move to take out the other extreme, and this opposite breakout often fails around 11:30 a.m. PST. This traps out the earlier traders who were positioning themselves for the breakout in one direction and traps in the new breakout traders who entered on the breakout in the other direction. Most trading range days close somewhere in the middle.

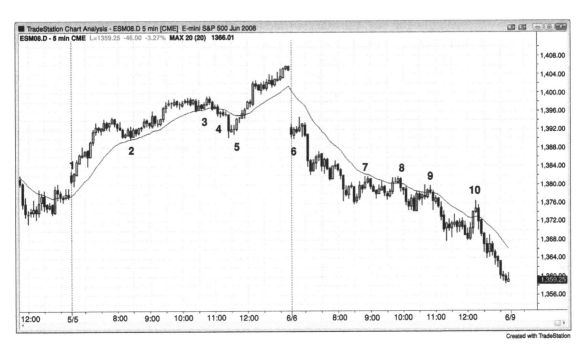

FIGURE 15.1   Late Stop Runs

In Figure 15.1 there are two 20 gap bar setups that formed on late stop runs. Bar 5 was the entry after the 11:25 a.m. PST stop run, and it was also a second entry on a moving average gap setup (a second moving average gap bar long setup, after the first entry above the bar after the bar 4 bear spike). Notice how strong the bear trend bar was with a large body and a close near its low. This bear breakout bar made the weak hands think that the market had turned into a bear trend. Smart traders looked at this as a great buying opportunity and expected it to be an exhaustive sell climax and a failed breakout. This type of stop run usually breaks the major trend line, and, since it is usually followed by a new extreme in the trend, it often sets the stage for a trade in the opposite direction in the first hour of the next day (here, a higher high after the break of the bull trend line). It formed a double bottom bull flag with the bar 2 start of the bull channel.

On both days, the moving average gap fades developed after two or more tests of the moving average. After the countertrend traders were able to bring the market back to the moving average multiple times, they developed the confidence to press their bets, resulting in a gap bar beyond the moving average. However, the first such breakout beyond the moving average usually fails and provides a great fade for the expected trend resumption.

On the first day, the market tried to reverse down at 7 a.m., presumably on a report. Since the day was a trend from the open bull trend at that point, the one-bar sell-off was the first pullback in a trend from the open day, and therefore a buy setup. The failed reversal was followed by a three-bar bull spike and then a channel.

On the second day, the 7 a.m. reversal succeeded and became a three-bar bear spike that was followed by a bear channel.

On the second day the market tried to reverse up from a final bear flag at noon, but the reversal failed at the bar 10 moving average gap short setup.

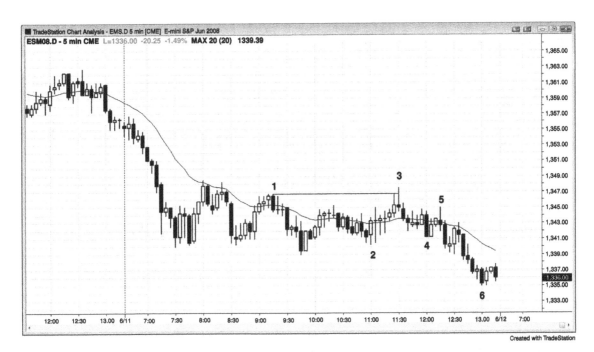

FIGURE 15.2 Late Bull Trap

On a bear trend from the open in Figure 15.2, followed by an inability to get above the moving average, traders were expecting an 11:30 a.m. PST bull trap, and it occurred today exactly on time. Bar 3 was also the first moving average gap bar in a bear trend. Usually, the trap is a strong countertrend leg, getting hopeful longs to buy aggressively, only to get forced into liquidation as the market quickly reverses back down. Today, however, the rally from bar 2 was composed of large overlapping dojis, indicating that traders were nervous in both directions. If there was no conviction, then how could traders get trapped? Well, the bar before bar 3 attempted to form a double top bear flag, and bar 3 spoiled it by going above the bar 1 high. This made many traders give up on the bear case, forcing the shorts to liquidate, and it trapped some bulls into longs on the breakout. The momentum leading to the breakout was weak, so there were probably not too many trapped bulls. However, by failing to form a perfect double top with bar 1, it trapped bears out. Since it was a trap, there was fuel for the short side as those bears who were trapped out now had to short lower and chase the market down, and those trapped bulls had to sell out of their longs. The weakness of the down leg from bar 3 is consistent with the weakness of the up leg from bar 2, but the result was as expected—a close on the low of the day. This was a bear trend resumption day, but since the resumption started so late and it followed a tight trading range with strong two-sided trading (large, overlapping bars with big tails), it resulted in a smaller leg than the sell-off at the open.

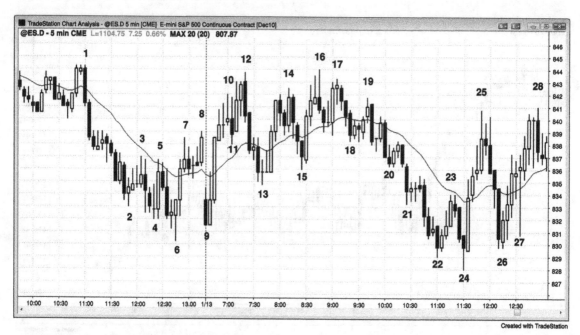

FIGURE 15.3   Late Trap on Trading Range Day

There is often an 11:30 a.m. PST trap on trading range days as well (see Figure 15.3). Here, after spending a couple of hours in the upper half of the day's range, the market ran through the low of the day, trapping out the bulls and trapping in new shorts. The market gave a second entry high 2 long above bar 24 on the 11:35 a.m. bar. The market made two attempts to break out below the bar 9 low of the day and failed, so it was likely to try the opposite direction. Most trading range days close somewhere in the middle.

The day opened as a trend from the first bar bull trend and pulled back below the bar 10 signal bar at 7:00 a.m., which was likely on some kind of report. Since there were three large sideways bars with prominent tails, this represented a small trading range and buying above it was risky. So the market broke briefly to the downside on the report, trapping bears in, and then it broke to the upside above bar 11, trapping bulls in and bears out; it then turned down a second time at bar 12. When there are trapped bulls and bears, in or out, the next signal is usually good for at least a scalp.

Deeper Discussion of This Chart

The rally into yesterday's close in Figure 15.3 was a reversal up from a wedge bottom and was likely to have at least two legs. The higher low reversal up at bar 9 was close enough to be a double bottom, and the bar 13 higher low at 7:40 a.m. PST was a double bottom pullback. Since the rally off the open was a strong spike up, the market was likely to try to form a channel after a pullback, but it failed with the bar 12 double top with bar 1. This was followed by several bear spikes over the next hour and ultimately a bear channel that reversed up at bar 24 at 11:30 a.m. The bar 22 reversal attempt at 11:00 a.m. failed. The market was in too steep a bear channel, so the first breakout of the channel was likely to be followed by a breakout pullback and a higher-probability long, and bar 24 was the signal bar. It was also the second attempt to reverse up from a new low of the day.

The push up to bar 12 created a wedge bear flag, with bars 5 and 8 being the first two pushes up. The market was too steeply up to short the bar 11 breakout of the tight bull channel up from bar 9, but shorting the breakout pullback to the bar 12 higher high was reasonable. It would be safer to wait for the bar 12 outside down bar to close, to see if the bears could own the bar. The close near the low confirmed the strength of the bears, so shorting below it on the beginning of the follow-through was a good entry.

CHAPTER 16

Counting the Legs of Trends and Trading Ranges

Trends often have two legs. If the momentum on the first leg after the reversal is strong, both the bulls and the bears will wonder if it will be the first of possibly many legs, creating a new trend. Because of this, both bulls and bears will expect that a test of the old trend's extreme will fail and the with-trend (with the old trend) traders will be quick to exit. For example, if there is a strong move up after a protracted bear trend, and this up move goes above the moving average and above the last lower high of the bear trend and contains many bull trend bars, both the bulls and the bears will assume that there will be a test of the low that will hold above the bear low. Once the momentum of this first up leg wanes, bulls will take partial or full profits and bears will short, just in case the bears are able to maintain control of the market. The bears are not certain if their trend is over and will be willing to initiate new short positions. The market will work down since buyers will be reluctant to buy until there is more bullish price action. As bulls come back in on the pullback that is testing the low, the new bears will be quick to exit because they don't want to take a loss on the trade. The buying by the bears covering their shorts will add to the upward pressure. The market will then form a higher low. The bears will not consider shorting again unless this leg falters near the top of the first up leg (a possible double top bear flag). If it does, the new bulls will be quick to exit because they won't want a loss, and the bears will become more aggressive since they will sense that this second leg up has failed. Eventually, one side will win out. This kind of trading goes on all day long in all markets and creates a lot of two-legged moves.

In fact, after the market makes a move of any size in one direction, it will eventually try to reverse that move and will often make two attempts at the reversal. This means that every trend and every countertrend move has a good chance of breaking down into two legs, and every leg will try to subdivide into two smaller legs.

When you are looking for a two-legged move and see one but the two legs are in a relatively tight channel of any kind, such as a wedge, they might in fact be subdivisions of the first leg and the channel may actually be only the first of two legs. This is especially true if the number of bars in each of the two legs looks inadequate compared to the pattern it is correcting. For example, if there is a wedge top that lasts for two hours and then a three-bar bear spike and then a three-bar channel, it is likely that the spike and channel together will be only the first leg down, and traders will be reluctant to buy heavily until after they see at least one more leg down.

Figure 16.1   COUNTING THE LEGS OF TRENDS AND TRADING RANGES   **255**

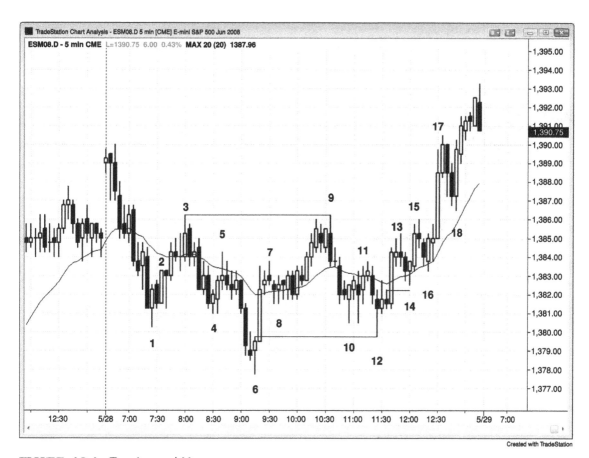

FIGURE 16.1 Two-Legged Moves

In Figure 16.1, the bear trend down to bar 6 occurred in two legs and the second leg subdivided into two smaller legs. The move up to bar 9 was also in two legs, as was the move down to bar 12. All spike and channel patterns are two-legged moves by definition, because there is a high-momentum spike phase and then a lower-momentum channel phase.

Bar 12 was a perfect breakout test of the start of the bull move. Its low exactly equaled the high of the bar 6 signal bar, running the breakeven stops of the bar 6 longs by one tick. Whenever there is a perfect or near-perfect breakout test, the odds are high that the market will make about a measured move (expect the move up from the bar 12 low to be equal in points to the move from bars 6 to 9).

There was a two-legged move up to bar 15, but when its high was surpassed, the market ran up quickly in a bull spike as the new shorts had to buy back their positions from the failed low 2 off the bar 15 short setup. Bar 9 had formed a double top bear flag with bar 3, and its failure on the rally up from bar 16 also contributed to the bull breakout.

FIGURE 16.2   Double Top Bear Flag

Apple (AAPL) was a well-behaved stock on the 5 minute chart shown in Figure 16.2. It formed a double top bear flag at bar 2 (1 cent below the high of bar 1), and the move down more than met the approximate target of twice the height of the trading range. Bar 2 was also the top of a two-legged move up to the moving average in a bear trend, forming a bear low 2 short at the moving average, which is a reliable entry in a trend. Trends in many stocks are very respectful of the moving average, which means that the moving average provides opportunities all day long to enter in the direction of the trend with limited risk. Four bars after bar 2 set up a double top pullback short.

Figure 16.3   COUNTING THE LEGS OF TRENDS AND TRADING RANGES   **257**

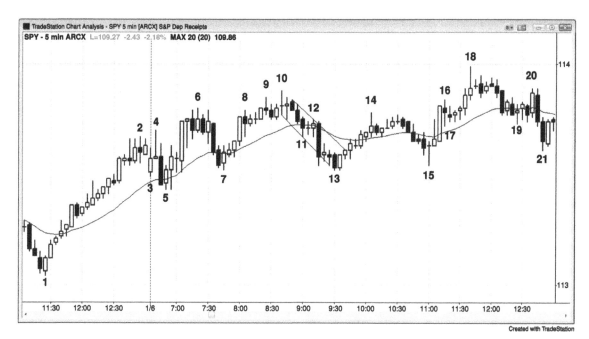

FIGURE 16.3   Wedge Top

In Figure 16.3, the SPY had a wedge top created by bars 4, 6, and 10, which is usually followed by a two-legged sideways to down correction. There was a three-bar bear leg that ended at bar 11 and a second leg down that ended at bar 13. This move was in a channel and would be just a single leg on a higher time frame chart. It was comparable in size to the leg up from bar 7 to bar 10 and therefore most traders would not be confident that it contained enough bars to adequately correct the large wedge. The market had a second sideways corrective leg to bar 15, slightly above the bar 13 low, creating a double bottom that was followed by a bull spike and channel up to a new trend high.

CHAPTER 17

Bar Counting: High and Low 1, 2, 3, and 4 Patterns and ABC Corrections

All markets are fractal. This is a mathematical concept that means that each segment of a market has the same general patterns as every lower and every higher time frame chart. If you remove the time and price labels from your charts, you will usually not be able to tell whether a chart is a 3 minute, 5 minute, 60 minute, or even a monthly chart. The only time that you can reliably approximate the time frame of a chart is when the average bar is only one to three ticks tall, because the chart will be mostly dojis and that only happens in small time frames or in markets with only minimal volume, and you should not be trading those.

Since every move on every chart will tend to be two-legged and every correction will also tend to be two-legged and every correction of every correction will tend to be two-legged, a trader who understands this tendency will find lots of opportunities.

A reliable sign that a pullback in a bull trend or in a trading range has ended is when the current bar's high extends at least one tick above the high of the prior bar. This leads to a useful concept of counting the number of times that this occurs, which is called "bar counting." In a sideways or downward move in a bull trend or a trading range, the first bar whose high is above the high of the prior bar is a high 1, and this ends the first leg of the sideways or down move, although this leg may become a small leg in a larger pullback. If the market does not turn into a bull swing and instead continues sideways or down, label the next occurrence of a bar with a high above the high of the prior bar as a high 2, ending the second leg. There needs to be at least a tiny trend line break between the high 1 and the high 2 to indicate that the trend traders are still active. Without this, do not yet look to buy, since the high 1 and high 2 are more likely just part of a channel down that is forming a complex first leg down.

In a strong upswing, the high 2 entry can be higher than that of the high 1, and in a strong downswing, a low 2 entry can be lower than that of the low 1. Incidentally, a high 2 in a bull trend and a low 2 in a bear trend are often referred to as ABC corrections, where the first leg is the A, the change in direction that forms the high 1 or low 1 entry is the B, and the final leg of the pullback is the C. The breakout from the C is a high 2 entry bar in a bull ABC correction and a low 2 entry bar in a bear ABC correction.

There is an important difference between a high 2 in a bull trend and a high 2 in a trading range, and between a low 2 in a bear trend and a low 2 in a trading range. For example, when there is a high 2 setup in a bull trend, it is usually at or above the moving average and the trend is strong enough for you to buy near the high of the day. You are buying a continuation pattern in a trend and therefore can buy near the top of the trend. However, when you are buying a high 2 in a trading range, you are usually looking to buy a reversal where the setup is below the moving average and near the bottom of the range. If you think that the market is in a trading range, it is risky to buy a high 2 above the moving average and near the high of the trading range. In fact, since this trade will likely fail, you should instead consider shorting using a limit order at or above the high of the high 2 signal bar. If the high 2 is likely to fail, why would it ever trigger? It triggers because the bears are looking to short above bars, and less so just below the highs of bars. They place limit orders to short at and above the high of the prior bar. With a relative lack of bears willing to short just below the high of the bar, the bulls are unopposed and are able to push the market above the high of the prior bar, hoping that lots of bulls will enter on buy stops. The high of the bar acts as a magnet, and the push above the bar is a small buy vacuum. The bulls find that there is an overwhelming number of bears waiting to short there. The result is that the high 2 triggers, but the market immediately turns down. Those bulls who bought over the last several ticks quickly see the lack of a rally above the high of the prior bar. Because the market is not doing what they expected, they exit and will not look to buy again for at least a few bars. Their selling out of their longs contributes to the sell-off. The opposite is true of a low 2 in a trading range. You should only look to sell a low 2 above the moving average and near the top of the trading range because you are trading a reversal and not a continuation pattern. You are trying to short the end of a leg up and are therefore trading against a small trend. If one forms near the bottom of a trading range and you believe that the market is now in a trading range and not in a bear trend, it is better to buy at or below the low 2 signal bar, expecting the low 2 to fail and form a type of double bottom. These expected failures usually happen when the market appears to be trending but you think that the market has instead entered a trading range.

A high 1 in a bull trend and a low 1 in a bear trend can have different risk/reward profiles depending on where each is in the trend. For example, if the market is bottoming and it forms a failed low 1, buying above the bar is taking the first high 1 entry of the new bull trend. The odds of success might be only 50–50, but the risk is small and the potential reward is large. You have a small chance of making a big profit. A high 1 long trade after the initial spike up in a new bull trend has a high probability of being at least a successful swing trade. The risk is small and the potential reward and probability of success are high. However, if the market is forming its third consecutive high 1 setup, the odds of a swing are small so traders should scalp. This means that the risk and potential reward are both small, and the probability is less than it was for the first high 1.

Some bull pullbacks can grow further and form a high 3 or a high 4. When a high 4 forms, it sometimes begins with a high 2 and this high 2 fails to go very far. It is instead followed by a bear breakout and another two legs down and a second high 2, and the entire move is simply a higher time frame high 2. At other times, the high 4 is a small spike and channel bear trend where the first or second push down is a bear spike and the next pushes down are in a bear channel. If the high 4 fails to resume the trend and the market falls below its low, it is likely that the market is no longer forming a pullback in a bull trend and instead is in a bear swing. Wait for more price action to unfold before placing a trade.

When a bear trend or a sideways market is correcting sideways or up, the first bar with a low below the low of the prior bar is a low 1, ending the first leg of the correction, which can be as brief as that single bar. Subsequent occurrences are called the low 2, low 3, and low 4 entries. If the low 4 fails (a bar extends above the high of the low 4 signal bar after the low 4 short triggered), the price action indicates that the bears have lost control and either the market will become two-sided, with bulls and bears alternating control, or the bulls will gain control. In any case, the bears can best demonstrate that they have regained control by breaking a bull trend line with strong momentum.

If the market is in a clear bull trend, do not look for low 1 or low 2 shorts, because those are setups only in bear trends and trading ranges. If the market is in a clear bear trend, do not look for high 1 or high 2 buys, because those are setups only in bull trends and trading ranges. In fact, if the market is in a bear trend, you can often look to short above the high of the prior bar because buying a high 1 in a bear trend is a low-probability trade. That means that if it has only about a 40 percent chance of being a successful long, it has about a 60 percent chance of hitting the protective stop before hitting a profit-taking limit order. If you are scalping on the 5 minute Emini chart, then there is a 60 percent chance that the market will fall and hit a two-point stop before it hits a limit order five ticks above the signal bar. So if there is a 60 percent chance it will fall two points before rising five ticks, this is a great setup for a short. Likewise, you can look to sell above the high of any bar in a strong bear trend or in a bear channel, and you can look to buy a low 1 in a bull trend and to buy below the low of any prior bar in a bull trend or in a bull channel.

As you are counting these pullbacks, you will often see the market continue its correction instead of reversing, in which case you have to change your perspective. If you thought that the market was in a trading range with simply a strong new high and then see a low 2 above the old high (a sell setup), but instead of falling, the market continues up, you should begin to look for high 1 and 2 buy entries. It is likely that the bull strength is sufficient for you to be trading only longs. You should defer looking for low 1 and 2 shorts until the bears demonstrate enough strength to make a tradable down move likely (like a bull trend line break followed by a failed test of the swing high).

Notice that in trading ranges, it is common to see a high 1, high 2, low 1, and low 2 all present in the course of 10 bars or so, even though a high 2 is bullish and a low 2 is bearish. Since the market is sideways, neither the bulls nor the bears are controlling the price action for more than a brief period, so it makes sense that each side will try to wrest control, and as each tries to assert itself, bull or bear patterns will form. It is very easy to see lots of high and low 1 and 2 patterns in trading ranges, and it is very important that you do not overtrade. When the market is mostly sideways with lots of overlap among the bars and the range is not a small flag in a very strong trend, most traders should step aside and not take any trades. Why is that? If you are looking for a high 2 or a low 2, you are looking to enter on a stop at either the top or the bottom of a tight trading range and you are doing the exact opposite of what the institutions are doing. When the market goes above the high of the prior bar in a tight trading range, they are taking profits on their longs or they are shorting, so you do not want to be buying. Your job is to follow what they are doing; it is not to ignore what they are doing and to fool yourself into believing that you have some magical setup that will make you a lot of money as long as you keep trading it. Tight trading ranges can form as small flags in very strong trends, and when they do it is reasonable to look to enter on a stop on the breakout of the range. For example, if there is a strong four-bar bear spike and there is no climax or strong reversal as the market goes sideways for 10 bars, it makes sense to go short on a stop below a bear trend bar. But if instead the day is a trading range day and the tight trading range is in the middle third of the day, most traders should never place a trade based on bar counting.

When the market is in a tight trading range, it often reverses direction repeatedly, so if you take every high 1, 2, 3, and 4 and also short every low 1, 2, 3, and 4, over the course of an hour you will lose all of the money that you made in the past week. In Chapter 22 on tight trading ranges, I discuss this in more detail. There are no magical setups, and every setup has an environment where the math gives it an edge, as well as other environments where it will lose. Trading based on bar counts requires a market that has swings. If the market is in a tight trading range, do not trade unless you are a very experienced trader and you are comfortable shorting above the high of the prior bar instead of buying there on a stop, and buying below the low of the prior bar instead of shorting there on a stop.

There are variations on this numbering, but the goal is still to help spot two-legged corrections. For example, in a strong bull trend, a two-legged pullback can form and have just a high 1 but functionally be a two-legged pullback. You can infer it from the appearance on the 5 minute chart, and you can confirm it by looking at a smaller time frame chart, although this is not necessary. It does not matter if you call it a high 1 on the chart in front of you, a high 2 variant, or a smaller time frame high 2, as long as you understand what the market is doing. If there is a bear close (or two), this can represent the first leg down even if the next bar does not extend above the high of the bear bar. If that next bar has a bull close but its high is still below the trend high, it then becomes the end of the first down leg if the next bar or so is again a bear trend bar. If the next bar extends below its low, look for a bar within the next few bars that extends above the high of its prior bar, ending the two legs down. View each bar as a potential signal bar, and place a buy stop at one tick above its high. Once filled, you now have a variant of a high 2. This entry bar is, strictly speaking, just a high 1, but treat it as a high 2. That bear bar at the start of the pullback was followed by a bar with a bull close. On a smaller time frame, this was almost certainly a small down leg followed by an up leg that became a lower high, and then finally another push down to where the high 2 ended the second leg.

Pullbacks often grow and evolve into larger pullbacks. For example, if there is a bull trend and a high 1 long entry fails to reach a new high and instead there is a lower high and then another leg down, traders will look for a high 2 setup to buy. If the high 2 triggers but the rally does not go very far and the market turns down again below the low of the high 2 signal bar, traders will then look to buy either a high 3 (a wedge or a triangle) or a high 4 pullback. Whenever there is a strong breakout below a high 2 or wedge (high 3) buy signal bar, the market usually will have at least two more pushes down. If the breakout below the high 2 signal bar is not strong and the entire move down has a wedge shape and reverses up from a trend channel line, then the high 3 is forming a wedge bull flag and is often a reliable buy setup. Remember, this is a pullback in a bull trend, and not a reversal attempt in a bear trend, where traders need a clear demonstration of bullish strength before looking to buy, as discussed in the section in book 3 on reversals. If the breakout below the high 2 buy signal bar reverses up after a second push down and the four pushes down are in something of a channel and does not look particularly strong, it is a high 4 buy setup. Some high 4 buy setups are simply high 2 buy setups on higher time frames, where the two legs each subdivide into two smaller legs. If the breakout below the failed high 2 has strong momentum and the entire pullback from the top of the selloff is in a relatively tight channel, then buying the high 3 is risky. Instead, traders should wait to see if there is a breakout above the bear channel and then a breakout pullback. Whenever a trader wonders if the channel down might be too strong to buy above a high 3 or high 4 signal bar, he should treat the setup like any other channel breakout, as was discussed in book 1. Wait to see how strong the bull breakout is before looking to buy. If the breakout is strong, then traders can look to buy a pullback. If it is so strong that it has a series of bull trend bars without a pullback, which can happen but is unusual, the market would have become always-in long and traders can buy for any reason, including on the close of any strong bull trend bar. Since the stop is below the bottom of the spike, which can be far away, the position size should be small. If instead the market falls below the low of the bar 4 signal bar, the market is likely in a bear trend and traders should start to look to sell rallies rather than to continue to look to buy.

The opposite is true in a bear rally. If the low 2 short fails and the market continues to rally, look at the momentum of the move up from the failed low 2. If it is not too strong and the market is in a channel, especially if it has a wedge shape, look to short the low 3, which would be a wedge bear flag. If the momentum up is very strong, like if there is a two- or three-bar strong bull spike up from the failed low 2, look for at least two more legs up and do not short the low 3. Short the low 4 only if the overall picture supports a short, and do not short if you believe that the market has now converted into a bull trend.

As is discussed in the chapter on reversals in the third book, when traders are looking for a reversal down, they often look for a high 1, high 2, or triangle (a high 3) pattern that they expect will fail and become the final flag of the bull leg, and then short above the buy signal bar. Since the breakout is a test of the high, it creates a double top (the breakout might form a lower high or a higher high, but since it is a second push up and it is turning down, it is a type of double top, as discussed in book 3). When a person shorts above a high 2 buy signal bar, he is expecting the market to trade down into a trading range or new bear trend. Since a double top is two pushes up, and the trader is expecting that it is at the top of a trading range or new bear swing, and is also a low 2 sell setup (selling below the low of the bar that created the double top). Almost every reversal down comes from some form of double top. If the top is after just a small leg up in a trading range, the double top will often involve only a few bars and be a micro double top. The same is true of most bottoms. They form from failed low 1 or low 2 or triangle breakouts, which create double bottoms and final flag reversals up. Since a trader is expecting a move up into a trading range or a new bull, a double bottom is also a high 2 buy setup, with the entry at one tick above the high of the bar that created the last push down to the double bottom.

High 3 and low 3 patterns should be traded like wedges (or a traditional triangle, if the pattern is mostly horizontal) because functionally they are the same. However, to keep the terminology consistent, it is better to call them wedges when they act as reversal patterns because by definition a high 3 is a pullback (a wedge bull flag) in a bull trend or trading range, and a low 3 is a wedge bear flag in a bear trend or a trading range. For example, if there is a bull trend or a trading range, a high 3 means that there were three legs down, and that sets up a buy signal above the high of the signal bar. If there is a bear trend, you are looking for low 1, 2, 3, and 4 setups and not high 1, 2, 3, and 4 patterns. If there is a clear wedge bottom in a bear trend, you should look to buy the reversal; but since it is in a bear trend, you should call this a wedge bottom and not a high 3. Likewise, if there is a bear trend or a trading range, a low 3 means that there were three pushes up and you should trade it like a wedge top. If there is a bull trend, you should not be looking for a low 3 to short, but shorting below a wedge top can be acceptable.

There is also a variation for a failed high/low 4. If the signal bar for the high 4 or low 4 is particularly small, especially if it is a doji, sometimes the entry bar will quickly reverse into an outside bar, running the protective stops of the traders who just entered. When the signal bar is small, to avoid a whipsaw it is often best to place your protective stop at more than one tick beyond the signal bar (maybe three ticks, but no more than a total of eight ticks from your entry in the Emini when the average range is about 10 points) and still to treat the pattern as valid even though technically it failed, albeit by only a tick or so. Remember, everything is subjective and a trader is always looking for something close to perfect, but never expecting perfection, because perfection is rare.

Be aware that complex corrections on the 5 minute chart often appear as simple high/low 1 or 2 corrections on higher time frame charts. It is not worth looking at the higher time frame charts since the trades are evident on the 5 minute chart and you risk distracting yourself looking for rare signals and missing too many 5 minute signals.

A high 1 buy setup is a failed attempt by the market to reverse down, and a low 1 short setup is a failed rally attempt in a bear trend. Because strong trends usually continue, reversal attempts almost always fail. You can profit by betting on the failure. You enter exactly where those trapped faders (traders trading against the trend) will exit with their losses. Their exit stop is your entry stop.

The most reliable high 1 and low 1 entries occur when there is a false breakout of a micro trend line in the spike phase of a trend, which is the strongest segment of the trend. Traders see a spike and start looking to buy a high 1, but they are overlooking the second critical component of a high 1 buy setup. The final component is a filter—do not take a high 1 following a significant buy climax, and don't take a low 1 short after a significant sell climax. Yes, you need a bull spike; but you also need a strong bull trend. One of the most common mistakes that traders make is that they trade on hope and buy every high 1, expecting a trend to follow. Instead, they have to force themselves to wait for the bull trend to form and then look for a high 1. If the bull spike is strong, but still below earlier highs on the chart, the market might still be in a trading range, which makes buying above a high 1 riskier. The high 1 buy setup could easily turn into the final flag of the rally before a big correction or a reversal. The bull spike that is racing up might be due to a buy vacuum test of the trading range high and not a new bull trend. If both the bulls and the bears expect the top of the trading range to get tested, once the market gets close to the top, the bulls will buy aggressively and relentlessly, confident that the market will make it up to the magnet that is just a little higher. The strong bears see the same thing and stop shorting. Why should they short now when they can sell at an even better price in a few minutes? The result is a very strong bull spike that leads to a reversal once it reaches around the top of the trading range, at which point smart traders would not be buying the closes of the strong bull trend bars or the high 1 buy setups. In fact, many would be shorting, using limit orders, since they expect that this break-out attempt will be like most strong breakout attempts, and will fail. For traders to buy a high 1, they need a strong bull spike *and* a bull trend, not simply a spike up within a trading range. Also, they should not buy the high 1 if the bull spike ended with too strong a buy climax.

The same is true for a low 1 short. Wait for the bear trend, not just a bear spike within a trading range, and then look for a spike with a low 1 sell setup. Don't simply short every low 1 after every spike, because most spikes occur in trading ranges, and shorting a low 1 at the bottom of a trading range is a losing strategy because the low 1 setup has a good chance of being the final flag in the leg down; the market might then have a large correction up or even a bull reversal. If traders are looking to buy a high 1 or short a low 1, they should do so only in the spike phase of a trend and not take the trade if there is evidence of a possible climax. For example, if you are looking to buy a high 1 setup, you are betting that the pullback will be minimal and have only one leg. Many high 1 setups are just one- or two-bar pullbacks after sharp three- to five-bar spikes, while others are four- or five-bar pullbacks to the moving average in extremely strong trends that have run for five to 10 bars, which can be a little too far, too fast. If you are buying such a brief pullback, you believe that there is tremendous urgency in the market and that this brief pullback might be your only chance to buy below the high of what you believe is a very strong bull trend. If the market goes sideways for five bars and has several small dojis, the market has lost its urgency and it is better to wait before buying. If a high 2 forms, it is a safer buy setup.

The most common reason for a trader failing to buy a high 1 pullback is that the trader was hoping for a larger pullback. However, it is important to get long when there is a strong bull trend, and traders should place a buy stop above the prior swing high, in case the pullback is brief and the bull trend quickly resumes. The same is true in a strong bear trend. If the three criteria for shorting a low 1 are present (a strong bear trend, a strong bear spike, and no strong sell climax), traders must get short. If they are deciding whether to place an order to short below a low 1 signal bar, they should place an order to short at one tick below the swing low. Then, if they end up not shorting the low 1 and the market races down, they will be swept into the strong bear trend. This is far better than watching from the sidelines and waiting for the next pullback. If they short the low 1, they can then cancel the order to short below the swing low.

If that high 1 is such a reliable buy setup in the spike phase of a strong bull trend, how could it possibly form when the institutions know that there might be an 80 percent chance of the trend resuming and being followed by a new high? Why would they ever allow the pullback if they believe the market will go higher? It is because they created the pullback. The spike was caused by many firms simultaneously buying relentlessly, which means that they were scaling into their long positions during their buy programs. At some point, each of those firms will start scaling out of its position, and once enough of them stop buying and begin to sell out of their positions, a bar will form with a low that is below the low of the prior bar. Many other firms will buy as the market falls below the other bar, but just for a scalp if the trend is not too strong. From this point on, firms will all be scaling out; because of this, the breakout above the high 1 setup often results in only a scalp. In the very strongest of trends, it is a swing trade and there might be one or two more high 1 setups at a higher level and then some high 2 buy setups; but in all cases, pullbacks are caused by institutions taking some profits from their lower entries. They are in the business of making money, which means that they have to take profits at some point, and when enough of them begin to take partial profits at one time, they create bull flags, like high 1, high 2, or larger pullbacks. The opposite is true in bear trends.

This is an important observation because you now see that you should buy a high 1 long setup only when the trend is very strong, which usually means only in the spike phase and only when the market is clearly in a trend. Finally, don't buy a high 1 after a climax or a reversal, and do not buy a high 1 pullback at the top of a trading range because the bull trend has not yet broken out. High 1 buy setups at the tops of strong bull spikes and low 1 short setups at the bottom of strong bear spikes are common in trading ranges and are usually traps. In fact, they are often good fade setups. For example, if a high 1 is setting up at the top of a trading range, especially if the signal bar is a doji bar, it is often sensible to place a limit order to short at or above the top of the high 1 buy signal bar. Since you expect the high 1 long to fail, you think that it will reverse and hit a two-point stop before it will go six ticks and fill your profit-taking limit order for a one-point scalp. When you expect a high 1 long failure, you believe that the probability of the protective stop being hit before the profit-taking limit order is filled is at least 60 percent. If you fade the high 1 by going short with a limit order at the high of the signal bar, you expect that it will not go six ticks up and you can therefore use a six-tick protective stop. Since you feel that it is a bad buy setup, you believe that it will fall seven ticks below your entry price, which is eight ticks below the long entry price of the bulls who bought on a stop at one tick above the signal bar. This means that you can scalp out of your short with a six-tick limit order and have at least a 60 percent chance of making six ticks while risking six ticks, which is a good trade. You can also place a limit order to go long at or below the low of a low 1 short signal bar if it forms at the bottom of a trading range and you believe that a low 1 short would fail.

If that high 1 at the top of the trading range was so strong, why was the spike not strong enough to break far above the trading range and have several bars of follow-through? The market is telling you that the spike is not very strong and you should therefore listen. Just because the spike has four bull trend bars does not make it the spike phase of a strong bull trend. Look at the entire chart and make sure that the spike is part of a strong trend and not just a trap at the top of a trading range. Remember, the market often has strong bull spikes at the tops of trading ranges because the strong traders step aside and don't sell until the market gets to the top of the range or even breaks out for a bar or two. The bulls then sell out of their longs to take profits and the bears sell to initiate new shorts. This vacuum sucks the market up quickly but it has nothing to do with a trend. Traders are very eager to sell but it does not make sense for them to sell if they think that the market will go up several more ticks to test the top of the range. Instead, they stop selling and wait for the market to get there; then they appear out of nowhere and the strong rally reverses, trapping beginners into buying near the high of the day. A high 1 is a buy setup only in a clear bull trend and not in a spike near the top of a trading range. A low 1 is a short setup only in a clear, strong bear trend.

High 1 and low 1 patterns are with-trend setups, so if one occurs within a pullback in a trend but in the direction of the pullback and not the trend, do not take the trade. Instead, wait for it to fail and then enter with the trend on the breakout pullback. For example, if there is a bull trend and then a four-bar-long bear micro trend line forms at or above the moving average, do not short the failed breakout above the trend line. You do not want to be shorting a bull trend at the bottom of a pullback near the moving average, which is commonly near the end of the pullback. Instead, look for this failure to fail and turn into a breakout pullback, which will be in the direction of the trend (up). There is a breakout above the bear micro trend line that failed. The failed breakout traded down briefly, but it failed to go far and it reversed up. Once it reversed up, the reversal up was a breakout pullback entry from the initial breakout above the micro trend line. However, if the bear leg has four or more consecutive bear trend bars and the failed micro trend line setup is below the moving average, it will likely be a profitable short scalp, even though the day may be a bull trend day.

Trends have trending highs and lows. In a bull trend, each low is usually above the prior low (a higher low) and each high gets higher (a higher high); in bear trends, there are lower highs and lower lows. In general, the terms *higher high* and *higher low* are reserved for situations in which a bull trend appears to be in place or in the process of developing, and *lower low* and *lower high* imply that a bear trend might be in effect. These terms imply that there will have been at least a minor trend line break, so you are considering buying a higher low in a bull trend (a pullback) or in a bear trend (countertrend but it may be a reversal) and selling a lower high in a bull trend or a bear trend. When trading countertrend, you should scalp most or all of your position unless the reversal is strong.

Once a high 2 long triggers in a bull trend or in a trading range, if the market then reverses and trades below the low of the pattern before reaching at least a scalper's profit, the high 2 buy has failed. Likewise, if there is a low 2 short entry in a bear trend or in a trading range and the market fails to reach at least a scalper's profit and instead breaks out above the top of the pattern, the low 2 sell has failed. The most common cause of a high or low 2 failure is that the trader is in denial about a trend reversal and is still looking for trades in the direction of the old trend.

A high or low 2 is one of the most reliable with-trend setups. If a trade fails, the pattern will usually evolve and get either one or two more corrective legs. For example, if the market is moving down in a pullback in a bull trend or in a trading range and forms a high 2, but within a bar or two a bar trades below the low of the signal bar, the high 2 has failed to reverse the market upward out of the bull flag. When that happens, the downswing will usually try to reverse up again in a high 3 or a high 4. The high 3 represents three pushes down and is therefore a variation of a wedge. If the market is more likely to continue lower, you would get stopped out of your long if you bought the high 3. However, if you simply always wait for a high 4, you will miss many good high 3 long trades. The market often gives traders a clue as to which scenario is more likely. That clue comes in the form of the momentum that follows the failed high 2. If the market does not significantly change its momentum from that of the down move, it is more likely that the market will reverse up on the high 3, creating a wedge bull flag buy signal (and the breakout below the high 2 becomes an exhaustion gap, instead of a measuring gap). If instead there is a large bear breakout bar or two, this increases the odds that there will be at least two more legs down, and traders should wait for the high 4 before looking to buy. In this case, the breakout bar is likely to become a measuring gap and lead to a measured move down. Whenever there is a strong spike, many traders will start the count over again and will expect at least two more legs down before they are willing to buy again. The reversal up after the first leg is the first attempt to break out above the steep bear trend line and is therefore likely to fail. The second attempt up is the breakout pullback from that breakout, and, since it is a breakout pullback (whether it is a lower low or a higher low), it is more likely to succeed. If the market reverses up from the high 4 after the failed high 2, usually the pattern is simply a complex high 2 where both legs subdivided into two smaller legs. This is usually evident on a higher time frame chart, where a simple high 2 will often be clearly seen. If that high 4 fails, the market is more likely now in a bear trend instead of just a pullback in a bull trend, and traders should then reevaluate the strength and direction of the market before placing any more trades.

The opposite is true in a rising leg in a bear trend or a trading range. If the low 2 triggers a short entry, but within a bar or two there is a bar that trades above the high of the signal bar and the momentum is unremarkable, a profitable low 3 setup (a wedge bear flag) is more likely. However, if there are a couple of large bull trend bars, then the breakout is strong and the market will likely have at least two more legs up, so traders should not short the low 3. Instead, they should wait to see if a low 4 sets up. If the momentum up after the low 3 is very strong, the market is likely in a steep bull channel and it is better not to short the low 4, which is the first breakout of the bottom of a strong bull channel. Instead, traders should wait to see if a higher high or lower high breakout pullback sets up. If so, this is a second-entry short and a lower-risk trade. However, if the bull channel is not very tight and there is some reason to look for a top, such as the low 3 being a small final flag or a second attempt to reverse down after moving above a swing high or a reversal from a higher time frame bear trend line, then traders can short the low 4. Low 4 signal bars are often small, and when they are, the market often quickly reverses up and runs the protective stops above the low 4 signal bar, and then once again reverses down into a good bear swing. Because of this, when there is a small low 4 or high 4 signal bar, use a money management stop of about two points in the Emini instead of a price action stop beyond the signal bar.

The key to understanding the concept of high/low 2 setups is to remember its intent. The idea is that the market will tend to make two attempts at anything, and in its attempt to correct, it frequently will try twice to reverse the trend. The advantage of buying a high 2 pullback in a bull trend is that there is very little thought involved and it is easy to do. The difficulty comes when a correction has two attempts but does not form a clear high or low 2. That is why it is necessary to look at variations—you can make money by trading two-legged pullbacks even when they don't offer a perfect high or low 2 setup.

The most obvious two-legged move has two clear swings with an opposite swing in between that breaks a minor trend line and usually forms a high 2 pullback in a bull trend or a low 2 in a bear trend (an ABC correction). However, there are less clear variations that provide just as reliable trades, so it is important to recognize these as well. Any time that you see a correction where you can infer two legs, then you have found an acceptable pattern. However, the further from the ideal it is, the less likely it will behave like the ideal.

A high 2 in a bull trend is more reliable than in a trading range. When there is a bull trend, the market has pullbacks along the way, which are created both by profit-taking bulls and by aggressive shorts. Most of the time, the top looks like it might be good enough for a scalp, and that draws in new bears who are hoping for a reversal. There might be a good-looking bear reversal bar, a wedge, a buy climax, or some other pattern that leads them to believe that the market has a reasonable chance of reversing, and they therefore short. If the market pulls back, they begin to feel confident. If the market forms a high 1 long, many will continue to hold short since they are hoping for a bear trend or at least a large correction in the bull trend, and they accept the high 1 as a possible lower high that will be followed by lower prices. When the market turns down from that lower high, they are feeling more confident. However, they will not hold on to their shorts if the market turns up a second time. If it does, that would be a high 2 long entry. The bulls will see the setup as two attempts to drive the market down where both failed, so they will buy the high 2 long. The bears will see it the same way, and if both fail, they will give up, buy back their shorts, and wait for another signal before shorting again. The relative absence of bears for the next bar or two and the renewed eagerness of the bulls make the high 2 a reliable setup in a bull trend. Most of the time, it forms at or near the moving average.

The opposite is true of a low 2 in a bear trend, where low 2 setups are more reliable than in trading ranges. The bear trend will have pullbacks, and invariably the start of the pullback will be just confusing enough to make the bulls wonder if it might be a trend reversal, so they begin to buy, and the bears will wonder if it might lead to a stronger correction up, so they begin to take profits, buying back some of their longs. The result of this buying by both the bulls and the bears is a rally, but at this point neither the bulls nor the bears know if it will be a reversal or just a bear flag. The early bulls might allow one move against them in the form of a low 1, since it might form a higher low, but they will not hold on to their longs if the market moves against them twice. They will exit on the low 2 and not buy again for at least a couple of bars. Also, the bears will short the low 2, so their shorting, coupled with the selling by the bulls (they are selling out of their longs) and the absence of new bulls, results in an imbalance in favor of the bears. Just like with a high 2 in a bull trend, a low 2 in a bear trend usually forms as a pullback to or near the moving average.

A three-push top is often a variation of a low 2, even though it is actually a low 3. Whenever the first leg is strong and disproportionately large or strong compared to the next two legs, you have something that looks enough like a wedge to behave like a wedge. The low 1 that follows that strong first leg is followed by two weaker legs that can often be seen as just one leg made of two smaller parts. The entry is on the low 3, at the completion of the wedge, but it can also be thought of as a low 2. However, the numbering becomes irrelevant because you are faced with a three-push pattern, and it should behave like a wedge reversal whether you choose to call the entry a low 3 or a low 2. Don't spend too much time on the intellectual side here. Remember, most really smart academics can't trade, so as ideal as intellectualism and perfection are, you will lose money if you fight the market and insist that it behave perfectly like it is often described in textbooks.

The opposite is true in three-push bottoms, where the second of the two legs can often be seen as breaking into two parts and you have what appears to be a high 3 but functions like a wedge and like a high 2. In other words, the market should go up for at least a scalp, regardless of how you choose to number the legs.

Some traders look for countertrend scalps against strong trends. For example, if there is a strong bear trend and then a bull reversal bar forms, overly eager bulls might buy above that bar. Since they are trading against a trend, they will often allow a pullback, like a low 1 short. They expect the low 1 short to fail and become a higher low, and they might hold long to see if that will be the case. However, if the market does not reach their profit target and instead forms a low 2 setup, most traders will not allow the trend to resume a second time and they will sell out of their longs as the low 2 triggers. If the low 2 does not trigger and the market has one more small push up and sets up a low 3, this is a wedge bear flag, and the longs will exit if it triggers. They know that there is a possibility that their trades still might work as long as the market does not fall below the small higher low, but they realize that the odds are too strongly against them. More experienced traders would not have bought that reversal and instead would have waited to short below the low 2 or 3 signal bar, which is a very strong setup in a bear trend. As the market falls below the higher low, the bear trend often accelerates as the final bulls give up and sell out of their losing longs. In general, if you ever buy early, always get out and even reverse if the market triggers a low 2 or 3 short, especially if there is a strong bear signal bar, because this is one of the most reliable sell setups. Similarly, if you short a strong bull trend, always get out if a high 2 or 3 triggers, especially if there is a strong bull signal bar, which creates one of the strongest buy setups. If you are emotionally able to reverse, you usually should.

Figure 17.1   BAR COUNTING   **273**

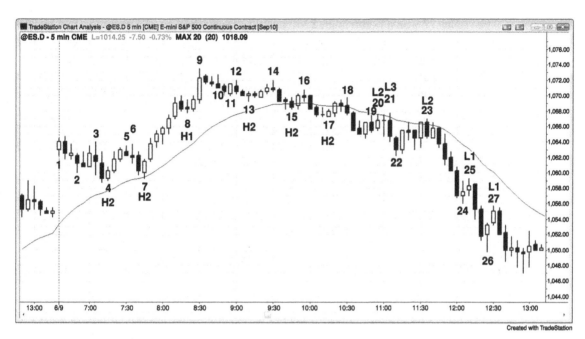

FIGURE 17.1   Bar Counting

Don't lose sight of the goal in bar counting. Focus on the pullbacks and not on the high 1s, high 2s, low 1s, and low 2s. Most of the time when the market is in a bull trend or in a trading range, you are looking to buy two-legged pullbacks, like the high 2s above bars 4, 7, 13, or 17 in Figure 17.1, and even then you should not mechanically buy every one. For example, there were two legs down to bar 15, the first being the channel down to bar 13. However, bar 15 was the fourth consecutive bear bar and it followed a strong bear trend bar two bars earlier. Also, the second leg was much smaller than the first so there might be more to go. When there are problems with a setup, it is better to wait.

Why wasn't bar 10 a good high 1 long setup? Because it was after a buy climax at the end of a bull leg and final flag (bar 8) and the market was likely to correct sideways to down for about 10 bars or more in two or more legs. Whenever there is a relatively large bull trend bar after the market has been trending up for a while, it might represent a temporary exhaustion in the trend. If a trend might be exhausted, it is no longer a strong bull trend and therefore a high 1 is not a good buy setup. This is also the reason why bar 11 was not a good buy setup. Since the market was still in the process of correcting after the buy climax, it was in a trading range phase and it is risky to buy a high 2 above the moving average in a trading range.

Bar 17 was a better high 2 long setup. It was the end of a complex two-legged correction where each leg subdivided into two legs, and the larger legs were of similar size and the small legs were of similar size, so the shape was good. Also, although in hindsight the market had converted into a bear trend, at this point there was still enough two-sided trading to consider it a trading range and therefore buying a high 2 was reasonable. The larger second leg down began at bar 14 and ended at bar 17, and the high 2 can be thought of in three ways: as being a high 4, as being a high 2 of the two larger legs where bar 13 was the high 1 end of the first leg, or as being a high 2 of the two smaller legs where bar 15 was the end of the first leg.

Although high 1s and low 1s are common, they rarely are good setups except in the strongest trends. Since a high 1 usually occurs near the top of a leg, you should buy it only if that leg is in the spike phase of a bull leg. Bar 8 is an example of a good high 1 because it formed in a strong bull trend that had six consecutive bull trend bars and each bull body had little, if any, overlap with the body of the bar before it. Almost all high 1s in bull spikes and low 1 pullbacks in bear spikes will be micro trend line breakouts.

Similarly, bars 25 and 27 were good low 1 short setups in a bear spike. There was a strong bear trend, a strong bear spike, and no strong sell climax, at least not at bar 24. Sometimes it is more descriptive to call the setup something other than a bar count setup, and bar 27 was a good example. Yes, it was a low 1 in a strong bear trend, but some traders would have been concerned about the strong bar 26 bull reversal bar. They would then have concluded that the bear trend was no longer strong enough to be shorting a low 1. However, they might have wondered if the market was starting to enter a trading range, because this was the second attempt to reverse up, and they might then have wondered whether bar 26 might actually be a high 2 at the bottom of an incipient trading range, where bar 24 set up the high 1. They would still have shorted below the bar 27 low 1, but not because it was a low 1. Instead, they would have shorted it because they saw it as a failed high 2 in a bear trend and they knew that the high 2 would have trapped bulls after that strong bar 26 reversal bar.

Since the market was in a strong bear trend at bar 25 and you could not buy above the high of the prior bar, you could have shorted above the high of the prior bar, bar 24, and you could have sold more below bar 25.

Deeper Discussion of This Chart

Bar 1 in Figure 17.1 was an attempt to be the start of a trend from the open bull trend on a large gap up day, but it failed on the very next bar, which became a bull trap (it trapped bulls into a losing trade). Since that bear reversal bar traded above bar 1 and turned down, it can be thought of as a failed high 1. This makes bar 2 a high 2 long setup, but after that bull trap, it was better to wait for a second leg down and at least

Figure 17.1   BAR COUNTING   **275**

one good bull body before looking to buy again. Also, the move down to bar 2 was a micro channel and the breakout above the channel would be likely to have a pullback, so it was better to wait for that pullback before looking to buy. Do not worry about unclear bar counting like this; instead, focus on the goal of finding a two-legged pullback to buy. The point that is worth noting here is that on many days when the second bar of the day trades above the first and then the market trades down, that second bar often becomes a high 1 in a high 2 buy setup, and you should be ready to buy that high 2 if the setup looks good. Although the bar 2 high 2 led to a profitable scalp, it would have been a stronger buy setup if bar 2 had been a bull reversal bar, especially if its low had been below the moving average.

Bar 20 was a two-legged pullback to the moving average (the bull trend bar two bars earlier was the first push up) and therefore a reasonable short setup. However, the market traded above the entry and signal bars two bars later on bar 21. That formed a small third push up that trapped bulls in who bought a failed low 2, and trapped bears out who let themselves get stopped out above the high of the bar 20 short signal bar. This is an example of a wedge bear flag. Whenever the market is below the moving average, traders are looking for shorts, and when there are both trapped bears and bulls, the odds of a successful short signal go up. The bulls will stop themselves out, and their selling as they exit their longs will help push the market down further. The bears who were just stopped out will now panic and be willing to chase the market down, adding to the selling pressure.

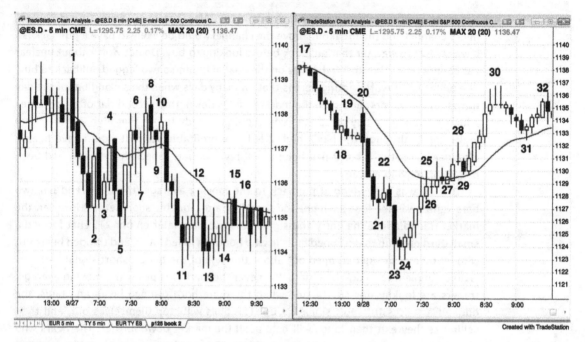

FIGURE 17.2   High and Low 1 Setups in Trading Ranges

The high and low 1 setups in the chart on the left in Figure 17.2 formed within a trading range and were not good trades. Those in the chart on the right were in clear bear and bull trends and were great setups. Just because the market has a strong bull spike and a high 1 buy setup does not mean that you should buy it, and you should never short a low 1 unless there is a strong bear trend.

By bar 7, the market had had five reversals, the range was small, and most of the bars overlapped with prior bars. The day was in a trading range and clearly not in a strong bull trend. Two bull trend bars formed a strong spike up from the lower low at bar 5, and it broke above the bar 4 lower high. Bulls were hoping that the day would break out to the upside and form a bull trend, and it could have, except for market inertia. Trends tend to keep trending and reversals usually fail; trading ranges keep going sideways and breakout attempts usually fail. Bar 7 was a high 1 buy setup after a strong bull spike, but it was in a trading range day. It also had a doji signal bar, which represents two-sided trading. This is a bad buy setup and, in fact, aggressive traders expected it to fail and shorted on a limit order at and above the bar 7 high.

Bar 9 was a high 2 setup above the moving average and in a trading range and therefore was likely to fail.

Figure 17.2   BAR COUNTING   **277**

Bar 11 was the fourth bear trend bar in a bear spike that broke to a new low of the day. However, this is a trading range day. It might become a trend day but it is not one yet and therefore a low 1 at the low of the day will likely fail, especially with a doji signal bar. Aggressive bulls bought at or below the low of bar 11, expecting the shorts to be trapped.

Compare those setups with those in the chart on the right. The market was in a trend from the open consisting of three large bear trend bars with small tails and little overlap, and broke far below yesterday's low. This was a clear, strong bear trend with lots of urgency. Bar 22 was a one-bar pullback, and traders aggressively shorted below this low 1 short setup. In fact, traders were so confident that the market would go below the low of the spike that many shorted on limit orders at and above the bar 21 high.

There was another sell climax to the low of the day, which is often followed by a two-legged correction and sometimes a trend reversal. Six bull trend bars created a rally to the moving average, and the bars had very little overlap, big bodies, and small tails. There was urgency to the buying, and everyone was waiting for a pullback from this strong bull spike in a possible new bull trend. There was a one-bar pause at bar 26, which set up a good high 1 long.

There was another six-bar spike up to bar 30 and then a six-bar pullback to the moving average at bar 31, where there was a bull signal bar and another valid high 1 buy setup.

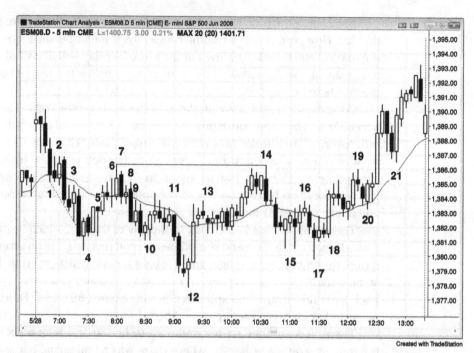

FIGURE 17.3   Bar Counting Is Sometimes Difficult

Figure 17.3 presents a chart of a difficult day to count (but fairly easy to trade) that shows many subtleties in counting the legs of pullbacks. When the first leg is steep and its correction is only a couple of bars long (like to the bar 2 pause), and then a high 2 setup forms, again after only a bar or two (like at bar 3), no significant trend line will be broken, so you should not be looking to buy a high 2. There is too much risk that this is a bear trend and not a trading range or a pullback in a bull trend, and therefore you should not be looking for high 1s and 2s.

Even though there have been two attempts to go up, the first attempt was too weak. You always want a show of strength before your buy setup. Otherwise, assume that the market is still in its first leg down. If the bar after bar 3 were to go above the bar 3 high, it would be an aggressive long entry, but the buy is always better if the rally after the first leg down (the high 1) shows more strength.

The market sometimes drops again and forms a high 3 after penetrating a trend channel line and reversing up. This is a wedge reversal (three legs and a failed breakout of a trend channel line) and one set up at bar 4. Note that neither bar 2 nor bar 3 went above their prior bars but they each effectively ended a small leg down. On a 1 minute chart, there was almost certainly a clear leg and small corrective rally that formed these 5 minute bull trend bars.

Figure 17.3

BAR COUNTING **279**

Bar 4 was a high 3 long entry bar, but it was also a bear trend bar. Since it was only the second bar of the up leg and the rally after a wedge bottom usually has at least two legs up, it was not a good low 1 short setup. Remember, all of these reversal attempts are more reliable when they follow a break of a longer and stronger trend line. If no meaningful trend line is broken on the prior leg (like the bar 2 reversal attempt), then the next leg's reversal attempt will not have much conviction (bar 3), and you should wait for additional price action like the wedge bottom at bar 4 before considering buying.

Bar 5 can be viewed as a low 1 or as a low 2, but when the market is correcting up from a climax bottom (a wedge is a type of climax), make sure to allow it to correct sideways to up before looking to short again. There is no strict rule about what constitutes an adequate correction, but in general the correction should have two clear legs and have at least about half as many bars as the wedge. The sell-off was also a spike and channel bear trend, so the leg up should test close to the start of the channel at bar 2.

Bar 6, strictly speaking, was a low 2, but since there was no meaningful bull trend line break at the low 1, you would not be shorting it. The market was still in a tight channel, so you should not be looking for a low 1 or low 2 short. Channels can have many pullbacks as the channel progresses, but they usually have at least three legs before there is a breakout and a reversal. Bar 7 was the third push up. It was a second-entry short on the moving average test, it formed a double top with the bar 2 top of the channel, and it was the first bar of a two-bar reversal. Shorting below the bear bar that followed was a reasonable trade. However, the market had been in a tight trading range since bar 6 so most traders should not have been trading; instead, they should have waited for the breakout and then begun to look for trades.

Bar 8 was a high 1, but it occurred after six sideways bars at the top of a weak rally and not in a strong bull spike.

Bar 10 was also a high 2 entry above a bull bar at the bottom of a trading range, and an acceptable long entry.

Although bar 11 was a high 1 variant because it did not extend above the prior bar, it was also a low 2 short setup below the moving average. The low 1 setup was the 2 bar reversal from two bars earlier, and that also set up a failed high 2 (bar 10 was the high 2 entry bar). It was the second attempt to create a failure of the bar 10 high 2 long, and most traders who bought above bar 10 would exit on this second failure. This is one of the reasons why a low 2 short below the moving average works. It is exactly where premature longs will exit, and as they sell out of their longs, they add to the selling pressure and they will not buy again for at least a bar or two.

Bar 12 was a bull reversal bar and a high 2 (bar 11 was the high 1) in a quiet day and it was the new low of the day, making it a high-probability trade for at least a scalp. If there was no high 1, the move down would have had about six trending bear bars and traders would have to wait for a breakout pullback (a second entry) before considering a long trade. Bar 12 was the end of a measured move (approximately) in a larger two-legged pullback, with the first leg ending at bar 10, and the end of an even larger measured move from the high of the day with a first leg ending at bar 4. Finally, bar 12 was a reversal up from a bear trend channel overshoot. The line is not shown, but it is anchored on the low of the bar before bar 10 and was created as a parallel of the bear trend line down from bar 7.

Bar 13 could have been the start of a tight trading range because it was the third consecutive small doji. By two bars later, the tight trading range was clear, so most traders should no longer have been using bar counts for setups. However, experienced traders could view bar 13 as a push down, and the two bear bars over the next four bars as two more pushes down; they could then view this tight trading range as a wedge bull flag (discussed in Chapter 18) and then look to buy the breakout, expecting a bull channel after the strong bar 12 bull spike. Since at this point the day was basically in a trading range and this tight trading range was in the middle of the day's range, bar counting was unreliable. However, since there had just been a strong spike up, it was reasonable to look to buy above a bull trend bar, regardless of what the bar count was.

Bar 14 was a low 2, ending the second leg up, with the spike up from bar 12 being the first leg up. It was also a double top bear flag with bar 7 and therefore the second failed attempt to run to the high of the day. On a trendless day and after a double top bear flag, you should look for two legs down. The first leg ended with the bar 15 high 1, which was followed by two small legs up, ending with the bar 16 low 2 at the moving average.

The second leg down ended with the high 2 at bar 17, but bar 17 was a bear trend bar following a bear trend bar, and it followed a first leg down to bar 15 that was very strong. It was still a valid buy but the uncertainty resulted in a second-chance entry at the bar 18 high 2. This second entry developed because enough traders were sufficiently uncomfortable with the first entry to make them wait for a second setup. It was also an ii pattern variant based on bodies only. In later chapters, you will learn that it is also a double bottom pullback long setup. Bar 17 formed a double bottom with either the bar before or the bar after bar 15, and the sideways bar before bar 18 was the pullback.

The low 2 at bar 19 was after strong upward momentum, but it was still a valid short. However, it resulted in a five-tick failure at bar 20 (described later; it means that the move down from bar 19 reached only five ticks and therefore left many shorts still trapped without a scalper's profit).

Bar 20 formed a failed low 2, which trapped shorts and was therefore a good entry, especially when the upward momentum had been strong. When a failed low 2 occurs, it is usually followed by either a low 3 wedge or a low 4. It was also a high 2 above the moving average and within a trading range, but the market

Figure 17.3   BAR COUNTING   **281**

was in the channel phase of a bull spike and channel trend, and therefore it was a with-trend buy setup, even though it was still below the top of the trading range. Spike and channel trends are discussed in Chapter 21 in book 1 on trends.

Since the bull spike up from bar 20 was so strong, at least two more legs up were likely, and buying the high 1 at bar 21 was a reliable trade. It was possible for this leg down to evolve into a two-legged pullback having a bar with a low below the low of bar 21 (forming a high 2 buy setup), but the odds were against it. There was simply too much strength.

FIGURE 17.4   The SDS Is Helpful in Analyzing the SPY

On the left in Figure 17.4 is the 5 minute Emini and on the right is the 5 minute SDS, an exchange-traded fund (ETF) that is the inverse of the SPY (an ETF that is comparable to the Emini) but has twice the leverage. On the Emini chart, there was a high 2 at bar 5 following a bull trend line break at bar 1 and then a higher high at bar 3 that tested the old trend high. This was a possible trend reversal. The downward momentum was strong and the high 1 at bar 4 was weak. It poked above the small bull micro trend line from the bar 3 high and immediately reversed down, indicating that the bulls were weak, not strong. It would have been unwise to buy the high 2 at bar 5 unless it showed exceptional strength, like having a strong bull reversal signal bar and not having a two-bar bear spike just before it. Also, the signal bar was too large, forcing a trader to buy high in a weak market, and the signal bar was a doji bar that was almost entirely within the prior two bars (both were bear trend bars).

When there are three or more bars with a lot of overlap and one or more is a doji, it is best to wait for more price action before initiating a trade. The bulls and the bears are in balance and any breakout will likely fail (like the high 2 buy signal at bar 5), and you certainly shouldn't be buying a breakout above its high, in particular in a bear leg, especially since most trading ranges are with the trend and the prior leg was down.

Figure 17.4   BAR COUNTING   **283**

Whenever you are wondering if a signal is strong enough, it is helpful to study the chart from different perspectives, like using a bar chart or an inverse chart. In general, just the fact that you feel that you need further study should tell you that it is not a clear and strong signal and therefore you should not take the trade.

Even if you were tempted to buy the high 2 on the Emini chart, virtually no one would be looking to sell the bar 5 low 2 on the SDS chart on the right, because the upward momentum was so strong. Since these charts are essentially just the inverse of one another, if you would not buy on the SDS, you should not sell on the Emini.

Note that bar 7 on the Emini was a high 4, which is usually a reliable buy signal. However, in the absence of any bullish strength in the high 1, 2, or 3, you should not take the trade. A bar count alone is not sufficient. You need prior strength in the form of a relatively strong move that broke at least a minor trend line. This is an example of a high 4 that was formed by a spike down and then a wedge channel (bars 4, 5, and 7 ended the three pushes down).

Notice that earlier there was a strong bull trend and that low 2 shorts were bad trades until after the market broke the bull trend line. There was not a strong downward surge, but the market went sideways for about 10 bars, indicating that the bears were strong enough to hold the bulls at bay for a protracted period. This show of strength by the bears was necessary for a trader to feel confident to short the final flag breakout to the bar 3 new high of the day.

Bar 4 was an acceptable micro trend line short on the Emini chart even though the day had been a bull trend day. After the final flag to the higher high at bar 3, you needed to consider that the trend might have switched to down. There should have been at least two bear legs after this type of reversal—both the bulls and bears would be expecting it. Also, the entry was above the moving average, which is what you want to see when selling below a low 1 signal bar.

Once the market appeared to be in a bear trend and the momentum down was good, you could short a high 1, 2, 3, and 4 by placing a limit order at or a few ticks above the high of the prior bar. Bars 4, 5, and 6 were examples of entry bars for those shorts, and they were also signal bars for selling more at one tick below their lows.

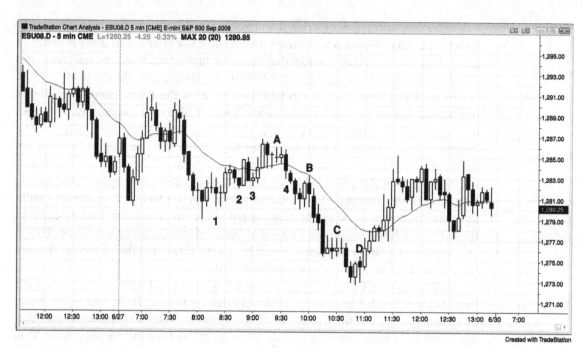

FIGURE 17.5 A Failed Low 2 Often Ends Up as a Low 4 Short

In Figure 17.5, bar 2 was a failed low 2, so one or two more legs up were to be expected. Even though the breakout above bar 2 was not strong, the channel up was too tight to short the low 3. A low 4 ended the bear rally and another one ended the sell-off to the low of the day. It does not matter that the bar A high 1 occurred before the low 4 of the prior leg.

Bar 1 was a micro trend line low 1 short that was good for a scalp. However, the small doji at 8:00 a.m. PST and the doji signal bar for that low 1 short meant that the market was becoming a possible tight trading range. This made the trade risky and it was probably better not to take the trade.

Bar B is a good example of a low 1 short on a pullback to the moving average after a strong move through the moving average. It is also a micro trend line failed breakout short.

Figure 17.6

BAR COUNTING **285**

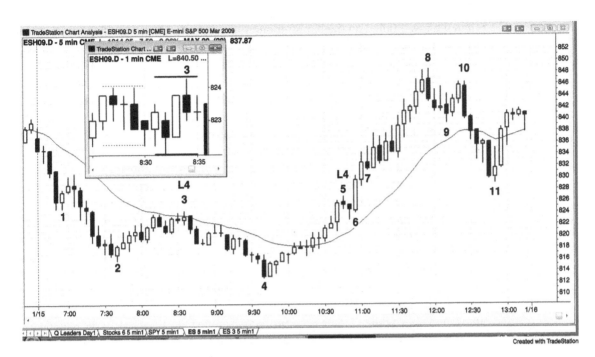

FIGURE 17.6 Failed Low 4

Two failed low 4 shorts illustrate important observations, as shown in Figure 17.6. The low 4 that triggered the short entry at bar 3 had a small doji bar for its setup. When this is the case, always put the stop at two or three ticks above the high of the signal bar because the market often quickly runs one tick above the signal bar to run stops just after you enter your short, as it did here. Look at the inset of the 1 minute chart. The 5 minute signal bar was made up of the five 1 minute bars between the dashed lines, and the entry bar was made up of the five bars between the solid lines. You can see that the market triggered the short in the second minute of the entry bar but then ran above the signal bar by one tick in the fourth minute before selling off down to bar 4.

The second low 4 was triggered by the bar 5 setup. The rally up to bar 4 was almost all bull trend bars, and it followed the bar 4 lower low that formed after breaking a major bear trend line. The trend had changed to a bull trend, and you should no longer have been looking for bear rallies, nor should you have been looking to short low 1s, 2s, 3s, or 4s, which are setups in trading ranges and in bear trends. This is especially true in the absence of bear strength on the move up from bar 4, like a break of the bull trend line. In fact, instead of looking for a reversal to short, you should have been looking for a pullback to buy and you could even have placed a limit order to buy at or below the low of bar 5. Look what happened when the low 4 failed on the bar after entry. As expected, everyone finally accepted the reality that this was a bull market, and the market shot up nonstop to bar 8, which was about a measured move of the height of bar 4 to bar 5, the entire low 4 pattern. The breakout created a measuring gap between the high of the breakout point (the bar 5 high) and the breakout pullback (bar 7). This type of measuring gap is discussed in Chapter 6 on gaps.

Notice that bar 7 was the first of three attempts to reverse back down, and therefore it was a magnet for any pullback from any additional rally. It was the start of the bull channel after the two-bar breakout spike above the failed low 4. The two-legged move down to bar 11 (following the bull trend line break and the bar 10 lower high) hit below the lows of all three of those earlier bear reversal bars, as is commonly the case. In the face of such a strong rally, it is hard to believe that the market could have come back down to those levels, but if you know how to read price action, you would have been more surprised if it did not, especially after such a climactic move up. Bar 7 was followed by a tight trading range, but this was in a strong bull market. Although the tight trading range made bar counting less reliable, since it was a strong bull market, traders should have been looking to buy above bull bars, while placing their protective stops below the low of the signal bar.

Incidentally, bar 7 and the two bear reversal bars that followed in the next four bars constituted three pushes down. When they failed with a breakout made up of two bull trend bars, there was another measuring gap above the wedge that led to a measured move up, and the high of the day exceeded it by a couple of ticks (failed wedges often lead to measured moves).

There was a high 1 buy setup that formed a couple of bars after bar 8, and although it was in a strong bull spike and in a bull trend, it was after a buy climax and therefore not a good buy setup. The market was in a parabolic bull channel after the two-bar bull spike at bar 6.

Figure 17.7

BAR COUNTING   **287**

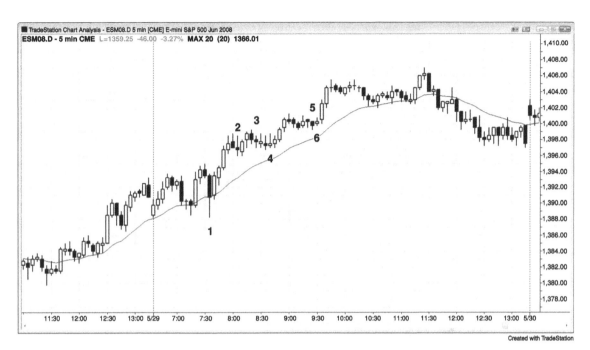

FIGURE 17.7   A Low 2 in a Bull Trend Is Not a Short

A low 2 setup is not enough reason to take a countertrend trade in the absence of a prior strong trend line break. In fact, it will almost always fail and turn into a great with-trend entry, like a high 2 buy, as happened at bars 4 and 6 in Figure 17.7. A low 2 is a setup in a trading range or a bear market and never in a bull trend, and this is a bull trend so traders should not be looking for low 2 setups. Before shorting a strong bull trend, you first need the bears to show that they have already been willing to be aggressive. You look to short their second attempt at pushing the market down, not their first, since the first usually fails. When the bull trend is very strong, you can even consider buying below the low of the prior bar, expecting any low 1 or low 2 to fail. For example, you could place a limit order to buy below the reversal bar that formed before bar 2, or you could buy on bar 5 as it fell below the low of the prior bar, expecting the low 2 to fail. In general, it is safer to buy on a stop above the high of the prior bar; but when the bull trend is strong, you can pretty much buy at any time and for any reason, and buying below the low of the prior bar is logical since you have to expect most reversal attempts to fail.

By bar 4, the market was in a tight trading range so bar counting was getting confusing. You should ignore it at this point and, since the bull trend was so strong, just look to buy on a stop above any bull bar, like the bar after bar 4.

FIGURE 17.8 Failed Low 2

As shown in Figure 17.8, today had a gap down breakout and then a breakout pullback to a double top just below the moving average at bar 2, and this was followed by a new low. At this point, traders did not know whether the two legs down to bar 3 ended a move or there was more to come (the first leg was from yesterday's close down to bar 1). Although the bar 4 low 2 short reached its scalper's profit target and therefore could not technically be a failure, the break below the trend line and the reversal up made it likely that the market would behave like a failed low 2; it would have at least two more legs up and then attempt to form a low 4 bear setup.

There were a couple of problems with the low 2 short at bar 4. First, it followed a trend line break (the rally up to bar 2), which meant that bar 3 could be the low of the day (a bad place to be shorting) since the high or low of the day usually develops in the first hour or so. Next, the low 2 was too far from the moving average and therefore not a good moving average test. Normally, second tests of the moving average are closer to the moving average or penetrate it more than the first, and the first test at bar 2 was clearly closer. Many traders won't feel comfortable entering with the trend unless the pullback touches or comes within a tick or so of the moving average. When the reversal begins before this happens, it will be missing the fuel that those shorts would have provided.

Bar 6 formed a low 4 setup and was the second push above the moving average. However, this rally had many overlapping bars and several dojis, indicating that the bulls and the bears were fairly balanced and a big, fast move down was unlikely.

Figure 17.8

BAR COUNTING **289**

Therefore, trading at this point might not be worthwhile for traders who prefer high-probability trades with big profit potential. The solution? Either wait for more price action, knowing that good setups will always come if you can be patient, or take the short but be prepared to allow for a pullback, like the one on the bar after entry.

Bar 9 was the fifth consecutive overlapping bar, and at this point the market was in a tight trading range. Bar counting in a tight trading range is too uncertain, and most traders should not be taking trades on that basis until after a breakout.

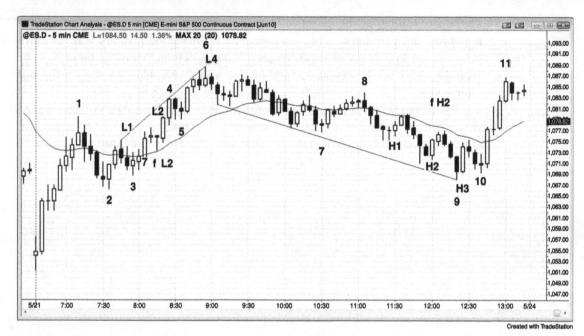

FIGURE 17.9 A Failed Low 2 Can Evolve into a Low 3 or Low 4

A failed low 2 can lead to either a wedge top (a low 3) or a low 4 top, depending on the momentum up from the failed low 2. Sometimes it can just turn into a bull trend. The breakout above the failed low 2 in Figure 17.9 was by two bull trend bars with large bodies and small tails, and the move up from bar 3 was in a tight channel. It was also a channel that followed the very strong spike from the open up to bar 1. Also, the low 2 reversed up after just a single bar. This strong bull momentum made shorting below the bar 5 ii pattern too risky. It was reasonable to expect this low 2 to fail since it was in the early stages of a bull channel, and channels often have pullbacks that trap traders in the wrong direction. The strength of the bulls was good up to this point, as seen by the tightness of the channel, the number of bull trend bars, and the lack of much overlap between adjacent bars. These are signs of a solid bull channel, and therefore a low 2 should be expected to fail.

Even though the market did not trade below bar 5 to trigger the low 3, it was still the third push up from bar 2 so it served the same purpose as a low 3. Since the momentum on the breakout was strong, two more legs up should be expected. The bar before bar 6 poked slightly above the trend channel line and had a bear close, and bar 6 tested the line again. This was a reasonable low 4 short setup for at least two legs down.

Figure 17.9   BAR COUNTING   **291**

Later in the day, a high 2 failed but turned up after a high 3 (a form of wedge) instead of a high 4. The moves up from the high 1 and high 2 each lasted several bars, indicating some strength by the bulls. Although the breakout below the failed high 2 was strong, it was an exhaustive sell climax. The increasing size of the bodies of the bars in the bear spike was a sign of exhaustion, and it occurred at the trend channel line and in the area of the bar 2 low. Since bar 2 was the start of a bull channel, it was a magnet that should be expected to be tested, as it was here. After the test, the market usually rallies to at least about 25 percent of the height of the developing trading range. Since the three-bar bear spike down to bar 9 represented strong bearish momentum, there was a possibility of at least one more leg down. Because of the sell climax, the odds favored at least two legs sideways to up. This made buying the bar 10 higher low a good probability trade, especially since the odds favored an attempt at a trading range after the test of the bar 2 bottom of the bull channel.

Deeper Discussion of This Chart

Today, as shown in Figure 17.9, opened with a failed breakout, reversing up after the gap down breakout. There was a strong bull trend bar spike and then a tight channel up to bar 1; the entire move was likely a bull spike on a higher time frame chart. When the momentum is strong like this, the odds favor at least a second leg up after a pullback, and that made it reasonable to look for buy setups once the market pulled back to the area of the bar 2 start of the bull channel.

This was also a trend from the open bull day, and bar 2 was the setup for the first pullback long. Bar 3 was a breakout pullback buy setup from the breakout of the bull flag from bar 1 to bar 2.

Traders saw the entire leg down from bar 6 as likely a pullback in a bull trend. The high 2 was close enough for that bottom but traders were not sure. In any case, they were looking to buy. Also notice that every new low down from the bar 6 high quickly reversed. Traders were buying the new lows, so buyers were active all the way down. Although the move down from the failed high 2 was strong, it was three bear bars of increasing size and was a small sell climax. A trader could buy above bar 9 and assume that the bar 9 low would hold (the wedge low), but it was better to wait for a pullback, which came with the bar 10 higher low. This led to a strong rally into the close as the bulls from the open resumed their buying.

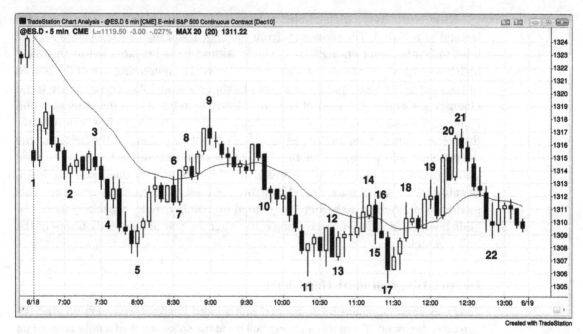

FIGURE 17.10 High 2 Variant

In Figure 17.10, the bar 16 doji had a large tail on the top, which indicates that the market moved up and down within that bar. That up move was the end of the first leg down, and therefore bar 17 should act like a high 2, which it did.

Bar 12 was a low 2 short setup below the moving average, but the market was beginning to form a trading range and therefore this was not a reliable short. In fact, it made more sense to buy at the bar 12 low, but this is something that only experienced traders should attempt. Whenever there is a sell signal just below the moving average and the signal bar is large and mostly overlaps two or more bars, the market is in a small trading range and shorting at the bottom is usually a losing strategy.

Deeper Discussion of This Chart

The day opened with a large gap down in Figure 17.10 and was therefore a bear breakout. Although bar 1 was a bear trend bar, it could still be the first bar of a trend from the open bull trend day, although this is less likely than if it had been a bull trend bar. Traders bought above the high of bar 1 for the failed breakout rally. The rally went for only two bars and then the bears shorted below the second bull bar and below the two-bar reversal (the low of that bear entry bar) for the breakout pullback short and a possible

Figure 17.10   BAR COUNTING   **293**

trend from the open bear day. A large gap down has an increased chance of being a bear trend day, and traders should try to take all reasonable short setups for a swing down.

Bar 4 was the third push down on the day, but it was the third bar of a bear spike and therefore not a reliable signal bar for a long. Traders should wait for a breakout and then a pullback before going long. The next bar was a bull trend bar that traded above bar 4 and formed a two-bar reversal, but the market did not trade above the top of the two bars; it instead broke out to the downside. The three bear bars before bar 2 had enough momentum so that many traders would restart the count and would consider bar 2 to be the first push down.

When bar 4 formed, some traders saw it as the third push down whereas others saw it as only the second, and no one knew which group of traders would be correct. When in doubt, stay out and wait for a second signal.

Bar 5 was a bull reversal bar and the second bar of a two-bar reversal; it was also the third push down in the channel that began with the bar 2 bear spike. The spike is often the first push, as it was here. At this point, the spike and channel bulls bought, expecting two pushes up, and the wedge traders who reset the count with the bar 2 spike also bought this third push down. The traders who wondered if bar 4 was the third push were looking for a breakout pullback and saw bar 5 as a lower low breakout pullback. All traders at this point believed that all of these factors were at play and the odds were good for a two-legged rally.

Bar 5 was followed by a four-bar bull spike up to the moving average, and this might have been the end of the first leg up.

Bar 6 was a setup for a low 2 short but since a second leg up was likely, it was better not to take a short scalp and instead look for a lower high long setup or a breakout of this bull flag. Bar 6 and two bars before it were bear bars forming two small legs down; they therefore set up a high 2 buy above the high of bar 6.

Bar 8 was a small doji, but it might have been a setup for a final flag short for a failed breakout of that four-bar bull flag that ended with bar 6. However, the move up to bar 8 from bar 5 was in a fairly tight bull channel, and therefore it was unclear if bar 8 was the second leg up. When in doubt, wait for a second signal. The bar after bar 8 was a bear trend bar, which was a good entry bar for the bears who shorted, but they would buy back their shorts above the bear trend bar. Many traders went long above bar 6 since there were trapped bears and this was also now a failed low 2, where bar 6 was the first push down.

Bar 9 was a bear reversal bar, a second-signal moving average gap bar where bar 8 was the first setup, and the top of a bear wedge. The top of the spike up from bar 5 was the first push up, and bar 8 was the second. A wedge reversal usually has at least two legs down, and it did here. The first ended at bar 11 and the second at bar 17. The bulls who were looking for two legs up from the wedge bottom at bar 5 were satisfied that the spike up from bar 5 was the first leg up and the channel up from the bottom of bar 6 was the second leg up.

The three bars after bar 10 tried to form a double bottom with the bar 7 bottom of the bull channel but failed.

Bar 10 was a bear spike, and it was followed by a climax channel down to bar 11.

Bar 11 was a doji bar but it followed a sharp move down from bar 9, and the market was likely to go sideways before reversing up because of that bear momentum.

Bar 12 was a low 2 short, but it was a large signal bar and there was a lot of overlap with the three prior bars; therefore this was likely to be a bear trap and not a good short setup. The failed low 2 led to a six-bar bull spike up to bar 14, but there was a lot of overlap between adjacent bars, and the move up was in a very tight channel. Even though the channel sloped up, its tightness increased the chances that any downside breakout would not go very far and the market would get pulled back up into the area of the channel. This was therefore a possible final flag, and that could lead to a bull reversal.

The market spiked down to bar 17, and bar 17 was a large bear trend bar and therefore a sell climax.

The bull inside bar that followed was a good setup for at least a two-legged rally based on the final flag reversal, the third push down on the day (this created a large wedge bull flag with bar 5 and bar 11), and the second lower low attempt to reverse up from breaking below the bar 5 low of the open.

Bar 17 was also a shrinking stair since it fell below bar 11 by two ticks and bar 11 fell below bar 5 by six ticks. This is a sign that the bear trend was losing momentum.

Bar 19 was a low 2 setup, but the upward momentum was too strong and the signal bar too weak to take a short. The entry bar was a strong bear trend bar, but the market immediately reversed up. Alert traders would have expected the low 2 to fail, and they went long above this bear entry bar.

Bar 20 was the third push up from the bar 17 low and a strong bear trend bar but the short never triggered. The market had one more push up to bar 21, and the reversal down was seen by some traders as a low 4, and by other traders as a wedge top with bar 18 being the first push and bar 19 being the second. Other traders saw it as a large low 2 where bar 14 was the first push up.

Figure 17.11   BAR COUNTING **295**

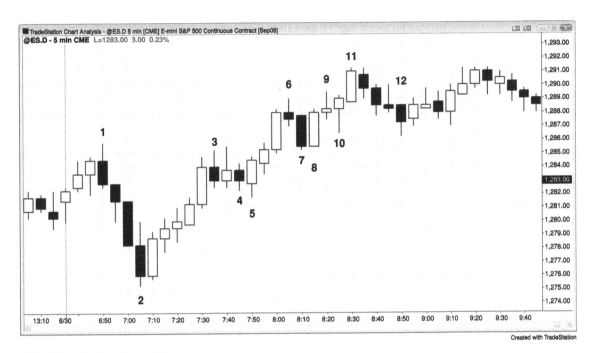

FIGURE 17.11 High 2 Variant

In Figure 17.11, bars 3 and 4 created a two-legged correction in a bull swing, even though the bar after bar 3 was the end of the up leg. Because it was a two-legged correction, bar 4 is a high 2 long signal bar.

Bar 7 was a bear trend bar so it was not a reliable high 1 signal bar, but bar 8 formed a two-bar reversal with it and the chances of a successful trade were greater if you bought above the bar 8 bull trend bar than if you bought above the bar 7 bear trend bar. Although some traders saw bar 7 as a low 2 entry after the bar 3 first leg up, the move up was so strong that this may have been a bull trend; therefore, shorting a low 2 was a low-probability trade.

Bar 8 was a failed low 2 buy setup and a high 1 long.

Some traders would have shorted below bar 9, but the bull channel was too steep and the signal bar too weak to be taking shorts at this point.

Bar 10 was a high 2 long (bar 8 was the high 1) because it followed two attempts to sell off at the high of the day (bars 7 and 10). A sequence of two attempts down is the same as a two-legged correction, so it was a high 2 long setup. It was also a failed low 2 buy setup and there were likely trapped bears who bought back their shorts above bar 10. Also, some of the shorts from the bar 8 signal would have allowed one push up, but almost all would have covered on a second push up. That is one of the reasons that high 2 buy setups are so reliable in bull trends.

Some traders saw bar 12 as a high 1 buy setup whereas others saw it as a high 2 buy setup where the doji bar before it signified the end of the first small push down. Since the move up to bar 11 was a wedge channel, it was likely to have a two-legged sideways to down correction, so buying here was not a high-probability trade. Bar 12 broke the bull trend line and could have been followed by a lower high or a higher high; in either case, bears would likely have looked to short the rally for at least a scalp down.

All of this analysis is loose, but its objective is important. Traders need to look for two-legged pullbacks because they set up excellent with-trend entries. Also, do not look for a low 2 short setup in a bull trend.

Figure 17.12

BAR COUNTING   **297**

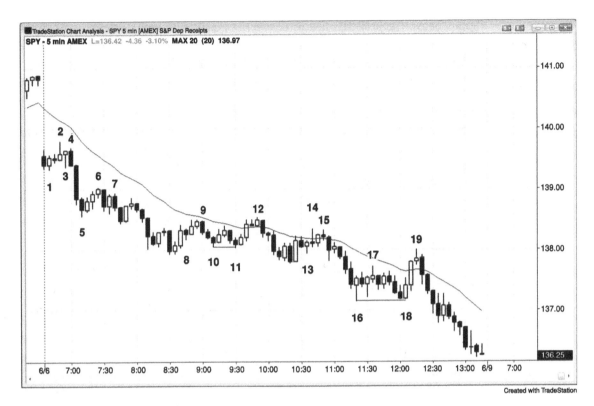

FIGURE 17.12   Low 2 Variants

The chart of the SPY presented in Figure 17.12 demonstrates lots of variations in low 2 setups, but if you think about each one, each was the logical end of a two-legged bear correction. Since the chart is clearly bearish (below the falling exponential moving average), traders were looking for opportunities to enter shorts, so anything that resembled a low 2 was good enough.

Bar 3 was a low 1 and its high was taken out by bar 4, making bar 4 a second attempt up and a setup for the low 2 short that triggered on the next bar.

Bar 6 was a low 1 setup, and two bars later there was a bull trend bar, indicating an up leg. Bar 7 was the signal bar for the short on the following bar, even though it was a lower entry than the low 1. It was still a two-legged correction.

Bar 8 was a small bear inside bar in an upward correction, and it therefore constituted a tiny correction, ending the first leg up. Bar 9 followed another bull trend bar (actually two), so it was the second attempt down and effectively a low 2 short near the moving average.

Bar 11 was lower than bar 10, so it was the start of the move up to bar 12. Why was the bar after the bar 12 top a low 2? The low of the bar 12 bull outside bar dipped below the prior bar just after bar 12 opened, although you cannot tell from this chart, but you can tell for certain by looking at a 1 minute chart (not shown). This made bar 12 a low 1. An outside bar breaks out of both sides of its prior bar; you do not know which side it broke through first, although the direction of its body is usually reliable (for example, a bull body usually indicates that the upside breakout occurred second, since its direction is up into its close). The bar after bar 12 broke below bar 12, so it was the second time in this leg up from bar 11 that a bar broke below the low of the prior bar and was therefore a low 2 short at the moving average. Bar 12 was also a low 2 short setup because bar 9 was a first move up and bar 12 was a second move up.

Bar 13 was a low 1 short entry bar (and a low 2 where the bear bar three bars earlier was the low 1), but after two strong bull trend bars, this was too risky to take since more of an upward correction was likely.

Once there was a second leg up (bar 14 had a higher high, so it was clearly a small second leg), any bar that had a low below the prior bar was a low 2 short. Bar 15 turned into a low 2 short signal bar even though it was a small swing high that was below the high of the two legs up (it was a lower high in what should be expected to be at least two legs down). Also, as discussed in the next chapter, bar 15 was also a wedge bear flag entry based on three pushes up where bar 14 was the third push up and the two bull trend bars before bar 13 were the first two pushes up.

Bar 17 was a low 2 setup but it followed two bull reversal bars with large tails so traders were beginning to buy in this area. This made shorting here risky, and it was likely that there would be more buyers below the bar than sellers. The more certain you are that the market is in a tight trading range, the less certain you will be about your bar counting. In general, it is better not to take trades based on bar counts in tight trading ranges unless you are very confident with your count, which means that you believe that the count is clear enough to warrant a trade.

Bar 18 was a double bottom with bar 16 and a high 2 based on the two small pushes down from bar 17.

Deeper Discussion of This Chart

As shown in Figure 17.12, the day had a large gap down and was therefore a bear break-out. The first bar was a bear trend bar and a possible high of the day; consequently, it was an acceptable short setup. However, the market reversed up into a failed breakout long setup on the next bar, and the day could have become a trend from the open bull trend day. The large gap down still favored the bears unless the bulls clearly took control of the market with a strong bull spike and follow-through.

Once the market traded below bar 2, the market then had both a spike down and a spike up after the first bar of the day, and the day's range was less than a third of the

Figure 17.12   BAR COUNTING   **299**

recent average daily range. This put the opening range in breakout mode for a possible trend day, and traders placed buy stops above the high of the day to go long on the upside breakout, and sell stops to go short below the bar 1 low spike for a downside breakout. The large bear trend bar that broke below bar 1 shows how aggressively the traders shorted. The sell-off was probably attributed to a 7:00 a.m. PST report. However, it is more likely that the institutions were already planning to short today and very unlikely that they were flooded with phone calls from their large clients who heard the bearish report and now suddenly decided to sell. The institutions were already looking to short but were hoping for a rally on the report so that they could short higher. The report convinced them that they were not going to get that rally so they had to short after the report, and they continued to short all day long.

Bar 18 was the end of a bear trend bar breakout of a tight trading range and likely to reverse up because of the magnetic pull of tight trading ranges, which often become final flags.

Bar 19 was the first moving average gap bar in a bear trend and therefore a good short. It is a good example of a bear trap that often occurs in the final hour or two of a bear trend day. It was at the top of a strong bull spike that broke above the bar 17 swing high and trapped bulls in and bears out. All bull spikes are climaxes and breakouts, and they sometimes fail and lead to reversals down instead of reversals up. At the time the spike was forming, emotional traders who were afraid that they were missing a major reversal bought as that second bull trend bar formed, as it broke above the bar 17 lower high, and as the bar closed on its high. Strong bears were simply stepping aside and letting the bulls go. These bears knew that the odds were high that there would be an attempted bull reversal before the day was over, and they waited for a strong bull trend bar to form. Once they saw it, they believed that the market would not hold up there very long, so they aggressively shorted. Since both they and the bulls knew that the bears controlled the day, the bears were confident of being able to again drive the market to a new low of the day. The bulls scalped out of their longs because they did not believe that the reversal up had enough of the ingredients of a strong bull reversal. There was no prior strong break of the bear trend line, and the market was unable to hold above the moving average at any point in the day.

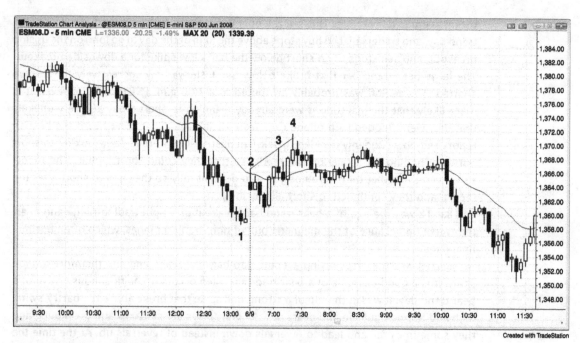

FIGURE 17.13   A Spike and Channel Is a Two-Legged Move

When there is a spike and channel pullback, the spike can be thought of as the first leg up and the channel as the second. In Figure 17.13, the gap opening up to bar 2 was the spike, which was the first of three pushes up. Bull channels often have two more pushes up before correcting, and the entire pattern formed a wedge top in this chart. Most patterns have multiple interpretations, and some traders base their trades on one whereas other traders rely more on another. The move up to bar 4 was seen by some traders as a wedge top and by others as a two-legged correction where the gap spike up to bar 2 was the first leg and the two-legged channel up to bar 4 was the second leg.

CHAPTER 18

Wedge and Other Three-Push Pullbacks

When a pullback forms in a bull trend, it is a bull flag, and when it occurs in a bear trend, it is a bear flag. It is often contained between a converging trend line and trend channel line. When this is the case and it is horizontal, it is a triangle, which can break out in either direction. However, when it is falling in a bull trend or rising in a bear trend, it is called a wedge, and, like all pullbacks, it will usually break out in the direction of the trend. Like other types of triangles, it has at least five legs, but unlike a typical triangle, the second leg often exceeds the prior swing point. It can be just a simple three-push wedge pattern or a channel after a spike. It can also assume an irregular shape that looks nothing like a wedge but has three countertrend pushes, which is all that is needed to qualify as a triangle, or, if it is sloping, a wedge type of triangle, or simply a wedge.

A wedge *pullback* is a with-trend setup, and traders can enter on the first signal, as soon as the market reverses back into the direction of the trend. Wedges can also be reliable *reversal* patterns, but unlike a wedge pullback, a wedge reversal is a countertrend setup and it is therefore usually better to wait for a second entry. For example, unless a wedge top is extremely strong, traders should wait for the bear breakout and then assess its strength. If it is strong, they can then look to see if there is a breakout pullback short setup, which they can short. The pullback can come as either a higher high or a lower high. If the breakout is weak, traders should expect it to fail and then look for a buy setup, so they can enter on the failed bear breakout for a resumption of the bull trend.

If a wedge reversal forms in a bull trend, the wedge is pointed up, unlike a wedge pullback in a bull trend, which is pointed down. A wedge bottom in a bear trend is pointed down, unlike a wedge bear flag, which is pointed up. Also, wedge flags are usually smaller patterns and most last about 10 to 20 bars. Since they are with-trend setups, they don't have to be perfect, and many are subtle and look nothing like a wedge or any other type of triangle, but have three pullbacks. A reversal usually needs to be at least 20 bars long and have a clear trend channel line to be strong enough to reverse a trend.

Wedges can also form in trading ranges, and when they do they usually share characteristics of wedge flags and wedge reversals. If the wedge is strong and there is clear two-sided trading, entering on the first signal is usually profitable. However, whenever you have any reasonable doubt, wait for a second signal. Wedge reversals are discussed in detail in the chapter on trend reversals in book 3.

When a wedge occurs as a pullback in a trend and the trend then resumes, its breakout reverses the countertrend action back into the direction of the trend. Remember, a wedge is usually the end of a trend, and a pullback is a small trend (but it is in the opposite direction of the larger trend), so it makes sense to view a wedge pullback as similar to a wedge reversal. In general, if a wedge is sloping up and to the right, whether it is a pullback in a bear trend or a top in a bull trend, it can be thought of as a bear flag even if there was no prior bear trend, since it will usually break out to the downside. This is because the behavior of its breakout and the follow-through after the breakout are indistinguishable from those of bear flags in strong bear trends. If it is sloping down and to the right, it can be thought of as a bull flag whether it is an actual bull flag or at the bottom of a bear trend, and it usually results in an upside breakout. As is discussed later, a low 3 is functionally the same as a wedge top and in fact often is an actual wedge, and a high 3 should be traded like a wedge bottom.

A strong trend sometimes has a three-legged pullback midday that lasts a couple of hours and lacks much momentum. Sometimes it is a spike and channel pattern, which is a common type of wedge pullback. The channel often has parallel lines instead of a wedge shape, but it still is a reliable with-trend setup. It does not matter whether you call it a pullback, trading range, triangle, flag, pennant, wedge, or anything else because the exact shape is irrelevant and all of these pullback variations have the same significance. What is important is that the third swing traps countertrend traders into a bad trade because they mistakenly assumed that the third leg was the start of a new trend. This is because most pullbacks end with two legs and whenever there is a third leg, traders wonder if the trend has reversed.

FIGURE 18.1   Wedge Bear Flag and Expanding Triangle

A strong trend is often followed by a three-swing pullback that typically has low momentum. In Figure 18.1, bars 4, 6, and 8 are the tops of the three pullbacks after the bar 3 new low, and each was a bull trending swing (higher lows and highs). Since there were many bars that overlapped the prior bars, many bars with tails, and many bear trend bars, the upward momentum was weak. This will make traders short each new high.

There was also an expanding triangle (bars 1, 2, 3, 8, and 9). The long entry setup was the inside bar after bar 9, but this was the final bar of the day. However, the next day gapped up above the signal bar (don't buy on the gap up; take an entry only if the entry bar opens below the high of the signal bar and then trades through your buy stop), so there was no entry until the bar 10 breakout pullback the next day.

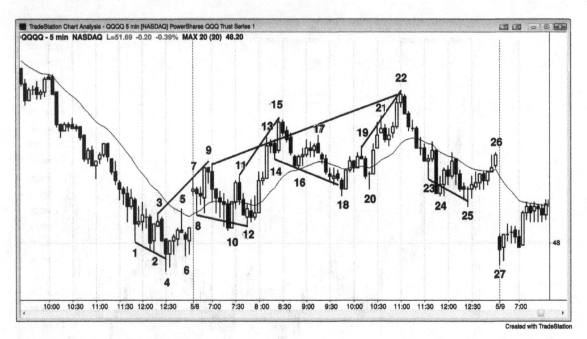

FIGURE 18.2   Wedge Bear Flag

As shown in Figure 18.2, bars 9, 15, and 22 formed a large bear flag and formed the middle leg of a three-swing sequence in the 5 minute QQQQ, which unfolded over three days (a bear trend, followed by a three-push rally, and then a test of the bear trend's low). Even though the upward momentum was good, it was actually minor compared to the size of the prior bear trend, whose low almost certainly would be tested. The test of the low occurred on the open of the third day. The wedge up to bar 22 was just a large bear flag and it could easily be seen as such on a 15 or 60 minute chart.

The wedge reversal attempt at bar 4 was too small to lead to a major reversal, and traders could have only scalped it and only after a higher low. However, the bar 6 higher low occurred too late in the day to trade.

As the market entered the large trading range, there were many wedge pullbacks that led to tradable scalps. Since the market was in a trading range, traders could enter on the reversal and they would not have to wait for a second signal. However, when a wedge is steep, it is usually better to wait. For example, the bars 11, 13, and 15 wedge was in a fairly tight bull channel and some traders might have preferred to wait to short below the bar 17 high for the expected second leg down.

Bars 14, 16, and 18 formed a wedge bull flag after the strong rally to bar 15, and traders could have bought above bar 18. However, since it was the seventh down bar in a row, other traders would have preferred to wait to buy above the bar 20 higher low.

Figure 18.3   WEDGE AND OTHER THREE-PUSH PULLBACKS   **305**

FIGURE 18.3   Gap Up and Wedge Bull Flag

As shown in Figure 18.3, the large gap up in Apple (AAPL) was effectively a steep bull leg (a bull spike). This was followed by three pullbacks, the third of which was a failure swing (it failed to go below the prior low). It can be called a wedge for simplicity's sake, although it does not have a good wedge shape. The gap up was the spike, and the sideways move to bar 3 was the pullback that led to the bull channel. This is a variant of a trend resumption day where here the first bull leg was the gap opening.

Deeper Discussion of This Chart

As shown in Figure 18.3, traders should swing part or all of their longs from the bar 3 entry, expecting approximately a measured move up equal to about the height of the gap spike (the low of the last bar of yesterday to the high of the first bar of today). The measured move could also be a leg 1 = leg 2 type, with bar 3 being the bottom of the second leg up.

FIGURE 18.4   Wedge Bear Flag

In Figure 18.4, Lehman Brothers Holdings (LEH) had a large reversal day at bar 1, which was on huge volume and was widely reported as strong support and a long-term bottom.

Bar 8 was the end of a wedge pullback (bars 4, 6 or 7, and 8) and of a small three-push pattern (bars 6, 7, and 8). It was also a double top bear flag with bar 2 (bar 8 was 24 cents higher, but close enough on a daily chart).

Bar 1 was a sell climax, which is a spike down followed by a spike up. The market often then goes sideways as the bulls continue to buy and attempt to generate a bull channel, and the bears continue to sell as they try to create a bear channel. Here, the bears won and the bulls had to sell out of their longs, adding to the selling pressure. The stock soon traded below the huge bar 1 reversal bar, and LEH, the third largest investment bank in the country, went out of business within a few months.

Bar 1 is an example of a one-bar island bottom, where there was an exhaustion gap before it and a breakout gap after it.

Figure 18.5   WEDGE AND OTHER THREE-PUSH PULLBACKS   **307**

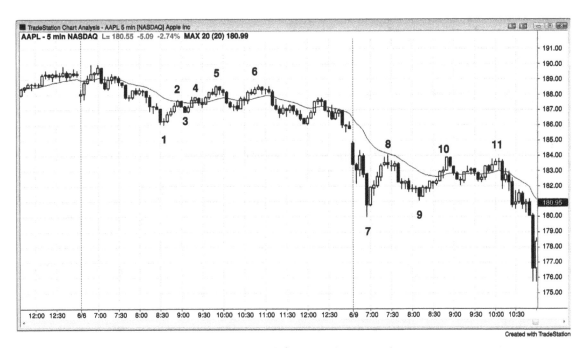

FIGURE 18.5   Higher High Breakout Pullback from Wedge Bear Flag

As shown in Figure 18.5, there was a two-legged correction up to bar 6 and the first leg ended at bar 5. Bar 5 was a wedge, but, as is often the case, it is effectively two legs, with the second one being made of two smaller legs (bars 4 and 5). The move to bar 1 was a small spike and then bars 2, 4, and 5 were three pushes up in a channel. The sell-off from bar 5 was a breakout below the bull channel, and the pullback from that breakout was the higher high at bar 6.

There was a second three-legged correction up from bar 7. It doesn't matter if you see this as a triangle or as two legs, one from bars 7 to 8 and the other from bars 9 to 11 with the second leg being made of two smaller legs. Three-legged corrections are common in trends, and sometimes they are really just two legs with the second leg having two smaller legs. When it gets this hard to think about it, stop thinking about anything other than the trend and the market's inability to get much above the moving average. Look for short entries and don't worry too much about counting legs if those thoughts are giving you an excuse to avoid placing orders.

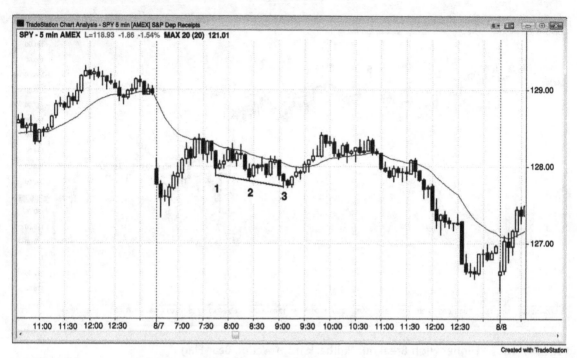

FIGURE 18.6   Spike and Channel as Wedge Bull Flag

Sometimes a pullback can be a small spike and channel pattern, creating a wedge bull flag (see Figure 18.6). Here, there was a bull move up and then a small spike down to bar 1, which was the first push of the spike down, and it was followed by two more pushes down. Channels after spikes often end with three pushes, and this one became a wedge bull flag and a higher low on the day. There was a second push up from bar 3, and it was about the same size as the rally off the low of the open (a leg 1 = leg 2 measured move).

Do not be too eager to buy the high 2 after the second leg down when both the first and second pushes down have strong momentum. A strong first spike down often means that you should allow for a possible wedge correction. Wait for a pullback from the breakout above the high 2 signal bar (here, the two-bar reversal at bar 2). That second-entry setup can be a higher low or, as it was here, a lower low, which formed a wedge bull flag.

As with all spike and channel patterns, the minimum target is the start of the channel, which was the high following bar 1, and there was enough room for at least a long scalp. The market exceeded the minimum target and tested the high of the opening rally where it formed a large double top bear flag, which led to a bear trend into the close.

Figure 18.7   WEDGE AND OTHER THREE-PUSH PULLBACKS   **309**

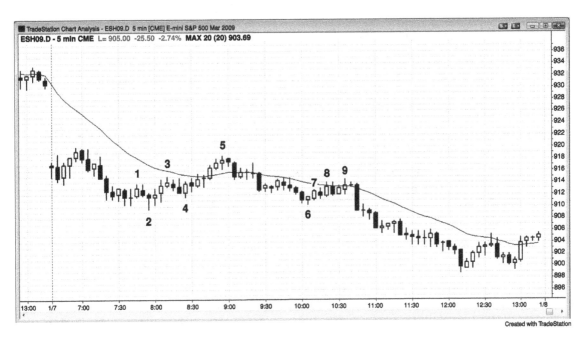

FIGURE 18.7 Wedge Flags

Three-push pullbacks often set up reliable with-trend entries (see Figure 18.7).

Bar 1 was a low 2, and it became the first of three pushes up in a bear rally. It does not matter that bar 2 was below the low of the bar that led to the bar 1 push up, and in fact this is a common occurrence when a final flag evolves into a larger pattern. Here, that larger pattern was a three-push-up bear rally that ended in a first moving average gap bar at bar 5. It was also a small spike and channel bull trend where the move to bar 3 was the spike and the rally from bar 4 to bar 5 was the channel. A small spike and channel is often a two-legged rally, and since it followed the bar 1 push up, those two legs were the second and third legs of a wedge bear flag.

The gap down on the open was a bear spike, and the move down to bar 2 was the channel. Bar 5 tested the top of the channel and formed a double top with it.

Bars 7 to 9 formed a three-push pullback that was a slightly rising tight channel that stalled at the moving average. In general, only very experienced traders should consider placing trades in tight trading ranges because they are difficult to interpret and that lowers the odds of any successful trade.

Bar 9 formed a double top bear flag with the fourth bar before bar 6, which was the start of a bear channel after a bear spike.

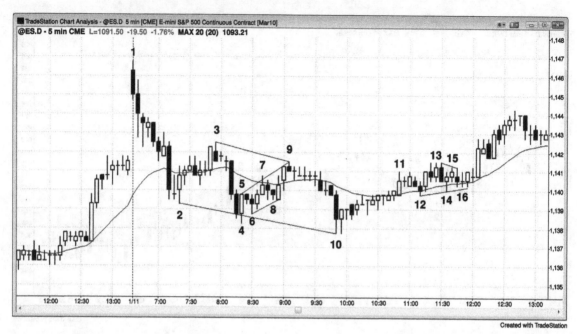

FIGURE 18.8   Three-Push Patterns

There are several wedge pullbacks in the 5 minute Emini chart presented in Figure 18.8. The three pushes down on bars 2, 4, and 10 created a typical wedge reversal pattern, but since it was a large correction in a bull trend that topped out at bar 1, it was a wedge pullback. The pullback lasted long enough to constitute a small bear trend, but that bear trend was just a pullback in a larger bull trend.

Bars 5, 7, and 9 were three pushes up in a channel and formed a correction of the brief strong move down from bar 3 to bar 4. You can use the extremes of the bars or the tops or bottoms of the bodies to draw the lines. Since the shapes of wedge pullbacks are so often irregular, inexact trend lines and trend channel lines are the rule and not the exception.

Bars 12, 14, and 16 formed three pushes down in a sideways correction in the rally up from bar 10. Triangles are a form of three-push pattern. Note that the high of bar 13 exceeded the bar 11 high. The rally after the first push down often exceeds the swing high that just preceded it.

Once bar 9 became a bear reversal bar, you could have drawn a best fit trend channel line with the bar 5 high, and it does not matter that the bar 7 high was above the line. Similarly, once the market formed the bull inside bar after bar 10 and set up the wedge bottom buy, you could have connected the bottoms of bars 2 and 10 to highlight the wedge, and it is irrelevant that the bar 4 second push down was below the line.

Figure 18.9   WEDGE AND OTHER THREE-PUSH PULLBACKS   **311**

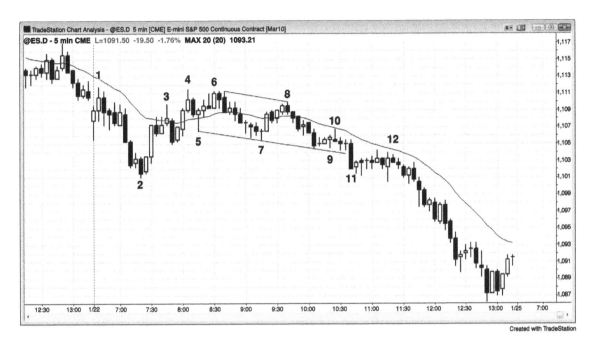

FIGURE 18.9   Failed Wedge Bull Flag

In Figure 18.9, the 5 minute Emini tried to form a wedge bull flag but failed. Bars 5, 7, and 9 were three pushes down, setting up a wedge bull flag long, but there was no reliable signal bar to go long around bar 9. This would have created a double bottom with the pullback after bar 3. Instead of forming a strong bull reversal setup, the market entered a small, tight trading range. The bar 11 downside breakout signaled the failure of the wedge bottom and set up the possibility of about a measured move down. Bar 11 became the spike for a protracted bear channel into the close.

CHAPTER 19

Dueling Lines: Wedge Pullback to the Trend Line

W hen a pullback is contained by a trend channel line and it ends at a higher time frame support or resistance line, this is a dueling lines pattern, and it often results in a reliable trade in the direction of the larger trend. It is a short-term trend (a pullback) ending at the long-term trend's support (in a bull trend) or resistance (in a bear trend). All pullbacks end in dueling lines patterns, although the support or resistance line is not always obvious. Any type of support or resistance can be the area where strong hands will come in and put an end to the pullback. Whenever traders see a pullback approaching a trend line, a trend channel line, a moving average, a prior swing low or high, or any other key price level, they should be alert for a setup that will lead to the end of the pullback and the resumption of the trend. When they see the setup, they are in a position to make a great trade. Remember, trading is becoming increasingly controlled by mathematics, and pullbacks end for a reason. A pullback in a bull trend always ends at a support level, and a pullback in a bear trend always ends at a resistance level, and therefore all pullbacks are dueling lines patterns. However, I reserve the term for those pullbacks where the support or resistance is seen by the trader, so that he can anticipate the possible trend resumption and place a trade. The most reliable form is when the pullback is in a channel and it has a wedge shape or three pushes, and the signal bar for the end of the pullback is a bar that pokes through the trend line and reverses. For example, if there is a bull trend and it is having a wedge bull flag pullback that is ending at the bull trend line, the trend channel line below the wedge bull flag is falling and it is intersecting the rising bull trend line exactly as the pullback is setting up a buy signal. The support line could be a horizontal line, like across a prior swing low, and this could set up a double bottom buy signal as the wedge is ending. The support could also come in the form of the moving average. When this happens, look to enter in the direction of the trend if there is an adequate setup.

As another example, look at a bear channel to see if there is a leg up within the channel. If so, look to see if that leg has three pushes. If the small bear rally is testing the bear trend line as it is also testing the trend channel line drawn across its highs, the odds are good that the leg up will end and the market will reverse down to test the lower end of the channel. If the market does turn down at this point, it is doing so because of the simultaneous testing of two resistance lines, even though one is rising and the other is falling, and having two types of resistance affecting the market at the same time increases the chance of a profitable trade.

Figure 19.1   DUELING LINES: WEDGE PULLBACK TO THE TREND LINE   **315**

FIGURE 19.1 Dueling Lines Pullback

All pullbacks end in dueling lines patterns, even if the long-term support is not readily seen. A pullback is a small trend in the opposite direction from the larger trend. All pullbacks always end for a reason, and a bull pullback always ends at some longer-term support, like a trend line, a measured move, or a prior swing high or low. In Figure 19.1, a bear trend channel line drawn between bars 3 and 5 created support for bar 6. All swing points should be considered when drawing trend lines and trend channel lines, even those from a prior trend. Bar 3 was a swing low in a bull trend, and bar 5 was a swing low in the correction of a possible new bear trend. The move down to bar 6 became just a large two-legged correction in the bull market. There were dueling lines at bar 6 (a bull trend line and a bear trend channel line of opposite slopes) and the market reversed up at the intersection, as is common. Since the move down to bar 6 was steep, it was reasonable to wait for the second entry at the bar 7 higher low, buying on a stop at one tick over its high.

A bear trend channel line could also have been based on a trend line drawn across the two swing highs that followed the bar 4 high, and then anchored to bar 5. The goal is to look at the overall shape and then choose any trend channel line that contains the price action. Then, watch how the market reacts after penetrating the line.

Deeper Discussion of This Chart

Bar 6 was a wedge bull flag in Figure 19.1. There was also a double top bear flag before the move down to bar 6, and a double top bear flag after a bull top can be thought of as a lower high that has two peaks.

Figure 19.2   DUELING LINES: WEDGE PULLBACK TO THE TREND LINE   **317**

FIGURE 19.2 Dueling Lines

As shown in Figure 19.2, bar 5 tested the bear trend line and as it did there was an overshoot of a smaller bull trend channel line (from bar 3 to bar 4), resulting in a short scalp off the dueling lines pattern. There was a second entry at the bar 6 nominal higher high. Since the move up to bar 5 was so strong, it is not surprising that after the market broke below the steep bull channel and tested the moving average, it had a breakout pullback to the higher high at bar 6. The channel is not shown, but it is the one that followed the bull spike up to bar 3.

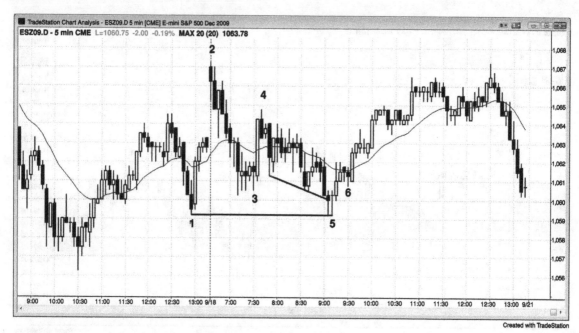

FIGURE 19.3 Dueling Lines Variant

Figure 19.3 is a variant of dueling lines where the long-term support came in the form of a horizontal line at a prior swing low and the result was a double bottom. This led to a reversal up from the new low of the day on this trading range day. The sell-off on the open was a bear spike, and the move from bar 4 to bar 6 was a channel.

Deeper Discussion of This Chart

The market broke out above a swing high in Figure 19.3, but the first bar of today was a bear trend bar and set up a failed breakout short. This was also an expanding triangle top, using either yesterday's 11:05 or 11:55 a.m. PST bar for the first push up. There was a spike up to bar 4, followed by a lower low pullback to bar 5, which formed a double bottom bull flag with bar 1. This led to a three-hour rally (the channel up from bar 5 after the bar 4 bull spike) and then a sell-off into the close. Even though it was a trading range day, it appears as a bear trend day on the daily chart because it opened near the high and closed near the low.

CHAPTER 20

"Reversal" Patterns: Double Tops and Bottoms and Head and Shoulders Tops and Bottoms

Since trends are constantly creating reversal patterns and they all fail except the final one, it is misleading to think of these commonly discussed patterns as reversal patterns. It is far more accurate to think of them as continuation patterns that rarely fail but, when they do, the failure can lead to a reversal. It is a mistake to see every top or bottom as a great reversal setup, because if you take all of those countertrend entries, the majority of your trades will be losers and your occasional wins will not be enough to offset your losses. However, if you are selective and look for other evidence that a trend might reverse, these can be effective setups.

All head and shoulders tops and bottoms are really head and shoulders continuation patterns (flags) because they are trading ranges and, like all trading ranges, they are much more likely to break out in the direction of the trend and only rarely reverse the trend. The same is true for double tops and bottoms. For example, if there is a head and shoulders top in a bull market, a breakout below the neckline will usually fail and the market will most likely then reverse up and have a with-trend breakout to the upside, above the right shoulder. The pattern becomes a triangle if it is mostly horizontal or a wedge bull flag if it is slightly sloping down. The three pushes down are the down legs after the left shoulder, the head, and the right shoulder. The right shoulder is an attempt to form a lower high after the move down from the head breaks the bull trend line. Since the move down from the head usually breaks below the bull trend line, the right shoulder becomes a lower high breakout pullback. Also, if there is a bear market that is forming a trading range and that trading range assumes the shape of a head and shoulders top, a break

319

below the neckline is a with-trend breakout of a bear flag and is likely to lead to lower prices.

Similarly, head and shoulders bottoms also are with-trend setups. A head and shoulders bottom in a bear trend is usually a triangle or a wedge bear flag and should break out to the downside, below the right shoulder. A head and shoulders bottom in a bull market is a bull flag and should break out to the upside, above the neckline.

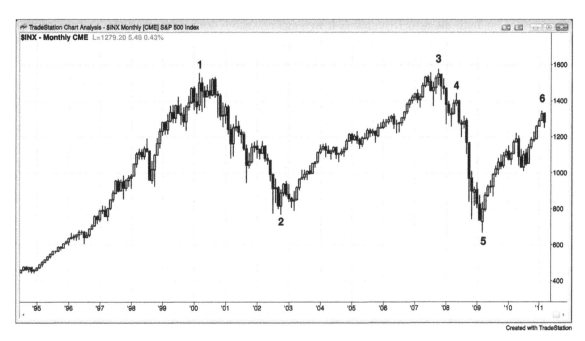

FIGURE 20.1   Monthly S&P Cash Index in a 12-Year Trading Range

There was a large double top in the monthly Standard & Poor's (S&P) cash index as shown in Figure 20.1. In the summer of 2007 when the market tested the 2000 high, all of those traders who had bought in the area of bar 1 wanted their money back. They had ridden through devastating losses down to bar 2. However, by bar 3 they had recovered those losses and did not want to risk another sell-off. They exited their positions and did not want to buy again until after a significant pullback. With a large block of buyers out of the market, short sellers took control and drove the market down. As so often happens, when traders want to buy a pullback, the pullback is so deep and violent that they change their minds, and this absence of buying sometimes causes the selling to accelerate. The cause is obviously much more complicated than this because there are countless participants acting for countless reasons, but this is a component.

The market often finds support in the area of the previous low. Here, the shorts who sold in the area of bar 2 were now back to around breakeven, and their exit led to a bounce. At this point the market was in a trading range, which could last a short or long time. Once a breakout arrived, it could be up or down. The standard entry of a double top is on a sell stop just below the low of the dip between the two tops. However, that is rarely successful because 80 percent of breakouts fail. That dip was bar 2 and the breakout below its low came six years later and failed.

With the rally from bar 5, it was clear that the double top was leading to a trading range and not a bear breakout. Very few traders who saw this as a large double top waited to short below bar 2. Most would have shorted around bar 3 or around the bar 4 lower high and low 2 that formed seven months later.

Over the next few years, the market could test down to around bar 5 after a double top pullback short setup, or even a head and shoulders top where the left shoulder is only slightly below the head. Since most tops fail, it is likely that it would then be followed by a rally, and the entire pattern would be a large wedge bull flag. This would then be followed by a breakout of the top of the pattern and an approximate measured move up over the next decade or two.

Incidentally, there were a couple of successful small double tops. The lower high that followed the bar 1 wedge formed a double top with bar 1. Also, the second push up to the bar 3 wedge was a double top with bar 3, even though it was a little lower than the bar 3 high.

Figure 20.2

"REVERSAL" PATTERNS   **323**

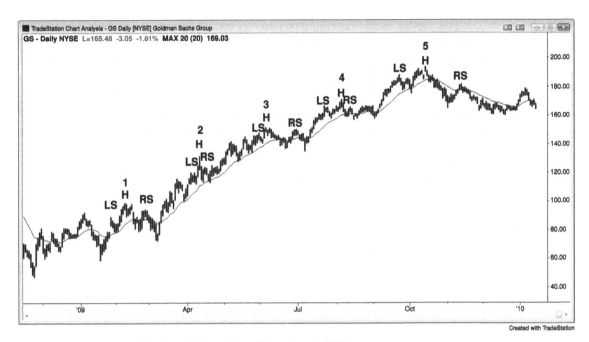

FIGURE 20.2   Most Head and Shoulders Tops Are Bull Flags

There were multiple head and shoulders tops on the Goldman Sachs (GS) daily chart shown in Figure 20.2. Head and shoulders formations have likely cost more beginning traders money than just about any other pattern, and this is probably due to so many pundits calling them reversal patterns when they are almost always continuation patterns. Head and shoulders tops are really triangles or wedge bull flags and are reliable buy setups. They are wedges because they have three pushes down, one after the left shoulder, a second after the head, and the third after the right shoulder. Since they are horizontal trading ranges in a bull trend, it makes sense that they should behave like any other trading range in a bull trend and lead to a bull breakout. Sometimes, like all continuation patterns, they fail to lead to a with-trend breakout and a reversal follows, and it is therefore misleading to attach terms like *top*, *bottom*, or *reversal* to them. These terms make traders look to do the opposite of what they should be doing, and it is therefore better not to use them. When you see one setting up in a bull trend, it is better to think of it as a wedge bull flag and call it that, because then you are looking to buy a pause in a bull trend, which is a profitable strategy. You should not call it a head and shoulders top since it is almost certainly not a top. Likewise, if you see a head and shoulders bottom forming in a bear trend, it is more accurate to instead call it a triangle or a wedge bear flag because this will make you look to short, which is the best way to make money in a bear trend.

The market is always trying to reverse, and the reversal attempts usually end when they are on the verge of reversing the always-in direction. All of the head and shoulders tops above are perfect examples. Many broke to the downside, but that is not enough for traders to believe that the trend has reversed. Traders also want to see follow-through. Since experienced traders know that most downside breakouts will not have follow-through, they look at these bear breakouts as great buying opportunities. Just as overly eager weak bears are shorting the strong bear trend bars that break below the necklines, triggering the head and shoulders top "reversal," the strong bulls step in and buy aggressively, correctly believing that the bear reversal will likely fail and simply become a bull flag.

Figure 20.3

"REVERSAL" PATTERNS **325**

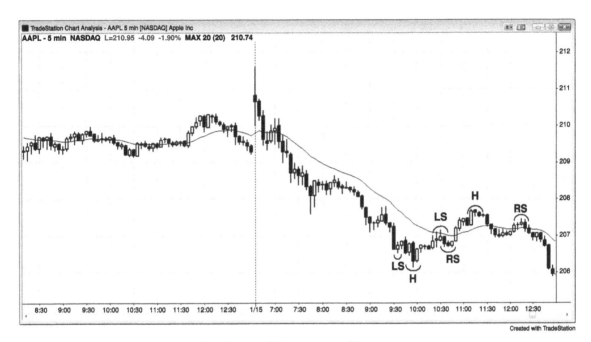

FIGURE 20.3 Head and Shoulders Top and Bottom Bear Flag

There was a failed head and shoulders bottom and a head and shoulders top bear flag in Apple (AAPL), as shown in Figure 20.3. The market was in a trend from the open bear trend and attempted to form a head and shoulders bottom (left shoulder, head, right shoulder), which, as expected, failed to reverse the market and instead evolved into a larger bear flag. The third push up of the wedge bear flag became the head of a head and shoulders top bear flag. The head of that head and shoulders top was the end of a two-legged rally that ended at a first moving average gap bar at 11:15 a.m. PST. The market tried to form a higher low after that head, but it failed and the small rally became the right shoulder, which was a breakout pullback from the channel up to the head. The breakout led to the test of the bear low, which was expected after a first moving average gap bar in a strong bear trend.

PART IV

Trading Ranges

The broadest and most useful definition of a trading range is that it is simply an area of two-sided trading. It can be as small as a single bar (a doji bar) or larger than all of the bars on your screen. It can be mostly horizontal, which indicates that the bulls and bears are in balance, or it can be slightly sloping. If it slopes up, the bulls are more aggressive. If it slopes down, the bears are stronger. If it slopes too much, it should be considered to be a trend channel and not a trading range. It can have very large swings lasting many bars or it can be very tight with each swing lasting only a bar or so, creating a narrow channel. When it is horizontal, the lines that contain it are support and resistance lines, with the support line below and the resistance line above.

The term trading range is usually applied to any section of a chart that is not trending and is mostly horizontal, but using the broader definition is more useful to traders because once you know that there is two-sided trading, you can look for opportunities to trade in both directions. Many beginners are too eager to look for reversals and can't resist trading them before the market is likely enough to transition from a trend to a trading range. However, once there is enough evidence that the transition is taking place, there are often high probability countertrend scalp and even swing setups. The key is to wait for enough evidence before taking them. Some patterns are usually not thought of as trading ranges but actually fit the broader definition of any area of the chart where there is two-sided trading taking place, which is most of the time. A trend has brief spikes where there is little two-sided trading, but most of the price action in a trend has some two-sided trading taking place and is therefore some type of trading range.

A pullback is a trading range where traders believe that the trend will soon resume. A traditional trading range is an area where there is uncertainty and the trend could resume or reverse, but most attempts to break out fail. A rising channel in a bull and a falling channel in a bear are sloping trading ranges, since both have two-sided trading, but the trend traders are more aggressive than the countertrend traders. They are also the first leg in a trading range that is not yet evident. For example, after the market spikes up in a strong series of large bull trend bars with only small tails and very little overlap, it soon enters a phase where there is more overlap of the bars, larger tails, some bear bodies, a shallower slope, and some pullbacks, even if they last for only a single bar. This is a bull channel, but all channels are basically trading ranges because they represent two-sided trading. If the channel is steeply up and the pullbacks are small, the bears are there but are getting overwhelmed by the bulls. A channel is made of a series of small trading ranges, each followed by a small breakout that leads to another small trading range. As the channel matures, the swings become larger as the bulls become less aggressive and the bears more aggressive. There will be a break below the channel and then usually a test to the bottom of the channel. At that point, the market had a leg up (the bull channel) and a leg down (the test of the bottom of the channel), and most traders will see the overall pattern as a trading range. It might form a double bottom bull flag or, at some point, the bears will take control and there will be a spike down and the process will reverse.

Here are some characteristics that are commonly found in trading ranges:

- There is a sense of uncertainty about the direction of the impending breakout. In fact, uncertainty is the hallmark of a trading range; whenever most traders are uncertain, the market is in a trading range (trends have a sense of certainty and urgency). Usually, however, a trading range is ultimately a trend resumption setup, which means that it is just pullback on a higher time frame chart.
- Almost all of the trades look like they are no more than 55 percent certain.
- There are both legitimate bull and bear setups forming at the same time.
- There are several changes in direction on your screen.
- The overall price action is mostly horizontal, with the bars on the left and right edges of the screen in the middle third of the screen vertically.
- Most of the bars are in the middle of the screen, and there are sharp reversals near the top and bottom.
- The market runs stops repeatedly, often with strong trend bars, but then reverses direction on the next bar. For example, the market will have two bear trend bars that fall below a strong swing low, but then the market reverses up on the next bar.
- There are many bull and bear trend bars but few instances where there are three or four consecutive bull trend bars or bear trend bars.

- Many bars have prominent tails.
- Many bars overlap 50 percent or more of the bar before.
- There are many areas where there are three or more bars that each overlap by 50 percent or more of the range of the prior bars.
- There are many dojis, which can be large or small.
- The moving average is relatively flat.
- The price action off the screen to the left was also in a trading range.
- There was just an impressive buy or sell climax.
- The vacuum effect is present, resulting in strong bull spikes at the top and strong bear spikes at the bottom, with both failing to break out and instead reversing back into the range.
- Many legs subdivide into two smaller legs and then reverse into a two-legged move in the opposite direction.
- Low 1 and low 2 short setups at the bottom and high 1 and high 2 buy setups at the top usually fail.
- Signal bars often look weak, even for second entries.

Any area of two-sided trading, even if it lasts for only a single bar, is a trading range. When you refer to a trading range as a pullback, you believe that the odds are favorable that the trend will soon resume and you will, therefore, likely be taking trades only in the direction of the trend. Every trader will have different criteria, but, in general, if you are about 60 percent or more certain that your trade will soon be followed by a resumption of the trend, then you believe that the pattern is a pullback. If instead you are less certain that your trade will be followed by a breakout, then the pattern is a trading range. A trading range is just a pullback that has lasted so long that it has lost its short-term predictive power, and 80 percent of the breakout attempts up or down will fail. If you buy near the bottom, the market will probably trade to the top, but instead of breaking out, there will be a sell setup and the market will return to the area of your long entry. If you short near the top, the market will probably trade down far enough to scalp a profit, but then rally back again to around your entry price. Ultimately, the odds favor that the trend that preceded the trading range will resume because it is simply a pullback on a higher time frame chart; however, if it lasts for days on the chart that you are trading, you will miss many trading opportunities if you simply place that single with-trend trade and wait for the breakout. Although you can trade it as a pullback on a higher time frame chart, most traders find it easier to make money if they watch and trade only a single chart, even though they are aware of setups on higher and lower time frame charts.

With a pullback, you should usually look to trade only in the direction of the trend, unless the pullback is likely to be large enough for a countertrend scalp. Most traders should still wait for the with-trend setup because countertrend scalping is a losing strategy for everyone except the most experienced traders. If you trade countertrend, you should do so only if you believe that the market will enter a trading range instead of just a pullback. With a trading range, you can trade in both directions, knowing that most breakout attempts up and down will fail. However, if there is a particularly strong setup at the bottom of a trading range in a bull market, you can consider swinging all or just part of your trade. Likewise, if there is a strong sell setup at the top of a trading range that followed a strong bear trend, you should swing part or all of your short position.

The final leg down in most trading ranges in bull markets is a bear channel, which is a last-ditch attempt by the bears to create a top and a new bear trend. A bear channel is a bull flag. Bulls can buy the reversal up from the bottom of the trading range or on the breakout pullback that usually follows soon afterward. When the trading range is in a bull market, the rallies tend to be stronger than the pullbacks, especially as the trading range nears its end. In addition, each pullback functions as a flag. The next rally is a breakout from that bull flag, and the next pullback is a breakout pullback setup, as well as another bull flag. One of those bull flags will be the final one, and its breakout will become the next leg up in the resumption of the bull trend. Since all trading ranges are pullbacks on higher time frame charts, that breakout will also be the breakout of that higher time frame bull flag. The opposite is true of trading ranges in bear trends, where the final leg is usually a bull channel, which is a bear flag.

Channels usually eventually evolve into trading ranges, and traders are always looking for the earliest signs of the transitions, because a channel is a trend, and traders are less willing to trade against it than they are in a trading range, where traders trade in both directions. Once traders believe that it has become a trading range, there will be spikes and channels in the opposite direction. Sometimes the trend will reverse (most reversal patterns are trading ranges), but more likely, the market will be in a trading range for at least 10 or 20 more bars.

Every channel has two-sided trading and is usually the start of a trading range. However, as long as the highs and lows keep trending, the channel is still in effect and the market has not yet converted to a trading range. For example, in a rising channel, the bulls will buy all pullbacks aggressively when the market gets near the most recent higher low, because they want everyone to see the market as still in a channel, which is a type of bull trend, and not in a trading range. This will make other traders more likely to buy, the rally more likely to continue, and their profit grow. Sometimes the market will fall below a minor higher low and find buyers. This new low is the basis for a new, flatter trend line (from the bottom of the channel) and a less steep, broader channel. It indicates that the price action is becoming more two-sided and therefore more like a trading range, but still in a channel. Once the market clearly enters a trading range, traders will start selling rallies, which will reduce the ability of the bulls to keep pushing the market higher and limit their ability to profit. As long as they can keep the market trending up, they know that most traders will only look to buy. The market will often pull pack to the most recent higher low and set up a double bottom bull flag. This is acceptable to the bulls because they know that it is a bullish setup and that the market will expect about a measured move up if the setup triggers (by trading above the high of the signal bar). At least they then have an idea of how much higher the rally might go, and this will give them a profit-taking target.

When the market is in its spike phase of a trend, it is very one-sided and pullbacks are created by institutions taking profits, not by them trading in the opposite direction. As pullbacks get deeper, countertrend traders begin to scalp. Once pullbacks grow into trading ranges, more countertrend traders are scalping and some are scaling into shorts. The with-trend traders become less confident about how much further the trend can go, and they transition from swing trading into more scalping. That is why in a trading range, scalping by both the bulls and bears is dominant. Both are buying low and selling high. The buying at the bottom is being done by bulls initiating longs and bears taking profits, and the selling at the top is by bears shorting and bulls taking profits. Since a trader's job is to follow the institutions, he too should be scalping, and buying near the bottom and selling near the top of the range. Whenever the market is in a trading range, traders should immediately think, "Buy low, sell high, and scalp."

Trading ranges have two-sided trading, where the bulls are stronger near the bottom and the bears are stronger near the top. Every rally in a trading range is essentially a bear flag and every selloff is effectively a bull flag. Because of this, traders trade the top of the range the way they trade a bear flag in a bear trend. They sell above and below bars, and above resistance and below support areas. They sell above bars, including strong bull trend bars, and above every type of resistance, because they see each move up as an attempt to break out of the top of the range, and they know that most breakout attempts fail. They sell below bars and below every type of support, because they see each move down as equivalent to a breakout of the bottom of a bear flag in a bear trend. They expect that attempts to break above the trading range will fail, that the bear flag breakouts will succeed, and that the market will soon reverse down and test the bottom of the range.

They trade the bottom of the range the way they trade a bull flag in a bull trend. They buy above and below bars, and above resistance and below support areas. They buy below bars, including strong bear trend bars, and below every type of support, because they see each a move down as an attempt to break out of the bottom of the range, and they know that most breakout attempts fail. They buy above bars and above every type of resistance, because they see each move up as equivalent to a breakout of the top of a bull flag in a bull trend. They expect that attempts to break below the trading range will fail, and that the bull flag breakouts will succeed, and that the market will soon reverse up and test the top of the range.

When the chart is trending, the trading ranges are relatively small and better described as pullbacks since they are just brief pauses in the trend and are followed by a test of the trend's extreme. If no test comes and the market reverses, what at first appeared to be a pullback has evolved into a reversal pattern. If the chart is composed of upswings and downswings across the entire screen, then neither the bulls nor the bears are dominant and they are alternating control over the market and the chart is then in a trading range. Each swing is a small trend that is potentially tradable, especially on a smaller time frame. On a larger time frame, the trading range will be a pullback in a trend. For example, a 5 minute chart that is a large trading range will likely be just a pullback in a trend on the 60 minute chart, and a 60 minute trading range will be a pullback on a daily or weekly chart.

Many traders use descriptive names like flags, pennants, or triangles, but the name is irrelevant. All that matters is that two-sided trading is taking place. The market is in breakout mode and at some point it will break out in either direction into another trend. Both the bulls and the bears believe that this price area is an area of good value, and both are initiating trades. Value exits at extremes. The market is either too cheap, as it is at support, or too expensive, as it is at resistance. The middle of a trading range is also an area of value for both the bulls and the bears, because both see it as an extreme. The bulls believe that the market is bottoming and therefore at a low, and the bears see it as topping and at a high. If the market drops a little, the bears will sell less and the bulls will become more aggressive at this better, more extreme price. This will tend to lift the market back toward the middle of the range. If the price goes up near the top of the range, the bulls will buy less, since they will see the market as a little expensive. The bears, in contrast, will be even more eager to sell at these better prices.

Even a steep channel represents breakout mode. For example, if there is a steep bull channel, the market can break out of the top of the channel and the trend can accelerate to the upside. When this happens, the breakout usually fails after one or two attempts and usually within about five bars, and if the market reverses back into the channel, it usually pokes through the opposite side of the channel and often is followed by a larger correction or a reversal. Even if a breakout spike lasts several bars, there is usually a pullback soon that tests the channel, and it often reenters the channel, breaks out of the other side, and then is followed by at least a two-legged correction and sometimes a trend reversal.

On a 5 minute Emini chart, when the market is in a relatively tight trading range where the swings are only two to four bars long before the market reverses toward the other side of the range, there is often much more going on than what appears to be happening. It is easy to ascribe the price action simply to random drift with light trading; but if you look at the volume, you will often discover that the bars are averaging 10,000 contracts or more. This is not light trading. What is probably happening is that many institutions are running buy programs while other institutions are running sell programs within the range. When the market gets near the top of the range, the sell programs are selling more aggressively; when it is near the bottom, the buy programs are overwhelming the sell programs. Neither side can win. At some point, either the buy programs will overwhelm the sell programs at the top of the range and the market will break out into a rally, or the sell programs will overwhelm the buy programs at the bottom of the range and the market will have a bear breakout. However, the trading range might have a dozen or more up and down swings before that happens, and since those dozen or so breakout attempts fail before one finally succeeds, it is far better to bet against them than to enter on each breakout attempt. It is important to understand that breakouts are common on every chart but most fail, as was discussed in Part I in the chapter on breakouts.

Trading ranges are always trying to break out, and because of this, the swings toward the top and bottom often have strong momentum with one or two, and sometimes three or four, large trend bars with small tails. On a test of the bottom of the range, the bears are trying to generate enough momentum to intimidate the bulls and attract other sellers so that there will be a breakout with follow-through. However, as the down leg begins, the bulls see the building downward momentum and are anticipating what the best price will be where they can buy aggressively again. The bears are also looking for a good price to take profits. What could be better than a couple of large bear trend bars that break below a swing low, especially if it is at another support area like a trend line or measured move target? Both the bulls and the bears wait for the market to test the bottom of the range, not caring if it undershoots it or overshoots it. As the market is falling toward the bottom of the range and the bulls and the bears expect it to go further to make a clear test, they have no incentive to buy when they believe they can buy even more cheaply if they wait a little more. When these institutional traders have stepped aside like this, there is a relative imbalance in the market, and the momentum often picks up as the market falls. This is the vacuum effect and it quickly sucks the market to the bottom of the range. Some large program traders trade momentum, selling aggressively when the momentum is strong and continuing to sell until the momentum down stops. This creates large bear trend bars that then are followed by a reversal up. It is common to see a large bear trend bar or two as the market tests the low of the range. Once it reaches a support level, which is usually a small measured move target, the buyers come in and aggressively buy. The bears buy back their shorts for a profit and the bulls buy new longs. This stops the momentum, causing the momentum traders to also stop selling and begin to buy back their shorts. With so many large traders buying aggressively and relentlessly, the market begins a swing up.

If you are an institutional bull or bear, this is perfect. You want to buy now that the market is at the bottom of the range, and what could be better than an overextended bear bar for your signal to buy? You believe strongly that the market will be going up, and here you have the market spiking down, showing extreme bearish strength. This is a great opportunity to buy since you believe the value is excellent and you know that if you are right, it will be at this low price only briefly. The institutional traders will appear out of nowhere and will buy aggressively. Some will buy on the close of that last big bear trend bar, whereas others will wait to see if the next bar is a pause bar. They will be even more confident if it has a bull close. If it is a pause bar, they will see that as more evidence that the bears are unable to follow through on their selling and are therefore weak. They might also wait for the market to trade above the high of the prior bar and actually reverse. There will be large bulls and bears buying at all of these signs and on all time frames, and they will have every imaginable signal telling them to enter.

Some of the profit-taking bears scaled in lower as the market fell. This made their average entry price fall as well, enabling them to aggressively buy back all of their shorts before the market reverses up to their average entry price to make sure that they have a profit when they exit. Since the shorts are buying and not selling and the bulls are now buying aggressively, there is a relative buy imbalance and the market again moves up toward the top of the range. The opposite happens at the top of the trading range, and strong bull trend bars often lead to selling by both the bulls taking profits and the bears initiating new shorts.

This is why trading ranges always race toward the top and toward the bottom and they always look like they are about to break out, only to reverse. It also explains why most breakouts of trading ranges fail and why there are bull trend bars that break out of the top and bear trend bars that break out of the bottom. The closer the market gets to the top or bottom of the range, the more traders believe that it will exceed the old extreme, at least by a tick or two. The top and bottom of a trading range have a magnetic pull that gets greater as the market gets closer to the top or bottom because large traders who expect the market to reverse are just waiting for the best price and then they suddenly enter aggressively, reversing the market. This is true for all trading ranges, including bull and bear channels, triangles, and bull and bear flags.

Never get trapped by the strong momentum surges toward the top or bottom of a trading range. You need to be following what the institutions are doing, and what they are doing is selling strong bull trend bars at the top of the range and buying strong bear trend bars at the bottom, exactly when the market looks like it has the strength to break out. Only traders who are very experienced reading charts should fade the market on the close of breakout bars. Almost all traders are more likely to be successful if they wait to enter on a stop as the market reverses back into the range. Also, they should take the trade only if the signal bar is not too large, because they need to be entering near the extreme of the range and not in the middle.

Eventually a breakout will be successful, but the prior five to ten attempts will all look very strong and fail. Because of this math, it is far better to expect failure. When a successful breakout happens, look to enter the new trend on a pullback or even during the breakout if it looks strong enough, and the overall context makes a breakout likely to succeed. But until then, follow the institutions; as soon as they are able to create a reversal (a failed breakout) near the top or bottom of the range, take the reversal entry. In Part I, the chapter on breakouts discusses how successful breakouts typically appear.

Since a trading range in a bull trend is a bull flag, and it is just a pullback on a higher time frame chart, a trader could buy the breakout on a stop and use a protective stop well below the bottom of the trading range. The chance of any one breakout being successful is about 20 percent, but the chance that the market will eventually break to the upside is about 60 percent. However, it might break to the upside and to the downside several times before the bull trend resumes, so if traders buy a breakout and do not want to get stopped out, they need to place their protective stops far enough below the trading range so that the repeated failed downside breakouts will not stop them out. Few traders are willing to risk that much and wait that long, so the majority of them should not buy most trading range breakouts. Sometimes a breakout above a trading range in a bull trend is a good entry on a buy stop, but only when the bull trend clearly has started to resume before the breakout. Even then, it is usually better to enter within the trading range as the bull trend is resuming or to wait for the breakout and either buy after the breakout, once it is clearly strong, or buy a breakout pullback, when one eventually forms.

The media makes it sound like traders oscillate between fear and greed. That is probably true for beginners, but not for experienced traders, who rarely feel either. Another pair of emotions is much more common with them, and also much more useful: uncertainty and urgency. A trend is an area of certainty, or at least relative certainty. Your personal radar can tell you if the market is more likely in a trend instead of a strong leg within a trading range. If you have a sense of uncertainty, the market is more likely in a trading range; if instead you have a sense of urgency and you are hoping for a pullback, then the market is more likely in a trend. Every trend is made of a series of spikes and trading ranges, and the spikes are brief. When they exist, there is a directional bias to the probabilities. This means that during a spike in a bull trend, the odds of the market moving X ticks higher before it moves X ticks lower are more than 50 percent, and can be 70 percent or more if the trend is strong. Both the bulls and the bears agree that the market needs to move to a new price level, where uncertainty will return. A trading range is that area of uncertainty, and whenever you are uncertain about the direction of the market, it is likely in a trading range. Within the middle of a trading range, the probability of the market moving up or down X ticks is about 50 percent most of the time. There are brief fluctuations in this probability, but most of them last for too few ticks to be traded profitably. This search for uncertainty is the basis of measured moves. The market will continue its higher-probability directional move until the odds fall below 50–50, meaning that a reversal is likely (the odds are greater that the market will now move in the opposite direction). Most of the time, that will occur at some area of support or resistance, like a prior swing point or trend line or trend channel line, and most of the time it will be in the area of some measured move. The reversal is a move toward what will become the middle of a trading range where there is a 50 percent chance of the market moving up or down X ticks before it goes X ticks in the opposite direction.

When you are completely neutral about a trading range, the directional probability of an equidistant move is 50 percent, and the market is around what will become the middle of the range. As the market works toward the top of the range, the odds favor the market going down, and the directional probability is 60 percent or more that the market will fall X ticks before it goes up X ticks. Near the bottom of the range, that is reversed, and the directional probability favors a rally. If there has been a strong bull trend leading up to the range and there has not been a clear top, then there is a directional bias in favor of the bulls, even when the market is in the middle of the trading range. If the trend was very strong, then the directional probability in the middle of the range might be 53 to 55 percent, although it is impossible to ever be certain. Just be aware that trading ranges are continuation patterns on higher time frame charts, and if there was a strong bull trend leading up to it and no clear top, the odds of an upside breakout are greater. Following a strong bull trend, when the market falls to the bottom of the range, the directional probability of an equidistant move is greater than at the bottom of a trading range that formed after a bear trend, so instead of 60 percent in favor of a rally, maybe it is 70 to 80 percent. In fact, the odds of a rally that is twice or three times X ticks before a sell-off of X ticks might even be 70 percent or higher. For example, if the trading range is 50 ticks tall and you bought above a bull reversal bar on a two-legged pullback to the bottom of the range, and the bar is eight ticks tall, there might be a 70 percent chance of the market rallying 20 or 30 ticks before hitting your stop 10 ticks below your entry. Likewise, near the top of the range, the directional probability of an equidistant move is less than in a trading range that followed a bear trend, and instead of a 70 percent to 80 percent chance of the market falling X ticks before rallying X ticks, those odds might be more like 60 percent. Again, no one can ever know the exact odds, but it is helpful to be aware of the bias because it should influence you when you are thinking about taking a trade. You should be more inclined to buy near the bottom of a trading range in a large bull market than you are to short at the top.

Neither the bulls nor the bears know the direction of the breakout, but both are comfortable trading within the range; and because of the tendency of bulls to buy less and bears to sell more at the top of the range and to do the opposite at the bottom, the market spends most of the time somewhere in the middle. This area of comfort has a magnetic pull, and whenever the market moves from it, the market gets drawn back into it. Even if there is a successful breakout that runs several bars, it usually will get pulled back into the range, and that is the basis for final flags, which are discussed in book 3. It is also common to see a breakout in one direction that runs for several bars, then a reversal, then a breakout in the opposite direction, and then a pullback into the range. The magnetic effect of a trading range can affect the market for several days, and it is common to see the market trend away from a strong trading range, like a relatively tight range that lasted 10 or more bars, only to come back into the range two or three days later.

What causes either the bulls or the bears in a trading range to change their perspective, eventually allowing a breakout to succeed? Rarely, there will be a news item like a Federal Open Market Committee (FOMC) report that is expected at a specific time in the middle of the day, but most of the time the breakout is unanticipated. There will always be a news-related reason for the breakout given on TV, but most of the time it probably is irrelevant to what is taking place. Once the market breaks out, CNBC will find some pundit who will confidently explain how it was the direct result of some news item. If instead the market broke out in the opposite direction, the pundit would then argue the opposite interpretation of the same news item. For example, if the market broke out to the upside on an FOMC interest rate cut, the pundit would argue that lower rates are good for the market. If it broke to the downside on the same rate cut, the pundit would argue that the rate cut is proof that the Federal Reserve thinks the economy is weak and therefore the market is overpriced. Both explanations are irrelevant and have nothing to do with what just took place. Nothing is ever that simple and, in any case, it is irrelevant to a trader. Most of the volume every day is generated by programs; there are dozens of big ones running before and during the breakout, and they are designed independently of one another by different firms that are each trying to take money from the others. The logic behind the programs is unknowable and therefore irrelevant. All that matters to traders is the net result. As a trader, you should follow the institutions, and if they are driving the market up, you should follow them and be a buyer. If they are driving the market down, you should follow them and be a seller.

Almost invariably, the breakout will be unfolding over the course of 10 or more bars before it finally succeeds, which might be an hour before the news was released. The market has already made up its mind about the direction of the breakout, no matter what the news will be, and if you can read the price action, you can often position yourself before the breakout occurs.

For example, if the bulls begin to become impatient because they thought that the market should have broken out of the upside by now, they will start to sell out of their longs. This will add to the selling pressure of the bears. Also, those bulls will likely want significantly lower prices before looking to buy again, and their absence of buying at the bottom of the range will remove buying pressure; the result will be that prices will fall down in a bear trend to a lower level where the bulls see value again, and another trading range will form. In an upside breakout, the opposite happens. Bears are no longer willing to short within the range and they will buy back their shorts, adding to the buying pressure of the bulls. They will look to short again only at a significantly higher price, which creates a thin area where the bulls move the market up quickly in a bull breakout. The market will continue to move up quickly in a bull trend until it reaches a level where the bears once again believe that there is value in shorting and the bulls start to take profits on their longs. Then, two-sided trading will resume and another trading range will form.

If the sideways price action has lasted for about 5 to 20 bars and is very tight, then a trader has to be particularly careful because the bulls and bears are in very tight balance. Trading breakouts in this situation can be costly since every brief up move is sold aggressively by the bears and the new bulls are quick to exit. This results in tails at the tops of the bars near the top of the range. Likewise, every sharp move down is quickly reversed, creating tails at the bottoms of the bars near the bottom of the range. There are, however, ways to profitably trade this type of market. Some firms and many traders are scaling into longs and out of shorts every few ticks lower and doing the opposite every few ticks higher. However, this is tedious and minimally profitable at best for individual traders, and they will find themselves too tired to trade well once a successful breakout finally occurs.

In general, all trading ranges are continuation patterns, meaning that they more often than not break out in the direction of the trend that preceded them. They also tend to break out away from the moving average. If they are below the moving average, they usually break to the downside, and if they are above it, they tend to break out to the upside. This is especially true if the trading range is adjacent to the moving average. If they are far from the moving average, they may be setting up a test back to the moving average. If a bull swing pauses in a trading range, the odds favor the ultimate breakout taking place to the upside. However, there may be several failed breakouts of the top and bottom before the final breakout, and sometimes the market breaks out countertrend. Also, the longer a trading range continues, the greater are the odds that it will become a reversal pattern (accumulation in a bear trading range, distribution in a bull trading range). This is because the with-trend traders will become concerned that they are failing to make the trend resume, and they will begin to cover their positions and will stop adding to them. Because of these uncertainties, traders need to be careful and look for low-risk price action setups. Trading ranges on a 5 minute chart that last for hours with many big, hard-to-read swings can be small, clean, and easy-to-read trading ranges on a 15 or 60 minute chart, so it sometimes is helpful to look at higher time frames. Many traders, in fact, trade higher time frame charts.

The chart on your screen is in a trading range most of the time, with the bulls and the bears in general agreement about value. Within the trading range, there are small trends; and within those trends, there are small trading ranges. When the market is trending, the bulls and the bears are also in agreement about value, and the agreement is that the value area is somewhere else. The market is moving quickly to a trading range where both bulls and bears feel there is value, and they will fight it out until it becomes clear that one side is right and the other is wrong, and then the market will trend again.

Some trading range days are composed of two or three large trending swings; during the swings, the market behaves like a strong trend. However, the first reversal usually does not begin until after the first hour or so, and a trend day is usually underway before then. When a trend starts too late, there is a good chance that the day will be a trading range day and that there will be at least a second reversal and a test of the middle of the range.

The middle third of the day, from around 8:30 a.m. until 10:30 a.m. PST, can be difficult for traders on days that are not clearly trending (in other words, most days). If the market is trading in the approximate middle of the day's range (or just the middle of a trading range within the day's range) and it is now in the middle of the day's trading hours, the chance of a tight trading range with overlapping bars, big tails, and multiple small reversals is significant, and most traders would be wise to trade sparingly. It is usually better to forgo any less than perfect entry under these circumstances and instead wait for a test of the high or low of the day. A trader who is not yet successful should not trade when the market is in the middle of the day while it is also in the middle of the day's range. This change to one's trading alone can mean the difference between being a loser and a winner.

Sometimes there will be an extremely great-looking pattern setting up midday in the Emini and you will get one tick of slippage on the entry. If the market does not race to your profit target within seconds, the chances are high that you have been trapped. In this case, it is almost always better to place a limit order to get out at breakeven. Whenever something looks too good to be true, so obvious that everyone will look to enter, the odds are high that it is exactly as it appears to be—not true.

Whenever there is a spike up and then a spike down, or vice versa, the market has formed a climax reversal, which is discussed in the third book. A spike is usually followed by a channel; but since there have been spikes in both directions, the bulls and bears will continue trading aggressively as they try to overpower each other and create a channel in their direction. This two-sided trading that usually takes place after a climax is a trading range, and it can be as brief as a single bar or can last for dozens of bars. The eventual breakout will usually lead to a measured move that approximates the height of the spike.

A trading range can sometimes appear to be a reversal setup but in fact be just a pause in the trend. For example, if there is a strong bull trend on the 60 minute chart and the 5 minute chart has a strong spike down that lasts several bars, which is followed by a pullback rally that lasts several bars and then a second spike down for several more bars, the pattern might look strongly bearish on the 5 minute chart, but it could be a simple high 2 or double bottom buy setup on the 60 minute chart. This is especially true if the ABC ends at the 60 minute moving average. You do not have to look at the 60 minute chart, but you should always be aware of the direction of the trend that preceded the trading range. This will give you more confidence to place the trade, which here is a large high 2 buy pattern and not the start of a new bear trend.

Sometimes the low of a bear trend day, especially a climactic one, can come from a small trading range that has large bars, often with large tails or large reversal bodies. These reversals are less common at tops, which tend to be less climactic than bottoms. These trading ranges are often other signals as well, such as double bottom pullbacks or double top bear flags.

Even though trading ranges are flags on higher time frame charts and usually break out in the direction of the trend, some break out in the opposite direction. In fact, most reversal patterns are some type of trading range. A head and shoulders pattern is an obvious one. A double top and a double bottom are also trading ranges. This is discussed further in the chapter on trend reversals in book 3, but it is important to realize that most trading ranges within trends break out in the direction of the trend and do not lead to reversals. Therefore, all reversal patterns are actually continuation patterns that occasionally fail to continue and instead reverse. Because of this, it is far better to look for with-trend entries when you see a reversal pattern than to look for reversal entries. This means that if there is a bull trend and it is forming a head and shoulders top, it is far better to look for a buy signal as the market tries to break out to the downside than it is to short on the breakout.

All trends contain trading ranges of different sizes and some trends are predominantly trading ranges, like trending trading range days, which were discussed earlier in book 1, Chapter 22. You should be aware that the market often tries to reverse the final trading range in the last hour or so, so if the day is a bear trending trading range day, look for a buy setup at the low of the day going into the final hour or two of the day.

Some experienced traders are good at knowing when a trend is evolving into a trading range, and they will scale into countertrend trades once they believe it is happening. For example, if the day is a bull trending trading range day and the breakout has reached the area of the measured move based on the height of the lower trading range, and if the rally has been in a relatively weak bull channel, bears will begin to short above prior swing highs. They will also watch for a relatively large bull trend bar and short its close or above its high, since it could be a buy climax and be the end or near the end of the bull channel and, therefore, near the top of a trading range. Only very experienced traders should attempt this, and most of those traders will trade small enough so that they can scale into their short positions if the market continues higher. If it does go higher and they scale in, some would take profits on their entire position once the market pulls back to their first entry. Others will exit the first entry at breakeven and hold the remainder for a test of the bottom of the channel. As the bull channel is progressing, beginners will see only a bull trend, but experienced traders will see the first leg of a developing trading range. Once the day is over and beginners look back, they will see the trading range and agree that it began at the bottom of the bull channel. However, as that bull channel progressed, beginners did not realize that the market was in both a bull channel and a trading range. As beginners, they should not be shorting in a bull trend, and should consider trading in a trading range only if there is a strong signal, preferably a second signal. The experienced traders who shorted were scalping because they saw the market as entering a trading range and not reversing into a bear trend. When the market is in a trading range, traders should generally only be scalping until the next trend begins, at which point they can once again swing part or all of their trades.

The single most difficult aspect of trading in a trading range is the trading range dilemma. Since most breakouts fail, your profit goals are limited, which means that you are scalping. However, when you reduce your reward yet keep your risk the same, you need a much higher probability of success to satisfy the trader's equation. Otherwise, you are trading a strategy that is guaranteed to eventually blow your account (i.e., drop it to below the minimum margin requirements for your broker to allow you to place trades). The dilemma is that you have to scalp, but scalping requires a very high probability of success, and that high degree of certainty cannot exist for long in a trading range, where by definition uncertainty prevails. If the range is particularly tight, the chance of success is even smaller. One way to improve your chance of success is to enter with limit orders as the market is going against you. For example, some traders will short above a weak-looking high 1 or high 2, or above a swing high or bull trend bar at the top of the range. They might also buy below a weak low 1 or low 2, or a swing low or bear trend bar at the bottom of the range. Another approach is to take a smaller initial position and scale in if the market goes against you.

If the range is large enough, most traders try to short small bear reversal bars at the top of the range and buy small bull reversal bars at the bottom of the range, especially when there are second entries, like shorting a low 2 at the top of the range or buying a high 2 at the bottom of the range. Remember, although both high 2 and low 2 setups are valid in trading ranges, traders trade them differently from when they form in trends. When there is a bull trend, traders will buy a high 2 near the top of a leg, but when there is a trading range, they will buy a high 2 only if it is at the bottom of the range. Similarly, bears will short a low 2 at the bottom of a bear trend but they will short a low 2 in a trading range only when it is at the top of the range.

Since a trading range is simply a horizontal channel, you trade it like any other channel. If the swings are small, you scalp; if they are large, you can scalp or swing some of your position to the opposite end. If the trading range is very large and has lasted several days, entire days can be strong trends and still be within the trading range. When that happens, trade the day like any other trend day. If the swings are very small, the trading range is a tight trading range, which is discussed Chapter 22. The tighter the range, the fewer trades you should take. When the range is a tight trading range, you should rarely take any trades.

When the market is in a trading range, look to buy near the bottom of the range and short near the top. In general, if the market has been going down for about 5 to 10 bars, only look to buy, especially if the market is near the bottom of the range. If the market has been going up for five to 10 bars, only look to short, especially if it is near the top of the range. Trade in the middle of the range only if the swings are large enough to make a profit. For example, if the trading range is 10 ticks tall, you do not want to buy six ticks above the low of the range, since the odds of the market going six ticks further up are not great and that is what you would need to make a four-tick profit. If the trading range is six points tall, you can buy a higher low and enter in the middle of the range since there is room above to make a scalper's profit before the market encounters the resistance of the top of the range. The chapter on channels in book 1 discusses how to trade them, and since a trading range is simply a horizontal channel, the techniques are the same.

Most of the bars will be in the middle of the range, and the market spends very little time at the extremes. When it is at the extremes, it usually got there with a strong trend bar, making many traders believe that the breakout will be successful and strong. There will often be three or more large, overlapping bars with a signal bar forcing bulls to buy near the high tick, and this usually is a trap. For example, suppose the market just raced to the bottom of the range with a couple of strong bear trend bars but has been sideways for a couple of bars, sitting just below the moving average; now there is a strong bear reversal bar, but it mostly overlaps the prior bars, and the entry price would be within a tick or so of the bottom of the bear flag. In this situation, don't take the trade. This is usually a bear trap, and it is much better to place a limit order to buy at the low of that bear reversal bar than to place a stop order to go short at one tick below its low. Take this fade only if you are experienced with your read.

The best entries are second entries at the top or bottom of the range where the signal bar is a reversal bar in your direction that is not too large and does not overlap the prior bar too much. However, the appearance of the signal bar is less important for trading range reversals than for trend reversals. Short setups at the top of the range often have signal bars with bull bodies, and buy setups near the bottom of the range often have bear bodies. A strong reversal bar is not usually mandatory unless a trader is looking to take a reversal trade in a strong trend.

Most traders will lose money if they scalp, even if they win on 60 percent of their trades. This is especially true if their risk is about twice as large as their potential reward. This means that traders have to be very careful with trading range trades. Given that 80 percent of breakout attempts fail, a trading range trader has to have limited goals, and many of the best trades will be big scalps or small swings. For example, if the average daily range in the Emini has recently been approximately 10 to 15 points, the average protective stop will be about two points. If traders are shorting below a strong bear signal at the top of a trading range that is at least six points tall, especially if they are taking a second signal, they have at least a 60 percent chance of making two points while risking two points. This results in a minimally profitable trader's equation and is therefore a successful strategy. If it appears that the move could fall four points, traders might take a quarter to half off at two points and try to swing the remainder for about four points. They might move the stop to breakeven after taking two-point partial profits, or they could tighten it from two points to maybe one point (four ticks) or five ticks. At that point, they are risking five ticks to make four points, and even if the chance of success is only 40 percent, they have a winning trader's equation. Some traders who took partial or full profits at two points will place limit orders to short again at their original entry price, but risk only about five ticks this time. They might try for two to four points on their trade, depending on the overall market. If the entry bar or the following bar becomes a strong bear bar, they will be inclined to hold for a larger move.

If the trading range is only three or sometimes even four points tall, entering on stops is usually a losing strategy. The trading range is then a relatively tight trading range, which is discussed later, and only very experienced traders should trade it. Most of the trades require limit order entries, and beginners should never buy when the market is falling or sell when it is rallying, because they invariably will choose situations in which the move will go so far that they will become frightened and exit with a loss.

Regardless of how tall the range is, if you are looking to trade and the leg that is testing the top or bottom of the range is a tight channel, it is better to wait for a breakout pullback, which is a second entry. So if the market has been going up for 10 bars and is near the top of the trading range, but these 10 bars are in a micro channel, do not short below the low of the prior bar—the upward momentum is too strong. Instead, wait to see if there is a pullback from this micro channel breakout. The pullback can be any test of the top of the channel, including a lower high, double top, or a higher high. Then look to short below the low of the prior bar and place a protective stop above the high of the signal bar. The setup is more reliable if that signal bar is a good bear reversal bar, especially if it is not too large. If it is too large, it will likely overlap one or more bars too much and will have you shorting too far below the high of the range. When this happens, it is usually better to wait for a pullback before shorting.

Any short setup is also more reliable if there is other evidence of strong bears entering the market within the prior 10 bars, like two or three bars around this level with large tails on top, or several recent bars with strong bear bodies. This represents building selling pressure and increases the chances that the trade will be successful. Similarly, if you are looking to buy at the bottom of the range and there are a few bars at this level with large tails on the bottom or several bars with bull bodies, then the bulls are becoming aggressive, and this buying pressure increases the chances of a profitable long trade. If there is support or resistance like a dueling lines pattern near your entry, the odds of a successful trade increase.

Trading ranges always look like they are breaking out, but the majority of breakout attempts fail. The extremes are often tested by large trend bars, and, if you are an experienced trader, you can fade the close of one of these bars. Although it is safer to wait for the breakout to fail before entering (breakouts and failures were discussed in Part I), if you are confident that the trend bar is just running stops beyond a swing high or low, you can enter of the close on the bar, especially if you can scale in if the market goes against you. For example, if the market has been in a quiet trading range for the past three hours and just formed a two-legged move down below a prior swing low, and the close was on the low of the bar, you can consider buying at the market on the close of the bar. If most of the up legs have had more momentum than the down legs, the odds are better, and they are better still if the trend bar is testing a trend line, a trend channel line, a measured move target, or other support level.

Since not all of the swings reach the extreme of the range, you can consider scaling into a trade. For example, if the market has been going up for eight bars and is forming a low 3 below the top of the trading range, you can consider shorting the low 3 setup and using a wide stop of maybe four points in the Emini on a day when the average range has been about 10 points. If the low 3 succeeds and you have a profitable trade, you exit. If the low 3 fails, it is likely that there will soon be a low 4 and that it will be successful. If so, you can scale into the trade by shorting a fixed number of ticks above your entry, or above the high of a prior bar or swing high, or on a stop on the low 4 signal. You can then exit both short positions near the bottom of the range or maybe at the entry price of the first short. This entry would then be a breakeven trade and the second, higher entry would be profitable. Scaling in and out of trades is discussed in Chapter 31.

Because trading ranges are two-sided, pullbacks are common. If you take a trade in a trading range, you have to be willing to sit through a pullback. However, if the trading range might be turning into a trend, you should exit if the market goes against you and wait for a second signal. Your odds of success are greater if you have the ability to scale in as the market goes against you.

If the market is at the bottom of the range and the downward momentum is weak and the market reverses up for a bar or two, it might be setting up a low 1 short. Since you should short a low 1 setup only in the spike phase of a bear trend and not in a trading range, it is unlikely that this low 1 would be profitable. You then believe that the odds are that a short below the low of the prior bar would go up eight ticks before it falls six ticks. That means that it makes sense to place a limit order to buy at or a couple of ticks below the low of the prior bar, expecting a failed low 1 short and a higher low. Also, if you believe that the market is forming a bull channel, you expect the low 2 to fail as well, and you therefore can place a limit order to buy at or below the low of the low 2 signal bar. You can do the opposite near the top of the range as the market is turning down and forming low-probability high 1 and high 2 buy setups. Place a limit order to short at or just above the high of the high 1 or high 2 signal bar.

Since the legs in a trading range often subdivide into two smaller legs, you can fade the breakout of the prior leg. Buying a breakout above a swing high usually yields a profitable trade only in a strong bull trend, and shorting below a swing low is usually profitable only in a strong bear trend. If the market just pulled back from the first leg down in a trading range, the odds of a successful short trade where you enter on the breakout of the bottom of that first leg are small. Instead, you can consider placing a limit order to buy a few ticks below that low for a scalp up.

Because most breakout attempts fail, never overstay any trade hoping for a successful breakout. Look to exit longs on scalp profit targets or on tests of the top of the range, and take profits on shorts on limit orders that give a scalper's profit or exit on a test of the bottom of the range. Never rely on martingale trading. This is discussed in Chapter 25, but it is a gambling technique where you double or triple the size of your next trade if you just lost on your prior trade. If you keep losing, you keep doubling or tripling the size of your prior trade until you win. Almost invariably when you are thinking about this, the market is in a tight trading range and will likely have four or more consecutive losers; you would therefore abandon the approach because it would require you to trade far more contracts than you can handle emotionally, and this will leave you with a huge loss. A breakout or a winning trade is never overdue, and the market can sustain unsustainable behavior much longer than you can sustain your account. Be fussy and take only reasonable entries, and never base any entry on the idea that the market is overdue for a good trade.

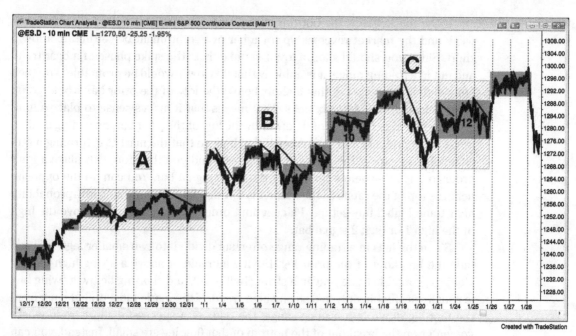

FIGURE PIV.1 Most of the Bars on Any Chart Are within Trading Ranges

The market is composed of trading ranges separated by brief trends, and each trading range is made up of smaller trends and trading ranges. Figure PIV.1 is a 10 minute chart of the Emini that shows about six weeks of price action. If a trader were watching only a 5 minute chart with about a day and a half of data, it would be easy to overlook the big picture. Some of the days were small trading range days, but those days were in the context of a large bull market. The large trading ranges are labeled with letters and the small trading ranges with numbers (the numbers refer to the trading ranges and not the bars). Although trading ranges repeatedly try to break out of the top and bottom and 80 percent of those attempts fail, when the breakout does come, it is usually in the same direction as the trend that preceded it. Most reversal patterns are trading ranges, like the rightmost trading range (13), but most reversal attempts turn into flags and break out in the direction of the trend.

While the market is in a trading range, traders can take trades in both directions, looking for small profits on each trade, but when there is a strong buy setup at the bottom of a trading range in a bull trend, a trader can swing part or all of the trade. For example, within the large B trading range, there were three pushes down, creating a triangle, and each push down tested the top of the large A trading range. The small 8 trading range also had a double bottom, and it was a bull flag down from the 6 trading range. A day trader might have swung a long into the close of the day, but traders willing to hold a position overnight saw that this was a good buy setup for a trade that could last several days.

Notice how the final leg down of most trading ranges is a bear channel, which is a last-ditch attempt by the bears to create a top and a new bear trend. A bear channel is a bull flag. Bulls can buy the reversal up from the bottom of the trading range or on the breakout pullback that usually follows soon afterward. The opposite is true of trading ranges in bear trends, where the final leg is usually a bull channel, which is a bear flag.

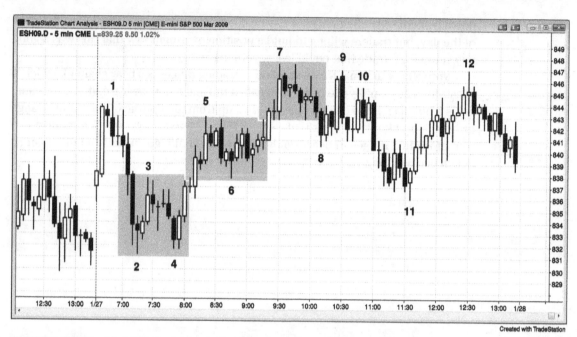

FIGURE PIV.2   Multiple Early Reversals Often Lead to a Trading Range Day

Multiple reversals in the first couple of hours usually result in a trading range day. Big traders often come into the day expecting a trading range day, and when enough do, their scalping and reversing often result in one forming. As shown in Figure PIV.2, today broke out but then reversed down at bar 1 and reversed up at bar 2. The reversal failed at bar 3, but the attempt at a bear channel failed at bar 4, and the market reversed up again. The bull spike up to bar 5 had two pauses along the way, indicating hesitancy. After the spike up, the market went sideways for about 10 bars and had many small reversals within the bull flag, as well as five bear bodies, again showing that the market was very two-sided, which is the hallmark of a trading range. Bar 7 was a bull trend bar to a new high of the day, but was immediately followed by a bear inside bar instead of two or three more bull trend bars. The market then had several large dojis; two of them had big tails on the top, showing that traders aggressively sold into the close of the bars (selling pressure). This shows that the bears were very strong at the high of the day, which is what commonly happens in a trading range. The directional probability of an equidistant move rose in favor of the bears. In this case, the odds of a two-point move down before a two-point move up might have been 60 percent. Although it is impossible to know exactly, traders believed that the shorts had the edge. Most traders suspected at this point that the day was a trading range day and the odds of a move down below the middle of the range were good. If traders shorted at any point after bar 7 and risked about two to three points, they probably had about a 60 percent chance of the market testing below the midpoint of the day, which was five to eight points lower, depending on where they shorted. Risking two points to make five points with 60 percent certainty is a great trade.

The middle of the day on a trading range day is a magnet and usually gets tested repeatedly during the day, including after the breakout to a new high. Also, since trading range days usually close in the middle of the day's range, look to fade tests of the extremes, like at bars 7, 9, 10, and 12. Traders were shorting above swing highs, like above bars 1, 3, and 5, and they were adding on, maybe at one or two points higher. If they added on, many traders would have exited some or all of their positions when the market returned to the original entry price. This would be a breakeven trade, but they would have a profit on their higher entries. If the market immediately went their way, they would scalp out of most or all of their positions because on trading range days it is better to scalp unless you are shorting at the very top or bottom of the day, where you can swing part of your position for a test of the middle of the day or even a test of the opposite extreme. Bulls bought below bars 6 and 8, and many were willing to scale in lower.

In general, doing the opposite of what you would do on a trend day is effective, especially if you can scale in. Once traders believe that the day is a trading range day, they will place trades based on that belief. Instead of looking to buy a high 1 or high 2 near the high, it is better to short above those signal bars. Instead of looking to short a low 1 or low 2 near the bottom of the range, it is better to buy below those bars. Traders enter on limit and market orders. Some look at a smaller time frame chart, wait for a reversal bar, and then enter on stops on the reversal. Traders will be scalping all day, expecting just about every move to not go far before reversing again. They will short above the high of prior bars and add on higher, and they will buy below the low of prior bars and add on lower. They will also fade large trend bars near the top and bottom of the developing range. The bulls saw the large bull trend bar that formed two bars before bar 1 as a brief opportunity to take profits at a high price. The bears also doubted there would be follow-through buying and shorted. Both the bulls and the bears sold at the close of the big bull trend bar, above its high, on the close of the two bear bars that followed, and below the low of the bear bars.

Once the market formed a large bear trend bar before bar 2 that tested below the day's low and near the low of yesterday, both the bulls and the bears started buying. The bears were buying back their shorts, and the bulls were initiating new longs. Both bought on the close of the bar and below its low. Bar 2 had a large tail on the bottom, showing that traders were eager to buy. The next bar had a bull close, and they bought that close and above its high. Traders sold on the close of the bar 7 breakout to a new high, even though it was a bull trend bar. They were confident that the day was a trading range day, so they waited to short until the market went above the opening high. As the market was going up, they believed that a new high of the day was likely, and since they thought the market would go a little higher, it did not make sense for them to short when they could do so at an even better price a few minutes later. This absence of the strongest sellers created a vacuum that sucked the market up quickly. Since they were confident that the new high would fail, they were very happy to sell on the close of a strong bull trend bar. The bulls were selling out of their longs to take profits, and the bears were selling to initiate new shorts. Both wanted to sell when the market was at maximum strength, since they believed that it should head down. Traders sold on the close of the bear inside bar that followed bar 7 and below its low. The next bar was a small doji bar, which was a weak high 1 buy setup, and many traders sold above its high, expecting it to fail. They also sold below the low of the high 1 entry bar, since it was then a one-bar lower high. Two bars later, they saw the doji signal bar for the high 2 buy setup as a weak signal, and sold above its high. Once the high 2 entry bar closed near its low, they sold below its low, since this was a failed high 2 sell signal.

The strong bull trend bar was a high 4 entry bar, but it was also a big bull trend bar near the high of a trading range day. The bull scalpers sold out of their longs, and the bears shorted on the close of the bar and below the bar 9 lower high two-bar reversal (this made the move down to bar 8 a final flag).

Once the market fell to the middle of the range, and especially after it broke below the bar 6 swing low, the bulls thought the breakout would fail. Most breakouts fail in general, and this is especially true on trading range days, and in the middle of the day and in the middle of the range. Traders started buying the bear closes and the pushes below the lows of the prior bars. By bar 11, the consensus was clear and the market created a bull reversal bar, signifying urgency to the upside. There was no one left who was willing to short down there, so the market had to go up to find a price that the bears once again believed offered value for shorting. This price is where they aggressively shorted earlier in the day, and their renewed selling created the double top at bar 12.

Bar 12 had a bull body, which is a bad signal bar for a reversal trade, but in a trading range (or at the end of a bear rally in a bear trend), signal bars are often not strong, but are still acceptable. At least it had a tail at the top, a small bull body, and a close in the middle.

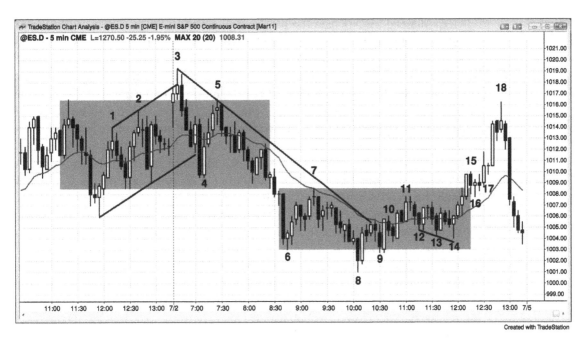

FIGURE PIV.3 Swing Trades in Trading Ranges

In Figure PIV.3, there are two trading ranges where traders could have swung part of their position for a possible breakout into a trend. In the upper range, traders could have shorted below the low of bar 3, which was the signal bar for the wedge reversal of the high of yesterday. Since the move down to bar 4 broke below the bull trend line, the market might then form a lower high and then a reversal into a bear trend. This allowed traders to short again below the low of bar 5, well before the breakout below the bottom of the trading range.

The market then formed a lower trading range. The bar 11 rally to the top of the range broke the bear trend line, so traders should be looking for a lower low or higher low and then a possible trend reversal up. The market formed a wedge bull flag at the bar 14 higher low, and bar 14 was a strong bull reversal bar. This allowed bulls to buy several bars before the breakout actually took place. There were high 1 breakout pullback long setups at bars 16 and 17.

In general, the stronger the trend, the more important the signal bar is for a reversal trade. Trading range signal bars are often less than perfect. Acceptable short setups can have signal bars with bull bodies. Likewise, acceptable long setups can have signal bars with bear bodies. Examples include bars 3, 5, and 7, the bar after bar 11, and bar 18.

Experienced traders saw the breakout down to bar 6 as a likely evolution of a trading range day into a trending trading range day. Aggressive bulls bought the close of bar 8, since it was a large bear trend bar in the area of a measured move down in what they thought was likely a developing lower trading range. Other bulls bought as bar 8 fell below the low of bar 6, and others bought at a fixed number of ticks below bar 6. Some bought at one point below and tried to buy more at two, three, or even four points below. Some thought that the breakout might be a five-tick failed breakout and used that as their reason to buy four ticks below. A few traders sold the breakout below bar 6 and reversed to long at their scalper's profit target, one point below their entry price. Others bought on bar 8 as it fell through the trend channel line (not shown) created by yesterday's low and bar 6, or after the market bounced a few ticks up from the bar 8 low after falling below the trend channel line. Since these bulls believed that the market was evolving into a trending trading range day and was forming the lower trading range, they were in scalping mode, as most traders are when the market is in a trading range. The swings today were relatively large, so many bulls were scalping for three or four points instead of just one or two. They needed to be adequately rewarded for taking relatively risky (lower-probability) trades, where the risk was large (the bulls who were scaling in were probably risking four to six points). Since experienced traders believed that the market was in a trading range, bear scalpers were shorting rallies near the top of the developing trading range, like around bar 7 or bar 11. Since bar 14 was a possible start of a test back into the upper range and was followed by several bull trend bars, most bears would have stopped looking to short at that point.

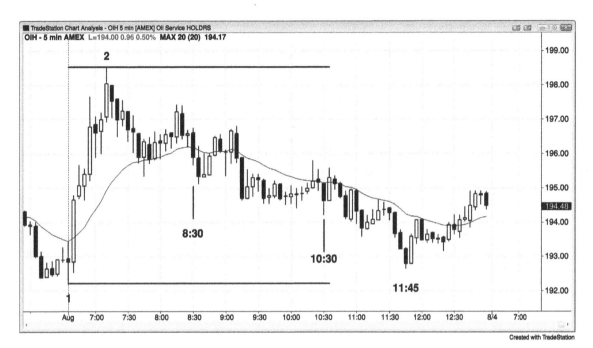

FIGURE PIV.4 Middle Third of the Range and of the Day

When the day is not a clear trend day, traders should be very careful during the middle third of the day when the market is around the middle third of the day's range. In Figure PIV.4, there are lots of overlapping bars, small dojis, and tiny failed breakouts, making the price action difficult to read. This is a barbwire type of tight trading range and is discussed more in Chapter 22. With experience, a trader can be successful trading under these circumstances, but the vast majority of traders would more likely give back most or all of the profit that they made in the first couple of hours. The goal is to make money, and sometimes your account is much better served by not placing trades and instead waiting for strong setups. In the chart, the sideways action lasted until 11:45 a.m. PST, which is relatively late in the day. The time parameters are only guidelines. The overriding factor is the price action, and on trading range days the best trades are fades of the highs and lows of the day, but this takes patience.

FIGURE PIV.5 Spike Up and Then Down Usually Leads to a Trading Range

Whenever the market has a spike up and then a spike down, or vice versa, it tends to enter a trading range as the bulls and bears both fight to create follow-through in their direction. In Figure PIV.5, Eli Lilly (LLY)'s daily chart shows a sharp up move that ended at bar 2 and was followed by a sharp down move. There was no clear buy pattern; instead there was a low 2 breakout pullback entry at bar 4. Bars 6 and 7 were short signal bars following brief bear trend line breaks (bar 6 was a first moving average gap bar). The bar 8 low of this spike and channel bear trend was not quite a measured move, and was followed by a test of the bar 4 start of the bear channel.

A sharp move up and then down, like the move up to bar 2 and then down, is a climactic reversal and a two-bar reversal on some higher time frame chart. It is a single reversal bar on an even higher time frame chart. Bar 8 was a sell climax and a two-bar reversal, and the move would be a single reversal bar on some higher time frame chart. It was followed by a trading range, which grew into a bull channel.

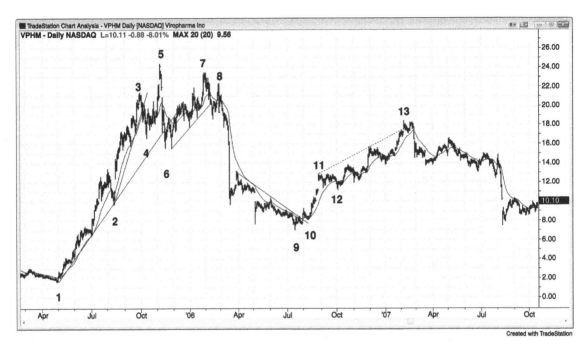

FIGURE PIV.6 Pullbacks Can Grow into Trading Ranges

Strong trends are followed by pullbacks that can grow into trading ranges and sometimes reversals, as shown in Figure PIV.6. Here, the daily chart of ViroPharma Inc. (VPHM) had a strong bull trend followed by a strong bear trend, and the entire chart evolved into a large trading range. A big move up followed by a big move down is a buy climax and is usually followed in turn by a trading range as the bulls and the bears continue to trade, both trying to generate follow-through in their direction.

At some point after the bar 1 bottom, the momentum traders controlled the market and drove it much higher than the fundamentals warranted. There was then a sharp move down to bar 9, where there was a three-push pattern (a wedge variant) that resulted in the spike and channel up to bar 13, effectively creating a large trading range. Bar 13 was an overshoot of the trend channel line, and the attempted breakout above the channel failed. Spike and channel bull trends, no matter how strong they appear, are usually followed by a test of the beginning of the channel, which was the bar 12 low.

Bar 10 was a breakout pullback higher low second chance to get long.

After many momentum players dumped their longs on the rally up from the bar 4 trend line break, the bulls were able to drive the market to a new high at bar 5, but this area found aggressive sellers who were able to break the major bull trend line as they pushed the market down to the bar 6 low, setting up a large reversal down from the bar 7 lower high test of the bar 5 trend high. The reversal down came off of the three pushes up to bar 7. At this point, the momentum players were out and looking for another stock. The rally up to bar 7 had several swings, indicating two-sided trading and therefore less momentum than in the prior rallies and in the sell-off down to bar 6. It became the pullback that led to the bear channel that followed the spike down to bar 6.

The market continued to sell off until value traders thought that the fundamentals were strong enough to make the stock a bargain around bar 9. Bar 9 was also a three-push-down buy. It could also have been near some Fibonacci retracement level, but that is irrelevant. You can just look and see that the pullback was deep, but not so deep that the force of the rally from bar 1 was totally erased. The bulls still had enough force left to rally the stock, especially since the value traders were back in play. They felt that the stock was cheap based on fundamentals, and their intention was to keep buying as the stock continued to drop (unless it dropped too far).

The final leg down in a trading range in a bull market is often a bear channel, as it was here. Some traders saw the entire move from bar 3 to bar 9 as a wedge bull flag, which is a bear channel. Others saw the bear channel as starting at bar 5, bar 7, or after the large bear spike that followed bar 8. That bear spike led to three pushes down and a wedge bear channel. Traders bought above bar 9 and on the breakout pullbacks at bars 10 and 12.

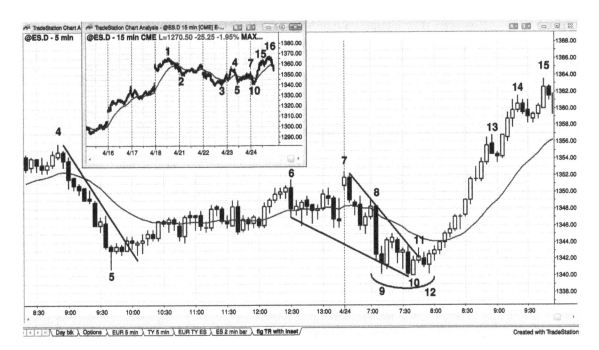

FIGURE PIV.7 A Trading Range Can Be a Reversal Setup

A trading range can be a reversal setup, especially when there are tails at the bottoms of the bars and two-bar reversals, which are reversal bars on a higher time frame chart. As shown in Figure PIV.7, yesterday had a bear spike and then the remainder of the day was a low-momentum bull channel. All bull channels are bear flags, and this one broke out to the downside on today's open. However, the market made three attempts (bars 8, 9, and 12) to break below yesterday's low and found buyers instead of sellers each time. The small trading range from bar 9 to bar 12 led to a reversal up instead of a downside breakout. The failed low 2 at bar 12 was the setup for today's strong bull trend.

Although a trader only needs to look at one chart to trade successfully, it is usually helpful to be aware of the big picture. The market was in a large trading range for four days, as shown in the inset of the 15 minute chart. The numbering is the same, but the 15 minute chart began before and ended after the 5 minute chart and has some additional numbers. Since there was a bull trend before the four-day trading range formed, traders were looking for an upside breakout. The final leg of a trading range in a bull market is often a bear channel, which is the last attempt by the bears to reverse the market down. Most reversal patterns are trading ranges, but most fail, like this one did. There were several possible choices for the start of the channel (bars 6, 7, and 8), and different traders saw each as the most important.

However, they all agreed that bars 10 and 12 were reasonable buy setups. Bar 10 was a second attempt to reverse up after breaking below yesterday's low, and bar 12 was a breakout pullback from the bar 11 break above the bear trend line, as well as a higher low. The strong bull trend bars were signs of buying pressure, which is always good to see when looking to buy.

Deeper Discussion of This Chart

As shown in Figure PIV.7, yesterday's bull channel from bar 5 to bar 6 broke the bear trend line, and today's lower low was therefore a possible trend reversal.

Yesterday's bear flag became the final flag in the bear trend (but the bear trend was in a large four-day trading range in a bull market). Whenever there is a relatively horizontal bear flag, or a sloping one that is in a tight channel, it will have a magnetic pull on the market, and this often prevents breakouts from going very far. The tight trading range is an area of comfort for both bulls and bears, and both see the price level as an area of value. Traders were aware of this and were looking for signs of a reversal up after the breakout. The failed low 2 at bar 12 was also a double bottom pullback buy setup. Other traders saw it as a triple bottom or a triangle reversal. Most reversal patterns have multiple interpretations, and different traders prefer to describe them in their own particular way. It does not matter what you call it, because all that matters is that you were aware of the possible reversal and looked for some reason to get long.

FIGURE PIV.8   Buy Climax, Then Trading Range

The FOMC report was released at 11:15 a.m. PST, and the 5 minute Emini formed a large bull outside bar at bar 1 in Figure PIV.8, but its high was never exceeded. It was followed by a large bear trend bar, setting up a buy climax, which is usually followed by a trading range. The trading range can be as short as a single bar or can last for dozens of bars. It did not take long for the bears to overwhelm the bulls and create a four-bar bear spike. Even though reports can be volatile, the price action is reliable; so don't get caught in the emotion, and just look for sensible entries.

Bar 5 began a trading range that had large two-bar reversals and tall dojis. Whenever a trading range forms with multiple large reversals at an extreme of the day, it is usually better to look for a reversal entry than a with-trend setup. The big, overlapping bars and tails indicated two-sided trading, and when there is strong two-sided trading, it is not prudent to be buying at the high of the day or selling at the low. The tight trading range that began at bar 5 was composed of large bars, bars with tails at the bottom, and two-bar reversals, all indicating that the bulls were willing to become aggressive. This was an area of strong two-sided trading and therefore an area where both the bulls and the bears felt there was value. There-fore, if the price drifted down in a downside breakout, the buyers would see the lower prices as an even better value and they would buy aggressively. The bears saw value in the range and were less willing to short below it. The relative ab-sence of bears and the increased buying by the bulls usually causes breakouts to fail; the market generally rallies back into the magnetic area, and sometimes the market reverses.

All spikes are also breakouts and climaxes. The four-bar bear spike that began with bar 3 had shrinking bodies, indicating waning momentum. The sell climax was followed by a one-bar pause and then another large bear trend bar at bar 4, which created consecutive sell climaxes. When the emotional sellers have sold twice in a short period of time, there are usually very few traders left who are willing to sell at the low prices, and a bottom is often near. There was a third sell climax into the close and then a rally on the open the next day.

Deeper Discussion of This Chart

Bar 2 in Figure PIV.8 was a high 2 long entry bar but there was a problem with this setup. Whenever there are three or more bars that almost completely overlap and they are just above the moving average and there is a buy signal where the entry would be close to the top of this trading range, the odds favor it being a bear trap. If you took any trade, it made more sense to short above the high of the prior bar because this was a small, tight trading range, and most trading range breakouts fail. Yes, it was a high 2, but one that should never be bought.

Bar 3 was a failed high 2, so there were trapped bulls at the high of the day. It was also a strong bear trend bar, setting up a good short entry. Since the market was in a trading range at this point, those two small pushes up made bar 3 a low 2 short setup. Since it was near the high of the day, it was a good place to be looking for shorts. Finally, it was a double top bear flag after a large bear trend bar, and a climactic reversal.

Bar 6 was a low 1 short setup, but it followed consecutive sell climaxes, and the risk that the market would form a two-legged sideways to up correction was significant. The odds favored a higher low and a second corrective leg, but the bars were large enough to provide room for a short scalp, despite the likely higher low.

Bar 7 was the first bar of a two-bar reversal, and it was better to buy above the higher of the two bars and not simply above the bull bar. This was an example of how overly eager bulls get trapped. Since the market at this point had several big sideways bars, it was in a trading range and it was better to look for shorts near the top of the range and not to buy. Buy low, sell high is the best way to trade trading ranges.

Bar 8 trapped bulls into a bad high 2 long, and they would exit on the low 2 short below bar 8. The signal bar was small enough so that there was room for a short scalp, but after a pair of two-bar reversals and with a doji signal bar, this was a risky short.

Bar 10 was another bull trap that was bought by weak bulls at the top of a big, tempting doji. Again, smart bears would have looked for a small setup bar for a short entry because the bulls would have been forced to sell and there would have been no buyers left, making the market quickly reach the short scalp profit target. Since this was the third push up, it should have been expected to function like a wedge top, and it was followed by a bear leg into the close. Since this was a trading range, there was nothing for reversal patterns to reverse, and buying above tall bars near the top of the range was likely to result in trapped bulls. Smart bears were still shorting above the high of the prior bar and below the lows of small bars near the top of the range.

This trading range became a final flag that reversed up on the open of the next day with a high 2 entry on the third bar of the day. In fact, you can view the entire day up to the report as a final flag. The market broke to the upside just before the report and then sold off on bar 1 on the report, and once again tried to break to the upside from the trading range. When the market tries something twice and fails both times, it usually then tries the opposite. This made a downside breakout likely after the bar 1 buy climax.

The large bear trend bars that followed bar 10 created the third consecutive sell climax, which had a high probability of being followed by at least a two-legged rally, but sometimes instead there is just a two-legged sideways correction.

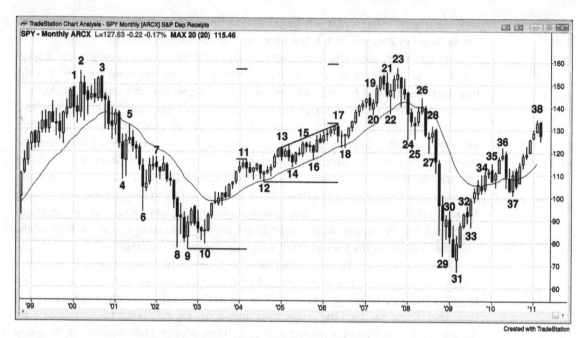

FIGURE PIV.9 Trading Ranges Leading to Reversals

Sometimes a trading range can lead to a trend reversal instead of a continuation, as it did four times on the monthly SPY chart shown in Figure PIV.9. Reversal patterns are discussed more fully in book 3. The purpose of this chart is to demonstrate that trading ranges can be reversal patterns.

Bars 4, 6, and 8 or 9 were three pushes down, and the low 2 short setup that formed two bars after bar 9 led to a higher low instead of a new low. Bars 4, 6, and 8 were all large bear trend bars, and they therefore formed three consecutive sell climaxes. That means that on all three bars, traders were aggressively selling at any price instead of on pullbacks. These were traders who were desperate to sell. Although they were mostly longs who were finally giving up, some of them were late, weak bears who had decided that there were not going to be any significant pullbacks. They were upset that they had missed so much of the bear trend, and they were determined not to miss any more, so they shorted at the market and on small pullbacks. Once these emotional bears shorted and the emotional bulls gave up and sold, there were very few traders left who were willing to sell at the bottom of the bear trend. After three sell climaxes, traders would have shorted only if there was a significant rally that had a good short setup. They got the rally, but they did not get a short setup until the move up went on for so long that it became a new bull trend that lasted five years.

Bar 8 and the bar after it both had large tails on their lows. Bar 9 was a bull reversal bar that was the second bar of a two-bar reversal, which was a reversal bar with a tail on the bottom on a higher time frame chart. Bar 10 and the bar before it also had prominent tails at their lows. This meant that bulls were buying going into the close of all of these bars and they were overwhelming the bears at this price level. The bulls thought this area was a great value for longs, and the bears thought it was too low to short aggressively. Some traders saw bars 8, 9, and 10 as a triple bottom, and others saw it as a head and shoulders bottom. Others thought that bars 8 and 9 formed a double bottom and bar 10 was a successful test of the low, and some saw the move above bar 9 as a breakout and then the move down to bar 10 as a higher low breakout pullback. It never matters what words you use to describe what is going on as long as you see that the market is telling you that the bulls are taking control. After three sell climaxes and such a long bear trend, the odds favored at least a two-legged pullback to the moving average and possibly to the beginning of the channels at bars 5 and 7. The entire move down from bar 2 was in a channel, and a bear channel is a bull flag. Channels often reverse after the third push down, so smart traders knew that this trading range from bar 8 to bar 10 might have been a reversal instead of a bear flag.

The push up from bar 20 and the move down to bar 22 comprised a buy climax, despite the bull close of bar 22. Once the market reversed down from the double top at bar 23, the bears were hoping that bar 23 was a higher high pullback after the bear spike down to bar 22, and they kept shorting as they tried to create a channel or spike down. The bulls kept buying and were hoping for a trading range and then another leg up. The bar 24 bear spike was convincing enough so that most traders thought that lower prices were more likely than higher prices over the next several bars.

The bulls tried again to create a bottom at bars 24, 25, and 27, but this was right after a reversal down from a spike and channel top, which was likely to have two legs down and test the bar 12 bottom of the channel. Also, bar 24 was the spike down that turned the market into a probable bear swing. There was likely to be follow-through in the form of some type of bear channel because the bar 24 breakout below the bar 22 neckline of the double top was so strong. Bar 25 was relatively small compared to the down bars and had a bear body. There was another spike down to bar 27, which made the downward momentum too strong to be buying above bar 27, especially since bar 27 was only a small doji bar and not a strong bull reversal bar. With the momentum down being so strong, buyers would not have been willing to buy above a lower low, but they might have been willing to buy above a strong higher low had one formed. The buyers gave up two bars later, and the market collapsed in sell climaxes down to bar 29 and bar 31.

The bar before bar 29, and bars 29 and 31, had large tails at the bottoms, again showing that the buyers were aggressively buying into the close of each bar. This was a small three-push-down pattern (this was clear on the daily chart), and the spike down from bar 30 was a sell climax after a huge sell climax down to bar 29. Consecutive sell climaxes usually lead to a pullback, at least to the moving average, lasting at least 10 bars and having at least two legs, and sometimes they can lead to a trend reversal. This buying was coming in just below the price level where the bulls bought aggressively at the bottom of bars 8, 9, and 10. The market was trying to reverse up from the breakout below that swing low, which is something that is common in trading ranges. In fact, the entire chart was a large trading range, despite the several strong trends that lasted as long as five years. Since most breakout attempts fail, buying should have been expected when the market fell below the bar 9 low.

Deeper Discussion of This Chart

As shown in Figure PIV.9, traders began to flip to always-in short as the market fell below the bars 1, 2, 3 head and shoulders top. Some started shorting below the bar 3 bear trend bar and two-bar reversal that formed the lower high. Others shorted for a variety of reasons as the spike grew down to bar 4. Even though bar 5 was a bull reversal bar and a breakout above a two-bar reversal, it was the first attempt to break out above the tight bear channel down from bar 3 and therefore was likely to fail. The bulls needed more strength in the form of several bull trend bars before they would become aggressive. The bears saw bar 5 as a micro channel low 1 short and were hoping for a measured move down. The bottom at bars 8, 9, and 10 was just below a measured move down from the open of the bar 3 start of the spike to the close of bar 4, the final bear trend bar in the spike. This also contributed to the profit taking by the shorts in that area as well as to the buying by the bulls.

Bar 10 was a double bottom pullback buy setup.

On the rally up to bar 11, the always-in trade flipped to long for more and more traders as the rally progressed. By the time the market paused at bar 12, just about everyone was convinced that the bull momentum was so strong that more of a rally was likely. Once the always-in trade flips, traders should try to get into the market. If there is no pullback, then buy at least a small position and use a wide stop, like below the bottom of the spike. That was what the institutions were doing. They were buying in pieces all the way up because they were not certain when a pullback would come, but they were certain that prices would be higher in the near term and wanted to be sure to profit from the strong trend. If they had waited for a pullback, it might have occurred after many more bull trend bars, and the entry on that pullback might have been well above where prices were at the moment.

As a general rule, as soon as traders decide that there is now a bull trend underway, they should buy at least a small position at the market or on a tiny pullback within the bar or a pullback on a lower time frame chart, because the directional probability of an equidistant move is probably at least 60 percent. For example, if they believed that the always-in trade flipped to long on that second bull trend bar after bar 10, they should have assumed that there was at least a 60 percent chance of the market going up for a measured move up. Traders measured the height from the bar 9 bottom to the bar 11 top of the bull spike and added that to the top of the bar 11 spike. SPY traders also measured from the open of the first bar of the spike (the bar after bar 10) to the close of the second bar of the spike. If the SPY traders bought at the close of that second bull trend bar, they would have put their stops below the low of the first bull trend bar (one bar earlier), and their risk would have been about 12 points. As the spike continued to grow, the measured move target continued to grow, yet the risk would have been fixed at 12 points, and at some point they could have moved their stops to breakeven. If they held until the market reversed down at bar 17, they would have made about 50 points with an initial risk of 12 points, and a breakeven risk after the first few bars following their entry. As the trend progressed to new highs, they could have trailed their stops to below the most recent swing low. For example, after the market rallied above bar 11, their stops would then have been below bar 12, and they would have been protecting about nine points of profit.

After the spike grew for two or three more bars, traders could have taken some profits, moved their stops to breakeven, and assumed that the directional probability of the spike going up for a measured move equal to its height was about 60 percent or more before the market fell below the low of the spike.

The rally up to bar 11 was a bull spike, and the channel up to bar 17 had three pushes and a wedge shape. This could have been the end of the channel, but the market broke out to the upside instead of to the downside. Usually, upside breakouts of bull channels reverse back down before about five bars, but this one continued for about 10 bars. It is common to see the market rally for a measured move up if the breakout of a wedge top is to the upside. Bars 13, 15, and 17 formed a wedge top, and the bar 23 high was just below that measured move from the bar 12 low to the bar 17 high. Also, bull spikes often lead to measured moves based on the open or low of the first bar to the close or high of the last bar. The bar 23 top of the bull leg was a measured move up, adding the number of points between the low of bar 9 to the high of bar 11 to the high of bar 11. Bulls usually look to take partial or complete profits at measured move targets, and aggressive bears will begin to short at that level.

Bar 23 was an expanding triangle top with bars 19 and 21.

Bars 20, 24, and 27 formed a wedge bull flag, but it was weak because of the number and size of the bear trend bars. When the market broke below the bar 27 bottom of the wedge, it fell for more than a measured move down.

The entire rally from bar 10 to bar 23 was a bull channel and therefore a bear flag. Other traders thought that the channel began at bar 12. In both cases, traders believed that the market should test down to at least the area of the bar 12 low. The tails on bars 24, 25, and 27 showed that there was some buying, but the momentum down was so strong that the bulls were unable to reverse the market. The move down from bar 23 to bar 27 had very few bull bodies and they were relatively small, and the move was in a relatively tight bear channel. Bulls would not have bought the first breakout above that bear channel and instead would have waited for a breakout pullback in the form of a higher low, and they would have wanted to see several strong bull trend bars before they would have been willing to become aggressive. Compare this bottom to the top at bar 23. The market did not become always-in down until the strong, convincing bar 24 bear breakout, and many bears would not have shorted until there was a lower high. The market formed a low 2 lower high test of the moving average at bar 26, and the move down was dramatic.

The inside bar after the bar 29 sell climax was a good candidate for a final flag, especially since the breakout was another sell climax. This was another factor in the bar 31 reversal.

CHAPTER 21

Example of How to Trade a Trading Range

When the market is in a trading range, traders should be guided by the maxim "Buy low, sell high." Also, think of your trades as scalps and not swings. Plan to take small profits and do not hold on hoping for a breakout. The rallies to the top usually look like they will become successful breakouts into a bull trend, but 80 percent of them fail, and 80 percent of the strong sell-offs to the bottom of the range fail to break out into a bear trend. Try to keep your potential reward at least as large as your risk so your winning percentage does not have to be 70 percent or higher. Since the market is two-sided, there will often be pullbacks after you enter and before you exit, so do not take a trade if you are unwilling to sit through a pullback. If the market has been going up for five to 10 bars in a trading range, it is usually far better to look only for shorts and to take profits on longs. If it has been going down for a while, look to buy or to take profits on shorts. Rarely enter on stops in the middle of the range, but it is sometimes reasonable to enter on limit orders there.

Among the best trade setups, beginners should focus on entries that use stops so that the market is going in their direction when they enter:

- Buying a high 2 near the bottom of the range. These are often second attempts to reverse the market up from the bottom, like a double bottom.
- Selling a low 2 near the top of the range. These are often second attempts to reverse the market down from the top, like a double top.
- Buying at the bottom of a trading range, especially if it is a second entry after a break above a bear trend line.

- Shorting at the top of a trading range, especially if it is a second entry after a break below the bull trend line.
- Buying a wedge bull flag near the bottom.
- Selling a wedge bear flag near the top.
- Buying a bull reversal bar or reversal pattern like a final flag (discussed in book 3) after a break below a swing low at the bottom of the range.
- Selling a bear reversal bar or reversal pattern like a final flag (discussed in book 3) after a break above a swing high at the top of the range.
- Buying a breakout pullback after an upside breakout near the bottom of the range (for example, if the market starts up and pulls back, look to buy above the high of the prior bar).
- Selling a breakout pullback after downside breakout near the top of the range (for example, if the market starts down and pulls back, look to sell below the low of the prior bar).

Entering using limit orders requires more experience reading charts, because the trader is entering in a market that is going in the opposite direction to the trade. Some traders trade smaller positions and scale in if the market continues against them; but only successful, experienced traders should ever attempt this. Here are some examples of limit or market order trade setups:

- Buying a bear spike at the market or on a limit order at or below the low of the prior swing low at the bottom of the range (entering in spikes requires a wider stop and the spike happens quickly, so this combination is difficult for many traders).
- Selling a bull spike at the market or on a limit order at or above the high of the prior swing high at the top of the range (entering in spikes requires a wider stop and the spike happens quickly, so this combination is difficult for many traders).
- Buying at the close or below the low of a large bear trend bar near the bottom of the range, since it is often an exhaustive sell climax and the end of the sell-off in a trading range.
- Selling at the close or above the high of a large bull trend bar near the top of the range, since it is often an exhaustive buy climax and the end of the rally in a trading range.
- Buying at or below a low 1 or 2 weak signal bar on a limit order at the bottom of a trading range.
- Shorting at or above a high 1 or 2 weak signal bar on a limit order at the top of a trading range.
- Buying a bear close at the start of a strong bull swing.
- Selling a bull close at the start of a strong bear swing.

Figure 21.1   EXAMPLE OF HOW TO TRADE A TRADING RANGE   **369**

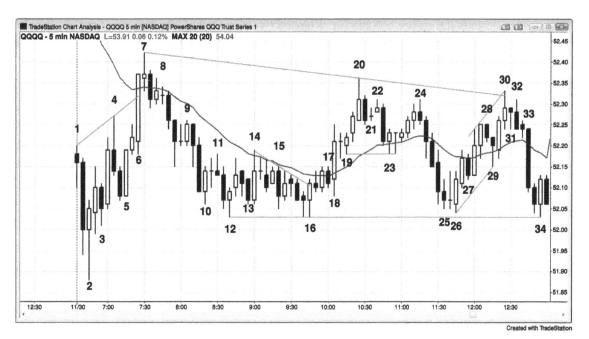

FIGURE 21.1   Fading Extremes for Scalps in Trading Ranges

There are many ways to trade a trading range day like the one in QQQ shown in Figure 21.1, but, in general, traders should look to fade the extremes and only scalp. Although there are many signals, traders should not worry about catching all of them or even most of them. All a trader needs is a few good setups a day to begin to become profitable.

I have a friend who has traded for many decades and who does extremely well on days like this. I have watched him trade the Emini in real time, and he would take about 15 profitable one-point scalps on a day like this, all based on fades. For example, in the bar 10 to bar 18 area, he would try to buy with limit orders below everything, like as the market fell below bar 10, as bar 13 went below the bear bar before it, and as bar 15 fell below the bar before it, and he would have added on as it fell below bar 13. He would have bought more as the market dipped below bar 15, and he would have tried to buy if the market fell below bar 12. It is important to remember that he is a very experienced trader and has the ability to spot trades that have a 70 to 80 percent chance of success. Very few traders have that ability, which is why beginners should not be scalping for one point while risking about two points. At a minimum, they should take trading range trades only where they believe the probability of success of an equidistant move is at least 60 percent. Since they would have to risk about two points on this chart, they should trade only if they are holding for at least a two-point profit. That means that they should look to buy near the bottom of the range and short near the top.

If traders bought near the bottom of the range, they should look to take profits near the top of the range. They should also look to initiate shorts near the top of the range and take profits on those shorts when the market moves toward the bottom of the range. Reversing is too difficult for most traders, and instead they should use profit targets for exits and then look for a trade in the opposite direction. For example, if they bought on bar 16 as it went above the high of the prior bar and triggered the double bottom bull flag entry, they could have a sell limit order to exit with a 10, 15, or 20 cent profit on the move up to bar 20. After they exited, they could then look for a short setup, like below the bar 22 lower high or below the bar 24 lower high. The latter was a better setup because it had a strong bear reversal bar and it was a double top bear flag with bar 22.

So when did traders conclude that this was a trading range day? Everyone is different, but there are often clues early on, and as more accumulate, traders become more confident. There were signs of two-sided trading right from the first bar, and other signs accumulated on just about every following bar. The first bar of the day was a doji, and that increased the chances of a trading range day. The market reversed up at bar 3 but had weak follow-through on the move up to bar 4. The first three bars had tails at their lows, and bar 2 overlapped about half of the prior bar. Bar 3 was a reversal down immediately after the long entry, and the next bar was a reversal up. The market reversed down again at bar 4 and up again at bar 5, and down again at bar 7 at the moving average. Whenever the market has four or five reversals in the first hour, the odds of a trading range day increase.

Bar 6 was a strong bull trend bar but there was no follow-through. It stalled at the moving average, and the next bar was a doji instead of another strong bull trend bar with a close well above the moving average. The next bar was a bear trend bar, and the two bars after also failed to close above the moving average. The bulls were not in control, despite a strong rally, so the market was two-sided.

Bar 2 was the start of a two-bar bull spike, and it was followed by a three-push bull channel up to bar 7. Since bar 2 was a strong bull reversal bar after a gap down and a sell-off, it was a good opening reversal and a possible low of the day. The day could have become a strong bull trend day but instead went sideways. However, it never dropped below the entry bar low.

Bar 2 was the first bar of a two-bar bull spike, and bars 4 and 7 were the second and third pushes up in a wedge channel after the spike. A channel in a spike and channel pattern is the first leg of a trading range, so most traders assumed at this point that the market would be in a trading range for at least the next 10 to 20 bars and maybe for the rest of the day. They looked to buy a two-legged sell-off that would test the bar 3 or bar 5 low, since those bars formed the bottom of the bull channel. Even if they believed that the day might become a trend day, they

Figure 21.1   EXAMPLE OF HOW TO TRADE A TRADING RANGE   **371**

saw it as a trading range for the time being and were therefore only scalping. Their scalping reinforced the trading range, because when lots of traders are selling near the high and buying near the low, it is very difficult for the market to break out into a trend.

Traders would have bought above bar 2 for at least a test of the moving average. Some traders would have shorted the bar 4 bear reversal bar at the new high of the day, but most would have assumed that the buying pressure from the bar 2 reversal bar, the two-bar bull spike, and the bull bar before bar 4 was strong enough for the market to test the moving average, even if there was a pullback. Because of this, many traders placed limit orders to buy at and below the bar 4 low, and they would have put their protective stops below the long entry bar after bar 2 or even below the bar 2 signal bar low. Some would have used a money stop, like around the height of an average bar so far today, maybe 10 to 15 cents. Some traders might have thought that the bears could have made a 10 cent scalp down from bar 4. That would require a 12 cent move below bar 4, so they might have used a 13-tick stop. They would have assumed that the short would have been a scalp, and therefore the bears would have had limit orders to buy back their shorts at 11 cents below the bar 4 low so that they could scalp out 10 cents on the shorts that they had entered on a stop at one tick below bar 4.

Alert traders would have placed a stop order to go long above the bear entry bar after bar 4 since they knew that the bar 4 signal bar was strong enough to entice shorts, and those shorts would be worried about a reversal up to the moving average. They would have their protective stops above their entry bar and not look to short again until the market reached the moving average. This made buying above that entry bar a great long scalp.

The bulls doubted that the bar after bar 5 was a reliable short, so they placed orders to buy one tick above, at, and below its low, expecting it to be a failed lower high. Only the long limit orders at one tick above the low got filled, which means that the bulls were very aggressive. The result was a strong bull trend bar up to the moving average. This was a strong bull breakout, but traders wondered why it stopped at the moving average instead of going far above. They needed to see immediate follow-through or they would suspect that this was going to be a failed breakout above the opening high. Maybe bar 6 was just a buy vacuum caused by the strong traders temporarily stepping aside. If they assumed that the market was going to test the moving average, it made no sense for them to sell just below the moving average. The absence of strong bulls and bears allowed the market to race up. However, once the market reached the area where they thought it was likely to stop, they appeared out of nowhere and sold aggressively, overwhelming the weak bulls. The strong bulls sold out of their longs for a profit, and the strong bears sold to initiate new shorts. Bears who saw the day as a likely trading range day would have had limit orders to sell as bar 6 moved above the moving average, while others would have shorted its close. Some would have been willing to scale in higher, especially after the weak follow-through on the next bar.

As the market traded down, it was clear to most traders that both the bulls and the bears were strong and that the market was likely to remain two-sided as both sides fought for control. This meant that a trading range was likely. When the market got near the top, the bulls became concerned that it was too expensive to buy and the bears saw it as a great value to short. This made the market fall. The bears who were eager to short near the top were not interested in shorting near the bottom, so selling dried up. The bulls who were willing to buy in the middle saw the bottom of the range as an even better value; they bought there aggressively, lifting the market back up.

Bears were willing to short below the bar 7 test of the moving average. If the bulls were strong, there should have been a strong move above the moving average and not this stall. Bar 7 made bar 6 look more like exhaustion than a strong breakout. Other bears shorted below the bar 8 ii pattern or below the bear bar that followed bar 7. The two-bar bear spike from the ii was reasonably strong, but it had a tail at its low, indicating some buying. At this point, the market had a strong spike up from the low of the day to bar 7 and now a strong spike down. Traders were expecting a trading range.

Bar 9 was a bull trap. Most traders saw the doji inside bar before it as a bad buy signal after the bear spike, and many placed limit orders to go short at the high of the doji bar. They were looking for a pullback to the area of the bottom of the bull channel around the bar 5 low. This was also in the area of the bar 2 signal bar high, which was a magnet for a breakout test. The bulls wanted a double bottom bull flag to develop in the bar 3 or bar 5 low area, but they also wanted the original entry bar low to hold (the low of the bar after bar 2). Otherwise, they would have probably given up on the belief that there was still a chance of a bull trend day.

Bar 10 was the third push down from the bar 7 high, and it was a strong bull trend bar. Bulls were concerned that the move down was in a tight channel and that the first breakout attempt might fail. Many bulls would have waited for a breakout pullback before buying. Some who did buy bought a smaller position, in case the market traded down closer to the bar 3 low, and they planned to buy more on a second signal up, which they got at bar 12. Others thought that many traders would have a 10 cent stop on their longs, so they placed a limit order to buy more 10 cents down, exactly where those weak bulls would be exiting. They then would put a protective stop on their entire position at maybe 10 more cents down, below the entry bar after bar 2, or even below bar 2. The traders who were willing to risk to a new low of the day might have traded even smaller to allow for a second scaled-in long about 10 cents below their first.

The bar 12 bull reversal bar was an approximate double bottom with the bar 3 or bar 5 low, and it was a second signal. This made it a high 2 near the bottom of

Figure 21.1   EXAMPLE OF HOW TO TRADE A TRADING RANGE   **373**

the trading range. It was the fourth push down from the high of the day, and some traders saw it as a high 4 bull flag. The bear spike down after bar 8 was the first push down for many traders, and bar 12 was the third. Many spike and channel patterns end in a third push like this and then try for a two-legged rally to test the top of the bear channel, which was around the bar 9 high. Some traders thought that the move down to bar 12 was in too tight a channel to buy, and they would have waited for a clear second signal. Many would not have bought until they got a relatively small bar near the bar 12 low. These traders could have bought on bar 16 for the double bottom bull flag. Bar 14 was strong enough to break above the bear channel, and then the market had a two-legged pullback. Bar 16 was also the entry for a wedge bull flag where bar 10 was the first push down and bar 12 was the second. Others saw bar 13 as the first push down and bar 15 as the second. It was also a descending triangle, and bar 16 was the breakout to the upside. Since it was a strong breakout bar, traders were looking to buy a breakout pullback. They would have limit orders to buy at or below the low of the prior bar and they would have been filled on bar 18. Others would have bought the close of the bear bar 17 since they thought that a breakout pullback and a higher low were more likely than a failed breakout and a move below the bar 16 bottom of the trading range.

Traders used that same logic and bought below the bar after bar 12, believing that it was a bad low 2 short since it was at the bottom of the trading range, and it was after the second reversal up where both reversals had good buying pressure (good bull reversal bars). Some would have bought on the close of the bear bar after bar 12 or on the bear close of bar 13, expecting the bar 12 low to hold. Others would have bought above bar 13, thinking that there were trapped bears and therefore the market could move up quickly as the bears covered.

Since this was a tight trading range, it was an area where both the bulls and the bears saw value. Both were comfortable initiating trades there. In an established area of value for both the bulls and the bears, breakouts usually cannot go too far before the market gets pulled back into the range. It has a strong magnetic pull, and bears will short more heavily above, while bulls will buy more heavily below.

Bar 18 was a large bull trend bar that broke out above the trading range of the past hour or so. However, since the overall day was in a larger trading range and the market was now in the middle of that larger range, traders were hesitant to buy. This resulted in the ii pattern. Some traders bought the bar 12 close and the breakout above bar 12. Others bought during the ii and above the bar 19 bull inside bar. Traders tried to buy on limit orders at and below the low of the inside bar after bar 18 but they did not get filled. This made them more willing to buy the breakout above bar 19. They saw that their buy orders did not get filled below and thought that this was a sign of urgency by the bulls.

The bar 18 breakout spike was followed by a small parabolic climax to bar 20 where a two-bar reversal down set up. The entry was below the lower of the two bars and it was not triggered until three bars later. Traders who believed that the day was a trading range day were looking to short a strong rally to near the high of the day. Bar 21 was a small doji and therefore a weak high 1 buy setup, especially after a buy climax. Bears shorted above its high. Others shorted below bar 22, where the bulls were selling out of their longs. They had bought at the top of a trading range, hoping for a bull breakout, and when it did not happen, they were quick to exit. As they did, they triggered the two-bar reversal short at the bar 20 high.

The market fell to the moving average and formed a high 2 buy signal with a bull reversal bar. This is a very reliable setup in a bull trend, but most traders still saw the day as a trading range day. Many bought above bar 23 with the hope that the day would become a bull trend, but they planned to exit quickly if there was not a strong bull breakout. They were concerned that the bar after bar 23 was a doji inside bar, because they wanted a sense of urgency, not hesitation.

They exited their longs, and bears shorted below the bar 24 bear reversal bar, which formed a double top bear flag with bar 22. Some saw it as a low 2 short with bar 22 and others saw it as a wedge top where bar 20 was the first push up and bar 22 was the second.

There was a strong bear spike to the bottom of the trading range, but bar 25 had a small bear body, indicating hesitation. The bulls were unable to create a breakout, and the result was only a trading range. The trading range failed to resist the magnetic pull of the bar 10 to 16 tight trading range. If this was a strong bear trend, the market would not have hesitated once it got back into the tight trading range from earlier in the day. Instead, it would have fallen below it in a series of strong bear trend bars. This told traders that the bears were not strong and that this might just be a sell vacuum. Strong traders might have stepped aside, expecting a test of the bottom of the range. Once the market got there, they began buying aggressively and relentlessly, the bulls initiating new longs and the bears taking profits on their shorts. They were determined to keep the market above the trading range low. Bar 26 was a high 2 at the bottom of the trading range and a strong bull reversal bar. Bar 25 was the high 1 setup. The bars 25 and 26 area formed a double bottom bull flag with the bars 12 to 16 area. This second bottom was also the breakout pullback from the bar 10 to bar 17 tight trading range.

Bar 26 had good follow-through on the next bar, and traders expected this test down to fail. Some bought the close of the bar 27 bear trend bar. Others placed limit orders to buy at and below the bar 27 low. The buying was so aggressive that the market could not even get to the bar 27 low. Alert traders saw this and quickly placed orders to buy on a stop above the bar 27 high. This resulted in a breakout formed by two bull trend bars.

Bar 28 was a bear inside bar, but the move up from bar 26 was in a tight channel so the first attempt down should fail. Bulls placed limit orders to buy at and below

Figure 21.1   EXAMPLE OF HOW TO TRADE A TRADING RANGE   **375**

the low of bar 28. The move down to bar 26 was a large two-legged move where bar 23 ended the first leg. This was a large bull flag, and the move up to bar 28 was the breakout. Bar 29 was the pullback from that breakout, and it was also the failed breakout of the bottom of the micro channel from bar 26 to bar 28.

Bar 30 was a dueling lines pattern, and bulls took profits as the market went above the two lines, creating the tail at the top. Others exited on the weak close and still others below the bar 31 two-bar reversal top.

Bar 31 was a doji and therefore a weak high 1 signal bar. Also, the spike from bar 26 to bar 30 was not strong enough to be buying a second high 1 (bar 29 was the first), and the day was a trading range day, not a clear bull trend day. Bears saw this as a bad high 1 at the top of a trading range and they shorted at the bar 31 high.

Other bears shorted below the bar 32 bear reversal bar. Some saw bars 30 and 31 as a two-bar reversal and others ignored bar 31 and saw bars 30 and 32 as a two-bar reversal. It was also a micro double top. The market went up on bar 30, down on bar 31, then up again on bar 32, and then down by the close of the bar. The market also made three pushes up on the day where bars 7 and 20 were the first two, so the day was a large triangle. The entry bar after bar 32 broke below the bull trend line from bars 26 and 29 (although not shown), and the market sold off sharply into the close on the second bar below the trend line.

There were many bull triangles between bars 10 and 16. Since the pattern was forming above the bottom of the bull spike up to bar 7, many traders thought that there might be a channel up that would test the bar 7 high at a minimum. There were also several bull spikes in this trading range, creating buying pressure and evidence for the bulls that the market was trying to form a higher low. Since none of the triangles was perfectly clear, not all traders agreed that any one was strong enough to make the market always-in long. Bars 10, 12, and 16 were three pushes down and formed a descending triangle. Bars 13, 15, and 16 were also three pushes down and a triangle. Some traders thought of it as a wedge bull flag. Another wedge bull flag was formed by the bear bar that formed two bars after bar 14, bar 15, and bar 16.

CHAPTER 22

Tight
Trading Ranges

A tight trading range is a common pattern that has been called many different things, but none of the terms is adequately descriptive. It is any sideways channel of two or more bars with lots of overlap in the bars, multiple reversals, many dojis, prominent tails, and both bull and bear bodies, and it can extend for a dozen or more bars. Most stop entries result in losses and should be avoided. If the average daily range in the Emini has been about 10 to 15 points, then any trading range that is three points tall or smaller is probably a tight trading range. A range of four and sometimes five points can sometimes behave like a tight trading range as well if the bars are large.

The bulls and the bears are in balance, and traders are waiting for a breakout and then the market's reaction after the breakout. Will the breakout continue, maybe after a small pullback, or will the pullback grow into a reversal and soon be followed by a breakout through the opposite side of the trading range? Just because the market is sideways, do not assume that the institutions have mostly stopped trading. The volume within each bar usually remains high, although less than that of the bars of the trend that preceded it. The bulls and the bears are both aggressively initiating new trades as they both fight to create a breakout in their direction. Some traders are scalping in and out, but others are adding to their positions and eventually reach their maximum size. Eventually one side wins and the other side gives up, and a new trend leg begins. For example, if there is a tight trading range that lasts a long time and many bulls have reached a position size that they do not want to exceed, then when the market begins to test the bottom of the range, there are not enough bulls left to lift the market back to the middle or top of the range. The market then begins to break to the downside, and these bulls who cannot or will not increase the size of their large positions only hope that there are other bulls with enough buying power to reverse the bear breakout. With each new lower tick, more bulls sell out of their longs and take their losses, and they will not consider buying again for at least several more bars. This selling pushes the market down further, causing more bulls to sell out with losses. The selling can accelerate as the remaining bulls give up, sell out, and wait for another possible bottom. This process occurs in all trading ranges, and also contributes to the late breakouts in trending trading range days. For example, if there is an upside breakout, it is in part because there are too many bears who are no longer able or willing to increase the size of their positions, and not enough left to resist the next test of the top of the range. The market breaks out, and the bears begin to buy back their shorts and become unwilling to sell again for at least several bars. The lack of selling by the bears, along with their buying as they cover their shorts, creates a one-sided market that forces the remaining bears to buy back their shorts. This short covering, along with buying by the bulls, often leads to a protracted bull swing.

Failed breakouts and reversals are common. It is usually better not to enter on the breakout; instead, wait for strong follow-through and then enter at the market, or wait for a breakout pullback and then enter in the direction of the trend, or wait for a failed breakout and then enter in the opposite direction. Although no one knows what algorithms are being used by the quants at high-frequency trading (HFT) firms, the huge volume taking place and the small moves with lots of reversals could easily be the result of programs trying to scalp one to four ticks repeatedly. The mathematicians do not need to even look at a chart. They design programs to capitalize on small movements, and a tight trading range looks like a perfect environment for a smart programmer.

Every pullback in a tight trading range is due to a micro buy or sell vacuum, just as occurs near the top and bottom of all trading ranges. Many bulls and bears will look to buy at a certain number of ticks below the high, whereas others will look to buy at a certain number of ticks below the low of the prior bar. These are traders who want to buy, but not at the current price. The bears want to buy back their short scalps, and the bulls want to initiate buy scalps. The absence of these buyers at the current price causes the market to get sucked down. Once it reaches their price, they suddenly buy aggressively, causing the reversal up. The bears take profits on their shorts and the bulls initiate longs. Once the market gets near the top of the range, the process reverses. The bulls sell out of their long scalps as they take profits, and the bears initiate new shorts. This same process occurs in every type of channel, whether it is horizontal (like a tight trading range) or sloped (like a channel after a spike).

The math is against a trader entering and exiting on stops in a tight trading range, but determining when the trader's equation is favorable for a limit order entry is too difficult for most traders. The best choice for most traders is simply to wait for the breakout and then decide if it is likely to succeed or fail, and then to look for trades. This is the same for a tight channel, which is just a sloping tight trading range. Although the market spends most of its time in channels, whether they are sideways trading ranges or sloping channels, trading within a channel is especially difficult when the channel is tight. When a channel or trading range is tight, only the most consistently profitable traders should trade, and these traders will enter using limit orders. Most traders should enter almost exclusively on stops. Since that is exactly the opposite way to trade tight channels, most traders should not trade them. Instead, they should simply wait for a spike or for a broader channel before trading again.

A tight trading range is usually a continuation pattern, but if it forms after a climactic reversal, even a small one, the market has an equal probability of breaking out in either direction. This is because the climactic reversal has generated momentum in the opposite direction and you will not know whether this opposite momentum will continue and lead to a breakout or the momentum of the prior trend will resume. Absent a climactic reversal, if a tight trading range forms after a trend leg, the probability that the breakout will be in the direction of the trend can be as high as 55 percent if the trend was strong. However, it is probably never higher than that, or else the market would not have formed the tight trading range. If the trend was less strong, the probability might be only 53 percent. Even if the market breaks out against the trend, the pattern usually evolves into a larger trading range, and the odds still ultimately favor a with-trend breakout. Remember, all trading ranges are just pullbacks on higher time frame charts. However, if a trader enters in the direction of the trend during a tight trading range and uses a very wide stop, allowing for the evolution into a taller trading range, the trader's equation becomes difficult to determine. The risk, reward, and probability become hard to assess, and whenever that is the case, it is better not to trade. Therefore, using a wide stop and holding for a long time is usually not a good strategy. If a trader enters with the trend in a tight trading range, expecting the trend to resume, but the market breaks out in the wrong direction, it is usually better to exit and wait for a larger trading range to develop before trying again to take a with-trend swing trade.

Because a tight trading range is a trading range, the chance of the market selling off when it is near the top of the range or rallying when it is near the bottom of the range is 60 percent or higher. However, because the range is tight, there is usually not enough room to make a profitable trade and, therefore, this probability is meaningless. It is better to just assume that the probability of the breakout being to the upside is 51 to 55 percent if the range followed a bull leg, and that the probability of the breakout being to the downside is 51 to 55 percent if the range followed a bear leg.

A tight trading range trumps everything, and that especially means all of the great reasons for taking any trade. It does not matter what else you see on the chart.

Once the market enters a tight trading range, the market is telling you that it has lost its direction and that the probability of the breakout in either direction is never more than about 55 percent. Since it is still a trading range, there is a slightly greater chance that the trend that preceded it will resume, but traders should assume that the odds are still only between 51 and 55 percent, depending on how strong the prior trend was and whether there was a strong reversal prior to the tight trading range. A tight trading range is made of lots of reversals, and each comes from a failed breakout attempt. There will be many "great" buy and sell signal bars, and some will have strong supporting logic. For example, if there is a great short signal that triggers, but the market forms an even better bull reversal bar within a bar or two, the bulls might think that the bears were trapped by a strong signal and will therefore be unwilling to short again for at least a couple of bars. This means that there are fewer bears near-term and the market has a high probability of having a successful bull breakout that runs for several bars. The logic is sound, but you need to go back to the mantra, "A tight trading range trumps everything." This includes every wonderful, logical reason you have for taking a trade. The reversals show that the institutions are selling on limit orders above bars and buying on limit orders below bars. Your job is to follow what they are doing, and you should never do the opposite. Entering and exiting on stops in a tight trading range is a losing strategy. Since you cannot profitably scalp for one to three ticks in a tight trading range the way the high frequency trading firms are doing, you have to wait. They create most of the volume in these tight ranges, and they are trading in ways that you cannot trade profitably. You have to wait, which can be extremely difficult to do. Sometimes a tight trading range can extend to 20 or more bars, and it then truly becomes a setup with no predictive value. Since guessing is never a sensible approach to trading, price action traders have to wait for the breakout before deciding what to do. In the majority of cases, there is a failure within a bar or two of the breakout, and the odds of a profitable trade are higher if you base your entry on the failure rather than on the breakout. In most cases, the reversal attempt fails and becomes a breakout pullback. Once there is a pullback from the breakout, enter in the direction of the breakout on a stop as the breakout resumes. In a bull breakout, wait for the pullback bar to close and then enter on a buy stop at one tick above its high. If the expected pullback bar instead leads to a reversal and plunges through the opposite side of the tight trading range, or if one of the next couple of bars falls through the bottom of the range, you can enter short on a stop at one tick below the tight trading range, or you can wait for a breakout pullback to short.

Because the move after the breakout from a protracted tight trading range on a trading range day is often not strong, the market frequently remains largely trendless for the rest of the day. However, the market behaves very differently if there was a strong trend leading up to the tight trading range, because the day will often become a trend resumption day. Here, there is a strong trend for the first hour or so and then a tight trading range that can last for several hours, and finally a breakout from the range in the direction of the original trend. This breakout often leads to a second trend that will be about the same number of points as the first leg. Less often, the breakout will be in the opposite direction and reverse most or all of the earlier trend.

Tight trading ranges usually have setups in both directions within them, but most traders should not take any trades once they believe that the market has entered a tight trading range. If they just entered a position and the pattern grows into a tight trading range, the best option is to try to get out at breakeven or maybe with a tick loss, and then wait for the breakout before deciding on your next trade. For example, if traders shorted because they thought there was a 60 percent chance that the market would fall 10 ticks before rallying 10 ticks but now the market is in a tight trading range, the math has changed. The traders now have only about a 50 percent chance of success, and as long as their risk and potential reward are unchanged, they now have a losing strategy. Their best recourse is to exit at breakeven and, if they are lucky, they might be able to get out with a tick or two of profit.

No matter what patterns you see, and there are always great-looking ones as they are setting up, you have to factor in the probability, which is 50 percent for an equidistant move. You can trade profitably only if the chance of winning times the potential reward is significantly greater than the chance of losing times the risk, but since a tight trading range is such a strong magnet, the moves are small within it, breakouts usually fail, and even when a breakout succeeds, it usually does not go far before the range sucks the market back into it. This makes the chance of making two or three times your risk very small; therefore, any breakout strategy, like buying above a bar or shorting below a bar, will lose over time.

Since a tight trading range is a channel, it can be traded like any other channel, but because the moves are small and take many bars to reach a profit target, it is very tedious, and most traders should avoid any trading once they believe that the market has entered a tight trading range. Sometimes a tight trading range has enough points from top to bottom to short a small bear reversal bar at the top for a scalp or to buy above a small bull trend bar at the bottom. Aggressive traders are buying below the low of the prior bar or shorting above the high of the prior bar, and are scalping out with a small profit. If there was a trend leading up to the tight trading range, the with-trend trades are more likely to be winners and a part can be held for a swing. For example, if the market enters a tight trading range after a strong rally and the range is holding just above the moving average, bulls will be buying below the lows of the prior bars. Although they can scalp out near the top of the range, they can also hold a part of their position for a swing up. Other traders (mostly HFT firms) scale into longs below the middle of the range and every one or two ticks lower. Shorts sell above the middle of the range and every tick or two higher. Both take profits around the middle of the range, exiting at breakeven on their earliest entry and with a profit on their later entries.

Since traders should focus on only the very best setups, they should always avoid the worst; and a tight trading range is the worst. Tight trading ranges are the single biggest problem for beginning traders and by far the most important obstacle that prevents them from trading profitably. For example, new traders remember that bar counts have been very reliable during the trends of the past few days so they start using them for entries within the range, expecting a breakout soon, but one never comes. They see every reversal as a new signal, and each one looks good at the time they place their order. There might be a strong bear reversal bar breaking out of a good-looking low 2 short setup. But it is still within the tight trading range and follows 14 bars that overlap, and the moving average is flat. Within the range, there might have been six prior reversals and none moved far enough to make even a scalper's profit. After an hour or so, the traders become depressed because they see that they have just lost on six consecutive trades. Even though the losses were small, they are now down seven points and there is only an hour remaining in the day. In a couple of hours, they gave back everything that they had earned over the past three days, and they promise themselves that they will never make that mistake again. Invariably, though, they do it again in two days, and then at least a couple of times a week for months until there is too little margin left in their accounts to trade.

That original money in their accounts was a gift to themselves. They were giving themselves an opportunity to see if they could create a new, wonderful life for themselves and their families. However, they repeatedly allowed themselves to break the most important rule in trading by trading within a tight trading range. They were arrogant to believe that their ability to read the market was strong. After all, they had made money for three consecutive days, and they had to be skillful to accomplish that. They believed that a winner was overdue after six consecutive losers, so the law of averages was on their side. Instead, they should have accepted the reality that a winner is never overdue, and the market usually continues to do what it just did. That means a seventh loser is more likely than a winner, and there will not likely be very good trading for the rest of the day. Yes, they traded those big swings of the past few days extremely well, but the character of the market changes from day to day, and that requires you to change your approach.

Traders often do not accept that the market has entered a tight trading range until they lose on two or three signals within four or five bars, and even once they do, they make even more costly mistakes. There is a natural tendency to assume that nothing can last forever and that every behavior regresses toward a mean. If the market has three or four losing trades, surely the odds favor that the next one will be a winner. It's just like flipping a coin, isn't it? Unfortunately, that is not how markets behave. When a market is trending, most attempts to reverse fail.

When it is in a trading range, most attempts to break out fail. This is the opposite of coin flips, where the odds are always 50–50. In trading, the odds are more like 70 percent or better that what just happened will continue to happen again and again. Because of the coin flip logic, most traders at some point begin to consider game theory.

The first idea that they consider is a martingale approach where they double or triple the size of their next trade after each loss. If they try it, they soon see that the martingale approach is really the martingale paradox. If you start with one contract and then after a loss you trade two contracts, and you keep doubling your position size after each consecutive losing trade, you know that eventually you will win. Once you do, that large final bet will recover all of your earlier losses and bring you back to breakeven. Better yet, triple the size of your trade after each loser so that once you finally win, you will end up with a net profit, despite your earlier losses. Martingale approaches are mathematically sound but paradoxically impossible to apply. Why is that? If you start with one contract and double after six consecutive losses, you would then be trading 32 contracts. If you trade every reversal, you will have six consecutive losers at least once a week and often more than six. The paradox is that a trader who is comfortable trading one contract would never trade 32 contracts, and a trader who is comfortable trading 32 contracts would never start with one.

Traders next consider waiting for three (or even more) consecutive losers before taking a trade because they believe that a string of four consecutive losing scalps does not happen too often. In fact, it happens almost every day, and the market often has six or even more consecutive reversals that fail; when that happens, the market is always in a tight trading range. Once they discover just how common six or seven consecutive losers are, they abandon that approach.

Once you see that the market is in a tight trading range, don't trade. Instead, simply wait for good swings to return, and they will, usually by the next day. Your job is not to place trades. It has to be to make money, and you cannot make money every month if you continue to lose more than you make. If the market appears to be swinging up and down and you take a trade, but the market then begins to form small, overlapping dojis within the next few bars, assume that the market is entering a tight trading range, especially if it is now the middle third of the day. Try to get out at breakeven or with a small loss and just wait for swings to return, even if you have to wait until tomorrow. You cannot afford to give back money based on the assumption that losers are part of trading. You must restrict your trading to the very best setups, even if that means that you don't trade for hours at a time.

An alternative to trying to get out at breakeven is to hold but use a wide stop beyond the range, but this is a less sound approach mathematically. The worst alternative is to take several entries within the pattern and sustain losses, even small ones. If you bought in a tight trading range in a bear trend and the market formed a low 2, you should exit and possibly reverse to short. If you shorted in that bear tight trading range and the market then formed a high 2, you should exit and possibly reverse to long, but only if the signal bar is a bull bar at the bottom of the range and there is enough room to the top of the pattern for a scalper's profit. However, this is rarely a good trade and only very experienced traders should attempt it. It is very difficult to watch the market for a couple of hours and not take a trade, but that is far better than incurring three or four losses and running out of time in the day to get back to breakeven. Be patient. Good setups will return before long.

An important type of tight trading range usually occurs in the middle of the day, in the middle of the day's range, and usually near the moving average, but it can occur at any time and in any location. It is called barbwire because of the spiky appearance of the large dojis and tails. If you see three or more bars that largely overlap and one or more of them has a tiny body (doji), this is barbwire. As a guide for how much overlap is enough, look at the second of the three bars. Usually the bars are relatively large, which signifies more emotion and more uncertainty. If more than half of its height is within the range of the bars before and after it, you should view the three bars as barbwire. Until you are a strong trader, don't touch barbwire or you will be hurt. The small body indicates that the market moved away from the bar's open, but traders with an opposite opinion moved it back by the close of the bar. Also, sideways bars where one bar overlaps much of the prior bar mean that no one is in control of the market, so you should not bet on the direction.

As with all trading ranges, the odds favor a with-trend breakout, but barbwire is notorious for sharp whipsaws and repeated losses for overly eager breakout traders. Barbwire often has both a failed low 2 and a failed high 2 before there is a successful breakout. In general, when barbwire forms adjacent to the moving average, it will usually break out in the direction away from the moving average. So if it forms just above the moving average, the odds favor a bull breakout, and if it forms just below the moving average, there will usually be a bear breakout. In the less common situation where it is straddling the moving average, you have to look to other aspects of price action to find tradable setups. Since all tight trading ranges are areas of agreement between the bulls and the bears, most breakouts fail. In fact, when a tight trading range occurs in a trend, it often becomes the final flag in the trend, and the breakout often reverses back into the tight trading range. The reversal usually leads to at least a two-legged pullback and sometimes even a trend reversal.

It is important to consider the move just prior its formation. If the barbwire develops in a pullback to the moving average but stays mostly on the with-trend side of the moving average, it is just part of the pullback and there will usually be a with-trend breakout. For example, if there is a 10-bar pullback to the moving average in a bull trend and then barbwire forms, with several bars poking through the moving average, but the pattern is mostly above the moving average, look for a bull breakout. Even though you might want to consider the 10-bar move down to the moving average as a new bear trend, if the pattern is mostly above the moving average, the bulls are in control and it is likely just the end of a bull pullback to the moving average.

However, if the pullback goes through the moving average and then the barbwire forms mostly on the opposite side of the moving average, this pullback has enough strength so that either a second leg is likely or you misread the chart and the trend might have already reversed. In either case, the breakout will likely be in the direction of the move that led to the pattern, rather than in the direction of the larger move that was in effect prior to this moving average pullback. For example, if there was a bear trend and now there is a 10-bar rally that poked above the moving average and is forming barbwire that is mostly above the moving average, the odds favor a bull breakout. The barbwire is a bull flag in the move up and not the end of a bear flag in the larger move down.

As difficult as barbwire can be to trade, if you analyze the bars carefully, experienced traders can trade it effectively. This is important because it is sometimes followed by a protracted trend move, especially when it is acting as a breakout pullback. For example, suppose the market is selling off to the bottom of a trading range and barbwire forms; if a low 2 develops just below the moving average and the signal bar is a strong bear reversal bar, this can be a strong short setup. The odds favor a successful breakout if the tails within the barbwire are not too prominent, there was a strong reversal at the top of this bear leg, and there are reasonable targets well below the barbwire.

Sometimes barbwire forms at the end of a several-bar spike in the first hour. When it happens in an area of support in a bull trend, it can become a reversal pattern and the low of the day. When this happens after a bull spike in the first hour at an area of resistance, it can become the high of the day. Barbwire less often forms reversal patterns later in the day.

The cardinal rule for trading in barbwire is to never enter on a breakout. Instead, wait for a trend bar to break out of the pattern. The trend bar is the first sign of conviction but, since the market has been two-sided, the odds are high that the breakout will fail, so be ready to fade it. For example, if there is a bull trend bar that breaks out to the upside by more than a couple of ticks, as soon as the bull trend bar closes, place an order to go short at one tick below the low of that breakout bar. Sometimes this short entry will fail, so once short and once the entry bar closes, place an order to reverse to long at one tick above the high of the short entry bar, which would become a breakout pullback buy entry. It is unusual for the second entry to fail. Do not fade the breakout if it has two or more consecutive trend bars, because that increases the odds that the breakout will be successful.

This means that any attempt to reverse back into the barbwire will probably fail and set up a breakout pullback. Once the market begins to form trend bars, either the bulls or the bears will soon be in control. When a with-trend breakout fails within a few bars and the market reverses, the barbwire is then the final flag of the prior trend.

You can also fade small bars near the top and bottom of barbwire if there is an entry. For example, if there is a small bar near the high, especially if it is a bear reversal bar, look to scalp a short with an entry order to sell at one tick below the low of that bar on a stop. You can also look for 3 minute small bars to fade as well. You should rarely, if ever, fade off 1 minute bars, because the 3 and 5 minute bars provide better winning percentages.

Since barbwire can have many spikes before there is a successful breakout, experienced traders sometimes place limit orders to buy below the low of the prior bar if that low is near the bottom of the range but not if it is in the middle or top of the range. Bears will short above the high of the prior bar with an entry near the top of the range, rather than at the high of a prior bar where the high is in the bottom half of the range. The more prominent the spikes are, the more likely this is to work. Also, it is more effective if the bars are at least as large as the average bars of the day. If the bars are too small and the range is too tight, then the odds of a successful scalp are less, and traders should wait to place trades. This is tedious work, and most experienced traders usually wait for moves with a higher probability of success and more profit potential. Since the volume is often good within barbwire, high-frequency trading firms are likely active, as they are in all tight trading ranges, scalping for one to three ticks. Computers do not get tired, so tedium is not an issue for them.

If barbwire is at the end of a pullback to the moving average in a strong trend, you need to take the second entry in the direction of that strong trend. For example, if there is a pullback to the moving average in a bull trend, you would buy a high 2 even if it is forming within barbwire. This is especially true if the signal bar is a bull reversal bar and if dojis and tails are not too prominent in the barbwire. You must look at the entire chart and see the bull trend. Do not simply look at the prior 10 bars and conclude that the market is now in a bear swing, which is not realistic if the market is holding above a rising moving average in a strong bull trend.

Whenever you are not certain, the best course is always to wait, which is difficult to do when you feel like an entry is overdue. However, that is what a smart trader always does because it simply does not make sense to trade low-probability setups. One very good rule is that if there is a trading range setting up and it is near the moving average, never look to buy if the bars are mostly below the moving average, and never look to sell if the bars are mostly above the moving average. This one rule will save you an enormous amount of money over the years.

Micro channels sometimes have barbwire behavior. For example, on a bear trend day, it is common to see a small rally within a micro channel. Then there might be a downside breakout that fails within a bar or two. This is not a buy setup since it almost always will be below a falling moving average on a bear trend day and you need to be looking for short setups only when the market rallies for five to 10 bars. Wait for the failed breakout to form a higher high or a lower high breakout pullback and then look to go short below that bar. You will be shorting exactly where the trapped bulls who bought above the bar that broke below the bull channel will be taking their losses. These patterns often have tails and can be barbwire, and they trap countertrend traders, just like barbwire.

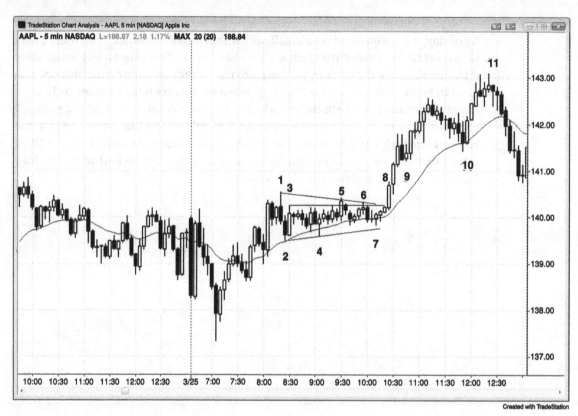

FIGURE 22.1 Tight Trading Range

By bar 4 in Figure 22.1, it was clear that the market had entered a tight trading range. Bar 1 was the second attempt to reverse down within three bars and was followed by the bar 2 attempt to reverse up in a two-bar reversal. Three changes in direction within five bars are a strong sign that the market was now strongly two-sided. When the market formed a small doji after bar 3, traders had to suspect that it was likely entering a tight trading range. When the next two bars were also dojis, a tight trading range was in effect.

Both bars 5 and 6 failed to break out of the top, and the tight trading range evolved into a triangle, which is also usually a with-trend pattern. Since the last trend was up from the low of the day, an upside breakout was likely, especially since all of the bars were holding above the moving average. After two failed break-outs, the odds were much higher that a third breakout would succeed. Also, bar 7 was a high 2 pullback from the bar 5 high, which had some momentum. An aggressive trader would have bought the high 2.

The next logical buy was a breakout above the high 2 of bar 5, the first failed breakout. You could also have bought at one or two cents above the high of the day. In general, buying a tight trading range breakout is a low-probability trade. However, the trading range followed a strong bull reversal off the low of the day, and the market could not close more than a tick below the moving average for two hours, which indicated that the bulls were very strong.

The highest-probability entry was the first pullback at bar 9, which reversed up after taking out the bear reversal bar's low by only one tick, trapping shorts in and longs out.

Another high-probability buy was the high 2 at the moving average at bar 10. The entry was above bar 10, the second bar of the two-bar reversal. There was a breakout of the bear micro channel two bars earlier, so bar 10 was also a lower low breakout pullback buy setup. High-probability trades often result in smaller gains, but by definition they usually have a much higher chance of success.

FIGURE 22.2 Tight Trading Range in Both Bull and Bear Legs

Sometimes a tight trading range can be a pullback in both a bull trend and a bear trend. In Figure 22.2, was the tight trading range from bar 6 to bar 8 a bull flag in the rally up from bar 3 to bar 4, or was it a bear flag in the bear trend down to bar 3? Both are logical possibilities, and whenever there is both a valid bull and bear interpretation, there is uncertainty, which means that the market is in a trading range and in breakout mode.

After breaking the bear trend line on the rally to bar 4, Lehman Brothers (LEH) formed a higher low at bar 6 and then entered a tight trading range. Since the move down to bar 3 was a wedge, it was likely to be followed by at least a two-legged sideways to up correction, especially after the reversal up from yesterday's low. Even though trading range breakouts usually fail, an upside breakout here could have had a second leg up that might have been as large as the leg from bar 3 to bar 4. It could even have been a trend reversal, especially since there was so much earlier bull strength on the move up to bar 1. Upside targets included the bar 4 final

Figure 22.2   TIGHT TRADING RANGES   **391**

lower high, the swing highs after bar 2 and bar 3, a measured move up where the second leg was as tall as the first, and even a test of the bar 1 bull spike.

The move up to bar 4 was contained fairly well in a channel and was therefore probably just the first of the two sideways to up legs. It also had bull bodies that were more prominent than the bear bodies, which was a sign of buying pressure. Bar 6 formed a double bottom with the third bar after the bar 3 low. Traders knew that if the bar 6 low was to hold, the market could have made a measured move up above bar 4 that equaled the height of the bar 6 low to the bar 4 high. Aggressive bulls were buying in the tight trading range because of the great risk/reward ratio. They were risking about 20 cents to below the bar 6 low to make a dollar or more on a 50–50 bet, which was a great trade.

The market became clearly always-in long by the close of bar 8, and even more certain when the next bar was a strong bull trend bar. Bulls were buying at the market, on tiny pullbacks, above prior swing highs, and on the closes of each of the three bars in the bull spike. There was now about a 60 to 70 percent chance of approximately a measured move up from the open of the first bar of the three-bar spike to the close of the third bar, and the market ultimately rallied beyond that target.

The first pullback after the breakout was the small bull inside bar at bar 9, so buying the high 1 at one tick above the high of bar 9 was a high-probability long.

The rally to bar 10 was about a 65 percent retracement of the bear trend down from bar 1. Fibonacci traders would call the rally to bar 10 a 61.8 percent pullback and say that it was close enough, but every pullback is close enough to some Fibonacci number, making the Fibonacci numbers essentially meaningless most of the time.

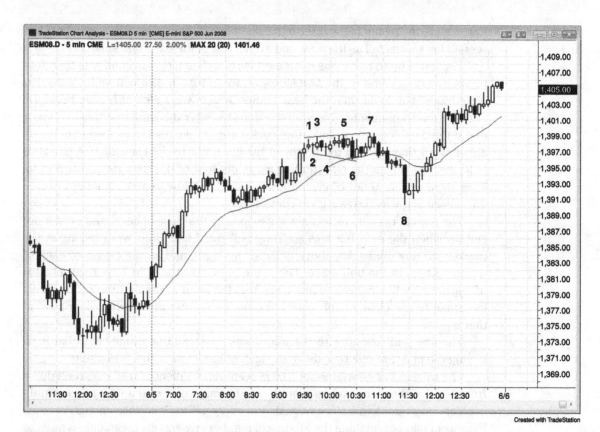

FIGURE 22.3 Tight Trading Range Evolving into Larger Trading Range

Although a tight trading range in a bull trend is a trading range and therefore a bull flag, it breaks to the downside first in about 45 to 49 percent of cases. The pattern then sometimes evolves into a larger trading range, which usually breaks out in the direction of the trend (in Figure 22.3, up). Most traders who bought in the tight trading range after bar 1 should have exited either on the breakout below bar 5 or below the bear inside bar after bar 7, and almost all would have exited on the downside breakout below bar 6. The alternative was to hold long and use a wide stop. However, even though the market did not fall below the 8:25 a.m. PST swing low from three hours earlier, a trader would have had to risk seven or more points to stay long. Most bulls who bought in the tight trading range would have instead taken a loss before the bar 8 low formed. At the time of their entry, the required risk that would have allowed for a larger trading range was too great, and the probability of reaching a big enough profit target to make the trader's equation profitable was too low for them to hold long. When that is the case, it is better to exit and then look for another trade in either direction. The trader's equation was reasonable for

Figure 22.3   TIGHT TRADING RANGES   **393**

traders who took a small loss and bought again above the bull bar that followed the bar 8 failed bear breakout. Here, they were buying a double bottom and therefore a possible bottom in a larger trading range in a bull trend.

By bar 3, barbwire was present because of three sideways bars with at least one being a doji. This meant that most traders should wait for a breakout and assess if it looked strong or likely to fail. Aggressive, experienced traders could have bought below the low of the prior bar, shorted above the high of the prior bar, bought above small bull reversal bars at the bottom, and shorted below small bear reversal bars near the top.

Bar 6 was a bear trend bar breakout followed by an ii setup at the moving average that led to a long scalp. The market had not touched the moving average in over 20 bars. The market was getting close, and the bulls thought that a touch was likely after the market missed it by a tick a couple of hours earlier. Since the bulls believed that the market would fall to the moving average, they were unwilling to buy just above it, and their refusal to buy left the market one-sided. The result was that the market fell quickly in the form of a strong bear spike to the moving average, where the bulls reappeared and bought aggressively.

Bar 7 was a failed bull trend bar breakout following the first failed breakout to the downside, and opposite failures are second entries and therefore especially reliable. The two-bar reversal at bar 7 set up a small expanding triangle short. Bar 5 was also an expanding triangle short, but at that point the range was too tight for a scalp down.

Expanding triangles are intensely two-sided and therefore have a magnetic pull on breakouts, causing most to fail, like at bar 6 and bar 7. Even after a successful breakout, the market often gets drawn back because it is an area where both the bulls and the bears believe there is value in initiating positions. Bar 8 was a large bear trend bar that became just another failed breakout.

Deeper Discussion of This Chart

In Figure 22.3, bar 8 was a sell climax, a failed breakout, and a double bottom with the bottom of the bull channel that began around 8:15 a.m. PST, and the bar after it was a first moving average gap bar setup (it was actually the second attempt, since the first was four bars earlier).

FIGURE 22.4   Stop Entries in Barbwire Are Costly

The chart presented in Figure 22.4 seems innocuous enough, right? But if you look carefully at the barbwire from bar 1 to bar 2, there were eight consecutive reversals that failed to reach a scalper's profit. Once you see overlapping bars near the moving average, you need to be very careful. In general, it is best to consider only with-trend entries (here, longs, since the pattern is mostly above the exponential moving average), and only if you can buy near the bottom of the pattern or after one side is clearly trapped. Although the tails are not as big and the bodies are not as small as in most barbwire patterns, overlapping bars at the moving average create a dangerous situation.

On a 15 minute chart, this 5 minute barbwire is simply a high 2 pullback to the moving average, and it is certainly reasonable to trade off the 15 minute chart when there is a 5 minute barbwire pattern. The best approach for most traders is simply to wait and not trade until after the pattern has broken out and a new pattern sets up. In some cases, like here, there is no low-risk setup. Bar 2 was a bad short since traders were shorting below a large signal bar at the bottom of a trading range in a bull day. Also, a bear reversal bar in a tight trading range has nothing to reverse, so it does not function as a reversal bar. Here it was the

Figure 22.4   TIGHT TRADING RANGES   **395**

first bar of a two-bar reversal up. The outside up bar was the second and the entry was above the high of the outside up bar, which was the higher of the two bars. Just because something looks like a reversal bar does not mean that it will function like one. Also, something can function like a perfect two-bar reversal even if it does not look like one. Traders who are constantly thinking about what is going on can catch these trades. It is likely that the chart would look different on other time frames—that the bear reversal bar would not exit and the two-bar reversal would look perfect. However, you never have to look for the perfect time frame if you understand what is happening on the chart in front of you.

FIGURE 22.5   Stop Entries Would Have Yielded 10 Consecutive Losers

Ten consecutive losing scalps should be a warning to traders who think they can make money by trading in barbwire. This is an extreme example of the trouble that traders can have if they choose not to work hard to understand price action and instead decide to trade entirely mechanically, reversing at each bar that reverses the prior bar. In Figure 22.5, bar 1 was a long scalp that would have resulted in a loss. If traders reversed to short on bar 2, they would have lost again. If they kept reversing after each loss, they would have had 10 consecutive losing entries, the last occurring at the bar 10 short. If their first position size was a single contract and they used a martingale approach of doubling their position size after each loss so that when they finally won they would be back to breakeven, that 11th entry would have required them to trade 1,024 contracts, and what one-lot trader would ever be able to do that? If they took a more aggressive martingale approach and decided to triple their position size after each loss so that when they finally had a winning scalp they would have a profit despite all of the earlier consecutive losers, their second trade would be for three contracts, their third would be for nine, and their 11th entry would be for 37,179 contracts! That is why martingale techniques are not practical. If your account is big enough to trade 1,024 contracts, you would never bother trading just one contract on your first trade, and if you are comfortable starting out with just one lot, you could never trade 1,024 contracts.

Figure 22.5   TIGHT TRADING RANGES   **397**

On this summer Friday, there were also eight consecutive losers starting at the long at bar A and ending with the short at bar B.

Traders could instead begin trading after four or five losers and increase their odds of success and reduce their overall risk, but this should be done only rarely and only by traders who can read price action quickly and accurately. Smart traders would avoid this approach in barbwire, especially when it grows into a protracted tight trading range. Anyone blindly doubling up after consecutive losers is gambling and not trading, and gambling is entertainment, which always involves a fee. None of the 10 losing trades had a strong enough setup to be traded in barbwire, and therefore it would have been better to wait. You cannot sustain repeated losses in barbwire and hope that your winners from earlier in the day will keep you profitable. They won't, and your account will inevitably shrink to the point that there is no longer enough margin to trade and it will become a blown account.

Once you become an experienced trader, you can consider buying below the lows of bars and below swing lows near the bottom of the range and shorting above the high of the prior bar or a swing high near the top of the range, but this is tedious and requires an intensity that most traders cannot consistently maintain.

FIGURE 22.6 Sloping Tight Trading Range

When a tight trading range slopes slightly up or down, it is still a tight trading range and it should be treated the same way. The bulls and bears are in close balance, and generally it is best to wait for failed breakouts and breakout pullbacks. In general, all tight trading ranges are continuation patterns, like the small one that ended at bar 1 in Figure 22.6.

The range that started at bar 2 was after two sharp bear legs and should be expected to be protracted and likely to lead to two up legs (the move to bar 3 became the first of the two legs). These patterns are difficult to trade and often have false breakouts. It is wise to trade them minimally, if at all, and simply wait for the inevitable clarity that will reappear. This was a micro channel, and the odds were high that once the breakout came, it would fail. The market broke to the downside, only to reverse back up into the close.

Figure 22.6   TIGHT TRADING RANGES   **399**

Deeper Discussion of This Chart

All trading ranges, especially tight ones, are magnets, and breakouts usually get pulled back into the range. When a horizontal trading range occurs after a trend has been underway for 20 or more bars, that trading range is often the final flag in the trend. The breakout often fails and the market returns to the price level within the range. Sometimes there is a trend reversal.

The two-legged pullback to the moving average that ended around bar 1 in Figure 22.6 became a final flag, and the market was drawn back up to that price area by the close.

The tight trading range that ended at bar 3 was also a final flag, and the breakout was to a higher low. The market then reversed up above the tight trading range for the second leg up after the sell climax at the low of the day.

Many traders saw the move down to bar 2 as simply a large two-legged sell-off. They also thought that the trading range that ended around bar 1 could be a final flag. After the sell climax at the low of the day, many expected two legs up and a test back into that trading range. Since the move was countertrend, they were willing to hold their long positions that they bought on the second entry above bar 2, and they did not exit during any of the times that a bar fell below the low of the prior bar. After a couple of strong bull trend bars, they began to trail their protective stops below the lows of the strong bull bars and soon were able to move their stops to around breakeven.

FIGURE 22.7 Barbwire with an ioi Pattern

In Figure 22.7, bar 1 was a large outside bar followed by a doji inside bar. Even though an ioi pattern is often a reliable breakout setup, here the tails on the recent bars are too prominent. When there are three sideways bars and at least one of them is a doji, no one is in control and the best approach is to wait for one side to gain control, as evidenced by a trend bar that clearly breaks out. If the breakout looks weak and sets up a reversal, then look to fade the breakout. Most trend bars coming out of these patterns fail and become setups in the opposite direction. This entry also frequently fails, which is a signal for a second trade. It is unusual for this second entry to fail. This type of bar counting is difficult for most traders to do in real time, and they are more likely to make money if they wait for clarity.

Bar 2 broke out of the ioi pattern, but buying above large overlapping bars, especially in barbwire, is usually a bull trap. In fact, an experienced trader will often place a limit order to go short at or above the high of that inside bar, expecting the bull breakout to be a trap and for the market to quickly reverse down.

So with the bulls trapped above bar 2, did it make sense to short below bar 2, since those bulls would have to sell out of their longs? You are faced with the same problem. Whenever there are three or more large bars and one of them is a signal bar forcing you to buy at the top of the tight trading range or to short at the bottom, the odds are that you will lose money because it is likely that the institutions are doing the opposite.

The bar after bar 3 was a bull inside bar and was setting up a high 2 long, where bar 2 was the high 1. The bar was not as large as the prior several bars, and you were buying above a bull trend bar that was testing the moving average, which is normally a good trade. Although this was a reasonable trade, the market was still in barbwire and it was better to wait for a second signal or a breakout pullback. Bar 5 was a bull trend bar at the moving average; it was the second entry within three bars, and it was at the same price as the first entry. All of these factors increased the odds of success. By the close of the bar, the bulls were happy to see a large bull breakout bar with no tail on the bottom and a small tail on the top, and the odds favored at least a measured move up from the open to the close of the bull spike. The entry bar was followed by another very strong bull trend bar.

FIGURE 22.8 Barbwire Failed Breakout

When barbwire forms in the middle of the day's range, almost invariably next to the 20-bar moving average, it is best to enter on a failed breakout. In Figure 22.8, the market broke out of the top in a high 2 and immediately reversed to break out of the bottom in a failed high 2. Traders shorted on the breakout below the tight trading range, on the close of the bar, and below its low. However, you had to be thinking about the possibility of a failed upside breakout to be able to place the sell order. Remember, that upside breakout was a strong bull trend bar at some

Figure 22.8

TIGHT TRADING RANGES **403**

point in the first minute or two, and that bullish strength made lots of traders think exclusively about getting long. Those traders let themselves get trapped out of the short trade. You must constantly be thinking, especially when the market is starting to move. Not only must you look for a way to get in, but you must also always think about what happens if the initial move fails and then quickly goes the other way. Otherwise, you will miss great trades, and traps are among the best.

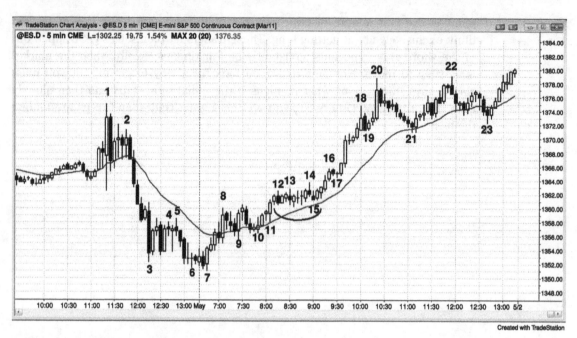

FIGURE 22.9 Tight Trading Range as a Flag

When a tight trading range forms at an extreme of the day after a breakout, it usually becomes a continuation pattern. Look for a with-trend entry, which sometimes happens after a false breakout in either direction. By bar 13 or so in Figure 22.9, most traders believed that the market was entering a tight trading range after the breakout above the top of the bar 8 bull spike. Bulls bought at and below the low of the prior bar and held some or all of their position for a likely upside breakout. Most of the bars within the tight trading range had bull bodies, and the range was holding above the moving average; both of these were signs of buying pressure and favored an upside breakout. Even though the bars were small and sideways, the volume usually remained heavy. Many of the bars had 5,000 to 10,000 contracts traded, which represented about $100 million of stock every minute.

There was a spike up to bar 8 after a lower low and then a breakout formed by six bull trend bars to a new high at bar 12. The market entered a tight trading range and broke out to the upside on bar 14, but the breakout immediately failed. However, the reversal down lasted only one bar and became a breakout pullback long setup that led to a strong bull trend. The bar 14 reversal trapped bulls out and bears in; and when both sides are trapped, the next move usually lasts for at least several bars.

Figure 22.10   TIGHT TRADING RANGES   **405**

FIGURE 22.10   Tight Trading Range Bear Flag

A tight trading range can be a reliable flag in a trend. In Figure 22.10, bar 1 was the entry from a low 2 short pattern within barbwire after a spike down to a new low of the day. It was a two-legged sideways breakout pullback. The bars were relatively large and overlapping, the tails were prominent, and there were a couple of dojis within the pattern.

The market formed a long tight trading range that ended with a two-legged sideways test of the moving average at bar 2. There was a bear reversal bar, which is always desirable when shorting a low 2 at the moving average in a bear trend.

Figure 22.10

Also, the bar was small and at the top of the tight trading range, so the risk was small. Since it was an entry in a trend, the potential reward was large.

If you look carefully at the pattern, there was additional support to the trade because it was a sideways low 4, although that was not particularly important here. There was a five-bar-long, two-legged sideways correction, and then a correction down (four bars, two legs), and then a second two-legged rally (six bars, sideways to up), ending with a small break above the moving average.

Figure 22.11   TIGHT TRADING RANGES   **407**

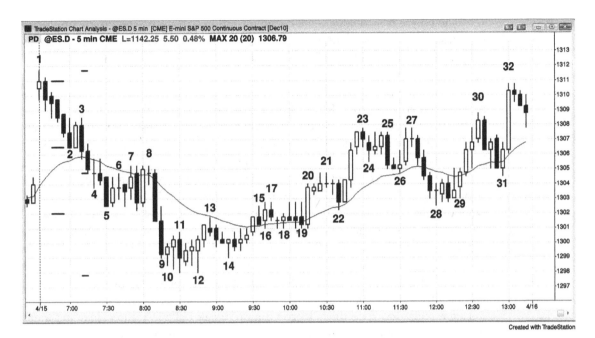

FIGURE 22.11 Barbwire Reversal

In Figure 22.11, barbwire formed at the bottom of each of the two legs down to the bar 10 low of the day. The first one became a bear flag, and the second was a reversal.

Today opened above yesterday's high but immediately formed a strong five-bar spike down to just above the moving average. The always-in position was clearly down, meaning that the market probably would trade below the bar 2 low before it traded above the top of the bear spike. The reality is that the odds were more like 90 percent than just 51 percent, given the strong momentum and the pause just above the magnets of the moving average and yesterday's close.

The move down to bar 5 was within a tight bear channel, and therefore it was too risky to buy the first attempt to break out above the channel. This first leg down tested yesterday's close, but the momentum down was so strong that the odds were good that the market would test down further, probably to the area of yesterday's low. Even though the large overlapping bars, dojis, big tails, and two-bar reversals indicated that the bulls were beginning to buy, there was no strong buy setup within the barbwire.

Bar 8 was an expanding triangle short setup at the moving average. Expanding triangle bear flags have three pushes up and usually a low 3 signal bar, as occurred here at bar 8.

Since there is strong two-sided trading within barbwire, when barbwire forms after a sell-off it often becomes the final flag of the bear trend. The market usually works its way back into the barbwire price area because both the bulls and the bears agree that there is value in initiating trades there.

When the market fell below the value area, the bulls saw the lower prices as an even better value, and the bears saw it as representing worse value. The result was that the bulls bought aggressively and the bears stopped shorting. Well, then, why was the breakout below the barbwire created by the two strongest bear trend bars of the day? This was because once the first barbwire failed to form a bottom on the test of yesterday's close, the next level of support was yesterday's low. The bulls were very eager to buy but were waiting until they believed that the market would likely not fall any further, and they came back into the market during the barbwire that began at bar 10. This was the third consecutive sell climax of the day (the move down to bar 2 and the sell-off from bar 3 to bar 5 were the first two). After three consecutive sell climaxes, the market usually corrects sideways to up for at least 10 bars and with at least two legs. Sell climaxes are emotional and usually indicate bulls desperate to get out at any price, even at the market, during a collapse. Once there were no more weak bulls left, the remaining longs were willing to hold through even more selling, and once there were no bulls left to sell out, the market had a buy imbalance. Also, the bears became very hesitant to short further after three consecutive sell climaxes and would now short only after a significant pullback.

Bar 11 was an ioi pattern with a bull inside bar setting up an acceptable long for aggressive bulls, especially if they were willing to scale in lower. Most traders should have instead waited for a higher low before going long. The bar 14 higher low had a bull body and was a pullback from the bar 10 and bar 12 double bottom.

Deeper Discussion of This Chart

Whenever the market has large trend bars, those bars are spikes, climaxes, and break-outs. The breakout component often leads to a measured move projection where the bears will take partial or complete profits, and aggressive bulls will begin to buy. In Figure 22.11 the breakout below bar 2 occurred with a five-bar bear spike from bar 3 to bar 5. The market tested the breakout with the four bars from bar 7 to bar 8, and the space between the bar 2 low breakout point and the bar 7 breakout test was a gap, which could become a measuring gap. The move from the bar 1 high to the middle of the gap often projects to a level where the market might find support. Here, the market fell below

Figure 22.11   TIGHT TRADING RANGES   **409**

that target. There are always many possible choices for measured move projections and many are not obvious. The move from the high of the day to the middle of the bar 4 doji within the measuring gap gave a projection that was one tick below the low of the day. Once the market fell below the first target, traders would look for other possible targets. If they found one that was logical, it would give them more confidence that the bottom for at least an hour or two was in.

The spike from the bar after bar 1 to the bottom of bar 2 could also have led to a measured move. The open of the first bar to the close of the final bar is often the height for the projection, and the low of the first barbwire pattern missed the target by a tick.

FIGURE 22.12   Barbwire as a Low 2

The market in Figure 22.12 was in a small range for the first three hours, so a break-out was likely. Bars 1, 2, and 3 were sideways and overlapping. Since bars 1 and 2 were dojis, this was a barbwire pattern. However, bars 3, 4, and 5 had good bodies and small tails. This meant that the market was transitioning from barbwire into an ordinary low 2 short setup in a bear trend, and it led to a two-bar bear spike and then a tight bear channel. Most bulls who were scaling in would have sold out of their longs on a low 2 short in a bear trend, especially if there was a bear signal bar. They then usually don't look to buy again for at least a couple of bars. This is why low 2 shorts are so effective in bear trends. The bulls step aside, and the bears become more aggressive.

CHAPTER 23

Triangles

Triangles are trading ranges and therefore channels, since they are an area of price action contained between two lines. The minimum requirement for a trading range to be called a triangle is that it has three pushes up or down. Since they have either higher lows or lower highs, or both in the case of an expanding triangle, they also have some trending behavior. Wedges are triangles that are either rising or falling. When they are just barely sloped, traders refer to them as triangles, but when the slope is greater, they usually call them wedges. A bull or bear flag can be a wedge and will usually just become a continuation pattern. Wedges can also occur at the end of a trend and form a reversal pattern. Because they behave more like flags or reversal patterns than like traditional triangles, they are discussed in those sections rather than here.

An expanding triangle is contained between two diverging lines, both of which are technically trend channel lines because the upper line is above the highs in a bull trend (higher highs) and the lower line is below the lows in a bear trend (lower lows). An oo (outside-outside) pattern, where an outside bar is followed by a larger outside bar, is a small expanding triangle. A contracting triangle is contained between two trend lines, since the market is in both a small bear trend and a small bull trend. An ii pattern is usually a small triangle on a lower time frame chart. An ascending triangle has a resistance line above and a bull trend line below; a descending triangle has a support line below and a bear trend line above. A wedge is an ascending or descending channel where the trend line and trend channel line converge, and it is a variant of a triangle and therefore also a type of channel. All triangles have at least three legs in one direction and at least two in the other, and every pattern that has three legs and is sideways or sloped and shaped like a wedge is a triangle. Unlike trend channels and trading ranges that can extend indefinitely, when the market is in a triangle, it is in breakout mode, meaning that a breakout is imminent. The breakout can be strong or weak; it can have follow-through and result in a trend, or it can fail and reverse, or it can simply go sideways and evolve into a larger trading range.

Like all trading ranges, a triangle is a pause in a trend, and the breakout is usually in the direction of the trend that preceded it. A triangle in a bull trend usually breaks out to the upside, and a bear triangle usually breaks out to the downside. Wedges can be more complicated. A bear wedge is a downward-sloping wedge and, like all bear channels, is a bull flag. When a downward-sloping wedge occurs within a larger bull trend, an upside breakout is in the direction of the larger trend, as expected. However, a large bear wedge can fill the entire screen, in which case the bars on the screen are in a bear trend. The upside breakout is then a reversal and a breakout against the trend on the screen. Whether or not there is a clear, large bull trend just off the left side of the screen is irrelevant. Any down wedge will behave like a large pullback in a bull trend, which means that it will behave like a bull flag. An upside breakout is a reversal out of the bear trend on the screen, but it is in the expected direction, since every bear channel, whether or not the lines converge and create a wedge, functions like a bull flag and should be thought of as a bull flag. Most, in fact, are bull flags on a larger time frame chart.

Every trading range with three pushes is functionally identical to a triangle. Most are triangles, but some don't have a clear triangle shape. However, since they behave exactly like triangles, they should be traded as if they were perfect triangles. Because they are more complex than one-push pullbacks (high 1 and low 1 pullbacks) and two-push pullbacks (high 2 and low 2 pullbacks), they represent stronger countertrend pressure. Since traders in the opposite direction are getting stronger, these patterns tend to occur late in trends and swings, and often become final flags. If a triangle has more than three pushes, most traders begin to refer to the correction as a trading range.

If a pattern is sloping and has three pushes, many traders erroneously see it as a wedge and look for a reversal. However, as discussed in Chapter 18 on wedges, if the three-push pattern is in a tight channel, the pattern will usually function like a channel and continue indefinitely, and not function like a wedge and reverse. If a wedge has three pushes, that alone is not a reason to trade in the opposite direction, however. When traders are not certain if the wedge is about to reverse, they should not enter on the breakout. For example, if there is a down channel that is fairly steep and the trend and trend channel lines are convergent but fairly close together, traders should not buy the first reversal up or the bull breakout of the wedge. They should wait until the bull breakout occurs and then evaluate its strength. If the breakout is strong (the characteristics of strong breakouts are discussed in Chapter 2), they should wait for a pullback and then enter at the end of the pullback (a breakout pullback buy). If there is no pullback for several bars, then the market is forming a strong bull spike and has almost certainly become always-in long in the eyes of most traders. They can then trade it like they would any other strong breakout. They might buy the close of a bar, buy above the high of the prior bar, buy any small pullback on a limit order, or wait for a pullback.

Since most triangles are relatively horizontal, the bulls and the bears are in balance, which means that they both see value at this price level. Because of this, breakouts often do not go very far before reversing back into the range, and triangles are often the final flag in a trend. If the breakout fails, the market usually gets drawn back into the trading range and sometimes breaks out of the opposite side and becomes a two-legged correction or even a trend reversal. This trading range behavior is discussed more in the Part IV discussion on trading ranges.

Since ascending, descending, and symmetrical triangles have the same trading implications, it is not necessary to distinguish one from another, and they can all be referred to as triangles. All of these triangles are mostly horizontal. They tend to break out slightly more often in the direction of the trend that preceded them, but not enough to place a trade on that basis alone. Since each is a type of trading range, each is an area of uncertainty, and it is better to wait for the breakout before placing a trade. However, when the pattern is tall enough, you can trade it like a trading range and fade the extremes, looking to buy near the bottom and sell near the top. The breakouts often fail and, like breakouts from any channel, if the market reverses back into the channel, it usually tests the opposite side. If it breaks out in either direction, the breakout usually leads to a measured move approximately equal in points to the height of the channel. If it goes beyond that, the market is likely in a trend.

Expanding triangles can be reversal patterns at the end of a trend or continuation patterns within a trend. Once they break out, the breakout often fails and the market then reverses, breaks out of the other side, and forms an even larger expanding triangle. The expanding triangle reversal then becomes a continuation pattern, and an expanding triangle continuation pattern then becomes a reversal. For example, if there is an expanding triangle at the bottom of a bear trend, it is a reversal pattern. Once the market rallies and breaks out of the top of the triangle, the breakout often fails and the market then turns down again. The result is a large expanding triangle bear flag. Sometimes an expanding triangle can lead to a major reversal, but usually it behaves more like a trading range and evolves into some other pattern. They are discussed more in the chapter on trend reversal patterns in book 3.

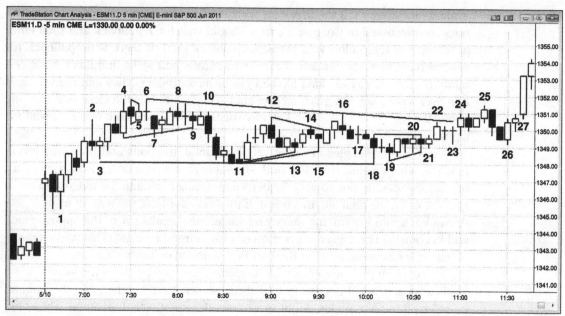

FIGURE 23.1 There Are Many Ways to Draw Triangles

Most traders think of a triangle as simply a trading range that has three or more pushes up or down. If it starts to have more than five pushes, most traders stop using the term *triangle* and just call the pattern a trading range. It does not matter what you call it, because all trading ranges behave similarly.

Most ii patterns, like at bar 5, bar 24, and the bar before 25 in Figure 23.1, should be thought of as small triangles, since most are triangles on smaller time frame charts.

The lows of bars 4, 7, and 9 were three pushes down in a sideways pattern and formed a triangle. The highs of bars 4, 6, and 8 formed three pushes up and therefore also created a triangle.

The lows of bars 3, 11 (or either of the two bars before it), and either 13, 15, or 18 formed three pushes down, and some traders saw each as a triangle. Bar 26 was a two-bar reversal breakout pullback buy setup from the bar 24 breakout of the large triangle from bar 3 to bar 18.

The lows of bar 18, bar 19, and the bar after bar 20 formed three pushes down. The high of the doji bar after bar 18, the bull bar after bar 19, and bar 20 formed three pushes up and created a triangle. Bar 23 was the pullback from the bar 22 breakout above the triangle.

Figure 23.2

TRIANGLES   **415**

FIGURE 23.2 Triangles

The daily chart of Intel (INTC) presented in Figure 23.2 had many triangles, which are rarely ever perfect. Triangle A was a rising wedge. The breakout had no momentum, and the pattern evolved into a tight trading range. When the market breaks out of a rising wedge in a rally but goes sideways instead of down, it is a sign of strength, and the bulls are likely to return. If the bears see a rising wedge in a bull trend and they are unable to reverse the market down, they will soon buy back their shorts and wait before shorting again. This makes the market one-sided, and the upside breakout continues to a price where the bears are willing to short once again and where the bulls will be comfortable taking profits by selling some or all of their longs.

Triangles B and E were both descending triangles, and B broke out to the upside. Triangle E first broke out to the upside, and the breakout failed. It then broke out to the downside, and again the breakout failed.

Triangle C was an expanding triangle. Traders could have shorted at the bar 3 high. Expanding triangle tops usually evolve into expanding triangle bottoms and vice versa, and this one did as well. Traders could buy above the bar 3 low.

Triangle D was an imperfect symmetrical triangle. Since symmetrical triangles are just trading ranges, traders could have looked to buy tests of the bull trend line below and short tests of the bear trend line above.

PART V

Orders and Trade Management

Simply knowing how to read charts does not mean that you can make a living as a trader. You need a plan for getting into and out of trades, and you have to constantly make decisions about every position that you are holding.

CHAPTER 24

Scalping, Swinging, Trading, and Investing

A n investor is someone who buys stocks based on fundamentals and plans to hold the stocks for six months to many years, allowing time for the beneficial fundamentals to be reflected in the price of the stock. Investors will often add to their positions if the stock goes against them, since their belief is that the stock is a value at the current price. A trader is someone who trades off daily charts and short-term fundamental events like earnings reports and product announcements with the intention of capturing a quick move, lasting from one to several days. Traders will take partial profits at the first pause and then move their stops to breakeven on the balance; they are not willing to have a profit turn into a loss. Traders are sometimes referred to as scalpers, but that term more commonly is used to refer to a type of day trader. Incidentally, it is important to keep to your time frame. A common cause of losses is putting on a trade, watching it become a loser, not exiting at your planned stop, and instead convincing yourself that it is fine to convert the trade into an investment. If you put it on for a trade, exit it as a trade and take the loss. Otherwise, you will invariably hold it far too long, and the loss will become many times larger than your original worst-case loss. On top of that, it will be a constant distraction and interfere with your ability to place and manage other trades.

In the eyes of a trader or investor using daily to monthly time frames, all day trading is scalping. However, to day traders, scalping is holding a position for one to 15 minutes or so and usually exiting on a limit order at a profit target in an attempt to capture one small leg on whatever time frame the scalper is using for trades. In general, the potential reward (the number of ticks to the profit target) is about the size of the risk (the number of ticks to the protective stop). The scalper does not want any pullbacks and will quickly exit at breakeven if the trade comes back before the target is reached; the scalper is therefore comparable to a trader on the daily charts. Intraday swing traders will hold a trade through pullbacks. They try to capture the two to four larger swings of the day, holding each position from 15 minutes to an entire day. Their potential reward is usually at least twice as large as their risk. They are comparable to an investor on the daily charts, who is willing to hold a position through pullbacks.

In the 1990s, the media and institutional investors ridiculed day traders, who were mostly scalpers, as gamblers who served no useful purpose. The critics totally ignored one important function that all traders provide, which is increasing liquidity and therefore reducing bid-ask spreads, making trading cheaper for everyone. A good deal of the criticism was probably due to the established institutional investors on Wall Street. They believed that they owned the game and they were kings, and they did not respect anyone who did not play it their way. They worked hard for their MBAs and thought that it was unfair that a high school dropout could theoretically make a fortune after spending just a few months learning simple trading techniques. The institutions enjoyed the awe that their feats garnered from the adoring public and at some level resented the attention that these uneducated upstarts were getting. Once HFT firms became the biggest volume traders on the Street and were producing far better performance records than the traditional institutional investors, the media took notice and began to give them more attention and respectful awe than the dinosaurs who had ruled the Street since its creation. HFT firms are the ultimate day traders and have made day trading respectable. CNBC's *Fast Money* has traders every day who often scalp, and are presented as admirable, successful traders. Now, the general feeling is that it is very difficult to make money as a trader, and if you are able to do it, you deserve a lot of respect, especially from other traders. It does not matter how you trade. All that matters is performance, and this is how it should be in a capitalistic society. Successful investors, traders, intraday swing traders, and scalpers all deserve the same respect and admiration, because all are doing something special, and doing it very well takes an extraordinary talent and a lot of hard work.

As discussed in Chapter 25 in the section on the trader's equation, swing traders take the opposite side of all scalps, but they also take the other side of trades by traders swinging in the opposite direction. A scalper has a reward about the same size as his risk and a high probability. There cannot be a scalp in the opposite direction with the same risk, reward, and probability. For example, the market cannot have a 60 percent chance of going up two points before going down two points at the same time that it has a 60 percent chance of going down two points before going up two points. Look at a bull trend. If a bullish trader buys at one tick above a strong signal bar in a reliable pullback in the Emini and his entry price is 1254, then his two-point stop is 1252 and his profit target is 1256. The bull would only take the trade if he thought that it probably would probably work, which implies that he had to be at least 60 percent certain, which means that the chance that the market would fall to 1252 and that his stop would be hit is be 40 percent or less. If a bear scalper took the other side of the trade and shorted at 1254.00, his stop is at 1256 and his profit target is 1252. Since the chance of the market falling to 1252 is 40 percent or less, the bear has a 40 percent chance or less of making his profit. In fact, it is almost always going to be less, because for his profit taking limit order to get filled, the market usually has to go one tick beyond it, which is even less likely because it is a bigger move.

Because of the mathematics, the person taking the other side of a scalp has to have a lower probability of success. Since in a very efficient market, institutions control the price action, every trade that takes place has to be one where one or more institutions are willing to take one side and one or more other institutions are willing to take the other (nothing is absolute, but this is pretty close). This means that the person taking the other side of a reasonable scalp has to have a reward greater than his risk if he is to have a profitable trader's equation (you have to assume that he does because he is an institution or someone taking a trade that an institution is also willing to take). This makes him a swing trader. Since the probability of swing trades is often 40 percent or less, a swing trader can take the opposite side of a scalper's trade and still have a positive trader's equation. If the probability of the market falling two points is 40 percent, the swing trading bear who is trying for more than two points has to have less than a 40 percent chance of success. However, if he manages his trade correctly, he can still make a consistent profit using this strategy. For example, from the discussion following on scaling into trades, you will see that he could be using a much wider stop than two points, and he might be willing to scale in several times if the market goes higher. If so, his probability of success can be 60 percent or higher. Once the market finally falls, he could exit his entire position at his original entry price of 1254. If he exited his entire position at his original short entry price, he would be out at breakeven on his first entry and have a profit on all of the later shorts that he placed at higher prices.

To scalp the 5 minute Emini chart effectively, with the current average daily range between eight and 15 points, you have to risk about two points, and your profit target is usually between one and three points. On one-point scalps, you have to win on over 67 percent of your trades just to break even. Although this is achievable for some traders, it is unrealistic for the majority of them. As a general rule, take a trade only where the potential reward is at least as large as the risk and where you are confident about the trade. If you are confident, one guideline is to assume that you believe that the chance of success is at least 60 percent. In the Emini, a two-point stop is currently (with an average daily range of 10 to 15 points) the most reliable stop for most trades based on a 5 minute chart, and that means that your profit target should be at least two points as well. If you do not think that two points is a realistic target, then don't take the trade. Incidentally, I had a friend many years ago who used to trade 100 Emini contracts at a time, scalping two ticks on about 25 trades a day. Since he lived in a 12,000-square-foot house, I assume that he was doing well. However, this is in the realm of high-frequency trading and virtually impossible for most traders to do profitably. A have another friend who once told me about a mutual acquaintance who made millions on Wall Street as an attorney and lost almost all of it as a trader. He probably assumed that he was much smarter than all of his clients who were making millions as traders and that he should have been able to do at least as well. He scalped 100 Emini contracts and lost $2 million over the first couple of years. He might have been smart, but he was not wise. Just because something looks easy does not mean that it actually is easy.

The issue of cherry-picking crosses everyone's mind at some point. Instead of worrying about taking 20 trades a day and trying to make one point on each, what about just scalping the very best three trades of the day and trying to make one point on each? In theory it is workable, but the reality is that if you have waited so long for the perfect trade and you worked so hard for so long to learn what is necessary to spot such a great trade, you have to make sure that you are adequately rewarded. One point is not enough. For example, if you believe that you are about to buy one of the best one or two setups of the day, you should assume that the market will agree that the setup is strong. That means that the always-in position will probably become clearly always-in long, that there will likely be at least two legs up to some kind of measured move or magnet area, and that the move should last at least 10 bars. Instead of scalping out for one point while risking two points, it makes much more sense to exit after a minimum of two points and maybe even four points. If you cannot handle this emotionally and you find yourself exiting at breakeven on the first pullback, you might try putting in a one cancels the other (OCO) bracket order as soon as you get long in which you have a two-point protective stop and a two-point profit-taking limit order. As soon as one gets filled, the other gets canceled automatically. Then go for a walk and come back in about an hour. After you've done this a few times, you might try using a three- or four-point profit target instead of two points and you might soon discover that you are averaging four points' profit per day on these trades.

Some scalpers scalp all of their trades, but many traders will scalp or swing, depending on circumstances. Implicit in the concept of scalping for this second group of scalpers is that they are not trading in the direction of a clear always-in situation. If they are scalping, they must believe either that there is no clear trend or that their trade is countertrend; otherwise they would be swinging. Even if the market has been trending and traders enter on a pullback, if they scalp, they believe that the trend is about to end, at least for a while. For example, if they buy a bull flag but exit with only a scalp, they suspect that the market is about to enter a trading range. If they believed otherwise, they would hold their position for a larger profit.

Whenever a trader sees the market pull back three or four ticks after a signal, it is a sign that big traders believe that the market is not likely to go far. Because of this, the trader will consider only trading range trades or countertrend trades, rather than trend trades. Since this means that the market is probably in a trading range, experienced traders will tend to scalp rather than swing, and look to buy low, sell high.

When traders are trading countertrend, they will sometimes trade a smaller position, like half size, because they are willing to add on if the market goes against them. If they do, they might get out once the market gets back to their first entry price. They would then have a breakeven trade on the first entry and a scalper's profit on the second. Whenever traders scalp, their profit target is often about half of the size of the minimum target for a swing, but the risk is usually the same. This means that their reward is about the same size as their risk, and they therefore need to have at least a 70 percent chance of success or else this approach is a losing strategy. Scaling in can help increase the odds, but the trade-off is more risk because your position size is larger. As easy and tempting as scalping appears to be, it is a very difficult approach to trade profitably.

If you swing part of your trade using a breakeven stop after taking partial profits at a couple of points, this reduces the required winning percentage. If you move your stop from the signal bar extreme to the entry bar extreme (one tick beyond both) after the entry bar closes, and then to breakeven after a five-tick move, this further reduces the required winning percentage to be profitable on the day. Finally, some scalpers use a wider stop of three to five points and add on as the market moves against them, and then use a wider profit target, and this again further reduces the required winning percentage. In general, if you see a setup that you feel is a very high-probability trade, the trade will likely be a scalp instead of a large swing. This is because whenever there is such an obvious imbalance, the market will correct it quickly, so a very high-probability, relatively low-risk situation cannot last more than a bar or two.

Swing traders use the same setups and stops as the scalpers, but focus on the few trades each day that are likely to have at least a two-legged move. They can usually net four or more points on part of their position on each trade and then move their stop to breakeven on the balance. Many will let the trade go against them and add on at a better price. However, they always have at least a mental stop and, if the market gets to that point, they conclude that their idea can no longer be valid and they will exit with a loss. Always look for where scalpers will have their stops, and look to add on to your position at that location, if the pattern is still valid. If you bought what you perceived to be a reversal, consider allowing the market to put in a lower low and then add on at the second entry. For example, with a reliable stock like Apple (AAPL), if you are buying what you perceive to be near the low of the move and the overall market is not in a bear trend day, consider risking two to three dollars on the trade and adding on at a one- to two-dollar open loss. However, only experienced traders who are very comfortable in their ability to read price charts and in their ability to accept a large loss if their read is wrong should attempt this. On most days, the market should go your way immediately, so this is not an issue.

Swing traders can take a position and keep adding the same size position with each subsequent signal, after they have a reasonable profit. The stop on the entire position is the stop of the most recent addition, which usually means that they will have a profit on their earlier entries, even if they lose on their final entry. They would also exit before their trailing stop was hit if the market generated a signal in the opposite direction.

Everyone wants a very high winning percentage, but very few people ever develop the ability to consistently win on 70 percent or more of their trades. This is why so few traders can make a living scalping for one or two points in the Emini, although just about everyone tries it for a while when starting out. For most traders to be successful, they have to learn to accept a lower winning percentage and develop the patience to swing trade, allowing pullbacks along the way. Even if traders are very successful scalpers, unless they are also willing to swing trade occasionally, they will usually not participate in some protracted trends where the probability of a successful trade is often 60 percent or less. Many very good traders sit quietly during these times and simply wait for a high-probability scalp, missing a good part of what is often a protracted move. This is an acceptable way to trade, because the goal of trading is to make money, not to be constantly placing trades.

When the Emini has an average daily range of 10 to 15 points, there will usually be at least one trade a day where a trader can enter on a stop and exit on a limit order with a four-point profit. Since 99 percent of the days have at least a five-point range, theoretically a trader could enter and exit on limit orders and make four points, but that is impossible for anyone to do consistently on small range days. In general, it is easier for traders to spot setups where they can enter on stops and exit on either limit orders or trailing stops. There is at least one four-point swing on 90 percent of the days, and about five four-point swings occur in about 10 percent of the days. Most days have one to three swings where a trader can make four points from a stop entry. If a trader is making 10 to 15 trades a day, then most of the trades are scalps. However, strong scalpers will know when a setup has a reasonable chance of becoming a swing of four to 10 points and will usually swing a quarter to a half of their positions in those situations. Once they exit the scalp portion, if there are additional entries as the market continues in their swing direction, they will usually put scalps back on when additional setups develop.

Swing trading is much more difficult than it appears when a trader looks at a chart at the end of the day. Swing setups tend to be either unclear, or clear but scary. Most swing setups have a 40 to 50 percent chance of leading to a swing that will reach the trader's profit target. In the other 50 to 60 percent of trades, either traders will exit before the target is reached if they believe that the target is no longer reasonable, or their protective stop will be hit. Most swing traders enter on reversals, because they need to get into the trade early if they hope to make four or more points. When a trend is especially strong, they can often make four points by entering on a pullback or even on the close of a bar in a strong spike, but these situations arise only a couple of times a week. Most swing traders try to buy some kind of double bottom, short some kind of double top, or enter on some other reliable opening reversal setup in the first couple of hours of the day. They often have to enter on several reversals before one turns into a big swing, but they still usually make money, on balance, on the trades that do not reach a four-point target. Those trades end up as scalps. For example, if a trader bought a double bottom in the first hour, and then after six bars the market set up a reasonable double top, the trader might reverse to short, maybe making a point or two on the long. Just as a scalper sometimes swings, most swing traders end up with lots of scalps. Once swing traders believe that their premise is no longer valid, they exit, often with a scalp.

After swing traders see a reasonable setup, they have to take the trade. Swing setups almost always appear less certain than scalp setups, and this lower probability tends to make traders wait. When there is a strong signal bar, it usually comes as part of a very emotional reversal, and a beginning trader is still thinking that the old trend remains in effect. Beginning traders are typically unprepared for this. They might be thinking that the old trend is still in effect, and they might have lost on several earlier countertrend trades today and don't want to lose any more money. Their denial causes them to miss the early entry. Entering on the breakout or after the breakout bar closes is hard to do, because the breakout spike is often large, and traders have to quickly decide to risk much more than they usually do. This is why they often end up choosing to wait for a pullback. Even if they reduce their position size so that the dollar risk is the same as with any other trade, the thought of risking two or three times as many ticks frightens them. Entering on a pullback is difficult because every pullback begins with a minor reversal, and they are afraid that the pullback might be the start of a deep correction. They end up waiting until the day is almost over and then finally decide that the trend is clear, but now there is no more time left to place a trade. Trends do everything they can to keep traders out, and that is the only way they can keep traders chasing the market all day. When a setup is easy and clear, the move is usually a small, fast scalp. If the move is going to go a long way, it has to be unclear and difficult to take, to keep traders on the sidelines and force them to chase the trend.

Swing traders should always be wondering if they should exit the trade early, before their profit target is reached. One way to help decide is to imagine that you are flat and think about whether you should enter at the market with a swing-size position and a protective stop exactly where a swing trader who is in the market would have his stop. If you would not take that trade, then you should exit your swing position immediately. This is because holding your current swing trade is identical financially to initiating a new trade of the identical size at that price and with that stop.

Most swing traders will scalp out if the trade is not unfolding as desired, and most scalpers will swing part of their position when they are entering on the best setups, so there is a lot of overlap in what both do. The fundamental difference is that the scalper will take far more trades, and most of those trades are not likely to yield more than a scalper's profit, whereas a swing trader tries to only take the trades that are likely to have at least two legs. Neither way is superior to the other, and traders choose the method that best suits their personalities.

As discussed in the section on the trader's equation in Chapter 25, swing trades are usually less certain than scalp trades. This means that the probability of success is less. However, a trader who is swinging is looking for a large profit, and the profit is usually at least twice as large as the risk. This larger potential profit compensates for the lower probability of success and can lead to a favorable trader's equation. The biggest swings come from breakouts of trading ranges and from reversals, and most reversal patterns are trading ranges. This is where uncertainty is highest, and the probability of success is often 50 percent or less. A swing trader needs to look for a setup where the reward is sufficiently larger than the risk, to compensate for the lower probability of success. Scalps are much more certain, but a high degree of certainty means a conspicuously large imbalance in the market, and a large imbalance is quickly noticed and neutralized by traders. The result is that the market quickly returns to a state of confusion (a trading range). Scalpers have to be fast in deciding to take the trade and in taking profits, because the move will usually come back to the entry price within a few bars.

Swings last a long time because of uncertainty, which is usually a critical component of any trade that lasts for many bars and covers many points. This is the wall of worry that is often mentioned in a strong bull trend, and it works in an opposite form in a strong bear trend. The difficulties of trend trading are discussed in the first book. Trends begin as small or large spikes, and then evolve into small or large channels. When the breakout is small, traders are uncertain if there will be follow-through. When it is big and strong, the uncertainty takes a different form. Traders are unsure of how much they have to risk to stay in the trade, and if the trader's equation is favorable because of the large risk. They see the large spike and realize that they might have to risk to the opposite side of the spike. This increased risk results in a much smaller position size. They then chase the market as it enters a channel, because their initial position was smaller than they wanted it to be. The channel then has the uncertainty of being a two-sided market. At the end of the day, beginners will look at the chart and see a strong trend, and wonder how they missed it. The reason is that all big moves are uncertain as they are unfolding, and this traps traders out of the strongest trends. It also often traps traders into countertrend trades, resulting in repeated losses. Even a beginner has a sense of probabilities and senses that the trend is a low-probability event, which it is. The strongest trends happen only a few times a month, so beginners know that the odds of today growing into one of those strong trend days are small. They end up either denying it and getting trapped out or fighting it and taking repeated losses. Instead, they need to learn to accept it and follow what the market is doing. If it is relentlessly going up, even though it looks weak, they need to buy at least a small position, and swing it.

Trade management for swing trading is identical to that for always-in trading, which is discussed in the third book, except that swing traders tend to scale out as the trade goes their way. A truly always-in trader holds on to the position until there is an opposite signal, and then reverses to a trade in the opposite direction. For most traders, swing trading entries and stops are identical to those in trend trading, which was discussed in book 1. One important difference is that most swing traders treat exits in a trading range differently from those in a trend. In a trend, they are more likely to let part of their positions run until there is an opposite signal, but in a trading range, they are much more likely to exit the remainder of their positions near the extreme of the trading range. At that point, they decide whether the move was weak enough and the reversal pattern strong enough so that they should look for an opposite swing, or instead the swing was strong enough so that they should wait for a pullback and reenter for a second leg in their original direction.

When the average daily range in the Emini is 10 to 15 points and a trader can usually use a two-point protective stop without getting stopped out of most good trades, many swing traders will take partial profits at two to four points, depending on the situation. If traders think that the market is in a trading range and they are buying a reversal up at the bottom, the probability of an equidistant move is usually 60 percent or more. Since they are risking two points, they then have a 60 percent chance of making two points before the stop is hit. This results in a minimally acceptable trader's equation, and therefore a trader can take partial profits at two points. If traders believe that the trading range is tall enough for them to make three or four points, they might take partial or full profits at that level. Other traders will take partial profits on longs at resistance levels, like minor reversals at measured move targets, above prior swing highs, and on bear trend line and bull trend channel line overshoots and reversals (failed breakouts). They will take partial profits on shorts at comparable support levels. All traders exit their final positions whenever there is a strong reversal signal. Remember, they will exit partially or fully on a weak reversal signal, but not usually reverse. This is because traders use different criteria for exiting than for entering a trade. They require a stronger signal before they enter, but will take partial or full profits on a weaker signal in the direction opposite to their position. There are many ways to profitably trade swing trades, and the only major issue is the trader's equation. As long as the math makes sense, then the approach is profitable and therefore reasonable.

It is reasonable for an experienced trader to be primarily a scalper when trading Eminis, looking for two to four points (when the average daily range is about 10 to 15 points), and a swing trader when trading stocks. If you are one of those extremely rare traders who can win on 80 percent or more of your trades, then you can scalp some Emini trades for a one-point profit. Exit part or all of your trade on a limit order after four ticks of profit, which usually requires the move to extend six ticks beyond the signal bar (the entry is on a stop at one tick beyond the signal bar; then you need four more ticks for your profit, and your limit exit order usually is not filled until the price moves one tick beyond your target). Four ticks in the Emini is one point, which is equivalent to a 10 cent (10-tick) move in the SPY (ETF contract).

So what should a beginner do? Most traders will lose money if they scalp for a profit target that is smaller than their risk, even if they win on 60 percent of their trades. Beginners will often be wrong about what they think is a 60 percent setup. Many of their trades will actually be only 50 percent certain at best, although they seemed much more certain at the time that the beginning traders took them. They will probably think that they just need a little more experience to increase their winning percentage up to 70 or 80 percent, where they know that math would then be on their side. The reality is that they will never become that good, because very few of the best traders ever get there. That is the simple truth.

At the other extreme is swing trading for a profit that is at least twice as large as his risk. Most of these setups are only 40 to 50 percent certain, but that is enough to have a favorable trader's equation. On most days, there are a couple of setups a day, and sometimes five or more, and most are usually major trend reversals (discussed in book 3). If a trader is willing to take low probability trades (the reward has to be at least twice as big as the risk, as discussed in Chapter 25), he needs to take every reasonable setup because the math is against him if he cherry picks. The trader's equation for these trades is positive for a basket of them, but the odds are that any one trade will lose since the probability is less than 50 percent. The probability is low because the setup looks bad, and the trade often looks weak even after the entry and usually has several pullbacks before a strong trend finally begins. Many traders instead prefer to wait for the trend to begin so that the probability will be 60 percent or higher, although there is less profit remaining in the trade. Many swing setups are strong, with probabilities of 60 percent or greater. When that is the case, each trade has a positive trader's equation and cherry picking is mathematically acceptable. Also, the math is good for either a swing or a scalp. Most traders starting out will experiment with both swing trading and scalping and just about everything else, like different time frames and indicators, to see if they can be successful and if a particular style better suits their personalities. There is no one best way, and any approach where there is a positive trader's equation is good. Many traders try to catch five to 10 tradable swings a day where the probability of making a profit that is at least as large as the risk is 60 percent or greater. When they do, they usually look for micro double tops to short and micro double bottoms to buy. If a trader thinks that a setup is strong and will likely yield a reward that is at least as large as his risk, then it has a probability of success of at least 60 percent (Chapter 25 discusses the mathematics of the directional probability of an equidistant move). This allows the trader to have a stop that is the same size as his profit target and still have a favorable trader's equation. Although this is the style that most successful traders adopt, most beginners should instead first look for strong swing trade setups, even though the chance of success is often only 50 to 60 percent. This is because when the reward is two or more times the size of the risk, the trader's equation is even stronger, despite the smaller probability of success. In the Emini, when the average daily range is about 10 to 15 points, look for trades with a good chance of a four-point (twice the size of the initial risk) or more swing, and exit some or all at four points. With experience, a trader can scalp out part for two to four points and then swing the balance. If he focuses on these setups, he is giving himself a reasonable chance to become a profitable trader. If a trader finds that he often exits too soon, he should consider placing his OCO orders (one to take profit at two to four points, the other to get stopped out with a loss of two points or less), walk away, and come back in an hour. He might be surprised that he has suddenly become a successful trader. Once the trend is established, look for additional entries in the direction of the trend, scalping most for two points while risking about two points and, if the trend is very strong, swinging some. As simple as this sounds, trading is never easy because you are competing against very smart people in a zero sum game, and what looks so obvious at the end of the day is usually not very obvious at all in real time. It takes a long time to learn to trade profitably and even once you do, you have to stay sharp and maintain your discipline every day. It is challenging, but that is part of the appeal. If you become successful, the financial rewards can be huge.

When it comes to stocks, there is much more variability in the size of the profit targets. For a $500 stock with an average daily range of $10, it would be foolish to scalp for 10 cents, because you would likely have to risk about two dollars, and your winning percentage would have to be over 95 percent. However, scalping for 10 cents might be worthwhile in QQQ especially if you are trading 10,000 shares.

It is relatively easy to look for swings in high-volume stocks (at least three million shares per day, but preferably seven million or more) that have an average range of several dollars. You want minimal slippage, reliable patterns, and at least $1.00 profit per trade. Try to scalp for $1.00 and then use a breakeven stop on the balance; hold until the close or until a clear and strong opposite setup develops. You might be able to watch about five stocks regularly throughout the day and sometimes check on up to another five or so at different times during the day, but you will rarely ever trade them.

An Emini scalper will likely be able to enter only a couple of stock trades a day, since Emini day trading takes so much attention. Also, if you only use bar charts for stocks, this allows you to put six charts on one screen. Just pick the one stock that is trending the best and then look for a pullback near the moving average. You can also trade reversals if you see a trend channel overshoot and reversal after there was a prior strong trend line break. If the Emini market is active, consider trading only 15 minute stock charts, which require less attention.

When you are anticipating a significant move or a new trend, or when you are entering on a pullback in a strong trend, exit 25 to 75 percent of your contracts at a scalper's profit that is equal to at least one to two times your initial risk, and then scale out of the remaining contracts as the market continues to go your way. Move your protective stop to around breakeven after you exit the scalp portion of your trade. Sometimes you will want to risk as many as four to six ticks in the Eminis if you feel strongly that the trade will remain good, and an exit and then a reentry approach would be at a worse price. A good trade should not come back to let latecomers in at the same price as the smart traders who got in at the perfect time. If the trade is great, all of the traders who missed the initial entry are now so eager to get in that they will be willing to enter at a worse price and will place limit entry orders at a tick or two worse than the original entry, keeping the breakeven stop of the original traders from being hit. However, sometimes the best trades come back to beyond the breakeven stop to trap traders out of what will become a huge, fast trend. When that seems like a possibility, risk a few extra ticks. Also, if it comes back and runs those stops and then immediately resumes the new trend, reenter or add to your swing position at one tick beyond the prior bar (in a new bull trend, this is one tick above the prior bar's high).

If the market touches the profit target limit order but does not go through it and the order is still filled, that means that there might be more trend pressure than is evident on the chart, and the chances increase that the market will go beyond the profit target within the next several bars. If you were long and the market was willing to buy your position back from you (you were selling on a limit to take profits) at the very highest tick of the leg, the buyers are aggressive and will likely reemerge on any pullback. Look for opportunities to get long again.

Similarly, if the market touches your profit target (for example, nine ticks beyond the signal bar) but you do not get filled, this can be a failure. If you were long and the market hit nine ticks above the signal bar and you were not filled, consider moving your stop to breakeven. Once this bar closes, if the context makes a reversal trade likely, consider placing an order to go short at one tick below this bar, because that is likely where most of the remaining long scalpers will get out, providing selling pressure. Also, they will not want to buy again until more price action unfolds, thus removing buyers from the market and increasing the odds that the sellers will push the market down enough for you to scalp out of your short. A five- or nine-tick failed breakout is common at the end of a protracted trend and is often the first sign of a reversal.

Although all stocks trade basically the same way, there are subtle personality differences between them. For example, Apple (AAPL) is very respectful when it comes to testing breakouts, whereas Goldman Sachs (GS) tends to run stops, requiring a wider stop.

Although it is theoretically possible to make a living by trading for one-point scalps in the Emini, risking four to eight ticks and using a smaller time frame chart like a one minute or 1,000 tick chart, it is like trying to make a living by panning for gold, trying to collects grains instead of nuggets. It is really hard work, it is only minimally profitable even when you do it well, and it is not fun. You have a much better chance of being successful and being able to trade happily for many years if you go for a larger profit and use a stop that is no larger than your profit target.

Figure 24.1

FIGURE 24.1   Swing Long after a Pullback from a Strong Rally

As shown in Figure 24.1, Baidu (BIDU) broke above the 15 minute trend line late yesterday and therefore was likely to have at least two legs up. It was possible that the second up leg ended at bar 5, but today's open was so strong that there likely would be an attempt to exceed it after a pullback. The drop to bar 7 was sharp, but bar 7 was a strong bull reversal bar that reversed the moving average gap, the gap up open, and the test of the bar 3 high (it ran the stops below that high and turned up sharply). For a $300 stock, you need a wider stop; so trade fewer shares to keep the risk the same, but use a larger profit target on the scalp portion of the trade. Two dollars is a reasonable initial target, and then move the stop to breakeven and exit by the close. Since this was a bull reversal from a bear spike and channel, there was a reasonable chance that the market might even test the bar 1 top of the bear channel.

Figure 24.1   SCALPING, SWINGING, TRADING, AND INVESTING   **433**

Very successful scalpers might have chosen not to participate in shorting during the four-bar bear spike down to bar 7 if they believed that the probability of any trade was under 70 percent. Traders who scalp exclusively will often sit quietly during weaker spikes if they think that the probability is not high enough for a scalp. The result is that they sometimes miss relatively big swings. However, this is still an acceptable approach to trading for the few traders who are able to win on 70 percent or more of their trades.

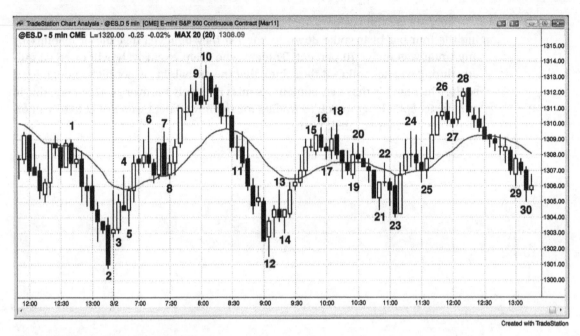

FIGURE 24.2 Swings Up and Down

Today (as shown in Figure 24.2) offered many opportunities for swing traders in both directions. The market fell almost 2 percent yesterday, but had been in a strong bull trend for months. The sell-off was just a poke below the daily moving average and was a pullback test the bottom of a bull channel in a 60 minute spike and channel bull trend. This meant that traders saw this as an area of support and thought that the sharp sell-off yesterday might have been just a sell vacuum and not the start of a bear trend. Both bars 3 and 5 were strong bull trend bars, and both followed attempts to test yesterday's low. The first bar of the day had a big tail on the top, which meant that it sold off into the close of the bar. However, instead of finding enough bears to drive the market below yesterday's strong bear close, the bulls were so strong that they did not allow the low 1 short to trigger. The bar 4 low 2 (some saw it as a low 1) triggered, but was strongly reversed up by bar 5. Traders thought that this was a possible low of the day and bought above bar 5 on a stop for a swing up. The double top at bar 7 never triggered, because it was a two-bar reversal and the trigger was below the lower of the two bars (the bull bar before bar 7), and not just below the bear bar. Some bulls took partial profits here (two to three points, depending on where they bought) as bars 6 and 7 were forming, and that long liquidation created the tails at the tops of the bars. The double top was followed by the bar 8 bull trend bar, setting up a high 2 buy signal above the moving

Figure 24.2   SCALPING, SWINGING, TRADING, AND INVESTING   **435**

average in a bull swing, which is a reliable buy setup. Some bulls took partial profits at two, three, or four points up from this entry, and others took full profits at three or four points. Many did not exit until the market gave a sell signal at the bar 10 two-bar reversal. As with many swing trades, the sell setup was not ideal because the momentum up from bar 8 was strong. This reduced the probability that a swing short would have been successful. However, if this was a trading range day, a bear had at least a 50 percent chance of the market testing the middle of the day's range, which was about five points below the entry price. With about a two-point risk, this yielded a good trader's equation.

This was the second leg up after a strong bear day and therefore a possible high of the day. Some bears shorted here, but other traders wondered if there might be another attempt up after such a strong rally. Once the market broke strongly to the downside in the bear bar before bar 11, traders gave up on the notion that the market might be forming a bull flag pullback to the moving average. Many traders shorted on this large bear bar, which is why it was a big bear breakout bar. Others shorted on the close of bar 11. Since it did not have a bull close, it confirmed the bear breakout. Still others chased the market down and shorted on the bear bars that followed. Since traders knew that the market might form a double bottom near yesterday's low, this sell-off could have been a sell vacuum instead of a bear trend. This made many traders hesitant to short near the support of the low of today and yesterday.

Bar 12 was a strong bull reversal bar with a low just above the low of yesterday, and therefore a signal bar for a double bottom long. It also followed the largest bear body of the day, which was an exhaustive sell climax and sell vacuum, and not the start of a bear trend. Smart bears took profits here, but many took partial profits at two, three, or four points from their entry prices, anticipating the double bottom and expecting the day to become a trading range day. Their expectation was based on their correct assumption that 80 percent of breakout attempts up and down fail, no matter how strong the spikes appear. Strong bulls also bought the sell vacuum, initiating new longs. Remember how strong the bulls appeared to be in the rally to bar 10, only for the move to be seen later as just a buy vacuum and not a new bull trend.

There was a second entry long after the failed bar 13 low 1 short at the bottom of the developing trading range, and then a bull reversal bar higher low at bar 14. Many bulls went long again here for a swing up. The spike up to bar 15 was strong, so traders expected another rally attempt after a pullback, and most would have considered this premise to remain valid as long as the market held above the bottom of the bull spike. Some traders put their protective stops below bar 14, while others used the bar 12 low. If they bought near the top of the spike, their risk was large and therefore their position size had to be small. Beginning traders would have had a hard time buying above either bar 12 or bar 14 because the sell-off was so steep. However, the day appeared to be a trading range day. Therefore, experienced traders were willing to buy a setup that might have only about a 40 to 50 percent chance of success, like the one at bar 12, which they believed had the potential to make about five points while risking about two. Bar 14 probably had a 60 percent chance of success, but the reward at that point was now a little less. Both setups had favorable trader's equations, even though beginners would have had a difficult time taking them.

Aggressive bears shorted below the bar 18 two-bar reversal, which was a double top and a lower high on the day. Other traders were instead waiting to buy a pullback.

Bar 19 appeared to be a high 2 buy entry, but since the bar before it was not a good buy signal bar, most traders would not have bought as bar 19 went outside up. Most would have waited for a pullback before buying. Some would have bought above bar 19 because it had a strong bull body, and the breakout above its high would have been a sign of confirmation of its bull breakout above the bar before it. Instead of a breakout pullback, the market broke to the downside.

Bar 21 was a strong bull reversal bar and a high 3 buy setup. However, since the market was still in the bear channel from bar 18, many bulls preferred to wait for a second entry, which came with the high 4 two-bar reversal at bar 23. Some bought the high 4 and others bought above the bull bar that followed bar 23. They saw this as a bull flag following the spike from bar 12 to bar 16, and they expected a second leg up, maybe to a leg 1 = leg 2 measured move up. Some traders who bought above bar 21 were aware that the market might form a lower low pullback from the breakout above the top of the bar, and this is what happened. Because of this possibility, many traded a smaller position size and used a wide protective stop, like maybe below bar 14 or bar 12, or maybe three to five points. Those traders then put on the remainder of their longs on the second entry above the bar 23 two-bar reversal. Some longs took partial profits at fixed intervals, like two, three, or four points, while others waited for price action profit targets, like below the bar 26 second leg up or below the bar 28 wedge rally (bars 24, 26, and 28 were the three pushes up).

Aggressive bears shorted below bar 28 or below the bear bar that followed it, looking for a test of the bar 25 bull channel that followed the spike up from bar 23. They took profits at two, three, and four points, or just above, at, or below the bar 25 bull channel low, or just before the close of the day.

CHAPTER 25

Mathematics of Trading: Should I Take This Trade? Will I Make Money If I Take This Trade?

I have a friend who has traded for over 30 years, and I think that he makes 10 or more points in the Eminis pretty much every day. He once told me that he believed that the average beginner should be able to make at least six points a day. I told him that I disagreed—that most beginners would be happy to consistently make two points a day. I left the conversation realizing that there are traders who have been wildly successful for so long that they have completely forgotten what it was like to be in the losing camp. However, the conversation also made me realize that, with enough experience, traders' good habits can become so much a part of who they are that trading becomes essentially effortless. But in every case, mathematics still has to be the basis of what they are doing. In fact, **trading is entirely about math**, and all successful traders understand probabilities and the trader's equation extremely well. The math changes with every tick, which is a barrier to those who don't understand what is going on and a great advantage to those who do.

Beginning traders are constantly looking for the perfect trade, one with a clear setup, high probability of success, low risk, and a large reward. At the end of the day, they wonder why they couldn't find one. Surely those trades exist, because how else are the big traders getting rich? What they don't realize is that making money is very difficult, because the market is filled with smart people who are trying to take money from each other. This prevents anyone from ever having a huge advantage. As soon as a perfect setup begins to form, everyone trades it and it quickly disappears, because there is no one willing to take the opposite side. The traders who missed the perfect setup don't want to chase it, and will enter only on a pullback. Once the market begins to pull back after not going very far, all of the traders who entered on what they thought was perfection are now holding losing trades. They quickly dump their positions and the perfect trade now goes in the opposite direction.

To make money as a trader, you need an edge, which means a mathematical advantage based on the size of your risk and reward, and on the probability of your profit target being reached before your protective stop is hit. Edges are rarely large, so whenever one of the three variables is unusually good, it will be offset by one or both of the other variables being bad. For example, if the potential reward is much larger than the risk, meaning that the risk is relatively small, the probability is usually small. If the probability is high, the reward is small and the risk is often high. The edge that traditional firms have is that they trade enough volume to have a vote on the direction of the market, and they have many trading systems running simultaneously and many traders trading independently, which smooths out their equity curve. Their goal is a small reward, usually 10 percent to 20 percent profit per year, with a relatively small risk and a high probability of success (they expect to make money by the end of the year more than 70 percent of the time). The edge of the high-frequency trading (HFT) firms is that they have a highly reliable statistical advantage, which is probably only 5 percent or less (a chance of winning of less than 55 percent is about a 5 percent advantage over a 50–50 pure luck system), but they apply it millions of times each week. This gives them a casino advantage. If a casino has only one customer, and he bets a billion dollars on a single bet, the casino has a 47 percent chance of going out of business on that bet. However, with a huge number of bets of ordinary sizes, the math greatly favors that their edge will result in a consistent profit. The same is true for a HFT firm. Since many are trying to make just a tick or two on each trade, their reward is tiny and their risk is relatively large on each trade, but the reliability of their success is high. Most of them probably have a 90 percent chance or better of making a profit every day, which means that their probability of success is high. The edge that day traders can have is an exceptional ability to read charts, resulting in a high winning percentage, which can be 70 percent or more. When combined with a profit target that is at least as large as the risk, they can make a very high return on their equity. Most of the very best traders in the world are discretionary traders, using subjective evaluations to make their decisions. Why would a superstar continue to work at Goldman Sachs, sharing his rewards, when he can go out on his own and open a hedge fund or trade for himself? Very few would, and that is why the world's greatest traders go out on their own, and it is also the great lure for all of us. There are countless examples on Wall Street of well-known traders earning billions of dollars a year from discretionary trading. Some hold positions for months or years at a time, like Warren Buffett, whereas others are day traders, like Paul Rotter, the "Eurex flipper." Day traders have many options in the trade-offs among risk, reward, and probability, and some are willing to accept a lower probability of success, say 40 percent, in exchange for a reward that is three or more times the risk.

Here are some examples of situations where a trader has an edge:

Probability of success of 70 percent or better (reward has to be at least half as big as risk just to break even):
- Scalps, but since most traders cannot consistently pick trades with a 70 percent chance of success, they should trade a scalp only if the reward is at least as large as the risk. For example, if you believe that a two-point stop is needed in the Emini, take the trade only if at least a two-point reward is reasonable.

Probability of success of 60 percent or better (reward has to be at least as big as risk to break even):
- Buying a high 2 pullback to the moving average in a bull trend.
- Selling a low 2 pullback to the moving average in a bear trend.
- Buying a wedge bull flag pullback in a bull trend.
- Selling a wedge bear flag pullback in a bear trend.
- Buying a breakout pullback from a breakout of a bull flag in a bull trend.
- Selling a breakout pullback from a breakout of a bear flag in a bear trend.
- Buying a high 1 pullback in a strong bull spike in a bull trend, but not after a buy climax.
- Selling a low 1 pullback in a strong bear spike in a bear trend, but not after a sell climax.
- Shorting at the top of a trading range, especially if it is a second entry.
- Buying at the bottom of a trading range, especially if it is a second entry.
- Trend reversals:
  - After a strong break of the trend line, look for a reversal after a test of the trend's extreme where there is a good reversal signal bar. Traders are looking to buy a higher low or a lower low at a bottom, or to short a higher high or a lower high at a top.
  - Strong final flag reversal.
  - Buying a third or fourth push down in a bear stairs pattern for a test of the low of the prior push down.
  - Selling a third or fourth push up in a bull stairs pattern for a test of the high of the prior push up.
- Entering using limit orders; this requires more experience reading charts, because the trader is entering in a market that is going in the opposite direction to the trade. However, experienced traders can reliably use limit or market orders with these setups:
  - Buying a bull spike in a strong bull breakout at the market or at the close of the bar, or on a limit order at or below the low of the prior bar (entering in spikes requires a wider stop and the spike happens quickly, so this combination is difficult for many traders).

- Selling a bear spike in a strong bear breakout at the market or at the close of the bar, or on a limit order at or above the high of the prior bar (entering in spikes requires a wider stop and the spike happens quickly, so this combination is difficult for many traders).
- Buying a bear breakout at around a measured move, if the breakout is not too strong—for example, if the range is about four points tall in the Emini, buying on a limit order at four points below the range, risking four points, and expecting a test of the breakout point. Only very experienced traders should consider this.
- Selling a bull breakout at around a measured move, if the breakout is not too strong—for example, if the range is about four points tall in the Emini, selling on a limit order at four points above the range, risking four points, and expecting a test of the breakout point. Only very experienced traders should consider this.
- Buying at or below a low 1 or 2 weak signal bar on a limit order in a possible new bull trend after a strong reversal or at the bottom of a trading range.
- Shorting at or above a high 1 or 2 weak signal bar on a limit order in a possible new bear trend after a strong reversal or at the top of a trading range.
- Buying at or below the prior bar on a limit order in a quiet bull flag at the moving average.
- Shorting at or above the prior bar on a limit order in a quiet bear flag at the moving average.
- Buying below a bull bar that breaks above a bull flag, anticipating a breakout pullback.
- Selling above a bear bar that breaks below a bear flag, anticipating a breakout pullback.

Probability of success of about 50 percent (reward has to be at least 50 percent greater than risk to break even):
- The initial entry when scaling into a position in a trading range.
- Buying or selling in a tight trading range, expecting a breakout that would result in a profit that is several times greater than your risk.
- Shorting a lower high in a trading range when the trend might be reversing down, or buying a higher low when the trend might be reversing up. Since the entry is in the middle of the trading range, the probability is 50 percent, but the reward is usually twice the risk.

Probability of success of 40 percent or less (reward has to be at least twice the size of risk):
- Buying at the bottom of a bear trend or shorting at the top of bull trend where the reversal trade allows for a small risk and a very large reward—for example, shorting a rally to a clear resistance level, entering on a limit order at one tick

below the resistance, and having a protective stop at one or two ticks above it. There are several examples in the chapter on entering on limit orders.

Probability of success of 40 percent to 60 percent, depending on circumstances (reward has to be at least twice the size of risk to break even when the probability is only 40 percent):

- Buying a breakout test in a bull trend on a limit order as the market is falling, or shorting a breakout test in a bear trend on a limit order as the market is rising.
- Buying below a low 1 or 2 signal bar, even if it is not weak, on a limit order (a potential higher low) in a new bull trend or at the bottom of a trading range, or shorting above a high 1 or 2 signal bar, even if it is not weak, on a limit order (a potential lower high) in a new bear trend or at the top of a trading range. For example, if the market might be completing a wedge reversal top in a bull trend and pulls back for a bar or a few bars, shorting above the high 1 and high 2 signal bars is shorting in what you hope is a new bear swing.
- Fading magnets, like shorting at a measured move up in a bull trend or buying at a measured move down in a bear trend.
- Buying a sell climax around the close of an unusually large bear trend bar in an area of support in an overdone bear trend (climaxes are discussed in book 3).
- Selling a buy climax around the close of an unusually large bull trend bar in an area of resistance in an overdone bull trend.

Beginning traders quickly learn that trading trends appears to be an excellent way to make money. However, they soon discover that trading trends is actually just as difficult as any other type of trading. For them to make money, someone else has to lose it. The market is a zero-sum game being played by countless smart people on both sides. This guarantees that the three variables in the trader's equation will always keep the edge small and difficult to assess. For a trader to make money, he has to be consistently better than half of the other traders out there. Since most of the competitors are profitable institutions, a trader has to be very good. In a trend, the probability is often smaller than a beginner would like, and the risk is larger. In a trading range, the risk is not great, but neither is the probability or the reward. In a reversal, although the reward can be large, the risk is often big as well and the probability is small. In a scalp, the probability is high, but the reward is small compared to the risk.

THE TRADER'S EQUATION

Even though most traders don't think about a trade in mathematical terms, all successful traders use the trader's equation, at least subconsciously. You will often hear pundits on television talk about the risk/reward ratio when they are deciding whether to take a trade. This is unfortunate because it overlooks an equally important variable, probability. To take a trade, you must believe that the trader's equation is favorable: the probability of success times the reward has to be greater than the probability of failure times the risk. When a pundit says that a trade has a good risk/reward ratio, he simply means that it has an edge or a mathematical advantage, if you manage your trade correctly. Implicit in his recommendation is that the trade will "probably" work, meaning that he believes that there is better than a 50 percent chance that you will make a profit. Although they don't think of their comments this way, this is what they must believe if they are successful traders, because there is no way to be successful without considering all three variables.

With any trade, you set the reward and risk because the potential reward is the distance to your profit target and the risk is the distance to your stop. The difficulty in solving the equation is assigning a value to the probability, which can never be known with certainty. In general, if you are uncertain, assume that you have a 50 percent of winning or losing, and if you are confident that the signal looks good, assume that you have a 60 percent chance of winning and a 40 percent chance of losing. Don't even worry about how far the move might go. Simply evaluate whether the setup looks good, and if it does, assume that the probability of a move up of any size has a 60 percent chance or better compared to a move down of the same size. This is the probability (or directional probability) of an equidistant move and is discussed later in this chapter. If the potential reward is many times larger than the risk, many traders will also consider taking a trade that is unlikely to be successful. When that is the case, they should assume that the probability is 40 percent. If the probability of success is much less than that, very few traders would ever consider taking the trade, no matter how great the potential reward is.

It is important to understand the implications of these probabilities. Otherwise, it is easy for a beginning trader to become upset when the market does something that he thinks is improbable, or even impossible. No matter how confident you feel, the market will often do the exact opposite of what you believe that it should. If you are 60 percent confident that the market will go up, that means that in 40 percent of the cases it will instead go down, and you will lose if you take the trade. You should not ignore that 40 percent any more than you would dismiss someone 30 yards away who is shooting at you, but who has only a 40 percent chance of hitting you. Forty percent is very real and dangerous, so always respect the traders who believe the opposite of you.

If you don't take a trade because you think that the probability is only 50 percent and you only take trades where you think the probability is 60 percent, then in half of the cases you will miss a good trade. This is just part of trading and a consequence of the edges being as small as they have to be in a zero-sum game with a huge number of very smart people, where half of them believe the exact opposite of the other half. Never get upset or confused by the market doing anything.

Simply accept that anything is possible, even if you do not understand why it is happening. No one ever really understands why, and the reason is never important. You make money from math, not from reasons, so if someone takes trades only when the trader's equation is strongly favorable, that trader is in a good position to consistently make money.

You have to remain in your comfort zone if you expect to trade profitably for many years. Some traders like trades where the reward is several times greater than the risk, and they are willing to win on only 30 to 40 percent of their trades. This approach has a favorable trader's equation, but most trades have a reward that is only about as large as the risk. This means that these traders will choose to miss most trades that take place every day because they don't believe that the reward is large enough to justify the low probability of success. Other traders will only trade high probability setups, and are willing to accept a reward that is only as large as the risk. However, very often when the market is trending, the pullbacks are small and the probability of the setups is often less than 50 percent. For example, if there is a weak bear channel with prominent tails, there might be a sell signal at the bottom of the channel. The market looks like the odds favor the formation of a trading range, but bears who are willing to short at the bottom, looking for a swing that is two or three times as large as their risk, will do very well. The traders who only want high probability trades will sit and watch the bear continue for 10 or 20 bars as they wait for a high probability reversal setup to buy or pullback to short. This is also an acceptable approach to trading. Some traders are comfortable in all environments and adjust their style to the market. This allows them to trade profitably all day long, which is the goal of every trader. The reality is that most good traders have a particular style and wait for setups consistent with that style.

Scalpers seek relatively small profits compared to the risk that they incur (they should go for a reward that is at least as large as the risk), and need a high probability of success to create a positive trader's equation. Don't assume that this means that they will only trade flags, because many will also trade strong breakouts. With a strong breakout, the stop theoretically is beyond the spike, which can be far away (for example, in a four bull trend bar breakout, the initial stop is theoretically below the low of the first bar, although most traders would not risk that much). However, since the breakout is strong, there is a 60 percent chance or better of an equidistant move. This means that they can take a trade with high risk, because the reward is equally high and the probability is also high. To keep their dollars at risk the same as it is for their other trades, they have to trade smaller volume.

One of the most important decisions that traders make all day long is whether the bulls or the bears will win at the high or low of the prior bar. For example, if there is a strong bull trend bar, will there be more bears selling to initiate shorts, and bulls selling out of their longs and taking profits around the high and close of the bar, mostly using market and limit orders, or will there be more bulls initiating new longs and bears buying back their shorts, mostly using stop orders? Similarly, at the low, will there be more buying or more selling? Traders try to assess the probability of making enough of a profit to offset the risk that they need to assume in a trade. Their goal is to make money over time, and they know that they will often lose. However, for them to be profitable in the long run, they need to be taking trades that have favorable (positive) trader's equations.

Once you see a possible setup, the first thing you have to do is determine how far away your protective stop has to be. Once you know your risk, you can decide on the number of shares or contracts that you can trade, keeping your total risk to within your normal limits. For example, if you normally risk $500 when you buy a stock, and you think that you would need to have your protective stop on the trade in question at about $1.00 below your entry price, then you can trade 500 shares. You then decide on what the probability of the trade is. If you cannot tell, then you assume that it is 50 percent. If it is 50 percent, then your potential reward should to be at least twice the size of your risk to make the trade worth taking. If you cannot reasonably expect to make $2.00 on that long, don't take the trade. If the chance of success is 60 percent, then your reward has to be at least equal to your risk, and if that $1.00 profit target is unreasonable, don't take the trade. If you do take the trade, make sure to use at least a $1.00 profit target, since that is the minimum that you need to have a positive trader's equation when the risk is $1.00 and the probability is 60 percent.

Every trade needs a mathematical basis. Assume that you have to risk two points in the Emini and you are considering a short setup. Is it 60 percent certain that you can make two points before losing two points? Is there a 70 percent chance of making one point, or a 40 percent chance of making four points? If the answer to any of these is yes, then there is at least a minimum mathematical reason to take the trade. If the answer to all of them is no, then consider the same three possibilities for a long. If the answer is yes for any of the three choices, then consider taking the trade. If the answer is no for both the bulls and the bears, then entering on a stop is not a good approach at the moment, and the market is unclear. This means that it is in a trading range, and experienced traders can look to short above bars and buy below bars with limit orders.

There are three variables to the trader's equation, and traders might focus on one over the other three because of their personalities. For example, a trader who needs a high winning percentage to be able to stay focused for the entire day will tend to look for trades where that is possible and would therefore have to be willing to accept relatively less reward and more risk. When the probability is high, the imbalance is conspicuous and the market will neutralize it quickly. The result is that the move usually lasts for only a few bars, and therefore the reward generally has to be small. Because the probability is often high and risk is small for a good scalp setup, traders will often trade their largest position size when taking a strong scalp. At the other extreme are traders who want their reward to be much larger than their risk, and to achieve that goal, they will have to be comfortable winning on only about 40 percent of their trades. When the probability is low, traders often trade smaller and some look to add on as the market goes their way. It is therefore common for a swing trader to take a smaller initial position than a scalp trader. Someone else might be risk averse and want a minimal risk on each trade. To get that, the trader has to accept some combination of lower reward and lower probability of success. There are other traders who take whatever trade is present and trade it appropriately, based on the context. When the probability is relatively high, they will take profits sooner. When the most important feature of the trade appears to be the reward that it offers, they accept that the probability will be less and that they have to be willing to swing more of their position to make the strategy work over time. Many trades are in between these extremes and have about a 50 percent chance of success. Whenever a trader takes one, he should always try for a reward that is about twice the size of his risk, to keep the trader's equation positive.

Even though a low-probability trade can have a potential reward that is much larger than the risk and therefore be a great trade, there is an inherent problem for most traders. Because swing trades have a large reward, by definition, they must also have either relatively low probabilities or large risks. A trade cannot exist with a high probability of making a large reward relative to the risk. Why not? Remember, there has to be someone who will take the other side of your trade, and since institutions control the market, then you have to believe that an institutional trader is willing to trade against you. If your probability of success is 80 percent, his is 20 percent. If your reward is six points, his risk is six points. If your risk is two points, his reward is two points. So if you think that you have an 80 percent chance of making six points while risking two points, then you believe that there are institutional traders willing to take the opposite side of your trade, where they have a 20 percent chance of making only two points while risking six points. Since that is virtually impossible in a huge market, you have to assume that your assessment of the variables is wrong and the trade is not nearly as good as you think. No institution has to be willing to do the exact opposite of what you are doing, but the market, which is composed of all institutions and is basically a single big institution, does. So some combination of institutions has to be willing to do the opposite of everything that you do, and if your trade is so great, then theirs is horrible, and the market would never allow it to develop. Yes, there are many naïve people who would be willing to take the other side of your trade because of their misread of the market, but the market is very efficiently controlled by institutions, and they would never let an edge get that large. You should assume that both sides of virtually every trade that takes place is being placed by an institution, or by an individual placing a trade that an institution would take if that individual did not place the trade. Individuals place lots of trades, but they cannot move the market, no matter how ignorant they are willing to be with their orders. Their orders can only get filled if an institution is willing to place the same order. For example, if the Emini is at 1264 and you are long with a protective sell stop at 1262, your stop cannot get hit unless there is an institution who is also willing to sell at 1262. This is true for virtually all trades. If the market is going up strongly, why would any institution ever be willing to sell below the market? Because many bought much lower and are looking for reasons to take profits. If they believe that the market falling to 1262 is a reason to take partial profits, they will sell there. If the market hits your stop, it is not because it was running stops on the little guys. It is because there were institutions who believed that selling at 1262 was a mathematically sound decision.

As any trade starts to move in the direction of having high probability, high reward, and low risk, institutions would act quickly to take advantage of it, preventing the edge from ever becoming very big. Also, the firms on the losing side of the edge would act fast to increase their edge. The market would move fast and far in the form of one or more large trend bars (a spike) in the direction of that profit target, greatly increasing the risk (the size of the required stop) before the setup became strong. The weak signal or the low probability makes most swing trades difficult to take. No one is going to give you money, and trading is always going to be difficult. If you see easy money, you are reading the market wrong and will soon find yourself giving your money to someone else.

Ninety percent or more of all trading in large markets is done by institutions, which means that the market is effectively a collection of institutions. Almost all are profitable over time, and the few that are not soon go out of business. Since institutions are profitable and they are the market, every trade that you take has a profitable trader (a part of the collection of institutions) taking the other side of your trade. No trade can take place without one institution willing to take one side and another willing to take the other. Seventy percent of all volume is generated by computer algorithms, and the small volume from individual traders is not enough to deter the program trading from its path. The small volume trades made by individuals can only take place if an institution would be willing to take the same trade. If you want to buy at a certain price, the market will not get to that price unless one or more institutions also want to buy at that price. You cannot sell at any price unless one or more institutions are willing to sell there, because the market can only go to a price where there are institutions willing to buy and others willing to sell. If you trade 200 Emini contracts, then you are trading institutional volume and are effectively an institution, and you will sometimes be able to move the market a tick or two. Most individual traders, however, have no ability to move the market, no matter how ignorantly they are willing to trade. The market will not run your stops. The market might test the price where your protective stop is, but it has nothing to do with your stop. It will only test that price if one or more institutions believe that it is financially sound to sell there and other institutions believe that it is profitable to buy there. At every tick, there are institutions buying and other institutions selling, and all have proven systems that will make money by placing those trades.

Whenever a trader is taking a scalp, the trader on the other side is probably a swing trader. However, many swing traders will also take the opposite side from other swing traders. Good scalpers cannot not take the other side of trades placed by other good scalpers because the risk and reward are about the same for both directions, and only one can have a high probability of success. The scalper has a high probability of success, so the trader on the opposite side has a low probability of success. Since he is an institutional trader, you have to believe that his methodology is sound and profitable over time. How can that be if you are making money doing the opposite of him in a zero sum game? Because you are not. Your entry is the opposite, but your management is not. Let's say that you are using a two-point profit target and a two-point stop in the Emini and you are shorting above a weak high 1 buy signal bar at the top of a trading range, correctly believing that you have better than a 60 percent chance of success. The institutional trader is buying as you are selling and his risk might also be two points, which is the opposite of your reward (he gets stopped out where you take your profits), but his reward is far greater than your risk. Your protective stop is two points. That is where you will buy back your short for a loss. However, that is not where he will sell out of his long. His target is probably several times greater, so he can have a positive trader's equation, despite a low probability of success. He might also be using a very wide stop and scaling into his trade, both of which could increase his probability to 60 percent or more, even though the probability of success on his initial entry might be only 40 percent. If you think about it, low probability trades could not exist if there was no way to manage them to get a positive trader's equation, because no institution would ever take them and they would never trigger. They can only trigger if an institution is willing to take them, and an institution would not take them unless there was a way to trade them profitably. Institutions have many ways to manage their trades to ensure a positive trader's equation, including scaling in or out, using a wide stop, hedging, and swinging the trade for a reward that is sufficiently larger than the risk, so that they can offset the low probability.

The spectrum of market activity is from intensely one-sided, like during the spike phase of a strong trend, to extremely two-sided, like in an extremely tight trading range. Most of the time, it is in between, with periods of more one-sided trading alternating with periods when two-sided trading is more dominant. This can easily be seen in a trading range, where trend bars represent one-side trading, and reversals and tails represent two-sided trading. When the market is in a bull trend and moves above the high of the prior bar, it is breaking out, and when it moves below the low of the prior bar, it is pulling back. The opposite is true in a bear trend, where a breakout is a move below the low of the prior bar and a pullback is a move above the high of the prior bar. When the market is extremely one-sided, like during the spike phase of a strong trend, pullbacks are mostly due to profit taking. For example, if the market is in a strong bull spike made of five bull trend bars and it then trades below the low of the fifth bar, it does so because bulls who bought lower are selling out of part of their positions to take some profits. Remember, there has to be an institution taking the other side of every trade, and he will only do so if it is part of a profitable strategy. There also is a sell vacuum that sucks the market below that bar. It is due to all of the bulls who are eager to either initiate longs or add to their longs, and they have been placing limit orders at and below the lows of the prior bars, hoping to get long at a small discount. These bulls are eager to get long, but only at a better price. If the prior bar is six ticks tall, many of these bulls will only begin buying at six ticks below the high of the bar or lower (in other words, at the low or below the bar). This means that there is a relative absence of buyers from one to five ticks down, and the price can get sucked down quickly to find buyers, which it will succeed in doing around the low of the bar. Remember, the bulls who are taking profits are selling out of part of their longs and they need buyers to take the other side of their trade. Once the profit takers decide to take partial profits, they need to be willing to sell at a price where there will be enough traders willing to buy. Once the market gets high enough, the only traders willing to buy will be those waiting for the market to fall below the prior bar. If enough bulls want to take profits, the market will have to drop below the prior bar for them to be able to exit part of their longs. Other bulls will only begin to take profits on their longs if the market moves below the prior bar, so they will sell out on a stop at one tick below the bar. The bulls who are eager to buy will take the other side of the profit taking bulls. There will be very few bears shorting below the low of that bar, so the move down is not due to bears who are looking to swing a short. Although some firms might be scaling into shorts by shorting on a stop below the prior bar, it is not logical that this would be a significant factor in the first pullback in a strong spike. When the market is extremely one-sided, firms looking to short know that the probability may be 80 percent or higher that they can soon short higher, so it does not make sense for them to short here.

Since small pullbacks in strong trends are mostly due to profit taking, there is usually no good way for the bears to make profits by shorting below the low of the prior bar as the first pullback is forming in a strong bull trend, or for a bull to make money by buying above the high of the prior bar as the first pullback is forming in a strong bear trend. However, when the market breaks above the high of the prior bar in a bull trend or below the low of the prior bar in a bear trend, there is a profitable way to manage both a long and a short trade. If there is no way for both the buyers and the sellers to make money above the high of the prior bar in a strong bull trend, the market would not trade there, because it can only get there if one institution can make a profit by buying up there and another can make a profit by selling. The selling up there is a combination of profit taking by bulls and shorting by bears, and as the market becomes increasingly two-sided, the shorting by bears becomes a bigger part of the volume. If there is no way for both the buyers and sellers to make money when the market moves below the prior bar in a strong bear trend, the market will not trade below the bar. Why would an institution ever take a trade that is a losing strategy? They never would. Neither the buying firm nor the selling firm has to make money on every trade, but every trade has to be part of a winning strategy or else they would not take them.

If institutions are smart, profitable, and responsible for every tick, why would they ever buy the highest tick in a bull trend (or sell the lowest tick in a bear trend)? It is because that is what their algorithms have been doing profitably all of the way up, and some are designed to continue to do it until it is clear that the bull trend is no longer in effect. They lose on that final buy, but make enough on all of their earlier trades to offset that loss. Remember, all of their systems lose between 30 and 70 percent of the time, and this is one of those times. There are also HFT firms that will scalp for even a single tick right up to the high tick of a bull trend. The high is always at a resistance level, and many HFT firms will buy a tick or two below resistance to try to capture that final tick, if their systems show that this is a profitable strategy. Other institutions are buying as part of a hedge in another market (stocks, options, bonds, currencies, etc.) because they perceive that their risk/reward ratio is better by placing the hedge. The volume is not from small individual traders, because they are responsible for less than 5 percent of the volume at major turning points.

The more two-sided the market is, the more likely every breakout and pullback has both institutional bears and bulls initiating trades (rather than one side simply taking profits, like in the first pullback in a strong spike). They are doing so based on strategies that they have tested and shown to be profitable over time. Hundreds of millions of dollars are at stake, so everything is closely scrutinized and has to be effective. The people who own that money will demand that the trading have a sound mathematical basis, or else they will move it to a firm whose trading does. When there is mostly two-sided trading going on, which is most of the time, there are buyers and sellers entering on every breakout and every pullback, and since institutions are profitable, all of them are using profitable strategies, even though many have probabilities of success of 40 percent or less.

In the example of that one-bar pullback in the strong bull spike, if there is a breakout above the high of that bar, it will be mostly due to eager bulls who are pressing their bets as they add to their longs or initiate new longs. They are buying from someone willing to sell, and those sellers are a combination of profit taking bulls who bought lower and aggressive bears who are beginning to short. Initially, the bears will only be scalpers, expecting only small pullbacks. Some HFT firms will scalp for a profit of only a tick or two, and there is often a high probability setup that will allow them to do so, even above a strong high 1 buy signal bar in a strong trend. Many are using algorithms based on tick charts, which can show tiny patterns that are invisible on the 5 minute chart. As the market becomes more two-sided and a trading range begins to develop, bears will begin to sell rallies (some will scale in as the market goes higher), like above weak high 1 or high 2 buy signal bars at the top of the range or channel, and look to hold for a swing down. The more two-sided the market becomes, the more bears begin to swing and the more bulls stop swinging and begin to scalp. Eventually most of the swing trading bulls will have taken their profits, at which point most of bulls will be scalpers. When the buy signal bars become weaker, scalpers lose interest in buying because the probability drops, and they will only take high probability trades. Once the bull scalpers and most of the swing bulls stop buying, and the shorting is being done more by swing trading bears than bear scalpers, the trend reverses.

Even when the market is entering a trading range, there are still some bulls buying those low probability (around 40 percent) buy setups like the weak high 1 and high 2 signal bars at the top of the range. They are swing traders running algorithms that have been proven to be profitable over time when taking these low probability swing trades. They know that the probability of success is falling as the market becomes more of a trading range. However, they also know that their systems are profitable, even if the probability of success is 40 percent or less. Some of their winners will be many times larger than their stops, more than making up for the losers that they experience 60 percent of the time. Their programs can also scale in lower, and their lower entries can be larger. This enables them to get out at breakeven or even with a small profit, if they consider their initial premise to be no longer valid and they want to get out of the trade. On most days, you win by shorting the high of that bad high 1 buy signal bar at the top of a trading range or weak bull channel. However, there are a few days a month when the market will trend up strongly and create a series of low probability buy signal bars (like dojis or bear trend bars for signal bars), and each one will be followed by a huge rally where the reward is many times greater than the risk. On these days, those swing trading programs that buy these low probability setups can make a fortune that is great enough to more than make up for all of those little losses. The scalpers, on the other hand, often miss much of these trends, because they are unwilling to trade the low probability setups. When the market is trending up strongly, most scalpers will see the strength and avoid shorting above weak buy signal bars. They know that selling at the top of a bull trend is risky. "Risky" simply means that the trader's equation is bad, and the risk from trading against a trend is that any low probability with trend setup can result in a huge move. Low probability is usually the flip side of high reward, just as high probability usually means that the reward is small (a scalp). Because they see the bull trend, they want to buy. However, since the buy signals look weak, they therefore are relatively low probability setups. The scalper then ends up not buying, and missing a trend that can last for hours and cover many points. The scalper will wait for deeper pullbacks to buy, and will occasionally buy a strong breakout that he thinks will have follow-through for a bar or so, but he will make far less money on this type of trend day than will a swing trader. A good scalper will make more money than a swing trader on most other days. Remember, since the scalper is taking high probability trades and has far more setups to choose from because his profit goal is smaller, he theoretically has far more profitable trades than the swing trader, which means a smoother equity curve and more profitable days.

Whenever you trade a low probability system, the *system* has a positive trader's equation, but the chances of winning on any one trade are small. Each individual trade has a small chance of success, but if you take all of the setups, the trader's equation for the group is positive. This means that you cannot cherry pick among trades that have a low probability of success, no matter how much larger the reward is than the risk. People have an uncanny ability to pick all of the bad cherries and none of the good ones, and often miss that one great trade that is needed to overcome their earlier losses. They end up talking themselves out of taking the low probability trades that result in huge profits, and into taking all of the losers, which always look easier to take. The result is that they lose money. To trade a low probability system, you have to take every strong signal, because if you cherry pick, you will invariably pick the wrong cherries, and will often miss that one great trade that you need to overcome your earlier losses. Most traders are usually unable to take every trade. This exposes them to this risk, and makes low probability trading so difficult to trade profitably.

At the other extreme is high probability trading, where a trader sacrifices the size of his reward for a much higher chance of winning on every trade. If a system has a probability of 60 percent or higher and a reward that is at least as large as its risk, then every individual trade has a positive trader's equation. Traders don't need to average every trade with a bunch of other trades to be profitable. Each trade has a positive trader's equation, so traders can cherry pick all they want and still make money, and it does not matter if they miss 10 good trades in a row. If a trader misses many trades, but manages to take a few high probability trades, his chance of being profitable is still good. Because of this natural tendency to not take every trade, if traders find themselves cherry picking among swing trades, they should consider that most traders should focus on taking more high probability trades. I, in fact, have a friend who trades the 10-Year U.S. Treasury Note Futures, and he wants the smallest possible risk on each trade. To achieve that, he trades a 50 tick chart where many of the bars are only two ticks tall, and looks to risk just three or four ticks on each trade. He tries to make eight or more ticks on his trades and, since he is a very good chart reader, he wins on 90 percent of his trades, or so he told me. I assume that means he does not necessarily reach his eight-tick target on all of his trades, and that many of his winners have just a tick or two of profit. He might even count his breakeven trades in his win column if he thinks that losing on 10 percent is the same as winning on 90 percent. In any case, his emphasis is on risk and he assumes that his winning percentage and his reward will take care of themselves if he picks his trades carefully.

A high-frequency trading firm might place hundreds of thousands of trades every day on a basket of several thousand stocks, and the trades are based on statistics rather than fundamentals. For example, if a firm found that it is profitable to sell a one-tick rally for a one-tick profit and a three-tick risk when a stock falls on six consecutive ticks, they might use that as one of their programs. Just how effective do you think their strategies are? They have the smartest mathematicians designing and testing them, so you'd think that they surely have to win 70 percent of the time or more. I seriously doubt that is the case, though, because their programs are competing against algorithms at other firms, and it is highly unlikely that an edge that large could last more than a very short time before other firms spot it and neutralize it. Everything is a trade-off, and their goal is to have an extremely reliable system with which they will make money almost every day. If a firm is making 500,000 trades a day, trying for a one- or two-tick profit on each trade, I doubt it is winning on 70 percent of its trades. I doubt it because edges are fleeting and small and it is extremely unlikely that they could find 500,000 trades every day where the chance of success is 70 percent. I suspect that their winning percentage is 55 percent or less. Remember, a casino's edge is about 3 percent, yet casinos make money every day. How can that be? If you are 99 percent certain that your edge is real, and the game is played thousands of times, the math overwhelmingly favors that you will win. The same is true for a high-frequency trading firm. It is accepting a small edge and a relatively large risk in exchange for consistent profits. Wouldn't the HFT firm make more money if it traded setups that are 70 percent certain? Obviously it would, if it could prove mathematically that the setups actually were 70 percent certain. This means that it cannot, but that does not mean that these setups don't exist. They do, but they are subjective and obviously very difficult to program. This subjectivity gives individual traders an edge. If they develop the ability to make subjective judgments and the ability to not make many mistakes, they have an edge. With so many smart people trading, edges are always going to be small and subjective, and it will always be very difficult to consistently capitalize on them; but it can be done and it is the goal of every trader.

The earlier you enter, the more profit you stand to make, but your probability of success is less. Some traders prefer a higher winning percentage, and they are willing to enter a little later if they can be more certain that their trade will be profitable. For example, if the market might be reversing up, a trader might buy. Another trader might wait for a couple of strong bull trend bars and a clear always-in long buy signal before buying. The trade is more certain, but the trader, having missed part of the move, stands to make less. The trader paid for the better odds with some of the potential profit, in the belief that it was a good trade-off. Some traders feel more comfortable with a very high winning percentage, even if that means that they make less on the trade. Other traders prefer a potential reward that is many times greater than the risk, even if that means that they might win only 40 percent of the time. The higher the probability of success, the more obvious the setup is. When a setup is particularly obvious, a lot of smart traders will take it, and the imbalance will last for only a bar or two. The market will quickly reach the expected target and then either reverse or enter a trading range. That is why the best scalps have limited profit potential but a high probability of success. However, since most traders are unable to consistently pick only the high-probability scalps, they should stick to trades where the potential reward is at least as great as the risk and the probability is about 60 percent.

At any given moment, there are countless possible combinations of reward, risk, and probability, and traders need to have a clear plan. They cannot use the probability of making two points while risking two points if they really are planning on exiting with a one-point profit. The minimum probability needed to make a trade mathematically sound is different for the two trades, and traders sometimes will mix the two scenarios up if they are overly eager to take a trade. This is a common problem for traders starting out, but it is a sure path to a blown account. You need to get the most you can out of a good trade, because you will always lose the most possible on a bad one, and you need the big profits to make up for those losses.

Is there ever a situation where the probability of success is 90 percent or higher? One occurs on every trade and is a part of a profitable strategy. For example, if you are long and the market touches your profit taking limit order but does not fill it, you will still hold long, at least briefly, because you think that the chances are good that your order will be filled very soon. Your stop might be below the low of the prior bar, about six ticks away. For you to continue to hold long for that one extra tick of profit while risking six ticks means that you believe, at least at that moment, that you have a 90 percent chance of success. If you hold onto your position, then you believe that "chances are" that your order will be filled before your stop is hit. Although most traders never think about the actual math, they cannot continue to think that the trade is good unless the probability of success is about 90 percent. They are right, at least at that instant. If the market quickly pulls back three ticks, you are then risking three ticks to your stop as you try to make three ticks to your limit order, and you are no longer 90 percent certain.

There is another situation where a trader can be 90 percent or more certain of a move, but it is not a sensible trade. For example, at any time in the day, there is likely a 95 percent certainty that the market will go up one tick before it goes down 200 ticks and a 95 percent certainty that it will go down one tick before it goes up 200 ticks. However, you would never risk 200 ticks to make one tick, no matter what the odds of success were. One loss would wipe out 200 winners, which means that you need a 99.5 percent chance of success just to break even, and you would have to execute flawlessly 200 times in a row.

Likewise, is there ever a sound mathematical strategy where the chance of success is only 10 percent? Yes, for example, if the market is in a strong bear trend and has a rally up from a higher low but is now falling again, traders might place limit orders to buy at one tick above the earlier low and protective stops one tick lower. The chance of success might be only 10 percent, but if the market has a strong reversal up, they might make 10 points on their half-point risk. This means that if they took the trade 10 times, they might lose 18 ticks on their nine losers and make 40 ticks on their one win, and have an average profit per trade of 2.2 ticks.

Remember, your decision about whether to take a trade needs to incorporate probability, risk, and reward, and not just one or two of the variables. In general, whenever the probability of a trade is very high, you should trade most or all of it as a scalp. This is because extremely high-probability situations will not last more than a bar or two before the market corrects them. If something seems very certain, you can be fairly sure that it won't last long enough for a swing trade. The lower the chance of success, the greater the reward has to be relative to the risk. The best trades are trades where the chance of success is 60 percent or more, and the reward is at least as large as the risk and preferably about twice as big. These trades occur every day in most markets, but you have to anticipate them before they set up, and you have to take them once they do set up, and manage them well.

Once you find a setup, you next must decide whether you should take the trade. The decision is based on a mathematical calculation that requires three inputs: risk, reward, and probability. Unfortunately, there is a natural tendency to consider only the probability. Many beginning traders will see a setup that they feel has a 60 percent chance of being a successful scalp, and they may be right, but they still lose money. How can that be? It is because the decision has to be based on more than just probability. You have to consider how much you stand to gain and how much you have to risk to achieve that gain. Remember, you need the probability of success times the reward to be greater than the probability of failure times the risk. For example, if you are watching the Emini today and see a low 2 just below the falling moving average in a strong bear market, and you decide from your experience that shorting it has about a 70 percent chance of leading to a two-point profit target limit order being filled before a two-point stop is hit, then you have a 70 percent chance of making two points and a 30 percent chance of losing two points. If you take this type of trade 10 times, you will make $7 \times 2 = 14$ points and you will lose $3 \times 2 = 6$ points. Your net profit for the 10 trades is $14 - 6 = 8$ points, so your average profit is 0.8 point, or $40, per trade. If you have low commissions of about $5.00 round turn, then your actual average profit is about $35 per trade. That might not sound like much, but if you can do that twice a day and trade 25 contracts, that is about $1,700 a day and about $350,000 a year.

If instead you use a two-point stop and a four-point profit target and take a trade that you think is better than a 50–50 bet, let's still do the math using only a

50 percent probability. If you take 10 trades, you will win four points on five of those trades for 20 points of profit. You will lose two points on the other five trades for a 10-point loss. Your net profit then is 10 points in 10 trades and your average profit is about one point per trade. If you subtract out 0.1 point for your commission, you will average about $45 per trade. Obviously, there will be lots of trades that you will exit before your stop or profit target is hit, but it is reasonable to assume that those will approximately offset each other and therefore this formula is useful in guiding you in your trade selection. If you are very selective in your setups and take only trades that have a 70 percent chance of success, if you take 10 trades you will make $7 \times 4 = 28$ points and lose $3 \times 2 = 6$ points. Your profit after commissions will average about 2.1 points per trade.

Although you could try to exit using a market order, most traders who use profit targets exit on limit orders and will be filled at their exact price. You can control the risk and reward by your selection of a protective stop and a profit target. If you choose to use a 10-tick stop, that is your risk in most cases. You will sometimes encounter significant slippage, especially in thinner markets, and you have to factor that in as well. For example, if you are trading a small-cap stock and usually have about 10 cents of slippage on stop orders in that stock, and you are using a 50 cent protective stop, then your risk is about 60 cents plus your commission. If you trade the Emini and you are not entering just before a report, you usually will not have slippage but you will still have a commission that will be about 0.1 point.

The most difficult part of the equation is assessing the probability that your profit-taking limit order will be filled before your protective stop is hit. Although you know the risk and potential reward because you chose them, it is impossible to ever know the probability precisely. However, you can often make an educated guess. If you don't have any confidence in your guess, just use 50 percent since uncertainty means that the market is in a trading range and the probability of a move up is about the same as for a move down.

However, if you are buying at the top of a two-legged pullback to the moving average in a strong bull trend, the probability of success might be 70 percent. If instead you are buying in a strong bear market at the top of a trading range that is just below the moving average, your probability of success might only be 30 percent. That means that if you take 10 trades, you will lose $7 \times 2 = 14$ points. Since you have only three winners, those winners have to average five points each just to break even! As that is extremely unlikely, you should rarely consider this trade.

If you take a trade because you believe that you have a 60 percent probability of making 10 ticks before losing 10 ticks but then over the next few bars the market enters a tight trading range, your probability of success has now fallen to about 50 percent. Since it is now a losing strategy to risk 10 ticks to make 10 ticks if the chance of success is only 50 percent, you should exit the trade as close to breakeven as possible. If you are lucky, you might even be able to make a tick or two. This is part of trade management. The market changes with each tick, and if a successful strategy suddenly becomes a losing strategy, get out and don't rely on hope. Once your premise is no longer workable, just exit and look for another trade. You have to trade the market that you now have and not the one that you had a few minutes ago and not the one you hope will develop over the next few minutes. Hope has no part in trading. You are trading against computers that have no emotion and are coldly objective, and that is how you have to be as well.

So what about one-point scalps in the Emini where you are entering on stops? If you are risking two points to make one point, then you have to win twice as often as you lose just to break even. If you add in commissions, then you need to win 70 percent of the time to break even. To make a profit, you have to be right 80 percent or more of the time; even most experienced, profitable traders could not do that long-term. You then have to conclude that it is simply not a profitable strategy. If you do it, you will almost certainly lose over time, and since you have to be trading with the overriding goal of consistently making money, you cannot trade this way. Yes, there are probably a few trades a day where the probability of making one point before losing two points is more than 80 percent, and you could theoretically make a lot of money if you are a very good chart reader, if you are very disciplined, if you can spot the best setups in time to place the trades, and if you restrict your one-point scalps to those few setups. This can be a profitable strategy, but the barrier posed by all of those ifs is insurmountable for most traders. It is far better to look for fewer trades but those where you have to be right only 50 to 60 percent of the time to make a profit. One of the problems is that it is fairly easy to win on 60 percent of one-point scalps, and this high winning percentage reinforces your behavior and makes you believe that you are so close to being able to be successful. However, that 80 percent requirement is simply impossible to reach for most traders, no matter how close they get.

The probability, risk, and reward change for every trade on every time frame with each tick. For example, if traders bought a high 2 bull flag in the Emini and thought that it had a 60 percent chance of making two points before losing two points, all three variables change with every tick. If the market races up for six ticks with all of the pullbacks being only one or two ticks, the probability of their original premise being correct might now be 80 percent. Since they need only four more ticks to scalp out with two points of profit, their reward is now four ticks. They might raise their protective stops to one tick below the low of the current bar, even before the bar closes, and this might be only three ticks below their entry price. This reduces the risk of the original trade to three ticks. They now might have an 80 percent chance of making the remaining two ticks while risking three ticks, which is a great trader's equation. If they were flat and saw this happening, however, they should not buy at the market and risk three ticks to make two ticks. An institution that is trading momentum and paying minuscule commissions can profitably take that trade, but individual traders would almost certainly lose money because they could not execute the trade fast enough and correctly often enough to make it work. Also, commissions greatly reduce the profitability on almost all trades where the reward is less than one point. At every moment, there are traders holding long and short trades with every imaginable combination of risk, reward, and probability. Although a day trader is concerned with every tick, a trader trading off of the daily or weekly charts would ignore small movements, because they would be too small to have any significant impact on the trader's equation. If, instead of going up immediately after entry, the market falls four ticks, then the scalper has four ticks left of risk and 12 ticks for reward, which is a great risk/reward ratio, but the probability would have fallen greatly to maybe 35 percent. This is still a sound strategy, but not nearly as profitable over time. Because it still has a favorable trader's equation, the trader should not exit early, unless the original premise has changed and the probability becomes maybe 30 percent or less.

On the other hand, if the trader's equation ever becomes marginal, he should try to exit quickly with as much profit as he can. If the trader's equation becomes negative, he should get out immediately, even if he ends up with a loss. Traders regularly exit early with a smaller profit if the market is not behaving as well as they anticipated, and that is the proper thing to do. However, if you find yourself exiting most trades with a smaller profit than you originally planned to make, you will probably lose money. Why is that? It is because you solved the trader's equation using one profit target, but it is not the one that you actually planned to use, if you were honest with yourself. Your smaller target probably results in a less favorable trader's equation, and most likely a negative one, which means that your approach will lose money. Yes, exiting with a smaller profit target has a greater chance of success, but when you start using a profit target that is smaller than your risk, your probability has to be unrealistically high. So high, in fact, that you almost certainly cannot maintain it, which means that you will lose money.

Whenever traders are thinking about taking a trade, they have to find some combination of probability, risk, and reward that creates a positive trader's equation. For example, if they are buying a pullback in a bull trend in the Emini and have to risk two points, they then have to consider the probability of the move reaching their profit target. If the target is one point, they have to be 80 percent certain of success or else the trade will lose money over time. If they think that a two-point profit target is reasonable, they have to be 60 percent certain to have a positive trader's equation. If they think that the bull trend is very strong and that they can make four points, they only need a 40 percent chance of success to have a profitable strategy. If at least one of those possibilities makes mathematical sense, they can take the trade. Once they enter, every new tick changes all three variables. If they were only 40 percent certain when they entered that the market would reach four points, and not 60 percent certain of making two points or 80 percent certain of making one point, but the entry bar was very strong, they could reevaluate all of the potential profit targets. Once the entry bar closes, if it is a strong bull trend bar they can tighten their stops, which now might be only four ticks below their entry. They might now think that there is a 60 percent chance of making two points while risking those four ticks, and this means that scalping out for two points has become a reasonable choice. If they think that the chance of making four points is now 50 percent, then this also has a strong trader's equation, especially since their risk is now only four ticks, and they can continue to hold for four points.

Although it is so important to take trades only where the reward is at least as large as the risk, successful traders actually risk five or more times what they stand to gain many times a day. All traders who are trying to exit on profit-taking limit orders are scalpers once the market gets to within a few ticks of their orders, and was discussed earlier. For example, if traders have limit orders to take eight ticks (two points) of profit on a long in the Emini, and the market reaches six or seven ticks and they think that their orders will get filled, they will hold their positions a little longer to find out. However, they probably have protective stops that are four to six ticks below (either below the low of the most recent bar or at breakeven), so at the instant that the market comes to within a tick of filling their orders, they are risking about five ticks to make that one final tick. This is effectively an extreme scalp, but is it sound? Only if they have about a 90 percent chance of success. If not, they should exit, at least theoretically. In practice, if the market is rising and comes to within a tick of filling their limit orders, the trade might have about a 90 percent chance of success at that instant, especially if the momentum up is strong. Traders will usually hold to see if the next tick is up, filling their orders, or down. By holding on to their positions, they believe that their chance of success is 90 percent. They probably do not think of it in mathematical terms, but that has to be what they believe if they think it is worth holding on to the trade. It is worth it only if it makes mathematical sense, and that math must include a probability of 90 percent, because that is what is required to keep the trader's equation positive when the risk is about five times greater than the reward. If the market trades down for a couple of ticks, they are then trying for three ticks of profit and risking to the low of the prior bar, or breakeven, which at that point is about three or four ticks. The probability of success is probably still 70 percent or higher, making the trader's equation still positive, although not strongly so.

Programmers are aware of this and there are therefore algorithms out there that will buy once the market comes to within a tick or two of a logical target and then falls back for a couple of ticks. In these cases, they probably have to risk about three ticks to make three ticks. Their commissions are so small as to not be a factor in their decisions. High-frequency trading firm algorithms are probably buying at a tick or two below the obvious target, but they will probably exit if the market falls back for a couple of ticks. The programmers know that the math is terrible if the risk is several times larger than the potential reward, and will not allow that to happen (unless they are scaling in). All of these programs create buying pressure and increase the chances that the target will be reached.

The individual traders are holding long while risking five ticks to make one tick for only a fraction of a second, and for that brief moment they are betting that they have a 90 percent chance of making one more tick while risking five ticks (and they are probably right). Otherwise, they would exit. If they tried to exit at seven ticks of profit instead of eight and the market came to within a tick of filling this new profit-taking limit order, for that instant they are risking about four ticks to make one. They need about an 80 percent chance of success, or else they should exit. Why not exit with six ticks of profit? Their risk is always going to be to below the low of the prior bar, so they are always going to have to risk about four to six ticks to make that final tick. The extremely bad trader's equation, with a risk many times greater than the reward, exists for only a fraction of a second. Most traders are willing to take that brief risk, because they know that the trader's equation will be much better in a few seconds. Either traders will have their profit and no more risk, or the market will fall back for a few ticks and they would then be risking about three ticks to make three ticks on a bet that is usually 60 percent or higher.

Should an individual trader simply buy a one- or two-tick pullback on a limit order once the market comes to within a tick or so of a 10-tick move above a signal bar, risking to below the low of the most recent bar? (Most of the time, the market has to go 10 ticks above the signal bar for a trader to exit with eight ticks of profit.) The logic is sound, but this is probably as minimally positive a trader's equation as traders would ever find, and they would be wiser to look for stronger trades. Also, commissions become significant on tiny scalps, making it virtually impossible for an individual trader to make money from trading them. Does this mean that the trader who bought on a stop above the signal bar should exit as soon as the market pulls back a tick or two? It might be mathematically sensible, but most traders would simply hold the long, risking to no worse than breakeven, and allow the market a little more time to fill their profit-taking limit orders. Computers don't have the problems of dealing with emotions and needing time to think, but most algorithms probably would still hold, briefly risking the five or so ticks while trying to make the final tick or two.

Remember, once the market pulls back a couple of ticks, traders are trying to make three ticks from that point and might be risking only three ticks, and the probability of success is probably 60 percent or better. At that moment, they have a profitable trader's equation. Traders without a position might consider buying at that point, risking about three ticks to make three ticks, but commissions then become disproportionally large. For example, they might be paying a $5.00 round turn commission to make $37.50 (three ticks), reducing their net profit to $32.50 while risking $42.50 (three ticks plus the commission), or about 30 percent more than their potential profit. With the reward less than the risk, the trader's equation would probably be negative. At the extreme, if traders tried to scalp one tick with a risk that is the same size as their reward, even if their probability of success is 80 percent, they will lose money. This is because a $5.00 round turn commission makes the risk ($12.50 for one tick, plus a $5.00 commission, for a total risk of $17.50) much greater than the reward ($12.50 for one tick, minus a $5.00 commission, for a net profit of $7.50). From a practical standpoint, traders should stick to their original plan and rely on their stops. If the move up to their limit orders is labored, they might change their plan and try to exit with one point of profit, but most traders cannot read the market that quickly and are better off just relying on their bracket orders.

When the trader's equation indicates that a trade is bad, then it is often good for traders who are fading the move with limit orders. For example, if entering on a low 1 short setup using a stop entry order would result in a losing trader's equation, traders should consider instead buying at the low of that short signal bar. If the traders who shorted on a stop below the low 1 signal bar had about a 50 percent chance of making four ticks while risking eight ticks, their strategy would be a loser over time. If different traders bought at the low 1 low, they, too, would have about a 50–50 chance of the market going up seven ticks to the stop of those short traders before falling six ticks to the short traders' profit target. If they risked six ticks and used a six-tick profit target, they would have a breakeven strategy. If they chose an especially weak-looking low 1 setup, like a doji signal bar at the bottom of a trading range, their probability of success might be 70 percent and their strategy would be profitable. This is discussed more in Chapter 28 on limit orders.

Beginners often make the mistake of considering only one or two of the variables in the equation, being in denial about the probability, or even fooling themselves into believing that their risk is smaller or their reward is larger than they actually are. For example, if there is a strong bull trend on the 5 minute Emini and all of the buy setups have had entries within a few ticks of the high of the current leg, traders might be afraid that there is not enough room at the top of their computer screen for them to make a profit on a long, so they don't buy. They see so much room to the bottom of the chart that they think that shorting has a better chance of success. To minimize risk, they short on the 1 minute chart. After they are short, they place their protective stop at one tick above their signal bar, risking about six ticks to make a four-tick scalp. Yet they consistently lose money. How can that be when the risk is so small? They lose because they do not understand market inertia and the propensity of trend reversals to fail, and they erroneously assumed that the probability of success for their countertrend trade was better than 50 percent. In fact, when there is a trend, most attempts at reversing fail, so the odds of success are probably more like 30 percent. The 70 percent certain trade was the long, buying near the top of the bull trend!

These traders thought that they were risking six ticks and that the reward was the 40 ticks to the bottom of the chart, so even if the chance of success was only 30 percent, they would still make money. The reality is that if the market started down, they would have scalped out with just four ticks and never held for 40 ticks. They would instinctively sense that they had gotten away with something and would have quickly taken their small profit, especially if they had just lost on their prior three shorts. This means that they also erroneously used 40 for their reward in the equation when in fact they were really planning on taking only a four-tick reward. Also, if the market went up instead of down, they might cancel their stops and add on by shorting another contract at six ticks above their initial entry, thinking that a second entry was even more reliable in a market that had to be due for a pullback. Their risk is then 12 ticks from their first entry and six ticks from their second. This means that they also were wrong in their initial assumption of a six-tick risk. Their average risk has increased to nine ticks. They now want to get out of both shorts near their original entry price. When the market starts down, they begin to feel that it won't reach their target; so they get out of both trades at two ticks above their target, making two ticks on their second entry and losing two on their first. Their net profit is zero, so their average profit is also zero, meaning that the reward variable in the equation was zero. So instead of risking six ticks to make 40 ticks and having a 30 percent chance of success, which is a potentially profitable strategy, they risked nine ticks to make zero ticks in a trade with only a 30 percent chance of success. That is why their accounts are slowly disappearing.

Traders often fool themselves into taking low-probability trades by telling themselves that they will use a reward that is much larger than the risk, which is needed in low-probability trades, when they really expect to exit with a much smaller profit target. For example, if traders buy in the middle of barbwire and need to risk two points to below the signal bar, they have about a 50 percent chance of making two points before their stops are hit. That is a losing strategy. However, they know that if they hold for four points, the probability might fall to 40 percent, but they would then have a positive trader's equation. They then take the trade, and they are proud of themselves for carefully considering the math. However, once they have one or two points of profit, they exit, fearful that most barbwire break-outs do not go far. They are happy to have the small profit, but don't realize that if they traded this strategy 10 times they would lose money. They might actually take this type of trade 10 times over the next month, along with a hundred other trades, only to discover that they ended up down on the month. They will look back with confusion, remembering all of the smart things that they did, but they will be oblivious to the reality that they took many trades with positive trader's equations but managed them incorrectly and traded them in a way that had negative trader's equations. Traders must be honest with themselves. This is not a dream. The money is very real, and when you lose it, it is gone forever. If you take a trade with a favorable trader's equation, you must manage it correctly to make the math work for you instead of against you.

At every instant, there is a mathematical edge to buying and to selling, even during the strongest spikes. How can this be true? By inference. Most of the trading is being done by institutional computers, which are using algorithms that have been shown to be profitable over time. So even if the market is in a free fall, there are computers buying as the market is collapsing. Every short, no matter how large, has to have a buyer taking the opposite side of the trade. When the volume is huge, the buyers have to be institutions because there are simply not enough small traders to offset the huge volume of shorts. Some of the buy programs are buying because the programmers have statistical proof that enough big breakouts fail and reverse sharply so that they will make a profit by buying strong bear breakouts. Other programs are buying back their shorts from much higher prices. These programs see the rapid fall as a potentially brief opportunity to lock in a profit at a great price before the market reverses up. High-frequency trading firms are also buying for small scalps, and other firms are buying to hedge shorting in other markets. When the market is not in an unusually strong bull or bear spike, there are institutional buyers and sellers at every tick, which could happen only if there was proof that their strategies were mathematically sound, based on the trader's equation. Each firm has its own combination of risk, reward, probability, and expected duration for every trade, and many scale into and out of their trades. The market could not exist unless there was a large number of big participants, and the majority of them have to be profitable over time. Otherwise, they would go out of business and the market would cease to exist as the huge market that it is. That means that the majority of them are trading logical, sound strategies, and that they are making money, even when they sometimes buy in a bear trend or short in a bull trend. Individual traders lack the deep pockets to run complex strategies, but there are enough effective simple ones for experienced traders to make money over time.

For the strong (i.e., institutional) bulls to get filled, they need enough volume on the other side, which can only come from strong bears. It is reasonable to assume that both the strong bears and the strong bulls make money over time or else they would not be investing enough money for them to be considered strong. There are countless possible strategies, including hedging and scaling in and out, and different strong bulls and bears will be using everything imaginable to make money. However, even in the absence of complex strategies, it is common for mathematically sound long and short setups to coexist. For example, if there is a strong bull trend that is overdone and likely to pull back, a strong bull can buy at the market and hold throughout the pullback and then take profits once the market resumes the uptrend and reaches a new high. At the same time that the strong bull bought, a strong bear could have shorted and made money as the market sold off to the moving average. Another example is when the market is in a tight trading range.

Let's say that the Emini is in a range that is only five ticks tall. The probability of either an upside or a downside breakout is about 50 percent. If a bull bought in the middle of the range or a bear sold in the middle, each might have to risk only three ticks to make four or more ticks on a small breakout. Since each has a reward that is larger than the risk and about a 50 percent chance of success, they each have a mathematically sound trade, even if they took their trades at the same time, and even if each took the opposite side of the other's trade.

Math can be deceptive, and it is risky to place trades on math alone unless you fully understand probability distributions. For example, let's say that you test every trading day of the year over the past 10 years to see if it is likely that the close of any given date has a high probability of being above the open. If you discover that some day in the near future, perhaps March 21, has closed above its open in nine of the past 10 years, you might conclude that there is some market force operating, maybe related to the upcoming end of the quarter, that makes that day close up so often. That conclusion is erroneous, though, because you do not understand distributions. If you were to throw a deck of cards up in the air 10 times and then record which cards landed face up, you would discover that some cards landed face up nine out of the 10 times. Maybe the eight of hearts was one of them. Do you feel 90 percent certain that it will land face up on the 11th toss, or do you suspect that the odds are really 50–50 and that it was just luck that some cards were face up in eight or nine of the 10 tosses, and others were face up only one, two, or three times? If you toss a coin 10 times and it lands on heads eight times, are you willing give someone odds that it will land heads up on the next toss, or do you think it was just luck? The message is clear. If you test enough ideas or enough inputs in any system, you will discover that some have worked in eight out of 10 tests and others have failed in eight out of 10. That is just the distribution of outcomes under a bell curve and has nothing to do with actual likelihood, and that is why so many traders who design great back-tested systems lose money when they trade them in real time. What they believe is 80 percent likely is really only 50–50, and since that is the reality, they need a profit target that is much larger than their risk to have any chance at making money. But in a 50–50 market, the profit target always pretty much equals the risk, and therefore, at best, their system will lose at least commissions and not make money.

Most traders should look for trades where they can make a swing profit. When the Emini has an average daily range of about 10 to 15 points, a trader can usually risk about two points on a trade, and a swing trade is any trade where the profit is four points or more. Although the probability of success is usually only 40 to 50 percent for most of these trades, this type of trading gives most traders the best chance of making a living as a trader. There are usually about five setups a day, and traders will likely have to place at least three trades a day to make sure that they each catch at least one big winner. If they are patient and disciplined, they will be about breakeven on the trades that do not result in four or more points of profit. Some of those trades will be one- to three-point winners, while others will be one- to two-point losers. However, they need the four-point winners to make the system profitable. A trader who wants to take more trades a day will have to be willing to accept a smaller profit target, like two points, because there are rarely five to 10 trades in a day where a trader can make four points. However, there are usually that many trades where a skilled trader can make two points while risking two points. These traders, then, need to be right at least 60 percent of the time to be profitable. This is more difficult, but it is a reasonable goal for traders who are particularly good at reading price action.

In actual trading, most successful traders have routines and do not have to think about the math when they place trades. For example, if you only look for a couple of four-point swings a day and always use a two-point stop, and you have been profitable using this approach for a few years, you will likely just look at a setup and ask yourself if it looks good without thinking about the probability. You know from experience that taking these certain setups with a two-point stop and a four-point profit target leads to your account being larger at the end of the month, and you do not need to think about anything else. As a general rule, beginners should use profit targets that are at least as large as their protective stops, because they then need only about a 50 percent win rate to break even. No one should ever take a trade with a long-term goal of breaking even. However, that is one of the steps that traders must take en route to becoming profitable. Once there, they can then try to increase the probability of success by being more selective in their setups, and also by using a larger profit target. This could be all that they need to become consistently profitable.

There is another point about reversal signals. If a signal is not clear, you should not take it, but you can use it to exit part or all of a position that you currently are holding. For example, if you are long and the market is now trying to reverse, but there is too much recent strength to consider reversing to short, you should consider exiting part or all of your position. A weak reversal signal is a good reason to take profits but a bad reason to initiate a trade against the current trend.

In trading, the less you have to think about, the more likely you will be successful, so having some guidelines can make trading a little easier. If you believe that there is a directional probability of at least 60 percent for a move that is the same size as or greater than the risk required, you can use either your risk or your reward as a starting point. In a breakout that you believe will be successful and have follow-through, you usually have to be at least 60 percent certain to draw that conclusion, and therefore if you risk the same as or less than what you expect for your reward, you have a profitable strategy. For example, if you buy at the top of a strong $2.00 bull spike in Apple (AAPL), a reasonable risk is to the bottom of the spike. Since you are risking $2.00 and the spike often leads to a measured move up, you can take partial or total profits $2.00 higher. If this is more than you are comfortable risking, just trade fewer shares. You can also wait to buy a 50 cent pullback to reduce your risk to $1.50 while increasing the size of your potential reward to $2.50.

If there is a breakout of the top of a $3.00 trading range in AAPL and you think the breakout will be successful, then you can risk to the bottom of the trading range, which might be $4.00 below, or below the bottom of the spike that was the breakout, which might be $2.00. Since a measured move up using the height of the trading range is likely, you can look to take partial or full profits at $3.00 above the top of the range.

If AAPL broke below a trading range that is $3.00 high and there is support around $3.00 below, which is also the area of the measured move based on the height of the range, you can look to buy about $3.00 down from the breakout for a $3.00 rally that will test the breakout. If the move down is a strong $2.00 or $3.00 spike that will likely have follow-through in the form of a bear channel, you should not buy on a limit order and should instead wait either for a second entry to go long or for a pullback that you can short. However, if the sell-off below the trading range has two or three strong bull trend bars, lots of overlapping bars with tails, and two or three clear legs down, you can consider buying on a limit order $3.00 down and risking $3.00, since the odds of a test up to the breakout $3.00 above are probably at least 60 percent. If there is a second-entry buy setup and the signal bar is only 30 cents tall and its low is $3.00 below the breakout point, then you are risking only 32 cents and you have about a 60 percent chance of gaining $2.70 on a rally back up to the bottom of the trading range.

DIRECTIONAL PROBABILITY

Traders always want to find trades where they will probably make money. However, there is another type of probability that can help traders in their trade selection. At every moment, there is a probability attached to the direction of the next tick. Will it be higher or lower? For most of the day, the probability hovers around 50 percent, which means that the chance that the next tick will be higher is the same as the chance that it will be lower. This is the current directional probability of an equidistant move where the size of that move is one tick. In fact, the directional probability of an equidistant move of any size up versus down hovers around 50 percent for most of the day. So there is usually close to a 50 percent chance that the market will go up 10 ticks before it falls 10 ticks and a 50 percent chance that it will fall 10 ticks before going up 10 ticks. The same is true for 20 ticks or 30 ticks. It does not matter, as long as the size of the move is not too large relative to the chart you are viewing; also, the smaller the size of the move relative to the range over the recent five to 10 bars, the more accurate is the probability. Obviously, if you are looking at a stock trading at $10, the directional probability of a $20 move down is meaningless, because there is a zero probability that you will lose $20. However, with respect to moves that are within a reasonable range based on the chart, all traders use directional probabilities on every trade, although most never think of their trades in these terms. Traders might buy IBM in a pullback to the daily moving average because they believe that the odds favor a $5.00 rally before a $3.00 drop. By "the odds favor," they mean that they believe that there is well over a 50 percent chance that they will achieve their goal, or else they would not take the trade. They most likely believe that the odds are 60 percent or better. If traders are extremely bullish, they might believe that the odds are 70 percent that IBM will rally $10 before it falls $3.00, and if they are right, then they just made a great trade.

This last observation is important and correct. If IBM is in a wedge bull flag pullback at the moving average and at the bull trend line in a strong bull trend on the 5 minute chart, the directional probability of a 50 cent rally before a 50 cent sell-off might be 60 percent, but the odds of a $1.00 rally before that 50 cent sell-off might be only slightly less, like maybe 57 percent, and this gives traders a great edge and explains why entering on pullbacks is such a good strategy.

Similarly, if someone trades Eminis and is buying a strong reversal up off a long-term (maybe 50 to 200 bars) bull trend line after a final bear flag in a bear swing, this trader might believe that the odds are 60–40 that the market will rally four points to his profit-taking limit order before it falls 2 points to his protective stop. If the trader takes this trade 10 times, he nets four points six times for 24 points and loses two points four times for eight points, and the overall profit is 16 points, or 1.6 points per trade. This is a good average for a day trade where the risk is two points. One of the most common causes of losses is a failure to give enough thought to the mathematical basis for a trade.

Almost all traders should only take trades where the reward is at least as large as the risk, and the directional probability of an equidistant move (a move where the reward is the same size as the risk) is a good thing to consider before taking any trade. Is it likely that I will make at least as much as I stand to lose? In other words, is there a 60 percent chance or better of making two points on a buy setup in the Emini while using a two-point protective stop? Is there a 60 percent chance of making 1.00 by shorting AAPL when using a 1.00 protective stop? If yes, then the trade has a positive trader's equation and therefore is a reasonable trade. If not, then don't take the trade. Although there are many combinations of risk, reward, and probability that can result in a positive trader's equation, thinking in terms of the directional probability of an equidistant move is a good, quick way to help decide whether you should take a trade. When trading, things happen fast and are often unclear, so it is useful to have a logical framework that can reliably help you decide within the limited time that the market will give you. If you can answer "yes" to the question, then you can take the trade. You may end up wanting to hold for a reward that is greater than the risk, but the minimum starting point always should be a reward that is equal to the risk. If you can look at any setup and quickly believe that the setup is good, then you likely believe that the probability of making a profit that is at least as big as your risk is 60 percent, and therefore the trade has a positive trader's equation and is a reasonable trade.

When the directional probability of an equidistant move hovers around 50 percent, this means that if IBM is trading at $100 and you don't look at a chart and are totally oblivious of the fundamentals and the overall market, and you simply bought 100 shares of IBM and then placed a one cancels the other (OCO) order to exit either at $101 on a sell limit order or at $99 on a sell stop, whichever came first, you would have about a 50 percent chance of making a dollar and a 50 percent chance of losing a dollar. If instead you initially shorted the 100 shares and also used an OCO $1.00 bracket order (buying on a limit $1.00 below or buying on a stop $1.00 above), you would still have about a 50 percent chance of making a dollar and a 50 percent chance of losing a dollar. There are slightly better odds for the rally because IBM is a growing company. If it goes up about 8 percent a year, this comes out to about three and a half cents a day and only negligibly raises the odds in favor of the upside target, so it is still about a 50–50 bet.

You can make money buying or shorting, even when the directional probability of an equidistant move is 50 percent, by scaling into or out of your trade (discussed in Chapter 31). You can also make money when the directional probability of a large move in your favor is around 50 percent if that move is sufficiently bigger than your risk. You can make money even when the directional probability of an equidistant move is less than 50 percent if the amount that you stand to gain on your trade is big enough. For example, if you buy near the top of a trading range, the directional probability of the market rallying 10 ticks before falling 10 ticks might be only 30 percent (remember, most attempts to break out of a trading range fail). Suppose that a successful breakout would rally to a magnet 60 ticks higher and you are risking only 10 ticks on a trade with only a 30 percent chance of success; if you take this trade 10 times, you will expect to make 60 ticks on three trades for 180 ticks of profit and lose 10 ticks on seven trades for a 70-tick loss. Your net profit would be 110 ticks, or 11 ticks per trade.

The easiest situation for most traders is to look for setups where the directional probability of an equidistant move is above 50 percent, and most traders should focus on finding these fleeting setups. They are fleeting because the market will quickly recognize the imbalance, and the price will move fast to bring the market back to neutrality. The imbalance exists at every moment that the market is trending and when the market is at the top or bottom of a trading range, and these are times when there is an edge that most traders can see and use to trade profitably. For example, say you short a low 2 on a pullback to the moving average in a strong bear trend; just before you enter, the market is near the top of a small trading range (every pullback is a small trading range) and has about a 60 percent directional probability of an equidistant move going down rather than up. Let's say that the signal bar is six ticks tall, that you enter on a stop one tick below its low, and that your protective stop is one tick above the bar so your total risk is eight ticks. During this breakout, the directional probability of the market falling eight ticks to your profit target (if that is where your target is) before it hits your protective stop might be 70 percent or higher. This means that there is a 70 percent chance of you making eight ticks before you lose eight ticks. If you do this on 10 trades, you will expect to make 56 ticks and lose 24 ticks and will net 32 ticks, or 3.2 ticks of profit per trade, which is acceptable for a scalper.

How does this help traders who are starting out? It gives them a logical basis for deciding which trades to take. They should always begin by assessing risk. If the signal bar is 48 cents tall in AAPL, then the initial risk is 50 cents if they enter on a stop at one tick above the high of the bar and have a stop at one tick below. If they are trading the Emini and the bar is six ticks tall, the stop will be eight ticks from the entry price, and they should use a profit target that is at least eight ticks away. Beginners should never enter a trade with the expectation of making less than they are risking, so they would then assume that their reward is at least 50 cents in that AAPL trade (or eight ticks for that Emini trade). They are looking for an equidistant move (the stop and profit target are both 50 cents from the entry price). Finally, they look at the setup. If they think that it looks good, using any definition of good, they should assume that the chance of the market filling the profit-taking limit order before hitting the protective stop is at least 60 percent. As long as they are reasonably good at reading charts, their opinion that the setup looks good means that they think it is more likely than not to lead to a profitable trade. If it is good enough for them to hold that belief, it has to be more than 50 percent certain. If it is only 55 percent certain, they would likely not be confident. If they are confident, then they likely believe that it is at least 60 percent certain. They might sometimes be 58 percent certain and at other times be 80 percent, but their average level of certainty will be at least 60 percent, and they can therefore use 60 percent when evaluating the trader's equation. Since their probability is at least 60 percent and their potential reward is at least as large as their risk, the trader's equation is positive and they can take the trade. They know that they might lose as much as 50 cents in up to 40 percent of the trades (they will exit some trades early on a trailing stop with less than a 50 cent loss), but their average profit will be greater than zero. Because they are using 60 percent instead of 50 percent, they will still likely be positive, even after slippage and commissions are considered.

Even though a trading range is characterized by uncertainty, which means that both the bulls and the bears are actively trading because they both believe there is value at their entry price, the directional probability of an equidistant move can briefly be much higher that 50 percent as the market tests the extremes. For example, suppose the 5 minute chart of IBM has been in a trading range that is

$1.00 tall, and the top and bottom of the range have been repeatedly tested so that the range is well defined; if you buy above a small bull reversal bar at the bottom of the range, the directional probability of a 50 cent move up before a 50 cent move down is likely 60 percent or higher, and it may briefly increase to 70 percent if there is a sharp move up after you enter. As the rally moves toward the middle of the range, the directional probability quickly falls back to 50 percent, but where that exact middle is cannot be known in advance. The market usually has to overshoot it for traders to decide that it clearly has gone too far. The market takes a long time to home in on that 50 percent price, but it is quick to recognize when a swing has gone too far. This price will be at some resistance area and will become the top of the trading range. Once the traders have decided that the directional probability now clearly favors the bears, the market is likely at the top of the trading range. As IBM gets close to the top of the range, the probability of a move 50 cents higher before there is a 50 cent pullback might fall to 40 percent, meaning that the 50 cent move down is now more likely (in fact, it has a 60 percent probability if the chance of the move up occurring first is 40 percent). IBM will then move down and it will often overshoot the area of neutrality to the point that it clearly went too far and swing up and down in search of uncertainty and a neutral directional probability. This process of up and down moves continues until the bulls and the bears agree on an area of value. At that point the swings become small and a tight trading range or the apex of a triangle form, and this will ultimately be in the middle of the trading range. Once the bulls and the bears perceive that the value is bad for one side, the market will break out and trend again until it finds a new area of value.

When a trading range is very tight, like 20 cents in IBM, it does not matter if the directional probability briefly jumps to 70 percent if you stand to gain only 10 cents while risking 10 cents, because slippage and commissions then become important. This is a bad scalp. If they amount to 4 cents, then your 10 cent gain is actually only a 6 cent net gain. Even if the odds are 60 percent in your favor, if you take this trade 10 times, you will make 36 cents and lose 40 cents. Since you can never be certain of the probability, and high probabilities last only briefly, you will lose money if you take that trade. Only HFT firms can consistently make money in this situation because their infrastructure allows them to quickly place profitable trades with the objective of only a one-tick profit.

A tight trading range can sometimes offer a great swing trading opportunity based on mathematics if the breakout is likely to lead to a large move. A tight trading range is a breakout mode situation, and the breakout will usually lead to a move that is several times the height of the range. Since the odds of the breakout in either direction are about 50–50, depending on the circumstances, what happens if you buy within a couple of ticks of the bottom of the range and risk about five ticks, or if you short within a couple of ticks of the top of the range and risk about five ticks? If you hold for the breakout and use a profit target that is 15 to 20 ticks, you are risking five ticks to make 20 ticks and have a 50 percent chance of success. This is a great theoretical trade because if you take it 10 times, you will make 20 ticks on five trades and lose five ticks on five trades and have a net profit of 75 ticks, or 7.5 ticks per trade. However, most traders cannot handle the stress of holding a 50–50 trade for a long time, watching the market repeatedly go in their direction, only to reverse and go against them.

If you look at a Market Profile of a trading range, you will see that there is very little time spent at the top and bottom of the range, where the high probabilities exist, which means that you have to watch intensely for a long time and then act quickly when the market tests the top or bottom of the range, and this is much more difficult to do than it sounds. When the market tests the top of the range, it usually does so with one or more strong bull trend bars and they have enough momentum to make you consider the possibility that the breakout might succeed. Also, the reversal down is often with a large signal bar, so your entry is close to the middle of the range, where the directional probability is close to 50 percent.

When the market is testing the top or bottom of the range and threatening to break out, the probability of a reversal might be 60 percent or higher, but if a breakout occurs, the directional probably of a move of X ticks up or down changes rapidly over the next several bars. If the breakout bar is not too large and it stalls at a trend channel line and other resistance area, the directional probability of a failed breakout and a reversal might briefly increase to 65 percent. If the next bar is a strong reversal bar, that probability might become 70 percent. This means that the trader has an edge, but edges are always fleeting and usually fairly small. As soon as traders believe that there is a 60 percent or better certainty about the near-term direction, everyone enters, the market quickly moves back to an area of uncertainty, and the edge disappears. When you believe there is an edge, there is an opportunity and you have to enter quickly before it evaporates.

However, if the breakout bar looks strong, the chance of a reversal might drop to 50 percent; and if there is strong follow-through over the next couple of bars, then the directional probability of a reversal can fall to 30 percent, meaning that the directional probability of a move of X ticks in the direction of the spike compared to one in the opposite direction would be 70 percent. So if there is a three-bar spike up in AAPL that is breaking out of a bull flag and the spike is currently $2.00 tall, there is a 70 percent chance that AAPL will rally $2.00 more before it falls $2.00 to the bottom of the spike. If the spike grows to $4.00, then the probability of a further rally of $4.00 before the bottom of the spike is hit still is at least 60 percent. The trader who bought when the spike was only $2.00 tall now has $2.00 in profit, is risking $2.00 to the bottom of the spike, and has a 60 percent chance of making an additional $4.00. That is why it is so important to enter as soon as you are confident that there is a strong directional probability in your favor (in other words, once there is a clear always-in position) and you believe that it will continue in your favor for several more bars.

This is one of the most important ways to make money as a trader. It is stressful to make these decisions in real time when you are looking at a chart where the past five breakout attempts have failed and now you are faced with one that looks like it might succeed. Also, you might be lulled into complacency, and the inertia of doing nothing makes it difficult to quickly change into the mind-set of having to act quickly and aggressively. However, if you can train yourself to do this, you will be in a position to take one of the most profitable types of trades. Remember, edges are fleeting. Everyone sees them and the market works quickly to neutralize them, so you have to be fast. If you are finding it difficult to take these trades, then trade a very small size. For example, if you normally like to trade 500 SPY shares and risk 20 cents but the size of the breakout spike would require you to risk 40 cents, simply buy 100 shares at the market and place that 40 cent protective stop. This is like diving off of a very high diving board. You are terrified for those first few seconds and you tense up every muscle in your body and squeeze your eyes, hold your breath, and pinch your nose. But within seconds, the move is over and you feel safe. When you take these emotional breakout trades, the situation is similar, but you must learn to jump and trust that soon everything will be okay and you will be able to tighten your stop. Within a few bars, you might have a 40 cent open profit and a breakeven stop and you will have made your best trade of the day.

How can you trust that the directional probability of an equidistant move in a strong spike is actually 60 percent or more? Go back to that AAPL bull breakout. Once AAPL has a strong $2.00 bull spike after a very strong buy signal, the institutions are buying as the spike is growing. You can see that the pullbacks are small as the bar is forming. If it closes on its high and the market begins to form another bull trend bar and then another, the institutions on the buy side are much stronger than on the sell side, and the market will likely have more follow-through. If that initial $2.00 bull spike looked strong enough for you to conclude that the always-in position was now long, then you should conclude that the directional probability of an equidistant move is at least 60 percent. This is because the institutions believe that the initial stop is below the spike and most spikes continue for at least a measured move. If the spike is $2.00 tall, they are risking $2.00 to make $2.00 and they cannot do that profitably if the odds are only 50–50. They almost certainly would not take the trade unless they had some room for error, and that means that the probability of them making $2.00 instead of losing $2.00 is at least 60 percent. Would you take the trade if you thought that the probability was less than 60 percent? Probably not, and you should conclude that they feel the same way.

One of the benefits of entering early in a trend is that once the trend goes your way, the math greatly improves for your trade. If the spike grows to $3.00, your risk is still $2.00, but the odds of a measured move up before the bottom of the spike is tested are still at least 60–40. If the spike then grows to $4.00, there is still at least a 60 percent chance that AAPL will go up $4.00 more before it falls to below the bottom of the spike. At this point, you have $2.00 in profit and are still risking just $2.00, but the odds of the market going up $4.00 more are at least 60 percent. This means that you now have a 60 percent chance of making a total of $6.00 while just risking $2.00. At this point, you probably have already taken a partial profit and might have moved your protective stop to breakeven. This is why it is so important to enter a trend early, even if that means entering during the spike phase and not waiting for a pullback. This is what the institutions are doing, and so should you.

Although the math is different every day and in every market and on every time frame and it is impossible to know it in advance, on most charts most trades will have between a 40 percent and a 60 percent chance of success. The word *most* is also vague and it means about 90 percent of the time. This can be confusing, but it is important to your success. If you were to buy or sell for any reason at any time, you would have a 90 percent certainty that the chances of making a certain number of points are about the same as the chances of losing the same number of points. However, that other 10 percent of the time is critical because if you are confident that the market is not in that 40 percent to 60 percent band, then you have an edge. For example, if AAPL is in a strong spike down on the 5 minute chart, the chances of making $1.00 on your short before losing $1.00 might be 70 percent or more. The better you become at understanding price action, the better you will be at spotting brief imbalances like this. They come every day, on every chart, and on every time frame, but the keys are to learn to spot them and to patiently wait for them. Once you become proficient, you are in a position to make money as a trader.

The directional probability cannot stay far above 50 percent for long because there has to be an institution on the other side and it will quickly realize that its trader's equation is negative and change its position. During a strong spike, there is a high level of directional certainty. For example, if AAPL has a strong three-bar bull spike of $3.00 on the 5 minute chart, the probability of the market moving up $3.00 more before falling $3.00 may be 60 percent or higher. Once the spike ends and the channel begins, the probability slowly erodes as the market approaches its measured move target or whatever resistance level is exerting a magnetic pull on the market. En route to its target, the directional probability falls to about 50 percent, but once it gets to the target, the directional probability overshoots 50 percent and now actually favors a move down. Why is that? Because the market usually has to go too far before traders realize that it has overshot neutrality. The market is good at knowing when it has gone too far, but not very good at knowing when it has gone far enough. Traders are uncertain when the market is actually in the middle of the developing range, and they do not become certain that it is at the top of the range until that is clearly the case. The top of the channel is the start of the move down and the top of an incipient trading range. Whenever the market is at the top of a trading range, the directional probability of an equidistant move favors a sell-off, since most breakout attempts fail and reverse back down into the range. Therefore, the probability of a down move is maybe 60 percent, and once the market drops down into the middle of the developing trading range, the directional probability of an equidistant move again returns to about 50 percent. If the trend up was very strong, the odds probably favor an up move slightly when the market is in the middle of the range, and if the market drifts down to the bottom of the channel, the odds of an up move increase further, since the market is then at the bottom of a trading range where a downside breakout is unlikely.

The market often oscillates above and below the middle of the range as it tries to find neutrality and uncertainty. This is where both the bulls and the bears feel there is value for new positions. However, at some point one side will decide that there is no longer value there, and far fewer traders will take positions at this price in that direction. The market will then trend until it finds a new price where both the bulls and the bears feel there is value, which will be in another trading range.

Once the market initially reaches the top of the channel, if it is $3.00 above the bottom, the market now has about a 60 percent chance of falling $3.00 to the bottom of the channel before rising $3.00 more. You could choose any number, like $2.00 or $1.00; it does not matter, as long as it is not too large for the chart on the screen. The market has about a 60 percent chance of falling $1.00 before rising $1.00 and vice versa. The bottom of the channel is a magnet that usually gets tested and it is $3.00 below. Since the pullback to test the bottom of the channel usually has far less momentum than the spike that preceded the channel, the directional probability of the move up after a test of the bottom of the channel will be less than when the market was in the spike, and it might be comparable to that of the bull channel. If the slope of the correction down is shallow, the directional probability of an equidistant move at the bottom of the pullback (and therefore the bottom of the developing trading range) favors the bulls and may be 60 percent. You can never know for sure, but the leg down is some kind of trend, just like the channel up was a weak trend, and whenever there is a trend, the directional probability of it continuing is above 50 percent until it has gone too far. Once the pullback has reached a support level, the directional probability once again rises to about 60 percent for the opposite direction (a move up). If the support appears weak, the probability is less, but still greater than 50 percent for a bounce up. For example, there might be a 56 percent chance of AAPL rallying one dollar before falling one more dollar.

In any case, when the probability is close to 50 percent, your reward has to be greater than your risk for you to take a trade. If your risk is the same as your reward, the trade is theoretically breakeven if you execute it perfectly and ignore commissions. Since you can do neither, the system will lose money. For example, if your profit target is $1.00 and you increase your stop to any size, say $2.00, you will lose money if the probability of a $1.00 move up is the same as a $1.00 move down. Why is that? Let's say that you do this four times. In two of the times you do this, your $1.00 profit-taking limit order will be filled. However, in the other two trades, the market will fall $1.00 before hitting your $1.00 profit target. Now that it is down a dollar, the probability is still 50 percent that it will move up $1.00 before moving down another $1.00 and hitting your $2.00 stop. This means that in one of four trades you lose $2.00 and in two of four you make $1.00. That remaining trade is when the market falls about a dollar but then rallies back to breakeven. At that point, the process begins again and you have a 50 percent chance of making $1.00 and a 25 percent chance of losing $2.00. You can do the iterations an infinite number of times and you will come up with the same result, and that is that you are twice as likely to make $1.00 as you are to lose $2.00. This means that the expected net profit is zero. Once you subtract commissions and some money for human error, you will conclude that it is a money-losing approach. You can use even larger stops and repeat the math, but the result will be the same.

Why does a measured move target often work so precisely? Because it is the minimum needed by institutions to have a positive trader's equation, and they would not otherwise take the trade. Since they are profitable, the basket of all of their trades has a positive trader's equation, which means that, for the average dollar that they trade, the minimum move has to be at least a measured move. Alternatively, the probability has to be much greater than 60 percent, which is unlikely. The result is that many trades hit a target exactly because many firms will take profits there, knowing that if they do, they are doing the minimum necessary to make the basket of their trades profitable. Most targets fail because they are the minimum, and when a market is strong, firms will hold well beyond the target before taking profits.

There is one final point about the mathematics of trading, and I will take it from the mathematician Charles Lutwidge Dodgson, and that is that much of life is not what it seems. In fact, Dodgson is not what he seemed to be and is better known as Lewis Carroll. We work in an Alice in Wonderland world where nothing is really as it seems. Up is not always up, and down is not always down. Just look at most strong breakouts of trading ranges—they usually fail and up is really the start of down and down is really just part of up. Also, 60 percent is 60 percent in only 90 percent of the cases and can be 90 percent sometimes and 10 percent at other times. If a good setup is 60 percent, how can you win 80 percent or more of the time? Well, in a pullback in a strong trend just above support, a setup might work 60 percent of the time; but if you use a wider stop or if you can scale in as the market goes lower, especially if your subsequent entry is larger, you might find that you win in 80 percent or more of those 60 percent setups. Since 80 percent of trend reversal attempts fail and become simply pullbacks, these pullbacks often have an 80 percent chance of a profitable trade in the direction of the trend. Also, if you use a very wide stop and are willing to sit through a large drawdown for a couple of hours, that 60 percent chance of making two points before losing two points in the Emini might be a 90 percent chance of making four points before losing eight points. If you are flexible and comfortable with constantly changing probabilities and many probabilities coexisting, your chance of success is much greater.

Figure 25.1   MATHEMATICS OF TRADING   **475**

FIGURE 25.1   As a Spike Grows, So Does the Profit Target

The profit potential increases as the size of the spike increases. Although some traders think of spikes as beginning at the high of the first bar of the spike and ending at the low of the final bar of the spike, it is usually more reliable to look only at the bodies of the bars instead of the tails. If a measured move down goes beyond one based on the open of the first bar to the close of the last bar, then traders should look at how the market behaves at a measured move based on the high of the first bar to the low of the last bar.

In the chart on the left in Figure 25.1, when the spike was just a single bear trend bar that had a body that was five ticks tall, the projected target for the move down was five ticks below the close of that bar. In the chart on the right, the spike had grown to four bars, and the open of the first bar was 19 ticks above the close of the final bar. The projected target was then 19 ticks below the close of the final bar. If you bought early on as the spike was just forming, even though your risk remained constant since your stop stayed at one tick above the high of the first bar of the spike, your potential reward increased as the measured move target continued to fall. You could reduce your risk to breakeven after the market had one or two large bear trend bars, or even move your protective stop to just above the high of one of those bars. If you did, you would be locking in at least a small profit while still being in a good position to make a large profit.

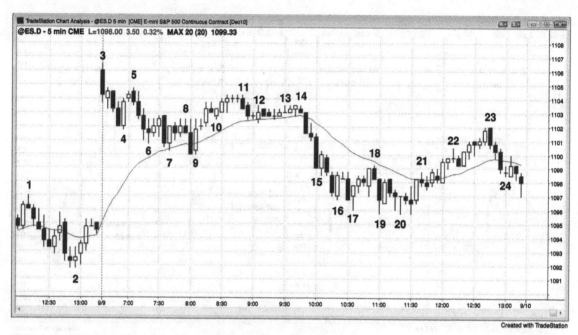

FIGURE 25.2   Look for Brief Moments of Higher Probability

Although the directional probability of an equidistant move up or down is usually around 50 percent, it is briefly higher many times during the day, and traders should look for trades when that happens. As shown in Figure 25.2, shorting anytime during the strong three-bar bear spike down to bar 15 had maybe a 70 percent chance that the market would fall X more points before rallying that same amount. Less obvious was the bottom at bar 20. The day was a trending trading range day, and the upper range between the bar 9 low and the bar 11 high was about four points. Since the lower range usually tests the bar 9 breakout point and the bottom range would likely be about the same height as the upper trading range, buying four or more points below bar 9 had perhaps a 60 percent chance of leading to a four-point rally before hitting a stop four points below. After the repeated bull reversal bars at bars 15, 16, 17, the bar after bar 19, and bar 20, the probability may have been as high as 70 percent. The bears made repeated attempts to push the market below yesterday's close and were failing. Each of these attempts represented buying pressure, which was cumulative. Once it reached a critical mass, the bulls would take over. After the first three or four bottom attempts, you could buy on a limit order at four points below bar 9, risk four points, and have an OCO limit order to take profits four points higher.

Shorting below bar 14 had only about a 50 percent chance of leading to a good swing trade, because it was in a tight trading range where the probability of a swing

Figure 25.2   MATHEMATICS OF TRADING   **477**

in either direction was only about 50 percent. The setup was a small wedge bear flag and a lower high after the two-bar bear spike at bar 11. There was strong selling earlier in the day, so maybe the probability of the downside breakout was slightly higher than 50 percent. The risk was less than two points, and the reward was the size of some kind of measured move down, like maybe a leg 1 = leg 2 move based on the move from bar 3 to bar 9, or the height of the bar 5 to bar 9 trading range. In either case, a trader had about a 50 percent chance of making about four points while risking about two points, which yields a sound trader's equation. Once the market broke out in the strong bear spike down to bar 15, traders held some of their positions for a measured move down based on the height of the bar 14 to bar 15 bear spike.

This was a trending trading range day, and it is a good example of why it was wise to pay attention to what type of day is unfolding. The trading range of the first half of the day was about half of the size of an average daily range. When a breakout occurs after the first hour or two, the market usually reaches about a measured move down and then bounces as it begins to form a lower trading range. Traders who understood this were more confident about buying between bars 16 and 20, and many traders were buying on limit orders at or below the most recent swing lows. That is why there were so many bars with tails down there. For example, after the bounce up at bar 19, aggressive traders placed limit or market orders to buy at, just below, or just above the bar 19 low. They went long at bar 20 and held for a test of the bottom to the upper trading range at the bar 9 low. Many would have used a protective stop that was about the same number of ticks as there were in the average recent bar.

Once the market began to develop strong bull bars from bar 16 to the bar before bar 18, the buying pressure was strong enough for traders to expect a test of the breakout below bar 9. They saw the space between the most recent tick and the bar 9 low as a gap and expected it to fill. It came to within three ticks on bar 18, but traders usually expect a test to come to within two ticks or less. With the market having had as much buying pressure as it had today, most traders believed that the market would trade above the bar 9 low. Some bought on limit orders at about a measured move down from the bar 9 low, based on the height of the trading range from the bar 9 low to the bar 11 high (it was about four points). Others began to buy below the low of the prior bar or below prior lows, like when the market fell below the bar 19 low. These traders might have used a risk equal to their reward, expecting about a 60 percent chance of success.

Had the bear breakout been very strong, traders would have done the opposite. They would have *shorted* in the area of the bottom of the bear spike and risked to above the spike, believing that there was about a 60 percent chance of reaching a reward equal to their risk. For example, some shorted around the bar 15 close and expected about a 60 percent chance of making as many ticks as they had to risk (one tick above the bar 14 high down to their entry price, or about four points). Once the market began to develop buying pressure several ticks above their profit-taking limit orders, they no longer saw their premise as valid. Even though they tightened their protective stops, they were not willing to risk two to three points to make that remaining point in the face of the buying pressure; they began to buy back their shorts, adding to the buying pressure. Since these bears just exited on a short trade that ended up weaker than they had expected, they would not have been willing to short again until after several more bars up. They would have considered shorting only at higher prices, like maybe at the bar 9 low, if there was a reasonable sell setup. At that point, the market was in a tight bull channel and likely to go higher, so not enough bears shorted there to turn the market down, and this led to the tight bull channel up to bar 23, where the market was vacuumed up to test the bar 12 low.

A scalper needs high probability trades to have a positive trader's equation, because his reward is often about the same size as his risk. However, some trends will have a series of weak buy setups at the top of bull channels (or weak sell setups at the bottom of bear channels) and therefore low probabilities of success. Many swing traders will still take the trades and often make many times their risk, but most scalpers will often miss trends that can last for 10 or more bars and cover many points. For example, a scalper might not buy above the bear doji that followed bar 21 or the bear reversal bar after bar 22, and find himself missing the rally up to bar 23. This can be frustrating to a beginning trader who watches the trend move up without a high probability pullback, but it is a mathematically sound decision. With experience, he will see that there were some high probability setups that he could have taken, like buying the close of either of the bull trend bars between bars 21 and 22, or buying at the bar 22 low, since the pullback was the first in a strong bull micro channel. There are a couple of days each month where a low probability buy setup at the top of a bull channel or a weak sell setup at the bottom of a bear channel can lead to a huge trend, and swing traders make big enough profits to offset the losses that they have on the majority of their other similar trades. They take many other trades as well, and some have a high probability of success.

Can a scalper make a profit with a stop larger than his target? Yes, but it requires trade management and most traders should not try it. For example, if he uses a one-point profit target and a two-point stop, and the market quickly fills his profit-taking limit order without any pullback, he actually risked only a couple of ticks to make four. If the market pulled back seven ticks before going his way, he then had to risk eight ticks and would then increase his profit target to at least the eight ticks he would need to have a profitable trader's equation, because the probability would likely still be around 60 percent.

Figure 25.3   MATHEMATICS OF TRADING   **479**

FIGURE 25.3 Scalpers Often Miss Trends When the Setups Are Not High Probability

Scalpers usually have a reward that is about equal to their risk, and this requires the setups to have at least a 60 percent probability of success. On some trend days, many of the setups don't look reliable enough, and the result is that scalpers often miss trends that can last 10 or more bars and cover many points. Swing traders, on the other hand, can be comfortable with setups that have a chance of success that is only 40 percent or less when the reward is many times larger than the risk.

Several of the setups in the move down from bar 18 probably did not have a 60 percent chance of success in the eyes of a lot of scalpers, and those scalpers would have missed most of the huge bear trend. Many would have chosen to trade little or not at all in the two hours between bars 18 and 25. Swing traders could have shorted below the bar 18 moving average gap bar, the bar 21 two-bar reversal and lower high, or the bar 28 double top lower high and bear flag, and made more than enough points to offset their relatively low probability of success. They could have added on below bar 31, even though it had a bull body and was the entry bar for a wedge long (bars 13, 25, and the small doji before bar 31 were the three pushes down). It was the first pullback in a six-bar bear micro channel in a bear trend, and it had a prominent tail on the top, increasing the chances that the market would trade down. The probability of the swing was still relatively low, but the potential reward was very large, because the market might have been breaking below a wedge bottom and could fall for about a measured move down, which it did.

Most scalpers would not have shorted below bar 18 because it had a bull body and was in a tight bull channel. Although the next bar had a bear body and therefore created a two-bar reversal, it had a prominent tail, making it a lower probability signal, especially after a strong rally that was in a tight bull channel.

Although bar 21 was a lower high, at that point in the day, most traders were looking for a second leg up after the strong bar 13 sell climax, so many scalpers would have been hesitant to short below the bottom of a triangle (bars 16 and 20 were the first two pushes down, and the doji bar after bar 21 might have become the third) or trading range, which is always a relatively low probability trade.

Bar 22 was a breakout pullback short but it followed a small doji, which might have been the start of the second leg up, so many scalpers would not have shorted at the bottom of what could have soon been the bottom of the second leg up.

All of the bear bars from bar 23 to bar 25 had prominent tails, which meant that traders were buying at the lows of the bars, and therefore the channel was weak. Scalpers don't like to short at the bottom of a weak bear channel.

The move up from the possible bar 25 lower low and bottom of the parabolic channel (after the three-bar bear spike down to bar 13, and the smaller spikes at bar 20 and two bars after bar 21) to bar 26 had four bull bodies, including a large bull trend bar. It was strong enough for many traders to see the market as having flipped to always in long, and be inclined to look for long setups, not shorts. Bar 27 was a strong bull reversal bar and two-legged higher low. The odds favored more sideways or up trading. Bar 28 had a bull body and was therefore not a strong sell signal bar. The next bar had a bear body and therefore created a two-bar reversal, but its low was far enough below the bar 28 low to make scalpers unwilling to short because there was too much risk of a double bottom with the bar 27 low.

Once the market had the strong breakout down to bar 29, scalpers might have shorted its close, or the close of the next bar, which confirmed the always-in flip to down.

Bar 31 was a breakout pullback, but had a bull body and prominent tails, which made scalpers suspect that the market might be entering a small trading range. The probability was great enough to make many not short below its low, but some would have. They also might have shorted as it moved above the doji bar and on the close, once they saw the large tail on the top, signifying selling pressure. With all of the difficult setups for scalpers, especially for shorting after the bar 18 high, there were still plenty of high probability opportunities for them to make money. They could have shorted below bars 2, 4, 6, 12, and maybe 21 (some would not have taken this short), and they could have shorted the closes of the bar after bar 6, the bar after bar 12, bar 29, bar 30, bar 31 and the bar after, and on limit orders above bar 1, bar 17, the bar after bar 20, the bar before bar 22, and the bar after bar 30. They could have bought above bar 3, bar 5, the bar after bar 13, the close of the bar after bar 25 or the bar after that, and above bar 27.

CHAPTER 26

Need Two Reasons to Take a Trade

S ome basic rules make trading easier because once a rule is satisfied, you can act without hesitation. One of the most important rules is that you need two reasons to take a trade, and any two reasons are good enough. Once you have them, place your order to enter, and once in, just follow basic profit target and protective stop-loss rules, trusting that you will be profitable by the end of the day. One important note is that if there is a steep trend, never trade countertrend, even if there is a high or low 2 or 4, unless there was first a prior significant trend line break or trend channel overshoot and reversal. Also, it is far better if the trend line break had strong momentum instead of just a sideways drift. Remember that bar counting setups are not trend reversal patterns. For example, a high 2 is an entry in a bull trend or at the bottom of a trading range and not in a bear trend, so if there is a steep bear trend, you should not be looking for high 2, high 3, or high 4 buy setups.

Learn to anticipate trades so that you will be ready to place your orders. For example, if there is a break below a major swing low and then two legs down, or an overshoot of a trend channel line, look for a reversal up; or if there is an ii breakout in an overdone leg, look for a reversal. Once you see an outside bar or a barbwire pattern, look for a small bar at the extreme for a possible fade trade. If there is a strong trend, be ready for the first moving average pullback, for any two-legged pullbacks to the moving average, and for the first moving average gap pullback.

There are only a few situations in which you need only one reason to enter a trade. First, anytime there is a strong trend, you must enter on every pullback that does not follow a climax or final flag reversal, even if the pullback is just a high 1 in a strong bull spike or a low 1 in a strong bear spike. Also, if there was a trend line overshoot and a good reversal bar, you can fade the move and expect the trend to resume. The only other time that only one reason is needed to enter a trade, whether in a trading range or in a trend, is when there is a second entry. By definition there was a first entry, so the second entry is the second reason.

Here are some possible reasons for entering a trade (remember, you need two or more):

- Good signal bar pattern, like a good reversal bar, a two-bar reversal, or an ii.
- Moving average pullback in a trend, especially if two-legged (a high 2 in a bull trend or a low 2 in a bear trend).
- Breakout pullback.
- Pullback in a clearly always-in market (a strong trend).
- Test of any kind of support or resistance, but especially trend lines, trend channel lines, breakout tests, and measured move targets.
- Dueling lines.
- High 2 buy setup in a bull trend or at the bottom of a trading range (whenever you see a double bottom, it is a high 2 buy setup).
- Low 2 sell setup in a bear trend or at the top of a trading range (every double top is a low 2 sell setup).
- Most bull reversals (bottoms) come from micro double bottoms, double bottoms, or final bear flag reversals.
- Most bear reversals (tops) come from micro double tops, double tops, or final bull flag reversals.
- Sideways to down high 3 pullback in a bull trend, which is a wedge bull flag.
- Sideways to up low 3 pullback in a bear trend, which is a wedge bear flag.
- High 4 bull flag.
- Low 4 bear flag.
- Weak high 1 or high 2 signal bar at the top of a trading range when you are looking for a short.
- Weak low 1 or low 2 signal bar at the bottom of a trading range when you are looking to buy.
- Failure of anything (the market reverses before going as far as expected):
  - A breakout of a prior high or low.
  - A flag breakout (final flags are discussed in book 3).
  - A reversal from an overshoot of a trend line or a trend channel line.
  - A failure to reach a profit target, like the market reversing at five or nine ticks in an Emini scalp.

FIGURE 26.1   At Least Two Reasons to Take a Trade

As shown in Figure 26.1, bar 2 was a two-legged pullback to the moving average (every double bottom is a high 2 buy setup) in a strong bull trend and was reason enough to go long. Another reason was that it was the first moving average touch in more than 20 bars in a trend from the open bull trend with a big gap up. It was also the first good trend line break, so a test of the high was expected.

Bar 3 followed the second failed attempt to break above bar 1. There was an ii setup with the second bar having a bear close. It was also a low 2 in a developing trading range, where the move up to bar 1 was the first leg up.

Bar 5 was a low 2 at the moving average in a bear swing after a strong three-bar bear spike. The market was likely to have a bear channel after the strong spike.

Bar 6 was a bear trend channel line overshoot and reversal and a breakout test of the tight trading range (a triangle) of the first hour. However, it was at the bottom of a three-hour bear channel, and channels can go very far and have many pullbacks along the way. It is almost always better to wait for a breakout pullback from the channel before taking a countertrend trade. That second entry came at the bar 7 higher low, which was a pullback after breaking above the trend line down from bar 5 (not shown).

Although bar 6 was a reversal bar, its close was barely above the midpoint and was therefore a weak signal bar.

FIGURE 26.2 Expanding Triangle

As shown in Figure 26.2, yesterday closed with a surge to bar 4, completing four legs of a developing expanding triangle, which needed one more new low to complete. If you were aware of that possibility, you would have looked for a long entry after a break below bar 3. Bar 5 dropped below bar 3, completing the expanding triangle bottom, and you just had to wait for an entry setup, which was one tick above the high of the bar 6 two-bar reversal and small higher low.

Figure 26.3   NEED TWO REASONS TO TAKE A TRADE   **485**

FIGURE 26.3 Two Reasons to Take a Trade

As shown in Figure 26.3, bar 1 was a second-entry short following a test of yesterday's high. The run-up was strong, and therefore it was better to wait for the second entry. Traders could have shorted as the bar fell below the low of the prior bar and became an outside down bar, or they could have shorted below the low of the bear bar from two bars earlier. In general, it is always more reliable to short below a strong bear bar.

Bar 2 was a high 2 following a large inside doji bar, but the down momentum was strong. When there is a tight bear channel after a strong bear spike, it is better to wait for a trend line break before buying. Likewise, bar 3 was a bad second long entry because it followed a strong bear trend bar, and you should have still been waiting for a bear trend line break before looking to buy.

Bar 4 was a low 2 at the moving average, but it followed four bars that almost entirely overlapped. In a tight trading range like this, you should never enter in either direction until after either one of the following events: a large trend bar breaks out of the pattern by at least three ticks and you have waited for that bar to fail, or there is a small bar that you can fade near the top or bottom of the trading range.

This was a two-bar reversal that overlapped at least one other bar, and the signal bar was large, forcing traders to short at the bottom of the trading range. As is discussed in book 1 in Chapter 5 on reversal bars, this was a likely bear trap and not a with-trend setup. Experienced traders would not have shorted there, and aggressive traders would have placed limit orders to buy at its low.

Many of these one-tick false breakouts like those at bars 2 and 3 occur in the first minute or two of a countertrend 5 minute entry bar. Breakouts that occur in the final minute of the bar tend to be more reliable because you then have momentum right at the end of the bar. The chances of it continuing into the next bar are greater than if it had occurred four minutes earlier and has since pulled back.

Trading low-probability trades will wipe out more than all of your gains.

FIGURE 26.4   Moving Average Pullback Short

When a stock is in a strong trend, it is reasonable to enter on a limit order on the first couple of tests of the moving average, or you can enter on the 1 minute chart with a price action stop entry at the moving average. In Figure 26.4, the 5 minute chart is the smaller chart, and the moving average on the 1 minute chart is the 5 minute moving average, but plotted on the 1 minute chart. At bars 1 and 2 in AAPL, a second entry off the 1 minute chart at the 5 minute moving average had about a 25 cent risk, and the price action entry off the 5 minute chart (insert) had about a 45 cent risk. You could also have shorted at the market on the first 5 minute close above the moving average and used about a 20 cent stop. Here, at bars 1 and 2 on the 5 minute chart, the market went only 4 cents above the close before reversing down. In general, it is better either to wait for the second 1 minute entry or to use the traditional 5 minute price action entry (on a stop below the bar that tests the exponential moving average), because there is very little gained by the other methods and they just involve more thought, which can distract you from your primary trading on a higher time frame chart, like the 5 minute.

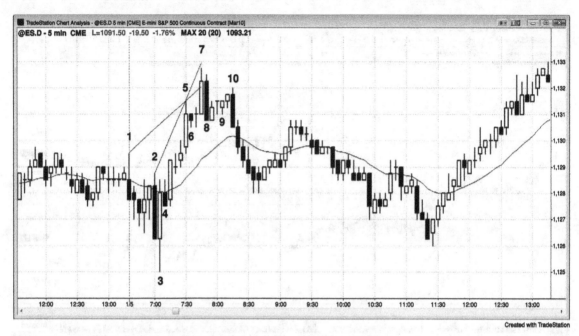

FIGURE 26.5 When a Channel Is Tight, Wait for a Second Signal

As shown in Figure 26.5, the Emini formed a wedge with bars 1, 5, and 7. The wedge formed by bars 2, 5, and 7 was a less reliable reversal setup because the channel was so steep. When there is a tight channel, it is better to wait to short a lower high, like the one that occurred at bar 10.

Bar 8 was a two-bar reversal, so the entry was below the lower of the two bars, which was below the bar 8 low and not just below bar 7. Most traders would have waited to short the bar 10 lower high instead of shorting as bar 8 fell below the low of bar 7. The reversal down was also from the small bar 6 final flag. Both wedge and final flag tops are usually followed by at least a two-legged sideways to down correction, and the high of the wedge usually will not be exceeded until after the correction is complete. Knowing this, it was reasonable to place a limit order to short at one or two ticks above the bar 9 iii pattern. The protective stop would have been above the high of bar 7 and that would have entailed a risk of six ticks. When there is a strong bear trend bar at a top, shorting below it is usually a good trade even if the entry occurs several bars later. Because bar 10 was such a strong bear trend bar and it closed below the bar 8 low, that is what happened here.

Figure 26.6   NEED TWO REASONS TO TAKE A TRADE   **489**

FIGURE 26.6 Buying New Lows in a Bear Trend

Even though the price action shown in Figure 26.6 is both a strong spike and channel bear trend and a trend from the open bear day and more money could have been made by shorting, experienced traders were buying each new low until the strong trend into the close. This is not for beginners, since this is very difficult to do emotionally until you have enough experience to be confident with what is going on. Beginners should only have been shorting in this clear bear trend.

One countertrend approach is to buy a half-size position on a limit order placed at the level of the prior swing low, and a second limit order to add on two points lower (you are trying to scale into your long position). If your one-point profit target is filled before the second buy order gets filled, you take your profit, cancel that other buy order, and look to buy a new swing low. For example, you would have been filled during bar 2 at exactly the low of bar 1, and you could have scalped out for a one-point profit. Your second order would not have been filled, and you would have canceled it at this point and looked to buy the next swing low. If you entered during bar 4 on a limit order located at the low of bar 3, you could have put your second half on two points lower and used a stop on the entire position two points below that second entry. Once the market rallied up to your original entry, you could have exited your entire position, having made a two-point profit on your lower entry and having been breakeven on your first buy.

This approach worked even at the end of the day, when the market entered a strong bear trend channel. If traders got long during bar 8 at the low of bar 7 and then bought more two points lower during bar 9, they could have gotten out during bar 10. The high of bar 10 was one tick above the low of bar 7, so they would have made two points' profit on their second entry and exited breakeven on the first.

CHAPTER 27

Entering
on Stops

A price action trader is looking for a reason to enter, and the bar that completes the setup is called a signal bar. The bar when you actually enter is called the entry bar. One of the best ways to trade using price action is to enter on a stop, because you are being carried into the trade by the market's momentum and therefore are trading in the direction of at least a tiny trend (at least one tick long). This is the single most reliable entry approach, and beginners should restrict themselves to it until they become consistently profitable. For example, if you are shorting a bear trend, you can place an order to sell short at one tick below the low of the prior bar, which becomes your signal bar after your order is filled. A reasonable location for a protective stop is at one tick above the high of the signal bar. After the entry bar closes, if it has a strong bear body, tighten the stop to one tick above the entry bar. Otherwise, keep the stop above the signal bar until after the market begins to move strongly in your direction.

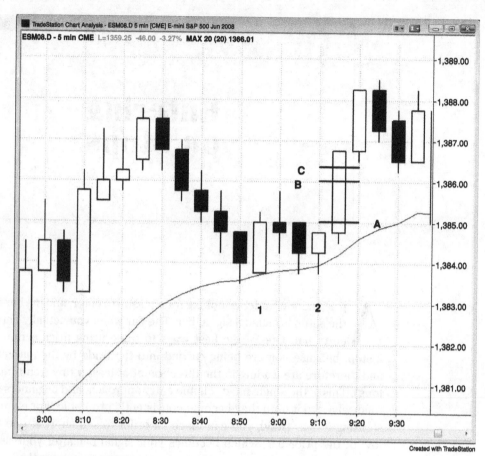

FIGURE 27.1   Need a Six-Tick Move to Make Four Ticks

It usually takes a six-tick move beyond the signal bar to net a four-tick scalp and a ten-tick move to make an eight-tick scalp in the Eminis. In Figure 27.1, the entry buy stop was one tick above the bar 2 signal bar's high at line A, where you would have been filled. Your limit sell order to take four ticks' profit on your scalp was four ticks above that, at line B. Your limit order usually won't get filled unless the market moves one tick beyond it. This was line C, and it was six ticks above the high of the signal bar.

CHAPTER 28

Entering
on Limits

Experienced traders will enter with stop or limit orders, depending on the situation. When the market is in a strong trend, entering on stops is a reasonable approach. When it is in more of a channel, they will be more inclined to look to enter on limit orders. For example, if there is a strong bull spike, traders will enter on stops above bars and at the market around the tops of bars. Once the market converts into its channel phase, it is still in a bull trend, but now the trend is weaker, and it can end at any time and test down to the bottom of the channel. Early on, traders will still look to enter on stops on high 1 and high 2 buy signals. After the channel has gone on for a while (maybe 10 or more bars), many experienced traders will switch to entering on limit orders at and below the low of the prior bar instead of on stop orders above the high of the prior bar. Once the channel goes on for a long time (maybe 20 bars) and approaches resistance areas, traders will stop looking to buy and will instead begin to sell at and above the high of the prior bar on limit orders. They will sell to take profits on longs, and some will scale into shorts. Once there is a bear breakout, the process begins in reverse. If the bear trend is strong, they will sell on stops below bars, but if the bear leg is weak, experienced traders will not short on stops near the low. Instead, they will prefer to short on stops on pullbacks, like below low 1 or low 2 setups near the moving average, and on limit orders at and above the high of the prior bar.

Until traders are consistently profitable, they should enter only on stops because then the market is going in their direction as they enter, and this increases the chances that they will have a profitable trade. Limit order entries can have just as good a probability of success, but it is more difficult to determine if the setup is strong, and this takes experience. It is also emotionally easier to see the trade immediately go your way than it is to see it go further against you, as often happens with a limit order entry. A limit order means that you are betting that the market is about to reverse direction. You might be right, but early. Therefore, many traders who enter on limit orders trade smaller sizes. They look to add on if the market continues against them and they still believe that it will soon reverse.

Here are some of the situations in which a limit order entry can be useful (examples of all of them are in the appropriate chapters of the three books):

- If you missed placing your stop entry order for the original entry by a few seconds and are trying to get in at the original price, place a limit order at the original price or a tick worse.
- Buy with a limit order located at the close of the prior bar if it was a strong bull trend bar in a strong bull spike.
- Sell with a limit order located at the close of the prior bar if it was a strong bear trend bar in a strong bear spike.
- Buy a small pullback in a strong bull spike before the bar closes, like placing a limit order to buy two ticks below the current high of the bar.
- Sell a small pullback in a strong bear spike before the bar closes, like placing a limit order to sell two ticks above the current low of the bar.
- When there is a bull breakout bar that could create a micro gap, buy just above the high of the bar before the breakout bar, which is the breakout point.
- When there is a bear breakout bar that could create a micro gap, sell just below the low of the bar before the breakout bar, which is the breakout point.
- Buy on a limit order at or below the low of the prior bar in a strong bull spike.
- Sell on a limit order at or above the high of the prior bar in a strong bear spike.
- Buy on a limit order at one tick above the bottom of an ii pattern in a strong bull trend, risking two ticks to make four or more ticks, since this has about a 60 percent probability.
- Sell on a limit order at one tick below the top of an ii pattern in a strong bear trend, risking two ticks to make four or more ticks, since this has about a 60 percent probability.
- When a bull trend bar that is not particularly large flips the market to always-in long, buy on a limit order at one tick above the high of the bar before it, anticipating a measuring gap (it is a sign of strength if the bar does not fall below the high of the bar before the bull breakout bar).
- When a bear trend bar that is not particularly large flips the market to always-in short, sell on a limit order at one tick below the low of the bar before it, anticipating a measuring gap (it is a sign of strength if the bar does not go above the low of the bar before the bear breakout bar).

- While the opening range is forming, if there are two consecutive bull trend bars with strong bodies, buy at the low of the previous bar, expecting the low of the bull spike to hold for at least a scalp up.
- While the opening range is forming, if there are two consecutive bear trend bars with strong bodies, sell at the high of the previous bar, expecting the high of the bear spike to hold for at least a scalp down.
- Buy a bear spike at the market or on a limit order at the bottom of a trading range.
- Sell a bull spike at the market or on a limit order at the top of a trading range.
- When there is a bear spike in a bull market and the bears need the next bar to be a bear bar to confirm a flip of the always-in trade to down, buy the close of the last bear trend bar in the spike before the follow-through bar forms, at and below the low of the bear trend bar, and at the close of the next bar if it does not have a bear body (and buy on a stop above its high). A pullback is more likely than a bear spike and channel.
- When there is a bull spike in a bear market and the bulls need the next bar to be a bull bar to confirm a flip of the always-in trade to up, sell the close of the last bull trend bar in the spike before the follow-through bar forms, at and above the high of the bull trend bar, and at the close of the next bar if it does not have a bull body (and sell on a stop below its low). A pullback is more likely than a bull spike and channel.
- When there is a large bear trend bar that is a likely sell climax at the end of a bear trend or pullback in a bull trend, buy at the close of the bar, below its low, and at the close of the next bar (and on a stop above its high).
- When there is a large bull trend bar that is a likely buy climax at the end of a bull trend or pullback in a bear trend, sell at the close of the bar, above its high, and at the close of the next bar (and on a stop below its low).
- When there is a pullback in a bull trend after a one-bar bull spike, buy on a limit order at a tick or two above the bottom of the bull spike, expecting a breakout pullback instead of a failed breakout.
- When there is a pullback in a bear trend after a one-bar bear spike, sell on a limit order at a tick or two below the top of the bear spike, expecting a breakout pullback instead of a failed breakout.
- When a second leg up is likely after a bull spike, buy on a limit order at a tick or two above the original signal bar high, even if the test comes dozens of bars later.
- When a second leg down is likely after a bear spike, sell on a limit order at a tick or two below the original signal bar low, even if the test comes dozens of bars later.
- Buy below the low of the prior bar in a bull channel, especially when the channel is in its early stages.

- Sell above the high of the prior bar in a bear channel, especially when the channel is in its early stages.
- Buy below the low of the prior bar and below the most recent swing low in a bear channel in its late stages after selling pressure has been building.
- Sell above the high of the prior bar and above the most recent swing high in a bull channel in its late stages after buying pressure has been building.
- Buy below the low of the prior bar in a bull micro channel, expecting the first breakout below the channel to fail.
- Sell above the high of the prior bar in a bear micro channel, expecting the first breakout above the channel to fail.
- When there is a spike and channel bull trend and a low-momentum pullback to the bottom of the channel, buy the test of the bottom of the channel.
- When there is a spike and channel bear trend and a low-momentum pullback to the top of the channel, sell the test of the top of the channel.
- Buy a bear close after at least a couple of strong bull trend bars at the start of a strong bull swing.
- Sell a bull close after at least a couple of strong bear trend bars at the start of a strong bear swing.
- Buy at or below the low of a prior swing low at the bottom of the range.
- Sell at or above the high of a prior swing high at the top of the range.
- Buy with a limit order a tick or two above the bottom of a bull ledge (a small trading range with a bottom created by two or more bars with identical lows).
- Sell with a limit order at a tick or two below the top of a bear ledge (a small trading range with a top created by two or more bars with identical highs).
- Buy at or below a low 1 or 2 weak signal bar on a limit order at the bottom of a trading range or in a new bull trend after a strong reversal up (a possible higher low).
- Short at or above a high 1 or 2 weak signal bar on a limit order at the top of a trading range or in a new bear trend after a strong reversal down (a possible lower high).
- In a strong bull trend, fade short scalps, since most will fail. When there is a strong bull trend and then a short scalp setup, buy on a limit order at two or three ticks above where the short scalpers are looking to take profits. For example, if there is a short setup in the Emini in a strong bull trend, look to buy on a limit order at about four ticks below the bear signal bar and risk about three ticks, expecting the sell-off to not reach the six ticks needed for the bears to make a one-point scalp.
- In a strong bear trend, fade long scalps, since most will fail. When there is a strong bear trend and then a buy scalp setup, short on a limit order at two or three ticks below where the bull scalpers are looking to take profits.

- In a very strong bull trend where the market has not yet dropped below the moving average by more than a couple of ticks, buy the close of the first small bear trend bar with a close that is a tick or two below the moving average.
- In a very strong bear trend where the market has not yet poked above the moving average by more than a couple of ticks, sell the close of the first small bull trend bar with a close that is a tick or two above the moving average.
- Buy at or below the prior bar on a limit order in a quiet bull flag at the moving average.
- Short at or above the prior bar on a limit order in a quiet bear flag at the moving average.
- Buy a bear close in a quiet bull flag at the moving average.
- Sell a bull close in a quiet bear flag at the moving average.
- Buy a moving average pullback in a strong bull trend, like a 20 gap bar buy setup.
- Sell a moving average pullback in a strong bear trend, like a 20 gap bar sell setup.
- Buy on a pullback to a steeply rising moving average and scale in at intervals below the moving average.
- Sell on a pullback to a steeply falling moving average and scale in at intervals above the moving average.
- Buy below a bull bar that breaks above a bull flag, anticipating a breakout pullback.
- Sell above a bear bar that breaks below a bear flag, anticipating a breakout pullback.
- When trying for a swing in a bull trend, buy or buy more on a breakout test, which is an attempt to run breakeven stops from an earlier long entry.
- When trying for a swing in a bear trend, sell or sell more on a breakout test, which is an attempt to hit breakeven stops from an earlier short entry.
- When there is a pullback to a possible double bottom bull flag, buy on a limit order around the prior swing low.
- When there is a pullback to a possible double top bear flag, sell on a limit order around the prior swing high.
- Scale into any trade where you believe that your premise is strong.
- If the market is in a stairs pattern, enter on a limit order for the pullback to the prior stair. For example, if the average daily range in the Emini is about 12 points and today is in a bear stairs pattern, consider placing a buy limit order at four points below the prior swing low for a rally up to test that swing low.
- In a trending trading range day, place a limit order at the extreme in anticipation of a test of the other side of the most recent trading range. For example, in a bull trending trading range day when selling pressure is building, consider shorting on a limit order located a tick or so below the measured move target (based

on the height of the lower trading range) for a test of the bottom of the upper range or a test into the lower range.

- In a trading range day during a bull spike near the top of the range, sell a bear close, especially if it is in the top half of the range of the prior bar and if it is a second attempt to reverse down.
- In a trading range day during a bear spike near the bottom of the range, buy a bull close, especially if it is in the bottom half of the range of the prior bar and if it is a second attempt to reverse up.
- In a bull trending trading range day, sell the close of, and above the high of, a large bull trend bar near the measured move target, especially if the bar is relatively large and, therefore, a possible buy climax, and if the last five to 10 bars had some selling pressure.
- In a bear trending trading range day, buy the close of, and below the low of, a large bear trend bar near the measured move target, especially if the bar is relatively large and, therefore, a possible sell climax, and if the last five to 10 bars had some buying pressure.
- In a bull trending trading range day where the range will be about 10 points, short on a limit order four to six points above the high of the lower range for a test of the breakout.
- In a bear trending trading range day where the range will be about 10 points, buy on a limit order four to six points below the low of the upper range for a test of the breakout.
- In a strong bear channel when the market is setting up a two-bar reversal up, short as the second bar rallies to the high of the first bar, risking a few ticks, expecting the market to not trade above the second bar and trigger the long.
- In a strong bull channel when the market is setting up a two-bar reversal down, buy as the second bar falls to the low of the first bar, risking a few ticks, expecting the market to not trade below the second bar and trigger the short.
- In a bull trend, buy a test of the bull trend line with a limit order (although it is usually better to buy above a bull reversal bar that tests the line).
- In a bear trend, sell a test of the bear trend line with a limit order (although it is usually better to sell below a bear reversal bar that tests the line).
- In a bull trend or a trading range, buy a falling wedge (a wedge bull flag) as the market tests the downwardly sloping trend channel line (although it is usually better to buy above a bull reversal bar that tests the line).
- In a bear trend or a trading range, short a rising wedge (a wedge bear flag) as the market tests the upwardly sloping trend channel line (although it is usually better to sell below a bear reversal bar that tests the line).
- In a bull trend where there is a pullback, which is a small bear trend, buy below a swing low, expecting the breakout to a new low to fail and become a high 2 or wedge bull flag buy signal.

- In a bear trend where there is a pullback, which is a small bull trend, sell above a swing high, expecting the breakout to a new high to fail and become a low 2 or wedge bear flag sell signal.
- In a bull trend, buy a 60 to 70 percent pullback from the current high, risking to a lower low, and taking profit at or above a new high (the reward is about twice the risk, the probability is about 60 percent).
- In a bear trend, sell a 60 to 70 percent pullback from the current low, risking to a higher high, and taking profit at or below a new low (the reward is about twice the risk, the probability is about 60 percent).

In general, when the market is in a bull trend, the bulls will expect every attempt by the bears to fail, and therefore look to buy each one. They will buy around the close of every bear trend bar, even if the bar is large and closes on its low. They will buy as the market falls below the low of the prior bar, any prior swing low, and any support level, like a trend line. They also will buy every attempt by the market to go higher, like around the high of a bull trend bar or as the market moves above the high of the prior bar or above a resistance level. This is the exact opposite of what traders do in strong bear markets, when they sell above and below bars, and above and below both resistance and support. They sell above bars (and around every type of resistance), including strong bull trend bars, because they see each move up as an attempt to reverse the trend, and most trend reversal attempts fail. They sell below bars (and around every type of support), because they see each move down as an attempt to resume the bear trend, and expect that most will succeed.

A market order is just a type of limit order where a trader is eager to get in or out of a trade and does not worry about saving a tick or two. Many traders who want to trade at the market just place a limit order on their price ladder, so many limit order trades are actually with the intent of entering or exiting at the market. For example, if the QQQ is at $51.10 and in a bull spike, traders who want to get long at the market will often hit a buy limit price on their price ladder that is above the offer, like at $51.14, and get filled at the market. Because of this, most of what I write about limit orders is applicable to market orders for traders who prefer to use market orders.

Something very important happens every time the market moves above the high or below the low of the prior bar. The market is breaking out of the range of the prior bar, but it is very important to realize that most attempts to break out fail. Unfortunately, beginning traders get caught up in the emotion of all breakouts and assume that the market is at the start of a big move. They don't understand that the breakout is a test. The market is searching for value, and the breakout is simply a contest between the bulls and the bears, and usually not the start of a big trend. The market runs this test every bar or two on every chart and in every time frame. A trader who used stop orders to buy above the high of every bar and short below the low of every bar would be taking every breakout and would lose money. Why? Because a stop entry is a breakout trade, and most breakouts fail. The market usually gets pulled back into the trading range, such as the body of the prior bar, and then decides where it will go next. Although stop entries and exits are the best choice for traders starting out, they have to be selective.

Let's say that the current bar just rallied to one tick above the high of the prior bar. Most individual traders would either do nothing, buy on a stop at one tick above the high of the prior bar, or sell on a limit order at the high of the prior bar. If the breakout is successful and the market runs far enough up for bulls to make their profits, then they made the right decision. However, if the move above the prior bar was just a buy vacuum, the market will soon turn down, and the bears will make a profit. If the trend is down, then many bears will wait for rallies to sell, and a favorite setup is a rally above anything, like a bear trend line, a prior swing high, or even simply the high of the prior bar. If there are enough strong bears waiting to short until the market moves above something, then this buy vacuum could easily lead to a one- or two-tick breakout above the high of the prior bar. Instead of the market finding a lot of strong bulls up there, it will find lots of strong bears who were waiting for the market to get just a little higher, like above the prior bar, before shorting.

The opposite is true for the bulls in an uptrend. They want to buy pullbacks, and if enough strong bulls believe that the bears will be able to push the market below the low of the current bar, why should they buy before that happens when they can soon buy lower? They simply step aside, place a limit order to buy at the low of the prior bar, and wait for the bears to push the market below the low of the current bar. That sell vacuum sucks the price down into their buy zone, and they buy aggressively, trapping the bears who will soon have to buy back their shorts (adding fuel to the rally), and the market quickly reverses up.

Most of the time, the probability for either buying on the stop above the prior bar or shorting on a limit order at the high of the prior bar is about 50 percent, but it is often 60 percent or more in favor of the stop or the limit order. With experience, traders can spot these 60 percent situations and place their orders in the direction that has the edge. Since most breakout attempts fail, successful limit order entries tend to be more reliable, but they are much harder to take because you are betting that a move will fail and reverse in your direction before hitting your protective stop. Until traders have a lot of experience, it is very stressful to wait for the market to reverse and go their way. Just as blindly entering on every stop signal is a losing strategy, blindly fading every one of those signals with a limit order in the opposite direction is also a losing strategy. On any given day, there might be about 10 reasonable stop entry setups and 20 or more limit order setups, although many are not obvious to inexperienced traders. Because there are so many reliable limit order setups, it is important for traders to be able to evaluate them.

When you are trying to enter on a limit order, you are trying to get in at a better price than the current price. For example, if you are looking to buy on a limit order, your order is below the current price and you need the price to fall for your order to get filled. Entering on stops is a safer approach in general because the market is moving in your direction as you enter, and the odds of follow-through are greater. For beginners, this is the best approach. However, there are many situations in which you can enter on a limit order instead of a stop. In fact, as mentioned, there are usually about twice as many limit order setups as there are stop entry setups, but they are riskier and usually harder to take because they are counter to at least the short-term trend. For example, if you just bought a second-entry setup in a pullback following a breakout above a bear trend line and a strong bull reversal bar, and the market tests the exact low of the entry bar a couple of times over the next one or two bars, consider placing a limit buy order to double your position at one tick above the low of the entry bar and risk just two ticks (to the original stop, just below the entry bar). You would likely not get filled if you tried to buy the low of the entry bar on a limit order, since the market usually has to trade through the limit price for the order to get filled. Everyone knows that there are many protective stops just one tick below that entry bar low—why isn't the smart money gunning for it? It is because if those stops are hit, the character of the market will have changed. Instead of being a strong second entry, the chart now has a failed second entry, and that is a with-trend setup and will likely result in two further legs down. If the smart money traders had loaded up on the bottom, they would not want to see the market drop for another two legs, so they will do exactly as you did: they will continue to accumulate longs to defend the bottom. Eventually, sellers will give up and start to cover, and as they do, the market will rise well beyond the scalper's target.

Entering on a limit order is trading countertrend to at least the short-term trend and, in general, can create needless anxiety that can interfere with your ability to trade later in the day. A strong spike alone is not a reason to begin to look to enter on a pullback using a limit order. For example, if there is a strong bull spike in the Emini to the top of a trading range or a possible buy climax at the end of a bull trend, traders might see it as a sign of strength and place limit orders to scale into longs at maybe one to four points lower. However, they need to consider the possibility that the bull spike was an exhaustive buy climax. When there is any doubt, a trader should not be buying on limit orders as the market is falling, because the sell-off might last for at least 10 bars and two legs, and it could be the start of a reversal down. A strong bull spike alone is not enough of a reason to buy a pullback on a limit order; traders need to consider the context of the bull spike. The opposite is true of bear spikes.

Furthermore, if the market rallied for a couple of hours but has now sold off for an hour with no sign of a bottom and you place a limit order to buy a Fibonacci 62 percent pullback or at a Bollinger, Keltner, or any other type of band, the market will be falling when you enter your long and you will therefore be trading against the current trend, hoping that the earlier trend will return. The market often bounces in the area of a 62 percent pullback, but not often enough or far enough to make it worthwhile compared to entering on a stop. If the market reverses up around that 62 percent retracement, just wait for the bar to close and look to see if it has a bullish close. If so, place an order to buy at one tick above its high. Then the market will be moving in your direction when you enter and the bulls will have demonstrated strength both by the bullish close and by their ability to push the market above the high of the prior bar. And you still have the 62 percent pullback in your favor. If the trade is good, it is now much more likely to be successful. Yes, you might miss a couple of ticks by waiting for the entry on a stop, but you will be avoiding far more losers and a lot of needless stress.

There are a few instances when entering on a limit order results in a winning percentage comparable to a good stop order entry. If for some reason you missed entering what appeared to be a great trade on a stop and within seconds you are able to place a limit order at the stop price or a tick or two worse, this can be effective. However, use it only for very strong trades because, in general, you do not want to be in a trade that let you in at a great price once you have already missed the original entry. Great trades rarely come back to bail out less astute traders.

In a strong bull trend, you cannot be looking to short a low 1 or a low 2, especially when the signal bar is weak. When there is a pause bar or a weak bear bar, many traders will step aside and wait until the market trades below that bar to buy. This creates a mini sell vacuum. Buying at or below the low of that bar is often a good trade with the expectation of a high 1 or high 2 trigger several ticks higher. Other traders will buy at fixed intervals below the high of the spike, like one or two points down, and this often coincides with the low of those low 1 and low 2 signal bars. Remember, in a strong bull trend, low 1 and low 2 signals do not exist and are only traps. Tops in strong bull trends become bull flags in about 80 percent of the cases. The opposite is true in strong bear trends, where shorting at or above the highs of high 1 and high 2 signal bars is often a good strategy.

If you are taking a reversal entry, especially in a trading range, there are frequently pullbacks along the way, often within a bar or two of entering. If you are confident in your reading of the price action, you can fade those pullbacks. These are usually low or high 1 or 2 setups that you believe will fail. For example, if there is a wedge bottom on a trading range day and you buy the reversal up, you can expect the low of the wedge to hold. You believe that the trend is now up, so you want to buy pullbacks. A pullback can be as small as a single bar. Since there will probably be two legs up, the first leg down should not go far. That low 1 short should fail and become a pullback in the new bull leg because the trend for the next 10 or more bars has reversed to up. The only time that a low 1 short is reliable is in the spike phase of a strong bear trend, and never after a reversal pattern. That low 1 short entry will likely fail to fall below the low of the wedge and will instead form a small higher low in the two-legged correction up. Because of that, you can place a limit order to buy at the low or one to three ticks below the low of that short signal bar, expecting a small higher low to form instead of a profitable low 1 short. You usually can risk as few as four ticks in the Emini.

As the reversal up continues, you might think that a low 2 short setup could form. However, since you believe that the trend has reversed into a bull trend, you expect that low 2 to fail as well and be followed by higher prices. You are still in the buy pullbacks mode, and that can include a small pullback, like a low 2. Here again you can place a limit order to buy at or below the low of the low 2 signal bar and risk about four ticks in the Emini. You are expecting this bear flag to fail to break out more than a few ticks, and instead to continue to work up into a bull channel. This is a type of final flag because it is the final flag of the bear trend. The bears thought of it as a bear flag, but when they are not able to break it below the bear signal bar by more than a tick or two, the flag will continue to grow up and to the right until traders realize that it has become a bull channel. At some point, when enough traders realize what is happening, the bears will cover and there will usually be an upside breakout and then a measured move up. Once the bears believe that either the market has reached the top of a trading range or the bull trend is in the process of reversing down, they will look for high 1 and high 2 signal bars and place limit orders to short at or just above the highs of those bars. They are looking to sell rallies, even very small ones like a high 1 or a high 2. Bulls will look to buy low 1 and low 2 entries at the bottom of a trading range, and at the bottom of a bear trend when they feel that the market is in the process of reversing into a bull swing.

As discussed in the chapter on trend reversals in the third book, most tops are some form of double top and involve a failed high 1, high 2, or triangle breakout, and that high 1, high 2, or triangle then becomes the final bull flag in the rally. When the leg up and top are small, the double top is a micro double top. When traders are anticipating a reversal, they will place sell limit orders at and above the signal bar for the bull flag, expecting it to fail. A bottom usually comes from a failed low 1, low 2, or triangle breakout, creating the final flag in the bear leg. When the double bottom forms over only a few bars, it is a micro double bottom. Traders expecting the flag to fail and lead to a reversal up will place limit orders to buy at and below the low of the sell signal bar.

Going back to that wedge bottom, if it ends with a large bull reversal bar and then there is a second strong bull trend bar with small tails, the odds of a two-legged rally are good. If the next bar is a small bull bar or a doji bar, then this is a weak setup for a low 1 short in any circumstance, and after a possible wedge bottom, it is especially likely to not lead to a profitable short. At a minimum, bears should wait for at least a low 2, but if the trend has reversed, that will also likely fail. Smart bulls will see the weak low 1 setup and expect it to fail to yield a scalper's profit for the shorts; they will place a limit order to buy at the low of the bar or maybe a few ticks lower, and risk maybe six ticks in the Emini. Traders do this in all markets all the time, and the locations of the limit order and protective stop depend on the market. For example, suppose the average daily range in Google (GOOG) has been $10 lately; if there is a reversal up from a bear wedge on the 5 minute chart and those first few bars extend $3 off the low, a trader might place a limit order to buy about 50 percent down at maybe $1.50 below the top of the first leg and maybe 50 cents or even a dollar below the low 1 signal bar, and then risk another $1.50 or $2.00, or to below the low of the wedge.

Entering on limit orders can also be effective in some barbwire patterns and in small trading ranges, where the bars are large and mostly overlapping and the pattern is largely horizontal. This is risky and requires quick decision making, and only the best and most experienced traders should attempt it.

Traders routinely fade all types of channels with limit and market orders, shorting at the top and reversing to long at the bottom. The safest channel is a trading range with clearly defined support and resistance that has been tested several times. Since false breakouts are common, traders who fade a test of the extremes by shorting at the resistance line above or buying at the support line below put their protective stops far enough beyond the line to allow for a failed breakout before the market reverses in their direction and tests the opposite side of the range. Traders do this in trend channels as well. For example, if there is a bull trend channel, they will short at the market or with a limit order when the market touches or gets close to the trend channel line, and they will short above the most recent swing high in the channel and scale in as the market goes higher. This is not a good strategy for the final couple of hours of the day because you will too often run out of time and have to cover a large short position for a loss.

Bulls will buy at the market or with a limit order on a test of the trend line at the bottom of the channel, and they will place a protective stop far enough below the line to allow for a small overshoot of the line. They will also buy with a limit order at or below the low of the prior bar. Since they are trading with the trend, they are more likely to swing their positions up and add on at subsequent setups. In a bull channel, you should not be looking for low 1, 2, 3, or 4 setups, because those are setups only in bear trends and trading ranges. If you see one in a bull trend, since the odds are that it will fail and hit the protective buy stop above, it makes more sense to take the opposite trade. Instead of looking to short below the low of the prior bar, place a limit order to buy at or below that bar. You will be buying where those bears will be shorting, and since they will likely lose, you will likely win.

If there are broader swings within the channel, like in a trending channel or stairs pattern, there is even stronger two-sided trading, so fading the top and bottom of the channel are even more reliable trades. All channel fading is especially reliable if a trader trades a small enough size to be able to scale in if the market goes further against the initial entry. For example, if the market is in a bear channel, you can buy on a limit order below each prior swing low and look to add on a little lower, using a wide stop. If the market reaches your profit target after the first entry, you take your profit. If instead the trend continues and your second limit order is also filled, you can exit both positions at the entry price of your first entry. You will then get out of your first entry at around breakeven and out of your second entry with a profit. There is one important caveat for traders who scale into countertrend trades, and that is that you should exit or reverse to the with-trend direction on the second move against you. This means that if you are scaling into shorts in a bull trend, exit or even reverse to long on a high 2, especially if it is near the moving average. Similarly, when scaling into longs in a bear trend and it sets up a low 2, especially if it is near the moving average, exit or even reverse to short if the low 2 triggers.

A scalper in the Eminis usually needs a six-tick move beyond the signal bar to scalp four ticks of profit. This is because the entry stop is one tick beyond the bar, and then you need four more ticks for your profit, and your profit target limit order usually won't get filled unless the market moves one tick beyond your order. Sometimes your order will get filled without the market moving through it, but when that happens, the market is usually strong and will likely move beyond that price within a few minutes of your fill. Similarly, to scalp 10 ticks in the QQQ, you usually need a 12-tick move.

When a setup looks weak, it is best to not take it and to wait for another opportunity. If it is weak, it will likely fail, and you should not take needless risk. Often a weak setup will have a second entry, in which case it becomes a strong setup.

Traders can also enter on limit orders on pullbacks to breakout areas if they believe that the breakout was strong and they expect that test to be successful. Breakout tests exist to see if traders will enter again where they entered earlier. For example, if the 5 minute Emini reversed up with a strong bull reversal bar after a final flag in a bear swing and the rally lasted for a couple of hours, it is common for the market to test down to within a tick or two of the high of that bull signal bar. Traders bought aggressively above that bar, and now the market is testing back down to that price level. If the bull trend is strong, buyers will return at that same price area and the bull swing will resume. Many institutions routinely have limit and market orders at that level, and it provides an excellent risk/reward ratio for traders. They might have to risk only four to six ticks and they might have better than a 50 percent chance of making four or more points. For examples, see Chapter 5 on failed breakouts, breakout pullbacks, and breakout tests.

Although most trades should be entered on stops, when there is a strong trend it is safe to enter anytime, and entering at the moving average on a limit order is particularly good in stocks, which tend to be well behaved. This allows for a smaller risk and greater potential reward and essentially no change in the winning percentage. In a bull trend, traders often risk to below the most recent higher low, so buying a pullback means that their protective stop is smaller. Similarly, in a bear trend, traders often put their protective stops above the most recent lower high and short on pullbacks.

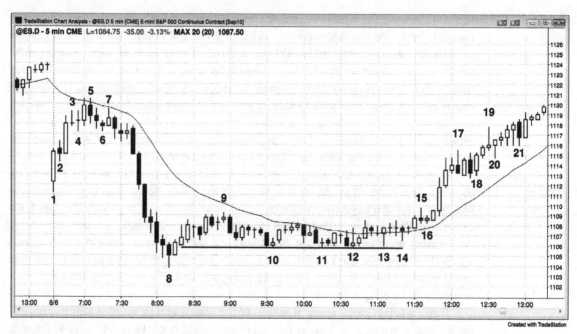

FIGURE 28.1   Limit Order Entries

The chart in Figure 28.1 shows several examples of good trades with limit order entries. The move up to bar 3 was strong and the market was pausing just below the moving average, which is a magnet. The market was close enough to be within the magnetic pull of the moving average. Since bar 3 was a doji and therefore a bad signal bar for a short after a strong up move, the market would likely not go down far before it pushed up again to test the moving average. Aggressive bulls could have bought at or just below bar 3 with a limit order for a test of the moving average, maybe risking six ticks.

After the bar 5 test of the moving average, the market was likely to correct sideways to down. Astute traders saw that the bulls were unable to create consecutive strong bull trend bars. This increased their willingness to go short. Bar 5 was a bear bar test of the bottom of the moving average. Since it was after a second buy climax (formed by the first and third bars of the day, which were large bull trend bars), two legs sideways to down were likely to follow. Therefore, shorting on a limit order at the bar 6 high or one tick above was a good risk/reward trade. Some bulls thought that a high 2 buy signal was likely so they placed limit orders to buy at and below the low of bar 5. However, given the two-sided nature of the recent bars, this was a risky strategy. Other traders saw the bear close on bar 5 and anticipated a low 2 short signal at the moving average. Just after bar 5 closed, they shorted at the market or on a limit order at the close of bar 5.

Figure 28.1   ENTERING ON LIMITS   **507**

As the market collapsed down from the moving average, traders shorted the closes of the three large trend bars, and they shorted on small pullbacks as the bear bars were forming. For example, many had limit orders to short one, two, or three ticks above the most recent low.

The opening range from bar 1 to bar 5 was about half the size of an average day's range, so once the market broke below bar 1, some traders would have looked at measured move targets for a possible low of the day. The bar 8 low was an exact measured move down from the open of bar 1 to the high of bar 5. Traders knew that the open of the day at this point was in the exact middle of the day's range, and that the market might try to test back up to the open before the close. This would create a doji bar on the daily chart with both the open and the close in the middle of the day. If the market could rally back up to the high, the day would become a bull reversal day. Some bulls were willing to go long on a limit order at one tick above the measured move target and then hold for a test of the open. The chance of a successful test of the open of the day was probably 30 percent to 40 percent. They could have used a protective stop of maybe a couple of points, and then they could have waited to see what happened. Since the sell-off was losing momentum, the odds were good that there would be enough profit takers for the market to bounce before their protective stops were hit. If the market fell below their entry price but did not hit their stops, they could have exited at breakeven if they felt that their premise was no longer valid. Once the market had the two-bar reversal up, they could have moved their protective stops to breakeven and then they could have waited patiently to see if the rally developed, which it did.

The bear spike down to bar 8 had seven consecutive bear trend bars. Traders who saw this as a sign of strength might have placed limit orders to scale into shorts at maybe one to four points higher. However, they needed to consider the possibility that the bear spike was an exhaustive sell climax. When there is any doubt, a trader should not be selling on limit orders as the market is rallying, because the rally might last for at least 10 bars and two legs, and it could be the start of a reversal up, especially under the current circumstances. A strong bear spike alone is not enough of a reason to sell a rally on a limit order. Traders have to look at the context of the bear spike.

The tight trading range at the low was a good example of how understanding the mathematics of trading can lead to a great trade. The range was too tight to be scalping with stop entries. You cannot buy above a bar or short below a bar and expect to consistently make profitable scalps when the range is this tight. However, there is a great opportunity for swing traders. The day was a trending trading range day and if it broke above the tight trading range, it would have had about a 70 percent chance of testing the bottom of the upper range at the bar 1 low. Once the double bottom bull flag was established by the move above bar 11, the bulls would defend its low. Therefore, buying one tick above it on a limit order and risking one or two ticks below it was a good risk/reward trade. Your limit order would have been filled on bar 12, which retested the bars 10 and 11 double bottom to the tick. You were risking about three ticks to make at least four points to the bar 1 low, or even about 12 points if the market reversed up and tested the high of the upper range, which it did. Since you were buying at the bottom of a tight trading range, you had a 60 percent chance of a test of the top of the range. However, you needed a successful upside breakout, and the chance of a breakout in either direction of a tight trading range is 50–50. So at the time of your purchase, you had a 50 percent chance of making four or more points while risking less than one point. This was a great risk/reward trade, but only traders who understood the math would have been able to see it that way.

Once the market started forming higher lows at bars 13 and 14, you could have trailed your protective stop to one tick below the most recent higher low. After the tests at bars 13 and 14 and then the breakout pullback at bar 16, the odds of at least a four-point move went up from maybe 50 percent to 70 percent. At that point, you had locked in a couple of ticks of profit and had a 70 percent chance of making at least four points, and maybe a 50 percent chance of the market going up to the top of the upper trading range. After the five bull trend bars started a breakout at bar 16, the market had at least a 60 percent chance of reaching a measured move up because that is typical when there is a strong spike breakout. The measured move would be based on the open of the bar after bar 16 to the close of the third bar of the spike and adding that to the close of that third bar. The strongest bodies of a spike often lead to a measured move. This meant that you had a 60 percent chance of making about another five points. You would have put your protective stop at the bottom of the spike, which would have protected about two points of your open profit.

Bar 17 was a bear reversal bar in a strong bull spike. Bulls expected that the market would form a successful high 1 buy setup after a one- or two-bar pullback. However, the high of that buy signal bar was likely to be higher than the low of the bar 17 sell signal bar, so aggressive bulls bought at the low of bar 17. The bar after bar 17 was a bull bar and the trend up was strong. If the bar after it was a bear trend bar, and it was, it would set up a two-bar reversal short. Since the bull trend was strong, aggressive bulls would have placed buy limit orders at the low of the bull bar. They would have expected that if the bear bar traded below the low of the bull bar, the two-bar reversal short would not fall below both bars of the two-bar reversal top and trigger on bar 18.

Since the market was clearly always-in long on the rally to bar 17 and the bear bar just before bar 18 was the second attempt to reverse down, many bulls thought that the market would soon resume up. They doubted that there would be follow-through, and as soon as bar 18 opened, they placed limit orders to buy at the close of the prior bar (the bear trend bar).

Figure 28.2

ENTERING ON LIMITS **509**

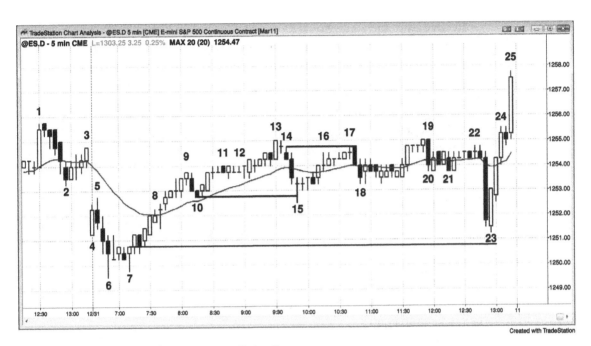

FIGURE 28.2 Limit Order Entries on Quiet Days

During quiet trading in late December, entering on limit orders is often the best approach. In Figure 28.2, the sell-off down to bar 6 had signs of buying pressure, like the bar 4 bull bar and the increasing size of the tails at the bottoms of the bars. This was therefore not a strong bear spike and consequently the low 1 breakout to bar 7 was likely to fail. Since bar 6 was also at the bottom of a two-day expanding triangle and a poke below a two-week-long bull trend line, traders were looking for a dueling lines buy setup. Aggressive bulls bought during bar 7 as it broke below the iii pattern, and more conservative traders bought above its high.

Most traders saw the market as always-in long by the close of the bull breakout bar before bar 8 and were therefore looking to buy pullbacks. Since the move up to bar 8 was in a bull micro channel, they believed that the first breakout below the low of the prior bar would fail and become a bear trap, even though some traders saw it as a low 2 short near the moving average. These bulls would have placed buy limit orders to buy at and below the low of the prior bar, and they would have been filled on the bar after bar 8.

Since the bar before bar 8 flipped the market to always-in long, bulls wanted the market to hold above the high of the bar before bar 8. Some placed buy limit orders at one tick above the high of that bar, and they were filled on the doji bar after bar 8. Some would have risked just two ticks. Others would have used a wider protective stop, and some would have added on lower. Even though the probability of success using a two-tick stop might have been only 30 to 40 percent, the potential reward was for a measured move up from this measuring gap, or at least a six-tick profit. The realistic worst case was a six-tick profit and a 30 percent chance of success, which is a breakeven strategy, and the best case was maybe a 60 percent chance of success and a 10- or 12-tick profit. This is an excellent result. Since the actual outcome was probably going to be somewhere in between and the math was therefore still good, this was a reasonable buy setup. The average daily range during this holiday trading was only about five to six points. Since the market has only a few days a year with a range less than five points, today's range should have become at least that large.

The move from bar 7 to bar 8 was a bull micro channel. Since the first breakout below a bull micro channel usually fails, bulls kept placing limit orders to buy at the low of the previous bar. They were filled on the bar after bar 8.

The micro channel continued up to bar 9, and the bulls were filled again on the next bar as it fell below bar 9. Some would have risked four to eight ticks on their longs, but others would have scaled in and bought more around four to six ticks below their first entry.

Although bar 11 was a possible final flag short and a higher high, most traders assumed that the momentum up was strong enough so that a bear leg was unlikely. Either the market would continue up or it would go down just a little, form a trading range, and then go on to a new high. Because the odds favored higher prices, they were willing to buy on limit orders at and below the low of the prior bar and were filled below bars 11 and 12.

The two-bar bear spike down from bar 14 might have flipped the market to always-in short for some traders, but most would have wanted to see strong follow-through selling on the next bar to confirm the breakout to the downside. Once they saw the doji close on the next bar instead of a strong bear close, they bought with limit orders around that close.

The market was likely to test the bar 10 bottom of the bull channel that followed the bar 7 to bar 9 bull spike. After that, a small trading range was likely as the market decided on its next move. Bears were shorting on the move up from bar 15 with a stop at one tick above the top of the bar 14 bear spike. Astute bears placed limit orders to short at one tick below the bar 14 high, with protective stops two ticks higher. They were filled on bar 17. Since their risk was only two ticks and they were shorting in a trading range, the chance of success for an equidistant move was at least 50 percent, and the chance of a four-tick move down before their two-tick stop was hit was probably also more than 50 percent. Since this was a trading range on a small day, these bears were in scalp mode and were happy to go for a one-point, four-tick profit. Their potential reward was twice the size of their risk and the probability was at least 50 percent, so the trader's equation was strong.

Figure 28.2

ENTERING ON LIMITS **511**

By bar 21, traders saw this as a trading range day and they expected breakout attempts to fail. Even though the strong bear spike after bar 22 was impressive, without follow-through selling and a bear close on the next bar it was likely to be a bear trap instead of a spike leading to a channel. Aggressive traders bought its close and also went long on a limit order at its low. They also saw that bar 23 was a test of the open of the day and of the original long above bar 7. They might have risked about four ticks for a swing trade up. Even if the probability was only 30 to 40 percent, the potential reward might have been four or five times the risk and therefore worth considering. More conservative traders bought above the bar 23 bull reversal bar that confirmed the failed bear breakout. They were buying higher above the bottom, and therefore their potential reward was less and their risk was more, but the greatly increased probability of success more than offset those problems.

When traders saw the strong close of the entry bar after bar 23, they bought on the close of the bar. Others waited until the next bar opened and then immediately placed limit orders to buy the close of the prior bar. When this next bar also became a strong bull trend bar, they repeated the process on bar 24.

The market was always-in long by the close of bar 24, so some bulls would have tried to buy the first bear close, which was on the next bar. However, the market never traded below the close of that bear bar, so most of their limit orders would probably not have been filled. This was a sign of urgency going into the close, and alert bulls would have also placed stop orders to go long above that bear bar because it was a breakout pullback buy setup. Many would not have been fast enough and would have chased the market up during the next bar, buying one- or two-tick pullbacks with limit orders as the bar was forming.

As the market was rallying up to bar 13, the trend was clearly up. Some traders placed limit orders to buy a Fibonacci 62 percent pullback, or any pullback of around 60 to 70 percent, with a stop below the bar 6 bull low. They were looking to buy where the reward would be about two or more times greater than the risk. Buying about two-thirds down for a test of the bull high was risking about one-third, making their target twice as large as their risk, which is always good. At the time they placed their orders, the trend was up, so buying a pullback had at least a 60 percent probability of an equidistant move (a move up equal to the size of their stop), and possibly a 60 percent chance of a new bull high (a reward twice as large as their risk). Entering on pullbacks to reduce risk is an approach used by many traders and has a strong trader's equation.

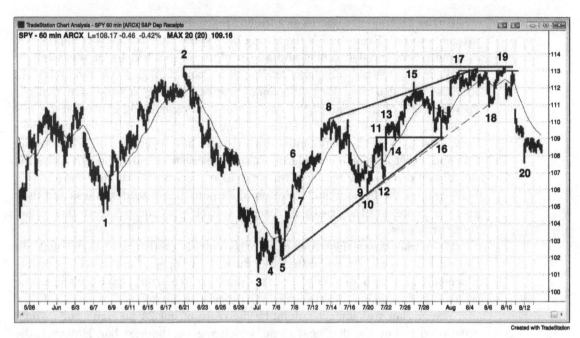

FIGURE 28.3 Limit Order Setups

This 60 minute chart of the SPY presented in Figure 28.3 shows many examples where institutions and traders almost certainly entered on limit or market orders. Bar 3 was a climactic bottom of a bear channel, which was a bull flag, and a possible expanding triangle bottom. Bar 1 was the second push down, and the swing low that preceded it was the first. After the bar 3 low, traders were so confident that the market was going higher on the leg down to bar 5 that they bought at the market and limit orders above the bar 4 low. Whenever a double bottom bull flag looks like this, it is because the bulls are so afraid of missing the new trend that they put their orders many ticks above the bar 4 low rather than at it or one tick above it. This led to a spike up to bar 6 and then a channel to bar 8. A trader could also have entered with a limit order in that area, risking about a point to below the bar 4 low and holding for a test of the tops of trading ranges in the channel at 105, 108, and maybe even 110. Each of these was the start of a channel down after a bear spike, and they were magnets. Traders were risking one point to make three to seven points and the probability was at least 40 percent, which made this a logical trade. Alternatively, they could have entered on a stop above the high of bar 5. This increased the probability of success to about 60 percent because they were then buying a confirmed bottom of a trading range (a double bottom). Their risk was to below the signal bar, which was about one point, and their first profit target was two points higher, again making for a sound strategy.

Bar 6 was the top of a strong bull spike and therefore the chance of any pullback being followed by a higher high was about 70 percent. Many traders therefore bought below its low. Other traders bought one tick above the bar 7 high 1 on a stop. When the market tested that price area again, they bought some at bar 9 but were not able to lift the market much. However, when bar 10 dipped below the bar 7 low, the bulls bought aggressively on limit and market orders (and stop orders).

Bar 14 was a small breakout test of the breakout above bar 11, and many traders bought there on limit orders, lifting the market.

The spike up to 13 was followed by the channel to 15 and then the test of the bottom of the channel at 16, where the market created a double bottom bull flag as it often does in a spike and channel bull trend. Buyers again bought at the market using limit orders at the same price as they did at bar 14, and this created a double bottom bull flag. Bar 16 dipped below the trend line from bar 5 to bar 10, and many traders bought this test at the market and with limit orders. They then redrew the trend line and bought again with limit and market orders when bar 18 tested it and tested below it. The buyers aggressively returned at the same price where they had bought on the breakout above bar 11 and the pullback to bar 14.

Bar 17 was a dueling lines short setup because the trend channel line across the top of the wedge was in the area of the bar 2 high, and a major swing high is always a resistance area. Traders repeatedly shorted below the resistance line over the next several days, and the market finally broke below the small double top formed by bars 17 and 19; this sell-off was also the start of the reversal down from the wedge top and large double top (bars 2 and 19). The market formed a trading range between bars 17 and 19, and traders repeatedly shorted tests of the top of the range, many doing so with limit orders.

The bull spike and channel up to bar 8 was so strong that higher prices were likely to follow. Although some traders buy at the market and on tiny pullbacks all of the way up, many traders only buy on pullbacks, like in the area of the bar 9 and bar 10 test of the bar 7 bottom of the bull channel. They buy on limit orders as the market is falling, as well as on stops above the high of the prior bar in areas of support. Since the trend was up, unless the market fell below the most recent higher low at bar 5, or below the bar 3 bottom of the swing, buying well below the bar 8 high would allow traders to use a smaller stop, reducing their risk. The trend is less certain after the sell-off to bars 9 or 10, reducing the probability of a profitable long swing, but the rally to bar 8 was stronger than the sell-off to bar 9, so the odds still favored the rally. Once the market turned up sharply to bar 11, the bulls raised their stops to below the bar 10 low. The sell-off to bar 12 was sharp, but held above the stop.

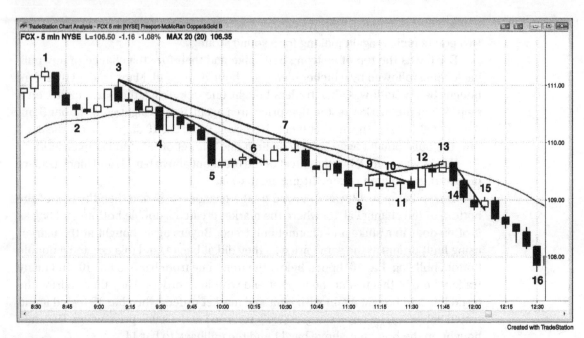

FIGURE 28.4   Fading Tests of Lines with Limit Orders

Many traders fade tests of trend lines and trend channel lines, but most traders make more money by entering on stops after the market reverses away from the lines. The trade-off is a little less profit for much more certainty, and this usually makes for a stronger trader's equation.

As shown in Figure 28.4, bar 6 was a test of the bear trend line in Freeport-McMoRan (FCX), and some traders shorted on a limit order as the market tested the line. This was a risky strategy in the three-bar tight trading range after the bar 5 sell climax, which was likely to have a two-legged correction. The market was within the magnetic pull of the moving average and was likely to test closer. A better strategy would have been to short on a stop at one tick below the bar 7 low 2 at the moving average.

Traders also shorted with limit orders on the test of the bear trend line from bar 9 to bar 10. A better strategy would have been to short below a low 2 signal bar, like the bar after bar 11, but that short never triggered. The market then had a wedge bear flag at the moving average at bar 13. Traders shorted with limit orders at the moving average and at the trend channel line, but a better strategy would have been to short below bar 13, or below a bear trend bar like the bar before or the bar after bar 13. When traders saw the bar 11 higher low, they expected any breakout above a swing high to fail. Some placed limit orders to short at one tick

Figure 28.4   ENTERING ON LIMITS   **515**

above bar 10. They also believed that there would be additional bears shorting at one tick below the moving average and that very few bulls would buy the breakout above the bar 10 swing high. Most attempts to reverse a bear trend fail and become bear flags. These aggressive bears shorted at the top of the bear flag, trusting that these high prices would not last long. Others entered as the market fell below the bar 12 bull trend bar, expecting remaining longs to sell out at that point and provide fuel for lower prices. These longs would have also been hesitant to buy again for at least a couple of bars, giving the bears short-term control over the market.

Bar 14 was the first bar of a three-bar bear spike, which created a bear micro channel. Traders could have shorted during bar 15 as it went above the trend line. Other traders shorted its close once they saw that it was going to be a weak bull breakout bar. Once bar 15 closed, many traders immediately placed limit orders at, just above, and just below its high. Since the next bar did not trade above bar 15, those who tried to short at or above bar 15 did not get filled. They then chased the market down, and many sold on a stop at one tick below the bar 15 low. This was the best entry, because traders saw the bear micro channel and believed more selling would follow, and they also saw that the market never went above bar 15. This told them that the traders who tried to short there were trapped out and would be eager to get short, and the next logical entry was on a stop below bar 15.

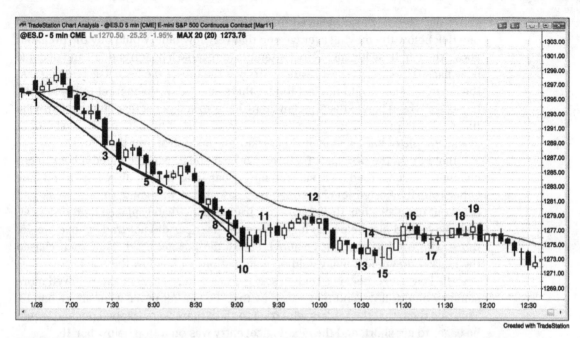

FIGURE 28.5   Trend Channel Lines Trap Early Bulls into Losses in a Strong Bear Trend

Buying at trend channel lines in a bear market, hoping for a wedge bottom, is a losing strategy. Whenever you find yourself repeatedly drawing trend channel lines as the market is falling, you are usually totally missing a strong trend and looking for trades in the wrong direction.

In Figure 28.5, bar 3 collapsed through the trend channel line drawn from bar 1 to bar 2, and traders who bought as the market fell to the line immediately found themselves trapped. Buying when the market is strongly always-in short is a losing strategy. Traders should look only for short trades and try to swing part of the position. A trader who bought as the market tested other trend channel lines at bars 6, 8, and 9 also likely lost money. Although a trader might have made money buying as bar 10 fell to the trend channel line, the risk was great and the probability and potential reward were small, so that was a bad strategy. However, buying above the strong bull inside bar that followed the large bar 10 sell climax was an acceptable long for a scalp up to around the moving average.

This was followed by a wedge bear flag short near the moving average at bar 12. Bar 12 was the second entry, and because it was a bear reversal bar close to the moving average, this was an especially reliable short setup in a strong bear trend.

CHAPTER 29

Protective and Trailing Stops

S ince most trades are only 60 percent certain at best, you always have to have a plan for that other 40 percent of the time when the trade does not do what you expect. You should not ignore that 40 percent any more than you should dismiss someone 30 yards away who is shooting at you but who has only a 40 percent chance of hitting you. Forty percent is very real and dangerous, so always respect the traders who believe the opposite of you. The most important part of your plan is to have a protective stop in the market in case the market goes against you. It is better to have the stop working, because many traders who use mental stops find too many reasons to ignore them when they are needed most, and they invariably allow their small loss to grow and grow. There are several approaches to placing stops, and any of them is fine. The most important consideration is that you have the stop order working in the market instead of just in your head.

The two main types of protective stops are money management stops, where you risk a certain number of ticks or dollars, and price action stops, where you get out if the market moves beyond a certain price bar or price level. Many traders use both or either, depending on the situation. For example, a trader who uses a two-point stop in the Emini for most of his trades might use a three-point stop if the bars are large. A price action trader who just went long might initially place a protective sell stop at one tick below the low of the signal bar. However, if the bar is unusually large, like six points tall, she might instead either trade far fewer contracts or switch to a money management stop of about three points. In general, using one method most or all of the time is best because then it is such a part of your routine that you will always have a protective stop working as soon as you enter any trade. This saves you from the distraction of having to think about what type and size stop you should be using in different situations when your focus needs to be on deciding whether to take the trade.

For most small scalps, traders do not want to see any pullbacks and will often exit as soon as one appears. However, if they believe that the market has entered a trend channel, they will usually allow small pullbacks. For example, if the day is a trading range day and the market just had a spike up off the low of the range and now might be forming a small bull channel that could test the top of the range, the profit goal of a trader who went long would be limited and therefore the trade would be a scalp. Since the market is in a bull channel, it will likely have pullbacks, which means that a bar might trade below the low of the prior bar by a few ticks, but not below the most recent swing low in the channel. Since the trader suspected that the market might enter a channel and he still went long, he has to be willing to hold through those pullbacks and keep his protective stop below the most recent swing low in the channel. Aggressive, experienced traders might even buy more on a limit order at the low of the prior bar, since they know that channels typically have one- or two-bar pullbacks yet continue to work higher.

If traders are buying for a swing, then they are expecting a bull trend. Since a bull trend is a series of higher highs and higher lows, it is reasonable to move the protective stop to below the most recent swing low after the market makes a new swing high. This is called a trailing stop. If the market trades up for five or 10 bars, pulls back to below the entry price, and trades up to a new swing high, traders will not want the market to trade below the low of that pullback and will move their protective stop to one tick below its low. Many traders would not want their stop to be tested a second time and would simply move their stop to breakeven.

Once traders see the market break out into what they believe will be a trending trading range day, they have to be ready to change their trading style as the market begins to form the second trading range. For example, if there is a bull breakout lasting a couple of bars followed by a one-bar pullback and then a weaker rally, the low of that pullback bar will probably become the low of the upper trading range. Since the market usually tests back into the breakout gap and often to the top of the lower trading range, the odds are that it will fall below the low of that pullback bar. Therefore, bulls should not trail their stops below that low, since they will get stopped out. If they were thinking about placing protective stops there, it makes more sense to exit on the close of a bull trend bar within the next several bars, so that they would be taking profits near the top of the developing trading range rather than below the bottom. Once the market evolves into a trading range, traders should no longer trade it as if it was still in a strong trend.

Some traders will allow pullbacks beyond the signal bar as long as they believe that their premise for a swing trade is still valid. For example, if they bought a high 2 pullback in a bull trend and the signal bar is about two points tall, they might be willing to hold on to their position even if the market falls below the low of the signal bar, thinking that it might evolve into a high 3, which is a wedge bull flag buy setup. Other traders would exit if the market fell below the signal bar and then buy again if a strong high 3 buy signal sets up. Some might even buy a position that is twice as large as their first because they see the strong second signal as more reliable. Many of these traders would have bought just a half-size position on the high 2 buy signal if they thought that the signal did not look quite right. They were allowing for the possibility of the high 2 failing and then evolving into a wedge bull flag, which might even look stronger. If this happened, they would then feel comfortable trading their usual full size.

Other traders trade half size when they see questionable signals, exit if their protective stop is hit, and then take the second signal with a full size if the signal is strong. Traders who scale in as a trade goes against them obviously do not use the signal bar extreme for their initial protective stop, and many look to scale in exactly where other traders are taking losses on their protective stops. Some simply use a wide stop. For example, when the average daily range in Eminis is less than about 15 points, a pullback in a trend is rarely more than seven points. Some traders will consider that the trend is still in effect unless the market falls more than between 50 to 75 percent of the average daily range. As long as a pullback is within their tolerance, they will hold their position and assume that their premise is correct. If they bought a pullback in a bull trend and their entry was three points below the high of the day, then they might risk five points. Since they believe that the trend is still in effect, they believe that they have a 60 percent or better chance of an equidistant move. This means that they are at least 60 percent certain that the market will go up at least five points before falling five points to their protective stop, which creates a profitable trader's equation. If their initial buy signal in the bull pullback came at five points below the high, then they might risk just three points, and they would look to exit their long on a test of the high. Since the pullback was relatively large, the trend might be a little weak, and this might make them take profits on a test of the trend high. They would try to get at least as much as they had to risk, but they might be willing to get out just below the old high if they were concerned that the market might be transitioning into a trading range or possibly even reversing into a bear trend.

Once the market finally begins to enter a trading range, traders should look to take at least partial profits around the high of the range, rather than relying on their trailing stops. This is because it is likely that the market will begin to have pullbacks that fall below prior swing lows. As soon as traders believe that their stops will likely get hit, it makes sense to exit before that happens, especially if they have already met most of their profit objectives.

The initial price action stop for most trades is one tick beyond the signal bar until the entry bar closes, when it is tightened to one or two ticks beyond the entry bar if the entry bar is strong. If the entry bar is a doji, then rely on your original stop. Remember that a doji is a single-bar trading range, and if you just bought, you don't want to exit (sell) below a trading range in what you think is a bull trend (or if you just shorted, you don't want to buy above a trading range in a new bear trend).

In fact, experienced traders can consider adding on at a tick or two below a small doji entry bar in a possible new bull trend (or above a doji entry bar in a new bear trend), relying on the initial stop location for the stop on the added contracts. They are buying below the low 1 short signal bar because they think that the market is going up, not down. A low 1 is a short setup at the bottom of a strong bear spike in a bear trend, or near the top of a trading range (in a trading range, it is better to wait to short a low 2), not at the bottom of a trading range or at the bottom of a new bull trend. Since a short down there is likely to fail, the two-point protective buy stop is more likely to be hit than is a six-tick profit-taking limit order placed below the low 1 signal bar. This means that buying below the low 1 signal bar will probably be followed by the market going up at least two points before falling six ticks. Since traders think this is a new bull trend or at least a trading range, they think that the market will go up at least three or four points, so this is a logical long trade.

If it is a bar in the opposite direction, then you have to make a decision. For example, say you just bought a pullback in a strong bull market and the signal bar was a strong bull reversal bar at the end of a two-legged pullback to the moving average. If the entry bar becomes a bear reversal bar, you should usually just keep your protective stop below the signal bar. However, if you were buying a reversal up in a strong bear trend, you should usually exit if the market falls below that bear entry bar. In some cases, you should even reverse to short, if the context makes sense. In general, you should not be buying in a strong bear trend if you believe that a failed long would be a short setup. Very few traders are able to reverse in such a situation, and if the bear trend is still strong enough so that shorting low 1 setups makes sense, then it is probably too strong to be looking for longs. Instead, a bull should wait for a strong rally and then look to buy a higher low pullback. Buying in a bear trend before there has been evidence that the bulls can control the market is a losing strategy. Since most bull reversals become bear flags, it is far better not to buy and instead to look to short, unless the reversal setup is especially strong (this is discussed in the chapter on trend reversals in the third book).

If the bars at the time of entry into any trade are too large, it is wiser to use a money management stop, like eight ticks on the Emini 5 minute chart, or about a 70 percent pullback (a couple of ticks beyond the Fibonacci 62 percent pullback). For example, in a long off a large bull signal bar, you would place the protective stop about 30 percent of the distance up from the bottom of the signal bar to the entry price. The size of the money management stop is in proportion to the size of the bars. After the market reaches the first profit target and partial profits are secured, move the protective stop to about breakeven (the entry price, which is one tick from the signal bar's extreme). The best trades will not hit a breakeven stop and will rarely ever go more than four ticks beyond the entry on the 5 minute Emini (for example, three ticks below the signal bar high after getting long).

If you are very confident in the reversal because of a large, strong reversal bar and a confluence of other factors, you can use a stop beyond that large signal bar and allow a pullback after entry, as long as it does not hit your stop. You might even allow a stop of a couple of points beyond your signal bar, but if you do, calculate your risk and reduce your position size to keep your risk the same as on your other trades. Also, if you are confident that a reversal is strong enough to make two legs likely, and if the market comes back through your original entry by a few ticks after you've scalped out part of your trade, you can hold through the pullback and rely on your original stop, despite being in a drawdown of several ticks. Otherwise (for example, in a new long) you will exit the swing portion at breakeven and then buy again above the high of the bar that ran your stop, giving up a couple of points or more of what you considered to be a very high-probability second leg.

If you are entering a quiet pullback that you believe is about to end and the bars are small, you might consider using your usual money management stop, even if it means that you are risking several ticks beyond your signal bar. For example, if the day is a bear trend day with a low-momentum bull channel up to the moving average that forms a low 4 short setup and the signal bar is a three-tick-tall doji bar, traders who believe that the pullback is about to end might risk their usual eight ticks, even though the stop would then be four ticks above the signal bar. Low 4 setups often form in tight channels, and the entry is a breakout below the tight channel. Tight channel breakouts usually have pullbacks, and sometimes they go beyond the signal bar. Here, a higher high breakout pullback would not be surprising. As long as the traders believe that their premise is still valid, they can allow the trade some room. Alternatively, they could exit if the market goes above the entry or signal bar and then sell again as the market turns down again; but if they are confident in their analysis, they can rely on their original eight-tick stop and allow the higher high pullback. In general, if you are in a losing trade, ask yourself if you would put the trade on now if you were flat. If the answer is no, then get out. If your premise is no longer valid, then exit, even with a loss.

When you are concerned that the market might be volatile and have large bars, you should trade only a fraction of your usual position size. Just cut your position size in half or down to a quarter and place the order. If you are buying and are confident that a low will hold, but a long trade would require a much greater money management stop than you typically use, you can use the larger stop and then wait. If the market hits your profit target without much of a pullback, take your profit. However, if it only goes a tick or so beyond your entry, pulls back almost to your stop, and then starts up again above your entry price, raise your profit target. As a general rule, the market will rally enough to equal the size of the stop that it required you to have to stay in the trade. So if the market dipped 11 ticks below your entry before reversing back up, a stop of only 12 ticks would have worked; therefore the market will likely go about 12 ticks or more above your entry price. It would be wise to place a limit order to exit with a profit at a tick or two less than this and, when it approaches the target, to move your stop to breakeven and wait to see if your profit target order gets filled. For example, suppose the pullback was 11 ticks, your stop beyond the signal bar was not hit (maybe it was 12 or even 18 ticks), and now the market is again going in your direction; calculate the total number of ticks that you would have had to risk to avoid being stopped out. At this point, you would have had to risk 12 ticks (one beyond the pullback). Now increase your profit target to one or two ticks less than the risk, or 11 ticks. You also should adjust your protective stop at this point to one tick beyond that pullback, so you are now risking 12 ticks.

When a protective stop is hit before making a scalper's profit, you were trapped into a bad trade, so reversing on the stop is occasionally a good strategy. This depends on the context. For example, a failed low 2 short is a good reversal into a long trade when you think that the market is reversing into a bull trend. However, a stop run in a tight trading range is not a reversal. Take time to make sure that you are reading the chart correctly before considering a trade in the opposite direction. If you don't have time to get right back in, wait for the next setup, which will always come before too long.

After studying a market, you will see what a reasonable stop is. For the Emini 5 minute chart when the average daily range is 10 to 15 points, eight ticks works well on most days. However, pay close attention to the maximum size stop required in the first hour, because this often becomes the best stop to use for the rest of the day. If the stop is more than eight ticks, you will likely be able to increase the size of your profit target as well. However, this provides a modest advantage at best unless the bars are exceptionally big.

There are a couple of common setups that usually require a large stop, which means trading a smaller position. Both involve entering around the close of a strong spike in a trend, but the two trades are in opposite directions. When there is a strong spike at the beginning of a trend and there are several consecutive trend bars, traders will enter in the direction of the trend as the bars are forming and as they close. For example, if there is a strong bull breakout that has two large bull trend bars, bulls will buy the close of the second bar and above its high. If it is followed by a third, fourth, and fifth consecutive bull trend bar, bulls will keep buying as the bull spike grows. The theoretical stop for all of their entries is below the bottom of the spike, which is far away. If traders used that for their stop, they need to trade a very small position size to keep their risk within their comfort zone. Realistically, most traders would consider scalping a larger position and using a smaller stop when they enter late in the spike. This is because a pullback becomes more likely, and it would allow them to then put a swing position on at a lower price and with a smaller stop, like below the signal bar.

The second situation when traders are entering during a large trend bar and need a large stop is when they are entering countertrend. For example, if there is a third consecutive sell climax without a significant pullback, and that third one has the largest bear trend bar of the day and closes near its low, aggressive bulls will buy the close of the bar, expecting it to be at or near the low of the swing; they will also expect a strong rally to follow. Reliable protective stop placement in this situation is never certain, but as a rule, since traders expect the rally to go at least to the high of the large bear trend bar and they are 60 percent certain of the trade, they should risk about as many ticks as there are in the bear trend bar. This is discussed more in the chapter on climaxes in book 3. If they are very experienced traders, this can be a reliable trade. The volume is often huge in these situations, which means that the institutions are buying heavily as well. The bears are taking profits on their shorts, and the bulls are aggressively buying. Both often wait for a large bear trend bar into support as a sign of exhaustion, and then buy heavily. Because they were expecting the bottom to form very soon, they stepped aside and stopped buying just above support, and this creates a sell vacuum in the form of the large bear trend bar.

There are many other special situations when a trader might use an unusually wide protective stop. I have a friend who looks for weak channels and scales in against them, expecting a reversal. For example, if the market is in a bull channel after a bull spike and the channel is not particularly strong, he places a limit order to go short at the prior swing high in the channel, using about a quarter of his normal position size, and adds on above the next two or three swing highs if the channel continues. When the average daily range in the Emini is about 10 to 15 points, his final stop is about eight points from his first entry and his target is a test of his first entry. Once the reversal is underway, if he thinks that it is strong, he will often swing part of his position below his original entry.

Traders can use wide stops when they are fading breakouts in stairs patterns or on trending trading range days. If the average range in the Emini is about 10 to 15 points and there is a breakout that runs about five points, a trader might fade the breakout and risk about five points to make five points, expecting a test of the breakout. In a typical situation, this trade has better than a 60 percent chance of success and therefore has a positive trader's equation.

Traders sometimes fade large trend bar breakouts of one-bar final flags at the ends of big trends, expecting that the trend bar is an exhaustive climax (this is discussed in the chapter on climactic reversals in book 3). For example, if there is a bull trend that has gone on for 30 bars or so with only small pullbacks, and then there is a large bull trend bar followed by a one- or two-bar pullback, bulls and bears will sell the close of the next bar if it is also a large bull trend bar. The bulls will sell to take profits, and aggressive bears will sell to initiate shorts. The bears will risk about the height of the bar (if the bar is 10 ticks tall, they will use about a 10-tick stop), and their initial profit target will be a test of the bottom of the bar. The next target is a measured move down.

I have another friend who routinely uses a five-point stop when entering on pullbacks in the Emini. He feels that he cannot consistently predict the end of a pullback and instead enters when he thinks that the trend is resuming. He just assumes that he sometimes enters early and that the pullback might go a little further before the trend resumes, and the wide stop allows him to stay in the trade. His profit target is a test of the trend's extreme, which might be three to five points away. If the resumption is strong, he will swing the trade, looking for five or more points. Although there are many variations to this approach, the average risk is generally about the size of the average reward, and since it is a with-trend strategy, the probability is at least 60 percent. This means that the strategy has a positive trader's equation.

Whenever traders use a wide stop, as soon as the market begins to turn in their direction they are usually able to tighten the stop and greatly reduce their risk. Once a swing trade reaches about halfway to the profit target, many traders will move their protective stop to break even. If the market moves strongly in their direction, the probability of success increases, the potential reward can remain the same or they might increase it, and the risk becomes smaller. This increases the strength of the trader's equation and is why many traders prefer to wait to enter until the market is able to get to this point. If, however, the reversal is very weak, although traders can tighten their stop and reduce their risk, their probability of success will be less and they might also reduce their reward (tighten their profit-taking limit order). If the trader's equation is weak enough, they might try to scalp out with a small profit and wait for another trade.

The goal is to make money, which requires a positive trader's equation. If the size of the bars requires a large stop, that is what you must use, but you also must adjust your target to keep the trader's equation positive. You should also reduce your position size.

In a big market, there might be a hundred institutions actively trading, each contributing about 1 percent of the total volume. Of the other 99 percent of the volume, only 5 percent is from individual traders. Institutions are going to try to take money from other institutions, which make up 94 percent of the market, not the 5 percent of dollars traded by people at home. Institutions could care less about us and are not out there running our stops, trying to devour the little guy. If your stop gets hit, it has nothing to do with you. For example, if you were long and your protective sell stop got hit, you should assume that it was because there was at least one institution that also wanted to sell at that price. Only rarely will enough small traders do the same thing to offer enough volume to attract an institution, so it is better to assume that the market will only trade at any price if there is both an institution willing to sell there and another willing to buy there.

Figure 29.1

PROTECTIVE AND TRAILING STOPS   **525**

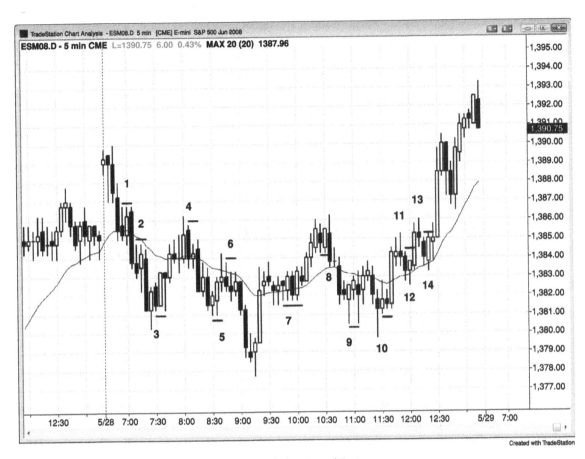

FIGURE 29.1   The Initial Stop Is Just beyond the Signal Bar

The initial stop is one tick beyond the signal bar in Figure 29.1. Once the entry bar closes, move the stop to one tick beyond the entry bar if the bar is strong. If the risk is too great, use a money management stop or risk about 60 percent of the height of the signal bar.

If you shorted on bar 1 on the breakout below the bear inside bar, the initial stop would have been above the signal bar. The bar 1 entry bar reversed up immediately after entry but did not exceed the top of the signal bar, so this would have eventually ended up as a profitable short scalp. Once the entry bar closed, if it is a bull or bear trend bar and not a doji bar, move the stop up to one tick above its high. In this example, the signal and entry bars had the same high, so the stop would not have to be tightened.

The bar before bar 3 was a bull reversal bar after three pushes down on the open. Although buying the first breakout of a tight bear channel is not usually a good trade, reversals in the first hour are usually reliable, especially when the prior day had a strong close (look at the steep slope of the moving average going into yesterday's close). The bar 3 entry bar immediately sold off but did not fall below the low of the signal bar, or below about 70 percent of its height (if you used a money management stop, thinking that this signal bar was too big to use a price action stop below its low). Once an entry bar closed, the protective stop should have been moved up to one tick below its low. If the market fell below its low, many traders would have gone short because this was a breakout pullback short setup. However, since this was not a strong bear spike, it was not a reliable low 1 short. Alternatively, a trader could have kept the stop below the signal bar, but when bottom picking in a strong bear trend, it is risky to hold a long if the market falls below a strong bear trend bar that is a low 1 short signal bar.

Two bars later, there was a pullback bar, but it did not hit the stop. It tested the entry bar low to the tick, creating a double bottom. Since this wedge bottom was likely to have two legs up, it was reasonable for an experienced trader to hold through the pullback that occurred two bars after entry and to rely on the stop below the entry bar. Otherwise, you would have been stopped out for seven ticks and then you would have bought above the high of the pullback bar to catch the second leg; your entry price would have been three ticks worse, so overall you would have been 10 ticks worse off.

The pullback to the moving average at bar 4 formed a double top with the bar 1 area, and it was a small wedge bear flag. Other traders would have seen it as a simple low 2 at the moving average. The initial protective stop for the short at the bar 4 low 2 was not hit, despite a pullback bar two bars after entry. The stop was above the signal bar, and you should not tighten to above the high of the most recent bar until after the market had moved about four ticks in your direction or until the market had a reasonably strong bear body. Give the trade time to work. Also, when the entry bar is a doji, it is usually safe to allow a one- or two-tick pullback. A doji bar is a one-bar trading range and it is risky to buy above a trading range, so don't buy back your short there. Rely on your original stop until the market has moved at least several ticks in your direction.

The bar 5 long immediately sold off to test the signal bar low (this was evident on the 1 minute chart, not shown) forming a micro double bottom and then a successful long scalp. Rely on your stop and ignore the 1 minute chart. When taking a 5 minute entry, rely on a 5 minute stop, else you will lose too often and be stopped out of a great many trades in your attempt to risk less per trade.

Bar 7 was a high 2 long after a strong bull spike. The market tested the stop below the signal bar but missed by one tick, and then tested the tightened stop below the entry bar, but neither stop was hit. The dojis prior to entry increased the risk of the trade, but with six closes above the moving average after the surge from a new low of the day, this was an acceptable long setup since you had to be expecting a second leg up.

Figure 29.1   PROTECTIVE AND TRAILING STOPS   **527**

The bar 8 ii pattern was a high 1 buy setup. However, it was not at the top of a strong bull spike in a strong bull trend and therefore it was not a good trade. In fact, it was at the top of a bull channel after the spike up from the low of the day; it was around a measured move up, and it might have been forming a double top with bar 4. Since most trading range breakout attempts fail, there was a 60 percent chance that the market would trade down and only a 40 percent chance that the breakout would be successful. It is impossible to know the probabilities with certainty, but 60–40 is a good rule of thumb when it comes to trading range breakout attempts. Aggressive traders would have shorted with a limit order at the high of the ii pattern, expecting it to be a bull trap. If a trader instead bought above the bar 8 ii pattern, the protective stop was hit on the entry bar; this would have been a good reversal, as are most failed ii patterns.

If you shorted the bar 11 swing high near the top of this trading range day, you could have reversed either on the bar 12 reversal bar that tested the moving average or on a buy stop at one tick above the entry bar that followed the bar 11 short.

The short from the bar 13 swing high, low 2 became a five-tick failure and a failed low 2. You should have reversed to long on bar 14 at one tick above the entry bar (the bar after the bar 13 signal bar) since there were trapped shorts, and you should have expected at least two more legs up. If you did not buy there, you should have bought on the bar after bar 14 because bar 14 was a two-bar reversal up and a high 2 buy signal above the moving average in a possible bull trend. Whenever traders are top picking and then see a high 2 buy signal at the moving average with a bull signal bar, they should always exit the short and reverse to long. If they were not short, they should go long. This was not a good short setup since this could have been setting up a pullback from the breakout of a large wedge bull flag. The strong bull trend bar two bars earlier was the breakout, and the three pushes down began with the bars around bar 7 (three bars before is a good choice), and then bar 9 and the bar before bar 10. The move up to bar 8 broke above the bear channel of the first couple of hours, and bar 10 was a second entry into the higher low after the break above the bear trend line. Some traders bought on bar 10 because they saw this as a head and shoulders bottom. Other traders bought with a limit order below the bar 13 low 2 since they saw this as a bull trend and not as a trading range, and a low 2 in a bull trend is a buy setup. A low 2 is a short setup only in a trading range or in a bear trend. When the market is in a bull phase, traders see a low 2 as a bear trap and will buy below it for the reversal up. Some traders would instead buy on a stop at one tick above the low 2 entry bar, waiting for confirmation that it would fail.

A trader who was swinging a long up from bar 12 would trail the stop to one tick below the most recent swing low after the market moved to a new high. So once the market rallied above the bar 13 swing high, the trader could move the protective stop up to just below the bar 14 higher low.

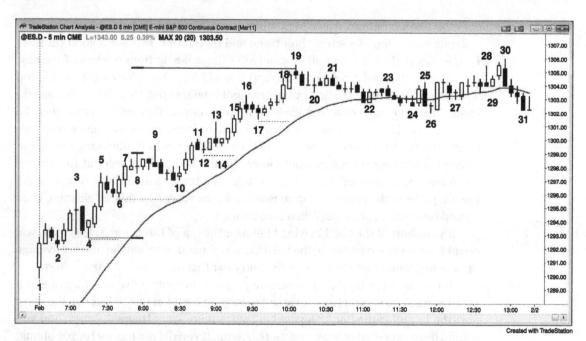

FIGURE 29.2   Trailing Stops in a Strong Bull Trend

In a strong bull trend, traders often trail their protective stops to below the most recent swing low just after the market makes a new swing high. Once the market looks like it will enter a trading range, traders should take some profits, and consider scalping for smaller profits.

Today, as shown in Figure 29.2, had a large gap up and a strong bull trend bar for the first bar of the day, and therefore had a good chance of becoming a bull trend from the open day. If traders bought above bar 2 or bar 4, they could have started to trail their protective stops as soon as bar 5 moved above the most recent swing high at bar 3. The three-bar bull spike up to bar 5 convinced most traders that the always-in direction was long and strong, so many traders wanted to let their profits run. Once bar 7 moved above bar 5, they could have tightened their protective stops to one tick below bar 6, and when the market moved above bar 9, they could have raised them to one tick below bar 10.

Traders know that trends usually have a larger pullback at some point, and many traders will take partial or full profits when they believe that a more complex pullback is imminent. A measured move target can often give an idea of where institutions might take profits, which means it is where a pullback could begin. Since the initial strong bull spike began at bar 4 and ended around bar 8, a measured move up from there would have been a level where profit taking was likely. The move up

Figure 29.2   PROTECTIVE AND TRAILING STOPS   **529**

from bar 10 to bar 19 also had three legs, and a three-legged move is a variant of a wedge (even when it is in a steep channel like this) and can be followed by a larger pullback. The initial target was the moving average. Bar 18 was a large bull trend bar and was followed by another large bull trend bar, and this two-bar buy climax followed a protracted trend. When this happens, the market often corrects for at least 10 bars and two legs, especially when it is far from the moving average, as it was here. When bar 19 became a bear reversal bar, many traders took profits. Other traders assumed that the first pullback would be followed by at least one more new high, and they held through the pullback. However, there was aggressive profit taking on bar 30 when the market moved above bar 19 near the close of the day, so many traders took profits at the new high and as the market turned down.

Today was a very strong bull trend day and was likely to have a test of the high after a pullback to the moving average. The bear channel down to bar 24 had low momentum and small bars. A trader who bought above bar 24 might have considered relying on the usual eight-tick stop, in case the breakout above the bear channel (all bear channels are bull flags) was followed by a lower low breakout pullback. The market broke strongly to the upside but immediately formed a big two-bar bear reversal. This was not a reliable short setup in a strong bull trend that was pulling back to the moving average. Experienced traders would have relied on their stops, even though the stops were several ticks below the signal bar. The stops would not have been hit and the traders could have then exited their longs near the high of the day. Alternatively, a trader could have exited below the bar 25 two-bar reversal and then bought again above the bar 26 micro channel breakout pullback.

A swing trader who bought during the strong bull trend at any point up to the bar 19 buy climax ideally would have used a protective stop below the most recent swing low, which means risking more than two points and using a wide stop. Once the bar 19 buy climax formed, the market was likely to enter a trading range and the trader would have switched to a trading range style of trading, which means scalping instead of swinging. Since the market was entering a trading range, it was likely to fall below prior swing lows and therefore it no longer made sense to keep protective stops there. Once a stop is likely to get hit because a trading range is forming, traders should exit their longs well before that happens. Astute traders would have exited on strength at the top of the likely developing range, like below bar 19. Aggressive traders would have begun to short at that point, looking for a scalp to the moving average.

Most swing traders would have trailed their protective stops below the most recent swing low. Instead of letting a swing trade run until the trend ends, some traders prefer to use profit targets. Those who do often move their protective stops to no worse than breakeven once the market has reached halfway to their profit targets.

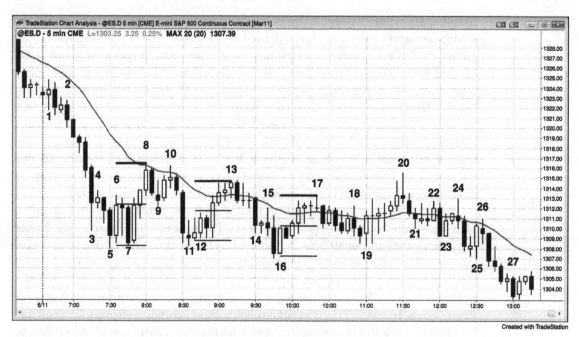

FIGURE 29.3   Reward Often Equals Risk

The market often rewards traders with as many ticks of profit as it forces them to risk. In general, it is risky to buy above large signal bars in a bear trend day, and the trades described here based on the chart shown in Figure 29.3 are questionable at best, but they illustrate a point.

If traders bought above bar 5, thinking that it was the second consecutive sell climax and the bottom of a parabolic move and therefore likely to be followed by a two-legged rally, their initial stops would have been below the bar 5 low. Bar 7 tested the low but did not hit the stops. However, once the market went above bar 7, the traders would have moved their stops to one tick below the bar 7 low, which was 16 ticks below the entry price. The market then rallied to exactly the bar 8 high, which was 16 ticks above the entry price (and a test of the moving average, where shorts came in). Traders who understood this tendency would have placed a profit-taking limit order at 15 ticks above their entry. Since they were buying at what they thought would become the bottom of a small trading range, they believed that they had at least a 60 percent chance of the market having an equidistant move up. This was a barely acceptable trade.

The same thing happened again on a long above the bar 12 and bar 16 strong bull trend bars. Once there was a pullback and then a move back up, traders saw

Figure 29.3   PROTECTIVE AND TRAILING STOPS   **531**

how much the market forced them to risk, and they could put a profit-taking limit order at one tick less than that risk.

A trader who shorted at any point during the bear spike from bar 2 to bar 3, and who planned to swing the trade, would have used a wide protective stop, possibly above the top of the spike. Most traders would have risked less than that, but they would also have risked two or three times as much as they would have on a scalp.

At bar 16, assume that a bull bought the reversal up from the third push down, looking for a final flag trend reversal. Since the channel down from 13 was tight, the probability of a successful long would have been higher if a trader waited to see if the breakout was strong, and then bought the strong spike or the pullback that followed. However, for the sake of illustration, assume that the trader simply bought above bar 16. He might have assumed that he had a 50 percent chance of the market breaking above the bar 13 high and reaching a measured move up, making his reward much greater than his risk, which was to below the bar 16 buy signal bar. However, he might have been concerned by the lack of urgency by the bulls on the move up to the bar 17 doji, and decided that his premise had changed. He might have become convinced that the market was simply making another lower low in a bear channel instead of a trend reversal, and then simply scalped out of his long. If he thought that the market was topping out, it would make no sense for him to continue to hold his long. If he thought that it might have a second leg up but not hit a breakeven stop, he might have moved his protective stop to breakeven. If he thought that the market might fall below his entry price but stay above the signal bar low and form a higher low, he could have kept his original stop, or he cold have exited and bought the breakout pullback to the higher low. Traders make these decisions constantly, and the better they get at making them, the better able they are to make money. If they always hold on to their original premise, even when the market is not doing what they expected, they will have a difficult time making money trading. Their job is to follow the market, and if it is not going where they believe it should, they should exit and look for another trade.

Swing traders allow pullbacks and patiently wait to tighten their stops until the trend is well underway. A swing trader who shorted below bar 20, expecting it to be a test of the top of the trading range that would lead to a resumption of the bear trend from the open, might have been looking for a reward that was at least twice as large as his risk. Once he saw the strong bear entry bar, he might have tightened his stop to above its high, or he might have left it above the bar 20 signal bar high until after it turned down from the bar 24 double top. The signal bar was three points (12 ticks) tall so his initial risk was 14 ticks. If his profit target was twice as large as his risk, he was looking to take profits at 28 ticks below his entry, or at 1,305.25, and his profit-taking limit order would have been filled two bars before bar 27. Bar 24 went one tick above the strong bear trend bar before bar 23, trapping out impatient weak shorts, but it did not get above the entry bar or the signal bar.

FIGURE 29.4   The Stop Size Is Often Set by the First Trade of the Day

The market rallied to above yesterday's high and then turned down, as shown in Figure 29.4. Traders who shorted below bar 1 would have placed an initial protective stop above bar 1. After the market turned down on bar 2, they could have calculated that the market went eight ticks against them before it went their way. That meant that the minimum initial protective stop that they would have had to use to stay in the trade was nine ticks, and they would have remembered that for the rest of the day.

If you bought the failed low 2 at bar 3 and placed the initial stop at one tick below the signal bar's low, you would have risked eight ticks. One-tick stop runs are common and you would have known that a nine-tick stop was needed earlier in the day, so it would have been wise to risk the extra tick. This was not a great buy because it followed a tiny breakout and the last seven bars were largely sideways. A second entry would have been better. Bar 4 was a high 2 buy setup, and the bull inside bar two bars later was a breakout pullback buy setup (the inside bar was the pullback from the high 2 long breakout); both of those were stronger setups.

Figure 29.4 PROTECTIVE AND TRAILING STOPS **533**

Once the bars become smaller, you can adjust the size of your stop to one that is appropriate for the current market conditions. However, the market often later in the day will have a trade that would require a larger stop. Don't worry if your stop gets hit and you take a loss. It is usually easier than constantly adjusting your stops, targets, and position sizes all day, and end up missing trades or making mistakes.

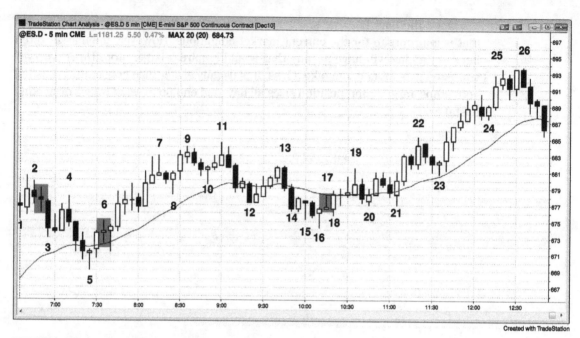

FIGURE 29.5 Don't Tighten Stops Too Soon

Don't tighten your protective stop after small doji bars that form within a few bars of entry. They are one-bar trading ranges, and it is common for the market to reverse beyond them for a tick or two. You do not want to get stopped out of a trade when your premise is still intact.

If traders shorted below bar 2 and saw the doji close of their entry bar, they should keep their protective stop above the signal bar high until the market makes a strong move in their direction. They could have scalped out part on the bar 3 plunge, and if they thought that the moving average was steep and there was a risk of a rally, they could then tighten it to breakeven or to one bar above bar 3. If they did, they would have been stopped out on bar 4, but it was still a sensible decision. However, on a large gap up day when there is a pullback that is close to the moving average, there is often a second leg down that tests closer; this often sets up the low of the day, as it did here at bar 5.

If traders bought above the bar 5 moving average gap bar and high 2 and wedge bull flag test, they could have moved their protective stop to breakeven on the swing portion of their trade once the entry bar closed and was clearly a strong bull trend bar. They would not have exited below the low of the bar 6 doji.

If they bought above the bar 16 bull reversal bar, thinking of it as a high 2 long or as a wedge bull flag (where either bar 8 or bar 10 formed the first push down), they would not tighten their stop after the entry bar became a doji. However, once bar 18 became a strong bull trend bar, they should move their stop to below its low.

CHAPTER 30

Profit Taking and Profit Targets

A ll pullbacks and reversals begin with profit taking. Experienced traders look to exit on strength, and then look to reenter on a pullback. For example, if a bull trend is just beginning and is especially strong, bulls will buy more as the market breaks above the most recent swing high. However, as the trend matures and develops more two-sided trading, they will no longer buy on a stop above the most recent swing high. Instead, as the rally weakens, they will look to take some profits above that high, or even a little below. If most bulls are taking profits around the previous high and not buying more on the breakout, the market will begin to have a pullback. This means that the bulls would rather buy at a lower price and they believe that there will be a pullback that will allow them to do this, so they are no longer willing to chase the market up, buying above prior highs. If the profit taking is very heavy and if there is aggressive, relentless shorting as well, the pullback will grow into a large correction (a trading range) or even a reversal. Bulls will also look to take profits on any sign of strength, like at the close and just above a large bull trend bar, or at the close of the next bar or two, especially if it is a small bar or has a bear close. They will take more profits below the low of the next bar. This is why so many large trend bars, which are breakout attempts, are followed by small bars and pullbacks, which means that the breakouts failed. Traders will also have a stop order below the low of the prior bar, below the most recent higher low, or at breakeven. This is because if the market reverses strongly before reaching their target, they might come to believe that they will be able to exit and then buy again at a better price. Bears initiating shorts see the same thing, and usually begin looking for scalps by selling at new highs or around the closes of strong bull trend bars. As the pullbacks get deeper, they will begin to swing parts of their positions. Initially, they usually get stopped out of the swing portions of their trades, but eventually they will get large swing profits as the corrections get deeper, or when the trend finally reverses.

Traders behave similarly in bear trends. Bears will short below swing lows when the trend is strong, but as it weakens, they will instead buy back their shorts around and below the most recent swing low, and look to short again higher. A bull scalper will buy new lows and scalp out on a small rally, around where the bears are shorting again. Both the bulls and the bears wait for a relatively large bear trend bar that breaks to a new low, at which point both will buy around its close. As the bear rallies get stronger, the bulls will be more willing to swing some of their positions. At some point, the market will transition into a large bull swing or trend, and the process will begin in the opposite direction. Understanding trend bars that create breakouts is one of the most important skills that a trader can acquire. Traders need to be able to assess whether a breakout is likely to succeed, whether it will be met with profit taking and a pullback, or whether it will be followed by a reversal. Each of these is discussed in detail elsewhere in the three books.

When you enter a trade, your goal is to have the market reach your profit target before it hits your protective stop. Unlike protective stops, which should always be working in the market whenever you are holding a position, profit targets can be either in the market or in your head. For example, if you are swing trading in a strong trend, you might take profits on some of your position along the way (this is scaling out of your trade) and you might choose to hold on to some of your position until there is a signal in the opposite position. Once that opposite signal triggers, you should exit. Very few traders have the ability to reverse a position by simultaneously exiting a profitable swing position and entering a new trade in the opposite direction.

Scalpers often have order cancels order or one cancels the other (OCO) orders working as soon as they enter. For example, they might buy AAPL for a 100 cent scalp and risk 50 cents when they buy a pullback where they are 60 percent or more certain that the trade will be successful. As soon as they enter, their initial order might automatically generate both a protective sell stop order at 50 cents below their entry price and a sell limit order at 100 cents above their entry price. Since this bracket order is OCO, as soon as one of the pair is filled, the other is automatically canceled. No matter how you manage your orders, you should check your account after every entry and exit to make sure that your current position and orders are what you think they should be. You don't want to be flat (have no position) and still have a buy limit order working when you thought that it should have been automatically canceled. Never assume that your broker's software will work as expected 100 percent of the time, or that you placed your trades and orders correctly. There is an inescapable failure rate with everything, and you should always confirm what you expect has been done after you believe it should have been done.

All trades should be made on the basis of the trader's equation, and beginning traders should look for trades where the probability of success is 60 percent or higher, and the reward is at least as large and preferably about twice the size of the risk, although a setup with that strong a trader's equation happens only a couple of times on an average day. For example, if the average daily range in the Euro FX Currency Futures or the foreign exchange (forex) equivalent, the EUR/USD, has lately been about 100 ticks (often referred to as pips), and there have been several 20-tick moves every day where a 10-tick protective stop would not have been hit, a trader might look to enter trends on pullbacks to the moving average, so that the probability of a winning trade is likely 60 percent or greater. The trader who carefully selects a setup has about a 60 percent chance of making 20 ticks while risking about 10 ticks, and this has an excellent trader's equation. In 10-Year U.S. Treasury Note Futures, if the average daily range has been about 32 ticks ($^{16}/_{32}$ of a point) and many signal bars have been four ticks tall, a trader could again look to enter on pullbacks to the moving average, risking about six ticks and using a profit target of eight ticks. This again has a strong trader's equation.

Trade management is different for scalps than it is for swings. A trader who is taking a scalp believes that the profit potential is limited either because there is no trend or because he is trading against the trend. Scalping in a trading range can be a profitable strategy, but only the most experienced traders should consider trading against the trend. The chances of making money are far greater if a trader can patiently wait for a pullback and enter in the direction of the trend, rather than hoping that a countertrend trade will be successful. Once you believe there is a trend, you must accept that 80 percent of reversal attempts will fail and evolve into flags. This makes it almost impossible for most traders to enter countertrend trades on stops and consistently make a profit. For example, if you think that a small bear reversal bar at the top of a strong bull trend will be followed by a pullback to the moving average, and you short on a stop at one tick below the low of the bar, you must realize that very smart bulls have limit orders to buy at the low of that bar, and the odds are on their side. If you are trading the Emini, you need the market to fall ten ticks below the low of that bar for you to make an eight-tick profit on your short, but most pullbacks in a strong bull trend will turn into high 1 or high 2 buy setups before that happens, and you will lose money. If you see that there is a strong trend and you want to buy a pullback, do not fool yourself into believing that you have enough talent to be able to profitably trade a short scalp as you wait for the buy setup to form. Invariably, you will lose money on the short scalp and not take the buy setup when it forms. You will be hoping for more down and be in denial that the pullback is about to end, and you will miss the long that might be good for several points of profit.

After the trend has turned into a trading range, then countertrend trading is really not countertrend, because the trend has temporarily ended. However, many traders try to pick the top of a bull trend or the bottom of a bear trend, believing that the market is about to enter a trading range and thinking that their risk is small, only to watch their accounts slowly melt away.

Whenever traders enter any trade, they need a plan to take profits, because otherwise the market will eventually turn on them and their profits will turn into losses. Trade management depends entirely on the trader's equation, and any combination of risk, reward, and probability that results in a consistent profit is an effective strategy. As a general rule, most traders should restrict themselves to high-probability trades where the risk is at least as great as the potential reward. Ideally, traders should look for setups where the chance of success is at least 60 percent and the potential reward is about twice the size of the risk, but usually they will have to settle for a reward that is about the same size as their risk, or maybe a little bigger. This most often happens in pullbacks in trends.

When swinging a trade in a strong trend, it is easy to take profits too early because it is so difficult to believe that the trade might run five or more times more than the size of your stop. However, when a trend is strong, that can be the case. If you believe that the trend is strong, it is reasonable to take about half of your position off after the market has gone your way for a distance equal to about twice the size of your original protective stop. For example, if your initial stop in the Emini was two points and you shorted in a strong bear trend near what you think will be the start of a big swing down, exit half of your position on a limit order at four points below your entry. At that point, trail your stop. You might take another quarter off at three times your original stop size, at six points, then let the last quarter run, and exit only if a strong buy signal develops or at the close of the day, whichever comes first. However, exiting the entire position at twice the risk is a reasonable approach if you are uncomfortable scaling out of a trade. You can always enter again on the next signal.

The trader's equation of every trade changes with every tick. If the trader's equation is still favorable but not as strong as it was, experienced traders will often either tighten their protective stops or exit with a smaller profits. If the trader's equation becomes marginal, traders should look to exit as soon as possible, with as big a profit or small a loss as they can. If it becomes negative, they should exit immediately at the market, even if that means taking a loss. One way to decide if you should exit your trade is to imagine that you are not holding a position. Then look at the market and decide if you think that it would be wise to enter at the market and use that protective stop. If you would not, then the trader's equation for your current position is weak or negative and you should exit.

Remember, a profit target is the flip side of a protective stop and is there to protect you from yourself. It forces you to take profits at a time when the trader's equation is still positive, and prevents you from holding too long and then exiting once the trade has come all of the way back to your entry price, or worse, once it has turned into a loser. Just as it is better for most traders to always use a protective stop that is actually in the market, it is also better to use a profit-taking limit order that is always in the market.

Figure 30.1   PROFIT TAKING AND PROFIT TARGETS   **539**

FIGURE 30.1   Pullbacks End at a Confluence of Support Types

When there is a trend, entering on a pullback to the moving average is a reliable approach where the probability of success is usually at least 60 percent and the potential reward is greater than the risk. In Figure 30.1, the strong four-bar bull spike up from bar 6 was followed by a sharp pullback to the moving average, where the bull inside bar after bar 11 was a reasonable signal bar for a long. Since the bar was four ticks tall, the initial risk was six ticks. Some traders saw the setup as a high 2, and others saw it as a tight wedge, where the lows of bars 8 and 10 were the first two pushes down. Fibonacci traders saw it as a 62 percent retracement, and it was also a breakout test of the bar 4 high, missing the breakeven stops by a tick. Whenever a pullback ends, there is usually a confluence of mathematically logical reasons for the location of the bottom of the pullback. Different firms will use different reasons, but when there are many present, enough firms will buy in the area so that they overwhelm the bears and the pullback ends.

The market was likely to find resistance at the bar 9 high, which bears saw as the start of the channel down following the spike down from bar 7 to the bar 8 low.

They were hoping for a double top bear flag, and many waited to short until the market tested the bar 9 high. This temporary loss of bears increased the chances that the level would be reached. The bar 9 high was exactly 10 ticks above the signal bar high, which is exactly how many ticks the bulls needed to be able to exit on a limit order with eight ticks' profit ($^4/_{32}$ of a point). Everything in major markets is mathematical because so much of the trading is done by computers and they have to rely on math for their decision making.

Figure 30.2　　　　　　　　　　　　　PROFIT TAKING AND PROFIT TARGETS　**541**

FIGURE 30.2　Buying Pullbacks in a Bull Trend

Buying pullbacks in the Euro FX Currency Futures (or the forex equivalent, the EUR/USD) is a reliable approach to trading. In the Euro, if traders carefully select their setups, they can often have a profit target that is about twice as large as their stop. Notice in Figure 30.2 how the bar 9 triangle breakout raced up without hesitation. The small bull inside bar was the buy signal and its high was just eight ticks above the low of the ledge, so the risk was 10 ticks. Since the inside bar was a buy signal, it was reasonable to buy as bar 9 went above it and became an outside bar. A trader could have had a profit-taking limit order located 20 ticks above the entry price, and would have been filled near the top of bar 10 (at the small horizontal black line).

The trader could then have bought the bar 14 double bottom (it was also a high 2 with the bar 12 high 1, and a breakout pullback from the breakout above the bar 12 small bull flag) and exited with 20 ticks of profit on bar 15, just above the bar 13 high. The bar 14 signal bar was 14 ticks tall, so the initial risk was 16 ticks. Since this was a pullback in a trend, the chance of success was assumed to be at least 60 percent.

Bar 19 was a bull reversal bar and the first pullback to the moving average in a strong bull trend. The bar was eight ticks tall, so the risk was 10 ticks and a trader could have exited just below the top of bar 20, which was exactly 22 ticks above the signal bar high. Since the limit order was 21 ticks above the signal bar high, the longs could have exited with their 20-tick profit. The market was likely in a trading range at this point, since bar 16 was a spike down (a doji top is a spike up and then a spike down, both within the same bar), and the move down to bar 19 was in a channel. The market was likely to test the top of the channel and form a double top, and the trading range was likely to grow, which it did. Because of this, it would have been better to scalp the long above bar 19. There was room for a 20-tick profit target to be filled below the top of the channel, so this was a reasonable location to exit the entire long scalp.

Traders could have bought again above the bar 21 two-bar reversal, since it was a double bottom with bar 19 and the first moving average gap bar (the first bar in the trend with a high below the moving average). The risk was 11 ticks, and traders could have exited with 20 ticks' profit just below the bar 22 high.

If traders bought the bar 9 triangle breakout, they could have changed their plan once they saw the strength of the two-bar bull spike. Instead of exiting their entire position at 20 ticks, they could have exited half there and then maybe place a limit order to exit another quarter at another 10 or 20 ticks higher. They could then have let the remainder run until the close of the day or until there was a clear short signal. The sell climax at bar 16 was likely to lead to a pullback to the moving average, and it would have been reasonable for traders to exit below bar 16 (or below the bear inside bar two bars later), and buy again at the moving average. However, if they had been scaling out and had only a quarter of their position left, they could have also held until the close, because they would have known that buyers were likely to return at the moving average, and they might have been able to push the market to a new high before the close.

The bar 21 long was still in a trading range, but it was a double bottom bull flag with bar 19; therefore there was a reasonable chance that the market might reach a new high before the close. Although a trader could have scalped out of his entire position at 20 ticks on the correct assumption that most attempts to break out of the top of a trading range will fail, this two-legged correction had a higher chance of leading to a successful breakout, and strong bull trend days often rally to a new high at the end of the day. A trader therefore could have swung a quarter to a half of his long, just in case.

CHAPTER 31

Scaling Into and Out of a Trade

Scaling into a trade simply means that you are entering again once you are already in a position, and scaling out means that when you exit, you exit only part of your position and look to exit the rest later. More traders are willing to scale out than are willing to scale in; in fact, many traders regularly scale out of trades. For example, if you exit part of your position for a scalp and then exit the balance for a swing, you are scaling out of your trade.

Scaling into a trade means that you are adding to your position. Institutions like mutual funds have to scale into and out of positions constantly because they receive new money and requests for redemptions every day. Individual traders commonly use scaling in when they enter in the direction of the trend during a pullback and when fading the extremes of a trading range, and when they dollar cost average. Scaling into a potential reversal is very risky; it is usually better to exit if the market goes against you and then look for a second entry.

You can scale in either as the trade moves against you or as it moves in your direction. If you scale in after you already have a profit, this is also referred to as adding to your position, or pressing your trade. For example, if the market is in a bull channel, bulls will add to their positions on every pullback as the market goes higher. The same is true of a strong bull spike. Many traders quickly add to their longs as the spike rapidly grows, bar after bar. Strong spikes always create brief opportunities when the trader's equation is exceptional, and some traders are adept at pressing their trades in these fast markets. Each additional purchase is usually at a higher price, and all of their earlier entries are profitable. Bears who are shorting in the bull channel as the market is going higher are scaling in above the highs of prior bars and adding on as the trade continues higher. Each earlier entry has a growing loss, but the bears expect that once the market reverses, they will have a net profit. I have a friend who is an expert at scaling into countertrend trades in channels in the Emini, looking for a reversal. He looks for the market to test the beginning of the channel, where he takes profits. For example, if the recent average range lately in the Emini has been about 10 to 15 points, and today has a spike and channel bull trend that has had a couple of pushes up and is not particularly strong, he would start to short on limit orders at the most recent swing high, and add to his position at the next one or two new highs in the channel, as long as each new entry was at least two points higher than the prior. Each of his one to three entries was for about 10 contracts. I chatted with him many times years ago as he took these trades, and the market never went much beyond his second or third entry before reversing and going his way, so the stop was never an issue in our conversation. However, I assume that it had to be at least a few points beyond his final entry. According to my math, I believe that he was willing to risk between $5,000 and $10,000 for his 30 contracts. I am telling this story not to advocate what he was doing, because very few people have the experience to trade like that. However, he is an interesting, real example of a trader who specializes in a particular type of scaling in and makes a living by doing it.

The key premise to scaling into a trade that is moving against you is that you believe that the market will soon turn in your direction and that you will be able to make a profit. You should never scale into a losing position unless you are confident about the big picture, and the best situation is when you believe that you are scaling into a growing pullback in a strong trend and with a clear always-in direction. Most traders never add to a losing position and instead let themselves get stopped out, and then look to re-enter if there is another signal. However, many traders feel that they can never be certain of the exact bottom or top of a trend or trading range, but are confident when the market is close to a reversal. Some of those traders take the reversal trade and use a wide stop. Others use a tight stop, and if the market goes against them, they get stopped out and then look for another entry. Scale in traders trade a much smaller position size initially and will add to their position if the market continues against them, as long as they believe that their premise remains valid. If the market goes their way immediately, many will look to build their position up to full size by pressing their bets. They were willing to scale in at either a better or worse price. For example, if they bought a reversal up from the bottom of a large trading range and were willing to scale in lower, but instead the market immediately goes their way, they might add to their position on pullbacks as the market continues to rally toward the top of the trading range. Other traders might trade half size, add the second half lower, and then look to exit the first half at breakeven on the reversal up, and swing the second half with a breakeven stop. If you are scaling into a losing position and you then decide that the big picture has changed and your premise is no longer valid, you must exit your trade and take your loss. Even if the market begins to turn your way, if you feel that your original target has become unrealistic, do not hold on and hope that your premise will once again become valid. You have to always trade the market that is in front of you and not the one that you want or the one that you had a few bars ago. The market changes with every tick, and if your original target is now unrealistic, look for a new target and get out there, even if that means that you will be taking a loss. For example, if you scaled into an always-in bull market and it then flipped to an always-in bear direction, you should exit and look for short trades instead of hoping that the always-in bull market will once again return. Hope is never a sound basis for holding a position, because the market is based on mathematics and not luck, fairness, emotion, karma, or religion.

"Never add to a losing position." That is one of the most fundamental rules on Wall Street. However, it is misleading because institutions do it all the time and it is part of many profitable strategies. How can that possibly be? It is because the adage refers to countertrend trades and the institutions are scaling into with trend trades. Whenever an institution feels that the market has gone too far up or down, it sees value in doing the opposite. Because no one can regularly pick exact turning points, many institutions enter in pieces over the course of many bars. They do not care if some of the entry signals form when their earlier entries have an open loss. As long as they see value and have a large position to build, they will work to fill it at the best possible price, regardless of whether it is above or below their earlier entries. This is similar to dollar cost averaging for an individual investor. If an investor has some cash and wants to buy stock, he might use 10 percent of the cash to buy on the first of each of the next 10 months, regardless of whether the later entries are at a lower price. Dollar cost averaging is a successful approach and more often than not requires an investor to add to a losing position. However, this is far different from a trader who buys at the bottom of a strong bear spike, thinking that there has to be a bounce soon. When the market falls straight down for two more bars, he buys more, and then more again even lower, as he attempts to lower his average cost. Soon, he is hoping for any bounce up to near his average entry price so that he can get out at breakeven. Invariably, his position has become so large that he decides that he has to get out on the next bear trend bar. That bar is usually a large sell climax and he exits with a huge loss, many times greater than the original profit he was trying to make from his buy scalp, and his exit is at the bottom of the market just before a huge rally.

There is a sound mathematical basis for scaling into or out of a trade, but many traders do it simply because they discovered that it works and they don't care about the reasoning. Professional traders do it on daily and weekly charts all the time. It works for day traders as well. If you are taking swing trades intraday on stocks that you do not follow constantly throughout the day and you are experienced at reading price action and confident that your entry is near the start of a swing, you can use a wide protective stop and look to add on if the market continues against you. Your initial trade could be a half or a third of your usual position size, and you can look to scale in one or two times as the market goes against you.

Scaling into a trade is usually best in a growing pullback in an always-in market (a clear trend), at least on a higher time frame, and in fading the extremes of a trading range. A trader can scale:

- Into longs on a small pullback from a strong bull spike (a pullback is a small countertrend channel).
- Into shorts on a small pullback from a strong bear spike.
- Into longs as a bear channel falls or into shorts as a bull channel rises.
- Into longs as a pullback falls further (pullbacks are small trends and therefore are in channels) or into shorts as a bear rally rises. For example, if there is a steeply rising moving average, bulls will scale into longs on a pullback below the moving average.
- At fixed intervals in pullbacks in any strong trend based on the size of the prior pullbacks and the recent average daily range.
- Into longs or into shorts in a trading range.
- Into a countertrend position during a breakout if a pullback to the breakout point is likely, like in a broad channel day, in a trending trading range day, or in a stairs pattern.

There are many ways to scale into or out of a position since there are so many variables, which include:

- *The number of times that you will scale in.* You can scale in one time or many times.
- *Sizes of your positions.* If you are allowing for the possibility of scaling in if the market goes against you, make sure to keep your initial positions small enough so that the risk on your final position is within your usual tolerance.
- *The number of shares entered at each level.* Your first entry can be for 100 shares, the second can be for 200, and the third can be for 500 or any number. However, most traders scale in with the same number of shares each time.
- *The prices of the different entries.* The steps don't have to be fixed, which means that you can scale into a long at 20 cents below the first entry and again at 30, 70, or any number of cents below that. Alternatively, you can enter at the first reversal signal and if the trend continues, you can scale in at the next reversal signal and maybe the one after that as well.
- *The risk.* This is how far your protective stop is from your average entry price.
- *The reward.* This is how far your profit-taking limit order is from your average entry price.

- *The probability.* It is never known with certainty, and it varies with the amount of risk, reward, and average entry price. For example, the probability of making 30 cents while risking 30 cents is greater than the probability of making 30 cents while risking 20 cents but less than the probability of making 30 cents while risking 40 cents.

Scaling involves uncertainty, which is inherent in channels and trading ranges where two-sided trading is taking place. The trader is betting that a short-term move is ending and that a larger move is about to begin. This is true even in a trading range, like when a trader is scaling into longs during a bear leg in the belief that the bigger picture is that of a trading range and that the small bear leg will probably fail to convert the trading range into a bear trend. Any combination of the variables that results in the chance of winning times the potential reward being greater than the chance of losing times the risk is a valid strategy. You always know the risk and the potential reward because you set them when you place your protective stop and your profit-taking limit order. You never know the probability with certainty, but you usually know when it is 60 percent or greater; if you are uncertain, then assume that it is 50 percent.

Whenever you scale in against a trend, as a general rule you should exit if the market makes a second move against you. This means that if you are bottom picking in a bear trend and the market forms a low 2 short, especially if it is near the moving average and has a bear signal bar, you should exit your longs and even consider reversing to short. If you still believe that a bottom is near, you can look to begin to scale in again lower. Also, it is risky to scale in against a trend in the final hour or so of the day, because you will too often find yourself holding a large losing position that you will have to cover by the close. Time is against you. Finally, it is risky to scale in against any strong trend. For example, if you believe that the market is in a strong bear trend, then you must believe it will soon be lower. If you believe that it will soon be lower, then it is too early to begin to buy. When a trend is strong, the only type of scaling in that you should consider is adding to your with-trend position.

There is a mathematical basis for scaling into and out of positions, but that does not mean that scaling in or out is the wisest use of your money. For example, suppose you believe that the chance that a stock now trading at $20 will fall to zero is 1 percent or less so you then buy 100 shares of a stock; if you scale in at each $5 drop, you would buy 100 more shares at $15, 100 more at $10, and 100 more at $5.00. You would then be long 400 shares with an average price of $12.50. Yes, the stock might not fall to zero, but you now need a 150 percent rally to get back to breakeven, and it is almost certain that you will make more money if you exit all of your shares at a loss and instead use the money to buy a stock that is in a strong uptrend.

Traders can also scale out of winning and losing trades. In that bull channel example, those bulls who were scaling into their longs as the bull channel went up would stop buying at some point and begin to take profits. If they took part of their trades off, they were scaling out of their trades. The bears might have decided that the reversal they were expecting would not be as strong as they originally thought and they might buy back some of the shorts that they just sold. If the market went another 10 ticks against them, they might buy back even more and look to short again higher. They were scaling out of their losing positions, although they might be planning to scale back in later.

One guideline that you can use to determine where to place your second entry is to think about how far away your protective stop would be if you were not scaling in. For example, if you were buying a pullback in a bull trend in Bank of America Corporation (BAC) and were thinking about using a 30 cent stop, you might instead buy more at that price and place a protective stop on your entire position 30 cents lower, or 60 cents below your first entry.

There are many ways to scale into a trade that is moving against you, and you can scale in any number of times. You can scale in at fixed intervals or at different support or resistance levels or at each subsequent reversal setup. You can make each subsequent entry the same size as the original or you can make them larger or smaller. The most important point is that if you are allowing for the possibility of scaling in, you have to have a plan at the outset. If you are not comfortable with creating a plan, do not scale into a losing position, even if you are buying a pullback in a strong bull trend or selling a bear rally in a strong bear trend. You must know where your final protective stop is and what your average entry price is, because you need to keep your total risk within your normal range. If you are not careful, you might find yourself holding your usual number of contracts but the stop is so far from your average entry price that your risk is several times greater than what you normally incur.

If traders are determined to try to scale into a trade, the least risky approach is to take a second entry if one appears while they are still in their trade and if their premise remains valid. For example, suppose they are long and the market goes sideways or a little down but not far enough to hit their protective stop, or a little up but not high enough to fill their profit-taking limit order; if the market creates another buy signal that has a good trader's equation, the traders can take that entry as well and treat their two entries as separate trades. They might have different stops and profit targets, but as long as each has a favorable trader's equation, the traders can treat them as separate trades and manage each based on its own characteristics. If a third good signal appears, they can buy again, but at some point their position becomes too complicated to be worth the effort. Since it is less stressful to just manage one trade at a time, most traders should not scale in, even if the subsequent signals look good.

Figure 31.1   SCALING INTO AND OUT OF A TRADE   **549**

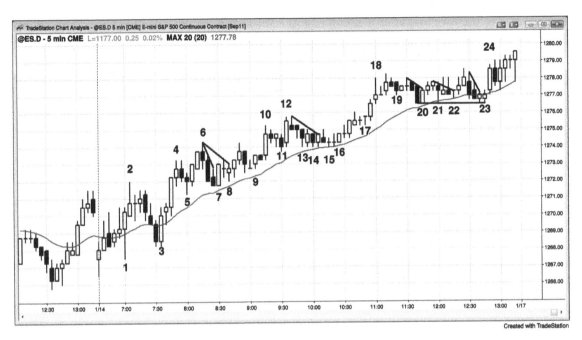

FIGURE 31.1 Scaling In Is Not for Most Traders

A beginning trader should not scale into trades because it can increase his risk to beyond his comfort level, and any mistake can result in a huge loss. However, an experienced trader might take a second or third entry on a pullback in a strong trend, or add to his position during each bar of a strong spike, like in the move up from bar 3 to bar 4.

Most traders saw the market shown in the chart in Figure 31.1 as strongly always-in long by the close of bar 4, which was a four-bar bull spike with very little overlap and big bodies. It followed earlier buying pressure on the open and again on the two-bar spike at bar 1. Bar 7 was a valid two-bar reversal and high 2 buy signal (where bar 5 was the high 1). Other traders saw bar 7 as a high 1 buy setup. The entry bar was the small doji bar after bar 7, and that constituted the breakout of the bull flag. The market then had a breakout pullback buy setup at bar 8, which was also a valid signal. Some traders saw it as a triangle with bars 6 and 7. The entry price was the same as that for the long above bar 7. Since the premise was still valid and bar 8 was even stronger evidence that the market was trying to go higher, a trader could have bought a second position on that signal. The two-bar rally from there was a five-tick failure and probably did not result in a fill of the profit-taking limit orders, but the bull trend was still intact and the protective stops were not hit. The move up, though, broke above another small bear trend line and was therefore another breakout of a bull flag. Bar 9 was the breakout pullback buy setup. Since the trend was still intact and this new setup also had a good trader's equation, the trader could buy a third position here and manage it as a separate trade, using the appropriate protective stop and profit target. The trader would have been able to scalp out of all three entries with a one-point profit on the bar 10 spike.

Bars 14, 15, and 16 provided a similar opportunity to scale into longs with three separate entries.

Bars 20, 21, 22, and 23 had four valid buy setups, and all four could have been exited with a one-point profit on the bar 24 bull spike.

Figure 31.2   SCALING INTO AND OUT OF A TRADE   **551**

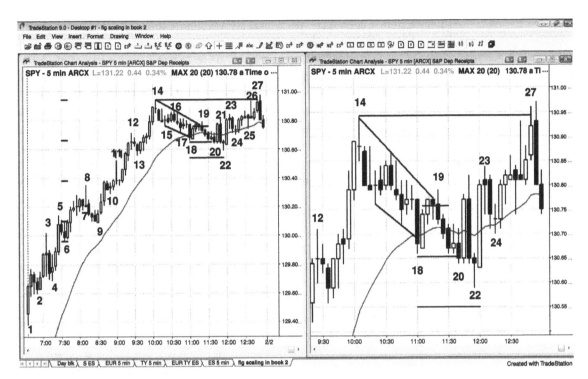

FIGURE 31.2 Scaling into Longs

As shown in Figure 31.2, the 5 minute SPY was in a strong bull trend, and bulls could have scaled into a long position during the bull spike from bar 9 to the bar before bar 14, or during the complex pullback from the bar 14 high. The chart on the right is a close-up of the one on the left, but only relevant bars of the pullback are labeled. Bulls could have bought the small wedge bull flag pullback to the moving average with the goal of taking profits at the old bull high (bar 14). They could have placed their buy stop at one tick above the bull inside bar that followed bar 18. Alternatively, they could have entered above the high of the two-bar reversal (the high of bar 18). If they bought 200 shares above the bull inside bar, they got long at $130.76. Their protective stop was one tick below the bar 18 low of $130.66, and they planned to take profits at a new high of the day on a limit order at $130.94, the high of bar 14. They were risking 11 cents to make 18 cents, and since this was a bull flag at the moving average, they probably had at least a 60 percent chance of success and a 40 percent chance of failure. In this case, they would have lost 11 cents when bar 20 fell below bar 18. Since they had bought 200 shares, they lost $22 plus commissions.

Other traders might have been equally confident that the trend was strong enough so that the pullback should be followed by a new high on the day, but they might have been concerned that the pullback to bar 18 was in a relatively tight channel. A channel is often just the first of two legs, and there was a reasonable risk that there might be a second leg sideways to down before the bull trend finally resumed. However, the trend was so strong that the market should not fall much below the moving average, if the trend was still good. Because of this uncertainty, the scale-in traders might have bought a half-size position above the bull inside bar after bar 18. Instead of stopping themselves out below bar 18, they might have bought the other half of their position there, 10 cents below their first entry. They could have then placed a stop on their entire position 11 cents lower, at twice the size of their initial protective stop. They would have been filled at $130.66 on bar 20, lowering their average entry price on their 200 shares to $130.71; the risk was then $130.55. They were risking 16 cents to make 23 cents, and since this was a bull flag, they had at least a 60 percent chance of success. The market reversed up strongly on the bar after bar 20, but quickly reversed down into a two-bar reversal. A beginner might have exited with a loss at that point, and might even have reversed to short. However, an experienced trader would never short at the bottom of a trading range in a bull trend and would have relied on a stop. The market reversed up again at bar 23 in a moving average gap bar buy setup and then worked higher to a new high on the day. The move up had several pullbacks, indicating that the bulls were not strong, and the market reversed down at the new high, where clearly many bulls, including the scale-in traders, took profits.

A bull who bought earlier in the day could have scaled out as the trend progressed. There were several reasonable chances to buy, like the high 1 setups at bars 2, 4, and 6. Let's say that a bull bought 400 shares at $130.10, one tick above bar 6, and placed a protective stop at one tick below at $129.96, risking 14 cents. There are many ways to take profits, and one popular one is at about twice the initial risk. The trader could have taken 100 shares off at 28 cents. This was during the spike up from bar 9 as it moved beyond bar 8. Other traders take partial profits at fixed intervals, like every 20 cents. A trader who did that would have exited on bar 8, which had a large tail on the top, indicating that many traders took partial profits there. Bulls should trail their protective stops at just below the most recent swing low, so this bull's stop was still below bar 6. Once the market moved above bar 8, the trader would have moved his stop to just below bar 9. He could have taken another 100 shares off at four times the initial risk, at $130.52, on the bull trend bar two bars before bar 12, as the market moved above bar 11. The bar 11 high was exactly $130.52, so many traders placed their limit orders at one tick below the obvious target. This is a type of failure and often leads to a bigger pullback, but here it led to a profit-taking tail at the top of the bar, and then only a small one-bar pause

Figure 31.2   SCALING INTO AND OUT OF A TRADE   **553**

in the trend. The trader could have continued to exit 100 shares at another 72 and 96 cents above the entry (or at 60 and 80 cents' profit), or could have exited the third 100 shares at the first sign that the market might have a larger pullback, like one tick below bar 14. He could then have looked to exit the final 100 shares before the close, maybe on a move to a new high of the day after the pullback. The final exit would have been on bar 27 at $130.94, 84 cents above the initial entry.

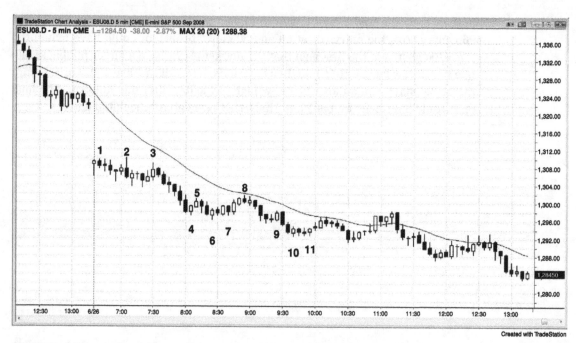

FIGURE 31.3 Institutions Scale In as the Market Goes against Them

When institutions buy at the bottom of a trading range, they will then buy more on every little dip to defend their stops as they try to turn the market up.

As shown in Figure 31.3, today had a big gap down so the day was likely to trend up or down. Following bar 3, the market sold off strongly into a lower range, and by the time bar 6 formed, the day was a trending trading range day. It is usually safe to buy near the bottom of every range and short near the top.

Bar 5 broke above a steep trend line. Bars 4 and 6 were strong bull reversal bars, with bar 6 setting up a second entry long (a lower low pullback from the breakout above the micro channel). The entry bar was a bear trend bar, which is a sign of weakness. If the market traded one tick below its low, this would have been a failure and the market would likely have dropped quickly down in one or two more legs (one more could set up a small wedge bottom). Since the smart money traders believed that this was a trending trading range day and they bought the second entry, they would defend it by continuing to add to their longs by buying down to the low of the entry bar. They did not want the market to go one tick lower, because they would then have a losing trade. The market missed those protective stops by one tick many times over the next 15 minutes, and patient longs were rewarded.

The day could also be viewed as a trend from the open bear trend, a small pullback bear trend, or a trend resumption bear trend, where the trading range from 8:00 a.m. PST until 11:00 a.m. was sloping downward, which was a sign that the bears were strong.

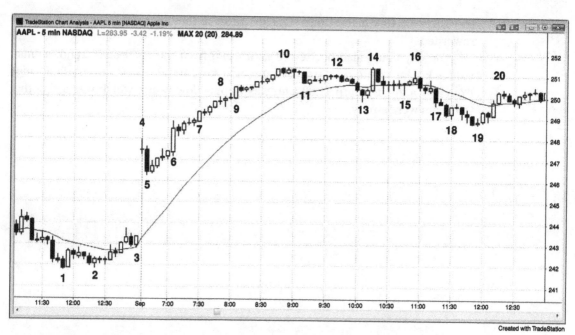

FIGURE 31.4   In Strong Bull Channels, Traders Scale In All the Way Up

When bulls are confident that the market is going higher and skeptical that there will soon be a pullback that would allow them to buy lower, they begin to buy at the market and keep buying all the way up. In Figure 31.4, Apple (AAPL) had a large gap up, then a pullback, and then a bull breakout at bar 6. The odds favored a bull trend day, and traders believed that even if there were a pullback, the market would soon reach a new high. Therefore, it made mathematical sense to begin buying at the market and on any tiny pullback, like maybe 10 cents. Traders and institutions continued to buy relentlessly but not with enough urgency or size to cause a huge bull trend bar and possible climactic reversal. They were scaling in all the way up to bar 10, because they believed that the first pullback would not go too far and it would be bought aggressively enough to push the market to a new high.

When the trend is this strong, you have to believe that the market will soon be higher. If you believe that it will soon be higher, it does not make sense to begin scaling into a short position, because if you wait, you can short at a better price. When a channel is strong, you should never scale in against the trend.

The market had about a $1.00 spike and channel bear pullback to the moving average at bar 13, where the bulls finally overwhelmed the bears. They pushed the market up to a nominal new high where even the traders who had bought at bar 10 could get out at breakeven. Many of those traders were momentum traders

Figure 31.4   SCALING INTO AND OUT OF A TRADE   **557**

who keep buying until the trend changes, and they were happy to add on at the bar 13 first moving average gap bar. They then exited their longs from bar 10 at breakeven, and their longs from bar 13 with a 60 cent profit.

Bulls might also have scaled in on the sell-off down to bar 19, believing that the bull trend was so strong that the pullback should lead to a test of the high. Bar 18 was a strong bull reversal bar, and bulls might have bought above its high. Since the bear channel was steep, these bulls knew that the market might fall further, but they wanted to be sure that they caught at least some of what they thought would be a trend resumption. Because the pullback might not have been over, some would have bought only a half-size position and would have looked to add on maybe 50 cents lower. They would have been filled on the move down to bar 19. Others would simply have looked for another bottom attempt and then bought more above the signal bar, like above the bar 19 high. Bar 19 was a large two-legged sideways to down correction where bar 13 was the first leg, and it was about a measured move down from the bars 10 and 14 double top. Although they might scale out of some of their positions on the test of their first entry at the bar 18 high, most would have held for a larger profit. They might have taken half off on the pause bar after the bull spike up to bar 20 and then moved the protective stop to breakeven on the balance.

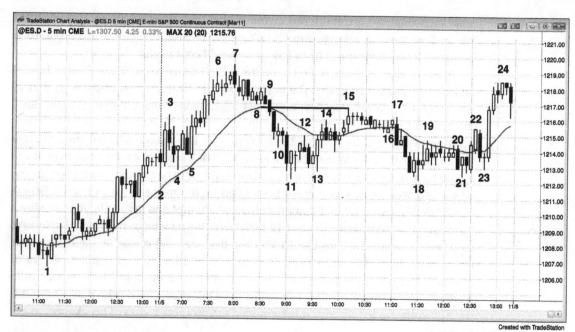

FIGURE 31.5 Scaling into a Pullback

When the moving average is steeply up, traders will buy a pullback to the moving average and scale in lower. In the chart shown in Figure 31.5, traders who had limit orders to buy a touch of the moving average got filled on bar 9, but unfortunately for them, the market spiked down. Many traders would have scaled in lower because they were confident that the market would soon rally back up to the moving average, and it often rallies all the way back to their initial purchase. The bar 15 high was exactly the price where the bar 9 longs bought the pullback to the moving average. Why did the market turn down at bar 15? Because many traders who scaled into longs on the sell-off to bar 11 sold out of their longs around breakeven for their initial entry, which was where bar 9 touched the moving average. They made a profit on their lower entries and got out at breakeven on their first entry. Their goal was a profitable long based on a steeply rising moving average, and once they achieved their goal, they sold out of their longs and there was no one left to buy.

When there is a possible reversal, many traders don't buy the first touch of the moving average. Instead, they will start to buy below the moving average. For example, the traders who bought at bar 9 might have scaled into additional longs at each one point lower. Other traders might instead have begun buying at one, two, or even more points lower and then could have scaled in at each one-point drop

Figure 31.5   SCALING INTO AND OUT OF A TRADE   **559**

from there for maybe two or three entries. They could have risked maybe half of the average range, or about five points below their first entry. For example, if they bought at 1,219 and again at 1,218, they could have exited both positions at their original price and made a point on their second entry and nothing on their first. If they were more aggressive, they could have taken profits at one point above their higher entry, at the moving average, or on the test of the bar 9 original moving average entry price.

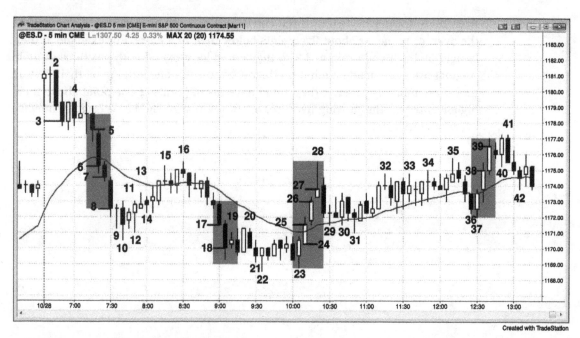

FIGURE 31.6 Scaling In during Spikes

Traders can enter or scale in during the spike phases of trends. As shown in Figure 31.6, today opened with a large gap up, but the first two bars were dojis, indicating that there was uncertainty about the high open. The bulls were not buying aggressively. They bought at the bottom of the two bars, creating tails, but if the market were to turn down, the bulls would have stopped buying if their two attempts failed. The strong bar 2 bear trend bar convinced the bulls that the market was going down. Traders shorted into its close, and the bulls exited on its close and on a stop below the first bar of the day. Once there was a strong bear bar on the next bar, bears were confident that a spike was underway and that there would be at least a measured move down. They shorted the close of bar 3. Since two-bar spikes are common in the first 30 minutes and are often followed by pullbacks, some bears would have kept their protective stops above bar 2 to allow for a possible lower high. Other bears saw bar 3 as such a strong bear trend bar and an entry bar (for traders who shorted below the bar 2 signal bar) that they would have put their stops above bar 3.

The next bar was a strong bull reversal bar, but since a lower high was likely after two strong bear trend bars, most traders would have held short. The market went one tick above the bar, trapping weak bears out and weak bulls in, and then reversed down at bar 4.

Figure 31.6   SCALING INTO AND OUT OF A TRADE   **561**

Some traders would have shorted on a stop below bar 4 and would have entered two bars later. The doji close of the entry bar would have made them nervous, but then the bear spike began.

Bar 5 had a strong bear body, so some traders would have shorted its close, and others would have shorted below its low.

Bar 6 was the second bar in the spike and had a large bear body. At this point, many traders saw it as a breakout from the opening range. The bulls finally gave up and the bears became very confident that the day's range would expand to the downside to reach around the average daily range of recent days. Traders shorted its close. Aggressive traders would have kept shorting closes until there was a bar with a large tail or a bull body. Even when one forms, it is the first pause or pullback and the market will usually go down again within a few bars so that the traders who had shorted the close of the bar before will still be able to make a scalper's profit. Once the pause bar forms after a spike of several bars, most traders stop entering on the close.

The market rallied to bar 16, and traders wondered if it might form a higher low and then have a second leg up. The bar 17 strong bear trend bar broke out below any possible bull flag and made traders think that a new low of the day was likely. Traders shorted its close and the close of the bar 18 follow-through bar. Bar 19 was a pause bar, so bears stopped shorting closes.

Bar 23 was a strong bull reversal bar and a two-bar reversal on the third push down of the day, and traders saw it as a possible wedge bottom or as a higher time frame wedge bull flag. Since its low was well above the low of yesterday, many traders saw the entire sell-off today as a bull flag. Some traders bought above its high, and other traders bought the close of the bar 25 entry bar. The market now had a two-bar bull spike after a good bottom, and traders knew it should have at least two legs up.

Bar 26 had another strong bull close, and traders bought the close.

Bar 28 had a large tail on the top, so traders stopped buying closes.

There was a wedge bull flag at bar 31, and the bulls assumed that this was the start of the second leg up.

The market broke below the bull channel from bar 31 to bar 35, and traders thought that the second leg up might have ended and the bear trend might be resuming. Some traders shorted the bar 36 close, but the market reversed up into a two-bar reversal at bar 37 and the bears would have exited. They would have thought that this was a bear trap and a false breakout of the bull channel, and they saw the market reversing up at a higher low (above bar 31) and wondered if the bull trend would resume.

Bulls bought above the two-bar reversal at bar 37 and again on the closes of bars 38 and 39. The next bar was a pause bar, so they stopped buying closes. The traders who bought on the close of bar 39 exited on the bar 41 bear bar. They bought for a scalp, and the market failed to go up on the next bar; it then failed again, so it was likely to go down.

So what do these spikes have to do with scale trading? Let's say that you are comfortable trading two contracts, scalping one for one point and swinging the other until the trend ends. If you took any of the early short entries on bars 2, 3, or 4, you would have scalped out one contract during bar 5. On the close of bar 5, you could put your scalp contract back and once again be short two contracts. You would have scalped one out during bar 8 and added it back on at the close of bar 8. Depending on where your first entry was, you might exit all on bar 12, or, if your original short was around bar 3, you might hold short with a breakeven stop.

As an alternative to adding just one contract on at the close of bar 5, you could short two more there and then be short three contracts, which is more than your usual risk, but put a breakeven stop on your first contract so that your total risk is the same as your usual total risk. You could repeat this again on the close of bar 7 and on the close of bar 8. At that point, your swing position would be four contracts, but you would have a breakeven stop on three. You would also have one scalp contract, so your total position size would be five contracts, but your total risk would be the same as you normally have when you trade two contracts.

You could use the same approach with the other spikes during the day. As long as you do not exceed your normal risk level that you would have on your usual two-contract size, there will be days when you can have five or more contracts on and make windfall profits.

Figure 31.7   SCALING INTO AND OUT OF A TRADE   **563**

FIGURE 31.7 Scaling In during Channels

Traders will scale into countertrend positions when the market is forming channels, but this is reliable only as long as the day is not a strong trend day. In Figure 31.7, the move down to bar 2 was about half of an average range, so the upside breakout that began at bar 6 could have led to a measured move up and then an upper range, creating a trending trading range day. The market would then be likely to come back down to test the bar 1 or bar 5 breakout points. Traders who understood this were willing to short above the bar 9 high and scale in higher. They could have added to their shorts either above other swing highs, like above bar 9, or at fixed intervals, like one and two points higher. They were shorting near the top of the channel, which is the ideal location for shorts. They could have taken profits at the breakout test that occurred on the spike down to bar 21.

Bulls would have scaled in below the low of the prior bar after the strong spike up to bar 7. They would have bought below the inside bar after bar 7 and again below bars 9, 11, and maybe 13. Since bar 13 was the third push up in the channel, and channels often correct for at least 10 bars after three pushes, most bulls would have been taking profits at this point instead of scaling in. Also, just as they would have scaled in below bars on the way up, they would have taken partial or full profits above the highs of prior bars, above swing highs, and at the closes of strong bull trend bars. All of these would have been near the top of the channel, which is where bulls tend to exit and bears tend to enter.

Bulls saw the move up to bar 13 as a sign of strength, and therefore they might have been willing to scale in on the bear channel down to bar 22. They might have first bought above the bar 19 bull reversal bar and then they could have added on at the second signal above bar 22, as the market tried to form a double bottom with the bar 8 bottom of the bull channel. Alternatively, they could have scaled in at fixed intervals, like one and two points below their original long entry above bar 19. They could have scaled out part at their original entry there and taken the rest off on the bar 26 test of the bar 18 top of the channel, or they could have scaled out at fixed intervals, like part at breakeven and then more at one point and then two points higher.

Figure 31.8   SCALING INTO AND OUT OF A TRADE   **565**

FIGURE 31.8   Entering Where Weak Traders Exit

The market often hits obvious protective stops to the tick and then reverses. If traders are just looking for a few major reversals a day, they have to be willing to use wider stops, because the market often hits round number protective stops located at two, three, four, or five points from the entry price to the tick and then reverses. If a trader shorted below bar 3 in Figure 31.8 and used a three-point stop, it would have been hit to the tick at the bar 9 high. However, if the trader was willing to scale in, he might have an order to short more exactly where the weak traders are getting stopped out. Because a three-point stop here was logical since it was the appropriate size for the recent price action and it was at a new high of the day, an astute trader looking to scale in would have placed a limit order to short more at 11 ticks above the first entry, one tick below the three-point stop.

A trader who bought the lower low at bar 13 or the second reversal up at bar 20 had the same experience with a three-point stop. It would have been hit to the tick. The alternative again was to scale in just shy of the obvious stop.

The initial trading range was about half of the size of an average day, so when traders saw the breakout down to bar 11, they knew that there was about a 60 percent chance or better that this would be a trending trading range day and that there would be a test of the bar 4 breakout point. Traders could have bought on limit orders at two, three, and four points below bar 4. They would have been filled on only their first order, and they could have exited with two points' profit on the move up to bar 12, which went a few ticks above the bar 4 breakout point.

Traders who saw the trending channels recognized that every breakout to a new low was followed by a pullback above the old low. Because of this, they could have planned to scale in below each low. Bar 13 was five ticks below bar 11, so traders would assume that the next new low would extend about five ticks below bar 13. Sometimes the next breakout is a little less and the market converts into a shrinking stairs pattern. They could have placed a limit order to buy about three ticks below the bar 13 low and an order to scale in one point lower and then again one point below that. Their scale orders would not have been filled, and they would have been able to make a point or two on their first entry. If they had scaled in, they could have exited the entire position at the first entry price and taken a breakeven trade on that first entry and a one-point profit on the second entry. Alternatively, they could have held out for more and made a point or two on the first and two or three points on the second.

They could have repeated the process as the market fell below bar 15. They might or might not have been filled on their second entry since the bar 21 low was exactly at the limit price, eight ticks below the bar 15 low.

If traders thought that the trading range from bar 11 to bar 17 would hold, they might have been willing to scale in on the sell-off with a first entry around bar 18. However, once the low 2 formed after bar 20, it was better to exit and possibly reverse to short and then look to buy again lower.

CHAPTER 32

Getting Trapped
In or Out
of a Trade

An entry stop can get you trapped into a bad trade, and a protective stop can get you trapped out of a good trade. It is reasonable to wonder how this can happen if most of the volume is generated by institutional computer orders—how can the institutional computers get it wrong so often? Those programs are often complex, and all of the institutions are using different methods. Some of the stop runs will be due to hedging or partial profit taking, while others will be due to scaling into a position, and most will have nothing to do with a 5 minute chart. It is simplistic to think that they are all getting it wrong and were trapped by a stop, or that the stop run was due to the relatively small volume that comes from individual traders. What appears on the chart is the distilled product of a huge number of traders who are basing their decisions on a huge number of different and unknowable reasons. The result is that individual traders sometimes get trapped into or out of the market. Most institutions are not trading tick by tick, and they are not concerned by these little moves because they know that the math behind their models is sound. They don't see these moves as traps; it is likely that most don't see them at all and instead rely on their models and on the orders that their customers want them to fill. High-frequency trading (HFT) firms, however, try to capitalize on any small move.

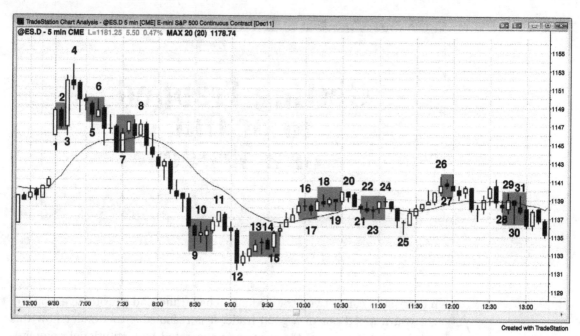

FIGURE 32.1   Trapped Traders

As shown in Figure 32.1, today was filled with setups that trapped traders into bad trades and out of good trades, but if you had carefully read the price action, you could have profited off each of these traps by placing limit orders to bet on the opposite direction.

Bar 2 was a bear trend bar on a gap up open and a possible high of the day, but with bar 1 being as strong as it was, it was probably better to wait for more information before shorting. Once the short triggered, alert traders would have bought above bar 2 on a stop, both because there were trapped bears and because the market went above a strong bull trend bar on a gap up day and the day could become a trend from the open bull trend day.

Bar 5 was the third bear bar in a spike down from a possible high of the day, so even if the market were to trade above its high, a lower high and a second leg down to the moving average were likely. A trader could have placed a sell limit order to go short at the bar 5 high and used a protective stop either at the high of the day or above the bear entry bar that followed the bar 4 sell signal.

The bear channel down to bar 7 was steep, so even though it was a high 2 pullback to the moving average and a bull trend bar, bulls would have been wise to wait for a breakout pullback before going long. Aggressive traders would have shorted with a limit order at the bar 7 high for a scalp.

Figure 32.1   GETTING TRAPPED IN OR OUT OF A TRADE   **569**

The move down to bar 9 was very strong, so buying the first attempt to rally was a bad trade. Traders could instead have placed a limit order to short at the bar 9 high, expecting a new low within the next few bars.

Bar 12 was a large bear trend bar and therefore a sell climax, and it followed the sell climax down to bar 9. The low 2 at bar 11 might have been the final flag in the bear trend before a larger correction ensued. Bar 13 was a low 1 short setup, but, since the market was no longer in a strong bear spike, this was a bad short. Traders could instead have placed a limit order to buy at the bar 13 low for a scalp.

Bar 14 was a weak low 2 short, since a correction lasting at least 10 bars was likely after the consecutive sell climaxes. Bulls could have bought the low of bar 14, expecting a failed low 2 and a breakout to the upside. Bar 15 became an outside up bar, trapping bears into the low 2 short. Because the bar was so quick to form, many bulls did not have time to understand what had taken place; they were trapped out and forced to chase the market up.

Bar 16 was a low 1 short setup after five bull trend bars and therefore likely to fail. Bulls would have bought at the low of the bar.

Bar 17 was a high 1 long setup, but the bull spike had bars with small bodies and tails. This was not a strong bull spike, and therefore the high 1 should fail. Bears shorted with limit orders at the high of bar 17.

Bar 18 was a low 2 short setup, but the market was still in a strong bull channel and now was going sideways for six bars. This low 2 was likely to fail, so bulls bought its low for a scalp.

Bar 19 was a failed low 2 and therefore a buy setup, but the market was beginning to go sideways and have small bars, and this would have made the third push up. Bears shorted at its high.

Bar 23 was a high 1 buy setup, but this was not a strong bull spike, so bears shorted at its high.

Bar 27 was a high 1 buy setup, but again the spike was not strong. The bars were small and the tails were prominent. Bears shorted at its high.

Bar 28 was a high 1 and a higher low in the middle of a trading range, and it formed after a strong bear reversal bar one bar earlier. Bears shorted at its high.

Bar 30 was a large doji bear reversal bar and a high 2 buy setup, but it was in the middle of a trading range and the large signal bar forced traders to buy near the top, which is never good. The doji bar was a weak signal bar. Bears shorted at its high.

About the Author

Al Brooks is a technical analysis contributor to *Futures* magazine and an independent day trader. Called the trader's trader, he has a devoted following, and provides live market commentary and daily chart analysis updates on his website at www.brookspriceaction.com. After changing careers from ophthalmology to trading 25 years ago, he discovered consistent trading success once he developed his unique approach to reading price charts bar by bar. He graduated from the University of Chicago Pritzker School of Medicine and received his BS in mathematics from Trinity College.

About the Website

This book includes a companion website, which can be found at:

www.wiley.com/go/tradingtrends

All of the charts provided in the book are included on the website for your convenience. The password to enter this site is: Brooks2.

Index